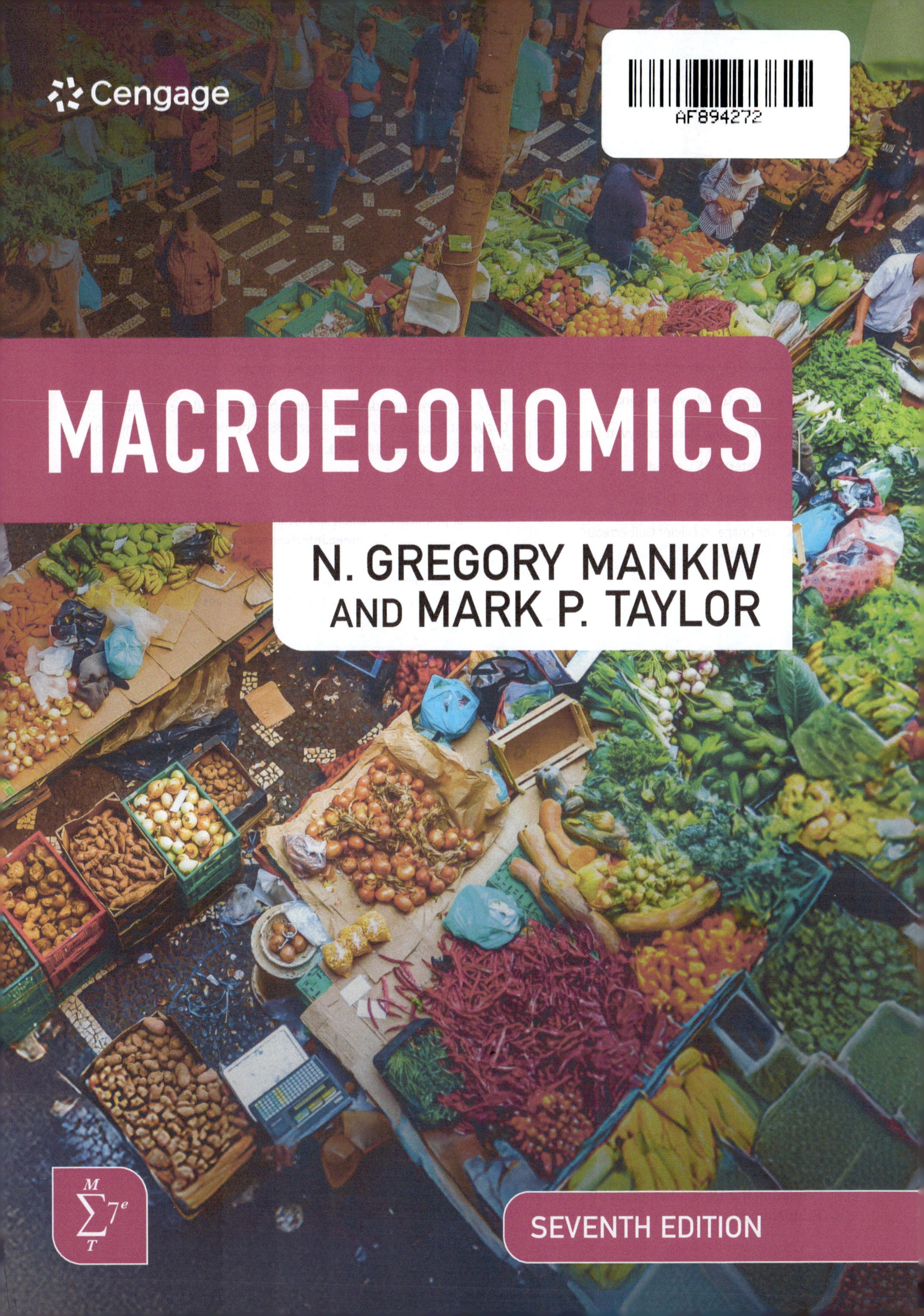

Cengage

MACROECONOMICS

N. GREGORY MANKIW
AND MARK P. TAYLOR

SEVENTH EDITION

Cengage

***Macroeconomics*, Seventh Edition**
US author: N. Gregory Mankiw
Adapting Authors: Mark P. Taylor, with contributor Andrew Ashwin

Publisher: Annabel Ainscow

List Manager: Birgit Gruber

Editorial Assistant: Kim Dodgshon

Marketing Manager: Louise Corless

Manager, GCPM: Jyotsna Ojha

Manufacturing Manager: Eyvett Davis

Typesetter: MPS Limited

Cover design: Cyan Design

Cover Image: © Olivier Guiberteau/ Shutterstock

WCN: 02-300-492

For product information and technology assistance, contact us at **emea.info@cengage.com**

For permission to use material from this text or product and for permission queries, email **emea.permissions@cengage.com**

British Library Cataloguing-in-Publication Data

A catalogue record for this book is available from the British Library.

ISBN: 978-1-8050-3050-8

Cengage Learning, EMEA
Cheriton House, North Way
Andover, Hampshire, SP10 5BE
United Kingdom

Printed in the United Kingdom by CPI Antony Rowe
Print Number: 01 Print Year: 2026

BRIEF CONTENTS

CONTENTS

ABOUT THE AUTHORS

AUTHORS

N. GREGORY MANKIW is the Robert M. Beren Professor of Economics at Harvard University. As a student, he studied economics at Princeton University and the Massachusetts Institute of Technology. As a teacher he has taught macroeconomics, microeconomics, statistics and principles of economics. Professor Mankiw is a prolific writer and a regular participant in academic and policy debates. In addition to his teaching, research and writing, Professor Mankiw has been a research associate of the National Bureau of Economic Research, vice president of the American Economic Association and an advisor to the Federal Reserve Banks of Boston and New York and the Congressional Budget Office. From 2003 to 2005, he served as chairman of the US President's Council of Economic Advisors and was an advisor to presidential candidate Mitt Romney during the 2012 US presidential election. Professor Mankiw's greatest accomplishment, however, was once being a clue on the TV game show *Jeopardy!*

MARK P. TAYLOR is the Donald Danforth, Jr Distinguished Professor of Finance at the Olin Business School at Washington University in St Louis, USA. He was previously Dean of the Olin Business School and, before that, Dean and Professor of Finance and Economics at Warwick Business School at the University of Warwick, UK. He obtained his first degree in philosophy, politics and economics from Oxford University and his Master's and Doctoral degrees in economics and finance from London University. Professor Taylor has taught economics and finance at various universities (including Oxford, New York, Bordeaux and Aix-Marseille) and at various levels (including principles courses and advanced undergraduate and postgraduate courses). He has also worked as a senior economist at the International Monetary Fund and at the Bank of England and as a managing director at BlackRock, the world's largest financial asset manager, where he ran a global investment fund based on macroeconomic analysis. His research has been extensively published in scholarly journals and he is today one of the most highly cited economists in the world.

CONTRIBUTING AUTHOR

ANDREW ASHWIN is an Associate Lecturer in the Department of Management in the Lincoln International Business School, at the University of Lincoln in the UK. Andrew teaches and supports students doing undergraduate degrees and MBAs in leadership and management across a range of modules and also taught commercial and operational management to students following master's degrees in the Lincoln Institute for Agricultural Technology. He has an MBA from the University of Hull and a PhD in assessment and the notion of threshold concepts in economics from the University of Leicester. Andrew is an experienced author, writing a number of texts for students at different levels, and journal publications related to his PhD research as well as working on the development of online learning materials at the University of Bristol's Institute of Learning and Research Technologies. Andrew was Chair of Examiners for a major awarding body for business and economics in England and is a subject specialist consultant in economics for the UK regulator, Ofqual. Andrew has a keen interest in assessment and learning in economics and received accreditation as a Chartered Assessor with the Chartered Institute of Educational Assessors. He has also edited the journal of the Economics, Business and Enterprise Association.

PREFACE

This seventh edition of *Macroeconomics* reflects the way in which the discipline continues to evolve amidst periods of great change and disruption for the UK, European and global economies. The conflicts in Ukraine and the Middle East present considerable challenges and cause disruption to global economies. Geopolitical tensions and political decision-making pose both new and old questions of economists. These all present challenges to the current knowledge base and understanding of economics, and we have tried to reflect some of these challenges in this new edition. Academics across the UK and Europe are engaged in a lively debate about the future direction of the subject, both in the way it is taught at the undergraduate level and how research into developing new knowledge should be conducted. This new edition seeks to reflect some of this debate while retaining a familiar look and structure. Readers should note that this edition adapts Greg Mankiw's best-selling US undergraduate *Principles of Economics* text to reflect the needs of students and instructors in the UK and European markets. As each new edition is written, the adaptation evolves and develops an identity distinct from the original US edition on which it is based. Responsibility for the UK and European edition lies with Cengage EMEA.

We have aimed to retain the lively, engaging writing style with the novice economics student in mind. The use of examples, the case studies and In the News articles help to provide some context to the theory and discussion throughout the text. The case studies and In the News articles are accompanied by questions which have been written to encourage you to think independently, to question and to be critical of received wisdom and what you read and hear about economic issues. We have also introduced a 'Critical Thinking' feature to this edition to encourage you to question assumptions and to ask further questions about what you read, hear and see, to help build your understanding.

MindTap provides a wealth of resources and support for the teaching and learning of economics at undergraduate level and includes assignable assessment tasks, videos, case studies and more to provide everything needed for undergraduate study in one place. Welcome to the wonderful world of economics – learn to think like an economist and a whole new world will open up to you.

ACKNOWLEDGEMENTS

We would like to thank the many reviewers who have provided expert advice either on this new seventh edition and/or on previous editions as the book has evolved over the years:

Yuting Bai, Lancaster University, UK
Michael Barrow, University of Sussex, UK
Brian Bell, King's College London and London School of Economics, UK
Keith Bender, The University of Aberdeen, UK
Karin Bergman, Lund University, Sweden
Annina Boogen, ZHAW School of Management and Law, Switzerland
Ioannis Bournakis, SKEMA Business School, France
Thomas Braeuninger, University of Mannheim, Germany
Klaas De Brucker, KU Leuven, Belgium
Zheng Chris Cao, Aston University, UK
Surja Narayan Datta, Oxford Brookes University, UK
Eleanor Denny, Trinity College Dublin, Ireland
David Duffy, Ulster University, Northern Ireland
Anna Maria Fiori, IESEG School of Management, France
Darragh Flannery, University of Limerick, Ireland
Massimo Filippini, ETH Zürich, Switzerland
Gaia Garino, University of Leicester, UK
Chris Grammenos, American College of Thessaloniki, Greece
Getinet Haile, University of Nottingham, UK
Christoph Harff, Hamm Hochschule, Germany
Luc Hens, Vrije University, Belgium
Giancarlo Ianulardo, University of Exeter, UK
William Jackson, University of York, UK
Colin Jennings, King's College London, UK
Sarah Louise Jewell, University of Reading, UK
Geraint Johnes, Lancaster University, UK
Arie Kroon, Utrecht Hogeschool, The Netherlands
Alan Leonard, University of Portsmouth, UK
Jassodra Maharaj, University of East London, UK
Paul Melessen, Hogeschool van Amsterdam, The Netherlands
Jarek Neneman, University of Lodz, Poland
Kristian Nielsen, Aalborg University, Denmark
Evan Pocher, The University of Aberdeen, UK
Katerina Raoukka, University of Cyprus, Cyprus
Jørn Rattsø, Norwegian University of Science & Technology, Norway
Alejandro Riaño, City, University of London, UK
Frédéric Robert-Nicoud, University of Geneva, Switzerland
Jack Rogers, University of Exeter, UK
Erich Ruppert, Hochschule Aschaffenburg, Germany
Noel Russell, University of Manchester, UK
Reto Schleiniger, Zürich University of Applied Sciences, Switzerland
Edward Shinnick, University College Cork, Ireland
Stanley Siebert, University of Birmingham, UK
Munacinga Simatele, University of Hertfordshire, UK
Robert Simmons, University of Lancaster, UK
Alison Sinclair, University of Nottingham, UK
Jan Egbert Sturm, ETH Zürich, Switzerland
Mouna Thiele, Hochschule Düsseldorf, Germany
Nikos Tzivanakis, Coventry University London, UK
Jovan Vojnovic, Edinburgh University, UK
Rolf Weder, University of Basel, Switzerland
Ansgar Wohlschlegel, Swansea University, UK
Klaus Zauner, City St George's, University of London, UK

DIGITAL RESOURCES

The Publisher also wishes to thank Panagiotis Giannarakis (University of Southampton, UK) for his updates to *Maths for Economics*, Vivek Prasad (University of St Andrews, UK) for his updates to the test bank, Anh Nguyen (Catholic University of Louvain, Belgium), Neil Reaich, Giancarlo Ianulardo (University of Exeter, UK) and Sangaralingam Ramesh (University College London, UK) for their contributions to the MindTap and other digital resources available for the new edition.

PART 1 INTRODUCTION TO ECONOMICS

1 WHAT IS ECONOMICS?

THE ECONOMY AND ECONOMIC SYSTEMS

Every day, billions of people around the world make decisions. They make decisions about providing for the fundamentals in life such as food, clothing and shelter and how they use non-work time for leisure and domestic tasks. Making these decisions involves interaction with other people, with governments and business organizations. At any time, individuals could be mothers, fathers, sons, daughters, carers, employers, employees, houseworkers, producers, consumers, savers, taxpayers or benefit recipients. Many, but not all, of these interactions are related to some sort of exchange, normally with the use of a medium of exchange such as money, and sometimes to a direct exchange of services, for example where a small firm supplying fencing does work for a farm in exchange for a supply of meat. Individuals purchase goods and services for final consumption and provide the inputs into production – land, labour and capital. We refer to these individuals collectively as 'households'. The organizations which buy these factors and use them to produce goods and services are referred to collectively as 'firms'.

The amount of interaction between households and firms – the amount of buying and selling which takes place – represents the level of **economic activity**. The more buying and selling there is, the higher the level of economic activity. Households and firms engaging in production and exchange in a particular geographic region are together referred to as the **economy**.

economic activity how much buying and selling goes on in the economy over a period of time
economy all the production and exchange activities that take place

Economics studies the interactions between households and firms in relation to exchange and the many decisions which are made in so doing. It also covers situations where some output is produced without the receipt of an income, such as the work done by unpaid carers and homemakers. It explores how people make a living; how resources are allocated among the many different uses they could be put to; and the way in which our activities influence not only our own well-being but also that of others and the environment.

The Economic Problem

There are three questions that any economy must face:

- What goods and services should be produced?
- How should these goods and services be produced?
- Who should get the goods and services that have been produced?

To satisfy these questions, economies have resources at their disposal which are classified as land, labour and capital.

- **Land** – all the natural resources of the earth. This includes mineral deposits such as iron ore, lithium, gold, rare earth metals such as cerium and lanthanum, and copper; oil and gas; fish in the sea; and all the food and raw materials produced from the land.
- **Labour** – the human effort, both mental and physical, that goes into production. A worker in a factory producing precision tools, an investment banker, an unpaid carer, a road sweeper, a teacher – these are all forms of labour.
- **Capital** – the equipment and structures used to produce goods and services. Capital goods include machinery in factories, buildings, tractors, computers, cooking ovens – anything where the good is not used for its own sake but for the contribution it makes to production.

Decisions around how these factors of production are used in combination, form an important basis of economics. Simplifying resources in this way is helpful in seeking to understand the basis of economic activity but equally hides the depth of the complexity around how these resources are used. Some of the biggest debates of our time are associated with how resources are used. Concerns over inequality and poverty, the environment, well-being and welfare are all linked in some way to decision-making about how resources are used.

> **land** all the natural resources of the earth
> **labour** the human effort, both mental and physical, that goes into production
> **capital** the equipment and structures used to produce goods and services

Scarcity and Choice

A basic assumption is that resources are ultimately scarce in relation to the demand for them. As members of households, we invariably do not have the ability to meet all our wants and needs. Our needs are the necessities of life which enable us to survive – food and water, clothing, shelter and proper health care – and our wants are the things which we believe make for a more comfortable and enjoyable life – holidays, different styles of clothes, smartphones, leisure activities, the furniture and items we have in our houses, and so on. Our demand for these wants and needs is generally greater than our ability to satisfy them. **Scarcity** means that society has limited resources and therefore cannot produce all the goods and services households demand. Just as a household cannot give every member everything they want, a society cannot give every individual the highest standard of living to which they might aspire. Because of the tension between scarcity and our wants and needs, decisions must be made by households and firms about how to allocate our incomes and resources to meet those wants and needs.

> **scarcity** the limited nature of society's resources

Economics investigates the issues arising due to the decisions that households and firms make as a result of this tension. In addition, we have to add into the mix the decisions made by government assumed to be acting on behalf of the people the government represents. A typical textbook definition of **economics** is 'the study of how society makes choices in managing its scarce resources and the consequences of this decision-making'. This definition can, however, mask the complexity and extent of the reach of economics. We might characterize households as having unlimited wants, but not everyone in society is materialistic, which the idea of unlimited wants might imply. Some people are more content with the simple things in life and their choices are based on what they see as being important. Decisions on resource use are invariably influenced by power relationships and equally choices are often influenced and determined based on power relationships. The choices that households, firms and governments make are not more or less valid but reflect the complexity of the subject. Some people choose to maintain their standard of living through crime. A decision to resort to crime has reasons and consequences, and these may be of as much interest to an economist as the reasons why firms choose to advertise their products or why central banks make decisions on monetary policy.

economics the study of how society manages its scarce resources

Some might point out that the very idea of scarcity should be questioned in some instances. In many countries, there are people who want to work but who cannot find a job. It could be argued that labour is not scarce in this situation, but job vacancies certainly are. Economists will be interested in how such a situation arises and what might be done to alleviate the issues that arise as a result of high levels of unemployment.

The study of economics, therefore, has many facets, but there are some central ideas which help define the field even though economics draws on related disciplines such as psychology, sociology, law, anthropology, geography, statistics and maths, among others. These central ideas provide themes around which this book is based and which form the basis of many first-year undergraduate degree courses.

HOW PEOPLE MAKE DECISIONS

The behaviour of an economy reflects the behaviour of the individuals who make up the economy. We will now outline some of the core issues which economics explores in relation to individuals making decisions. Remember that individuals form households, firms and governments.

People Face Trade-offs

Households, firms and governments must make choices. Making choices involves trade-offs. A **trade-off** is the loss of the benefits from a decision to forego or sacrifice one option, balanced against the benefits incurred from the choice made. When choosing between alternatives consideration must be given to the benefits gained from choosing one course of action but recognizing that there are benefits that could arise from the alternatives that will be sacrificed. To get one thing we like, we usually must give up another thing that we might also like. Making decisions, therefore, requires trading off the benefits of one action against those of another.

trade-off the loss of the benefits from a decision to forego or sacrifice one option, balanced against the benefits incurred from the choice made

To illustrate this important concept, we provide some examples below.

Example 1 Consider an economics undergraduate student who must decide how to allocate their time. They can devote a high proportion of their available time to studying, which will potentially bring benefits such as a better class of degree; they can devote a high proportion of their available time to enjoying leisure activities, which yield different benefits; or they can divide their time between the two. For every hour they study, they give up the benefits of an hour they could have devoted to spending time with friends or in the gym, watching TV, sleeping or working at a part-time job for some extra spending money. The student must trade-off the benefits from studying against the benefits of using their time in other ways.

Example 2 A firm might be faced with the decision on whether to invest in a new product or a new accounting system. Both bring benefits – the new product might result in improved revenues and profits in the future, and the accounting system may make it more effective in controlling its costs, thus helping its profits. If scarce investment funds are put into the accounting system, the firm must trade-off the benefits that the new product investment would have brought.

Example 3 When people are grouped into societies, they face different kinds of trade-offs which can highlight the interaction of individuals, firms and governments within society in general. An example is the trade-off between a clean environment and a high level of income. Laws that require firms to reduce pollution raise the cost of producing goods and services. Because of the higher costs, firms can end up earning smaller profits, paying lower wages, charging higher prices, or some combination of these three. Thus, while pollution regulations give us the benefit of a cleaner environment and the improved levels of health that come with it, they can have the cost of reducing the incomes of firms' owners, workers and customers.

Efficiency and Equity An important trade-off that has interested economists for many years is the trade-off between efficiency and equity. In economics, efficiency deals with ways in which society gets the most it can (depending how efficiency is defined) from its scarce resources. An outcome can be identified as being efficient by some measure, but not necessarily desirable. **Equity** looks at the extent to which the benefits of outcomes are distributed fairly among society's members. Often, when government policies are being designed, these two goals conflict. Because equity is about 'fairness' it inevitably involves value judgements. Differences in opinion lead to disagreements among policymakers and economists.

equity the property of distributing economic prosperity fairly among the members of society

There are some economists who dismiss the idea of a trade-off between equity and efficiency as a myth in some contexts, because the idea has been generalized to all situations. The historical context and origins of many economic ideas are important to understand. The origins of the equity and efficiency trade-off came from Arthur Okun in the 1970s. There are some economists who argue that improving equality can lead to improvements in efficiency – in effect that it is possible to have a bigger cake and to eat it.

Policies aimed at achieving a more equal distribution of economic well-being, such as the social security system, involve a trade-off between the effects of a benefits system versus the effects on the efficiency of the tax system that pays for it. A government decision to raise the top rate of income tax on what it considers 'the very rich' but to abolish income tax for those earning the minimum wage, is effectively a redistribution of income from the rich to the poor. It provides incentive effects for some in society to seek work but may reduce the reward for working hard, so some in society choose to work less or even move to another country where the tax system is less onerous. Whether the trade-off is a 'good' thing is dependent on the philosophy, belief sets and opinions of the decision-makers, and the power which they have in society. Recognizing that people face trade-offs does not by itself tell us what decisions they will or should make. Acknowledging and understanding the consequences of trade-offs is important, because people are likely to make more informed decisions if they understand the options they have available.

SELF TEST You will often hear the adage 'there is no such thing as a free lunch'. Does this simply refer to the fact that someone must have paid for the lunch to be provided and served? Or does the recipient of the 'free lunch' also incur a cost?

Opportunity Cost

Because people face trade-offs, making decisions requires comparing the costs and benefits of alternative courses of action. In many cases, however, the costs of an action are not as obvious as might first appear.

Consider, for example, the decision whether to go to university. The benefits include intellectual enrichment and a lifetime of better job opportunities. In considering the costs, you might be tempted to add up the money you spend on tuition fees, resources and living expenses over the period of the degree. This approach is intuitive and might be a way in which non-economists would approach the decision. An economist would point out that even if you decided to leave full-time education, you would still incur living expenses and so these costs would be incurred in any event. Accommodation becomes a cost of higher education only if it is more expensive at university than elsewhere.

This calculation of costs ignores the largest cost of a university education – your time. For most students, the wages given up to attend university are the largest single cost of their higher education. When making decisions it is sometimes more helpful to measure the cost in terms of what other options have had to be sacrificed rather than in money terms. **Opportunity cost** is the measure of the options sacrificed in making a decision. The opportunity cost of going to university is the wages from full-time work that you have had to sacrifice.

opportunity cost whatever must be given up to obtain some item; the value of the benefits foregone (sacrificed)

Calculating Opportunity Costs Opportunity cost is the cost expressed in terms of the next best alternative sacrificed – what must be given up in order to acquire something. As a general principle, we can express the opportunity cost as a ratio expressed as the sacrifice in one good in terms of the gain in the other. For example, if a person chooses to spend a sum of money on buying a pair of trainers (the gain), that same sum of money cannot be used to buy a ticket to a festival (the sacrifice). The ratio is:

$$Opportunity\ cost\ of\ good\ y = \frac{Sacrifice\ of\ good\ x}{Gain\ in\ good\ y}$$

Expressing the opportunity cost in terms of good *x* would give:

$$Opportunity\ cost\ of\ good\ x = \frac{Sacrifice\ of\ good\ y}{Gain\ in\ good\ x}$$

Opportunity cost can be expressed in terms of either good – they are the reciprocal of each other.

Thinking at the Margin

Decisions in life are rarely straightforward and usually involve weighing up costs and benefits. Having a framework or principle on which to base decision-making can help if we want to maximize benefits or minimize costs. Thinking at the margin is one such framework that economists adopt in thinking about decision-making. **Marginal changes** describe small incremental adjustments to an existing plan of action. Marginal analysis is based around an assumption that **economic agents** (an individual, firm, government or organization that has an impact in some way on an economy) are seeking to maximize or minimize outcomes when making decisions. Consumers may be assumed to seek to maximize the satisfaction they gain from their incomes, and firms to maximize profits and minimize costs. Maximizing and minimizing behaviour is based on a further assumption that economic agents behave rationally.

marginal changes small incremental adjustments to a plan of action
economic agents an individual, firm, government or organization that has an impact in some way on an economy

It is important to stop and consider what we mean by the term 'rational' in this context. When some economists use the term '**rational**' in the context of decision-making, it simply means the assumption that decision-makers can make consistent choices between alternatives. We will look at this in more detail later in the book, but at this stage we will express rationality based on decision-makers' ability to rank their preferences and do the best they can with their existing resources. Thinking at the margin means that decision-makers choose a course of action that takes into consideration marginal costs and benefits.

rational the assumption that decision-makers can make consistent choices between alternatives and do the best they can given their situation

The assumption of rational behaviour provides a framework around which decisions can be analyzed and has been a basic tenet of economics since the 1870s, with thinkers such as William Stanley Jevons and Carl Menger building on work by David Ricardo and Jeremy Bentham, which became part of the so-called marginalist school. The assumptions of rational economic behaviour have implications which have been subject to criticism. In studying economic models which rely on the assumption of rational behaviour, it is important to remember that if these assumptions are relaxed, outcomes might be very different. We will cover a number of economic models which are based on this assumption, because it provides a view into the way in which economic analysis has developed historically and how it is subject to evolution and change. It also provides a way of thinking about issues which can be contrasted with other ways of thinking when different assumptions are held.

People Respond to Incentives

If we assume the principle of rational behaviour and that people make decisions by comparing costs and benefits, it is logical to assume that their behaviour may change when the costs or benefits change. That is, people respond to incentives. The threat of a fine and the removal of a driving licence is designed to regulate the way in which people drive and park their cars; putting a price on the provision of plastic bags in supermarkets aims to encourage people to re-use bags and reduce the total number used.

There has been an increase in the amount of research conducted on incentives because the intentions of policymakers do not always lead to the outcomes expected or desired. A fine imposed on parents who are late picking up their children from day care centres might be expected to reduce the number of late pickups. One study in Israel (refer to Gneezy, U. and Rustichini, A. (2000) A Fine is a Price. *The Journal of Legal Studies* 29(1), 1–17), however, showed that far from reducing the number of late pickups, parents were willing to pay the fine and the number arriving late actually increased. Such consequences are referred to as 'unintended consequences'.

SELF TEST What sort of incentives might governments put in place to encourage workers to find work and get off welfare benefits? What might be the unintended consequences of the incentives you identify?

HOW PEOPLE INTERACT

Decision-making not only affects ourselves but other economic agents as well. We will now explore some issues which arise when economic agents interact with others.

Trade Can Make Everyone Better Off

The United States and China are competitors with Europe in the world economy because US and Chinese firms produce many of the same goods as European firms. It might be thought that if China increases its share of world trade at the expense of Europe this might be bad news for people in Europe. This may not be the case.

Trade between Europe and the United States and China is not like a sports contest, where one side wins and the other side loses (a zero-sum game). In some circumstances trade between economies can make all parties better off. Households, firms and countries have different resource endowments; individuals have talents and skills that allow them to produce some things more efficiently than others; some firms have experience and expertise in the production of goods and services; and some countries, like Spain, are blessed with plenty of sunshine which allows their farmers to grow high quality soft fruit. Trade allows individuals, firms and countries to specialize in the activities they do best. With the income they receive from specializing they can trade with others who are also specializing and can improve their standard of living as a result.

However, while trade can provide benefits and winners, there are also likely to be costs and losers. The economic development of some countries since the 1970s has meant that many people have access to cheap, good quality goods and services as a result of the export of these goods and services. For workers and employers in these industries in developed economies, the competition from developing countries might mean that they find themselves without work or must close their businesses. In some situations, it is difficult for these people to find alternative work, and whole communities can be greatly affected by the changes being experienced. They may not agree that 'trade can benefit everyone'.

The Capitalist Economic System

An **economic system** is the way in which resources are organized and allocated to provide for the needs of an economy's citizens to address the economic problem. In many countries of the world, a capitalist economic system based on markets is the primary way in which the three questions of the economic problem are addressed. A **capitalist economic system** incorporates the principles of the private ownership of factors of production to produce goods and services which are exchanged through a price mechanism. Production is operated primarily for profit.

economic system the way in which resources are organized and allocated to provide for the needs of an economy's citizens

capitalist economic system a system which relies on the private ownership of factors of production to produce goods and services which are exchanged through a price mechanism and where production is operated primarily for profit

Capitalist economic systems have proved capable of raising the standard of living of millions of people since the early 1800s. We can measure the standard of living in terms of the income that people earn, which allows them to purchase the goods and services they need to survive and enjoy life. While capitalist systems have increased living standards for many, it is not the case that everyone in society benefits equally. Capitalism has meant that some people and countries have become very rich whereas others remain poor. The existence of the profit motive provides an incentive for entrepreneurs to take risks to organize factors of production. This dynamism in capitalist systems leads to developments in technology and capital efficiency which help generate profits for the individuals and firms concerned. It also increases knowledge and information in society as a whole, which further contributes to economic development.

Critics of capitalist systems argue that they are inherently unstable and lurch from boom to bust. In addition, capitalist systems favour those who have acquired ownership of factor inputs and thus possess different degrees of economic power. Ownership of factor inputs can result in the exploitation of workers. Owners of factors of production can wield considerable economic and political power which can distort resource allocation. Karl Marx spent a large part of his life seeking to understand and analyze the capitalist system and developing theories to explain why it exploited workers and was unstable.

Markets Can Be a Good Way to Organize Economic Activity

The role of markets in capitalist economic systems is central. In a **market economy**, the three key questions of the economic problem are addressed through the decentralized decisions of many firms and households as they interact in markets for goods and services. Firms decide whom to hire and what to make. Households decide which firms to work for and what to buy with their incomes. These firms and households interact in the marketplace, where prices and, it is assumed, self-interest, guide their decisions.

market economy an economy that addresses the three key questions of the economic problem by allocating resources through the decentralized decisions of many firms and households as they interact in markets for goods and services

In a pure market economy (one without any government intervention) no one is considering the economic well-being of society as a whole. Free markets are assumed to contain many buyers and sellers of numerous goods and services, and all of them are interested, primarily, in their own well-being. Yet, despite decentralized decision-making and self-interested decision-makers, market economies have proven remarkably successful in organizing economic activity in a way that can promote overall economic well-being for millions of people, even though it is recognized there are inequalities that will arise.

Planned Economic Systems The inequitable distribution of wealth in capitalist societies which was witnessed in the countries that benefitted from the Industrial Revolution in the 1700s and 1800s led to the development of other economic systems. The most notable among these were **planned economic systems**, sometimes referred to as communist systems or *command economies*. Communist countries worked on the premise that central planners could guide economic activity and answer the three key questions of the economic problem. The theory behind central planning was that the government could organize economic activity in a way that promoted economic well-being for the country as a whole and led to a more equitable outcome.

> **planned economic systems** economic activity organized by central planners who decided on the answers to the fundamental economic questions

Today, most countries that once had centrally planned economies such as Russia, Poland, Angola, Mozambique and the Democratic Republic of Congo have abandoned this system and are developing more market-based economies. In China, a hybrid between a capitalist economy and central planning has emerged since the 1980s. During this time, China has embraced capitalism with many former state-owned industries being privatized, entrepreneurship encouraged and structural reforms implemented to help improve trade flows and the interconnectedness of regions across China. However, the state still plays a central role in the overall planning of the economy, a system that some have called 'state-led authoritarian capitalism'.

FYI

Adam Smith and the Invisible Hand

Adam Smith published *An Inquiry into the Nature and Causes of the Wealth of Nations* in 1776 and it is a landmark in economics. Smith's work reflected a point of view that was typical of so-called enlightenment writers at the end of the eighteenth century – that individuals are usually best left to their own devices, without government guiding their actions. This political philosophy provides the intellectual basis for the market economy.

Here is Adam Smith's description of how people interact in a market economy:

Man (sic) has almost constant occasion for the help of his brethren, and it is vain for him to expect it from their benevolence only. He will be more likely to prevail if he can interest their self-love in his favour, and show them that it is for their own advantage to do for him what he requires of them ... It is not from the benevolence of the butcher, the brewer, or the baker that we expect our dinner, but from their regard to their own interest...

Every individual ... neither intends to promote the public interest, nor knows how much he is promoting it ... He intends only his own gain, and he is in this, as in many other cases, led by an invisible hand to promote an end which was no part of his intention. Nor is it always the worse for the society that it was no part of it. By pursuing his own interest, he frequently promotes that of the society more effectually than when he really intends to promote it.

Smith suggested that participants in the economy are motivated by self-interest and that the 'invisible hand' of the marketplace guides this self-interest into promoting general economic well-being. Smith's use of the term 'self-interest' should not be interpreted as 'selfishness'. Smith was interested in how humans pursue their own self-interest *in their own way*. As the 2002 Nobel Prize in Economics winner, Vernon L. Smith, put it in his Prize Lecture, 'doing good for others does not require deliberate action to further the perceived interest of others'.

The term 'invisible hand' is widely used in economics to describe the way market economies allocate scarce resources, but interestingly, Adam Smith only used the phrase once in *The Wealth of Nations*. The phrase was also used in an earlier book, *The Theory of Moral Sentiments*. In both instances, Smith outlined the idea that self-interested individuals' actions could produce socially desirable results.

In the *Theory of Moral Sentiments*, the phrase is used to show how human desire for luxury can have the effect of providing employment for others, and in *The Wealth of Nations* the phrase is used in relation to investment choices. There are similarities in sentiment in both uses, but in the former case, Smith, it seems, was seeking to explore the political philosophy of the economic system he was writing about; a system that was very different in many respects from that which we witness today.

Governments Can Sometimes Improve Market Outcomes

An economy can allocate some goods and services through the price mechanism, but markets do not always lead to efficient or equitable outcomes. In some cases, goods and services would not be provided by a market system because it is not practicable to do so. In other cases market-based allocations might be deemed undesirable, with either too few or too many goods and services consumed or produced. The capitalist system and markets rely on laws and regulations to ensure that property rights are enforced.

Governments provide goods and services which might not be provided in sufficient quantities in a market system and set the legal and regulatory framework within which firms and households can operate ostensibly for the benefit of all in society. Government intervention in markets may aim to promote efficiency *and* equity. That is, most policies aim either to enlarge the economic cake, or change the way in which the cake is divided, or even try to achieve both. Market systems do not always ensure that everyone has sufficient food, decent clothing and adequate health care. Many public policies, such as income tax and the social security system, are designed to achieve a more equitable distribution of economic well-being.

When markets do allocate resources, the resulting outcomes might still be deemed inefficient. Economists use the term '**market failure**' to refer to a situation in which the market on its own fails to produce an efficient allocation of resources. One possible cause of market failure is an **externality**, which is the uncompensated impact, both negative and positive, of one person's actions on the well-being of a bystander (a third party). For instance, the classic example of a negative externality is pollution. Another possible cause of market failure is **market power**, which refers to the ability of a single person or business (or group of businesses) to unduly influence market prices or output. In the presence of market failure, well-designed public policy can enhance economic efficiency.

market failure a situation where scarce resources are not allocated to their most efficient use
externality the cost or benefit of one person's decision on the well-being of a bystander (a third party) which the decision-maker does not take into account in making the decision
market power the ability of a single economic agent (or small group of agents) to have a substantial influence on market prices or output

To say that the government *can* improve on market outcomes at times does not mean that it always *will*. Public policy is made by a political process that is also imperfect. Sometimes policies are designed simply to reward the politically powerful. Sometimes they are made by well-intentioned leaders who are not fully informed. One goal of the study of economics is to help you judge when a government policy is justifiable to promote efficiency or equity, and when it is not.

HOW THE ECONOMY AS A WHOLE WORKS

We started by discussing how individuals make decisions and then looked at how people interact with one another. We will now look at issues arising that concern the workings of the economy as a whole.

Microeconomics and Macroeconomics

Since roughly the 1930s, the field of economics has been divided into two broad subfields. **Microeconomics** is the study of how households and firms make decisions and how they interact in specific markets. **Macroeconomics** is the study of economy-wide phenomena. The Nobel Prize winning economist Ragnar Frisch is credited with being the first to use the two terms (along with the term 'econometrics' incidentally). The Cambridge economist Joan Robinson, an associate of Keynes, was one of the first to define macroeconomics, referring to it as 'the theory of output as a whole'.

microeconomics the study of how households and firms make decisions and how they interact in specific markets
macroeconomics the study of economy-wide phenomena, including inflation, unemployment and economic growth

Microeconomics might involve the study of the effects of a congestion tax on the use of cars in a city centre, the impact of foreign competition on the European car industry or the effects of attending university on a person's lifetime earnings. A macroeconomist might study the effects of borrowing by national governments, the changes over time in an economy's rate of unemployment or alternative policies to increase growth in national living standards.

Microeconomics and macroeconomics are closely intertwined. Because changes in the overall economy arise from the decisions of millions of individuals, it is impossible to understand macroeconomic developments without considering the associated microeconomic decisions. For example, a macroeconomist might study the effect of a cut in income tax on the overall production of goods and services in an economy. To analyze this issue, they must consider how the tax cut affects the decisions of households concerning how much to spend on goods and services.

Despite the inherent link between microeconomics and macroeconomics, the two fields are distinct. Because microeconomics and macroeconomics address different questions, they sometimes take quite different approaches and are often taught through separate courses.

An Economy's Standard of Living is Related to Its Ability to Produce Goods and Services

A key concept in macroeconomics is **economic growth** – the increase in the amount of goods and services produced in an economy over a period of time, usually expressed over a quarter and annually. One measure of the economic well-being of a nation is given by **gross domestic product (GDP) per capita** (per head) of the population, which is the average income per head of the population. If you look at GDP per capita figures, it becomes clear that many advanced economies have a relatively high income per capita, whereas in countries in sub-Saharan Africa, average incomes are much lower and, in some cases, significantly lower. For example, in 2022, the GDP per capita of Benin in West Africa was reported by the World Bank as being $1,303. In comparison, the GDP per capita of Germany was $48,718. Put another way, average incomes in Benin are around 2.67 per cent of those in Germany.

economic growth the increase in the amount of goods and services in an economy over a period of time
gross domestic product (GDP) per capita the market value of all goods and services produced within a country in a given period of time divided by the population of a country to give a per capita figure

Not surprisingly, this large variation in average income is reflected in various other measures of the quality of life and **standard of living**. Citizens of high-income countries typically have better nutrition, better health care and longer life expectancy than citizens of low-income countries, as well as more gadgets and more cars, among many other things.

standard of living refers to the amount of goods and services that can be purchased by the population of a country. Usually measured by the inflation-adjusted (real) income per head of the population

Changes in the standard of living over time are also large. Between 2015 and 2022, economic growth in Bangladesh, measured as the percentage growth rate of GDP, averaged around 6.6 per cent per year and in China about 5.9 per cent a year. In contrast, in Brazil, the economy only grew by around 0.3 per cent over the same time period, and in 2021 and 2022, the economy of Brunei Darussalam actually shrank in size by around 106 per cent each year (Source: World Bank).

Variation in living standards is attributable to differences in countries' **productivity** – that is, the quantity of goods and services produced by a worker (or other factor of production) per time period. In nations where workers can produce a large quantity of goods and services per unit of time, many people enjoy a high standard of living. In nations where workers are less productive, however, people endure a more meagre existence. Similarly, the growth rate of a nation's productivity is a significant factor in determining the growth rate of its average income.

productivity the quantity of goods and services produced from each hour of a worker or factor of production's time

The relationship between productivity and living standards also has profound implications for public policy. When thinking about how any policy will affect living standards, the key question is how will it affect the ability to produce goods and services? To boost living standards, policymakers need to raise productivity by ensuring that workers are well educated, have the tools and infrastructure needed to produce goods and services and have access to the best available technology.

The standard of living is not the only measure of well-being. In the UK, for example, the Office for National Statistics (ONS) publishes data on well-being through 41 different measures. These attempt to incorporate how people feel about their lives; whether they see what they do as worthwhile; their satisfaction with family life; how satisfied they are with their jobs and their health; where people live and how safe they feel; their involvement in sport, culture and volunteer work; and the extent to which they access the natural environment. In February 2025, for example, the ONS reported that the percentage of people reporting low satisfaction with their lives stood at 4.7 per cent in the third quarter of 2024. This represents around 1 in 20 of the UK population.

Prices Rise When the Government Prints Too Much Money

In Zimbabwe in March 2007 inflation was reported to be running at 2,200 per cent. That meant that a good priced at the equivalent of Z$2.99 in March 2006 would be priced at Z$68.77 just a year later. In February 2008, inflation was estimated at 165,000 per cent. Five months later it was reported as 2,200,000 per cent. In July 2008, the government issued a Z$100 billion note. At that time, it was just about enough to buy a loaf of bread. Estimates for inflation in Zimbabwe in July 2008 put the rate of growth of prices at 231,000,000 per cent. In January 2009, the government issued Z$10, 20, 50 and 100 trillion dollar notes – a trillion is 1 followed by 12 zeros. This episode is one of history's most spectacular examples of **inflation**, an increase in the overall level of prices in the economy. It is not the only example of inflation that went out of control, however. Weimar Germany in the early 1920s, the Balkans in the mid-1990s and, more recently, Venezuela in 2018, all experienced hyperinflation. In Venezuela, inflation accelerated rapidly in 2017, reaching over 65,000 per cent, and in April 2021 was reported by the Foreign and Commonwealth Office as over 2,300 per cent. In Argentina, the annual rate of inflation reached almost 300 per cent in April 2024.

inflation an increase in the overall level of prices in the economy

High inflation is a problem because it imposes various costs on society. Keeping inflation stable and at a low level is a goal of economic policymakers around the world. In almost all cases of high or persistent inflation, a causal factor is the growth in the quantity of money. When a government creates large quantities of the nation's money without any corresponding increase in output or productivity, the value of money falls. In the period outlined above, the Zimbabwean government was issuing money in ever higher denominations. It is generally accepted that there is a relationship between the growth in the quantity of money and the rate of growth of prices. The inflation in Argentina, for example, has been blamed on excessive government spending funded by printing too much money, the peso, in this instance. Households in Argentina took to seeking to exchange their increasingly depreciating pesos for US dollars as a means of insulating themselves from the effects of rising prices.

FYI

A Different Way of Thinking?

Some of the ideas we have presented here are based on an assumption that economic growth is desirable. With the constant striving for economic growth comes a number of challenges not least the problems for humanity that come as a side effect of growth. The mindset of going for growth is not the only way of thinking, however. The goal of growth has been challenged by some. Alternative ideas about how humanity lives and its goals have been put forward, two examples of which are de-growth and doughnut (or donut to use the US spelling) economics.

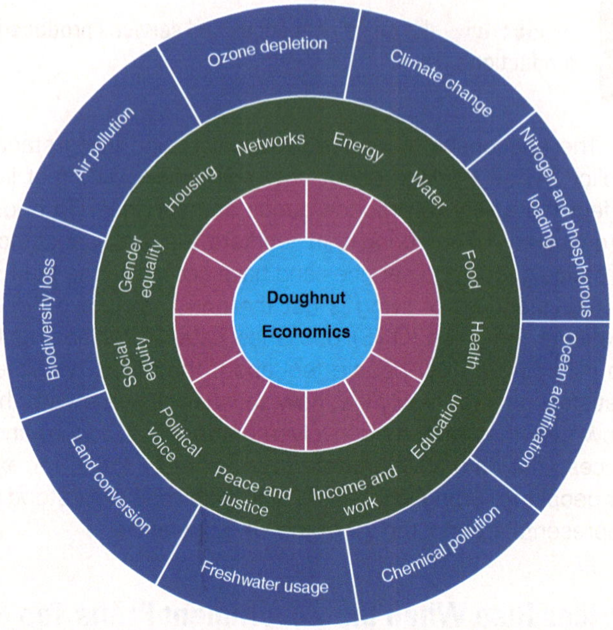

Source: Adapted from MIT open source code. Copyright © 2021 Jeremy Johnson

De-growth is an idea that has been around since the 1970s and its proponents argue that we need to reconsider the way we use our scarce resources. At the heart of de-growth is sustainability, using resources in a way that does not compromise resource use for future generations. Advocates of de-growth argue that humans should put human well-being above profit and that we could learn to live more simply. Do we really need all the 'stuff' many of us own? What really matters in our lives? Could people grow more of their own food? Should we focus housing policy on utilizing more empty properties instead of seeking to resolve housing shortages by building new homes, for example? According to Action on Empty Homes, there are over 1 million empty homes in England alone, that equates to 1 in every 25.

Doughnut economics also seeks to shift the debate from growth to thinking differently about how we live and use resources. The idea was introduced by Kate Raworth in a report for Oxfam in 2012. The doughnut consists of two concentric rings. Within the doughnut is a 'safe space for humanity' where key needs are satisfied such as water, energy, food, housing, equality, peace and justice, health, education, and so on. The outer edge of the doughnut identifies the various challenges that humanity faces, air pollution, biodiversity loss, chemical pollution, climate change, ocean acidification, and so on. Thinking about how we use resources can help in drawing humanity into the doughnut, into the 'safe space'. Rather than focusing on competition and individualism, humans need to think more cooperatively and with more care for each other. The ideas covered in doughnut economics are drawn from various strands of economic thought, including behavioural, complexity, institutional, feminist and ecological economics.

SELF TEST What is the difference between microeconomics and macroeconomics? Write down three questions that the study of microeconomics might be concerned with and three questions that might be involved in the study of macroeconomics.

SUMMARY

1 Key issues arising in individual decision-making are that people face trade-offs among alternative goals, that the cost of any action is measured in terms of foregone opportunities, that rational people make decisions by comparing marginal costs and marginal benefits, and that people change their behaviour in response to the incentives they face.

2 When economic agents interact with each other, the resulting trade can be mutually beneficial.

3 In capitalist economic systems, the market mechanism is the primary way in which the questions of what to produce, how much to produce and who should get the resulting output are answered.

4 Markets do not always give outcomes that are efficient or equitable. In such circumstances, governments can potentially improve market outcomes.

5 The field of economics is divided into two subfields: microeconomics and macroeconomics. Microeconomists study decision-making by households and firms and the interaction among households and firms in the marketplace. Macroeconomists study the forces and trends that affect the economy as a whole.

6 The fundamental lessons about the economy as a whole are that productivity is a key source of living standards and that money growth can be a primary source of inflation.

IN THE NEWS

Artificial Intelligence and the Digital Economy

Artificial intelligence (AI) refers to computer systems that simulate human intelligence and can perform tasks associated with problem solving and decision-making. Like humans, these computer systems can have the capability to learn from data generated from their operations and from new data inputted into the system to improve the efficiency of operations over time. AI has aroused interest, excitement, suspicion and fear in equal measure. Very few firms, households and governments will be immune to the effects of AI. There have been concerns expressed that AI could result in large numbers of jobs disappearing, or that it may contribute to increases in global inequality. At the same time, however, the technology could also result in an increase in productivity with a consequent increase in global economic growth.

© iStock/gorodenkoff

There is a great deal of misunderstanding and confusion around how far AI will impact our lives. This is not unusual when significant new technologies are developed.

As with the development of new technology over thousands of years, the main effects are on how they affect different resources and how resource use might change as a result. This, in turn, will impact the way in which policymakers, households and firms will behave and make decisions around the three key economic questions of: what goods and services should be produced, how should they be produced and who should get the goods and services that are produced? AI could result in a wide range of beneficial effects, for example in reducing instances of financial fraud, improving market trading, making supply chains more efficient, boosting the efficiency and effectiveness of healthcare provision, identifying errors in production processes, monitoring agricultural production and energy demand – the list can seem endless.

While there are undoubtedly benefits to AI, there are also costs. Those who have jobs that could be replaced by AI may end up on lower incomes, whereas those who have the skills to work with and exploit AI may end up on much higher wages. Organizations that have the opportunities to develop AI may be able to wield greater power over consumers and markets. The gap between the developed and developing world could widen. AI could be used by criminals or by

(Continued)

governments for nefarious purposes, and the safety and security of people around the world could be compromised. With AI estimated to soon demand an equivalent amount of energy to a medium-large developed country, and the climate crisis disproportionately affecting developing countries who are less likely to see the immediate benefits of AI systems, the widespread use of AI in its current state also raises serious ethical issues.

Critical Thinking Questions

1 Throughout human history, there have been revolutions in technology that have transformed economies and economic activity. Why should the development of AI be seen as anything other than another example of human technological development?
2 Many firms will be affected by developments in AI. Use an example to explain a possible trade-off that the owners of firms may have to consider in relation to the adoption of AI technology.
3 To what extent do you agree with the view that developments in AI increase the likelihood that in the future more decisions will be made 'at the margin'?
4 Explain the possible link between the development of AI and increases in productivity and economic growth.
5 Despite the claims for AI and for the digital economy in general, productivity across many developed economies has not increased but has been sluggish at best. Does this suggest that the hype around AI is over-emphasized?

References:

www.aatcomment.org.uk/trends/ai/beware-the-energy-costs-of-using-ai/, accessed 18 July 2025.

emeritus.org/blog/examples-of-artificial-intelligence-ai/, accessed 17 July 2025.

www.europarl.europa.eu/RegData/etudes/BRIE/2019/637967/EPRS_BRI(2019)637967_EN.pdf, accessed 17 July 2025.

www.imf.org/en/Blogs/Articles/2024/01/14/ai-will-transform-the-global-economy-lets-make-sure-it-benefits-humanity, accessed 17 July 2025.

QUESTIONS FOR REVIEW

1 What are the three economic questions which any society must answer?
2 Describe the main features of a capitalist economic system and explain why private property and a strong legal system are vital to the success of this system.
3 Give three examples of important trade-offs that you face in your life.
4 What is the opportunity cost of going to a restaurant for a meal?
5 Water is necessary for life. Is the marginal benefit of a glass of water large or small?
6 Why should policymakers think about incentives?
7 Why can specialization and trade help improve standards of living?
8 Explain the two main causes of market failure and give an example of each.
9 Why is productivity important?
10 What do you think are the main costs of inflation that is out of control on the population?

PROBLEMS AND APPLICATIONS

1 Describe some of the trade-offs faced by each of the following:
   a. A family deciding whether to buy a new car.
   b. A government deciding whether to build a high-speed rail link between two major cities in the north of the country.
   c. A company chief executive officer deciding whether to recommend the acquisition of a smaller firm.
   d. A university lecturer deciding how much time to devote to preparing for their weekly lecture.
2 In 2025, the youth unemployment rate in Spain was reported by the European Union as standing at around 26 per cent. Does this mean that labour is not a scarce resource in Spain?

3 You are trying to decide whether to take a holiday. Most of the costs of the holiday (airfare, hotel, foregone wages) are measured in euros, but the benefits of the holiday are psychological. How can you compare the benefits to the costs?

4 Many of the countries which had planned economic systems have transitioned to a more market-based economic system in the face of numerous problems. What do you think are the disadvantages of planned economic systems? How do market economies solve these problems? Can market systems solve all problems? What do you think are the advantages and disadvantages of the hybrid system that China has adopted?

5 You win €10,000 on the EuroMillions lottery draw. You have a choice between spending the money now or putting it away for a year in a bank account that pays 5 per cent interest. What is the opportunity cost of spending the €10,000 now?

6 Three managers of the van Heerven Coach Company are discussing a possible increase in production. Each suggests a way to make this decision.
FIRST MANAGER: We need to decide how many additional coaches to produce. Personally, I think we should examine whether our company's productivity – number of coaches produced per worker per hour – would rise or fall if we increased output.
SECOND MANAGER: We should examine whether our average cost per worker would rise or fall.
THIRD MANAGER: We should examine whether the extra revenue from selling the additional coaches would be greater or smaller than the extra costs.
Who do you think is right? Why?

7 Assume a social security system in a country provides income for people over the age of 65. If a recipient decides to work and earn some income, the amount they receive in social security benefits is typically reduced.
   a. How does the provision of this grant affect people's incentive to save while working?
   b. How does the reduction in benefits associated with higher earnings affect people's incentive to work past the age of 65?

8 Your flatmate is a better cook than you are, but you can clean more quickly than your flatmate can. If your flatmate did all the cooking and you did all the cleaning, would your household chores take you more or less time than if you divided each task evenly? Give a similar example of how specialization and trade can make two countries both better off.

9 Explain whether each of the following government activities is motivated by a concern about equity or a concern about efficiency. In the case of efficiency, discuss the type of market failure involved:
   a. Regulating water prices.
   b. Regulating electricity prices.
   c. Providing some people on low or no income with vouchers that can be used to buy food.
   d. Prohibiting the purchase of cigarettes by people aged 15 or under.
   e. Imposing higher personal income tax rates on people with higher incomes.
   f. Instituting laws against driving while using a mobile phone.

10 In what ways is your standard of living different from that of your parents or grandparents when they were your age? Why do you think these changes occurred?

2 THINKING LIKE AN ECONOMIST

INTRODUCTION

A perpetual debate in many economies revolves around the provision of health services. In the UK and many European countries, health provision is universal, meaning it is available to all regardless of their income or status and is free at the point of use. Of course, health provision is not 'free' – it is extremely expensive. If a government wants to increase spending on health, it must find a way of funding it. Assume that a government announces an increase in spending on its health service of €2.8 billion, to be funded by tightening the rules on corporate taxes to prevent large corporations avoiding their tax liabilities.

How would an economist think about this policy? An economist would want to know what the additional investment would be spent on, whether this additional spending would result in a more efficient health service and, crucially, how 'efficient' was being defined in this context.

Regardless of whether the economist has a personal view about whether the means of raising the funds are 'right', they would think about whether the amount of money raised through these measures would be sufficient. They would also consider whether tightening rules on tax avoidance would have consequences on the behaviour of economic actors who would be affected. Political parties might not foresee these changes in behaviour and this could compromise the intended outcome.

Ultimately, the economist would want to investigate the costs and benefits of such a policy, try to quantify those costs and benefits and offer an informed view of the consequences. It would not simply be a case of looking at the obvious costs and benefits. They would also investigate the hidden costs and benefits which might lead to an outcome or outcomes that may be very different from those the policy was designed to achieve.

Economics, like most other fields of study, has its own language, its own processes, its methods of discovery and its own way of thinking. As you embark on your study of economics you will have to learn lots of terms and concepts. Many of the concepts you will come across in this book are abstract. Abstract concepts are ones which are not concrete or real – they have no tangible qualities. We will talk about markets, efficiency, comparative advantage and equilibrium, for example, but it is not possible to physically see these concepts.

As you work through your modules you will find that it is not always easy to think like an economist. There will also be times when you are confused and find some of the ideas and concepts being presented to you running contrary to common sense (i.e. they are counter-intuitive). What you will be experiencing is perfectly normal and a part of the learning journey.

ECONOMIC METHODOLOGY

How do economists know what they know? How do we 'know', for example, that prices respond to changes in demand and supply, that prices rise when governments print too much money, that consumers prefer more to less or that trade can benefit everyone? What methods do they adopt to find out such information and arrive at theories? In this chapter we will discuss the methodology of economics. There is considerable debate about this methodology and, crucially, about the assumptions which underpin many of the theories and models used in the discipline. There has been, and probably will continue to be, a number of books and articles published which are critical of economics and economists. The effect of business decision-making on the environment, the impact of the 2007–9 Financial Crisis and the widening gap between the wealthy and those on low incomes are all topics that you will find covered in criticisms of economics and of economists whose ideas and theories are bound up with these issues. If you read some of these books and articles, you might be forgiven for wondering what on earth you have done in choosing to study such a bankrupt subject which is populated by automatons who ignore everything 'real' and blindly pursue their own narrow focus because it suits them to do so.

The reality is somewhat different. There have been debates and disagreements in economics for hundreds of years. Some of these disagreements are about the assumptions that are made in exploring economic phenomena. In other cases, there may be broad agreement on the direction of (for example) cause and effect, but the disagreement may be on the extent of the effects or the precise nature of the causes.

Economics as a Science

One of the debates about economics is the extent to which it is a 'science'. Science is a process. It is related to the discovery and creation of new knowledge and understanding but also relies on existing knowledge and understanding. Science is ongoing. The knowledge and understanding associated with the process are constantly evolving as new discoveries help improve our knowledge and understanding of the world around us.

Of course, we tend to think of science from the perspective of physics, chemistry and biology, which many people have studied at school. These subjects are referred to as 'natural sciences', because they are associated with the study of physical things and the natural world. When studying natural phenomena, it is often possible to conduct controlled experiments. This means that researchers can vary an object of interest and observe what happens to other variables and objects. The experiment can be repeated and data gathered, which can help to explain events and to establish cause and effect.

Other discipline areas cannot carry out experiments in the same way. Economics is one of those disciplines. Economics studies decision-making and the effect of decision-making on a wide range of topic areas, but central to the study are human beings. Controlled experiments, which can be carried out in the natural sciences, cannot be carried out in the same way in economics. Economics is referred to as a 'social science' because it deals with human beings as individuals and in groups. The process of knowledge creation and development in social sciences can take on different nuances compared to the natural sciences, but there are processes and methods which are common to both.

SELF TEST Can any discipline which deals with human behaviour truly call itself a 'science'?

Empirical Research

One of the developments in approaches to economics in recent years has been a greater emphasis on empirical research. **Empirical research** focuses attention on observation and experience, on measurable phenomena which allow conclusions to be drawn which are supported by verifiable evidence. This is very different from the development of knowledge which is based on theory or belief. It could be argued that much thinking in economics in the 19th century, for example, was driven by the development of theories based on beliefs. Theories of consumer behaviour, for example, were generated from assumptions about humans that were derived from intuitive beliefs about how they go about making consumption decisions. There is nothing inherently wrong with generating knowledge in this way, but the knowledge is only useful, it is argued, if the phenomena it seeks to explain are actually observed in everyday interactions.

empirical research knowledge generated through observation and experience of measurable phenomena which allow conclusions to be drawn, supported by verifiable evidence

Empirical research can provide evidence of whether a theory can accurately explain or predict the phenomena concerned. Such research may start out with a specific research question or questions. It is likely to include a review of the state of current knowledge in the field as part of a literature review and then presents a research design which explains the approach to the research, the process involved and how data will be gathered and analyzed. Knowing this allows others to replicate the research being undertaken to help with the verification (or otherwise) of the knowledge being created. Results are then presented which may be in the form of accepted statistical data that allows inferences or conclusions to be drawn about the research question or questions. These results can then be subject to discussion about the nature of the new knowledge, the consequences of the findings, limitations of the research and areas that require further research.

Empirical research allows any discipline to advance and refine knowledge. Empirical research can show that current knowledge and thinking in a discipline is inaccurate or even plainly wrong. It sets researchers on new paths of discovery and so is very much an iterative and evolutionary process. In physics, for example, researchers are seeking answers to the nature of matter. Theories have been developed over time that explain the forces that operate in our universe, but as knowledge has developed, more and more questions are generated which existing models of the universe cannot explain. Empirical research may help to provide answers to questions around the nature of matter and the extent to which existing models are able to explain our universe.

In economics, our understanding of labour markets, of how the economy works, of firm and consumer behaviour, among many other areas, have changed as a result of empirical research which has thrown new light on our existing knowledge and understanding. Such research does not mean that economics is 'broken' or 'bankrupt' any more than questions over the 'standard model' in physics mean that discipline is broken, but it can be seen as being a natural part of the evolution of a discipline. Economics is still relatively young as a field of study and we have much to learn. It has been more widely argued, however, that economists do need to embrace empirical research and the findings of such research into their teaching programmes and their textbooks to more accurately reflect the current state of knowledge and understanding of the phenomena we seek to explore and explain.

Models

Economics uses a lot of models. A model is a representation of reality which facilitates understanding of how something works. Models can be used as a means of helping understand the real world, for making informed decisions and judgements and as a benchmark for comparison.

Models are, of necessity, simplifications of reality and are not meant to represent every feature, nuance or aspect of the real world they are attempting to explain. It is often worth thinking of models which architects use to show how a building will look. The model will provide the observer with an image of what the eventual building will look like. It shows its key features and helps in understanding the scale of the building, how it integrates with its surroundings and its main structures. What the model does not do is incorporate every feature and aspect of the building as this is not necessary to develop a broad understanding of the building and its environment.

Similarly, economists use models to represent the world around them. We use models to represent how markets work, how the economy as a whole works, how consumers behave and how firms behave. These models are based on assumptions, some of which might not be fully accurate as a representation of how the real world works or how the economic agents which form part of the model behave. This does not necessarily detract from the value of the model in describing how the phenomenon under investigation works.

Economic models have several uses: they can be used for predicting or forecasting what might happen in the future as a consequence of a decision or policy, they might be developed to help explain or better understand economic phenomena, and they might be used to simulate an event and provide a comparison with what would have happened if the decision, policy or change had not happened (the **counterfactual**). Economists' models are often composed of diagrams and equations. By feeding in data, economists can use models to generate outcomes which provide some insight and form the basis of decision-making.

counterfactual analysis based on a premise of what would have occurred if something had not happened

Models are valuable in that they allow economists to manipulate variables which form part of the model and explore what might happen. Models in economics will always contain a number of variables. Some of these variables are determined by the model and some are generated within the model. For example, take the relationship between quantity demanded and price, where the quantity demanded (Q_d) is dependent on the price (P). Q_d is said to be the dependent variable. Its value will be dependent on the functional relationships in the model (the factors that affect demand) such as incomes, tastes and the prices of other goods. Q_d can be described as an **endogenous variable**. Price, on the other hand, is the independent variable – it affects the model (the quantity demanded) but is not affected by it. The price is not determined by, or dependent on, the quantity demanded. Price would be referred to as an **exogenous variable**.

endogenous variable a variable whose value is determined within the model
exogenous variable a variable whose value is determined outside the model

Models are inherently unstable the longer the time period being considered and forecast. Shocks occur which are impossible to factor into the building of models. These not only have short-term impacts but may also change longer-term dynamics. For example, the Covid-19 pandemic in the early 2020s and also ongoing major armed conflicts have imposed major shocks on the global economy and have had a fundamental impact on the ways in which governments think and behave and how economies have performed that could not have been envisaged before these events. One of the reasons why models of climate change are subject to debate and disagreement is that over time, the internal dynamics of models change in ways which render future predictions inherently unstable.

The so-called 'butterfly wing' effect, as described in chaos theory, highlights the complexity surrounding modelling in meteorology. The butterfly effect notes that a butterfly flapping its wings at a particular point in time and space creates small changes in conditions which can lead to significant changes in faraway places. For example, a flap of a butterfly's wings in New Mexico may be traced as the initial causal factor of a cyclone in China sometime in the future. Chaos theory further tells us that minor errors in measurements or assumptions can be amplified to such an extent that any predictions made by the model are rendered useless. In other words, the further into the future we are attempting to make forecasts and predictions, the more unstable our models become.

Cause and Effect One problem facing economists is separating out cause and effect. Observation and experience can lead to the identification of phenomena occurring which intuition would seem to suggest are related in some way. Does a change in price, for example, cause a change in the amount bought by consumers, or does quantity bought affect price?

To get a clearer picture, economists will utilize an important aspect which is common to other sciences, that of holding other variables in the model constant. The Latin term '***ceteris paribus***', meaning 'other things equal', is used to note when other factors that might affect outcomes are assumed to be constant. Research on the relationship between different variables, based on the principle of *ceteris paribus*, can lead to a conclusion which provides an answer to the nature of the relationships. The question which must be asked is: How do we know this 'answer' is correct?

ceteris paribus **(other things equal)** a term used to describe analysis where one variable in the model is allowed to vary while others are held constant

Take the case of the relationship between crime rates and unemployment. Is a rise in the crime rate, for example, *always* caused by a rise in unemployment, or are there other factors that can also influence the crime rate? How significant is the incidence of unemployment in determining crime rates? How do those who research such a relationship establish the facts of the case?

Human Values in Models Models can be developed, predictions made and conclusions drawn, but there are then human values to take into consideration. Many economists, for example, would agree that there is sufficient evidence to suggest that government stimulus in a period of economic downturn can help reduce the number of people unemployed. What might be the subject of more disagreement is the significance of the effect, or the value of the associated costs and benefits of such a policy.

Models of climate change may suggest that the increase in human-generated carbon emissions will contribute to a change in the global climate. There may be some who would disagree with this basic conclusion, partly because they dispute the 'facts' which form the basis for the model.

Models also allow **inferences** to be made. This means that conclusions, consequences or explanations can be drawn based on the evidence provided by the model. This is not to say that these conclusions are full and final; they are simply what may be reasonably and logically derived based on the manipulations of the model.

inferences conclusions or explanations derived from evidence and reasoning

The climate change model, for example, might infer a policy suggestion that significant measures have to be put in place to cut carbon emissions in the next 10 years to prevent the costs which our children and grandchildren will have to bear. There may be people who disagree on whether the cost of the current sacrifices required are outweighed by the value of the benefits that will occur 50 to 100 years into the future.

Manipulating Models Economists will often use models based on mathematical formulae. This allows the modeller to manipulate the numbers in the formula and identify the extent to which outcomes differ. When a model is manipulated, outcomes can be identified. The model may help to explain the mechanism or reasons why the outcomes identified occur. The outcomes from models can then be compared to actual data to see the extent to which the model is useful in explaining observed data and behaviour.

This is a perfectly normal part of the scientific process. Those critical of a model and its outcomes can provide refinements to the model which might better represent the phenomena it is meant to be describing or explaining. This is how knowledge is created, developed and improved upon. The explanatory power of models is dependent on how well they are built. If they are too simplified or the assumptions cannot be reasonably observed in the real world, then their explanatory power breaks down. In considering models, it can be helpful to keep in mind a quote made by British statistician George E. P. Box (1919–2013), who noted: 'All models are wrong but some are useful'.

SELF TEST Make a list of five benefits of modelling in economics and five limitations.

Types of Reasoning

One of the ways in which science discovers new knowledge is through asking questions. The consequences of asking these questions can be significant. For example, if Isaac Newton really did get hit on the head with an apple and, amidst his pain, asked the question: 'I wonder why apples fall to the ground?' the answers he generated have fundamentally changed the way we look at the world. Newton's work on gravity spawned many other questions and led Einstein to arrive at the theory of relativity. The theory of relativity in its turn was used to help in the development of global positioning satellites (GPS) which so many people in the world now use and rely upon in their cars, smartphones, watches and other gadgets.

When questions are asked, there are different routes which scientists take to explore those questions or, in some cases, arrive at the questions themselves. We can identify different types of reasoning which help clarify the process involved. There is no 'right' way of reasoning, but there is debate about which produces more reliable theories, which in turn have predictive power.

Deductive Reasoning Deductive reasoning begins with known 'facts' or 'truths' – things that we know to be true (or think to be true). It then works through a process of using these facts or truths to arrive at answers to the question we are interested in and, as a consequence, at new facts or truths.

The 'question' might take the form of a general statement or **hypothesis**, which is derived from the Greek (*hypotithenai*), meaning 'a placing under' or 'to suppose'. A hypothesis is an assumption, tentative prediction, explanation or supposition for something. To discover whether the hypothesis is true or correct, it must be tested. If the facts or known truths are applied to the hypothesis, then the conclusions drawn allow us to discover whether the hypothesis is 'true' or 'correct'.

hypothesis an assumption, tentative prediction, explanation or supposition for something

For example, you observe an animal you have not seen before and ask the question: 'I wonder if that animal is a bird?' The hypothesis or supposition would be that this animal is a bird. You observe that the animal has feathers. Based on the known truth that all birds have feathers, you can conclude that it is a bird.

The conclusion rests on the assumption that the facts or known truths used to arrive at the conclusion are indeed true; in this case, that all birds have feathers. If the fact or the premise used in our example was: all birds have feathers and fly, we might arrive at a conclusion which is unsound. This is because, while all birds have feathers, not all birds fly. This simple example serves to highlight one of the reasons why there can be disagreement in economics. The 'truths' or facts that are used in deductive reasoning might be disputed.

Let us look at a simple example in economics. Many countries have put in place legislation to establish a minimum wage as a means of protecting the lowest paid workers in society. What will be the consequences of this legislation? An economist might develop a hypothesis that a minimum wage will result in increased unemployment. In analyzing whether this hypothesis is 'true' or not, the economist might use the 'known facts' that when the price of something is set above equilibrium (the price at which demand and supply are the same), the quantity demanded will fall and the quantity supplied will rise, resulting in a surplus. In this example, the surplus will be a surplus of labour, that is more people willing to supply labour services compared to the demand by employers of those labour, services. Therefore, the conclusion is that a minimum wage will indeed result in unemployment.

Economists may use models of the labour market which are based on mathematical equations to help quantify the extent of the unemployment that will occur. These models are in turn based on the 'known truths' about the labour market and how it works. There is extensive debate around minimum wage laws, which is a particular source of disagreement among economists. Part of the reason for this is disputes over the 'known truths' and the parameters of the model, that is the way the variables are defined and quantified. This is one of the reasons why economics differs from the natural sciences, in that the models used are based on human behaviour and not on natural forces. Human behaviour tends to be unpredictable and not always fully understood, whereas factors in natural sciences may be more stable and 'easier' to define and quantify.

Inductive Reasoning Inductive reasoning begins with data and observation. The data or observation is analyzed. From this analysis, patterns are identified which may be patterns of behaviour. These patterns generate a question, or hypothesis, which explains the observed behaviour or pattern. This explanation or conclusion is then applied to all other instances of the phenomena. This is referred to as **generalization**. In generalizing, the researcher is offering a theory or explanation of events and phenomena. This theory can then be tested and verified, or could be shown to be inaccurate and amended, or a new theory could be proposed to replace the incorrect one.

One example of inductive reasoning in economics might be the observation that countries experiencing rapid and accelerating inflation (hyperinflation) also seem to have central banks which print large sums of money. The pattern seems to be that rapid increases in the money supply are associated with instances of hyperinflation. If there was only one instance of this pattern, it may be that the researcher could not

generalization the act of formulating general concepts or explanations by inferring from specific instances of an event or behaviour generalize to all instances. If this pattern was observed and verified by the data in a number of instances, however, it may be possible to arrive at a general theory which posits that hyperinflation is caused by rapid increases in the money supply. Other instances of hyperinflation can then be monitored, the data analyzed and the theory confirmed or rejected, depending on the nature of the evidence which arises from additional instances of this phenomena.

Inductive reasoning is thus empirical in nature – it refers to evidence to confirm or reject theories. For this reason, inductive reasoning is seen as a benchmark for developing knowledge and understanding. One of the challenges facing social sciences like economics in using inductive reasoning is that conclusions and generalizations can be made based on partial or incomplete data.

Given the nature of human beings, this is a particular problem for economics. If we observe patterns of behaviour for tens of thousands of households in Ireland, for example, and draw a general conclusion and theory of this behaviour, can we safely assume that this also explains similar behaviour across Europe or indeed the world? Identifying patterns in data means that the data must be collected, be available for study and be reliably complete. This is not always possible. Looking at data for gross domestic product for different countries online, for example, often highlights differences in results from one source to another. This may be explained by the way in which the data is collected, how it is processed, who is gathering and analyzing the data, and the statistical processes used.

Experiments in Economics

Although economists use inductive reasoning like other scientists, they do face an obstacle that makes their task especially challenging. Physicists, for example, can set up controlled experiments such as the Large Hadron Collider, which is seeking to recreate conditions that existed milliseconds after the Big Bang. The experiments being conducted are designed to help confirm existing theories and/or develop new ones to explain forces and matter and how the universe began. By contrast, economists studying inflation are not allowed to manipulate a nation's monetary policy simply to generate useful data.

Economists pay close attention to the natural experiments offered by history. The Covid-19 pandemic led to considerable economic disruption, but some economists were able to look at the economic effects of previous pandemics to assess the type of effects that could be expected and for how long these might persist. For economic policymakers, this provides information on which to base policy decisions. Those policy decisions might be fraught with challenges but do need to be made. Throughout this book, therefore, we consider many historical episodes. These episodes are valuable to study because they give us insight into the economy of the past and, more importantly, they allow us to illustrate and evaluate economic theories of the present.

Despite the challenges faced by economists in conducting experiments, there are two major fields that are worthy of note. Experiments in economics can be conducted in a 'laboratory', where data can be collected via observations of individual or group behaviour through questionnaires and surveys, interviews and so on, or through the collection and analysis of data that exists such as wages, prices, stock prices, volumes of trades, unemployment levels, inflation and so on. The data can be analyzed in relation to a research question and conclusions drawn which help develop new understanding or refine and improve existing understanding. The conclusions drawn from such experiments may be generalizable; in other words, the findings of the experiment can be extended outside the 'laboratory' to explain behaviour or economic phenomena and provide the basis for prediction.

One example of how laboratory experiments can help change understanding is the work of people such as Daniel Kahneman, Amos Tversky, Richard Thaler and Cass Sunstein, whose research has helped to provide insights into judgement and decision-making and has offered a different perspective on the assumptions of rational decision-making. Thaler, the 2017 Nobel Prize winner in Economics, for example, conducted a number of experiments to explore how individuals respond when faced with different questions on losses and gains in relation to a reference point. He found that prior ownership of a good, for example a ticket to see a football game, altered people's willingness to sell, even at prices significantly higher than they had paid.

Thaler's observations on the consistency of this behaviour across a number of experiments led him to coin the term *'endowment effect'* to explain the behaviour. It is now widely accepted that the endowment effect does exist and that it runs counter to the assumptions of rational behaviour in economics. Thaler worked with Kahneman and Tversky and extended the theory to distinguish between goods which are held for trade and those which are held for use. The endowment effect, they suggested, was not universal; it was more powerful when goods were held for use.

A second type of experiment in economics is *natural experiments*. A natural experiment is one where the study of phenomena is determined by natural conditions which are not in the control of the experimenter. Natural experiments can be exploited when some change occurs which allows observation to be carried out on the effects of this change in one population, and comparisons made with another population that is not affected. For example, in 2021, a large container ship, the *Ever Given*, got stuck in the Suez Canal in Egypt. It caused a major disruption to shipping that used that waterway. This event gave rise to the opportunity for economists to ask questions about the effects of the incident and why some countries' trade was affected more than others.

Typically, natural experiments make use of the statistical tools of correlation and regression to determine whether there is any relationship between two or more variables, and if any such relationship exists, what the nature and strength of the relationship is. From such analysis, a model can be developed which can be used to predict.

At the heart of such analysis is the extent to which a relationship between two or more variables can be linked to cause and effect. Just because two variables appear to have some relationship does not necessarily imply cause and effect. For example, a researcher might find that an observation of graduates in the workforce shows that their incomes are generally higher than those of non-graduates. Can the researcher conclude that having a degree will lead to higher income? Possibly, but not necessarily. There might be other factors that have an effect on income apart from having a degree. Trying to build a model which takes into account these different factors is an important part of the value of natural experiments.

CASE STUDY

The Basic Income Experiment

It is sometimes said that economists cannot conduct major experiments by intervening in economies, but it is possible to do so. One example is the idea of a universal basic income (UBI) where individuals receive a sum of money deemed sufficient to cover basic needs. Pilot programmes on UBI have been introduced in Wales, in Jarrow and East Finchley in England and in Finland. A two-year pilot was introduced in Finland in January 2017 to investigate the effect of the introduction of a basic income scheme. Some 2,000 participants were chosen at random to take part in the experiment. Other countries have also conducted small-scale experiments with a basic income, including Brazil, the Netherlands, Spain and South Korea.

The hypothesis being investigated was whether giving the unemployed a guaranteed basic income had an impact on mental and physical well-being and on their employment prospects. The income amount was the same for every individual regardless of their background or position and was paid periodically, for example every month. Unlike many unemployment insurance schemes, receiving basic income was not dependent on the individuals having to demonstrate that they were seeking employment. If an individual received a guaranteed basic income, would this help alleviate poverty and inequality, and encourage individuals to find work?

A number of similar experiments are in operation related to basic income. In Canada, for example, a basic income experiment was introduced in June 2017 in two cities and a town in Ontario. Two groups of people were selected. One group received a basic annual income of up to CDN$17,000 (around €11,100) and the other group received nothing. In the Canada experiment, the participants must be on a low income and, for those getting the basic income, if they find work their basic income is reduced by half.

Barcelona launched a basic income experiment in October 2017 which, like the Finland experiment, involved 2,000 participants, half of whom received between €400 and €525 per month over a two-year period. Unlike the Finland experiment, in Barcelona the money was given to households, not individuals, and those receiving the money were required to give something back in the form of attending support programmes to help them find work, as well as other community-based programmes.

In Finland, the 2,000 unemployed participants received €560 per month as a basic income. By having this guaranteed sum, the hypothesis was that individuals would likely be more flexible in seeking work, moving between jobs and taking part in the gig economy with all its potential uncertainties

(*Continued*)

The results of the experiment on the initial 2,000 participants were published in 2020. One of the arguments against a basic income is that if you give people money but do not insist they be actively looking for work (which is invariably the basis of unemployment insurance schemes), people will just get lazy and lose the incentive to find work. The results of the Finnish experiment seemed to reject this hypothesis. The Finnish experiment found that there was a small, but positive, impact on employment in the control group and that there was an improvement in the reported life satisfaction among the target group compared to a control group. The results of the experiment seemed to offer other beneficial outcomes, referred to as 'positive feedback loops', where incremental benefits can be magnified.

One of the challenges that was made clear in the Finnish experiment was the difficulties and complexities of the design of such polices. Wales, for example, announced early on that it would not be continuing the pilot when its term ended in 2025 because of the cost, despite initial suggestions of positive outcomes. However, experiments like this, and others, can help to improve knowledge and understanding of such phenomena and the extent to which the policies can be generalized.

If an individual receives a guaranteed basic income, would this help alleviate poverty and inequality, and encourage individuals to find work?

Questions:

1 Do you think the basic income experiment in Finland used a deductive or inductive approach? Explain.
2 How might the experimenters have assessed the degree of cause and effect given the results of the experiment in Finland?
3 Where do you think the hypothesis that giving people money reduces the incentive to find work arose from? Is the evidence from the Finland experiment sufficient to reject this hypothesis?

Theories

Theories can be used to explain something and to make predictions. The theory of indifference curves and budget lines can be used to explain consumer behaviour. The value of this theory is how reliable it is in predicting consumer behaviour. If we observe the way consumers behave and the outcomes predicted do not conform to the theory, it may be that new research must be conducted to offer refinements to the theory, or even that the theory needs to be consigned to history.

One of the criticisms of economics is that some theories commonly taught on undergraduate courses have been derived through deductive reasoning, but that the premises used as the basis for the conclusions drawn are inaccurate, or just wrong, and not supported by data and evidence. For example, the neo-classical theory of consumer behaviour makes assumptions that consumers act rationally, prefer more to less and make purchasing decisions based on pure self-interest. The premises for the theory were developed in the nineteenth century when the economy and society were very different. The historical context of many theories in economics should not be ignored.

Critics argue that these assumptions are not supported by evidence and data, and thus any predictions arising from such theories are unreliable or wrong. Supporters of such theories argue that they do contain useful insights into behaviour that allow valid predictions to be made. While they may not explain human behaviour in every instance, they still have some value. Models, they argue, are after all simplifications of reality and cannot hope to replicate every aspect of human behaviour.

Falsifiability

As hinted at earlier, one of the criticisms of economics in recent years has been that while it claims to be a science, it does not follow scientific principles, or at least only does so when it deems it convenient. In particular, critics have argued that many of the theories we will present in this book are no longer accurate and should be dismissed. Despite this – and critics would argue that this book is one of many that perpetuate the problem – these theories continue to form the basis for many undergraduate economics courses. Why do we continue to teach theories which are inaccurate or just wrong? Critics would argue that including these theories in an economics course is like physics courses continuing to teach a theory of the aether, a historical theory that 'space' was filled with some invisible substance which has subsequently been shown to be wrong.

In considering these debates, we can refer to the philosophy of science and one of its foremost exponents, Sir Karl Popper. Popper was born in Vienna in 1902 and in 1946 moved to the UK to teach at the London School of Economics. He was knighted in 1965, and his contribution to the philosophy of science was extensive and highly regarded.

One of Popper's important contributions was the principle of **falsifiability**. Popper based the idea on the fundamental assumption that it is not possible to know the truth of everything. Ideas and theories might be widely accepted and adopted, but ultimately, we cannot be 100 per cent sure that these ideas and theories are correct. Knowledge is always subject to evolution and development, and in the light of new evidence, our theories and ideas may change.

falsifiability the possibility of a theory being rejected as a result of the new observations or new data

Popper argued that it is not possible to prove beyond all doubt that a theory is 'true', but what is possible is that a theory can be proved as false. New evidence can arise, be discovered or produced that can prove a theory is false. Popper further argued that inductive reasoning is flawed because we cannot claim to know 'truth' from what invariably is limited observation. Just because we observe many instances of a phenomenon or behaviour does not mean that we can generalize to all instances of that phenomenon or behaviour. The famous example cited by Popper to exemplify this is that of the 'black swan'. An observer could record many thousands of instances of white swans and generalize that 'all swans are white'. However, it is not possible to make this conclusion, since not all swans have been observed. If one person subsequently observed a black swan, then the theory that all swans are white can be declared false.

Popper's view was that 'good' science should be based around the idea of falsifying theories rather than attempting to prove theories. The researcher should make it clear in their findings the conditions under which the theory being proposed can be falsified. This approach means that researchers who seek to defend a theory and find ways of proving it is true, even in the face of evidence to the contrary, are not adhering to the fundamentals of scientific method. A general principle behind scientific method, therefore, is that it should be possible to falsify a theory, and 'good science' should be centred on this and not on seeking to prove existing theories.

This debate is particularly relevant to economics because of the criticism that the subject has faced, particularly since the 2007–9 Financial Crisis. You may well find that some of your lecturers are fierce defendants of particular theories, or at the very least will seek to find ways in which a theory, or elements of a theory, can be adjusted or explained in the light of evidence which may suggest the theory is false. As you continue your studies, it is important to keep in mind the discussion in this section about the way we discover and verify new theories, knowledge and understanding about the subject.

Economics is a dynamic subject and the detailed research that many economists continue to undertake might hide the depth to which many take the criticisms of the subject. Popular criticism of the subject can be just that – an attempt to appeal to everyone, while many of us will confess to having little or no understanding of exactly what economists do, how they research the subject or the controls they put in place to improve the quality of the research and outcomes. It is worth bearing in mind that the modelling method allows economists to approach issues, research them, think about them and attempt to uncover new knowledge and understanding. This is not the same thing as saying the models themselves, whatever they be, are final truths and are more important than the method.

While this book will include many theories which have been the focus of some criticism, they are important in understanding the historical development of economics and how we have come to know what we know. However, it is also important to recognize that there is still much we do not know and much to be discovered. Economists know this.

Keeping an Open Mind Understanding the processes and debates around scientific method, as well as economic theories and their limitations, helps generate more questions and the search for better ways in which we can understand the economy and human behaviour. All we ask is that you keep an open mind and recognize that there can be some truths hidden in theories, even if they are not the full truths, and these theories and the discipline as a whole are subject to ongoing evolution. Economics is *a way of approaching problems and issues* rather than a set of definitive truths. The debate about how economists come to know things and present theories and models which claim to be predictive is one which continues to pervade the discipline.

The Cambridge economist Joan Robinson perhaps captured the debate very well when she wrote economics 'limps along with one foot in untested hypotheses and the other in untestable slogans ... our task is to sort out as best we may, this mixture of ideology and science' (Robinson, J. (1968) *Economic Philosophy*. Pelican).

As noted earlier, separating out cause and effect can be problematic. Observation and experience can lead to the identification of phenomena occurring which intuition would seem to suggest are related in some way. Empirical research can help provide a conclusion which provides an answer, for example whether a rise in the money supply does cause a rise in the price level. The questions which must be asked are: how do we know this 'answer' is correct? What are the factors that influence the price level? How significant is the role of the money supply in determining the price level? How was the research conducted, and what 'facts' and assumptions were used in carrying out the research and building the model? Can these facts and assumptions be accepted as an accurate representation of the 'truth', or are there interpretations of both which might impact on the conclusions drawn?

If facts and assumptions are accepted, then we must presume that those who collected them did so in an unbiased and unprejudiced way and that they were professionally competent and had sufficient expertise to be able to do so in a way we can trust. Separating out cause and effect can be informed by statistical tests but is also subject to interpretation. It is not always easy to establish cause and effect, particularly when controlled experiments are not possible, and this characterizes much of economics.

The Role of Assumptions

If you ask a physicist how long it would take for a cannonball to fall from the top of the Leaning Tower of Pisa, they would probably answer the question by assuming that the cannonball falls in a vacuum. This assumption is false; the building is surrounded by air, which exerts friction on the falling cannonball and slows it down. Yet the physicist will point out that friction on the cannonball is so small in relation to its weight or mass that its effect is negligible. Assuming the cannonball falls in a vacuum greatly simplifies the problem without substantially affecting the answer.

Economists make assumptions for the same reason: assumptions can simplify the complex world and make it easier to understand. To study the effects of international trade, for example, we may assume that the world consists of only two countries and that each country produces only two goods. The real world consists of dozens of countries, each of which produces thousands of different types of goods, but by assuming two countries and two goods, we can focus our thinking. Once we understand international trade in an imaginary world with two countries and two goods, we are in a better position to understand international trade in the more complex world in which we live.

The art in scientific thinking is deciding which assumptions to make. Suppose, for instance, that we were dropping a beach ball rather than a cannonball from the top of the building. Our physicist would realize that the assumption of no friction is far less accurate in this case: friction exerts a greater force on a beach ball than on a cannonball because a beach ball is much larger and lighter, so the effects of air friction may not be negligible relative to the weight of the ball because it is so light. The assumption that gravity works in a vacuum may, therefore, be reasonable for studying a falling cannonball but not for studying a falling beach ball.

Similarly, economists use different assumptions to answer different questions. Most economic issues will be affected by a number of different factors. If we try to model the issue taking into account all these factors, the complexity might lead to outcomes which do not help in developing an understanding of economic phenomena. In researching a phenomenon, economists may look at what happens when one factor changes, but all other factors assumed to have an effect are held constant. This is a core feature of neo-classical economic methodology. It might be assumed that the amount consumers wish to purchase is affected by the price of the good concerned, income, tastes and the prices of other related goods. Our understanding of consumer behaviour is simplified if we look at the effect on demand of a change in income and hold all other factors constant. This can be repeated with the other factors to generate some general principles about the demand for goods and services.

Assumptions must be tested to see the extent to which they are accurate and reasonable in the same way that it is deemed reasonable by the physicist to drop the assumption of friction when considering the effect of dropping a cannonball from the Leaning Tower of Pisa.

Fake News

The term 'fake news' has become widely used in recent years. One of the benefits of technology is that it provides access to more information than humans have perhaps ever experienced. One of the disadvantages, however, is that we need to be able to view the information we receive critically and to not accept everything we are told, read or watch without question. Fake news refers to stories or information presented as fact, the deliberate spreading of false information or distortions of stories designed to deceive. Often, fake news is spread by people who have not critically assessed the facts and is passed on via social media to (often) thousands or millions of others who in turn may not critically process the information.

Seeking to distinguish between fact and opinion has always been an important skill and thinking like an economist can help in this process and to get into the habit of questioning what we see, hear and read. Economic news and data are cited and quoted almost daily and are particularly pertinent during election campaigns, for example, where the electorate is bombarded with sometimes contradictory information, claims and data. A study by Assenza *et al.* (2024) analyzed a series of fake news items in the United States between 2007 and 2022 and found that it can lead to increased macroeconomic uncertainty, make unemployment worse and lead to reduced industrial production (Assenza, T., Collard, F., Feve, P. and Huber, S. (2024) *From Buzz to Bust: How Fake News Shapes the Business Cycle*. London: CEPR. Available at cepr.org/voxeu/columns/buzz-bust-how-fake-news-shapes-business-cycle, accessed 30 May 2025). Adopting an objective approach to information and adopting the principles covered in this section on economic methodology can help to identify instances of fake news and also reduce the negative effects that fake news can generate.

SCHOOLS OF THOUGHT

Given our preceding discussion on economic methodology, it might come as no surprise that there are different approaches to economics, and different perspectives.

These may be informed by assumptions and belief systems which influence the way issues are looked at, and the outcomes and policy implications which arise as a result. For example, in the latter part of the 1930s, the thinking about government involvement in the macroeconomy changed as a result of the ideas of John Maynard Keynes. 'Keynesian' economics became a dominant school of thought throughout the post-war period in a number of countries. We will look at the ideas of Keynes later in the book. Perhaps the dominant methodology is the *neo-classical* approach, which is sometimes referred to as 'mainstream economics'.

Neo-classical Economics

The neo-classical approach takes the view that the market is a central feature in generating well-being and in answering the three questions all societies have to face, which we looked at in the previous chapter. In analyzing markets and outcomes, the neo-classical approach assumes that decisions are based on rationality, that economic agents act out of self-interest and are autonomous. The neo-classical approach models behaviour through constrained optimization problems. This means that it is assumed economic agents seek to maximize or minimize outcomes but are subject to constraints. Individuals seek to maximize utility (the satisfaction derived from consumption) subject to the constraint of their income. Firms seek to minimize costs subject to the constraint of resources available and the price of those resources.

Critics of this approach argue that the assumptions are flawed, and that what is observed about human behaviour does not conform to the neo-classical view. They argue that such is the power of the neo-classical hold on economics that other views, so-called heterodox economics (where the term 'heterodox' means views at odds with the mainstream), find it hard to gain any ground. These differing views include feminist economics, Marxist economics and the Austrian school.

Feminist Economics

Feminist economics questions many of the assumptions of the neo-classical school. Economic well-being, they argue, is not simply provided through market exchange but also includes unpaid work carried out in the home. This housework, by both males and females, needs to have the recognition its significance to well-being deserves. Economic activity, therefore, needs to include a valuation of this unpaid work.

Feminist economists also research into other areas where there are gender and social inequalities, and they would argue that it is not possible to have value-free analysis and research into economic issues. For example, the idea that humans face a trade-off between work and leisure is misleading in that 'leisure' is associated with pleasurable activities which people choose to take part in. For many women, 'non-work' activity, that is work that is not paid, is not leisure at all and involves considerable work in caring for the home and family. To only assume that 'work' is valuable betrays a value judgement which relegates analysis of unpaid work below that of paid work.

Marxist Economics

Much of the analysis will be derived from the neo-classical approach, but there are other explanations for how markets and firms work. Marxist economics presents different explanations for essentially the same phenomena and has developed from the work of Karl Marx in the nineteenth century. Marx sought to analyze and understand the capitalist system and explain how and why production takes place and the circumstances under which different groups in society have economic power.

Marxist economics views firms and markets not as entities but as collections of humans, and it is these humans who make decisions. Some humans have control over the means of production and can exploit that power in ways which lead to different outcomes and which drive dynamism in economies. This dynamism can be self-destructive, however, and the competition between capitalists to attempt to retain control over the means of production is partly what generates booms and busts in capitalist economies. Neo-classical economists propose different explanations for the swings in the business cycle.

The Austrian School

The Austrian school originated in work carried out at the University of Vienna in the latter part of the nineteenth century. Academics at Vienna were of the belief that economic well-being is maximized when markets are allowed to do their work and that the government should have a minimal role in the economy (referred to as 'laissez-faire' roughly translated as 'to leave', or 'let it be'). Individual liberty is a fundamental principle in Austrian school economics.

The Austrian school is now not based in Vienna but has adherents in different parts of the world. Key figures in the Austrian school include Carl Menger, Eugen Böhm-Bawerk, Friedrich Weiser, Ludwig von Mises and Friedrich August von Hayek. Other influential economists such as the 1991 Nobel Prize winner in Economics, Ronald Coase, were said to have been influenced by the Austrian school (Coase was at the London School of Economics when Hayek was on the faculty and acknowledged the impact he made).

Austrian school economists look at the explanation for business cycles in the supply side of the economy rather than focusing on demand. Excess supply is what drives the economy into recession and this, in turn, can be caused by interest rates being too low, leading to too much investment and the availability of cheap money. It is this that triggers inflation. For Austrian economists, therefore, inflation is not the main problem or focus of policy; inflation is a symptom of imbalances in the financial sector of the economy. Economists from the Austrian school had been warning of too low interest rates and too high debt levels for many years in the early part of the twenty-first century and there are those who argue that it was these economists who correctly predicted the 2007–9 Financial Crisis and not mainstream economists. Critics of the Austrian school argue that it relies on narrative analysis rather than mathematical, statistical and empirical analysis, and so their claims cannot be tested and verified.

THE ECONOMIST AS POLICY ADVISOR

Often economists are asked to explain the causes of economic events and recommend policies to improve economic outcomes. Why, for example, is unemployment higher for teenagers than older workers and, given this situation, what should the government do to improve the economic well-being of teenagers? These two roles lead to important distinctions in the way in which we need to view statements and analysis. To answer the first question, the economist might use scientific method to offer an explanation, but the second involves a value judgement. This highlights the distinction between what are termed positive economics and normative economics.

Positive versus Normative Analysis

Suppose that two people are discussing minimum wage laws.

Pascale: *Minimum wage laws cause unemployment.*

Sophie: *The government should raise the minimum wage.*

Pascale's statement is making a claim about how the world works. Sophie is making a value judgement about a change she would like to see implemented.

Pascale's statement is referred to as a positive statement. **Positive statements** have the property that the claims in them can be tested and confirmed, refuted or shown to not be provable either way. It would be possible to conduct research to show whether there is any correlation between the imposition of minimum wage laws and a rise in unemployment. A positive statement does not have to be true – it is possible that the research might conclude that there is no link between minimum wages and unemployment.

positive statements claims that attempt to describe the world as it is

Sophie's is said to be normative. **Normative statements** have the property that they include opinion and make a claim about how the world ought to be; it is not possible to test opinions and confirm or reject them.

normative statements claims that attempt to prescribe how the world should be

Positive analysis incorporates the use of scientific methodology to arrive at conclusions which can be tested. Normative analysis is the process of making recommendations about particular policies or courses of action. It is perfectly possible to conduct both positive and normative analysis. For example, the statement: *the government should reduce the deficit as this will benefit the economy*, contains a normative statement – an opinion that the government ought to reduce the deficit. It also includes a positive statement: *a reduction in the government deficit will benefit the economy*, which is capable of being tested.

A key difference between positive and normative statements, therefore, is how we judge their validity. Deciding what is good or bad policy is not merely a matter of science; it also involves our views on ethics, religion and political philosophy.

Of course, positive and normative statements may be related. Our positive views about how the world works affect our normative views about what policies are desirable. Pascale's claim that the minimum wage causes unemployment, if true, might lead us to reject Sophie's conclusion that the government should raise the minimum wage.

WHY ECONOMISTS DISAGREE

If economics is classed as a science and adheres to scientific methods, why does there appear to be considerable disagreement among economists surrounding many different policy initiatives? There are two basic reasons:

- Economists may disagree about the validity of alternative positive theories about how the world works.
- Economists may have different values and, therefore, different normative views about what policy should try to accomplish.

Let us discuss each of these reasons.

Differences in Scientific Judgements

History shows us that there have always been disagreements between scientists about 'truth' and reality. In 1964, for example, Peter Higgs at the University of Edinburgh had his original paper on the theoretical model predicting what came to be known as the Higgs Boson, rejected by the journal *Physics Lectures,* which saw the theory as having 'little relevance to physics'. In 2012, the experiments at Cern in Switzerland confirmed the existence of the Higgs Boson, and in 2013, Professor Higgs was jointly awarded the Nobel Prize for Physics. Science is a search for understanding about the world around us. It is not surprising that as the search continues, scientists can disagree about the direction in which 'truth' lies.

Economists often disagree for the same reason. Economics is a young science, and there is still much to be learned. Indeed, there are some who argue that economics can never be a true 'science' because processes that are considered appropriate and necessary in natural sciences cannot be applied to economics because it deals with human behaviour. Humans cannot be subjected to the same controls and comparisons that can be used in physics, for example.

Economists sometimes disagree because they have different beliefs about the validity of alternative theories or about the size of important parameters. For example, economists disagree about whether the government should levy taxes based on a household's income or based on its consumption (spending). Advocates of a switch from an income tax to a consumption tax believe that the change would encourage households to save more, because income that is saved would not be taxed. Higher saving, in turn, would lead to more rapid growth in productivity and living standards. Advocates of an income tax system believe that household saving would not respond much to a change in the tax laws. These two groups of economists hold different normative views about the tax system because they have different positive views about the responsiveness of saving to tax incentives.

SELF TEST 'Sometimes, theories are worth defending. The experience of Peter Higgs is testament to this view.' Comment on this statement in relation to theories in economics and the principle of falsifiability.

Differences in Values

Anneka and Henrik both take water from the town well. To pay for maintaining the well, the town imposes a property tax on its residents. Anneka lives in a large house worth €2 million and pays a property tax of €10,000 a year. Henrik owns a small cottage worth €20,000 and pays a property tax of €1,000 a year.

Is this policy fair? If not, who pays too much and who pays too little? Would it be better to replace the tax based on the value of the property with a tax that was just a single payment from everyone living in the town (a poll tax) in return for using the well – say, €1,000 a year? After all, Anneka lives on her own and uses much less water than Henrik and the other four members of his family who live with him and use more water as a result. Would that be a fairer policy?

This raises two interesting questions in economics – how do we define words like 'fair' and 'unfair', and who holds the power to influence and make decisions? If the power is in the hands of certain groups in government or powerful businesses, policies may be adopted even if they are widely perceived as being 'unfair'.

What about replacing the property tax not with a poll tax but with an income tax? Anneka has an income of €100,000 a year so that a 5 per cent income tax would present her with a tax bill of €5,000. Henrik, on the other hand, has an income of only €10,000 a year and so would pay only €500 a year in tax, and the members of his family who do not work would not pay any income tax. Does it matter whether Henrik's low income is due to his decision not to go to university and take a low paid job? Would it matter if it were due to a physical disability? Does it matter whether Anneka's high income is due to a large inheritance from her family? What if it were due to her willingness to work long hours at a dreary job?

These are difficult questions on which people are likely to disagree. If the town hired two experts to study how the town should tax its residents to pay for the well, we should not be surprised if they offered conflicting advice.

This simple example shows why economists sometimes disagree about public policy. As we learned earlier in our discussion of normative and positive analysis, policies cannot be judged on scientific grounds alone. Economists give conflicting advice sometimes because they have different values.

SELF TEST Why might economic advisors to a government disagree about a question of policy such as reducing a budget deficit?

Decision-Making in Economics

It could be said that economics is the science of decision-making. The way that economists go about making or recommending decisions involves, first, identifying the problem or issue. For example, greenhouse gas emissions are a contributory factor in climate change. Note that this is a premise which is assumed to be true. One answer to this problem is a decision to cut the emissions of greenhouse gases. The next stage is to look at the costs and benefits involved in the decision. These costs and benefits are not just the private costs and benefits to individuals, firms and organizations; they will also include the costs and benefits to third parties who are not directly involved in the actual decision. For example, cutting greenhouse gas emissions means that resources will have to be diverted to new ways of production or different ways of producing energy. The private costs will be those borne by the businesses that will have to implement measures to adhere to the limits placed upon them. The social costs might include the impact on local people of the construction of wind farms or new nuclear power stations.

Having identified the costs and benefits, the economist then seeks to place a value on them to get some idea of the relationship between the costs and benefits of making the decision. In some cases, valuing costs and benefits can be easy, but many are much more challenging. The loss of visual amenity for a resident living near a wind turbine or the value of the possible loss of life from a nuclear catastrophe at a power plant, for example, may be very difficult to value. Economists have attempted to devise ways in which these values can be estimated, but they are not perfect.

Once the sum of the costs and benefits is calculated, the decision then becomes clearer. If the cost outweighs the benefit then making the decision may be unwise, but if the costs are less than the benefits, then it may mean the decision can be supported. Policymakers may want to look at the *extent* to which the costs outweigh the benefit, or the benefit outweighs the costs. Every day millions of decisions are made by individuals, businesses and governments. Can we safely assume that decision-makers compute the value of the costs and benefits of a decision to enable them to make an informed decision? While not every one of these decisions will be made using the exact processes outlined above, and many of us certainly do not stop to think about how we rationalize our decisions, nevertheless our brains do engage in computational processes as we make decisions, but they are mostly subconscious. Economists and psychologists are increasingly finding out more about how humans make decisions, which is helping improve our understanding of the models which we use to analyze consumer behaviour.

SUMMARY

- Economics is characterized by different methodologies and approaches, including neo-classical, feminist, Marxist and Austrian.
- There is a debate about whether economics is a 'science'. It does follow certain scientific methodologies, but it must be accepted that economists are working with human behaviour.
- Economists make assumptions and build simplified models to understand the world around them. Economists increasingly use empirical methods to develop and test hypotheses.
- Economists must try to distinguish between cause and effect, and this is not always easy to do.
- Research can be conducted by using inductive and deductive reasoning – no one way is the 'right way'.
- Economists develop theories which can be used to explain phenomena and make predictions.
- The principle of falsifiability is based on the assumption that we cannot know everything for sure and, as a result, researchers should clarify the conditions under which a theory can be proved false.
- Using theory and observation is part of scientific method, but economists must always remember that they are studying human beings and humans do not always behave in consistent or rational ways.
- Economists can conduct experiments in laboratory settings and use 'natural experiments' observing outcomes from changes in policy or when events occur.
- A positive statement is an assertion about how the world *is*. A normative statement is an assertion about how the world *ought to be*.
- Economists who advise policymakers offer conflicting advice either because of differences in scientific judgements or because of differences in values. At other times, economists are united in the advice they offer, but policymakers may choose to ignore it.
- Decision-making in economics can be made more informed by assessing the costs and benefits of a decision and attempting to quantify the costs and benefits to provide the basis for an informed decision.

IN THE NEWS

Tribal Economics

The debate about economics as a profession, about the use and value of models and the differences of opinion that the subject generates, continues to flourish. In January 2024 at the prestigious World Economic Forum in Davos, the President of the European Central Bank (ECB), Christine Lagarde, created some news headlines when she appeared to criticize the economics profession in a speech at an event entitled 'How to Trust Economics'. Lagarde is not a trained economist but a lawyer. She has, however, held several positions associated with economics as part of the French government and at the International Monetary Fund (IMF). Her leadership of the ECB has been criticized in some quarters with some reports suggesting the fact she is not a trained economist puts her at a disadvantage in running the ECB.

At Davos, Lagarde was quoted as saying, 'Many economists are actually a tribal clique ... [They] are among the most tribal scientists that you can think of. They quote each other. They don't go beyond that world. They feel comfortable in that world. And maybe models have something to do with it ... If we had more consultations with epidemiologists, if we had climate change scientists to help us with what's coming up, if we were consulting a bit better with geologists, for instance, to properly appreciate what rare earths and resources are out there, I think we would be in a better position to actually understand these developments, project better and be better economists.'

Lagarde was not alone in her criticism of economic models, particularly those used for forecasting. Maria Demertzis, a former Senior Fellow at Bruegel, a think tank, and part-time Professor of Economic Policy at the Florence School

(Continued)

of Transnational Governance at the European University Institute, speaking about the ECB's macroeconomic forecasting said, 'If you look at the track record of forecasting, it's abysmal. The fact that inflation returns to [below 2%] in two years' time is by construction. The models that they use force it to return to equilibrium and inflation to 2% in two years' time.'

The pandemic led to a change in behaviours of many people and some industries and firms experienced the benefits of these changed behaviours.

Critical Thinking Questions

1 Why do you think that it is important to 'trust' economics and economists? What does 'trust' mean in this respect?
2 Do you think it is important that the leader of a major institution like the ECB be a trained economist? Justify your reasoning.
3 What is wrong with being 'tribal scientists'? Are not scientists from all disciplines essentially 'tribal'?
4 Comment on the view that consulting with a wider range of professions and disciplines would improve economics.
5 Why do you think that Demertzis suggests that forecasting is 'abysmal' and what point do you think she is making in saying that the models used 'force inflation to return to equilibrium'?

Reference:

www.euractiv.com/section/economy-jobs/news/a-tribal-clique-lagarde-denounces-economists-at-davos/, accessed 14 July 2025.

QUESTIONS FOR REVIEW

1 How is economics like a science?
2 Why do economists make assumptions?
3 Should an economic model describe reality exactly?
4 What is meant by empirical study in economics?
5 Using an example, explain the difference between inductive and deductive reasoning.
6 Should economic theories be developed as a result of observation or before observation? Explain.
7 What is the difference between a positive and a normative statement? Give an example of each.
8 Why do differences in values lead to disagreements among economists?
9 Using an example, explain the difference between an endogenous and an exogenous variable.
10 Why do economists sometimes offer conflicting advice to policymakers?

PROBLEMS AND APPLICATIONS

1 Terms like 'investment', 'capital', 'interest', 'price' and 'cost' have different meanings in economics than they do in normal everyday usage. Find out what the differences are and explain why economists might have developed these different meanings.

2 One common assumption in economics is that the products of different firms in the same industry are indistinguishable. For each of the following industries, discuss whether this is a reasonable assumption:
   a. steel
   b. novels
   c. wheat
   d. fast food
   e. mobile phones (think carefully about this one)
   f. hairdressers.

3 A researcher in a university notices that the price of flights to holiday destinations tends to be much higher outside semester dates. They formulate a theory to explain this phenomenon. Has the researcher arrived at the theory by induction or deduction? What steps might the researcher take to apply scientific method to test the theory?

4 A politician makes a speech which is critical of the government's immigration policy, saying that it is too loose and encourages too many people to enter the country and take jobs away from local people. How might an economist go about assessing the validity of the politician's comments?

5 If models are not capable of representing the real world in any detail and rely too much on assumptions, then what value can they be?

6 Does the fact that there are different schools of thought in economics reduce its validity as an academic discipline?

7 Rival political groups argue about the value and effectiveness of speed cameras as a means of influencing driver behaviour and improving safety on the roads. An economist is asked to conduct research into the costs and benefits of speed cameras to help decision-making. What sort of factors will the economist have to take into consideration in such research, and what might be the challenges in identifying and quantifying the full range of costs and benefits?

8 If you were prime minister or president, would you be more interested in your economic advisors' positive views or their normative views? Why?

9 Would you expect economists to disagree less about public policy as time goes on? Why or why not? Can their differences be completely eliminated? Why or why not?

10 Consider a theory which states that an increase in interest rates will lead to an increase in savings. How would the principle of *ceteris paribus* be important in investigating the predictive power of this theory?

3 THE MARKET FORCES OF SUPPLY AND DEMAND

This chapter introduces the theory of supply and demand. It considers how buyers and sellers behave and how they interact with one another. It shows how prices act as a signal to both buyers and sellers to help them make decisions, which in turn contributes to the allocation of the economy's scarce resources. The model of the market based on supply and demand, like any other model, is based on a series of assumptions. These assumptions have been criticized on the basis that they are not reflective of reality and as a result the predictive power of the model is limited.

Others have argued that the model is sufficiently representative to have value and provides a useful benchmark for comparison with how many markets behave. At the very least, the model provides a framework to help shape thinking about how economic agents interact. Many undergraduate principles of economics modules will include the model of supply and demand as a central part of the microeconomics course and this chapter will cover this area. As we progress through the chapter and the analysis it is important to bear in mind the assumptions of the model.

THE ASSUMPTIONS OF THE COMPETITIVE MARKET MODEL

The terms *supply* and *demand* refer to the behaviour of people as they interact with one another in markets. A **market** is a group of buyers and sellers of a particular good or service. The buyers as a group determine the demand for the product and the sellers as a group determine the supply of the product.

market a group of buyers and sellers of a particular good or service

The market model represents a neo-classical explanation of how resources are allocated. This analysis was developed in the nineteenth century and follows on from the work of Adam Smith. One of the fundamental outcomes of the market model is that, if the assumptions hold, the resulting allocation of resources will be 'efficient'. What this means is that the price buyers pay for goods in the market is a reflection of the value (or utility) they get from acquiring the goods. In addition, the price producers receive is a reflection of the cost of production including an element of profit which is sufficient to keep them in that line of production. If consumers and producers are both maximizing benefits and minimizing costs, it is assumed that society must be maximizing welfare, because the goods and services produced are those which are most desirable and in demand.

The competitive model of supply and demand which leads to this 'efficient' outcome is based on the following assumptions:

1. There are many buyers and sellers in the market.
2. No individual buyer or seller is big enough or has the power to be able to influence price.
3. There is freedom of entry into and exit from the market.
4. Goods produced are homogenous (identical).

5. Buyers and sellers act independently and only consider their own position in making decisions.
6. There are clearly defined property rights, which means that producers and consumers consider all costs and benefits when making decisions.

You will find there are economists who believe that markets are the most effective way we have yet discovered to allocate scarce resources. This further implies that government intervention in markets should be kept to a minimum. There are others who say that the model is so flawed that there is a much bigger role for government to play in the economy. This diversity of opinion among economists was considered in the last chapter. Awareness of the difference between positive and normative economics is important in distinguishing the belief systems on which particular views are based and whether the outcomes claimed are testable.

Part of thinking as an economist is in teasing out the subtle (and sometimes not so subtle) belief systems and value judgements underlying statements and being prepared to subject such statements to critique and analysis. The market model has been criticized for just this point because it is based on a number of value judgements. Consumers attempting to maximize utility include an assumption that more is preferred to less and that this is desirable. Producers seeking to maximize profit will attempt to produce an output that minimizes cost and reduces waste to a minimum, and that this is also desirable. Whether these are indeed desirable is subject to considerable debate and they are essentially normative value judgements.

Competitive Markets

Competition exists when two or more firms are rivals for customers. In economics, however, in a **competitive market** (the terms *perfectly competitive market* or *perfect competition* are synonymous with *competitive market*) the assumptions outlined above lead to some important conclusions. Because there are many buyers and sellers in a perfectly competitive market, neither has any power to influence price. They must accept the price the market determines and they are said to be *price-takers*. Each seller has no control over the price, because other sellers are offering identical products. In addition, each seller only supplies a very small amount in relation to the total supply of the market.

> **competitive market** a market in which there are many buyers and sellers so that each has a negligible impact on the market price

Because products are homogenous, a seller has little reason to charge less than the going price. If they charge more, buyers will make their purchases elsewhere. Similarly, no single buyer can influence the price because each buyer purchases only a small amount relative to the size of the market. Buyers make their decisions based on the utility (or satisfaction) they gain from consumption. In so doing they are independent of the decisions of suppliers. Buyers and sellers make decisions independently and goods are homogenous. This implies that there is no need for advertising or branding and that both producers and consumers consider all costs and benefits, including the costs and benefits which may affect a third party, when making decisions. For example, producers will consider the costs to society of the pollution they create in production.

There are some markets in which the assumption of perfect competition applies to a degree. For example, consider the market for rapeseed oil, which is part of the market for agricultural products. Production of rapeseed oil across the European Union (EU) was around 30 million tonnes in 2024. Rapeseed is part of a global oil seed market which includes the production of soya beans, which account for around 61 per cent of total oil seed production (Source of data: Oilseeds and Protein Crops market situation, 30 May 2024, European Commission). In the EU agricultural market, there are about 9.1 million farms employing around 8.6 million people, although if counting part-time and seasonal workers, this figure is nearer to 17 million. No single seller can influence the price of agricultural products. Therefore each takes the market price as given and it is assumed that they can sell all their output at the market price (remember that the total output of individual sellers represents only a small fraction of total output).

The products produced in agricultural markets are broadly similar. Milk produced by one farmer is not that much different from that produced by another. It is important to remember, however, that even in markets where products might be perceived as being homogenous, there are differences in quality and use. For example, wheat can be produced at different qualities with some going for animal feed and some for bread making.

The characteristics of agricultural markets make them useful for using as examples in describing competitive markets. As we proceed to look in more depth at the market model, let us keep in mind a particular good, milk, to help focus our thinking. The market for milk fulfils many of the characteristics of a perfectly competitive market: milk is fairly homogenous, there are about 460,000 dairy farms and there are millions of buyers of milk across the EU.

SELF TEST What constitutes a market? List the main characteristics of a competitive market.

DEMAND

We begin our study of markets by examining the demand for goods and services.

The Demand Curve: The Relationship Between Price and Quantity Demanded

The **quantity demanded** of any good is the amount of the good that buyers are willing and able to purchase at different prices. Many things determine the quantity demanded of any good, but one determinant plays a central role: the price of the good. If the price of milk rose from €0.50 per litre to €0.75 per litre, less milk would be bought. If the price of milk fell to €0.35 per litre, more milk would be bought. Because the quantity demanded falls as the price rises and rises as the price falls, we say that the quantity demanded is *negatively or inversely related* to the price. This relationship between price and quantity demanded is referred to as the **law of demand**. It is called a 'law' because the relationship is observed so often in the economy. The label 'law' dates from the observations made in the eighteenth and nineteenth centuries. Alfred Marshall, in his 1890 work *Principles of Economics*, noted:

> *There is then one general law of demand: The greater the amount to be sold, the smaller must be the price at which it is offered in order that it may find purchasers; or, in other words, the amount demanded increases with a fall in price, and diminishes with a rise in price.*

quantity demanded the amount of a good that buyers are willing and able to purchase at different prices
law of demand the claim that, other things being equal (*ceteris paribus*), the quantity demanded of a good falls when the price of the good rises

CRITICAL THINKING POINT Consider the statement by Marshall. To what extent do you think this statement is based on empirical principles? Explain.

We can represent the relationship between the price and quantity demanded in a table such as the one shown in Figure 3.1. The table shows Rachel's willingness to buy litres of milk each month at different prices, holding constant other factors, such as her income, tastes and the prices of other goods. The willingness to pay determines the position of the demand curve and is related to the utility or level of satisfaction Rachel gets from consuming milk. If milk has a zero price, Rachel would be willing to buy 20 litres per time period. At €0.10 per litre, Rachel would be willing to buy 18 litres. As the price rises further, she is willing to buy fewer and fewer litres. When the price reaches €1, Rachel would not be prepared to buy any milk at all. This table is a **demand schedule**, a table that shows the relationship between the price of a good and the quantity demanded, holding constant everything else that influences how much consumers of the good want to buy.

> **demand schedule** a table that shows the relationship between the price of a good and the quantity demanded

The graph in Figure 3.1 uses the numbers from the table to illustrate the law of demand. By convention, price is on the vertical axis, and the quantity demanded is on the horizontal axis. The downwards sloping line relating price and quantity demanded is called the **demand curve**.

> **demand curve** a graph of the relationship between the price of a good and the quantity demanded

FIGURE 3.1

Rachel's Demand Schedule and Demand Curve

The demand schedule shows the quantity demanded at each price. The demand curve, which graphs the demand schedule, shows how the quantity demanded of the good changes as its price varies. Because a lower price increases the quantity demanded, the demand curve slopes downwards from left to right.

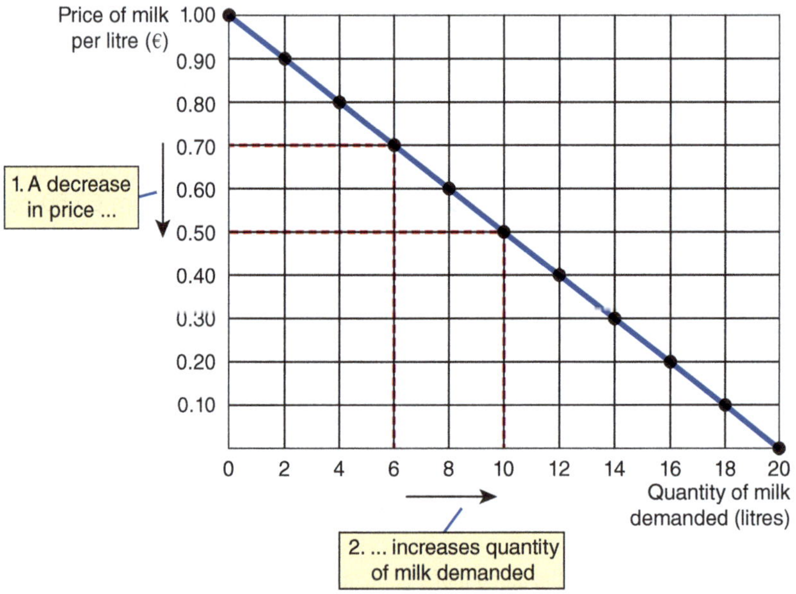

Price of milk per litre (€)	Quantity of milk demanded (litres per month)
0.00	20
0.10	18
0.20	16
0.30	14
0.40	12
0.50	10
0.60	8
0.70	6
0.80	4
0.90	2
1.00	0

Movement Along the Demand Curve

It is important to be clear about the terminology used when referring to market demand. A change in the price of a good, *ceteris paribus*, which results in a change in quantity demanded, is represented graphically as a *movement along the demand curve*.

If we assume that the price of milk falls, this will lead to an increase in quantity demanded. There are two reasons for this increase:

1. **The income effect.** If we assume that incomes remain constant, then a fall in the price of milk means that consumers can now afford to buy more with their income. In other words, their real income, what a given amount of money can buy at any point in time, has increased, and part of the increase in quantity demanded can be put down to this effect.
2. **The substitution effect.** Now that milk is lower in price compared to other products such as fruit juice, some consumers will choose to substitute the more expensive drinks with the now cheaper milk. This switch accounts for the remaining part of the increase in quantity demanded.

Market Demand Versus Individual Demand

The demand curve in Figure 3.1 shows an individual's demand for a product. The *market demand* is the sum of all the individual demands for a particular good or service.

The table in Figure 3.2 illustrates the demand schedules for milk of two individuals: Rachel and Lars. Assuming Rachel and Lars are the only two people in the market, the market demand at each price is the sum of the two individual demands.

Figure 3.2 shows the demand curves that correspond to these demand schedules. To find the total quantity demanded at any price, we add the individual quantities found on the horizontal axis of the individual demand curves. The market demand curve shows how the total quantity demanded of a good varies as the price of the good varies, while all the other factors are held constant.

Remember... A change in quantity demanded refers to the increase or decrease in demand as a result of a change in the price, holding constant all other factors influencing demand. A change in quantity demanded is shown by a movement along the demand curve.

SHIFTS VERSUS MOVEMENTS ALONG THE DEMAND CURVE

The individual and market demand curves shown are drawn under the assumption of *ceteris paribus* – other things being equal with the only variable changing being that of price. If any of the factors affecting demand change, *other than a change in price*, this will cause a shift in the position of the demand curve, which is referred to as a *change in demand*.

If the price of milk, for example, is €0.30 per litre, a family might buy 5 litres of milk a week. If their income rises, they can now afford to buy more milk and so might now buy 7 litres a week. The price of milk has not changed – it is still €0.30 per litre – but the amount of milk the family buys has increased. If this behaviour is reflected elsewhere in the economy by other families whose incomes have changed, then the market demand curve will shift to the right.

If any of the factors affecting demand other than price change, then the amount consumers wish to purchase changes whatever the price.

A Shift in the Demand Curve

If one or more of the factors influencing demand other than price changes, the demand curve shifts. For example, suppose a top European medical school published research that suggested people who regularly drank milk lived longer, healthier lives. The discovery would raise the demand for milk because consumers' tastes would be expected to change in favour of drinking more milk. At any given price, buyers would now want to purchase a larger quantity of milk and the demand curve for milk would shift to the right.

FIGURE 3.2

Market Demand as the Sum of Individual Demands

*The quantity demanded in a market is the sum of the quantities demanded by all buyers at each price. The market demand curve is found by adding horizontally the individual demand curves. At a price of €0.50, Rachel would like to buy 10 litres of milk, but Lars would only be prepared to buy 5 litres at that price. The quantity demanded **in the market** at this price, therefore, is 15 litres.*

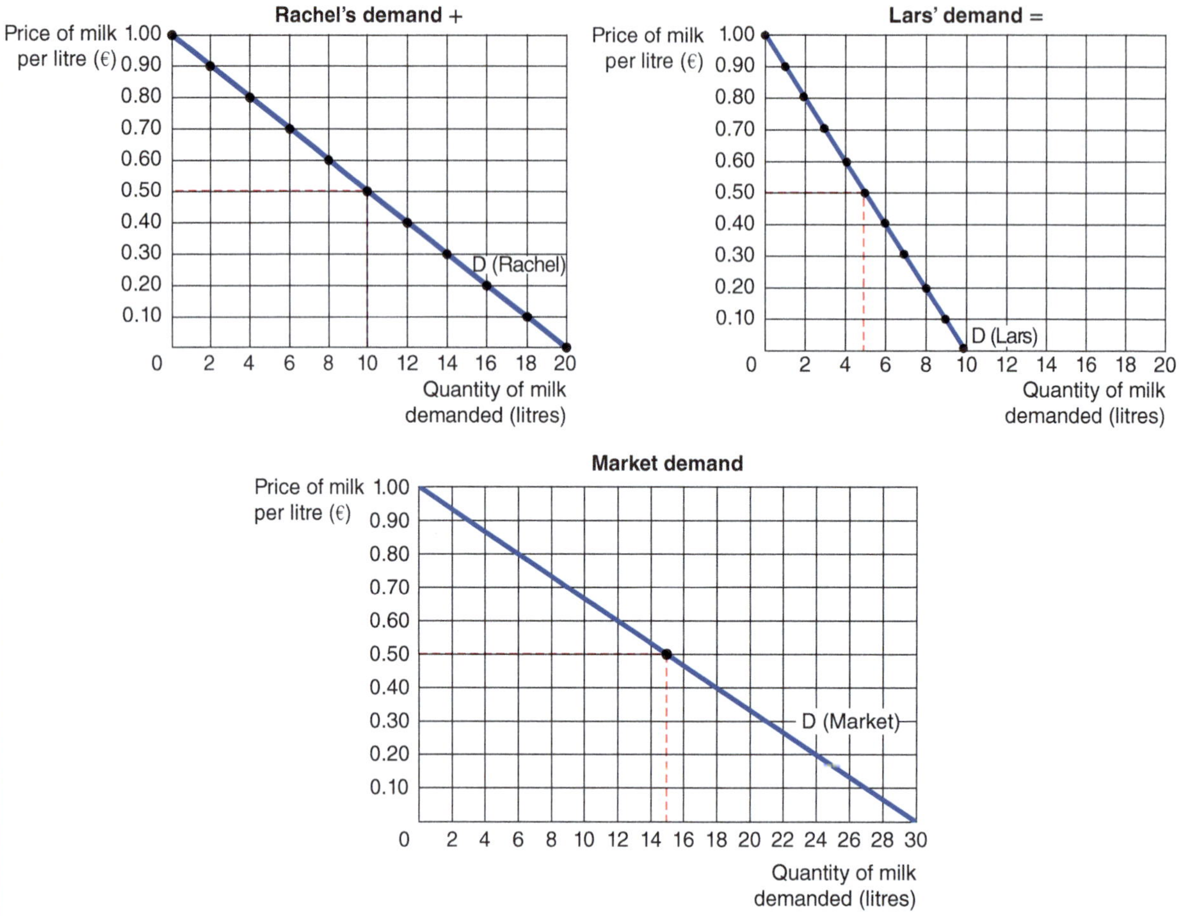

Price of milk per litre (€)	Rachel +	Lars =	Market
0.00	20	10	30
0.10	18	9	27
0.20	16	8	24
0.30	14	7	21
0.40	12	6	18
0.50	10	5	15
0.60	8	4	12
0.70	6	3	9
0.80	4	2	6
0.90	2	1	3
1.00	0	0	0

Figure 3.3 illustrates shifts in demand. Any change that increases the quantity demanded at every price, such as our imaginary research report, shifts the demand curve to the right and is called *an increase in demand*. Any change that reduces the quantity demanded at every price shifts the demand curve to the left and is called *a decrease in demand*.

FIGURE 3.3

Shifts in the Demand Curve

Any change that raises the quantity that buyers wish to purchase at a given price shifts the demand curve to the right. Any change that lowers the quantity that buyers wish to purchase at a given price shifts the demand curve to the left.

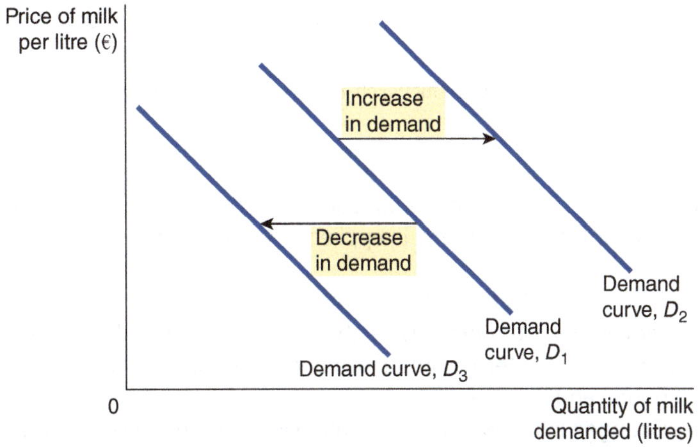

The following is a short summary of the main factors affecting changes in demand which cause a shift in the demand curve.

Prices of Other (Related) Goods Suppose that the price of milk falls. The law of demand says that you will buy more milk. At the same time, you will probably buy less fruit juice. Because milk and fruit juice are both refreshing drinks, they satisfy similar desires. When a fall in the price of one good reduces the demand for another good, the two goods are called **substitutes**. Substitutes are often pairs of goods that are used in place of each other, such as butter and spreads, pullovers and sweatshirts, and cinema tickets and film streaming. The more closely related substitute products are, the more effect we might see on demand if the price of one of the substitutes changes.

substitutes two goods for which an increase in the price of one leads to an increase in the demand for the other (and vice versa)

Now suppose that the price of breakfast cereals falls. According to the law of demand, more packets of breakfast cereals will be bought. When this happens, we might expect to see the demand for milk increase as well, because breakfast cereals and milk are used together. When a fall in the price of one good raises the demand for another good, the two goods are called **complements**. Complements are often pairs of goods that are used together, such as petrol and cars, computers and software, bread and cheese, strawberries and cream, and smartphones and apps.

complements two goods for which an increase in the price of one leads to a decrease in the demand for the other

SELF TEST What type of relationship do apps and smartphones have? If the price of smartphones increases, what would you expect to happen to the demand for apps? Sketch a diagram to illustrate your answer.

Income Changes in incomes affect demand. A lower income means less to spend in total, so you would have to spend less on some – and probably most – goods. Equally, if income rises, then it is likely that demand for many goods will also rise. If the demand for a good falls when income falls or rises as income rises, the good is called a **normal good**.

normal good a good for which, *ceteris paribus*, an increase in income leads to an increase in demand (and vice versa)

If the demand for a good rises when income falls, the good is called an **inferior good**. An example of an inferior good might be bus rides. If your income falls, you are less likely to buy a car or take a taxi and more likely to take the bus. As income falls, therefore, demand for bus rides tends to increase.

inferior good a good for which, *ceteris paribus*, an increase in income leads to a decrease in demand (and vice versa)

Tastes A key determinant of demand is tastes. If you like milk, you buy more of it. Understanding the role of tastes or preferences in consumer behaviour is taking on more importance as research in the fields of psychology and neurology is applied to economics.

The Size and Structure of the Population Because market demand is derived from individual demands, it follows that the more buyers there are, the higher the demand is likely to be. The size of the population, therefore, is a determinant of demand. A larger population, *ceteris paribus*, will mean a higher demand for all goods and services.

Changes in the way the population is structured also influence demand. Many countries have an ageing population and this leads to a change in demand. If there is an increasing proportion of the population aged 65 and over, the demand for goods and services used by this older population is likely to increase in demand as a result. Examples include: the demand for retirement homes, insurance policies suitable for older people, the demand for smaller cars and for health care services.

Advertising Firms advertise their products in many different ways, and it is likely that if a firm embarks on an advertising campaign, the demand for that product will increase.

Expectations of Consumers Expectations about the future may affect the demand for a good or service today. For example, if it was announced that the price of milk was expected to rise next month, consumers may be more willing to buy milk at today's price.

SELF TEST Make up an example of a demand schedule for pizza and graph the demand curve. Give an example of something that would cause the demand curve for pizza to shift to the right and to the left.

Remember... A change in any factor affecting demand, other than price, is referred to as a *change in demand*. A change in demand is represented graphically as a shift in the demand curve, either to the right (an increase in demand) or to the left (a decrease in demand).

A demand curve can be represented algebraically. For example, a demand curve might be represented by the demand function $P = 20 - Q_D$. This is an example of a linear equation. In mathematics, a linear equation is of the type $Q_D = a - bP$. Here, quantity demanded is the dependent variable and, in linear equations, the dependent variable is represented on the vertical axis. In economics, quantity demanded is shown on the horizontal axis. The demand curve is therefore a visual representation of the inverse demand curve where P is the subject of the equation. Using our inverse demand function we can find the quantity demanded at different prices given by this particular equation. If price were zero, our equation would be: $0 = 20 - Q_D$. Therefore, Q_D would be 20. If $P = 10$, then quantity demanded would be given by $10 = 20 - Q_D$. Q_D would therefore be 10.

SUPPLY

We now turn to the other side of the market and examine the behaviour of sellers. Once again, to focus our thinking, we will continue to consider the market for milk.

The Supply Curve: The Relationship Between Price and Quantity Supplied

The **quantity supplied** of any good or service is the amount that sellers are willing and able to sell at different prices. When the price of milk is high, selling milk is profitable, and so sellers are willing to supply more. Sellers of milk work longer hours, buy more dairy cows and employ extra workers to increase supply to the market. By contrast, when the price of milk is low, the business is less profitable, and so sellers are willing to produce less milk. At a low price, some sellers may even choose to shut down, and their quantity supplied falls to zero. Because the quantity supplied rises as the price rises and falls as the price falls, we say that the quantity supplied is *positively related* to the price of the good. As with demand, the pervasiveness of this relationship between price and quantity supplied led to it being called the **law of supply**.

> **quantity supplied** the amount of a good that sellers are willing and able to sell at different prices
> **law of supply** the claim that, *ceteris paribus*, the quantity supplied of a good rises when the price of a good rises

The table in Figure 3.4 shows the quantity that Richard, a milk producer, is willing to supply at various prices. At a price below €0.10 per litre, Richard does not supply any milk at all. As the price rises, he is willing to supply a greater and greater quantity. This is the **supply schedule**, a table that shows the relationship between the price of a good and the quantity supplied, holding constant everything else that influences how much producers of the good want to sell.

> **supply schedule** a table that shows the relationship between the price of a good and the quantity supplied

The graph in Figure 3.4 uses the numbers from the table to illustrate the law of supply. The curve relating price and quantity supplied is called the **supply curve**. The supply curve slopes upwards from left to right because, other things equal, a higher price means a greater quantity supplied.

> **supply curve** a graph of the relationship between the price of a good and the quantity supplied

FIGURE 3.4

Richard's Supply Schedule and Supply Curve

The supply schedule shows the quantity supplied at each price. This supply curve, which graphs the supply schedule, shows how the quantity supplied of the good changes as its price varies. Because a higher price increases the quantity supplied, the supply curve slopes upwards.

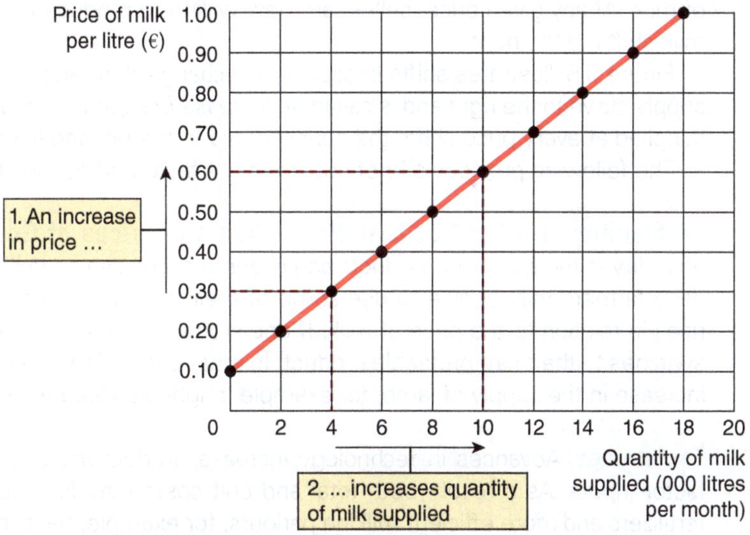

Price of milk per litre (€)	Quantity of milk supplied (000 litres per month)
0.00	0
0.10	0
0.20	2
0.30	4
0.40	6
0.50	8
0.60	10
0.70	12
0.80	14
0.90	16
1.00	18

A Movement Along the Supply Curve

As with demand, it is important to use the correct terminology and to understand the terminology to avoid making mistakes. If the price of a good rises, *ceteris paribus*, there is a *change in quantity supplied*. This is represented graphically as a movement along the supply curve.

Market Supply Versus Individual Supply

Just as market demand is the sum of the demands of all buyers, market supply is the sum of the supplies of all sellers. The table in Figure 3.5 shows the supply schedules for two milk producers – Richard and Megan. At any price, Richard's supply schedule tells us the quantity of milk Richard is willing to supply, and Megan's supply schedule tells us the quantity of milk Megan is willing to supply. The market supply is the sum of the two individual supplies (assuming Richard and Megan are the only suppliers in the market).

The graph in Figure 3.5 shows the supply curves that correspond to the supply schedules. As with demand curves, we find the total quantity supplied at any price by adding the individual quantities found on the horizontal axis of the individual supply curves. The market supply curve shows how the total quantity supplied varies as the price of the good varies.

Remember... A *change in quantity supplied* refers to the increase or decrease in supply as a result of a change in the price, holding constant all other factors influencing supply. A change in quantity supplied is shown by a movement along the supply curve.

Shifts in the Supply Curve

The supply curve will shift if factors affecting producers' willingness and ability to supply, other than price, change. For example, suppose the price of animal feed falls. Because animal feed is an input into producing milk, the fall in the price of animal feed makes selling milk more profitable. This raises the supply of milk. At any given price, sellers are now willing to produce a larger quantity. Thus, the supply curve for milk shifts to the right.

Figure 3.6 illustrates shifts in supply. Any change that raises quantity supplied at every price shifts the supply curve to the right and is called *an increase in supply*. Similarly, any change that reduces the quantity supplied at every price shifts the supply curve to the left and is called *a decrease in supply*.

The following provides a brief outline of the factors affecting supply *other than price*.

Profitability of Other Goods in Production and Prices of Goods in Joint Supply Firms have some flexibility in the supply of products and in some cases can switch production to other goods. For example, dairy farmers may decide to use some of their land to produce arable crops if the price of those crops rises in relation to the price of milk. If one crop becomes more profitable, then it may be that the farmer switches to the more profitable product. In other cases, firms may find that products are in joint supply. An increase in the supply of lamb, for example, might also lead to an increase in the supply of wool.

Technology Advances in technology increase productivity allowing more to be produced using fewer factor inputs. As a result, both total and unit costs may fall and supply increases. The development of fertilizers and more efficient milking parlours, for example, have increased milk yields per cow and helped reduce costs as a result. By reducing firms' costs, the advance in technology increases the supply of milk.

Natural/Social Factors There are often many natural or social factors that affect supply. These include such things as the weather affecting crops, natural disasters, pestilence and disease, changing attitudes and social expectations (for example, over the production of organic food, the disposal of waste, reducing carbon emissions, ethical supply sourcing, and so on), all of which can have an influence on production decisions. Some or all of these may have an influence on the cost of inputs into production.

Input Prices: The Prices of Factors of Production To produce any output, sellers use various inputs collectively referred to as land, labour and capital. Dairy farmers, for example, will use fertilizer, feed, silage, farm buildings, veterinary services and the labour of workers. When the price of one or more of these inputs rises, producing milk is less profitable and firms supply less milk. If input prices rise substantially, a firm might shut down and supply no milk at all. If input prices fall for some reason, then production may be more profitable and there is an incentive to supply more at each price. Thus, the supply of a good is negatively related to the price of the inputs used to make the good.

FIGURE 3.5

Market Supply as the Sum of Individual Supplies

The quantity supplied in a market is the sum of the quantities supplied by all the sellers at each price. Thus, the market supply curve is found by adding horizontally the individual supply curves. At a price of €0.50, Richard is willing to supply 8,000 litres of milk per month, and Megan is willing to supply 5,000 litres per month. The quantity supplied in the market at this price is 13,000 litres per month.

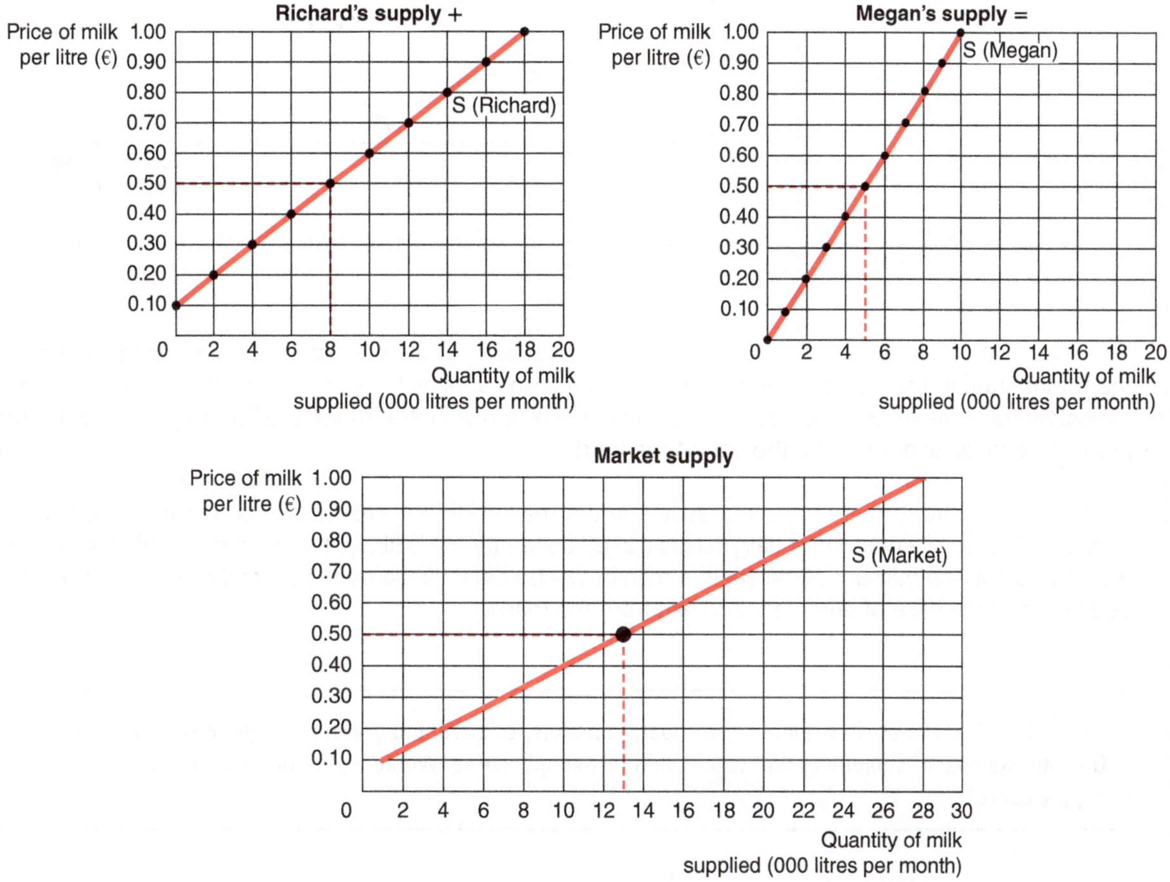

Price of milk per litre (€)	Quantity Supplied (000 litres per month) Richard +	Megan =	Market
0.00	0	0	0
0.10	0	1	1
0.20	2	2	4
0.30	4	3	7
0.40	6	4	10
0.50	8	5	13
0.60	10	6	16
0.70	12	7	19
0.80	14	8	22
0.90	16	9	25
1.00	18	10	28

FIGURE 3.6

Shifts in the Supply Curve

Any change that raises the quantity that sellers wish to produce at a given price shifts the supply curve to the right. Any change that lowers the quantity that sellers wish to produce at a given price shifts the supply curve to the left.

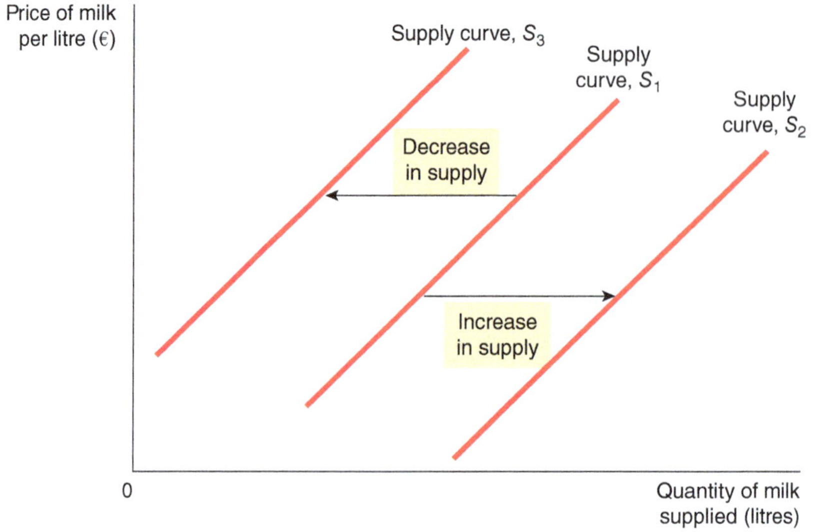

Expectations of Producers Output levels can vary according to the expectations of producers about the future state of the market. The amount of milk a farm supplies today, for example, may depend on its expectations of the future. If it expects the price of milk to rise in the future, the firm might invest in more productive capacity or increase the size of the herd.

Number of Sellers If there are more sellers in the market, then it makes sense that the supply would increase. Equally, if a number of dairy farms closed down, then it is likely that the amount of milk supplied would also fall. The number of sellers in a market will be determined by the profitability of the product in question and the ease of entry into and exit from the market.

SELF TEST Make up an example of a supply schedule for pizza and graph the implied supply curve. Give an example of something that would shift this supply curve. Would a change in price shift the supply curve?

Remember... A change in any factor affecting supply, other than price, is referred to as a *change in supply*. A change in supply is represented graphically as a shift in the supply curve, either to the right (an increase in supply) or the left (a decrease in supply).

As with a demand curve, a supply curve can be represented algebraically. In economics the inverse supply function is used, which represents price on the vertical axis and quantity supplied, the dependent variable, on the horizontal axis. A supply curve might be represented by the supply function $P = 8 + 2Q_s$. The constant, 8, gives the vertical intercept, the point at which the supply curve cuts the vertical axis. The coefficient of $2Q_s$ represents the slope of the supply curve given by the change in price divided by the change in quantity supplied (rise over run). The positive sign in the equation tells us that the supply curve slopes upwards from left to right. Using our inverse supply function we can find the quantity supplied at different prices given by this particular equation. If price were 16, our equation would be $16 = 8 + 2Q_s$. Rearranging would give $2Q_S = 8$. Therefore, Q_S would be 4. If $P = 20$, then quantity supplied would be given by $20 = 8 + 2Q_S$. Therefore, Q_S would be 6.

SUPPLY AND DEMAND TOGETHER

Having analyzed supply and demand separately, we now combine them to see how they determine the quantity of a good sold in a market and its price.

Equilibrium

Equilibrium is defined as a state of rest, a point where there is no force acting for change. Economists refer to supply and demand as being *market forces*. Figure 3.7 shows the market supply curve and market demand curve together. In the market model, the relationship between supply and demand exerts force on price. If supply is greater than demand or vice versa, then there is pressure on price to change. Market equilibrium occurs when the amount consumers wish to buy at a particular price is the same as the amount sellers are willing to offer for sale at that price. The price at this intersection is called the **equilibrium or market price**, and the quantity is called the **equilibrium quantity**. In Figure 3.7 the equilibrium price is €0.40 per litre, and the equilibrium quantity is 7,000 litres of milk bought and sold per day.

equilibrium or market price the price where the quantity demanded is the same as the quantity supplied
equilibrium quantity the quantity bought and sold at the equilibrium price

FIGURE 3.7

The Equilibrium of Supply and Demand

The equilibrium is found where the supply and demand curves intersect. At the equilibrium price, the quantity supplied is the same as the quantity demanded. Here the equilibrium price is €0.40 per litre of milk. At this price, sellers are willing to offer 7,000 litres of milk per day for sale and buyers wish to purchase 7,000 litres of milk per day.

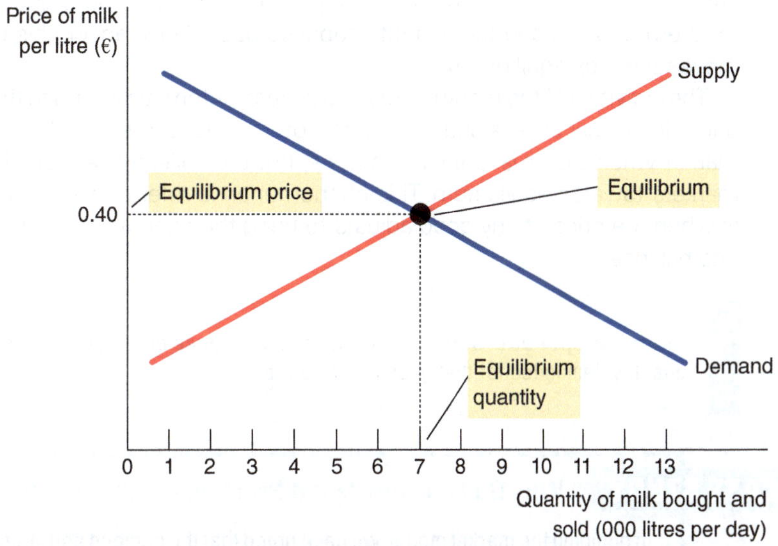

At the equilibrium price, the quantity of the good that buyers are willing and able to buy exactly balances the quantity that sellers are willing and able to sell. The equilibrium price is sometimes called the *market clearing price* because, *at this price*, everyone in the market has been satisfied. So, buyers have bought all they want to buy, and sellers have sold all they want to sell. There is no shortage in the market where demand is greater than supply and neither is there any surplus where supply is greater than demand.

The market will remain in equilibrium until something causes either a shift in the demand curve or a shift in the supply curve (or both). If one or both curves shift, at the existing equilibrium price there will now be either a **surplus** or a **shortage**. The market mechanism takes time to adjust. Sometimes it can be very quick (which tends to happen in highly organized markets like stock and commodity markets) and sometimes it is much slower to react. When the market is in disequilibrium and a shortage or surplus exists, the behaviour of buyers and sellers acts as a force on price.

surplus a situation in which the quantity supplied is greater than the quantity demanded at the going market price
shortage a situation in which quantity demanded is greater than quantity supplied at the going market price

A Surplus A surplus exists when the amount sellers wish to sell is greater than the amount consumers wish to buy at a price. When there is a surplus or *excess supply* of a good, suppliers are unable to sell all they want at the going price. Sellers find stocks increasing, so they respond to the surplus by cutting their prices. As the price falls, some consumers are persuaded to buy more and so there is a movement along the demand curve. Equally, some sellers in the market respond to the falling price by reducing the amount they are willing to offer for sale (a movement along the supply curve). Prices continue to fall until the market reaches a new equilibrium. The effect on price and the amount bought and sold depend on whether the demand curve or supply curve shifted in the first place (or whether both shifted). This is why analysis of markets is referred to as **comparative statics**, because we are comparing one initial static equilibrium with another once market forces have worked their way through.

comparative statics the comparison of one initial static equilibrium with another

A Shortage A shortage occurs if the amount consumers are willing and able to purchase at a price is greater than the amount sellers are willing and able to offer for sale. With too many buyers chasing too few goods, sellers can respond to the shortage by raising their prices without losing sales. As the price rises, some buyers will drop out of the market and quantity demanded falls (a movement along the demand curve). Rising prices encourage some producers to offer more goods for sale as it is now more profitable for them to do so and the quantity supplied rises. Once again, this process will continue until the market moves towards equilibrium.

The activities of the many buyers and sellers 'automatically' push the market price towards the equilibrium price. Individual buyers and sellers do not consciously realize they are acting as forces for change in the market when they make their decisions, but the collective act of all the buyers and sellers tends to push markets towards equilibrium. This phenomenon is referred to as the **law of supply and demand**, which is when the price of any good adjusts to bring the quantity supplied and quantity demanded for that good into balance.

law of supply and demand the claim that the price of any good adjusts to bring the quantity supplied and the quantity demanded for that good into balance

CASE STUDY Why Do Economists Put Price on the Vertical Axis?

In outlining the market model, we have noted that the demand and supply of a product is dependent on the price. Demand and supply are said to be the dependent variables and price the independent variable. In mathematics the relationship between variables is expressed as a function, such as $y = f(x)$. This states that the value of y is dependent on the value of x as specified by the particular function f. If the function is $y = x^2$, then the value of y will be equal to whatever value x takes, squared. The dependent variable is y and the independent variable is x. In a graphical representation of this function, the dependent variable y is shown on the vertical axis and the independent variable, x, is shown on the horizontal axis. This is standard representation in mathematics.

In economics, however, the way that the market model is represented is that price, the independent variable, is shown on the vertical axis, and demand and supply, the dependent variables, are shown on the horizontal axis. Why is this? As with many things in economics, the reason is historical, and it is not always easy to pin down exactly when and why the flipping of the axes occurred. One thing is certain – the convention has endured.

(*Continued*)

One initial point worth mentioning is that a sketch of a market (which is what supply and demand diagrams are) is just that – a sketch. Sketches are not mathematical representations of equations. It is entirely possible that a graph can be drawn which represents specific equations of course. It is important to distinguish between the way we sketch and use graphs today and the way that economists and mathematicians may have used these tools in the eighteenth and nineteenth centuries. It is also important to note that the use of diagrams is a means to describe and apply the basics of a model. Supply and demand diagrams are used to demonstrate how equilibrium is reached, for example when factors affecting supply and demand change among other things.

© Alamy/Historic Collection

Alfred Marshall popularized the use of diagrams in which price was on the vertical axis but was not the first to use diagrams.

It is often reported that British economist Alfred Marshall pioneered the use of diagrams in which price was on the vertical axis. Marshall used such diagrams in his *Principles of Economics* published in 1890, but he was not the first to use diagrams. Antoine-Augustin Cournot (1801–77) in his 1838 publication *Researches into the Mathematical Principles of the Theory of Wealth* used diagrams representing the relationship between price and quantity, but with price on the horizontal axis. Cournot used these diagrams to show how small changes in price can affect total revenue and thus implied the concept of price elasticity. Cournot further introduced supply curves to give the 'cross' undergraduate economists are all too familiar with to show how the imposition of a tax would affect price and quantity. Here, Cournot had price on the vertical axis and quantity on the horizontal.

Karl Henrich Rau (1792–1870) used a supply and demand diagram in his 1841 publication *Grundsätze der Volkswirtschaftslehre* (*Principles of Economics*) to analyze equilibrium in which price was on the vertical axis. In 1870, Fleeming Jenkin used diagrams to show applications of the 'law of supply and demand' which also had price on the vertical axis.

It was, however, Marshall who popularized the use of diagrams to model supply and demand with price on the vertical axis. In his 1890 book, many of these diagrams appeared as footnotes rather than as part of the text, leading historians of economic methodology to reason that he saw diagrams as an aid to understanding the economics rather than the primary source of understanding.

Marshall's text uses models as a means of showing what can happen in a market if demand and supply change. He used the model as a means of providing different 'experiments' to address questions. In doing so, he showed that the market outcome could be the same regardless of the way the model was manipulated, which would, in turn, imply that the model's predictions were stable.

Other explanations suggest that price can be the dependent variable in that changes in quantities can affect price. For example, if there is a drought, the supply of a product is affected negatively, which

(*Continued*)

impacts its price as a result of a shift in the supply curve. Quantity is not always determined by price, therefore. If each time a diagram was drawn, price was on a different axis to match the application being explored, it might become too confusing and the power of a diagram to aid understanding would be lost. Better, therefore, to be consistent and have price on the vertical axis.

Finally, in response to a question on the subject on his blog, Greg Mankiw notes that his Harvard colleague, Robert Barro, refers to an interpretation of demand and supply by the economist John Hicks. This interpretation derives from Marshall's construction of demand and supply. Hicks refers to 'demand price' and 'supply price' as how much an individual is willing to pay to secure additional units of goods and how much a supplier must be paid to provide additional output. In this construction, price is the dependent variable, hence the logic of putting it on the vertical axis.

Questions:

1. Why do you think quantity demanded and quantity supplied are dependent on the price and not the other way round?
2. To what extent do you think that sketches of supply and demand diagrams are an aid to understanding in economics?
3. Is the flipping of axes just another example of manipulation to serve its own ends in economics? Explain.

The Algebra of Equilibrium We have seen how demand and supply can be represented algebraically. In equilibrium, we know that demand equals supply. Algebraically, therefore, we set the demand and supply equations equal to each other and solve for P. Using our two examples, the demand function is given by $P = 20 - Q_D$ and the supply function as $P = 8 + 2Q_S$. In equilibrium, therefore, $20 - Q_D = 8 + 2Q_S$. Rearranging to collect all the Q terms on one side, we get: $3Q = 12$, thus $Q = 4$. Having solved for Q, we can substitute this into either the demand or supply function to find the equilibrium price. Using the demand function, this would be: $P = 20 - Q_D$, $P = 20 - 4$, therefore $P = 16$. As a check we can substitute $Q = 4$ into our supply function and get $P = 8 + 2Q_S$, $P = 8 + 8$, therefore $P = 16$.

PRICES AS SIGNALS

The main function of price in a competitive market is to act as a signal to both buyers and sellers.

Price as a Signal to Buyers

For buyers, price tells them something about what they must give up (usually an amount of money) to acquire the benefits that having the good will confer on them. These benefits are referred to as the utility or satisfaction derived from consumption and reflect the willingness to pay.

If an individual is willing to pay €10 to go and watch a film, then the model assumes that the value of the benefits gained from watching the film is worth that amount of money to the individual. But what does this mean? How much is €10 worth? Economists would answer this question by saying that if an individual is willing to give up €10 to watch a film, then the value of the benefits gained (the utility) must be greater than the next best alternative that the €10 could have been spent on. This reflects the trade-offs that people face and that the cost of something is what you have to give up in order to acquire it. This is fundamental to the law of demand.

At higher prices, the sacrifice being made in terms of the value of the benefits gained from alternatives is greater and so we may be less willing to do so as a result. If the price of a ticket for a film was €15, then it might have to be a very good film to persuade the individual that giving up what else €15 could buy is worth it.

Price also acts as a signal at the margin. Most consumers will recognize the agony they have experienced over making some purchasing decisions. Those 'to die for' pair of shoes, for example, may be absolutely perfect, but at €120 they might make the buyer think twice. If they were €100, then it might be considered a 'no brainer'. That extra €20 might make all the difference to the decision of whether to buy or not.

Economists and those in other disciplines such as psychology are increasingly investigating the complex nature of purchasing decisions that humans make. The development of magnetic resonance imaging (MRI) techniques, for example, has allowed researchers to investigate how the brain responds to different stimuli when making purchasing decisions.

Price as a Signal to Sellers

For sellers, price acts as a signal in relation to the profitability of production. For many sellers, increasing the amount of a good produced will incur some additional input costs. A higher price is required to compensate for the additional cost and to enable the producer to gain some reward from the risk they are taking in production. That reward is termed *profit*.

Rising Prices in a Competitive Market

If prices are rising in a free market, this acts as a different but related signal to buyers and sellers. Rising prices to a seller means that there is a shortage and thus acts as a signal to expand production, because the seller knows that it is more likely they will be able to sell what they produce.

For buyers, a rising price changes the nature of the trade-off they face. Rising prices act as a signal that more will have to be given up to acquire the good. They must decide whether the value of the benefits they will gain from acquiring the good is worth the extra price they have to pay and the sacrifice of the value of the benefits of the next best alternative.

For example, say the price of going to the cinema increases from €10 to €15 per ticket. Some cinema goers will happily pay the extra because they really enjoy a night out at the cinema. Some people, however, might start to think that €15 is a bit expensive. They might think that they could have a night out at a restaurant with friends, a meal and a few drinks for €15 and that would represent more value to them than going to the cinema. Some of these people would, therefore, stop going to the cinema and go to a restaurant instead. In this instance, the price signal to these people has changed.

What we do know is that for both buyers and sellers, there are many complex processes that occur in decision-making. While we do not fully understand all these processes yet, economists are constantly searching for new insights that might help them understand the workings of markets more fully. All of us go through these complex processes every time we make a purchasing decision. We may not realize it, but we do! Having some appreciation of these processes is fundamental to thinking like an economist.

ANALYZING CHANGES IN EQUILIBRIUM

So far, we have seen how supply and demand together determine a market's equilibrium. This in turn determines the price of the good and the amount of the good that buyers purchase and sellers produce. Of course, the equilibrium price and quantity depend on the position of the supply and demand curves. We use comparative static analysis to look at what happens when some event shifts one of these curves and causes the equilibrium in the market to change.

To do this we proceed in three steps:

1. We decide whether the event in question shifts the supply curve, the demand curve or, in some cases, both.
2. We decide whether the curve shifts to the right or to the left.
3. We use the supply and demand diagram to compare the initial and the new equilibrium, which shows how the shift affects the equilibrium price and quantity bought and sold.

To see how these three steps work in analyzing market changes, let us consider various events that might affect the market for milk. We begin the analysis by assuming that the market for milk is in equilibrium with the price of milk at €0.50 per litre and 13,000 litres being bought and sold per day. We then follow our three-step approach.

Example 1: A Change in Demand Suppose that one summer, the weather is very hot. How does this event affect the market for milk?

1. The hot weather affects the demand curve by changing people's taste for milk. That is, the weather changes the amount of milk that people want to buy at any given price.
2. Because hot weather makes people want to drink more milk, make refreshing milk shakes or producers of ice cream buy more milk to make ice cream, the demand curve shifts to the right. Figure 3.8 shows this increase in demand as the shift in the demand curve from D_1 to D_2. (What you must remember now is that demand curve D_1 does not exist anymore and so we have shown it as a dashed line.) This shift indicates that the quantity of milk demanded is now higher at every price. At the existing market price of €0.50 buyers now want to buy 19,000 litres of milk, but sellers are only offering 13,000 litres per day for sale at this price. The shift in demand has led to a shortage of milk in the market of 6,000 litres per day, represented by the bracket.
3. The shortage encourages producers to increase the output of milk (a movement along the supply curve). There is an *increase in quantity supplied.* But the additional production incurs extra costs and so a higher price is required to compensate sellers. As sellers increase the amount of milk offered for sale as price rises, consumers behave differently. Some consumers who were willing to buy milk at €0.50 are not willing to pay more and so drop out of the market. As price creeps up, therefore, there is a movement along the demand curve representing those consumers who drop out of the market.

FIGURE 3.8

How an Increase in Demand Affects the Equilibrium

An event that raises quantity demanded at any given price shifts the demand curve to the right. The equilibrium price and the equilibrium quantity both rise. Here, an abnormally hot summer causes buyers to demand more milk. The demand curve shifts from D_1 to D_2, which causes the equilibrium price to rise from €0.50 to €0.60 and the equilibrium quantity bought and sold to rise from 13,000 litres to 16,000 litres per day.

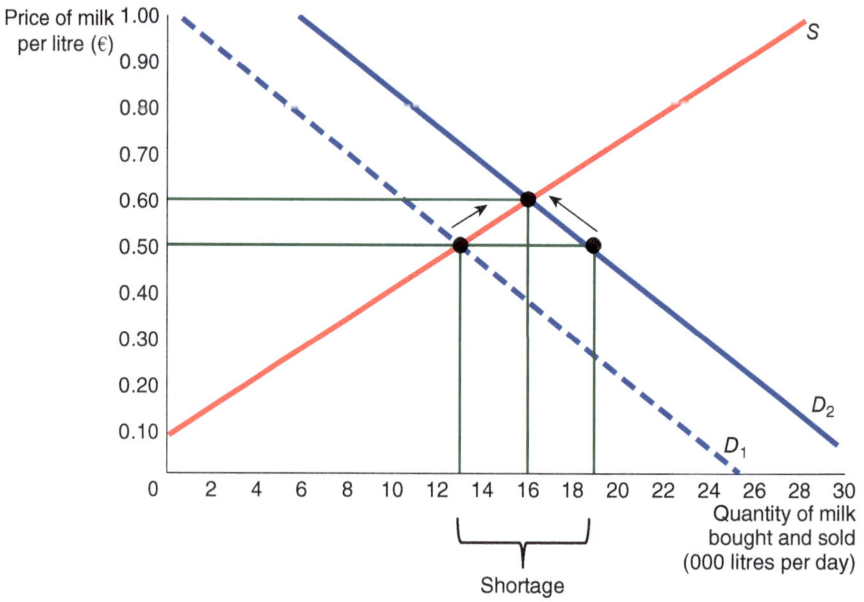

The market forces of supply and demand continue to work through until a new equilibrium is reached. The new equilibrium price is now €0.60 per litre and the equilibrium quantity bought and sold is now 16,000 litres per day. To compare our starting and finishing positions, the hot weather which caused the shift in the demand curve has led to an increase in the price of milk and the quantity of milk bought and sold.

Example 2: A Change in Supply Suppose that, during another summer, a drought drives up the price of animal feed for dairy cattle.

1. The change in the price of animal feed, an input into producing milk, affects the supply curve. By raising the costs of production, it reduces the amount of milk that firms produce and sell at any given price. Some farmers may send cattle for slaughter because they cannot afford to feed them anymore, and some farmers may simply decide to sell up and get out of farming altogether. The demand curve does not change because the higher cost of inputs does not directly affect the amount of milk consumers wish to buy.
2. The supply curve shifts to the left because, at every price, the total amount that farmers are willing and able to sell is reduced. Figure 3.9 illustrates this decrease in supply as a shift in the supply curve from S_1 to S_2. At a price of €0.50 sellers are now only able to offer 2,000 litres of milk for sale per day, but demand is still 13,000 litres per day. The shift in supply to the left has created a shortage in the market of 11,000 litres per day. Once again, the shortage will create pressure on price to rise as buyers look to purchase milk.
3. As Figure 3.9 shows, the shortage raises the equilibrium price from €0.50 to €0.70 per litre and lowers the equilibrium quantity bought and sold from 13,000 to 8,000 litres per day. As a result of the animal feed price increase, the price of milk rises, and the quantity of milk bought and sold falls.

FIGURE 3.9

How a Decrease in Supply Affects the Equilibrium

An event that reduces quantity supplied at any given price shifts the supply curve to the left. The equilibrium price rises, and the equilibrium quantity falls. Here, an increase in the price of animal feed (an input) causes sellers to supply less milk. The supply curve shifts from S_1 to S_2, which causes the equilibrium price of milk to rise from €0.50 to €0.70 and the equilibrium quantity to fall from 13,000 litres to 8,000 litres per day.

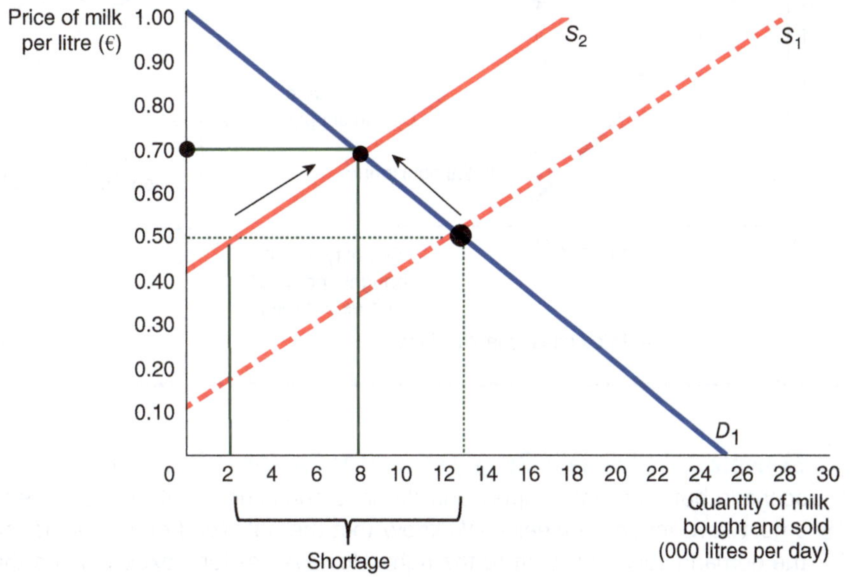

Example 3: A Change in Supply as well as Demand (i) Now suppose that the hot weather and the rise in animal feed occur during the same time period.

1. We determine that both curves must shift. The hot weather affects the demand curve for milk because it alters the amount that consumers want to buy at any given price. At the same time, when the rise in animal feed drives up input prices, it alters the supply curve for milk because it changes the amount that firms want to sell at any given price.
2. The curves shift in the same directions as they did in our previous analysis: the demand curve shifts to the right, and the supply curve shifts to the left. Figure 3.10 illustrates these shifts.
3. As Figure 3.10 shows, there are two possible outcomes that might result, depending on the relative size of the demand and supply shifts. In both cases, the equilibrium price rises. In panel (a), where demand increases substantially while supply falls just a little, the equilibrium quantity bought and

sold also rises. By contrast, in panel (b), where supply falls substantially while demand rises just a little, the equilibrium quantity bought and sold falls. Thus, these events certainly raise the price of milk, but their impact on the amount of milk bought and sold is ambiguous (that is, it could go either way).

FIGURE 3.10

A Shift in Supply as well as Demand (i)

The figure shows a simultaneous increase in demand and decrease in supply. In panel (a), the equilibrium price rises from P_1 to P_2, and the equilibrium quantity rises from Q_1 to Q_2. In panel (b), the equilibrium price again rises from P_1 to P_2, but the equilibrium quantity falls from Q_1 to Q_2.

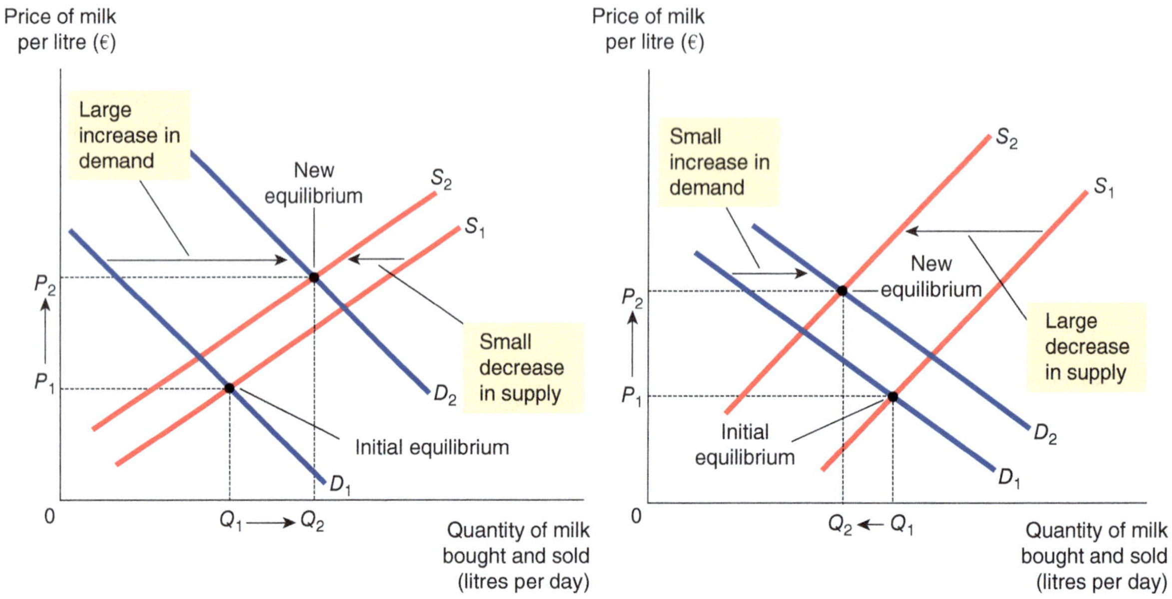

(a) Price rises, quantity rises

(b) Price rises, quantity falls

Example 4: A Change in Supply as well as Demand (ii) We are now going to look at a slightly different scenario but with both supply and demand changing together. Assume that forecasters have predicted a heatwave for some weeks. We know that the hot weather is likely to increase demand for milk and so the demand curve will shift to the right. However, sellers' expectations that sales of milk will increase as a result of the forecasts mean that they take steps to expand production of milk. This would lead to a shift of the supply curve to the right – more milk is now offered for sale at every price.

1. We determine that both curves must shift. The hot weather affects the demand curve because it alters the amount of milk that consumers want to buy at any given price. At the same time, the expectations of producers alter the supply curve for milk because they change the amount that firms want to sell at any given price.
2. Both demand and supply curves shift to the right as illustrated in Figure 3.11.
3. Figure 3.11 shows three possible outcomes that might result, depending on the relative size of the demand and supply shifts. In panel (a), where demand increases substantially while supply rises just a little, the equilibrium price and quantity both rise. By contrast, in panel (b), where supply rises substantially while demand rises just a little, the equilibrium price falls but the equilibrium quantity rises. In panel (c), the increases in demand and supply are identical and so equilibrium price does not change. Equilibrium quantity will increase, however. Thus, these events have different effects on the price of milk, although the amount bought and sold in each case is higher. In this instance the effect on price is ambiguous.

FIGURE 3.11

A Shift in Supply as well as Demand (ii)

In panel (a) the equilibrium price rises from P_1 to P_2, and the equilibrium quantity rises from Q_1 to Q_2. In panel (b), the equilibrium price falls from P_1 to P_2, but the equilibrium quantity rises from Q_1 to Q_2. In panel (c), there is no change to the equilibrium price, but the equilibrium quantity rises from Q_1 to Q_2.

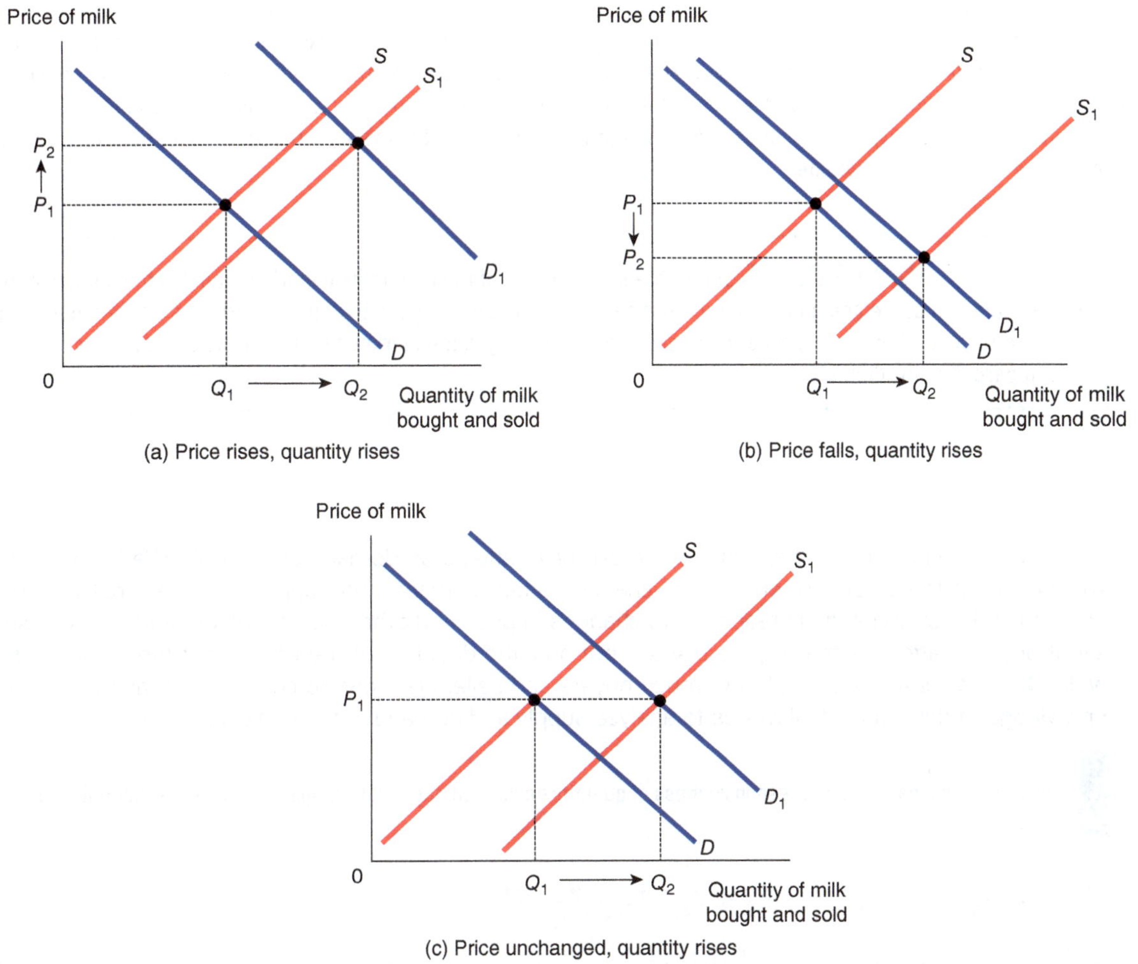

FYI

Experimental Economics

In the previous chapter we looked at the nature of models and the importance of empiricism. In this chapter so far, we have been explaining a model that purports to show how prices are determined in markets. If we spend time observing markets it is apparent that when shortages or surpluses arise, prices change as predicted by the model. When conflict broke out in Ukraine in 2022, there was an impact on the supply of grain. Grain exports from Ukraine were disrupted and, as supply decreased, prices rose. Similar observations can be made in many other instances. Is this sufficient to confirm the value and validity of the model? Perhaps, but science might require more rigorous analysis.

(*Continued*)

Economists have attempted to conduct experiments around competitive market behaviour and it is worth seeking out some examples of these. One such example is research conducted by Nobel Prize winning economist Vernon L. Smith. 'An Experimental Study of Competitive Market Behaviour' was published in *The Journal of Political Economy* in 1962. The experiments were carried out and refined over a period in the mid to late 1950s. The outcome of the research is interesting and you are advised to look at the article and read it. Perhaps more important is how Smith's work led to developments in experimental economics that became more widely utilized in subsequent years.

When reading the article, remember to try to adopt a critical approach. For example, what assumptions does Smith use? How valid are these assumptions? Consider Smith's background (and belief systems) and try to consider how this might have influenced his research. What else would you need to know to consider the research a useful contribution to the validity of the model of a competitive market? Are Smith's experiments replicable and do they arrive at the same sort of outcome?

CRITICAL THINKING POINT One of the assumptions of the competitive market model is that sellers can sell any amount at the going market price but cannot influence prices. In the analysis, we have noted that when a shortage or surplus occurs, sellers adjust prices according to the market situation. How do you account for this apparent contradiction?

ELASTICITY

So far, we have noted that changes in price can have effects on demand and supply. We have not been specific about the extent to which such changes affect demand and supply, however, that is how far demand and supply change in response to changes in price and other factors. When studying how some event or policy affects a market, we discuss not only the direction of the effects but their magnitude as well. **Elasticity** is a measure of how much buyers and sellers respond to changes in market conditions. Knowledge of this concept allows us to analyze supply and demand with greater precision.

elasticity a measure of the responsiveness of quantity demanded or quantity supplied to one of its determinants

THE PRICE ELASTICITY OF DEMAND

Businesses cannot directly control demand. They can seek to influence demand (and do) by utilizing a variety of strategies and tactics, but ultimately the consumer invariably decides whether to buy a product or not. One important way in which consumer behaviour can be influenced is through a firm changing the prices of its goods. Many firms do have some control over the price they can charge. As we have seen, however, in the assumptions of the perfectly competitive market model, this is not the case as the firm is a price-taker. An understanding of the price elasticity of demand is important in anticipating and analyzing the likely effects of changes in price on demand.

The Price Elasticity of Demand and Its Determinants

The **price elasticity of demand** measures how much the quantity demanded responds to a change in price. Demand for a good is said to be *price elastic* or price sensitive if the quantity demanded responds substantially to changes in price. Demand is said to be *price inelastic or* price insensitive if the quantity demanded responds only slightly to changes in price.

price elasticity of demand a measure of how much the quantity demanded of a good responds to a change in the price of that good, computed as the percentage change in quantity demanded divided by the percentage change in price

The price elasticity of demand for any good measures how willing consumers are to move away from the good as its price rises. Thus, the elasticity reflects the many economic, social and psychological forces that influence consumer tastes and preferences. Based on experience, however, we can state some general rules about what determines the price elasticity of demand.

Availability of Close Substitutes Goods with close substitutes tend to have more price elastic demand because it is easier for consumers to switch from that good to others. For example, butter and spreads are easily substitutable. A relatively small increase in the price of butter, assuming the price of spread is held fixed, causes the quantity of butter sold to fall by a relatively large amount. As a general rule, the closer the substitute the more price elastic the good is because it is easier for consumers to switch from one to the other. By contrast, because eggs are a food without a close substitute, we might expect the demand for eggs to be less price elastic than the demand for butter.

Necessities versus Luxuries Necessities tend to have relatively price inelastic demands, whereas luxuries have relatively price elastic demands. People use gas and electricity to heat their homes and cook their food. If the price of gas and electricity rose together, people would not demand dramatically less of them. They might try to be more energy efficient and reduce their demand a little, but they would still need hot food and warm homes. By contrast, when the price of a Louis Vuitton handbag rises, the quantity of these handbags demanded falls substantially. The reason is that most people view hot food and warm homes as necessities and a Louis Vuitton handbag as a luxury.

Of course, whether a good is a necessity or a luxury depends not on the intrinsic properties of the good but on the preferences of the buyer. Those for whom fashion accessories are vitally important in their lives may feel that being seen with a Louis Vuitton handbag is a necessity with inelastic demand. They may also feel that hot food and a warm place to sleep are less of a necessity, having a more price elastic demand as a result.

Definition of the Market The elasticity of demand in any market depends on how we draw the boundaries of the market. Narrowly defined markets tend to be associated with a more price elastic demand than broadly defined markets, because it is easier to find close substitutes for narrowly defined goods. For example, food, a broad category, has a fairly price inelastic demand because there are no good substitutes for food. Ice cream, a narrower category, has a more price elastic demand because it is easy to substitute other desserts for ice cream. Vanilla ice cream, a very narrow category, has a very price elastic demand in comparison because other flavours of ice cream can be considered very close substitutes for vanilla.

Proportion of Income Devoted to the Product Some products have a relatively high price and take a larger proportion of income than others. Buying a new suite of furniture for a lounge, for example, tends to take up a large amount of income. Buying an ice cream, however, might account for only a tiny proportion of income. If the price of a three-piece suite rises by 10 per cent, therefore, this is likely to have a greater effect on demand for this furniture than a 10 per cent increase in the price of an ice cream. The higher the proportion of income devoted to the product the greater the price elasticity is likely to be.

Time Horizon Goods tend to have more price elastic demand over longer time horizons. If the price of a unit of electricity rises much above an equivalent energy unit of gas, demand may fall only slightly in the short run. This is because many people already have electric cookers or electric heating appliances installed in their homes and cannot easily switch. If the price difference persists over several years, however, people may find it worth their while to replace their old electric heating and cooking appliances with new gas or clean energy appliances. In this instance, the demand for electricity would therefore fall.

Computing the Price Elasticity of Demand

Economists compute the price elasticity of demand as the percentage change in the quantity demanded divided by the percentage change in the price. That is:

$$\text{Price elasticity of demand} = \frac{\text{Percentage change in quantity demanded}}{\text{Percentage change in price}}$$

For example, suppose that a 10 per cent increase in the price of a packet of breakfast cereal causes the amount bought to fall by 20 per cent. Because the quantity demanded of a good is negatively related to its price, the percentage change in quantity will always have the opposite sign to the percentage change in price. In this example, the percentage change in price is a *positive* 10 per cent (reflecting an increase), and the percentage change in quantity demanded is a *negative* 20 per cent (reflecting a decrease). For this reason, price elasticities of demand are sometimes reported as negative numbers. In this book we follow the common practice of dropping the minus sign and reporting all price elasticities as positive numbers. (Mathematicians call this the *absolute value*.) With this convention, a larger price elasticity implies a greater responsiveness of quantity demanded to price.

In our example, the price elasticity of demand is calculated as:

$$\text{Price elasticity of demand} = \frac{20\%}{10\%} = 2$$

A price elasticity of demand of 2 reflects the fact that the change in the quantity demanded is proportionately twice as large as the change in the price.

Elasticity can have a value which lies between 0 and infinity:

- Between 0 and 1, elasticity is said to be price inelastic, that is the percentage change in quantity demanded is less than the percentage change in price.
- If elasticity is greater than 1 it said to be price elastic – the percentage change in quantity demanded is greater than the percentage change in price.
- If the percentage change in quantity demanded is the same as the percentage change in price then the price elasticity is equal to 1 and is called unit or unitary elasticity.

Relative Elasticities We have and will use the term 'relatively' elastic or inelastic throughout our analysis. The use of this term is important. We can look at goods, for example, both of which are classed as 'inelastic' but where one is more inelastic than the other. If we are comparing good x, which has a price elasticity of 0.2, and good y, which has a price elasticity of 0.5, then both are price inelastic. Good y is more price elastic in comparison, however. As with so much of economics, careful use of terminology is important in conveying a clear understanding.

Calculating Price Elasticity

In this next section we will describe two methods commonly used to calculate price elasticity. These are the midpoint or arc elasticity of demand and point elasticity of demand. Some institutions may focus on only one of these methods, in which case you can (if you wish) skip the method below which your institution does not cover.

Using the Midpoint (Arc Elasticity of Demand) Method If you try calculating the price elasticity of demand between two points on a demand curve, you will notice that the elasticity from point A to point B seems different from the elasticity from point B to point A. For example, consider these numbers:

$$\text{Point } A: \text{ Price} = €4 \text{ Quantity} = 120$$
$$\text{Point } B: \text{ Price} = €6 \text{ Quantity} = 80$$

The standard way to compute a percentage change is to divide the change by the initial level and multiply by 100. Going from point A to point B, the price rises by 50 per cent, and the quantity falls by 33 per cent, indicating that the price elasticity of demand is 33/50 or 0.66. By contrast, going from point B to point A, the price falls by 33 per cent, and the quantity rises by 50 per cent, indicating that the price elasticity of demand is 50/33 or 1.5 (to one decimal place).

The midpoint method overcomes this problem by computing a percentage change by dividing the change by the midpoint (or average) of the initial and final levels. We can express the midpoint method with the following equation for the price elasticity of demand between two points, denoted (Q_1, P_1) and (Q_2, P_2):

$$\text{Price elasticity of demand} = \frac{(Q_2 - Q_1) / [(Q_2 + Q_1) / 2]}{(P_2 - P_1) / [(P_2 + P_1) / 2]}$$

The numerator and denominator reflect the proportionate change in quantity and price computed using the midpoint method.

Using the example above, €5 is the midpoint of €4 and €6. Therefore, according to the midpoint method, a change from €4 to €6 is considered a 40 per cent rise, because $(6 - 4)/5 \times 100 = 40$. Similarly, a change from €6 to €4 is considered a 40 per cent fall.

The midpoint method gives the same answer regardless of the direction of change and facilitates the calculation of the price elasticity of demand between two points. In our example, when going from point A to point B, the price rises by 40 per cent, and the quantity falls by 40 per cent. Similarly, when going from point B to point A, the price falls by 40 per cent, and the quantity rises by 40 per cent. In both directions, the price elasticity of demand equals 1.

Using the Point Elasticity of Demand Method Rather than measuring elasticity between two points on the demand curve, point elasticity of demand measures elasticity at a particular point on the demand curve. Let us take our general equation for price elasticity given by:

$$\text{Price elasticity of demand} = \frac{\%\Delta Qd}{\%\Delta P}$$

where the Greek letter delta (Δ) means 'change'. To calculate the percentage change in quantity demanded and the percentage change in price we use the following equations:

$$\text{Percentage change in quantity demanded} = \frac{\Delta Qd}{Qd} \times 100$$

And:

$$\text{Percentage change in price} = \frac{\Delta P}{P} \times 100$$

We can substitute these two equations into our elasticity equation to get:

$$\text{Price elasticity of demand} = \frac{\Delta Qd}{Qd} / \frac{\Delta P}{P}$$

This can be rearranged to give:

$$\text{Price elasticity of demand} = \frac{P}{Qd} \times \frac{\Delta Qd}{\Delta P} \quad \textbf{(1)}$$

The slope of the demand curve is given by:

$$\text{Slope} = \frac{\Delta P}{\Delta Qd}$$

The ratio $\frac{Qd}{\Delta P}$ is the reciprocal of the slope of the demand curve, so the equation for the price elasticity of demand can also be written as:

$$\text{Price elasticity of demand} = \frac{P}{Qd} \times \frac{1}{\frac{\Delta P}{\Delta Qd}} \quad \textbf{(2)}$$

Using either equation 1 or equation 2 will lead to the same answer (the difference will be taking into account the negative sign, which as we have seen can be dropped when we are using absolute numbers).

Using calculus, the equation is:

$$\text{Price elasticity of demand} = \frac{P}{Qd} \times \frac{dQd}{dP}$$

This considers the change in quantity and the change in price as the ratio tends to the limit, in other words how quantity demanded responds to an infinitesimally small change in price.

The Variety of Demand Curves

Because the price elasticity of demand measures how much quantity demanded responds to changes in the price, it is closely related to the slope of the demand curve. The following heuristic (rule of thumb) is a useful guide *when the scales of the axes are the same*: The flatter the demand curve that passes through a given point, the greater the price elasticity of demand. The steeper the demand curve that passes through a given point, the smaller the price elasticity of demand.

Figure 3.12 shows five cases, each of which uses the same scale on each axis. This is an important point to remember, because simply looking at a graph and the shape of the curve without recognizing the scale can result in incorrect conclusions about elasticity.

In the extreme case of a zero elasticity shown in panel (a), demand is *perfectly inelastic*, and the demand curve is vertical. In this case, regardless of the price, the quantity demanded stays the same.

FIGURE 3.12

The Price Elasticity of Demand

The steepness of the demand curve indicates the price elasticity of demand (assuming the scale used on the axes are the same). Note that all percentage changes are calculated using the midpoint method and rounded.

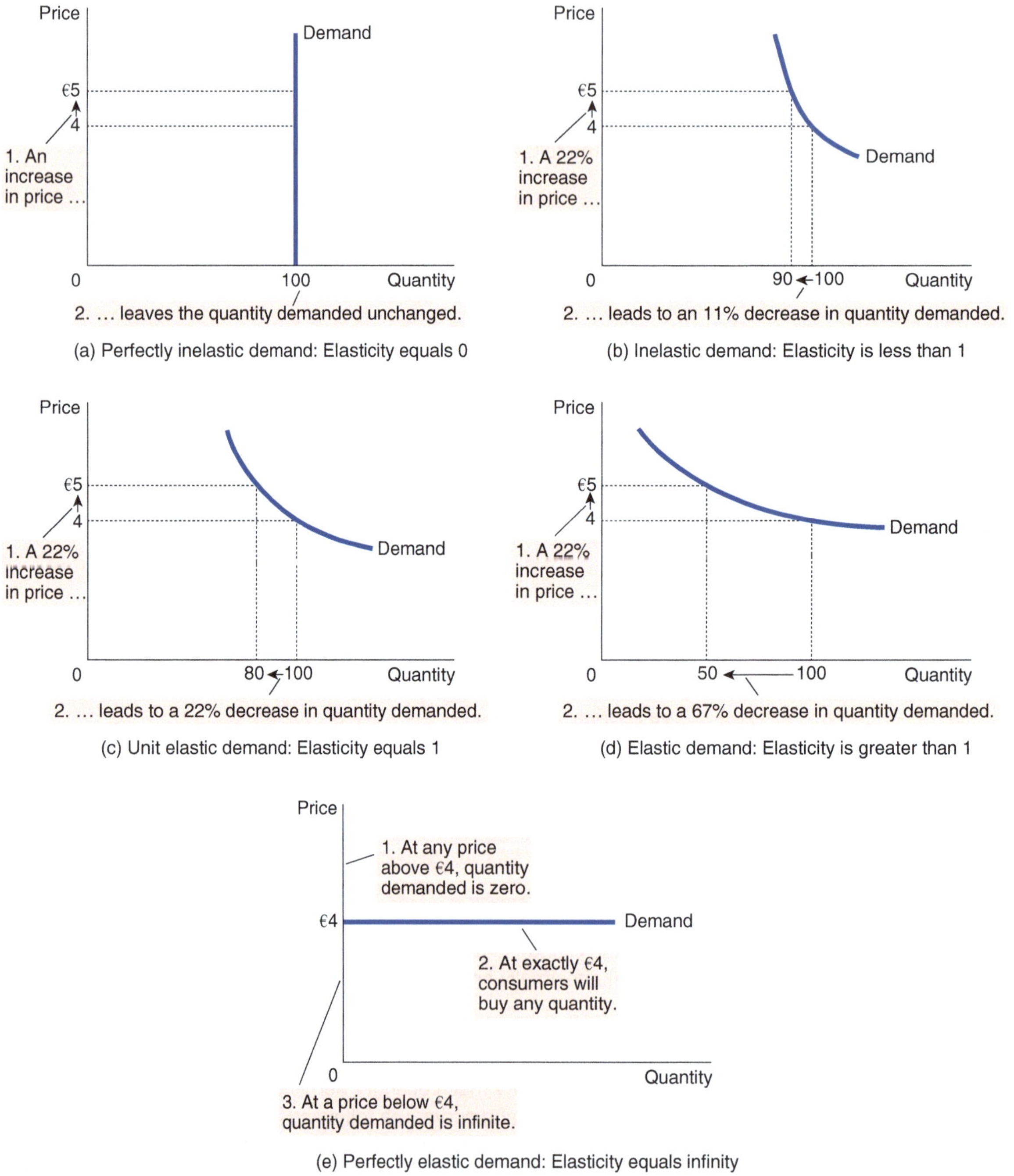

Panels (b), (c) and (d) present demand curves that are flatter and flatter, and represent greater degrees of elasticity. At the opposite extreme shown in panel (e), demand is *perfectly elastic*. This occurs as the price elasticity of demand approaches infinity and the demand curve becomes horizontal, reflecting the fact that very small changes in the price lead to huge changes in the quantity demanded.

Total Expenditure, Total Revenue and the Price Elasticity of Demand

When studying changes in demand in a market, we are interested in the amount paid by buyers of the good which will in turn represent the total revenue that sellers receive. **Total expenditure** is given by the total amount bought multiplied by the price paid. We can show total expenditure graphically, as in Figure 3.13. The height of the box under the demand curve is P and the width is Q. The area of this box, $P \times Q$, equals the total expenditure in this market. In Figure 3.13, where P = €4 and Q = 100, total expenditure is €4 × 100 or €400.

total expenditure the amount paid by buyers, computed as the price of the good times the quantity purchased

FIGURE 3.13

Total Expenditure

The total amount paid by buyers, and received as revenue by sellers, equals the area of the box under the demand curve, P × Q. Here, at a price of €4, the quantity demanded is 100, and total expenditure is €400.

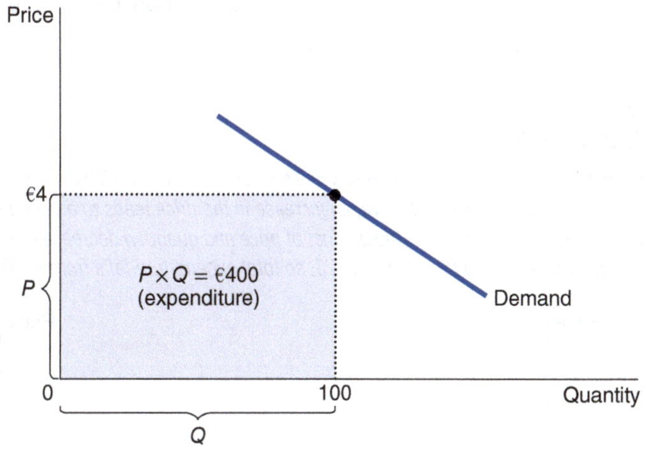

Business Decision-Making and Price Elasticity For businesses that are not price-takers, having some understanding of the price elasticity of demand is important in decision-making. If a firm is thinking of changing price, how will the demand for its product react? The firm knows that there is an inverse relationship between price and demand, but the effect on its revenue will be dependent on the price elasticity of demand. It is entirely possible that a firm could reduce its price and increase total revenue. Equally, a firm could raise price and find its total revenue falling. At first glance this might sound counter-intuitive, but it all depends on the price elasticity of demand for the product.

If demand is price inelastic, as in Figure 3.14, then an increase in the price causes an increase in total expenditure. Here an increase in price from €1 to €3 causes the quantity demanded to fall from 100 to 80, and so total expenditure rises from €100 to €240. An increase in price raises $P \times Q$ because the fall in Q is proportionately smaller than the rise in P.

If demand is price elastic an increase in the price causes a decrease in total expenditure. In Figure 3.15, for instance, when the price rises from €4 to €5, the quantity demanded falls from 50 to 20, and so total expenditure falls from €200 to €100. Because demand is price elastic, the reduction in the quantity demanded more than offsets the increase in the price. That is, an increase in price reduces $P \times Q$ because the fall in Q is proportionately greater than the rise in P.

FIGURE 3.14

How Total Expenditure Changes When Price Changes: Inelastic Demand

With a price inelastic demand curve, an increase in the price leads to a decrease in quantity demanded that is proportionately smaller. Therefore, total expenditure (the product of price and quantity) increases. Here, an increase in the price from €1 to €3 causes the quantity demanded to fall from 100 to 80, and total expenditure rises from €100 to €240.

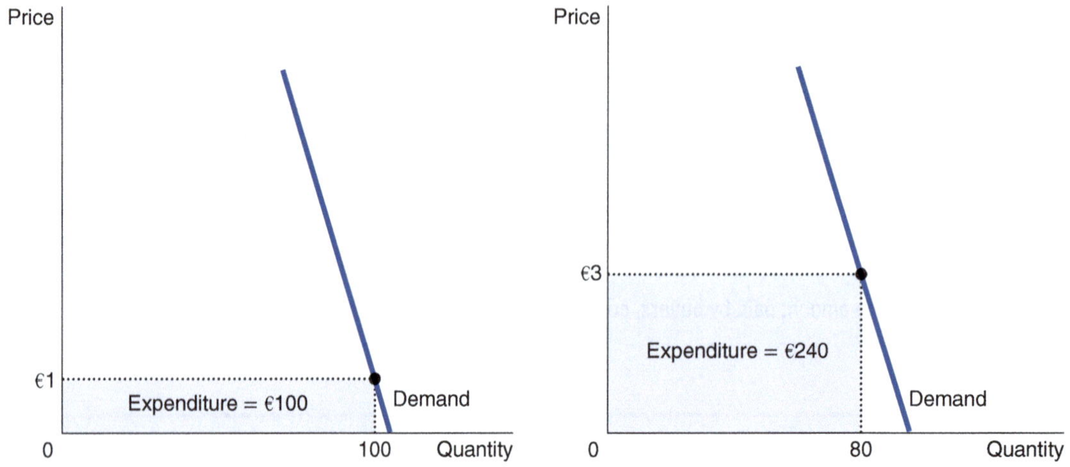

FIGURE 3.15

How Total Expenditure Changes When Price Changes: Elastic Demand

With a price elastic demand curve, an increase in the price leads to a decrease in quantity demanded that is proportionately larger. Therefore, total expenditure (the product of price and quantity) decreases. Here, an increase in the price from €4 to €5 causes the quantity demanded to fall from 50 to 20, so total expenditure falls from €200 to €100.

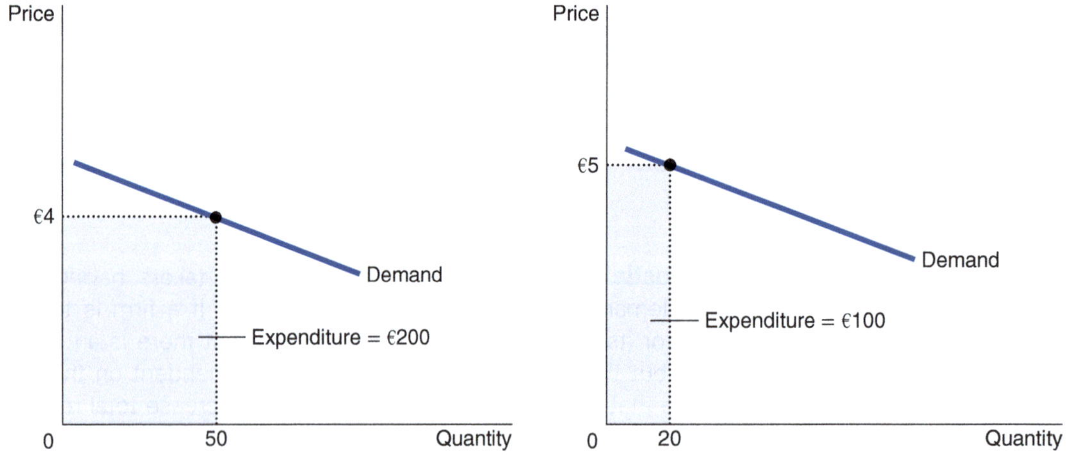

Although the examples in these two figures are extreme, they illustrate a general rule:

- When demand is price inelastic (a price elasticity less than 1), price and total expenditure move in the same direction.
- When demand is price elastic (a price elasticity greater than 1), price and total expenditure move in opposite directions.
- If demand is unit price elastic (a price elasticity exactly equal to 1), total expenditure remains constant when the price changes.

Elasticity and Total Expenditure along a Linear Demand Curve

Demand curves can be linear (straight) or curvilinear (curved). The elasticity at any point along a demand curve will depend on the shape of the demand curve. A linear demand curve has a constant slope. Slope is defined as 'rise over run', which here is the ratio of the change in price ('rise', or the change in the *y* axis) to the change in quantity ('run', or the change in the *x* axis). The slope of the demand curve in Figure 3.16 is constant because each €1 increase in price causes the same two-unit decrease in the quantity demanded.

FIGURE 3.16

Elasticity of a Linear Demand Curve

The slope of a linear demand curve is constant, but its elasticity is not. The demand schedule in the table was used to calculate the price elasticity of demand by the midpoint method. At points with a low price and high quantity, the demand curve is inelastic. At points with a high price and low quantity, the demand curve is elastic.

Price	Quantity	Total revenue (Price × Quantity)	% change in price	% change in quantity	Price elasticity	Quantity description
€7	0	€0	15	200	13.3	Elastic
6	2	12	18	67	3.7	Elastic
5	4	20	22	40	1.8	Elastic
4	6	24	29	29	1.0	Unit elastic
3	8	24	40	22	0.6	Inelastic
2	10	20	67	18	0.3	Inelastic
1	12	12	200	15	0.1	Inelastic
0	14	0				

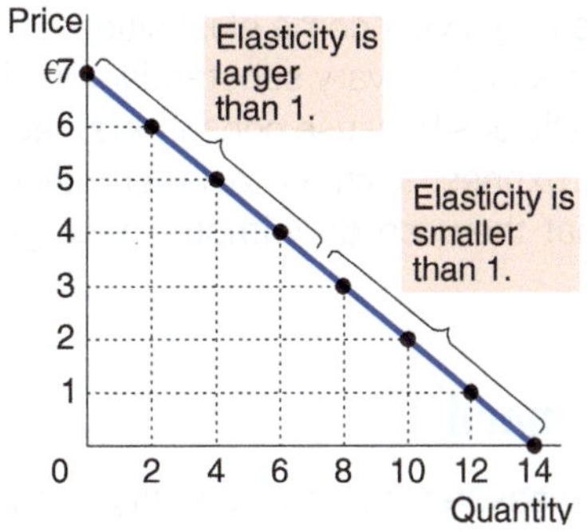

Even though the slope of a linear demand curve is constant, the elasticity is not. The reason is that the slope is the ratio of *changes* in the two variables, whereas the elasticity is the ratio of *percentage changes* in the two variables. The table in Figure 3.16 shows the demand schedule for the linear demand curve in the graph. The table uses the midpoint method to calculate the price elasticity of demand. At points with a low price and high quantity, the demand curve is price inelastic. At points with a high price and low quantity, the demand curve is price elastic.

The table also presents total expenditure at each point on the demand curve. These numbers illustrate the relationship between total expenditure and price elasticity. When the price is €1, for instance, demand is inelastic and a price increase to €2 raises total expenditure. When the price is €5, demand is elastic, and a price increase to €6 reduces total expenditure. Between €3 and €4, demand is exactly unit price elastic and total expenditure is the same at these two prices.

OTHER DEMAND ELASTICITIES

In addition to the price elasticity of demand, economists also use other elasticities to describe the behaviour of buyers in a market.

The Income Elasticity of Demand

The **income elasticity of demand** measures how quantity demanded changes as consumer income changes. It is calculated as the percentage change in quantity demanded divided by the percentage change in income. That is:

$$\text{Income elasticity of demand} = \frac{\text{Percentage change in quantity demanded}}{\text{Percentage change in income}}$$

income elasticity of demand a measure of how much quantity demanded of a good responds to a change in consumers' income, computed as the percentage change in quantity demanded divided by the percentage change in income

Many goods are *normal goods*: higher income raises quantity demanded. Because quantity demanded and income change in the same direction, normal goods have positive income elasticities. *Inferior goods*, where higher income lowers the quantity demanded, see quantity demanded and income move in opposite directions; inferior goods have negative income elasticities.

Even among normal goods, income elasticities vary substantially in size. Necessities, such as food and clothing, tend to have small income elasticities because consumers, regardless of how low their incomes, choose to buy some of these goods. Luxuries, such as caviar and diamonds, tend to have high income elasticities because consumers feel that they can do without these goods altogether if their income is too low.

The Cross-Price Elasticity of Demand

The **cross-price elasticity of demand** measures how the quantity demanded of one good changes as the price of another good changes. It is calculated as the percentage change in quantity demanded of good 1 divided by the percentage change in the price of good 2. That is:

$$\text{Cross-price elasticity of demand} = \frac{\text{Percentage change in quantity demanded of good 1}}{\text{Percentage change in the price of good 2}}$$

cross-price elasticity of demand a measure of how much the quantity demanded of one good responds to a change in the price of another good, computed as the percentage change in quantity demanded of the first good divided by the percentage change in the price of the second good

Whether the cross-price elasticity is a positive or negative number depends on whether the two goods are substitutes or complements. Substitutes are goods that are typically used in place of one another, such as Pepsi and Coca-Cola. An increase in the price of Pepsi induces some buyers to switch to Coca-Cola instead. Because the price of Pepsi and the quantity of Coca-Cola demanded move in the same direction, the cross-price elasticity is positive.

Conversely, complements are goods that are typically used together, such as smartphones and payment plans. In this case, the cross-price elasticity is negative, indicating that an increase in the price of smartphones reduces the quantity of payment plans demanded. As with price elasticity of demand, cross-price elasticity may increase over time. So, a change in the price of electricity will have little effect on demand for gas in the short run but much stronger effects over several years.

SELF TEST Define the price elasticity of demand. Explain the relationship between total expenditure and the price elasticity of demand.

PRICE ELASTICITY OF SUPPLY

The **price elasticity of supply** measures how much the quantity supplied responds to changes in the price. Supply of a good is said to be *price elastic* (or price sensitive) if the quantity supplied responds substantially to changes in the price. Supply is said to be *price inelastic* (or price insensitive) if the quantity supplied responds only slightly to changes in the price.

price elasticity of supply a measure of how much the quantity supplied of a good responds to a change in the price of that good, computed as the percentage change in quantity supplied divided by the percentage change in price

The Price Elasticity of Supply and Its Determinants

The price elasticity of supply depends on the flexibility of sellers to change the amount of the good they produce in response to changes in price. For example, seafront property has a price inelastic supply because it is very difficult to produce more of it quickly, that is supply is not very sensitive to changes in price. By contrast, manufactured goods, such as books, cars and television sets, have relatively price elastic supplies, because the firms that produce them can run their factories longer in response to a higher price, that is supply is sensitive to changes in price.

Elasticity can take any value greater than or equal to 0. The closer to 0 the more price inelastic, and the closer to infinity the more price elastic. The following subsections look at the key determinants of the price elasticity of supply.

The Time Period In most markets, a key determinant of the price elasticity of supply is the time period being considered. Supply is usually more price elastic in the long run than in the short run. Over very short periods of time, firms may find it impossible to respond to a change in price by changing output. In the short run, firms cannot easily change the size of their factories or productive capacity to make more or less of a good but may have some flexibility. For example, it might take a month to employ new labour and access more supplies of raw materials, and after that time some increase in output can be accommodated. By contrast, over longer periods, firms can build new factories or close old ones, employ new staff and buy in more capital and equipment. In addition, new firms can enter a market and old firms can shut down. Thus, in the long run, the quantity supplied can respond substantially to price changes.

Productive Capacity Most businesses, in the short run, will have a finite capacity. This is an upper limit to the amount that they can produce at any one time which is determined by the amount of factor inputs they possess. How far they are using this capacity depends, in turn, on the state of the economy. In periods of strong economic growth, firms may be operating at or near full capacity. If demand is rising for the product they produce and prices are rising, it may be difficult for the firm to expand output to meet this new demand and so supply may be price inelastic.

When the economy is growing slowly or is contracting, some firms may find they must cut back output and may only be operating at 60 per cent of full capacity, for example. In this situation, if demand later increased and prices started to rise, it may be much easier for the firm to expand output relatively quickly and so supply would be more elastic.

The Size of the Firm/Industry It is possible that, as a general rule, supply may be more price elastic in smaller firms or industries than in larger ones. For example, consider a small independent furniture manufacturer. Demand for its products may rise, and in response the firm may be able to buy in raw materials (wood, for example) to meet this increase in demand. While the firm will incur a cost in buying in this timber, it is unlikely that the unit cost for the material will increase substantially.

Compare this to a situation where a steel manufacturer increases its purchase of raw materials (iron ore, for example). Buying large quantities of iron ore on global commodity markets can drive up unit price and, by association, unit costs.

The response of supply to changes in price in large firms/industries, therefore, may be less elastic than in smaller firms/industries. This is also related to the number of firms in the industry – the more firms there are in the industry the easier it is to increase supply, *ceteris paribus*.

The Mobility of Factors of Production Consider a farmer whose land is currently devoted to producing wheat. A sharp rise in the price of rapeseed might encourage the farmer to switch use of land from wheat to rapeseed in the next planting cycle. The mobility of the factor of production land, in this case, is relatively high and so the supply of rapeseed may be relatively price elastic.

A number of multinational firms that have plants in different parts of the world now build each plant to be identical. What this means is that if there is disruption to one plant, the firm can more easily transfer operations to another plant elsewhere and continue production 'seamlessly'. Equally, they can expand supply by utilizing these plants more swiftly. Car manufacturers provide an example of this interchangeability of parts and operations. The chassis may be identical across a range of branded car models. This is the case with some Audi, Volkswagen, Seat and Skoda models. This means that supply may be more price elastic as a result.

Compare this to the supply of highly skilled oncology consultants. An increase in the wages of oncology consultants (suggesting a shortage exists) will not mean that a renal consultant or other doctors can suddenly switch to take advantage of the higher wages and increase the supply of oncology consultants. In this example, the mobility of labour to switch between different uses is limited and so the supply of these specialist consultants is likely to be relatively price inelastic.

Ease of Storing Stock/Inventory In some firms, stocks can be built up to enable the firm to respond more flexibly to changes in prices. In industries where inventory build-up is relatively easy and cheap, supply is more price elastic than in industries where it is much harder to do this. Consider the fresh fruit industry, for example. Storing fresh fruit is not easy because it is perishable, and so the price elasticity of supply in this industry may be more inelastic.

Computing the Price Elasticity of Supply

Computing the price elasticity of supply is similar to the process we adopted for calculating the price elasticity of demand. The two methods of calculating price elasticity of demand, the midpoint or arc method and the point elasticity method, also apply to supply.

The price elasticity of supply is the percentage change in the quantity supplied divided by the percentage change in the price. That is:

$$\textit{Price elasticity of supply} = \frac{\textit{Percentage change in quantity supplied}}{\textit{Percentage change in price}}$$

For example, suppose that a 10 per cent increase in the price of bicycles causes the amount of bicycles supplied to the market to rise by 15 per cent. We calculate the elasticity of supply as:

$$\text{Price elasticity of supply} = \frac{15}{10}$$
$$\text{Price elasticity of supply} = 1.5$$

In this example, the price elasticity of 1.5 reflects the fact that the quantity supplied moves proportionately one and a half times as much as the price.

The Midpoint (Arc) Method of Calculating the Elasticity of Supply As with the price elasticity of demand, the midpoint method for the price elasticity of supply between two points, denoted (Q_1, P_1) and (Q_2, P_2), has the following equation:

$$\text{Price elasticity of supply} = \frac{(Q_2 - Q_1)/[(Q_2 + Q_1)/2]}{(P_2 - P_1)/[(P_2 + P_1)/2]}$$

The numerator is the percentage change in quantity supplied computed using the midpoint method, and the denominator is the percentage change in price computed using the midpoint method.

Point Elasticity of Supply Method As with point elasticity of demand, point elasticity of supply measures elasticity at a particular point on the supply curve. Exactly the same principles apply as with point elasticity of demand, so the equation for point elasticity of supply is given by:

$$\text{Price elasticity of supply} = \frac{P}{Qs} \times \frac{1}{\frac{\Delta P}{\Delta Qs}}$$

Using calculus, the equation is:

$$\text{Price elasticity of supply} = \frac{P}{Qs} \times \frac{dQs}{dP}$$

The Variety of Supply Curves

Because the price elasticity of supply measures the responsiveness of quantity supplied to changes in price, it is reflected in the appearance of the supply curve (again, assuming we are using the same scales on the axes of diagrams being used). Figure 3.17 shows five cases. In the extreme case of a zero elasticity, as shown in panel (a), supply is *perfectly inelastic* and the supply curve is vertical. In this case, the quantity supplied is the same regardless of the price.

In panels (b), (c) and (d) the supply curves are increasingly flatter, associated with increasing price elasticity, which shows that the quantity supplied responds more to changes in the price. At the opposite extreme, shown in panel (e), supply is *perfectly elastic*. This occurs as the price elasticity of supply approaches infinity and the supply curve becomes horizontal, meaning that very small changes in the price lead to very large changes in the quantity supplied.

In some markets, the elasticity of supply is not constant but varies over the supply curve. Figure 3.18 shows a typical case for an industry in which firms have factories with a limited capacity for production. For low levels of quantity supplied, the elasticity of supply is high, indicating that firms respond substantially to changes in the price. In this region, firms have capacity for production that is not being used, such as buildings and machinery sitting idle for all or part of the day. Small increases in price make it profitable for firms to begin using this idle capacity. As the quantity supplied rises, firms begin to reach capacity. Once capacity is fully used, increasing production further requires the construction of new factories. To induce firms to incur this extra expense, the price must rise substantially, so supply becomes less elastic.

FIGURE 3.17

The Price Elasticity of Supply

The price elasticity of supply determines whether the supply curve is steep or flat (assuming that the scale used for the axes is the same). Note that all percentage changes are calculated using the midpoint method and rounded.

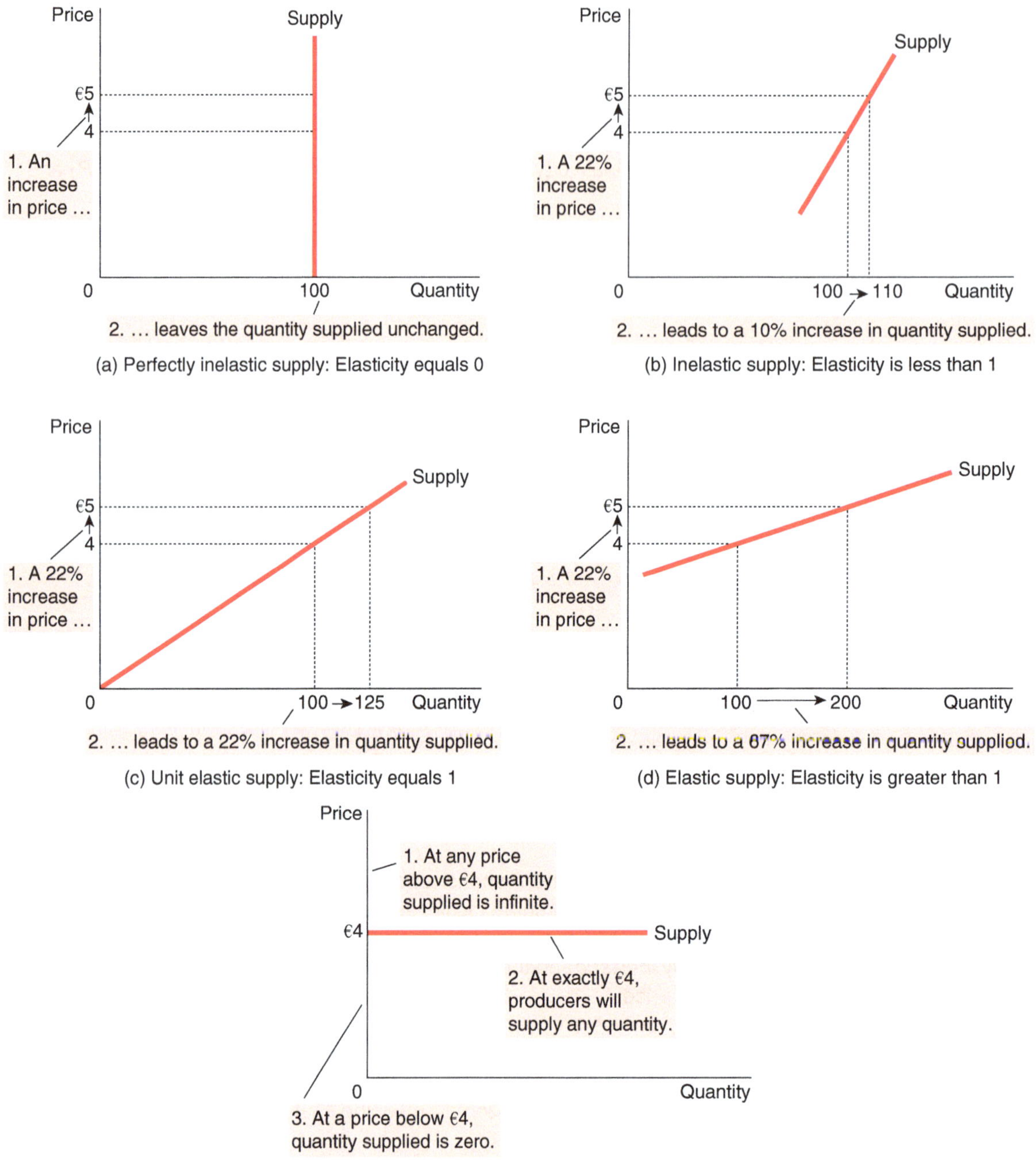

(a) Perfectly inelastic supply: Elasticity equals 0

(b) Inelastic supply: Elasticity is less than 1

(c) Unit elastic supply: Elasticity equals 1

(d) Elastic supply: Elasticity is greater than 1

(e) Perfectly elastic supply: Elasticity equals infinity

Figure 3.18 presents a numerical example of this phenomenon. In each case we have used the midpoint method and the numbers have been rounded for convenience. When the price rises from €3 to €4 (a 29 per cent increase, according to the midpoint method), the quantity supplied rises from 100 to 200 (a 67 per cent increase). Because quantity supplied moves proportionately more than the price, the supply curve has elasticity greater than 1.

By contrast, when the price rises from €12 to €15 (a 22 per cent increase), the quantity supplied rises from 500 to 525 (a 5 per cent increase). In this case, quantity supplied moves proportionately less than the price, so the elasticity is less than 1.

FIGURE 3.18

How the Price Elasticity of Supply Can Vary

Because firms often have a maximum capacity for production, the elasticity of supply may be very high at low levels of quantity supplied and very low at high levels of quantity supplied. Here, an increase in price from €3 to €4 increases the quantity supplied from 100 to 200. Because the increase in quantity supplied of 67 per cent (computed using the midpoint method) is larger than the increase in price of 29 per cent, the supply curve is elastic in this range. By contrast, when the price rises from €12 to €15, the quantity supplied rises only from 500 to 525. Because the increase in quantity supplied of 5 per cent is smaller than the increase in price of 22 per cent, the supply curve is inelastic in this range.

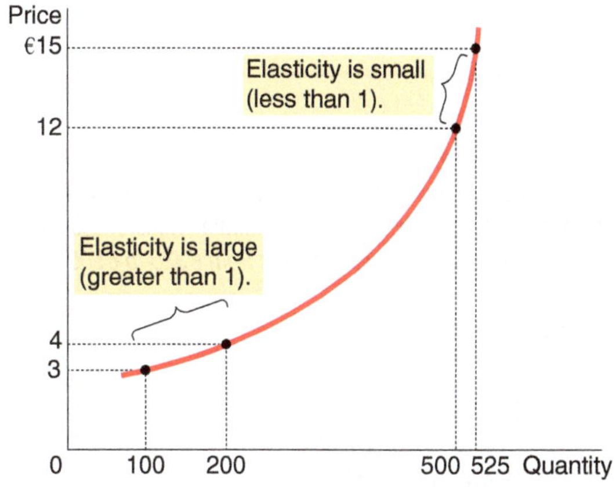

SELF TEST Define the price elasticity of supply. Explain why the price elasticity of supply might be different in the long run from in the short run.

Total Revenue and the Price Elasticity of Supply

When studying changes in supply in a market we are often interested in the resulting changes in the **total revenue** received by producers. In any market, total revenue received by sellers is $P \times Q$, the price of the good times the quantity of the good sold. This is highlighted in Figure 3.19, which shows an upwards sloping supply curve with an assumed price of €5 and a supply of 100 units. The height of the box under the supply curve is P and the width is Q. The area of this box, $P \times Q$, equals the total revenue received in this market. In Figure 3.19, where $P =$ €5 and $Q = 100$, total revenue is €5 × 100 or €500.

total revenue the amount received by sellers of a good, computed as the price of the good times the quantity sold

FIGURE 3.19

The Supply Curve and Total Revenue

The total amount received by sellers equals the area of the box under the demand curve, P × Q. Here, at a price of €5, the quantity supplied is 100 and the total revenue is €500.

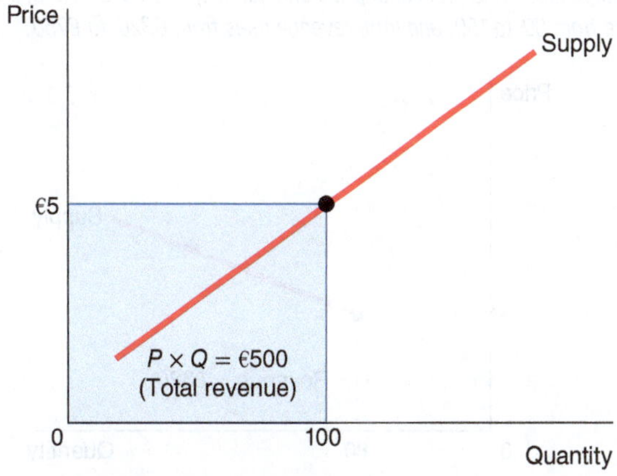

Total revenue will change as price changes, depending on the price elasticity of supply. If supply is price inelastic, as in Figure 3.20, then an increase in price which is proportionately larger causes an increase in total revenue. Here, an increase in price from €4 to €5 causes the quantity supplied to rise only from 80 to 100, and so total revenue rises from €320 to €500 (assuming the firm sells the additional supply).

FIGURE 3.20

How Total Revenue Changes When Price Changes: Inelastic Supply

With an inelastic supply curve, an increase in price leads to an increase in quantity supplied that is proportionately smaller. Therefore, total revenue (the product of price and quantity) increases. Here, an increase in price from €4 to €5 causes the quantity supplied to rise from 80 to 100, and total revenue rises from €320 to €500.

If supply is price elastic then a similar increase in price brings about a much larger than proportionate increase in supply. In Figure 3.21, we assume a price of €4 and a supply of 80 with total revenue of €320. Now a price increase from €4 to €5 leads to a much greater than proportionate increase in supply from 80 to 150 with total revenue rising to €750 – again, assuming the firm sells the additional supply.

FIGURE 3.21

How Total Revenue Changes When Price Changes: Elastic Supply

With a price elastic supply curve, an increase in price leads to an increase in quantity supplied that is proportionately larger. Therefore, total revenue (the product of price and quantity) increases. Here, an increase in the price from €4 to €5 causes the quantity supplied to rise from 80 to 150, and total revenue rises from €320 to €750.

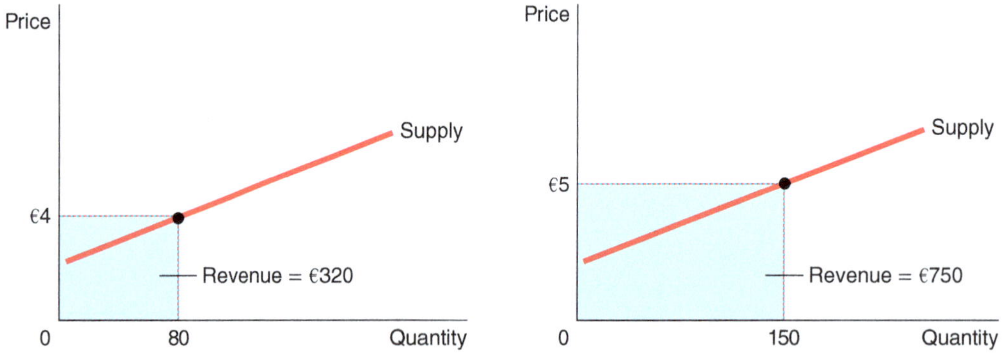

APPLICATIONS OF SUPPLY AND DEMAND ELASTICITY

Why is it the case that travel on the train at certain times during the day is a different price than at other times? Why, despite the increase in productivity in agriculture, have farmers' incomes gone down, on average, over recent years? At first, these questions might seem to have little in common. Yet both questions are about markets and the forces of supply and demand. An understanding of elasticity is a key part of the answer to these and many other questions.

Why Does the Price of Train Travel Vary at Different Times of the Day?

In many countries the price of a train journey varies at different times during the day and the week. Assume that a ticket for a seat on a train from Birmingham to London between 6.00am and 9.00am is around £85 (€100), whereas for the same journey leaving at midday the price is between £6 and £32 (€7.13 and €38.02). Train operators know that the demand for rail travel between 6.00am and 9.00am is higher than during the day time, but they also know that few commuters have choices about when they arrive at work or to meetings, conferences and so on.

An individual can use other forms of transport such as their car or a coach, but the train is often very convenient, so the number of substitutes is considered low. The price elasticity of demand for train travel early in the morning, therefore, is relatively low compared to at midday. In the morning, train operators know that seats on trains will be mostly taken and there will be very few left empty, whereas during the day it is much more likely that trains will be running with empty seats. Knowing that there is a different price elasticity of demand means that train operators can maximize revenue at these different times by charging different prices.

Figure 3.22 shows the situation in the market for train travel. Panel (a) shows the demand and supply for tickets between Birmingham and London between 6.00am and 9.00am. The demand curve D_i is relatively steep, indicating that the price elasticity of demand is relatively low. At a price of £80, 1,000 tickets are bought and as a result the total revenue for the train operator is £80,000.

FIGURE 3.22

Price Sensitivity in the Passenger Train Market

Panel (a) represents the market for train travel between 6.00am and 9.00am between two major cities. The demand for train travel at this time is relatively price inelastic – passengers are insensitive to price at this time because they have few alternatives and have to get into work and to meetings. The train operators generate revenue of £80,000 by selling 1,000 tickets at £80 each.

Panel (b) shows the market after 9.00am. Train operators face a different demand curve at this time and passengers are more price sensitive. If the train operator continued to charge £80, demand would be just 100 and revenue would be £8,000. If the train operator reduces the price to £40, demand would be 800 and the total revenue would be £32,000.

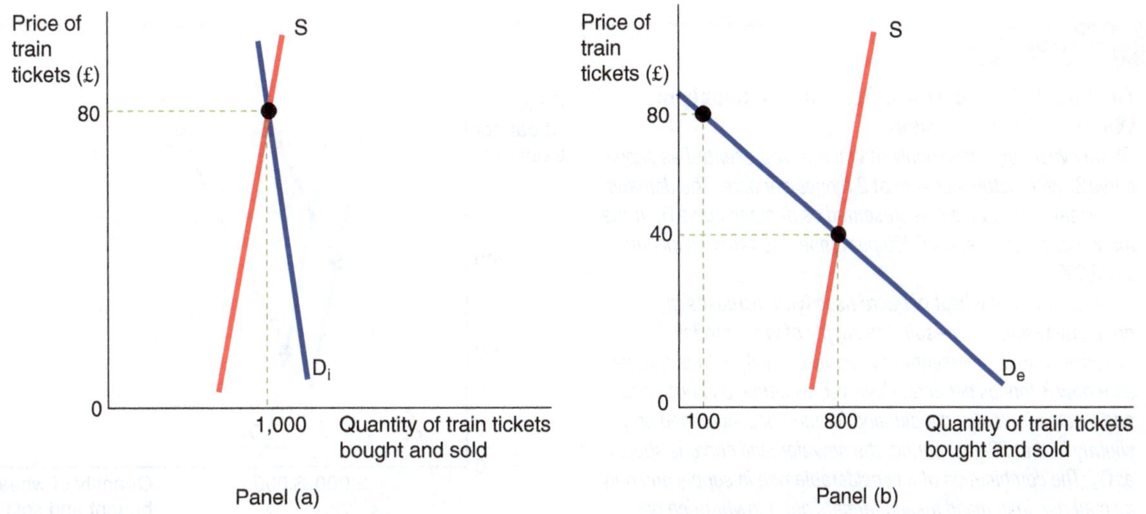

Panel (b) shows a demand curve D_e with a similar supply curve. *Ceteris paribus*, the train operator has the same number of trains available at all times during the day, but notice that the supply curve is relatively steep and therefore inelastic because although the operator has some flexibility to increase the number of trains available, and thus seats for passengers, there is a limit as to how far the capacity can be varied throughout the day.

If the train operator charged a price of £80 after 9.00am, the demand for tickets would be relatively low at 100. Total revenue, therefore, would be £8,000 and there would be many seats left empty. This is because the train operator effectively faces a different market during the day. Those who travel by train during the day may have a choice – they might be travelling for leisure or to see friends and they do not *need* to travel by train, unlike those in the morning who must get to work at a certain time.

These passengers are price sensitive – charge too high a price and they will not choose to travel by train, but offer a price that these passengers see as being attractive and which to them represents value for money and they may choose to buy a train ticket. If the train operator, therefore, sets the price for train tickets after 9.00am at £40, the demand for train tickets would be 800 and total revenue would be £32,000. If we assume that train operators are acting rationally, then they would prefer to generate revenue of £32,000 rather than £8,000, and so it would be more sensible for them to charge a lower price to capture these more price sensitive passengers.

Why Have Farmers' Incomes Fallen Despite Increases in Productivity?

In many developed countries, agricultural production has increased since the 1920s. One of the reasons is that farmers can use more machinery. Also, advances in science and technology have meant that productivity, the amount of output per acre of land, has increased.

Assume a farmer has 1,000 acres of land and grows wheat, and that 20 years ago each acre of land yielded an average of 2 tonnes of wheat. We say 'an average' because output can be dependent on factors outside the farmer's control such as the weather, pests, diseases and so on. Assume that the price of wheat is €200 per tonne. Twenty years ago, the average income for our farmer would be 2,000 tonnes × €200 = €400,000. *Ceteris paribus*, if productivity increases meant that average output per acre was now 3 tonnes per acre, income would rise to €600,000.

However, this assumes other things are equal. Research suggests that the demand for food is relatively price and income inelastic. Over the 20-year period we are assuming in our analysis, the demand for wheat may only have risen by a relatively small amount and is price and income inelastic. People may earn more money now than they did 20 years ago, but evidence suggests that as people's incomes increase, they spend a smaller proportion of income on food. This is called 'Engel's law'.

Figure 3.23 shows a representation of this situation. In the first time period, the supply curve, representing output per acre of 2 tonnes, intersects the demand curve D_1 at a price of €200 per tonne giving the farmer an income of €400,000.

FIGURE 3.23

The Effect of Increases in Demand and Supply of Wheat on Farm Incomes

Twenty years ago, the supply of wheat is represented as supply curve S_1 with output per acre at 2 tonnes per acre. The demand for wheat at that time is represented as demand curve D_1. If the market price of wheat is €200 per tonne, the farmer's income is €400,000.

The output of wheat per acre rises with increases in productivity and, as a result, the supply of wheat today increases and is represented by supply curve S_2 with output per acre now 3 tonnes per acre. However, as demand is both price and income inelastic, the demand for food has increased only slightly in that 20-year period; the new demand curve is shown as D_2. The combination of a considerable rise in supply and only a small rise in demand means farmers get a lower price per tonne and income is actually lower.

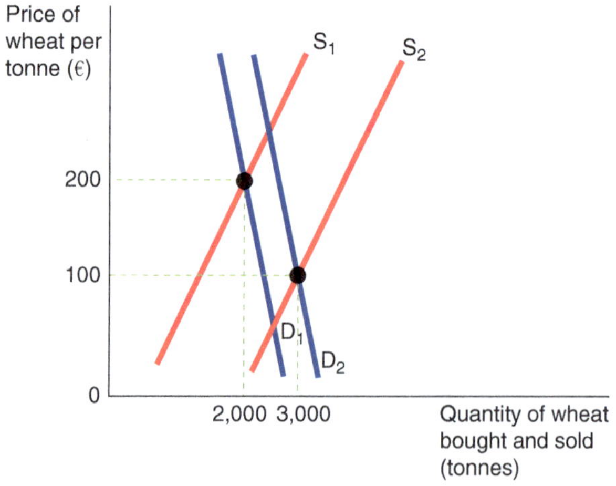

Twenty years later, the productivity improvements at the farm see the supply curve shifting to S_2 representing an average output per acre of 3 tonnes. However, over the 20-year period, demand has increased, but only by a small amount as people spend a smaller proportion of their income on food as they get richer. The fact that food is relatively price inelastic is indicated by the relatively steep demand curve, and the result is that the market price has fallen to €100 per tonne, with the farmer now selling 3,000 tonnes. The farmer's income has fallen to €300,000.

SELF TEST What must firms who charge different prices for the same product at different times be able to do for the pricing tactic to work? (Hint: can you use off-peak tickets for a train journey during peak hours?)

SUMMARY

- Economists use the model of supply and demand to analyze competitive markets. In a competitive market, there are many buyers and sellers, each of whom has little or no influence on the market price.
- The demand curve shows how the quantity of a good demanded depends on the price. According to the law of demand, as the price of a good falls, the quantity demanded rises. Therefore, the demand curve slopes downwards.
- In addition to price, other determinants of how much consumers want to buy include income, the prices of substitutes and complements, tastes, expectations, the size and structure of the population, and advertising. If one of these factors changes, the demand curve shifts.
- The supply curve shows how the quantity of a good supplied depends on the price. According to the law of supply, as the price of a good rises the quantity supplied rises. Therefore, the supply curve slopes upwards.
- In addition to price, other determinants of how much producers want to sell include the price and profitability of goods in production and joint supply, input prices, technology, expectations, the number of sellers, and natural and social factors. If one of these factors changes, the supply curve shifts.
- The intersection of the supply and demand curves determines the market equilibrium. At the equilibrium price, the quantity demanded equals the quantity supplied.
- The behaviour of buyers and sellers drives markets towards their equilibrium. When the market price is above the equilibrium price, there is a surplus of the good, which causes the market price to fall. When the market price is below the equilibrium price, there is a shortage, which causes the market price to rise.
- To analyze how any event influences a market, we use the supply and demand diagram to examine how the event affects the equilibrium price and quantity. To do this we follow three steps.
  - First, we decide whether the event shifts the supply curve or the demand curve (or both).
  - Second, we decide which direction the curve (or curves) shifts.
  - Third, we compare the new equilibrium with the initial equilibrium.
- In market economies, prices are the signals that guide economic decisions and thereby allocate scarce resources. For every good in the economy, the price ensures that supply and demand are in balance. The equilibrium price then determines how much of the good buyers choose to purchase and how much sellers choose to produce.
- The price elasticity of demand measures how much the quantity demanded responds to changes in the price. Demand tends to be more price elastic if close substitutes are available, if the good is a luxury rather than a necessity, if the market is narrowly defined or if buyers have substantial time to react to a price change.
- The price elasticity of demand is calculated as the percentage change in quantity demanded divided by the percentage change in price. If the price elasticity is less than 1, so that quantity demanded moves proportionately less than the price, demand is said to be price inelastic. If the elasticity is greater than 1, so that quantity demanded moves proportionately more than the price, demand is said to be price elastic.
- The price elasticity of supply measures how much the quantity supplied responds to changes in the price. This elasticity often depends on the time horizon under consideration. In most markets, supply is more price elastic in the long run than in the short run.

- The price elasticity of supply is calculated as the percentage change in quantity supplied divided by the percentage change in price. If price elasticity is less than 1, so that quantity supplied moves proportionately less than the price, supply is said to be price inelastic. If the elasticity is greater than 1, so that quantity supplied moves proportionately more than the price, supply is said to be price elastic.
- Total revenue, the total amount received by sellers for a good, equals the price of the good times the quantity sold. For price inelastic demand curves, total revenue rises as price rises. For price elastic demand curves, total revenue falls as price rises.
- The income elasticity of demand measures how much the quantity demanded responds to changes in consumers' income. The cross-price elasticity of demand measures how much the quantity demanded of one good responds to changes in the price of another good.

IN THE NEWS

Supply Chains

Models of the market such as those described in this chapter are relatively simple. Markets in real life are very complex even if the basic principles of the supply and demand model apply. The market for aircraft is a good example of a highly complex market. During 2023 and 2024, the US manufacturer Boeing faced a number of problems that hit output as well as demand. According to reports, the company delivered 83 aircraft to customers in the first quarter of 2024 compared to 130 in the same period in 2023. Its key rival in the aircraft supply market, Airbus, saw an increase in demand for its jets, but meeting that demand was proving challenging. The supply chain for aircraft production is complex and involves some 8,000 direct and 18,000 indirect suppliers from more than 100 countries. The fallout from the pandemic, the effects of Brexit and increased conflict combined have put pressure on supply chains which are impacting the ability of Airbus to meet its supply targets to customers. Shortages of component parts are delaying completion of aircraft. In addition, internal constraints need to be managed with reports that mandatory overtime at weekends is being considered in some manufacturing centres at Airbus.

Critical Thinking Questions

1 Assume the market for narrow body jet aircraft is in equilibrium with the price at £125 million each and the total bought and sold at 3,000 per year. Analyze the changes in the market using the supply and demand model based on an assumed fall in demand for aircraft from Boeing and a rise in demand of aircraft from Airbus. On what would the outcomes of your analysis depend?

2 The aircraft manufacturing industry is dominated by the two major suppliers, Airbus and Boeing. Does this mean that the model of markets developed in this chapter is irrelevant to this market?

3 Consider the factors that might influence the demand for aircraft as well as the supply using the basic model outlined in the chapter.

© iStock/aapsky

The complexity of supply chains in industries such as aviation highlights some of the challenges of using models in economics.

4 What do you think the price elasticity of demand and supply for aircraft might be? Explain your reasoning.

(*Continued*)

5 How are wider global issues impacting the elasticity of supply for aircraft? How might a firm like Airbus seek to manage the challenges it faces in meeting demand?

References:

www.airbus.com/en/sustainability/respecting-the-planet/responsible-supply-chain, accessed 10 July 2025.
www.proactiveinvestors.co.uk/companies/news/1048862/airbus-facing-supply-chain-shortages-according-to-reuters-report-1048862.html, accessed 10 July 2025.
www.reuters.com/business/aerospace-defense/airbus-seeks-mandatory-weekend-overtime-catch-up-delayed-a220-production-2024-06-12/, accessed 10 July 2025.

QUESTIONS FOR REVIEW

1 a. What are the demand schedule and the demand curve, and how are they related? Why does the demand curve slope downwards from left to right?
   b. What are the supply schedule and the supply curve, and how are they related? Why does the supply curve slope upwards?
2 a. Does a change in consumers' tastes lead to a movement along the demand curve or a shift in the demand curve?
   b. Does a change in price lead to a movement along the demand curve or a shift in the demand curve?
   c. Does a change in producers' technology lead to a movement along the supply curve or a shift in the supply curve?
   d. Does a change in price lead to a movement along the supply curve or a shift in the supply curve?
   In each case, explain your reasoning and use a diagram to illustrate.
3 Francine's income declines and, as a result, she buys more cabbage. Are cabbages an inferior or a normal good? What happens to Francine's demand curve for cabbages?
4 Define the equilibrium of a market. Describe the forces that move a market towards its equilibrium. Describe the role of prices in market economies.
5 Define the price elasticity of demand and the income elasticity of demand. How is the price elasticity of supply calculated? Explain what this measures.
6 a. List and explain some of the determinants of the price elasticity of demand. Think of some examples to illustrate the factors you cover.
   b. What are the main factors that affect the price elasticity of supply? Think of some examples to illustrate the factors you cover.
7 If the price elasticity is greater than 1, is demand elastic or inelastic? If the price elasticity equals 0, is demand perfectly elastic or perfectly inelastic?
8 Is the price elasticity of supply usually larger in the short run or in the long run? Why?
9 A business person reads that the price elasticity of demand for the product they sell is 1.25. If the person wishes to increase revenue, should they increase or reduce price? Explain.
10 What factors might affect the price elasticity of supply for a commodity such as rubber in the short run and the long run? Explain.

PROBLEMS AND APPLICATIONS

1 Explain each of the following statements using supply and demand diagrams.
   a. When there is a drought in southern Europe, the price of soft fruit rises in supermarkets throughout Europe.
   b. When a report is published linking a product with an increased risk of cancer, the price of the product concerned tends to fall.
   c. The United States announces that it intends to impose new sanctions on the Islamic Republic of Iran. The price of petrol in Europe rises and the price of a used Mercedes falls.

2 Using supply and demand diagrams, show the effect of the following events on the market for sweatshirts.
   a. A drought in Egypt damages the cotton crop.
   b. The price of leather jackets falls.
   c. All universities require students to attend morning exercise classes in appropriate attire.
   d. New knitting machines are invented.

3 Think about the market for cigars.
   a. Are cigars substitutes or complements for cigarettes?
   b. Using a supply and demand diagram, show what happens in the markets for cigars if a tax on cigarettes is increased.
   c. If policymakers wanted to reduce total tobacco consumption, what policies could they combine with the cigarette tax?

4 Consider the following events: Scientists reveal that eating oranges decreases the risk of diabetes, and at the same time, farmers in Spain use a new fertilizer which increases the yield of oranges per tree. Illustrate and explain what effect these changes have on the equilibrium price and quantity of oranges. Remember to note the relative size of the changes you describe and how these could affect outcomes.

5 Suppose that the price of tickets to see your local football team play at home is determined by market forces. Currently, the demand and supply schedules are as follows:

Price (€)	Quantity demanded	Quantity supplied
10	50,000	30,000
20	40,000	30,000
30	30,000	30,000
40	20,000	30,000
50	10,000	30,000

   a. Draw the demand and supply curves. What is unusual about this supply curve? Why might this be true?
   b. What are the equilibrium price and quantity of tickets?
   c. Your team plans to increase total capacity in its stadium by 5,000 seats next season. What admission price should it charge if it wants to maximize total revenue?
   d. What is the price elasticity of demand and supply for an increase in price from €30 to €40? (Use whatever method you think is most appropriate for this example.)
   e. As a result of the calculation made in 5d. above, what would you recommend the owners of the club do if there are consistently empty seats in the stadium and they want to maximize revenue?

6 Market research has revealed the following information about the market for chocolate bars: $Qd = 1{,}600 - 300P$, and the supply schedule is $Qs = 1{,}400 + 700P$. Calculate the equilibrium price and quantity in the market for chocolate bars.

7 Seafront properties along the south coast of France have a price inelastic supply, and cars have a price elastic supply. Suppose that a rise in population doubles the demand for both products (that is, the quantity demanded at each price is twice what it was).
   a. What happens to the equilibrium price and quantity in each market?
   b. Which product experiences a larger change in price?
   c. Which product experiences a larger change in quantity?
   d. What happens to total consumer spending on each product?

8 Suppose that business travellers and holidaymakers have the following demand for airline tickets from Munich to Naples:

Price (€)	Quantity demanded (business travellers)	Quantity demanded (holidaymakers)
150	2,100	1,000
200	2,000	800
250	1,900	600
300	1,800	400

a. As the price of tickets rises from €200 to €250, what is the price elasticity of demand for (i) business travellers and (ii) holidaymakers? (Use either the midpoint or point method in your calculations.)
b. Why might holidaymakers have a different price elasticity to business travellers?

9 Consider public policy aimed at smoking.
a. Studies indicate that the price elasticity of demand for cigarettes is about 0.4. If a packet of cigarettes is currently priced at €17 and the government wants to reduce smoking by 20 per cent, by how much should it increase the price through levying a tax?
b. If the government permanently increases the price of cigarettes, will the policy have a larger effect on smoking one year from now or five years from now? Explain.
c. Studies also find that teenagers have a higher price elasticity of demand for cigarettes than do adults. Why might this be true?

10 Explain why the following might be true: a drought around the world raises the total revenue that farmers receive from the sale of grain, but a drought only in France reduces the total revenue that French farmers receive.

PART 2 THE DATA OF MACROECONOMICS

4 MEASURING A NATION'S WELL-BEING AND THE PRICE LEVEL

Economics is divided into two branches: microeconomics and macroeconomics. Microeconomics is the study of how individual households and firms make decisions and how they interact with one another in markets. Macroeconomics is the study of the economy as a whole.

There are a number of areas of controversy in macroeconomics. Some of the disagreements of economists stem from economic history and different schools of thought, which have shaped thinking since the mid-1700s. It must be remembered that some of the most revered economic thinkers were people of their day, describing, analyzing and thinking about problems which were highly relevant at particular points in history. Economies and the context in which they operate do not stand still. What was relevant and prescient about the way an economic system was thought to have worked in one period of history does not necessarily mean that its mechanics and analysis can be transferred to other time periods. For example, the analysis of the causes of the Great Depression of the 1930s and the policy options which were appropriate to remedy some of the problems caused by the crisis, may have some similarities to the causes and consequences of the 2007–9 Financial Crisis. The issues faced by economies in the mid-2020s are different again from those which faced policymakers at the end of the 2010s. Given the differences, to what extent will policy measures used in, for example, 2010, still be relevant and applicable in 2030?

Before we look at measures of economic well-being, we are going to briefly introduce some key schools of thought which have applied analysis to the way the economy works. It is sensible to keep these in mind as we progress through the second half of the book and our study of macroeconomics.

MARXIST ECONOMICS

Karl Marx's analysis of economics and economic systems is based on the idea that 'modern' human history is dominated by class struggles and the exploitation of one class by another. This exploitation is based on economic power, slaves and slave owners, feudal lords and peasants, and ultimately, under a capitalist economic system, the bourgeoisie capital-owning class and the proletariat. Marx had an explanation for the tendency of capitalism to experience repeated crises.

At the heart of his argument is the labour theory of value. Marx suggested that over a business cycle, the rate of profit would decline. He saw equilibrium not in terms of market clearing but the tendency for rates of profit on capital to equalize to capitalists who are in constant competition with each other. This market competition prevents capitalists from taking all surplus value for themselves. Some of it must be reinvested to maintain the advantage over competitors. Some of this investment is in machinery, which Marx referred to as 'constant capital'.

Improvements in technology mean that this investment increases the ratio of constant capital to variable capital (labour). If this ratio increases at a faster rate than the ratio of surplus value to variable capital, there will be a tendency for the rate of profit to fall. Ultimately, this drive by capitalists to keep ahead of each other would drive some businesses out of the market. Unemployment (the reserve army of the unemployed) would increase as a result. Pressure on wages will cause wage rates to fall, causing the rate of profit to fall, and the process would begin over.

Ultimately, these crises would lead to workers taking to organizing themselves and ultimately taking the means of production into their own hands, possibly through revolution. One of the features of socialism, the social ownership and greater democratic control of the means of production, was a greater focus on equity as opposed to efficiency. This was a recognition that the outcomes of classical economic theory might be 'efficient' but not necessarily 'fair'. Marx was writing at a time when the amount of labour working in factories was extensive; it is perhaps no surprise that their latent power was to be feared. It is easy to see why the owning class was wary of the development of trade unions and organized labour. Marx's critique challenged the neo-classical orthodoxy and represented a challenge to the fundamental basis of the 'organized, civilized' society of the late nineteenth century.

THE AUSTRIAN SCHOOL

We have already encountered some of the economists associated with the Austrian School – Menger, Jevons and Walras. Menger wrote *Principles of Economics*, published in 1871, and argued that the analysis of economics, such as individual preferences and decisions at the margin, were universally applicable. This was much along the same lines that the classical economists had argued for using the 'law of demand and supply'. Menger's view was not accepted by other economists in Germany at the time, notably William Roscher, a professor at the University of Leipzig from 1848 until his death in 1894. It was, allegedly, some of Roscher's students who used the term 'Austrian school', as a means of insulting Menger and others on the faculty at the University of Vienna. Despite the insult, economists of the Austrian school have made significant contributions to economic thinking. Since the 1930s, however, the Austrian school has been associated with universities other than Vienna, for example Chicago. In particular, Ludwig von Mises, Friedrich Hayek (the Nobel Prize winner for Economics in 1974 who taught at the University of Chicago) and Friedrich von Wieser have been at the forefront of an intellectual tradition that is linked to the Austrian school.

The fundamental beliefs associated with the Austrian school are those of the power of free markets, private property, property rights and individual choice. These are tempered by an understanding of decision-making over time and under conditions of uncertainty. Austrian school economists recognize that ultimately individuals are the only ones that make choices, but in so doing generate unintended consequences. In analyzing choices, a focus on the process and relationships of exchange and bargaining is important. This reflects the idea that understanding human sciences like economics is not a case of being able to predict, but rather to understand. Recognition of the role of subjective views in economics is thus important in analyzing issues such as utility and opportunity cost.

Thinkers in the Austrian school tradition have made numerous contributions to macroeconomics, most notably in the field of monetary theory for which Hayek received his Nobel Prize. Austrian economists are noted for proposing free banking and the denationalization of money. Free banking would see the abolition of central banks, and a system where banks would compete in a free market, setting interest rates and issuing their own currency.

KEYNESIANISM

Keynesian economics is associated with the work of John Maynard Keynes (1883–1946). The very fact that a school of thought is named after him is perhaps a testament to the importance of Keynes. Keynes studied under Alfred Marshall and Arthur Pigou at Cambridge in the early 1900s, where he eventually ended up teaching. His most notable work, *The General Theory of Employment, Interest and Money*, published in 1936, has influenced subsequent generations of economists. It presented a challenge to neo-classical and Austrian school assumptions that free markets, left to their own devices, clear. Keynes suggested that there was no reason that, for example, labour markets should clear, and that the persistence of unemployment over a period could be due to demand deficiencies in the economy. Demand deficiencies could be corrected by government intervention in the economy, by using tax and spending instruments to boost aggregate demand (or to reduce it when the economy was overheating). Keynes' ideas were developed by other notable economists including Joan Robinson, John Hicks, James Tobin, Arthur Okun, Robert Solow and Paul Samuelson.

Some of these developments were christened 'New Keynesianism', in particular the work of Samuelson and Solow in developing the so-called 'neo-classical synthesis', which sought to explain the short-term failure of markets to clear because of sticky wages and prices. The attempt to explain Keynesian ideas in the context of neo-classical principles was coined 'bastard Keynesianism' by Joan Robinson.

A number of developed economies adopted Keynesian demand management policies after World War II, and unemployment remained relatively low and growth stable up until the late 1960s. At this point, global pressures began to have wider economic impacts. The collapse of the Bretton Woods system of fixed exchange rates against gold, and the oil price shocks caused by the tensions between Arabs and Israelis in the early 1970s, began to reveal fault lines in economies.

Some argued that demand management policies had led to complacency among firms and workers, who expected governments to always come to the rescue when economic times got hard. This, it is argued, led to a lack of competitiveness and an over-reliance on the state. In the 1960s, research by economists into the role of money and monetary policy, and the problems being experienced by a number of countries of accelerating inflation and rising unemployment (stagflation), led to the decline in the use of demand management policies. Keynesian ideas became eclipsed by monetarism. The 2007–9 Financial Crisis and the subsequent global recession led to a resurgence of interest in Keynes' ideas.

MONETARISM

Monetarism has become associated with a number of things, not least an assumption that all monetarists are advocates of free markets. This is not the case. Monetarism is essentially linked to a number of beliefs, most notably that in the long run increases in the money supply have no effect on real variables (so-called monetary neutrality), but in the short run this neutrality may not exist. Monetary neutrality implies that an increase in the money supply will, over a period, lead to an increase in the price level, but not in real variables such as output, consumption and relative prices. The idea that changes in the money supply would lead to changes in the price level was encapsulated in the Fisher equation of exchange.

One of the leading economists of the monetarist school was Milton Friedman, winner of the Nobel Prize for Economics in 1976. Friedman had challenged aspects of Keynes' ideas when he published *A Theory of the Consumption Function* in 1957, which developed the idea of the permanent income hypothesis. In other work, he researched price determination in individual markets, but his association with the revival of monetarism is perhaps what he will be remembered for. Friedman noted that 'inflation is always and everywhere a monetary phenomenon'. The subjugation of Keynesian demand management policies in the 1970s as inflation accelerated alarmingly in a number of developed economies, and the acceptance of Friedman's analysis of the role of the money supply, led to a greater focus on attempting to control the money supply as a means of controlling inflation.

In the UK and the United States, the respective governments announced targets for the growth in the money supply throughout much of the 1980s, but in the event failed to achieve these targets. The policy was abandoned in favour of exchange rate targeting and, later, inflation targeting.

THE NATURE OF MACROECONOMICS

The goal of macroeconomics is to explain the economic changes that affect many households, firms and markets simultaneously. Economists analyze the economy as a whole, as it provides an indication of the overall well-being. We can identify two measures of well-being. Subjective well-being refers to the way in which people evaluate their own happiness. Objective well-being refers to measures of the quality of life and uses indicators such as educational attainment, measures of the standard of living, life expectancy and so on. Many of the macroeconomic variables which economists study are inextricably linked with these definitions of well-being. Having a reasonable income means that people can afford to buy the necessities and luxuries in life which contribute to subjective well-being. Countries with higher national incomes can provide better quality education, more secure jobs, higher quality of housing, infrastructure and healthcare, among other things, which affect objective well-being.

One of the most common ways in which the well-being of an economy is measured is through *gross domestic product,* or simply GDP, which measures the total income of a nation. GDP is a widely reported macroeconomic statistic, but it has its critics, and the way the data are collected also has limitations. As with many things, what is considered a good measure of well-being depends on underlying belief systems and judgements. For example, GDP measures focus on incomes, with the implication that higher national income equates to an increased ability to acquire more goods and services, which in turn means increased well-being. This can be interpreted as being based on a consumerist value system, which may not take adequate account of factors which can also contribute to subjective and objective well-being. Some economists have pointed out that despite considerable increases in GDP since the late 1960s in many developed countries, reports of subjective well-being have not risen by the same amount. There may be a number of reasons for this, but it seems that what economists and politicians might use as a measure of the health and wealth of an economy is not perceived in the same way by the citizens of a country.

We will begin our investigation of measures of well-being by looking at national income. Given the caveats outlined above, this remains one of the most important ways in which well-being is reported and measured.

THE ECONOMY'S INCOME AND EXPENDITURE

Incomes are used as a measure of well-being because incomes can be used to purchase life's necessities and luxuries. Income is, therefore, equated with the standard of living. Recall that the standard of living is defined as the amount of goods and services that can be purchased by the population of a country. By this definition, those with higher incomes enjoy higher standards of living – better housing, better healthcare, fancier cars, more frequent and luxurious holidays and so on. The same logic can be applied to a nation's overall economic well-being. To judge whether an economy is doing well or poorly, we can look at the total income that everyone in the economy is earning. This is the task of GDP.

GDP measures two things at once: the total income of everyone in the economy and the total expenditure on the economy's output of goods and services. These two things are really the same because every transaction has two parties: a buyer and a seller. Every euro of spending by some buyer is a euro of income for a seller. For example, if Michael pays Astrid €20 to clean the windows at his house, Astrid is a seller of a service and Michael is a buyer. Astrid earns an income of €20 and Michael spends €20. Thus the transaction contributes equally to the economy's income and to its expenditure. GDP, whether measured as total income or total expenditure, rises by €20.

The Circular Flow of Income

You go to a cafe on campus in between lectures and buy a hot drink and a sandwich and either hand over €5 to the person behind the counter or use your phone, watch or a card to pay for the transaction. If you think about this transaction, it encapsulates the circular flow of income. Your expenditure is €5 and the cafe (the business) receives an income of €5. The €5 you have handed over represents the value of the goods you have purchased and which have been produced – the inputs and other resources that have been used in producing the hot drink and sandwich. This is the essence of the circular flow model. The equality of income and expenditure can be represented through the circular flow diagram in Figure 4.1. This is a model which describes all the transactions between households and firms in a simple economy. In this economy, the market for goods and services is where households and firms interact through firms providing goods and services which are bought by households. The spending by households on these goods and services represents the revenue of firms. The two also interact in the market for factors of production. Firms use the money they receive from the sale of goods and services to purchase the factors of production (land, labour, capital and enterprise) from households who provide these factor services. The factor incomes received by households (wages, rent, interest and profit) are used to pay for goods and services. In this economy, money flows from households to firms and then back to households.

FIGURE 4.1

The Circular Flow Diagram

Households buy goods and services from firms, and firms use the revenue from sales to pay wages to workers, rent to landowners, interest on capital and profit to owners of firms. GDP equals the total amount spent by households in the market for goods and services. It also equals the total wages, rent, interest and profit paid by firms in the markets for the factors of production. Leakages to the circular flow include taxes, savings and spending on imports whereas injections to the circular flow include government spending, investment and revenue generated from exports.

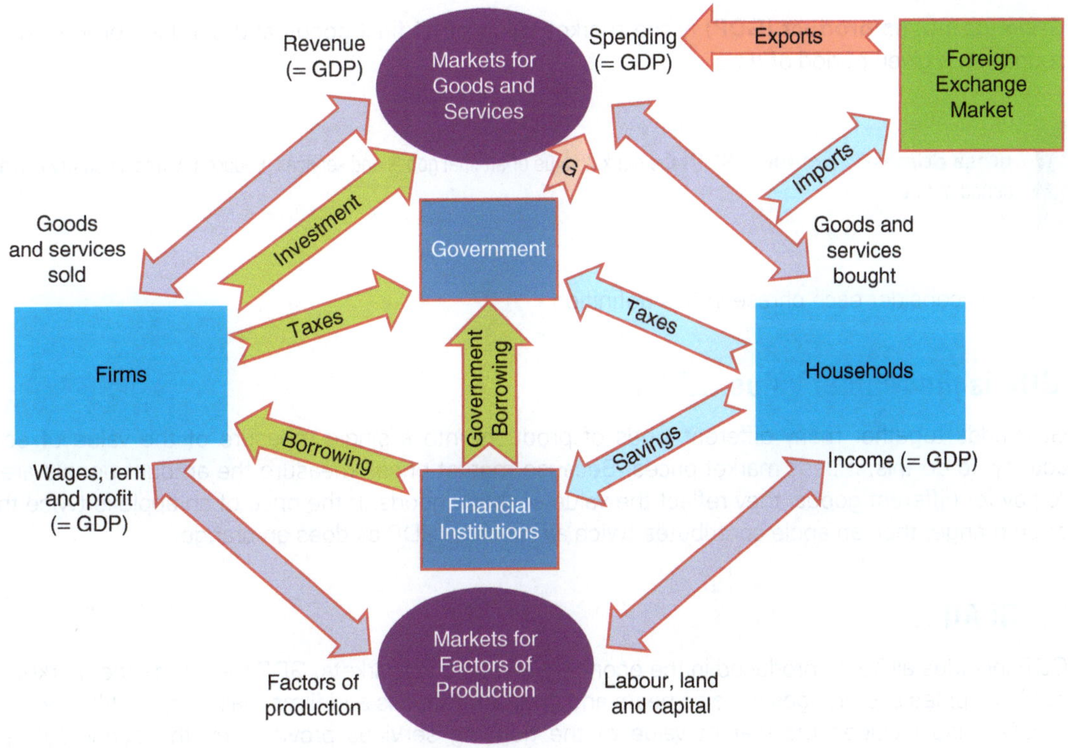

Not all of the incomes households receive are spent in the market for goods and services. Some of this income is subject to tax which is paid to the government. Some income will be saved, and the funds find their way into financial institutions in the form of pension saving, insurance and assurance and saving in bank accounts. Some of the income spent on goods and services by households leaves the economy in the form of spending on imports. Similarly, some of the income (Y) received by firms is paid to the government in business taxes. Taxes (T), saving (S) and spending on imports (M) are referred to as *leakages* from the circular flow.

Governments use tax revenue and borrowing from financial institutions to spend on government services and investment on infrastructure, education, health, defence and so on, representing government spending (G) which goes back into the circular flow. Firms make use of the funds provided by savers in financial institutions through borrowing to finance investment spending on new plant, equipment and expansion. This investment (I) finds its way back into the market for goods and services. Firms will also sell some of the goods and services they produce abroad, and so the revenue from exports (X) flows back into the system. Financial institutions also lend money overseas and firms overseas invest money into the country which is recorded as net capital outflow (NCO). Government spending (G), investment spending (I) and revenue from exports (X) are referred to as *injections* to the circular flow.

In theory, measuring GDP through income or expenditure will arrive at the same result. National income (NY), national expenditure and GDP are invariably used synonymously. A common measure of showing GDP is to add up the sum of expenditures in the economy – consumer spending (C), investment spending (I), government spending (G) and the difference between the amount paid out on imports (M) and that received in exports (X) (net exports: ($X - M$) or NX). This provides a measure of GDP given by the following equation:

$$GDP\,(NY) = C + I + G + NX$$

SELF TEST What two things are measured by GDP? How can it measure two things at once?

THE MEASUREMENT OF GROSS DOMESTIC PRODUCT

Gross domestic product (GDP) is the market value of all final goods and services produced within a country in a given period of time.

gross domestic product (GDP) the market value of all final goods and services produced within a country in a given period of time

Let us consider each phrase in this definition.

'GDP is the Market Value ...'

GDP adds together many different kinds of products into a single measure of the value of economic activity. To do this, it uses market prices. Because market prices measure the amount people are willing to pay for different goods, they reflect the value of those goods. If the price of an apple is twice the price of an orange, then an apple contributes twice as much to GDP as does an orange.

'... Of All ...'

GDP includes all items produced in the economy and sold in markets. GDP measures the market value of not just apples and oranges but also pears and grapefruit, books and films, haircuts, healthcare and so on.

GDP also includes the market value of the housing services provided by the economy's stock of housing. For rental housing, this value is easy to calculate – the rent equals both the tenant's expenditure and the landlord's income. Yet many people own the place where they live and therefore do not pay rent. The government includes this owner occupied housing in GDP by estimating its rental value. That is, GDP is based on the assumption that the owner, in effect, pays rent to themselves, so the rent is included both in their expenditure and income.

There are many goods and services that are traded, but not through official recorded markets, and these transactions may not appear in GDP figures. For example, vegetables bought at the greengrocer's shop or the supermarket are part of GDP, but vegetables grown in your garden are not. There are many trades which are carried out on a cash basis and hidden from the authorities. For example, a plumber might do a repair on a boiler, be paid in cash and not declare this as part of their income. A teenager child-minds for a couple on a Saturday night and gets paid in cash, but the value of this work is hidden from GDP figures. This type of activity is referred to as the 'informal', 'shadow' or 'black' economy. It is extremely difficult to measure the size of the shadow economy, but some studies put the number of people engaging in shadow work at 30 million in the EU, and anything up to a quarter of a country's GDP. Some estimates have put the size of the shadow economy in the UK at around £150bn (€190bn) a year and across Europe as a whole, around €2 trillion.

There are also transactions of goods and services in markets which are illegal. As such, these are unlikely to be declared to tax authorities. This can also affect the value of GDP. From September 2014, the UK's national statistical service, the Office for National Statistics (ONS), included estimates of the level of activity in illegal drugs and prostitution to bring the figures for the UK National Accounts in line with methods used across other EU countries. The ONS estimated that the average impact on the UK economy by including illegal drugs and prostitution amounts to around £11 billion (€12.3 billion) per year.

A number of economists have noted that calculations of GDP do not take into account the value of work carried out by homemakers, and neither is the value of childcare work carried out by grandparents, for example. Feminist economists, in particular, criticize the distinction between 'productive' work carried out in markets and 'unproductive work' which is not. The work done in supporting families in the home can contribute significantly to overall well-being and is the centre of most people's lives. This contribution is not considered in GDP calculations. As a result, it not only undervalues the true measure of well-being in the economy but also the value of women's productive contribution to the economy.

'... Final ...'

When a paper company sells paper to a greetings card company, the paper is called an *intermediate good,* and the card is called a *final good.* GDP includes only the value of final goods. The reason is that the value of intermediate goods is already included in the prices of final goods. Adding the market value of the paper to the market value of the card would be double counting. That is, it would (incorrectly) count the paper twice.

An important exception to this principle arises when an intermediate good is produced and, rather than being used, is added to a firm's inventory of goods to be used or sold at a later date. In this case, the intermediate good is taken to be 'final' for the moment, and its value as inventory investment is added to GDP. When the inventory of the intermediate good is later used or sold, the firm's inventory investment is negative, and GDP for the later period is reduced accordingly.

'... Goods and Services ...'

GDP includes both tangible goods (food, clothing, cars) and intangible services (haircuts, house cleaning, doctor's visits). When you stream a song by your favourite band, you are buying a good, and the purchase price is part of GDP. When you pay to hear a concert by the same band, you are buying a service, and the ticket price is also part of GDP.

'... Produced ...'

GDP includes goods and services currently produced. It does not include transactions involving items produced in the past. When you buy a new textbook for your economics course, the value of the textbook is included in the GDP of the country in which the publisher operates. When one person sells a used textbook to another person, the value of the used textbook is not included in GDP.

'... Within a Country ...'

GDP measures the value of production within the geographic confines of a country. When an Australian citizen works temporarily in the UK, their production is part of UK GDP. When a UK citizen owns a factory in Bulgaria, the production at their factory is not part of UK GDP (it is part of Bulgaria's GDP). Thus items are included in a nation's GDP if they are produced domestically, regardless of the nationality of the producer.

'... In a Given Period of Time'

GDP measures the value of production that takes place within a specific interval of time. Usually that interval is a year or a quarter of a year (three months). GDP measures the economy's flow of income and expenditure during that interval.

When the government reports the GDP for a quarter, it usually presents GDP 'at an annual rate'. This means that the figure reported for quarterly GDP is the amount of income and expenditure during the quarter multiplied by four. The government uses this convention so that quarterly and annual figures on GDP can be compared more easily.

In addition, when the government reports quarterly GDP, it presents the data after they have been modified by a statistical procedure called *seasonal adjustment*. The unadjusted data show clearly that the economy produces more goods and services during certain times of the year than during others (as you might guess, December's holiday shopping season is a high point in many countries, while the period before and after Ramadan is a high point for many Muslim countries). When monitoring the condition of the economy, economists and policymakers often want to look beyond these regular seasonal changes. Therefore government statisticians adjust the quarterly data to take out the seasonal cycle.

SELF TEST Which contributes more to GDP – the production of €1 worth of tin or the production of €1 worth of gold? Why?

FYI

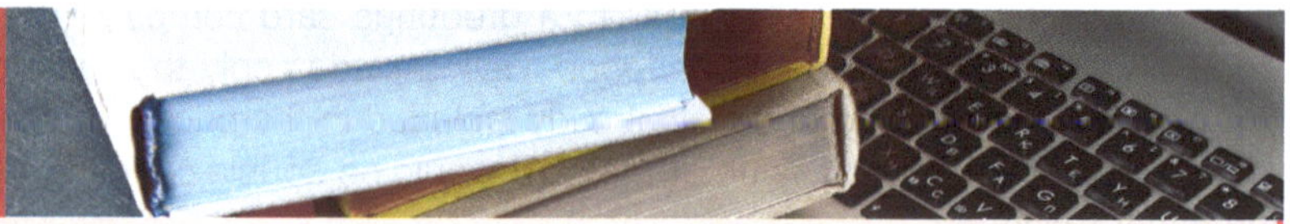

Other Measures of Income

When the ONS or Eurostat computes the GDP every three months for the UK and the EU respectively, they also compute various other measures of income to arrive at a more complete picture of what is happening in the economy. These other measures differ from GDP by excluding or including certain categories of income. What follows is a brief description of five of these income measures, ordered from largest to smallest, based on the UK:

- *Gross national product (GNP)* is the total income earned by a nation's permanent residents (called nationals). It differs from GDP by including income that domestic residents earn abroad and excluding income that foreigners earn in the domestic country, as we saw above. For most countries, domestic residents are responsible for most domestic production, so GDP and GNP are quite close.
- *Net national product (NNP)* is the total income of a nation's residents (GNP) minus losses from depreciation. *Depreciation* is the wear and tear on the economy's stock of equipment and structures, such as lorries rusting and computers becoming obsolete.
- *National income (NY)* is the total income earned by a nation's residents in the production of goods and services. It differs from net national product by excluding indirect business taxes (such as sales taxes) and including business subsidies. NNP and NY also differ because of a 'statistical discrepancy' that arises from problems in data collection.

(*Continued*)

- *Personal income* is the income that households and non-corporate businesses receive. Unlike NY, it excludes *retained earnings*, which is income that corporations have earned but have not paid out to their owners. It also subtracts corporate income taxes and contributions for social insurance. In addition, personal income includes the interest income that households receive from their holdings of government debt and the income that households receive from government transfer programmes, such as welfare and social security payments.
- *Disposable personal income* is the income that households and non-corporate businesses have left after satisfying all their obligations to the government. It equals personal income minus personal taxes and certain non-tax payments (such as parking tickets).

Although the various measures of income differ in detail, they almost always tell the same story about economic conditions. When GDP is growing rapidly, these other measures of income are usually growing rapidly; when GDP is falling, these other measures are usually falling as well.

THE COMPONENTS OF GDP

Spending in the economy takes many forms. At any moment, the Müller family may be having lunch in a Munich restaurant; Honda may be building a car factory on the banks of the Rhine; and the German army may be procuring weapons from German arms manufacturers. German GDP includes all of these various forms of spending on domestically produced goods and services. Similarly, each country in Europe will monitor the forms of spending and income to arrive at the GDP for that country.

Earlier we noted that national income could be described by the equation:

$$Y \equiv C + I + G + NX$$

Notice that we have used the three bar, 'identically equals' symbol, '≡', in this equation. This is because the equation is an *identity* – an equation that must be true by the way the variables in the equation are defined. In this case, because each euro or pound of expenditure included in GDP is placed into one of the four components of GDP, the total of the four components must be equal to GDP. For the most part we will follow normal practice in dealing with identities and use the usual equals sign, '='. Let us look at each of these four components more closely.

Consumption

Consumption is spending by households on goods and services. 'Goods' include household spending on durables, such as cars and appliances like washing machines and fridges, and non-durable goods, such as food and clothing.

consumption spending by households on goods and services, with the exception of purchases of new housing

'Services' include such intangible items as haircuts, entertainment and medical care. Household spending on education is also included in consumption of services (although you might argue that it would fit better in the next component).

Investment

Investment is the purchase of buildings, equipment and machinery that will contribute to future productive output. It is the sum of purchases of capital equipment, inventories and structures. Investment in structures includes expenditure on new housing. By convention, the purchase of a new house is the one form of household spending categorized as investment rather than consumption.

investment spending on capital equipment, inventories and structures, including household purchases of new housing

The treatment of inventory accumulation is noteworthy. When Sony produces a smartphone and, instead of selling it, adds it to its inventory, Sony is assumed to have 'purchased' the phone for itself. That is, the national income accountants treat the phone as part of Sony's investment spending. If Sony later sells the phone out of inventory, Sony's inventory investment will then be negative, offsetting the positive expenditure of the buyer. Inventories are treated this way because one aim of GDP is to measure the value of an economy's production, and goods added to inventory are part of that period's production.

Government Spending

Government spending includes spending on goods and services by local and national governments. It includes the salaries of government workers and spending on public works.

government spending spending on goods and services by local and national governments

The meaning of 'government spending' requires a little clarification. When the government pays the salary of an army general, that salary is part of government spending. What happens when the government pays a social security benefit to one of the elderly? Such government spending is called a **transfer payment** because it is not made in exchange for a currently produced good or service. Transfer payments alter household income, but they do not reflect the economy's production (from a macroeconomic standpoint, transfer payments are like negative taxes). Because GDP is intended to measure income from, and expenditure on, the production of goods and services, transfer payments are not counted as part of government spending.

transfer payment a payment for which no good or service is exchanged

Net Exports

Net exports equal the purchases of domestically produced goods and services by foreigners (exports), which generates a flow of funds into a country, minus the domestic purchases of foreign goods (imports), which result in funds leaving a country. A domestic firm's sale to a buyer in another country, such as the sale of Sony phones to customers in Europe, increases Japanese net exports.

net exports spending on domestically produced goods and services by foreigners (exports) minus spending on foreign goods by domestic residents (imports)

The 'net' in 'net exports' refers to the fact that the value of imports is subtracted from the value of exports. This subtraction is made because imports of goods and services are included in other components of GDP. For example, suppose that a UK household buys a £30,000 car from Volvo, the Swedish car maker. That transaction increases consumption in the UK by £30,000 because car purchases are part of consumer spending in the UK. It also reduces net exports by £30,000 because the car is an import (note it represents an export for Sweden). In other words, net exports include goods and services produced abroad (with a minus sign) because these goods and services are included in consumption, investment and government purchases (with a plus sign). Thus when a domestic household, firm or government buys a good or service from abroad, the purchase reduces net exports. However, because it also raises consumption, investment or government purchases, it does not affect GDP. The above example shows the importance of making sure that we focus on a particular country when discussing imports and exports because of the potential for confusion to arise.

Once GDP figures are published, they can be presented in different ways. One of the most common is GDP per head or per capita. GDP per capita is found by dividing the GDP of a country by the population of that country to express national income per head of the population. This measure is useful in comparing GDP across different countries.

CASE STUDY Revisions to GDP Figures

National or regional statistical services such as the ONS or Eurostat have very sophisticated systems for collecting and calculating national income data. The European system of national and regional accounts (known as ESA95) compiles data on the structure and developments of member state economies. It uses an agreed accounting framework which is recognized across the world to allow each economy to be described and to be able to draw accurate and reliable comparisons between different regions and economies or groups of economies. It is worth trying to imagine how challenging a task collecting all this data actually is. Just look around you whenever you are out at the amount of economic activity which is taking place – people buying and selling goods and services in shops, there are online transactions, people travelling on public transport, people using their cars for which they have bought insurance, fuel and paid for maintenance, road sweepers cleaning up litter, emptying bins and removing chewing gum from the pavements, police patrolling the streets and so on. Trying to collect all the data for the expenditures that are taking place is a massive task. Inevitably, any published GDP figure is provisional and statistical services continue to update the data they receive and publish revised figures on a regular basis.

Providing accurate data is important, because business, government and investment decisions are all made with the macroeconomic environment in mind. It is made very clear, therefore, that GDP data when published is subject to revision and these revisions can sometimes be significant. Initial figures for quarterly GDP are referred to as 'flash estimates' because they are based on a fraction of the total data used for final estimate. The ONS, for example, will provide at least two revisions to initial estimates. Once all the data are in, initial estimates can be confirmed or revised up or down. Announcements on GDP data, therefore, need to be looked at with some caution. One quarter's figures may not necessarily be a reliable indicator of the pattern of GDP over time.

© iStock/gordenkoff

Data flows in from the economy all the time and results in the necessity to revise GDP figures.

Questions:

1 Why do you think it is important to develop methods of collecting and calculating national income data that is subject to agreed accounting frameworks?
2 If national income statistics are subject to frequent revision, how useful can they be for decision-making by firms and households?
3 'Because national income statistics are always effectively "out of date", they should be used with caution in any economic analysis'. To what extent do you agree with this statement?

SELF TEST List the four components of expenditure. Which of these do you think accounts for the largest proportion of GDP in a country? Why?

REAL VERSUS NOMINAL GDP

Changes in total expenditure on goods and services from one year to another can be looked at in two ways:

1. The economy is producing a larger output of goods and services (a real increase).
2. Goods and services are being sold at higher prices (a nominal increase).

When studying changes in the economy over time, these two effects are separated. The focus is on a measure of the total quantity of goods and services the economy is producing that is not affected by changes in the prices of those goods and services.

To do this, economists use a measure called **real GDP**. Real GDP answers a hypothetical question: what would be the value of the goods and services produced this year if we valued these goods and services at the prices that prevailed in some specific year in the past? By evaluating current production using prices that are fixed at past levels, real GDP shows how an economy's overall production of goods and services changes over time. The GDP figures produced using this method are called **GDP at constant prices**. GDP figures produced without taking into consideration the change in prices over time are called **GDP at current or market prices** and are calculated by taking the output of goods and services and multiplying by the price of those goods and services in the reporting year.

real GDP the production of goods and services valued at constant prices
GDP at constant prices gross domestic product calculated using prices that existed at a particular base year, which takes into account changes in inflation
GDP at current or market prices gross domestic product calculated by multiplying the output of goods and services by the price of those goods and services in the reporting year

To see more precisely how real GDP is constructed, let us consider an example.

A Numerical Example

Table 4.1 shows some data for an economy that produces only two goods – apples and potatoes. The table shows the quantities of the two goods produced and their prices in the years 2026, 2027 and 2028.

TABLE 4.1 Real and Nominal GDP

	Prices and quantities			
Year	Price of apples per kg (€)	Quantity of apples (kg)	Price of potatoes per kg (€)	Quantity of potatoes (kg)
2026	1	100	2	50
2027	2	150	3	100
2028	3	200	4	150

Year	Calculating nominal GDP
2026	(€1 per kg apples × 100 kg) + (€2 per kg potatoes × 50 kg) = €200
2027	(€2 per kg apples × 150 kg) + (€3 per kg potatoes × 100 kg) = €600
2028	(€3 per kg apples × 200 kg) + (€4 per kg potatoes × 150 kg) = €1,200
Year	**Calculating real GDP (base year 2026)**
2026	(€1 per kg apples × 100 kg) + (€2 per kg potatoes × 50 kg) = €200
2027	(€1 per kg apples × 150 kg) + (€2 per kg potatoes × 100 kg) = €350
2028	(€1 per kg apples × 200 kg) + (€2 per kg potatoes × 150 kg) = €500
Year	**Calculating the GDP deflator**
2026	(€200/€200) × 100 = 100
2027	(€600/€350) × 100 = 171
2028	(€1,200/€500) × 100 = 240

To compute total spending in this economy, we would multiply the quantities of apples and potatoes by their prices. In the year 2026, 100 kg of apples are sold at a price of €1 per kg, so expenditure on apples equals €100. In the same year, 50 kg of potatoes are sold for €2 per kg, so expenditure on potatoes also equals €100. Total expenditure in the economy – the sum of expenditure on apples and expenditure on potatoes – is €200. This amount, the production of goods and services valued at current or market prices (i.e. the price existing in the reporting year), is called **nominal GDP**.

nominal GDP the production of goods and services valued at current prices

The table shows the calculation of nominal GDP for these three years. Total spending rises from €200 in 2026 to €600 in 2027 and then to €1,200 in 2028. Part of this rise is attributable to the increase in the quantities of apples and potatoes produced, and part is attributable to the increase in the prices of apples and potatoes.

To obtain a measure of the amount produced that is not affected by changes in prices, we use real GDP, the production of goods and services valued at constant prices. Real GDP is calculated by first choosing one year as a *base year*. We then use the prices of apples and potatoes in the base year to compute the value of goods and services in all of the years. In other words, the prices in the base year provide the basis for comparing quantities in different years.

Suppose that we choose 2026 to be the base year in our example. We can then use the prices of apples and potatoes in 2026 to compute the value of goods and services produced in 2026, 2027 and 2028. Table 4.1 shows these calculations. To compute real GDP for 2026 we use the prices of apples and potatoes in 2026 (the base year) and the quantities of apples and potatoes produced in 2026. (For the base year, real GDP always equals nominal GDP.) To compute real GDP for 2027, we use the prices of apples and potatoes in 2026 (the base year) and the quantities of apples and potatoes produced in 2027. Similarly, to compute real GDP for 2028, we use the prices in 2026 and the quantities in 2028. When we find that real GDP has risen from €200 in 2026 to €350 in 2027 and then to €500 in 2028, we know that the increase is attributable to an increase in the *quantities produced*, because the prices are being held fixed at base year levels.

The growth rate in real GDP takes the difference between GDP across the two time periods under consideration denoted by $GDP_t - GDP_{t-1}$, divided by GDP in year $_{t-1}$. Multiplying the result by 100 gives the percentage rate of growth in real GDP:

$$\text{Growth rate of real GDP in year } t = \frac{(GDP_t - GDP_{t-1})}{GDP_{t-1}} \times 100$$

The GDP Deflator

Nominal GDP reflects both the prices of goods and services and the quantities of goods and services the economy is producing. In contrast, by holding prices constant at base year levels, real GDP reflects only the quantities produced. From these two statistics we can compute a third, called the **GDP deflator**, sometimes also referred to as the *implicit price level*, which reflects the prices of goods and services but not the quantities produced.

GDP deflator a measure of the price level calculated as the ratio of nominal GDP to real GDP times 100

The GDP deflator is calculated as follows:

$$\text{GDP deflator} = \frac{\text{Nominal GDP}}{\text{Real GDP}} \times 100$$

Because nominal GDP and real GDP must be the same in the base year, the GDP deflator for the base year always equals 100. The GDP deflator for subsequent years measures the change in nominal GDP from the base year that cannot be attributable to a change in real GDP by measuring the current level of prices relative to the level of prices in the base year.

Imagine that the quantities produced in the economy rise over time, but prices remain the same. In this case, both nominal and real GDP rise together, so the GDP deflator is constant. Now suppose that prices rise over time, but the quantities produced stay the same. In this second case, nominal GDP rises but real GDP remains the same, so the GDP deflator rises as well. Notice that, in both cases, the GDP deflator reflects what is happening to prices, not quantities. Real GDP is found by taking the nominal GDP and dividing by the GDP deflator:

$$\text{Real GDP} = \frac{\text{Nominal GDP}}{\text{GDP deflator}}$$

Let us now return to our numerical example in Table 4.1. The GDP deflator is computed at the bottom of the table. For 2026, the base year, nominal GDP is €200, and real GDP is €200, so the GDP deflator is 100. For the year 2027, nominal GDP is €600, and real GDP is €350, so the GDP deflator is 171. Because the GDP deflator rose in year 2027 from 100 to 171, we can say that the price level increased by 71 per cent.

The GDP deflator is one measure that economists use to monitor the average level of prices in the economy. We examine another – the Consumer Prices Index – later in this chapter, where we also describe the differences between the two measures.

SELF TEST Define real and nominal GDP. Which is a better measure of economic well-being? Why?

Chain Linking

We have looked at measuring GDP through income and expenditure methods and said that in theory they are the same. GDP can also be measured by looking at the output or production method. The price of a product represents the value of the inputs that went into production. At each stage of the production process the value of output can be recorded – the value added. The ONS defines **gross value added** (GVA) as the 'contribution to the economy of each individual producer, industry or sector'. GVA is used as the measure of the output and income approaches to measuring GDP. Statistics offices usually classify output according to industry types – construction, agriculture forestry and fisheries, mining, services and so on.

gross value added the contribution of domestic producers, industries and sectors to an economy

The measure for GDP is a 'volume measure', measuring 'how much' has been produced. In the UK the ONS must produce a single measure of GDP. It does this by using the three approaches – income, expenditure and output – with the final figure reflecting the three measures. In theory these measures should all be the same, but the process of collecting information from millions of transactions means that in reality they would never be exact.

Imagine a situation, for example, where someone has some work done on their house – say the plastering of a room. The total price for the work paid by the owner of the house might be £1,500. This should represent the sum of the resources used in the job. The plasterer may declare to His Majesty's Revenue and Customs (HMRC is responsible for collecting UK taxes) that the work represented income of £1,200 (to evade paying income tax – illegal, but nevertheless it happens). The resources used might have included the plasterboard, plaster, electricity, buckets, nails, water, trowels and hawks, the vehicles to get to and from the builders' merchants, etc. It is easy to see how, even in such a simple example, it becomes incredibly difficult to keep track of every item involved!

The choice of which base year to use in calculating real GDP is also important. Up until early 2004, the ONS used a method referred to as 'fixed base aggregations'. For example, it might have compared the data using 1995 as the base year. However, as with any statistical data which use a base year in their compilation, this can lead to inconsistencies because circumstances change. Goods, for example, that were common in 1995 may not exist anymore and there might be some products that were not available at that time – Blu-ray DVDs, for example. In general, the more you can update the base year, the more accurate the statistics will be.

Fixed base aggregations in GDP statistics were used as follows. The growth of the different parts of the economy was given weights when trying to arrive at the final figure for GDP. This took account of their relative importance in the economy and a base year of 1995 was used to help determine these weights. These base years were updated every five years.

The method, known as **annual chain linking**, helps to overcome these problems. Rather than updating the base year every five years, this method does it every year, calculating the prices in previous years' prices (PYPs). You will see GDP tables expressed as 'GDP (CVM)', where CVM means Chained Volume Measures, as opposed to 'GDP in constant prices'. The ONS and other statistical services are constantly looking to update their methods to provide more reliable and accurate data, and this is one example of such a revision of methods.

annual chain linking a method of calculating GDP volume measures based on prices in the previous year

Table 4.2 shows an example of how the chain linking method works. We will use our previous example of an economy producing apples and potatoes in the years 2026 and 2027 with the following prices and quantities.

TABLE 4.2 Chain Linking

Year	Price of apples per kg (€)	Quantity of apples (kg)	Price of potatoes per kg (€)	Quantity of potatoes (kg)
2026	1	100	2	50
2027	2	150	3	100

2026 nominal GDP = (100 × €1) + (50 × €2) = €200

2027 nominal GDP = (150 × €2) + (100 × €3) = €600

If 2026 is used as the base year, the value of 2026 and 2027 production at 2026 prices is as follows:

2026: Nominal GDP = Real GDP = €200

2027: Real GDP = (150 × €1) + (100 × €2) = €350

$$\text{The percentage change in real GDP} = \left(\frac{350 - 200}{200}\right) \times 100 = 75\%$$

Chain-weighted real GDP uses average prices over the time period:

$$\text{Average price of apples between 2026 and 2027} = \frac{(€1 + €2)}{2} = €1.50$$

$$\text{Average price of potatoes between 2026 and 2027} = \frac{(€2 + €3)}{2} = €2.50$$

2026 GDP at average prices = (100 × €1.50) + (50 × €2.50) = €275

2027 GDP at average prices = (150 × €1.50) + (100 × €2.50) = €475

$$\text{Percentage change in chain-weighted GDP} = \left(\frac{(€475 - €275)}{275}\right) \times 100 = 72.7\%$$

$$\text{Implicit GDP deflator} = \frac{\text{Nominal GDP}}{\text{Real GDP}} \times 100$$

$$\text{In 2026, the implicit GDP deflator} = \frac{200}{200} \times 100 = 100$$

$$\text{In 2027, the implicit GDP deflator} = \frac{600}{350} \times 100 = 171.4$$

The percentage change in the implicit GDP deflator = 71.4%

With chain weighting, the base year is the mid-point between the two years.

$$\text{The 2026 chain-weighted GDP deflator} = \frac{\textit{Nominal GDP}_{2026}}{\textit{Real GDP at 2026 average prices}} \times 100$$

$$= \left(\frac{200}{275}\right) \times 100 = 72.7$$

$$\text{The 2027 chain-weighted GDP deflator} = \frac{\textit{Nominal GDP}_{2027}}{\textit{Real GDP at 2027 average prices}} \times 100$$

$$= \left(\frac{600}{475}\right) \times 100 = 126.3$$

$$\text{The percentage change in the chain-weighted GDP deflator} = \left(\frac{(126.3 - 72.7)}{72.7}\right) \times 100 = 73.7\%$$

In terms of analysis of the data it should make little difference, but recognizing it enables you to be more confident that the data are more likely to be accurate and reliable compared to the previous measures. The vast majority of official data are produced using chain-weighted measures.

THE LIMITATIONS OF GDP AS A MEASURE OF WELL-BEING

The use of GDP as a measure of well-being is well established. Yet some people dispute the validity of GDP as a measure of well-being. Critics of the use of GDP suggest that it is too focused on material possessions and income. They argue that there are many things that are not measured by GDP but contribute to the quality of life and economic well-being. These include the health of a country's children, or the quality of their education, or even the beauty of the poetry making up their literary heritage.

To counter this, it can be argued that GDP might not measure these things. However, nations with larger GDPs can afford better healthcare, better educational systems and can afford to teach more of their citizens to read and enjoy poetry. GDP does not take account of our intelligence, integrity, courage or wisdom, but all these laudable attributes are easier to foster when people are less concerned about being able to afford the material necessities of life. In short, GDP does not directly measure those things that make life worthwhile, but it does measure our ability to obtain the inputs into a worthwhile life.

It is widely recognized, however, that GDP is not a perfect measure of well-being. Some things that contribute to a good life are left out of GDP:

- **Leisure.** Suppose, for instance, that everyone in the economy suddenly started working every day of the week, rather than enjoying leisure at the weekends. More goods and services would be produced, and GDP would rise. Yet, despite the increase in GDP, we should not conclude that well-being had improved. The loss from reduced leisure would offset the gain from producing and consuming a greater quantity of goods and services.
- **Work in the home and volunteer work.** Because GDP uses market prices to value goods and services, it excludes the value of much activity that takes place outside of markets. In particular, GDP omits the value of goods and services produced at home. Volunteer work also contributes to the well-being of those in society, but GDP does not reflect these contributions.
- **The quality of the environment.** Imagine that the government eliminated all environmental regulations. Firms could then produce goods and services without considering the pollution they create, and GDP might rise. Yet well-being would most likely fall. The deterioration in the quality of air and water would more than offset the gains from greater production.
- **Distribution of incomes.** A society in which 100 people have annual incomes of €50,000 has GDP of €5 million and, not surprisingly, GDP per capita of €50,000. Likewise, a society in which 10 people earn €500,000 and 90 suffer with nothing at all would have GDP of €5 million. Few people would look at those two situations and call them equivalent. GDP per person tells us what happens to the average person, but behind the average lies a large variety of personal experiences. GDP does not tell us much about income distributions.

The Economics of Happiness

Despite the massive increase in wealth, incomes and access to material goods and services for many people in developed countries since the late 1960s, our perception of happiness has not really changed that much. Numerous surveys have highlighted relatively stable rates of 'happiness' in rich countries. Professor Richard Layard, one of a group of economists including Andrew Oswald, Stephen Nickell, Robert Skidelsky, Tim Besley, Will Hutton, and those behavioural economists that we have met before in this book, have studied this apparent paradox. Layard states that in relation to Western societies: 'on average, people are no happier than they were fifty years ago' (Layard, R. (2005) *Happiness: Lessons from a New Science*. London: Penguin).

Psychologists and economists have found that links between how people see their own happiness and other things that might influence their judgement are statistically strong. This also seems to apply across different countries. As a result, we might be able to conclude that there are a range of factors that can contribute to a definition of happiness. If you are fortunate enough to find yourself being able to boast of having these characteristics, or in some cases managing to avoid them, then you are more likely to be happy.

Layard identified some key factors that may contribute to 'happiness'. He suggested that some of the factors associated with promoting happiness include sex, socializing, relaxing, praying, worshipping or meditating, eating, exercising, watching TV and shopping, among others. Other studies have suggested that an individual's level of education, health, whether they are married, single or divorced, the level of income enjoyed, whether they are working/unemployed/retired, their aspirations, and whether they have experienced bereavement, can all be contributory factors.

From such characteristics, equations to statistically arrive at measures of well-being can be derived. These have been used by both economists and psychologists and have been found to be surprisingly reliable in statistical terms. One of the leading thinkers on the economics of happiness is Professor Andrew Oswald who is based at the University of Warwick. Oswald offers the following equation:

$$W_{it} = \alpha + \beta X_{it} + \varepsilon_{it}$$

In this equation, W_{it} is the reported well-being of an individual at a particular time period and X represents a collection of variables that are known to be characteristics affecting well-being at a particular time period. These could be economic, such as income, or demographic (such as gender). The final term is an error term, which is used to take into account unobserved factors that may have an impact on the final outcome.

One of the factors above that may be affecting happiness levels more than we might expect is aspirations. You are very likely, whatever your age, to have been regaled by your parents that things were different in their day and that 'people these days have so much more'. That is very true, but what might also be the case is that different generations are starting to expect more. If your parents have managed to reach middle age and have a comfortable car to drive around in, you might start to expect such a vehicle to be the norm and would hope it might be your first car, and so on.

Layard suggests that unhappiness results from society viewing how it is developing in terms of a zero-sum game. What he means by this is that we might increasingly view the scramble to gain money and status in terms of a competitive game that has a winner and a loser. If one person gets a high ranking job with a large salary and lots of status, it means that another person somehow loses out – either by not being able to get that same job, or in some sort of psychological way. Such a perception of life being a zero-sum game is a source of much unhappiness. This reflects the idea of *positional externalities*.

If we know something of the factors that can contribute to making someone 'happy' and also that our current measure is not the best at reflecting this, then it makes sense to look elsewhere for a measure of well-being. One such idea is to use something called the Measure of Domestic Progress (MDP). The MDP looks at many of the factors that we might associate with economic growth but takes into consideration the relative effects of economic growth and other things that GDP calculations do not consider. For example, there is an attempt to place a value on the amount of unpaid domestic work that is carried out, which is taken as being a positive factor in contributing to well-being. It also assigns a negative effect to various social and environmental impacts of growth such as pollution, depletion of natural resources, and costs of crime and family breakdown.

Other attempts to suggest more effective measures of improvements in well-being include such things as the Measure of Economic Welfare (MEW) developed by James Tobin and William Nordhaus, the Index of Sustainable Economic Welfare and the Genuine Progress Indicator.

Personal Well-Being Measures

To take into consideration some of the limitations of GDP and to make use of some of the research carried out on well-being, a number of national statistical offices now publish data which attempt to measure subjective and objective well-being. The ONS in the UK is one such body. It has published reports on personal well-being in the UK since 2012 using four 'high-level' measures and 41 headline measures. The report is produced through a survey which asks around 165,000 people a series of questions. The four 'high-level' measures are:

1. Overall, how satisfied are you with your life nowadays?
2. Overall, to what extent do you feel the things you do in your life are worthwhile?
3. Overall, how happy did you feel yesterday?
4. Overall, how anxious did you feel yesterday?

Answers are given on a scale of 0 to 10 with 10 being 'completely' and 0 being 'not at all'. The headline measures include areas such as personal health and finances, the environment, relationships, where people live, education and skills, the economy and governance. The ONS hopes that the reports offer a further insight into national well-being which supplements other data such as GDP measures. Given the report has only been published since 2012, the ability to identify longer-term trends is in its infancy, but one key factor that has been noted is that there is a relationship between reported well-being and the state of the economy, with unemployment being a particular contributor to low levels of well-being.

Other statistical offices such as Eurostat and the OECD are also developing well-being statistics which reflect the recognition that GDP figures alone do not offer a full picture of well-being. Eurostat's Quality of Life indicators include similar categories to the ONS reports and include data on material living conditions, work, health, education, leisure and social interaction, economic and physical safety, governance and basic rights, the natural and living environment, and the overall experience of life.

CRITICAL THINKING POINT To what extent do you think the obsession with GDP as a measure of economic well-being is unhelpful in improving decision-making of firms and governments and in improving standards of living? How do we define 'improvements' in this context and what would these improvements actually look like?

INTERNATIONAL DIFFERENCES IN GDP AND THE QUALITY OF LIFE

GDP data are used as a way of comparing well-being across different countries. Rich and less wealthy countries have vastly different levels of GDP per person. Data from World Economics show that in 2023, the average GDP per capita in PPP US dollars (we will discuss purchasing power parity (PPP) in greater detail in Chapter 9) in high-income countries was around $66,846 whereas in middle-income countries it was $20,845. Life expectancy at birth in high-income countries in 2022 was 80, whereas in low-income countries, the figure was 63. Data from World Population Review show that literacy rates in countries such as Niger were around 38 per cent in 2022, 73 per cent in Egypt in 2022 and 27 per cent in Chad in 2022, whereas in developed countries, the rates are almost 100 per cent.

These data show a clear pattern. In high-income countries people can expect to live longer, and almost all of the population can read. In less wealthy countries, people typically can expect to live much shorter lives, and the proportion of the population which is literate is relatively low.

Although data on other aspects of the quality of life are less complete, they tell a similar story. Countries with low GDP per capita tend to have more infants with low birth weight, higher rates of infant mortality, higher rates of maternal mortality, higher rates of child malnutrition and less common access to safe drinking water. In countries with low GDP per capita, fewer school age children are actually in school, and those who are in school must learn with fewer teachers per student. These countries also tend to have fewer televisions, fewer telephones, fewer paved roads and fewer households with electricity.

MEASURING THE COST OF LIVING

When people get their wages and buy the goods and services they need to live and enjoy life, the price of these goods and services determines how many goods and services can be bought. Over time, prices change, and it can be difficult to make comparisons of wages and prices over time. The **cost of living** refers to how much money people need to maintain certain standards of living in terms of the goods and services they can afford to buy. In the UK in 1900, for example, a copy of *The Times* newspaper was priced at 1.2p, a pint of beer or milk could be bought for less than 1p and a dozen fresh eggs was 6.9p. In 1930, the average house price in the UK was £590 and a loaf of bread was around 3p (these prices are expressed in decimal currency equivalents). At the turn of the twenty-first century, the average level of prices was 66 times the level of 1900. Because prices were so much lower in the early 1900s than they are today, it is not clear whether people enjoyed a lower or higher standard of living given average wages in 1900 compared to average wages today.

> **cost of living** how much money people need to maintain standards of living in terms of the goods and services they can afford to buy

Taking a snapshot of prices of goods and services in an economy at a particular point in time gives the **price level**. Looking at how the price level changes over time is the rate of change of the price level. To see how the price level changes and, therefore, to provide a way of comparing the cost of living over time, we need to find some way of turning money figures into meaningful measures of purchasing power. That is exactly the job of a statistic called the *Consumer Prices Index* (CPI).

> **price level** a snapshot of the prices of goods and services in an economy at a particular period of time

The CPI is used to monitor changes in the cost of living over time. When the CPI rises, the typical family must spend more money to maintain the same standard of living. Economists use the term *inflation* to describe a situation in which the economy's overall price level is rising and *deflation* when the overall price level is falling. The *inflation rate* is the percentage change in the price level from the previous period; if this is negative, the economy is experiencing deflation.

THE CONSUMER PRICES INDEX

The **Consumer Prices Index** (CPI) is a measure of the overall prices of the goods and services bought by a typical consumer. Each month, a government body (in the UK the ONS and in Europe, Eurostat) computes and reports the CPI. In the euro area, the measure of consumer price inflation is called the Harmonized Index of Consumer Prices (HICP). This essentially works in the same way as the CPI but measures the change, over time, in the prices of goods and services in the euro area. The term 'harmonized' in the title simply means that all countries in the euro area use the same methodology for collecting, analyzing and reporting on the data.

> **Consumer Prices Index** a measure of the overall prices of the goods and services bought by a typical consumer

How the Consumer Prices Index Is Calculated

To see how these statistics are constructed, we will consider a simple economy in which consumers buy only two goods – salad and burgers. Table 4.3 shows the five steps that the ONS and Eurostat follow. (We will use the ONS as the base for the example here, but the principle applies to the way price changes are measured in Europe as a whole.)

TABLE 4.3 Calculating the Consumer Prices Index and the Inflation Rate: An Example

This table shows how to calculate the CPI and the inflation rate for a hypothetical economy in which consumers buy only salad and burgers.

Step 1: Survey consumers to determine a fixed basket of goods		
4 salads and 2 burgers		
Step 2: Find the price of each good in each year		
Year	**Price of salad (€)**	**Price of burgers (€)**
2026	1	2
2027	2	3
2028	3	4
Step 3: Compute the cost of the basket of goods in each year		
2026	(€1 per salad × 4 salads) + (€2 per burger × 2 burgers) = €8	
2027	(€2 per salad × 4 salads) + (€3 per burger × 2 burgers) = €14	
2028	(€3 per salad × 4 salads) + (€4 per burger × 2 burgers) = €20	
Step 4: Choose one year as a base year (2026) and compute the CPI in each year		
2026	$\left(\frac{\text{€}8}{\text{€}8}\right) \times 100 = 100$	
2027	$\left(\frac{\text{€}14}{\text{€}8}\right)$ 3 100 5 175	
2028	$\left(\frac{\text{€}20}{\text{€}8}\right) \times 100 = 250$	
Step 5: Use the CPI to compute the inflation rate from previous year		
2026	$\left(\frac{(175 - 100)}{100}\right)$ 3 100 5 75%	
2027	$\left(\frac{(250\ 2\ 175)}{175}\right)$ 3 100 5 43%	

1. **Fix the basket.** The first step in computing the CPI is to determine which prices are most important to the typical consumer. If the typical consumer buys more salad than burgers, then the price of salad is more important than the price of burgers and, therefore, should be given greater weight in measuring the cost of living. The ONS sets these weights by surveying consumers and finding the basket of goods and services that the typical consumer buys. In the example in Table 4.3, the typical consumer buys a basket of four salads and two burgers.
2. **Find the prices.** The second step is to find the prices of each of the goods and services in the basket for each point in time. The table shows the prices of salad and burgers for three different years.
3. **Compute the basket's cost**. The third step is to use the data on prices to calculate the cost of the basket of goods and services at different times. The table shows this calculation for each of the three years. Notice that only the prices in this calculation change. By keeping the basket of goods the same (four salads and two burgers), we are isolating the effects of price changes from the effect of any quantity changes that might be occurring at the same time.
4. **Choose a base year and compute the index.** The fourth step is to designate one year as the base year, which is the benchmark against which other years are compared. To calculate the index, the price of the basket of goods and services in each year is divided by the price of the basket in the base year, and this ratio is then multiplied by 100. The resulting number is the CPI.

   In the example in Table 4.3, the year 2026 is the base year. In this year, the basket of salad and burgers costs €8. Therefore the price of the basket in all years is divided by €8 and multiplied by 100.

The CPI is 100 in 2026. (The index is always 100 in the base year.) The CPI is 175 in 2027. This means that the price of the basket in 2027 is 175 per cent of its price in the base year. Put differently, a basket of goods that costs €100 in the base year costs €175 in 2027. Similarly, the CPI is 250 in 2028, indicating that the price level in 2028 is 250 per cent of the price level in the base year.

5. **Compute the inflation rate.** The fifth and final step is to use the CPI to calculate the **inflation rate**, which is the percentage change in the price index from the preceding period. That is, the inflation rate between two consecutive years is computed as follows:

$$\textit{Inflation rate in year 2} = 100 \times \frac{(\textit{CPI in year 2} - \textit{CPI in year 1})}{\textit{CPI in year 1}}$$

In our example, the inflation rate is 75 per cent in 2027 and 43 per cent in 2028.

$$CPI_{year\ t} = \frac{\textit{Cost of basket of goods in year t prices}}{\textit{Cost of basket of goods in base year prices}}$$

The inflation rate is given by:

$$Inflation_{year\ t} = \frac{(\textit{Price index}_{year\ t}) - (\textit{Price index}_{year\ t-1})}{(\textit{Price index}_{year\ t-1})} \times 100$$

inflation rate the percentage change in the price index from the preceding period

Although this example simplifies the real world by including only two goods, it shows how statistics offices compute the CPI and the inflation rate. The offices collect and process data on the prices of thousands of goods and services every month. By following the five foregoing steps, this determines how quickly the cost of living for the typical consumer is rising. In addition to the CPI for the overall economy, statistics offices also calculate price indices for the sub-categories of 'goods' and of 'services' separately, as well as the **producer prices index** (PPI), which measures the prices of a basket of goods and services bought by firms rather than consumers. Because firms eventually pass on their costs to consumers in the form of higher consumer prices, changes in the PPI are often thought to be useful in predicting changes in the CPI.

producer prices index a measure of the prices of a basket of goods and services bought by firms

Problems in Measuring the Cost of Living

The goal of the CPI is to measure changes in the cost of living – how much people must pay to purchase goods and services. In other words, the CPI tries to gauge how much incomes must rise to maintain a constant standard of living. Assume that an individual in 2026 has an income of €120 per week and only buys burgers at €2 each. Their standard of living is 60 burgers a week. In 2027, burgers rise in price to €3 and so the standard of living, assuming income does not change, is now only 40 burgers a week. We would say that the individual's standard of living has fallen because they can now afford to consume fewer burgers. To keep their standard of living constant at 60 burgers, the person's income needs to rise from €120 per week to €180 per week. If the rise in incomes keeps pace with the rise in prices, then the individual's standard of living will remain constant. If incomes rise by a lower percentage than the CPI, then standards of living are being eroded. If incomes rise at a faster rate than the CPI, standards of living are improving, and people are better off.

The CPI, however, is not a perfect measure of the cost of living. Four problems with the index are widely acknowledged but are difficult to solve.

Substitution Bias The first problem is called *substitution bias*. When prices change from one year to the next, they do not all change proportionately: some prices rise more than others and some prices fall. Consumers respond to these differing price changes by buying less of the goods whose prices have risen by large amounts and buying more of the goods whose prices have risen less or perhaps even have fallen (and, of course, different consumers will respond to price changes in different ways because of the price elasticity of demand). Consumers substitute towards goods that have become relatively less expensive. If a price index is computed assuming a fixed basket of goods, it ignores the possibility of consumer substitution and, therefore, overstates the increase in the cost of living from one year to the next.

Let us consider a simple example. Imagine that in the base year apples are cheaper than pears, and so consumers buy more apples than pears. When the statistics office constructs the basket of goods, apples will be weighted more heavily than pears. Suppose that next year pears are cheaper than apples. Consumers may respond to the price changes by buying more pears and fewer apples. Yet, when computing the CPI, the statistics office uses a fixed basket, which in essence assumes that consumers continue buying the now expensive apples in the same quantities as before. For this reason, the index will measure a much larger increase in the cost of living than consumers actually experience.

The Introduction of New Goods The second problem with the CPI is the *introduction of new goods*. When a new good is introduced, consumers have more variety from which to choose. Greater variety, in turn, makes each euro or pound more valuable, so consumers need fewer units of currency to maintain any given standard of living. Yet because the CPI is based on a fixed basket of goods and services, it does not reflect this change in purchasing power.

For example, when video players were introduced, consumers were able to watch their favourite films at home. Compared with going to the cinema, the convenience was greater and the cost was less. A perfect cost of living index would have reflected the introduction of the video player with a decrease in the cost of living. The CPI, however, did not decrease in response to the introduction of the video player. Eventually, the ONS did revise the basket of goods to include video players, and subsequently the index reflected changes in their prices. As time has passed the index has had to be revised to take account of the decline in the video and the rise of the DVD, then Blu-ray DVDs and, nowadays, the increase in downloading and streaming of films.

Unmeasured Quality Change The third problem with the CPI is *unmeasured quality change*. If the quality of a good deteriorates from one year to the next, the effective value of a euro or pound falls, even if the price of the good stays the same. Similarly, if the quality rises from one year to the next, the effective value of a euro or pound rises. Statistics offices do their best to account for quality change. When the quality of a good in the basket changes, for example when a car model has more horsepower or gets better fuel mileage from one year to the next, statistics offices adjust the price of the good to account for the quality change. They are, in essence, trying to compute the price of a basket of goods of constant quality.

To take another example, in 2004 the ONS introduced digital cameras into the CPI for the first time. As well as the problems associated with introducing a new good into the index that we discussed earlier, digital cameras are also subject to very rapid technological progress. Features such as zoom and the number of megapixels keep on improving rapidly. The sale of digital cameras has now been impacted by the developments in camera technology which is incorporated into smartphones. Thus while the average price of a digital camera or a smartphone might remain the same over a period, the average quality may have risen substantially. The ONS attempts to correct for this by a method known as *hedonic quality adjustment*. This involves working out the average characteristics (e.g. screen size, number of megapixels, zoom features, etc.) of the average digital camera and adjusting the price when one of these average characteristics increases. Despite these efforts, changes in quality remain a problem, because quality is so hard to measure.

Relevance of the CPI The final problem with the index is that people may not see the reported CPI measure of inflation as relevant to their particular situation. This is because their spending patterns are individual and might not be typical of the representative pattern on which the official figures are based. For example, if an individual spent a high proportion of their income on fuel and their mortgage, the effect of price rises in gas, electricity, petrol, and a rise in mortgage rates would have a disproportionate effect on their experience of inflation. This different perception of inflation can have an effect on expectations, the importance of which we will see later.

Because of the different perceptions that people have about inflation and how it affects them, the ONS published a Personal Inflation Calculator (PIC) in 2007. The PIC allows users to be able to input their own details such as what their personal monthly expenditure is, how much they spend on food, meals out, alcohol, clothing and footwear, fuel for transport and so on. In addition, the calculator looks at what is spent on utilities such as water, council tax, vehicles, holidays and housing.

The PIC is designed to help people to develop more of an interest in how inflation is calculated and be more aware of how the reality of price rises in their lives might differ to the officially published figures.

FYI

What is in the CPI's Basket?

When constructing the CPI, the UK ONS tries to include all the goods and services that the typical consumer buys. Moreover, it tries to weight these goods and services according to how much consumers buy of each item. Every month the ONS collects around 180,000 prices of over 720 goods and services from around 140 areas throughout the UK that are supposed to be representative of the goods and services used on a regular basis. As buying habits change, the basket of goods and services must change also. Each year the ONS announces a revision to the basket of goods and services that make up the basis of inflation figures in the UK. The ONS must take into consideration not only how representative the sample of goods and services is but also any changes in importance in the typical household budget, and whether the replacement brands that shops bring in are of comparable quality.

Some goods and services that are not as representative any more are removed from the basket. This is measured by the amount spent on these goods and services. If consumer expenditure on items exceeds £400 million annually, then these are normally included in the basket, but if expenditure falls below £100 million, then there must be a very good reason put forward to keep these goods in the basket. In recent years this has included microwave ovens, which first made an appearance in the index in the 1980s. They are still popular, say the ONS, but their reliability and falling prices means that the amount spent on them has reduced. As a result, they have been removed from the basket. Other items that have dropped out include film for 35 mm cameras (the cameras themselves dropped out in 2007), top 40 CD singles and television repairs. As technology changes the way we live, the ONS says that people prefer to download music rather than buy singles, and households tend to replace TVs rather than get them repaired.

The goods and services that have come into the basket in recent years include gluten-free bread, air fryers, wild bird seed, e-cigarette refills and liquid, craft beers, protein powder, electric and hybrid cars, smartwatches, games consoles, online subscriptions and music streaming subscription.

The GDP Deflator versus the Consumer Prices Index

Recall that the GDP deflator is the ratio of nominal GDP to real GDP. Because nominal GDP is current output valued at current prices, and real GDP is current output valued at base year prices, the GDP deflator reflects the current level of prices relative to the level of prices in the base year.

Economists and policymakers monitor both the GDP deflator and the CPI to gauge how quickly prices are rising. Usually, these two statistics tell a similar story. Yet there are two important differences that can cause them to diverge.

The first difference is that the GDP deflator reflects the prices of all goods and services *produced domestically*, whereas the CPI reflects the prices of all goods and services *bought by consumers*. For example, suppose that the price of an aeroplane produced by Dassault, a French aerospace firm, and sold to the French Air Force rises. Even though the aeroplane is part of GDP in France, it is not part of the basket of goods and services bought by a typical consumer. Thus the price increase shows up in the GDP deflator for France but not in France's CPI.

As another example, suppose that Volvo raises the price of its cars. Because Volvos are made in Sweden, the car is not part of French GDP. But French consumers buy Volvos, and so the car is part of the typical consumer's basket of goods. Hence a price increase in an imported consumption good, such as a Volvo, shows up in the CPI but not in the GDP deflator.

This first difference between the CPI and the GDP deflator is particularly important when the price of oil changes. Although the UK does produce some oil, as with many parts of Europe, much of the oil used in the UK is imported from the Middle East. As a result, oil and oil products such as petrol and heating oil comprise a much larger share of consumer spending than they do of GDP. When the price of oil changes, the CPI changes by much more than does the GDP deflator.

The second and subtler difference between the GDP deflator and the CPI concerns how various prices are weighted to yield a single number for the overall level of prices. The CPI compares the price of a *fixed* basket of goods and services with the price of the basket in the base year. While, as we have seen, the ONS revises the basket of goods on a regular basis, in contrast, the GDP deflator compares the prices of *currently produced* goods and services with the prices of the same goods and services in the base year. Thus the group of goods and services used to compute the GDP deflator changes automatically over time. This difference is not important when all prices are changing proportionately. However, if the prices of different goods and services are changing by varying amounts, the way we weight the various prices matters for the overall inflation rate.

The inflation rate as measured by both the GDP deflator and the CPI do tend to move together.

SELF TEST Explain briefly what the CPI is trying to measure and how it is constructed.

CORRECTING ECONOMIC VARIABLES FOR THE EFFECTS OF INFLATION

The purpose of measuring the overall level of prices in the economy is to permit comparisons of monetary figures from different points in time. Now that we know how price indices are calculated, let us see how we might use such an index to compare a certain figure from the past to a figure in the present.

Money Figures from Different Times

To compare money figures over a period of time, we need to know the level of prices in both the historical year and the level of prices today. To compare money figures, we need to inflate the historical figure into today's currency. A price index determines the size of this inflation correction.

The equation for turning euro or pound figures from *year T* into today's euros or pounds is the following (assuming the price level today and the price level in *year T* are measured against the same base year):

$$\text{Amount in today's currency} = \text{Amount in year } T \text{ currency} \times \frac{\text{Price level today}}{\text{Price level in year } T}$$

A price index such as the CPI measures the price level and determines the size of the inflation correction. To illustrate, let us take an example of the salary for members of parliament in the UK. In 1947 this was £1,000 per year according to the House of Commons Information Office. Assume that the ONS reports the prices index (PI) for 1947 at 28.9 and for 2027, 1,018.6. Substituting these figures into the equation gives:

$$\text{Salary in 2027 £} = \text{Salary in 1947 £} \times \frac{\text{PI in 2027}}{\text{PI in 1947}}$$

$$\text{Salary in 2027} = £1{,}000 \times \left(\frac{1{,}018.6}{28.9}\right)$$

$$\text{Salary in 2027} = £35{,}230$$

We find that the salary paid to an MP in 1947 is equivalent to a salary in 2027 of £35,230. Assume that the basic annual salary of an MP in 2027 was £94,000. It seems that an MP in 2027 is considerably better off in terms of salary earned than their compatriots in 1947.

Indexation

As we have just seen, price indices are used to correct for the effects of inflation when comparing monetary figures from different times. This type of correction shows up in many places in the economy. When some money amount is automatically corrected for inflation by law or contract, the amount is said to be **indexed** for inflation. For example, many long-term contracts between firms and unions include partial or complete indexation of the wage to the CPI. Such a provision is called a *cost of living allowance*, or COLA. A COLA automatically raises the wage each year based on the CPI or other measure, at a particular point in time.

indexed the automatic correction of a money amount for the effects of inflation by law or contract

Income tax brackets – the income levels at which the tax rates change – are also often moved annually in line with inflation, although, in most countries, they are not formally indexed. Indeed, there are many ways in which the tax system is not indexed for inflation, even when perhaps it should be.

Real and Nominal Interest Rates

Correcting economic variables for the effects of inflation is particularly important, and somewhat tricky, when we look at data on interest rates. Savings deposited in an interest-bearing account provide a return based on the interest rate available. Conversely, when people borrow from a bank to fund purchases such as a car, interest is payable on the loan. Interest represents a payment in the future for a transfer of money in the past. As a result, interest rates always involve comparing amounts of money at different points in time. To fully understand interest rates, we need to know how to correct for the effects of inflation.

Let us consider an example. Suppose that Carla deposits €1,000 in a savings account that pays an annual interest rate of 10 per cent. After a year passes, Carla has accumulated €100 in interest. Carla then withdraws her €1,100. Is Carla €100 richer than she was when she made the deposit a year earlier?

The answer depends on what we mean by 'richer'. Carla does have €100 more than she had before. In other words, the number of euros has risen by 10 per cent. If prices have risen at the same time, each euro now buys less than it did a year ago. Thus her purchasing power has not risen by 10 per cent. If the inflation rate was 4 per cent, then the amount of goods she can buy has increased by only 6 per cent. If the inflation rate was 15 per cent, then the price of goods has increased proportionately more than the number of euros in her account. In that case, Carla's purchasing power has actually fallen by 5 per cent.

The interest rate that the savings account pays is called the **nominal interest rate**, and the interest rate corrected for inflation is called the **real interest rate**. We can write the relationship between the nominal interest rate, the real interest rate and inflation as follows:

$$r_t = i_t - \pi_t$$

The real interest rate in a particular time period (r_t) = nominal interest rate in that time period (i_t) – inflation rate in the same time period (π_t).

The real interest rate is the difference between the nominal interest rate and the rate of inflation. The nominal interest rate tells you how fast the number of pounds or euros in your bank account rises over time. The real interest rate tells you how fast the purchasing power of your bank account rises over time.

nominal interest rate the interest rate as usually reported without a correction for the effects of inflation
real interest rate the interest rate corrected for the effects of inflation

SELF TEST Why is it important to adjust for inflation when considering wage increases and the returns from any financial investment?

CONCLUSION

This chapter has discussed how economists measure well-being and the cost of living. Much of the study of macroeconomics we will look at in the rest of this book is aimed at revealing the long-run and short-run determinants of a nation's GDP. Why, for example, do most economies experience fluctuations in economic activity? Why are key macroeconomic measures such as inflation, unemployment, interest rates and exchange rates important in determining economic well-being? What can governments do to promote more rapid growth in GDP? What can policymakers do to reduce the severity of fluctuations in GDP? These are the questions we will take up shortly.

Despite the focus on GDP as a measure of economic well-being, we must not forget the limitations of this measure and that overall economic well-being may include many factors other than income.

When comparing figures in monetary or nominal terms from different times, it is important to keep in mind that a pound or euro today is not the same as a pound or euro 10 years ago or, most likely, 10 years from now. We have seen how economists measure the overall level of prices in the economy and how they use price indices to correct economic variables for the effects of inflation. This analysis is only a starting point. We have not yet examined the causes and effects of inflation or how inflation interacts with other economic variables. To do that, we need to go beyond issues of measurement. Having explained how economists measure macroeconomic quantities and prices, we are now ready to develop the models that explain long-run and short-run movements in these variables.

SUMMARY

- Because every transaction has a buyer and a seller, the total expenditure in the economy must equal the total income in the economy.
- GDP measures an economy's total expenditure on newly produced goods and services and the total income earned from the production of these goods and services. More precisely, GDP is the market value of all final goods and services produced within a country in a given period of time.
- GDP is divided among four components of expenditure: consumption, investment, government purchases and net exports. Consumption includes spending on goods and services by households, with the exception of purchases of new housing. Investment includes spending on new equipment and structures, including households' purchases of new housing. Government spending includes spending on goods and services by local and central governments. Net exports equal the value of goods and services produced domestically and sold abroad (exports) minus the value of goods and services produced abroad and sold domestically (imports).
- Nominal GDP uses current prices to value the economy's production of goods and services. Real GDP uses constant base year prices to value the economy's production of goods and services. The GDP deflator – calculated from the ratio of nominal to real GDP – measures the level of prices in the economy.
- GDP is one measure of economic well-being. It has limitations because it excludes many activities which occur illegally and does not take account of the benefits to well-being from work done outside markets such as looking after the home, rearing children, caring and volunteer work.
- Because of the limitations of using GDP, a number of governments are now supporting efforts to report on broader measures of well-being which include both subjective and objective reporting of how people feel about their lives and circumstances.
- The CPI shows the changes in the prices of a basket of goods and services relative to the prices of the same basket in the base year. The index is used to measure the overall level of prices in the economy. The percentage change in the CPI measures the inflation rate.
- The CPI is an imperfect measure of the cost of living for three reasons. First, it does not take into account consumers' ability to substitute towards goods that become relatively cheaper over time. Second, it does not take into account increases in the purchasing power of money due to the introduction of new goods. Third, it is distorted by unmeasured changes in the quality of goods and services. Because of these measurement problems, the CPI overstates true inflation.

- Although the GDP deflator also measures the overall level of prices in the economy, it differs from the CPI because it includes goods and services produced rather than goods and services consumed. As a result, imported goods affect the CPI but not the GDP deflator. In addition, while the CPI uses a fixed basket of goods, the GDP deflator automatically changes the group of goods and services over time as the composition of GDP changes.
- Money figures (e.g. in euros) from different points in time do not represent a valid comparison of purchasing power. To compare a money figure from the past to a money figure today, the older figure should be inflated using a price index.
- Various laws and private contracts use price indices to correct for the effects of inflation.
- A correction for inflation is especially important when looking at data on interest rates. The nominal interest rate is the interest rate usually reported. It is the rate at which the amount of money in a savings account increases over time. In contrast, the real interest rate takes into account changes in the value of the money over time. The real interest rate equals the nominal interest rate minus the rate of inflation.

IN THE NEWS

The Cost of Living

Global events such as the Covid-19 pandemic, conflict in eastern Europe and the Middle East, along with the challenges presented by climate change have all conspired to put strong upward pressures on prices in many countries. In the EU, for example, the inflation rate reached a high of 10.6 per cent in October 2022 before falling back to 2.1 per cent in September 2024. In the UK, inflation, as measured by the CPI, all items peaked at 11.1 per cent, also in October 2022, before falling back to 1.7 per cent in September 2024 but then accelerated to 2.3 per cent in October of that year and 2.6 per cent in December. The UK's Office for Budget Responsibility (OBR) had forecast that inflation in the UK would reach 2.6 per cent in 2025, partly as a result of measures introduced in the autumn budget of the Labour Government that came into power in the summer of 2024. It transpired that the 12-month CPI actually hit 3.5 per cent in April 2025 and 3.6 per cent in June 2025.

These relatively high inflation figures were associated with news headlines about a 'cost of living crisis'. When the December 2024 inflation figures were released in the UK, critics of the UK government noted that the cost of living crisis had not eased for many people and that the government was making decisions that contributed to increasing inflationary pressures. The government itself argued that it had to take 'difficult decisions' to help get the economy back on track after years of Conservative government 'mismanagement', and that it was intent on encouraging economic growth and 'putting more money in the pockets of working people'.

It is important to distance ourselves from the rhetoric of politicians and newswriters, especially as an economist, and to adopt a critical approach to the issues presented to us. When, for example, is the use of the word 'crisis' justifiable in relation to such issues? What do governments mean when stating that they commit to 'economic growth'? Who constitutes a 'working person' and what does it mean to 'put money in their pockets'?

To answer some of these questions we can look at the content covered in this chapter. We can apply our understanding of the issues around the data of macroeconomics, how we

© iStock/glegorly

When does the rate of change of prices become worthy of being called a 'crisis'?

(Continued)

measure economic growth and well-being, how we measure inflation and some of the challenges associated with doing so. We also need to ask other questions to understand and disentangle the rhetoric a little more. What other information do we need to provide a more informed view on these sorts of issues? What has happened to wages during the period being considered, for example? What has happened to interest rates? How many people suffer from accelerating inflation and is the impact on 'people' identical? How do we make sense of economic growth and inflation figures in relation to assessing how peoples' welfare and well-being are affected?

Critical Thinking Questions

1 How do global events, such as those cited in the article, affect economic growth and lead to increasing inflationary pressures?

2 Consider the peak inflationary figures mentioned in the article in the EU and the UK. How do we judge whether these sorts of figures are 'serious' and of concern?

3 How would you define the term 'crisis' and, given your definition, to what extent is the word appropriate for describing the rising inflationary pressures experienced in the EU and the UK in the first half of the 2020s?

4 What do you think governments mean when they say they want to 'boost economic growth'? Consider the issues raised in this chapter to critique the idea of 'boosting economic growth' and the assumption that this is desirable.

5 How would you define the term 'working people'? Has the term any practical and valuable meaning? How would you judge whether the well-being of 'working people' had improved over a period of time? How would you interpret the meaning of 'putting more money into peoples' pockets'?

References:

ec.europa.eu/eurostat/web/products-euro-indicators/w/2-17102024-ap, accessed 6 August 2025.
www.ons.gov.uk/economy/inflationandpriceindices/timeseries/d7g7/mm23, accessed 6 August 2025.

QUESTIONS FOR REVIEW

1 Explain why an economy's income must equal its expenditure.

2 What is meant by the term GDP per capita and how is it measured?

3 List the four components of GDP. Give an example of each.

4 Why do economists use real GDP rather than nominal GDP to gauge economic well-being?

5 In the year 2026, the economy produces 100 loaves of bread that sell for €2 each. In the year 2027, the economy produces 200 loaves of bread that sell for €3 each. Calculate nominal GDP, real GDP and the GDP deflator for each year (use 2026 as the base year). By what percentage does each of these three statistics rise from one year to the next?

6 What are the limitations of using GDP as a measure of well-being for a country?

7 What are the five stages of constructing a prices index?

8 Describe the three problems that make the CPI an imperfect measure of the cost of living.

9 Assume that the price of a bottle of wine in 1995 was €3.50 and in 2027 it is €8.50. Further assume that the price index in 1995 was 95 and in 2027 was 160. Was wine cheaper in 1995 than in 2027? Explain.

10 Explain the meaning of nominal interest rate and real interest rate. How are they related?

PROBLEMS AND APPLICATIONS

1 What components of GDP (if any) would each of the following transactions affect? Explain.
   a. A family buys a new refrigerator.
   b. Aunt Jane buys a new house.
   c. Aston Martin sells a DB7 from its inventory.
   d. You buy a pizza.
   e. The government builds a new motorway.
   f. You buy a bottle of Californian wine.
   g. Honda expands its factory in Derby, England.

2 Why do you think households' purchases of new housing are included in the investment component of GDP rather than the consumption component? Can you think of a reason why households' purchases of new cars should also be included in investment rather than in consumption? To what other consumption goods might this logic apply?

3 Below are some data from the land of milk and honey.

Year	Price of milk (€)	Quantity of milk (litres)	Price of honey (€)	Quantity of honey (jars)
2025	1	100	2	50
2026	1	200	2	100
2027	2	200	4	100

   a. Compute nominal GDP, real GDP and the GDP deflator for each year, using 2025 as the base year.
   b. Compute the percentage change in nominal GDP, real GDP and the GDP deflator in 2026 and 2027 from the preceding year. For each year, identify the variable that does not change. Explain in words why your answer makes sense.
   c. Did economic well-being rise more in 2026 or 2027? Explain.

4 Economists sometimes prefer to use GNP rather than GDP as a measure of economic well-being. Which measure should we prefer if we are analyzing the total income of domestic residents? Which measure should we prefer if we are analyzing the total amount of economic activity occurring in the economy?

5 Given the limitations of using GDP as a measure of well-being, should calculation of GDP be scrapped in favour of wider reporting of well-being such as objective and subjective well-being?

6 The participation of women in many European and North American economies has risen dramatically since the 1990s.
   a. How do you think this rise affected GDP?
   b. Now imagine a measure of well-being that includes time spent working in the home and taking leisure. How would the change in this measure of well-being compare to the change in GDP?
   c. Can you think of other aspects of well-being that are associated with the rise in women's labour force participation? Would it be practical to construct a measure of well-being that includes these aspects?

7 Suppose that people consume only three goods, as shown in this table:

	Tennis balls	Tennis racquets	Cola
2026 price (€)	2	40	1
2026 quantity	100	10	200
2027 price (€)	2	60	2
2027 quantity	100	10	200

   a. What is the percentage change in the price of each of the three goods? What is the percentage change in the overall price level?
   b. Have tennis racquets become more or less expensive relative to cola? Does the well-being of some people change relative to that of others? Explain.

8 Which of the problems in the construction of the CPI might be illustrated by each of the following situations? Explain.
   a. The increase in streaming films.
   b. The increased use of electric vehicle charging points at public sites.
   c. Increased purchasing of second-hand petrol and diesel cars.
   d. Increased use of digital cameras in smartphones.
   e. Reduced use of fuel-efficient cars after fuel prices fall.

9 Suppose the government were to determine the level of the state retirement pension in the UK so that it increased each year in proportion to the increase in the CPI.
   a. If the elderly consume the same market basket as other people, would such a policy provide the elderly with an improvement in their standard of living each year? Explain.
   b. In fact, the elderly consume more healthcare than younger people, and healthcare costs tend to rise faster than overall inflation. What would you do to determine whether the elderly are actually better off from year to year?

10 Suppose that a borrower and a lender agree on the nominal interest rate to be paid on a loan. Then inflation turns out to be higher than they both expected.
   a. Is the real interest rate on this loan higher or lower than expected?
   b. Does the lender gain or lose from this unexpectedly high inflation? Does the borrower gain or lose?

PART 3 THE REAL ECONOMY IN THE LONG RUN

5 PRODUCTION AND GROWTH

In this chapter we are going to look at what determines the level of economic growth. We have seen that there are disparities in incomes in countries and between countries. The average person in a wealthy country, such as the countries of Western Europe, has an income more than 10 times as high as the average person in a lower-income country, such as India, Indonesia or Nigeria.

The Nobel Prize winning economist Robert E. Lucas, spent some time looking at different growth rates and levels of poverty and inequality between countries. Lucas asked why countries have different growth rates and exhibited such wide variations in living standards. The news and social media bring these variations in standards of living sharply into focus. In some respects this makes us more aware of the vast differences in living standards than perhaps ever before. Indeed, in the 1990s, Lucas wrote: 'The consequences for human welfare involved in questions like these are simply staggering: once one starts to think about them, it is hard to think about anything else.' It is worth dwelling on Lucas' words. There are millions of people around the world for whom life is a daily struggle. Simply finding enough food and water to maintain life is a challenge. Contrast this with the lifestyles of many people in the developed world, and the moral implications of such a comparison are significant.

What explains these diverse experiences? How can the rich countries be sure to maintain their high standard of living? What policies should the poor countries pursue to promote more rapid growth to join the developed world? These are among the most important questions in macroeconomics. As we have seen, an economy's GDP measures both the total income earned in the economy and the total expenditure on the economy's output of goods and services. The level and growth of real GDP is one gauge of economic prosperity. Here we focus on the long-run determinants of the level and growth of real GDP.

ECONOMIC GROWTH AROUND THE WORLD

It is typical for analysis of economic growth to use the level of GDP in relation to the population. In particular, we can identify two concepts, GDP per capita and GDP per worker. GDP per capita takes the level of real GDP at a point in time and divides it by the population to get a measure of income per head of the population. This serves as a useful basis for comparison across countries. It is typical to present such data in US dollars.

$$\text{Real GDP per capita} = \frac{\text{Real GDP}}{\text{Total population}}$$

Similarly, we could look at real GDP in relation to the number of people employed in the population to give a measure of income per head of the working population:

$$\text{Real GDP per worker} = \frac{\text{Real GDP}}{\text{Number of people in employment}}$$

A glance at any historic GDP data of countries around the world shows a considerable difference in standards of living. Not only does GDP per capita vary considerably around the world but the rates of growth of GDP also vary. Countries with a relatively high per capita GDP often have relatively low levels of annual growth. The UK, for example, has had typical average growth rates of around 2 to 3 per cent since the 1960s. Germany, Norway and France have experienced growth rates around 3 to 3.5 per cent, whereas other countries such as the United Arab Emirates and China have seen periods of rapid growth. China's average growth since 1970 has been around 9 per cent. China is now the world's second largest economy behind the US, although its people still have a relatively low per capita income. Many of the developed countries in Western Europe have been able to sustain long periods of growth and while the average is not spectacular, the per capita incomes of people in these countries is much higher than some of the countries that currently experience high annual growth rates. Rich countries will not always be richer, and poor countries will not always be poor.

Countries like China and India have been able to experience rapid improvements in the standard of living for many people. In both countries, millions have been lifted out of poverty in the twenty-first century. By contrast, countries like Niger, the Central African Republic and the Democratic Republic of the Congo have remained among the least wealthy countries on the planet. The reason why growth in some countries accelerates whereas in others it languishes, and their people remain poor, is the subject of the next section.

FYI

The Magic of Compounding and the Rule of 70

Suppose you observe that one country has an average growth rate of 1 per cent per year while another has an average growth rate of 3 per cent per year. At first, this might not seem like a big deal. What difference can 2 percentage points make?

The answer is, a big difference. Even growth rates that seem small when written in percentage terms seem large after they are compounded for many years.

Consider an example. Suppose that two economics graduates – Milton and Janet – both take their first jobs at the age of 22 earning €20,000 a year. Milton lives in an economy where all incomes grow at 1 per cent per year, while Janet lives in one where incomes grow at 3 per cent per year. Calculations using the principle of compounding show what happens. After the first year Milton, earns an additional 1 per cent of €20,000 (€200). In year 2 he earns an additional 1 per cent of €20,200 (€20,402) and so on. To calculate compound figures over time we use the formula $M = P(1 + i)^n$ where M is the total value at the end of the period, P is the initial value, i is the rate of interest (or rate of growth) and n the number of years. After 40 years, therefore, Milton earns $20{,}000\ (1 + 0.01)^{40}$ which equals €29,777 a year.

Janet, on the other hand, 40 years later, earns €$20{,}000\ (1 + 0.03)^{40}$ which equals €65,240. Because of that difference of 2 percentage points in the growth rate, Janet's salary is more than twice Milton's.

An old rule of thumb, called the *rule of 70*, is helpful in understanding growth rates and the effects of compounding. According to the rule of 70, if some variable grows at a rate of x per cent per year, then that variable doubles in approximately $\frac{70}{x}$ years. In Milton's economy, incomes grow at 1 per cent per year, so it takes about 70 years for incomes to double. In Janet's economy, incomes grow at 3 per cent per year, so it takes about $\frac{70}{3}$ or a little over 23 years for incomes to double.

GROWTH THEORY

Over time, economic growth in most countries varies. Sometimes the economy experiences strong periods of growth and at other times growth is slower. Sometimes the economy shrinks! Over a period of time, a trend can be established which is usually expressed as a growth rate in percentage terms. Recall that real GDP growth is given by:

$$\text{Growth rate of real GDP in year } t = \frac{(GDP_t - GDP_{t-1})}{GDP_{t-1}} \times 100$$

Different countries have different trend growth rates. For a country to experience considerable improvements in living standards, sustained growth over a period of time is necessary. The annual growth does not necessarily need to be high, but it has to be consistent. What determines whether a country can maintain sustained growth over a period, and why some countries can grow faster than others, is a central feature of macroeconomics. Research into growth theory has resulted in Nobel Prizes for Simon Kuznets in 1971 and Robert Solow in 1987.

In 1956, Robert. M. Solow and Trevor Swan identified the rate of human and physical capital and population growth as being key determinants of economic growth. Over the years, economists have looked at other factors that may influence economic growth, which include the following:

- The level of macroeconomic stability in an economy.
- The type of trade policy that exists in a country (is the country outward-looking or does it tend to be insular?).
- The nature and quality of institutions and governance (i.e. how effectively the rule of law operates and how well governments can control corruption) in the country concerned.
- The extent to which violence, war and conflict exist in a country.
- Regional characteristics such as whether the country is part of Europe, North America, Asia or sub-Saharan Africa.
- Geographical factors such as physical resource endowments and climate.
- The extent to which a country is competitive in international markets.
- Internal factors such as the amount of productive land available.

The next section will cover the role of productivity in growth which can be referred to as the *neo-classical theory of growth*. Initially, we will look at the nature of the term *productivity*, which is central to neo-classical growth theory.

PRODUCTIVITY

Some of the concepts in this chapter discuss the production function and the concepts of marginal and diminishing marginal product. Your knowledge of these concepts will be useful in this section. The main difference is that we are now thinking on a macroeconomic level rather than a microeconomic one.

Why Productivity Is So Important

Let us begin our study of productivity and economic growth by developing a simple model based on an individual who finds herself shipwrecked on a desert island, who we will call Annie. Because Annie lives alone, she catches her own fish, grows her own vegetables and makes her own clothes. We can think of Annie's activities – her production and consumption of fish, vegetables and clothing – as being a simple economy. What determines Annie's standard of living? If Annie is good at catching fish, growing vegetables and making clothes, she lives well. If she is bad at doing these things, she does not live well. Because Annie can consume only what she produces, her living standard is tied to her productive ability.

Remember that *productivity* refers to the quantity of goods and services that a worker (or any factor of production) can produce in a specified time period. In the case of Annie's economy, productivity is the key determinant of her living standards and growth in productivity is the key determinant of the growth in living standards. The more fish Annie can catch per hour, the more she eats for dinner. If Annie finds a better place to catch fish, her productivity rises. This increase in productivity makes Annie better off. She could eat the extra fish, or she could spend less time fishing and devote more time to making other goods she enjoys.

The key role of productivity in determining living standards is as true for nations as it is for Annie. Recall that an economy's GDP measures three things at once: the total income earned by everyone in the economy, the total expenditure on the economy's output of goods and services, and the value of the output produced.

Like Annie, a nation can enjoy a high standard of living if it can produce a large quantity of goods and services. Western Europeans live better than Malians because Western European workers are more productive than Malian workers. Hence to understand the large differences in living standards we observe across countries or over time, we focus on the production of goods and services.

How Productivity Is Determined

To illustrate the determinants of productivity, we return to our example of Annie. Many factors will determine Annie's productivity. Annie will be better at catching fish, for instance, if she has more fishing rods, if she has been trained in the best fishing techniques, if her island has a plentiful fish supply and if she invents a better fishing lure. Each of these determinants of Annie's productivity – which we can call *physical capital*, *human capital*, *natural resources* and *technological knowledge* – has a counterpart in more complex and realistic economies. Let us consider each of these factors in turn.

Physical Capital Workers can be more productive if the capital stock is high. The stock of equipment and structures that are used to produce goods and services is called physical capital, or just *capital*. For example, when carpenters make furniture, they use saws, lathes and drill presses. More and better quality tools, such as electric circular saws and precision routers, allow work to be done more quickly and more accurately. A carpenter with only basic hand tools can make less furniture each week than a carpenter with sophisticated and specialized woodworking equipment.

An important feature of capital is that it is a *produced* factor of production. Capital is an input into the production process that in the past was an output from the production process. The carpenter uses a lathe to make the leg of a table. Earlier the lathe itself was the output of a firm that manufactured lathes. The lathe manufacturer in turn used other equipment to make its product. Thus capital is a factor of production used to produce all kinds of goods and services, including more capital.

Human Capital A second determinant of productivity is human capital. Human capital is the economist's term for the knowledge and skills that workers acquire through education, training and experience. Human capital includes the skills accumulated in early childhood programmes, primary school, secondary school, university or college, and on-the-job training for adults in the labour force.

Although education, training and experience are less tangible than lathes, bulldozers and buildings, human capital is like physical capital in many ways. Like physical capital, human capital raises a nation's ability to produce goods and services. Like physical capital, human capital is a produced factor of production. Producing human capital requires inputs in the form of teachers, lecturers, libraries and student time. Indeed, students can be viewed as 'workers' who have the important job of producing the human capital that will be used in future production.

Natural Resources A third determinant of productivity is **natural resources**. Natural resources are inputs into production that are provided by nature, such as land, rivers and mineral deposits. Natural resources take two forms: renewable and non-renewable. A forest is an example of a renewable resource. When one tree is cut down, a seedling can be planted in its place to be harvested in the future. Oil is an example of a non-renewable resource. Because oil is produced by nature over many thousands or even millions of years, there is only a limited supply. Once the supply of oil is depleted, it is impossible to create more (at least not for thousands of years).

> **natural resources** the inputs into the production of goods and services that are provided by nature, such as land, rivers and mineral deposits

Differences in natural resources are responsible for some of the differences in standards of living around the world. The historical success of the United States was driven in part by the large supply of land well suited for agriculture. Today, some countries in the Middle East, such as Kuwait and Saudi Arabia, are rich simply because they happen to be on top of some of the largest pools of oil in the world.

Although natural resources can be important, they are not necessary for an economy to be highly productive in producing goods and services. Japan, for instance, is one of the richest countries in the world, despite having few natural resources. International trade makes Japan's success possible. Japan imports many of the natural resources it needs, such as oil, and exports its manufactured goods to economies rich in natural resources.

Technological Knowledge The fourth determinant of productivity is **technological knowledge** – the understanding of the best ways to produce goods and services. Most Europeans and North Americans worked on farms in the 1870s, because farm technology required a high input of labour to feed the entire population. Today, thanks to advances in the technology of farming, a small fraction of the populations of Western Europe, the United States and Canada can produce enough food to feed their entire populations. This technological change made labour available to produce other goods and services.

technological knowledge society's understanding of the best ways to produce goods and services

Technological knowledge takes many forms. Some technology is common knowledge. After it starts to be used by one person, many other people become aware of it. For example, once Henry Ford successfully introduced production in assembly lines in the United States, other car makers and industrial producers throughout the world quickly followed suit. Other technology is proprietary – it is known only by the company that discovers it. Only the Coca-Cola Company, for instance, knows the secret recipe for making its famous soft drink.

Other technology can be proprietary for a short time. When a pharmaceutical company discovers a new drug, the patent system gives that company a temporary right to be its exclusive manufacturer. When the patent expires, however, other companies are allowed to make the drug. All these forms of technological knowledge are important for the economy's production of goods and services.

It is worthwhile to distinguish between technological knowledge and human capital. Although they are closely related, there is an important difference. Technological knowledge refers to *society's* understanding about how the world works. Human capital refers to the resources expended transmitting this understanding to the *labour force*. To use a relevant metaphor, knowledge is the quality of society's textbooks, whereas human capital is the amount of time that the population has devoted to reading them. Workers' productivity depends on both the quality of textbooks they have available and the amount of time they have spent studying them.

Technical progress means that the *quality* of physical and human capital is improved, so for any given quantity of capital and labour, the average productivity of both is higher, meaning that a higher output can be produced from the economy's factors of production. In essence, technical progress can help to counterbalance the effects of diminishing marginal product. If additional factors are employed but the total productivity of those factors increases, then the economy can experience growth.

Given the aggregate production function $Y = A \times f(K, L)$, where A is the rate of technological progress, if the capital/labour ratio is constant, factor productivity can rise if there is an increase in technological progress. For example, if technological progress increases by 0.5 per cent a year, then $A = (1 + 0.005)$. Average labour productivity can increase by 0.5 per cent even if the ratio of capital to labour stays constant. If this is the case, then the production function will actually shift upwards (or the production possibilities curve will shift outwards), reflecting the ability of the economy to produce more of every good.

CRITICAL THINKING POINT Productivity in a number of developed nations has either fallen or remained stagnant in recent years. Is it possible that we have reached a plateau in productivity in developed nations and that it will not be possible to increase productivity substantially in the near future?

THE DETERMINANTS OF ECONOMIC GROWTH

The Solow and Swan growth theory (hereafter referred to simply as the Solow model or theory) establishes some key elements of the determinants of economic growth. The assumptions of the model are that there are constant returns to scale, a closed economy with no government sector, (so $Y = C + S$), and that increases in capital and labour are subject to diminishing marginal product.

Recall that the output level denoted by the letter Y (GDP), is determined by the level of technology (A), and the quantities and productivity of labour and capital (K and L). The resulting aggregate production function can be represented as in Figure 5.1. GDP is on the vertical axis and the physical capital stock is on the horizontal axis. Assuming technology is given, an increasing physical capital stock is associated with a rising GDP. GDP rises relatively quickly at first but then slows due to the law of diminishing marginal product. The level of investment in capital stock is shown by the line I. This investment is dependent on the savings ratio in the country, and a higher savings rate will be associated with an increase in capital accumulation. Levels of physical capital stock are associated with levels of GDP. If the capital stock is K_1, for example, GDP will be Y_1. The distance between the level of GDP at K_1 and the investment level is consumption, and the remainder is investment.

FIGURE 5.1

The Aggregate Production Function and Investment

The aggregate production function is determined by technology and capital and labour productivity for a given level of physical capital stock. The savings rate determines the level of investment. At a level of capital stock K_1*, GDP is* Y_1*. The level of consumption at* Y_1 *is the difference between the aggregate production function and investment.*

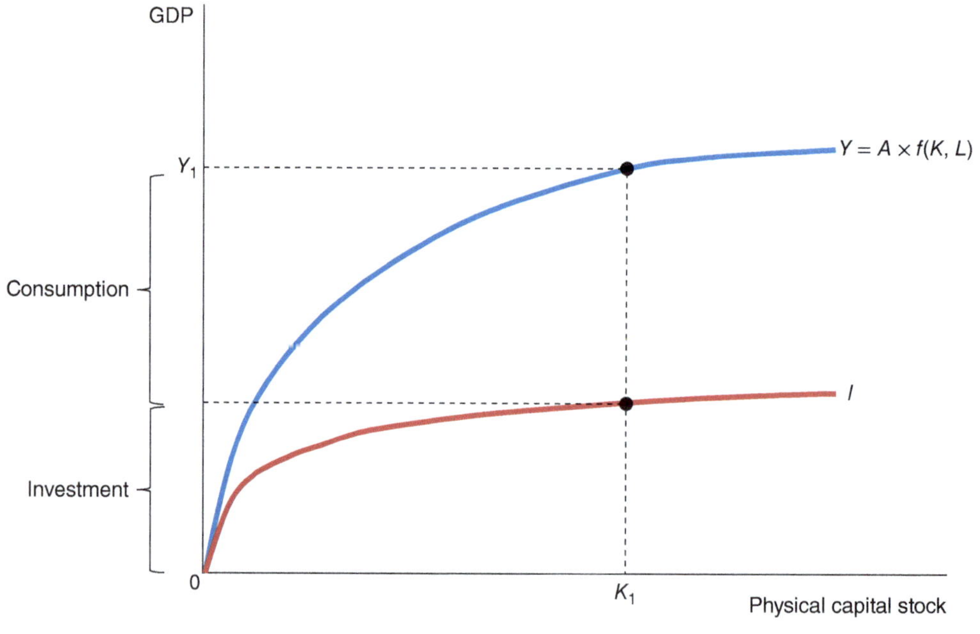

Long-Run Equilibrium

For an economy with a given level of physical capital, the growth path will be dependent on the level of technology, the productivity of labour and capital, and the savings rate which determines investment in physical capital. Some investment is spent on replacing worn out and obsolete capital, termed depreciation. If physical capital lasts for an average of 15 years, then the depreciation rate will be $\frac{1}{15}$ or 6.7 per cent (rounded up). The depreciation rate is assumed to be relatively constant as a proportion of the amount of physical capital. These three elements of the growth model are represented in Figure 5.2. This time the vertical axis is output per worker given by GDP (Y) divided by the number of workers, L, $\frac{Y}{L}$. The horizontal axis is the capital–output ratio or capital per worker given by the amount of physical capital, K, divided by the number of workers, L, $\frac{K}{L}$.

The ratio of capital to labour is one factor determining labour productivity. One of the reasons put forward for the rapid growth in countries like South Korea and Vietnam is that not only have they a supply of relatively cheap labour, but both countries have invested in capital and as a result labour productivity is relatively high. In comparison, average incomes in many African countries remain very low. The main difference is that in these African countries, investment in capital stock is low and, as a result, labour productivity is also very low. In addition to the aggregate production function, $Y = A(K, L)$, and investment (I), which is determined by the savings rate, we have included the depreciation rate, δK. The depreciation rate is assumed to be a constant proportion of capital per worker.

Let us now look at what happens if a country finds itself with a capital per worker level of K_1 in Figure 5.2.

FIGURE 5.2

Steady-State Equilibrium

The long-run equilibrium is given where spending on investment is equal to the depreciation rate. This is associated with a capital–output ratio which is constant at K. If the economy is at any other capital–output ratio, the economy will move towards the steady-state equilibrium.*

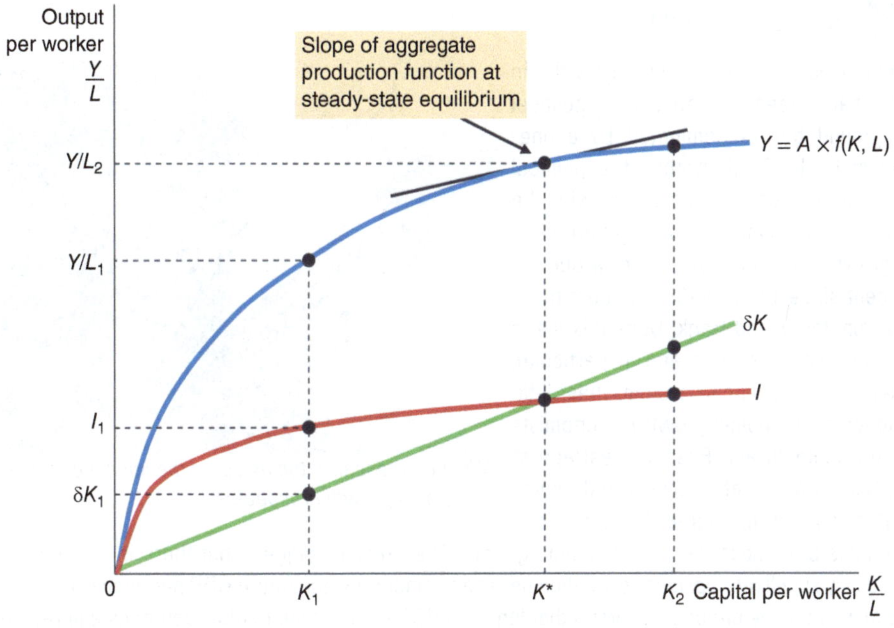

At K_1, investment per worker is higher than depreciation per worker and so the capital–output ratio, or capital per worker, rises. As capital per worker rises, output per worker increases from the initial level of $\frac{Y}{L_1}$. The economy will continue to grow until it reaches a capital–output ratio of K^*. At this ratio, investment spending is equal to the depreciation rate and the capital–output ratio will remain constant. Solow called this the **steady-state equilibrium**. This capital–output ratio gives an output per worker of $\frac{Y}{L_2}$.

If the capital–output ratio was K_2, spending on depreciation would be higher than investment and the capital–output ratio would fall, pushing the economy back towards the steady-state equilibrium at K^*. This steady-state equilibrium will be associated with a particular growth rate in the economy given by the slope of the aggregate production function shown by the tangential line in Figure 5.2.

steady-state equilibrium the point in a growing economy where investment spending is the same as spending on depreciation and the capital–output ratio remains constant

The Solow model provides a means of understanding the transition of economies over time. Less developed economies will have lower capital–output ratios. Investment in capital will increase the capital per worker and lead to growth. In Figure 5.2, the growth rate at the capital–output level K_1, is higher than that at the steady-state equilibrium, K^* as indicated by the steeper slope of the aggregate production function at the output per worker level of $\frac{Y}{L_1}$. However, investment is determined by the savings ratio. In less developed countries this may be relatively low because incomes are low. For those on low incomes, the priority is likely to be more on feeding the family and surviving rather than saving. In addition, less developed countries may not have sufficiently developed financial institutions to funnel savings, and problems of governance and corruption can often mean these economies continue to remain poor and do not transition to more sustained growth associated with the steady-state equilibrium.

SELF TEST List and describe four determinants of a country's productivity.

CASE STUDY Democracy and Growth

What can research tell us about the impact of a political system on growth prospects?

Strong levels of economic growth in China have been set against a political background that is dominated by a one-party state. In Saudi Arabia, the political system is an absolute monarchy with the King, head of state and the government. Its growth rate has averaged around 5 per cent since the mid-1980s according to data from the World Bank. Does this mean that the political system and in particular, a democratic political system, has little influence on economic growth? Economists Daron Acemoglu and Pascual Restrepo at MIT, Suresh Naidu at Colombia and James A. Robinson from Harvard, researched the effects of democracies on economic growth. Their results suggest that there is 'an economically and statistically significant *positive* correlation between democracy and future GDP per capita'. Further, they were able to quantify the effect by showing that long-run GDP in the 25 years after countries embrace democracy increases by between 20 and 25 per cent. The explanation for how democracies arrive at this impact on growth includes the opening up of economies, investment in schooling, particularly at the primary school level, better healthcare, improved methods of collecting and using taxes which can be used to provide public goods, and lower levels of social unrest. Countries in the research included many who have transitioned to democracy since the 1980s. These include Albania, Argentina, Bhutan, Czechia, Ghana, Honduras, Hungary, Liberia, Mali, Nicaragua, Niger, Pakistan, Poland, Sierra Leone, Slovenia, South Africa, Thailand, Türkiye and Zambia.

Questions:

1. What do you think is meant by the phrase, 'an economically and statistically significant positive correlation between democracy and future GDP per capita'?
2. Consider the explanations put forward by the researchers regarding this correlation. How do these explanations link to the discussions in the chapter so far on the causes of increases in productivity and growth?
3. Do the findings of the research imply that countries that are not democracies are doomed to lower than possible growth rates compared to those that are democracies? Explain.

Reference:

Acemoglu, D., Naidu, S., Restrepo, P. and Robinson, J.A. (2015) *Democracy Does Cause Growth*. MIT.

CAUSES OF GROWTH

The Solow model provides a way of predicting that the capital–output ratio of economies will eventually converge to the steady state. The evidence does not fully support the predictions of the model and this is due in part to its assumptions. In particular, steady-state equilibrium will be dependent on an economy's characteristics – its population, the level of physical and human capital, the savings rate, the depreciation rate, the proportion of the labour force in work and the level of technology. Rather than using the model to compare economies with very different characteristics, it may be more valuable to understand growth by comparing groups of economies with similar characteristics. We can use the model developed so far to understand more complex interactions in economies which will influence growth.

Changes in the Savings Rate

An increase in the savings rate can increase investment and the capital–output ratio. If we assume the economy starts at the steady-state equilibrium shown as K^* in Figure 5.3, investment will now be higher than spending on depreciation and this will increase the capital–output ratio moving the economy to a new steady-state equilibrium at K^{**}.

FIGURE 5.3

An Increase in the Savings Rate

An increase in the savings rate from I to I_1 leads to an increase in investment above the depreciation rate and increases the capital–output ratio. The economy moves to a new steady-state equilibrium of K^{**}.

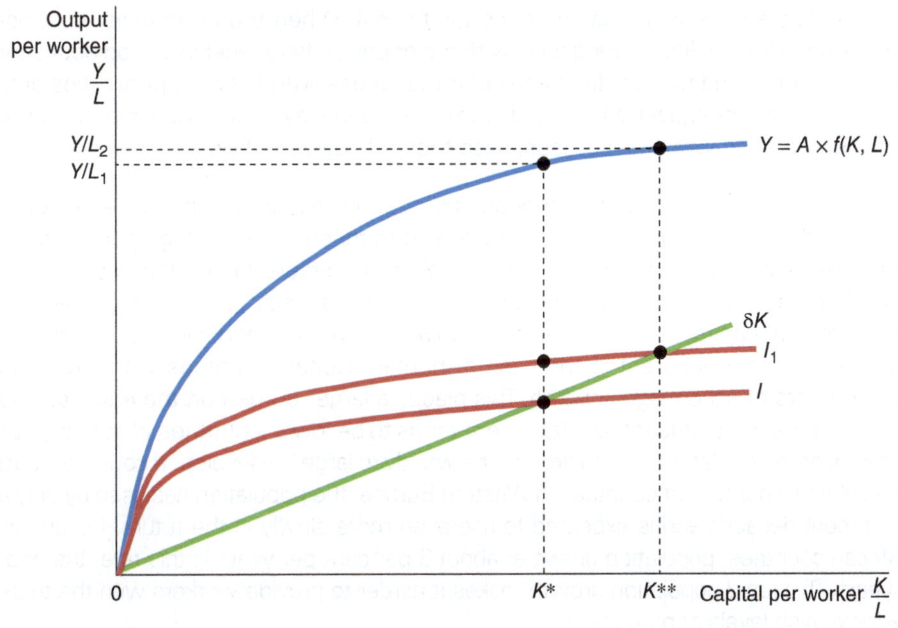

An Increase in the Population

If the population grows at the same rate as income, then GDP per capita will remain constant. The reality is that population growth varies depending on the country. In many countries, the population is rising and the reasons can be complex. The **birth rate**, the number of people born per thousand of the population, can be rising *ceteris paribus*, or the **death rate**, the number of deaths per thousand of the population, could be falling *ceteris paribus*. Or there could be a mixture of the two. In the UK and many European countries, the death rate is falling. More people are living longer and the birth rate is relatively constant, meaning that the population is rising. A rising population, however, does not mean that the labour force is increasing. An ageing population could mean that the labour force is shrinking. In addition, the **migration rate**, the difference between the number of people entering a country from abroad and the number leaving, can also influence the overall level and makeup of the population.

birth rate the number of people born per thousand of the population
death rate the number of deaths per thousand of the population
migration rate the difference between the number of people entering a country from abroad and the number leaving

One argument put forward in support of immigration to the UK, for example, has been that those people coming into the country are bringing with them skills which help increase productivity. If this is the case, then the aggregate production function could shift upwards reflecting the improved productivity of labour given the level of technology and the amount of capital available. Research and analysis of this issue is an important macroeconomic topic, particularly given the immigration issues which have affected many countries in Europe.

The Solow growth model shows that if the labour force is rising, then for the capital–output ratio to remain constant, investment must cover depreciation and provide more capital. If investment does not keep pace with the rise in the population, people will become poorer. In part, this helps to explain why many less developed countries experience continued high levels of poverty, because their population rises but investment fails to keep pace. Policymakers have tried to curb population growth by education on birth control and, in the case of China, by legislation which limited couples to having one child only. This law was introduced in 1979 and only reversed in October 2015.

Another way in which a country can influence population growth is to invoke the use of incentives. Bearing a child, like any decision, has an opportunity cost. When the opportunity cost rises, people will choose to have smaller families. In particular, with the opportunity to receive a good education and desirable employment, women tend to want fewer children than those with fewer opportunities outside the home. Hence policies that foster equal treatment of women are one way for less developed economies to reduce the rate of population growth and, perhaps, raise their standards of living.

Dilution of the Capital Stock Some modern theories of economic growth emphasize the effect of population growth on capital accumulation. According to these theories, high population growth reduces GDP per worker because rapid growth in the number of workers forces the capital stock to be spread more thinly. In other words, when population growth is rapid, each worker is equipped with less capital. A smaller quantity of capital per worker leads to lower productivity and lower GDP per worker.

This problem is most apparent in the case of human capital. Countries with high population growth have large numbers of school-age children. This places a larger burden on the education system. It is not surprising, therefore, that educational attainment tends to be low in countries with high population growth.

The differences in population growth around the world are large. In developed countries, such as the United States, the UK and a number of countries in Western Europe, the population has risen by only about 1 per cent per year in recent decades and is expected to rise even more slowly in the future. In contrast, in many low-income African countries, population grows at about 3 per cent per year. At this rate, the population doubles every 23 years. This rapid population growth makes it harder to provide workers with the tools and skills they need to achieve high levels of productivity.

Promoting Technological Progress Although rapid population growth may depress economic prosperity by reducing the amount of capital each worker has, it may also have some benefits. Some economists have suggested that world population growth has been an engine of technological progress and economic prosperity. The mechanism is simple. If there are more people, there is a greater probability that some of those people will come up with new ideas that will lead to technological progress, which benefits everyone.

The economist Michael Kremer has provided some support for this hypothesis in an article titled 'Population Growth and Technological Change: One Million BC to 1990', which was published in the *Quarterly Journal of Economics* in 1993. Kremer begins by noting that over the broad span of human history, world growth rates have increased as world population has. For example, world growth was more rapid when the world population was 1 billion (which occurred around the year 1800) than it was when the population was only 100 million (around 500 BC). This fact is consistent with the hypothesis that having more people induces more technological progress.

Kremer's second piece of evidence comes from comparing regions of the world. The melting of the polar ice caps at the end of the ice age around 10,000 BC flooded the land bridges and separated the world into several distinct regions that could not communicate with one another for thousands of years. If technological progress is more rapid when there are more people to discover things, then larger regions should have experienced more rapid growth.

According to Kremer, that is exactly what happened. The most successful region of the world in the year 1500 (when Columbus re-established technological contact) comprised the 'Old World' civilizations of the large Eurasia–Africa region. Next in technological development were the Aztec and Mayan civilizations in the Americas, followed by the hunter–gatherers of Australia, and then the primitive people of Tasmania, who lacked even fire-making and most stone and bone tools.

The smallest isolated region was Flinders Island, a tiny island between Tasmania and Australia. With the smallest population, Flinders Island had the fewest opportunities for technological advance and, indeed, seemed to regress. Around 3,000 BC, human society on Flinders Island died out completely. A large population, Kremer concludes, is a prerequisite for technological advance.

At first sight this conclusion does seem to be at odds with casual empirical observation of the modern world. As we previously noted, in many wealthy, developed countries population growth has been only about 1 per cent per year in recent decades, while in many low-income countries, such as those of sub-Saharan Africa, population growth is much higher. If Kremer is right, then higher population growth should help these low-income countries grow. The point is that Kremer was really analyzing *world* economic growth, or rather, economic growth in isolated regions of the world. Nowadays, in a very low-income country, it is unlikely that technological advances will be made that are not already known in developed countries. The problem is not lack of technological progress but difficulty in applying technology because of the scarcity of human capital and perhaps because of problems arising from political instability and corruption. Moreover, because many talented people from less developed countries tend to emigrate to wealthy, developed countries where they may work, for example, as scientists or entrepreneurs, population growth in less developed countries may actually enhance economic growth in developed countries.

An Increase in Technology

Increases in technology can be a public good. Assuming the technology is not protected, and even if it is this tends to be for a limited time, it is freely available to everyone to exploit. The aggregate production function shows that even if capital and labour remain constant, an increase in technology will increase income because both capital and labour become more productive. This can be seen in the developments in computer technology since the start of the century. In 1997, widespread availability of the internet was in its infancy and the capacity and functionality of the mobile phone was very different. The computing power many people routinely carry around with them every day in 2025 is staggering. In 1965, Intel engineer Gordon Moore predicted that the processing power of computers would double every two years. While the rate of change has slowed in recent years, the pace of change has been largely in line with Moore's prediction, such that it has been dubbed 'Moore's law'.

The application of technology to business has led to increases in productivity and different ways of doing things. Innovation often occurs because someone muses on problems and finds ways of resolving those problems and thus builds on existing knowledge. Not only does technology mean that the effects of diminishing marginal product can be offset, but it leads to proportional increases in productive capacity. If labour and capital productivity is measured as an index and year X is 100, a 5 per cent increase over one year means productivity rises to 105. A further 5 per cent increase in year X+2 would see the productivity index rising to 110.25. Increases in technology can lead to exponential increases in productivity and GDP. In 1960, for example, the Office for National Statistics (ONS) reports that output per worker in the UK, using 2012 as the base year for the index, was 35.8. In 2014 the index stood at 101.6.

FYI

Thomas Malthus

Thomas Robert Malthus (1766–1834), an English minister and early economic thinker, is famous for his book entitled *An Essay on the Principle of Population as It Affects the Future Improvement of Society*. In it, Malthus argued that an ever increasing population would continually strain society's ability to provide for itself. As a result, humans were doomed to forever live in poverty.

Malthus's logic began by noting that 'food is necessary to the existence of man' and that 'the passion between the sexes is necessary and will remain nearly in its present state'. He concluded that 'the power of population is infinitely greater than the power in the earth to produce subsistence for man *(sic)*'. According to Malthus, the only check on population growth was 'misery and vice'. Attempts by charities or governments to alleviate poverty were counterproductive, he argued, because they merely allowed the poor to have more children, placing even greater strains on society's productive capabilities.

Fortunately, Malthus's dire forecast was far off the mark. Although the world population has increased about sixfold over the past two centuries, living standards around the world are, on average, much higher. As a result of economic growth, chronic hunger and malnutrition are less common now than they were in Malthus's day. Famines occur from time to time, but they are more often the result of an unequal income distribution or political instability than an inadequate production of food.

Where did Malthus go wrong? He assumed – correctly – that world population would rise exponentially, since as more people are born and survive, more and more people are born as their children, and so on. He also assumed – incorrectly – that the amount of food produced could rise only linearly, by increasing the amount of land under cultivation with productivity remaining constant. Growth in humankind's ingenuity over the years has offset the effects of a larger population. Pesticides, fertilizers, mechanized farm equipment, new crop varieties and other technological advances that Malthus never imagined have allowed each farmer to feed ever greater numbers of people. Even with more mouths to feed, fewer farmers are necessary because each farmer is so much more productive than Malthus ever imagined.

Summary

Our look at the Solow growth model provides some insight into the causes of growth and provides some indications about where policymakers might direct their focus if increases in economic growth and growth per capita are considered desirable policy objectives. The aggregate production function provides a model for showing how income/output can grow when more inputs of capital and labour are used. It also shows how improvements in technology can make those factor inputs more productive. Key to growth is the accumulation of capital stock. A higher capital stock, *ceteris paribus*, will help generate higher output. Capital accumulation is made possible by investment from saving. If the savings rate leads to investment that is higher than spending on depreciation, the economy will move towards its steady-state equilibrium. Increases in the savings rate, in itself, do not generate increases in output per capita because of the diminishing marginal product of labour and capital. Improvements in technology can offset the effects of diminishing marginal product and generate both increased output and output per capita. The way in which the size and structure of the population changes is a factor that must be taken into account in whether increases in output lead to an increase in GDP per capita.

The Solow growth model allows predictions to be made about how countries grow. The transition to steady-state equilibrium has been researched and a number of studies suggest that many countries do move towards a state where long-run growth rates are similar. Such research includes Barro and Sala-i-Martin (Barro, R.J. and Sala-i-Martin, X. (1992) 'Convergence'. *Journal of Political Economy*, 100: 223–51), Mankiw, Romer and Weil (Mankiw, N.G., Romer, D. and Weil, D.N. (1992) 'A Contribution to the Empirics of Economic Growth'. *Quarterly Journal of Economics*, 107: 407–37), and Evans (Evans, P. (1996) 'Using Cross-Country Variances to Evaluate Growth Theories'. *Journal of Economic Dynamics and Control*, 20: 1027–49).

ENDOGENOUS GROWTH THEORY

The Solow growth model suggests that investment in capital alone cannot increase growth per capita because of diminishing marginal product, and that capital accounts for only around a third of contribution to output. Long-run growth is generated by changes in technology. In the Solow model, technology is exogenous in that the level of technology is not affected by either capital accumulation or changes in the population.

What the Solow model does not do is offer an explanation as to what determines the level of technology and technological changes. As noted above, and given our definition of technology, technology can be viewed as a public good which has the characteristic of being non-rival. As knowledge and ideas develop, these become publicly available and can be used by anyone. One person's use does not prevent anyone else from using that same knowledge or idea. If technology is a public good, then what incentive is there for anyone to innovate and come up with new ideas if they are not able to profit from them?

Paul Romer sought to investigate why improvements in technology occur, and the resulting model he developed is referred to as endogenous growth theory.

Endogenous growth theory is a theory of long-run economic growth which results from the creation of new knowledge and technology which impacts on everyone and makes them more productive as a result. The rate of economic growth in the long run is determined by the rate of growth in total factor productivity, and this total factor productivity is dependent on the rate at which technology progresses.

endogenous growth theory a theory that the rate of economic growth in the long run is determined by the rate of growth in total factor productivity. This total factor productivity is dependent on the rate at which technology progresses

Earlier in the chapter we looked at how technology has changed at a rapid rate since the 1960s. An important element of such exponential changes in technology is innovation and investment by firms into research and development (R&D). Much of this innovation and R&D might be carried out by firms in the expectation of gaining a competitive advantage. Recall that competitive advantage is the advantages over rivals which are both distinctive (i.e. not easy to copy) and defensible (that the firm can prevent others from copying their ideas). It is assumed, therefore, that the incentives firms have to innovate and invest in R&D are driven by the profit motive. If technology does have the characteristic of being non-rival, then this has policy implications. Policies must be developed to encourage firms to innovate, perhaps through extending intellectual property rights and to provide wider social benefits through improvements in education.

In the Solow model, capital accumulation is generated through saving and improvements in human capital through education. Capital accumulation, however, is not simply a case of increasing capital at a constant rate. When firms invest in new equipment, there may be increases in the knowledge required to operate and utilize that new equipment effectively and efficiently, which in itself increases intellectual capital and offsets diminishing marginal product. For example, if a firm invests in a new accounting system, its workers must be trained in its use, which increases their human capital. If they leave the firm, they take their knowledge and skills with them, which benefits other firms. In using the new system, some workers may identify ways in which the system can be tweaked to benefit the particular characteristics of the business itself. This can be fed back to the developers of the system to incorporate in subsequent versions in addition to improving productivity in the firm itself. Intellectual capital, therefore, grows through innovation, which in turn affects productivity.

As innovation develops, new technologies replace old ones and new skills are needed which render existing skills obsolete. In 1942, Austrian economist Joseph Schumpeter developed the idea of **creative destruction** to describe this process. The implication of this process is that as technology changes over time, there will be winners and losers. Some firms will go out of business and workers may have to retrain to secure new skills, and the process can be highly damaging to those involved. However, ultimately, if growth is to be secured, society will have to accept that R&D and innovation are both contributors to the rate at which creative destruction happens and are essential to increases in technology. Finding ways to encourage investment in R&D becomes a core focus of government policy.

creative destruction the process where new technologies replace old ones and new skills are needed which render existing skills obsolete

ECONOMIC GROWTH AND PUBLIC POLICY

So far, we have determined that a society's standard of living depends, in part, on its ability to produce goods and services. Furthermore, its productivity depends on physical capital, human capital, natural resources and technological knowledge. Let us now turn to the question faced by policymakers around the world: what can government policy do to raise productivity and living standards?

The Importance of Saving and Investment

We introduced the role of the savings ratio in relation to investment earlier in the chapter. Investment is necessary to sustain and increase the capital stock. Because capital is a produced factor of production, a society can change the amount of capital it has. If today the economy produces a large quantity of new capital goods, then tomorrow it will have a larger stock of capital and be able to produce more of all types of goods and services. Thus one way to raise future productivity is to invest more current resources in the production of capital.

When considering the accumulation of capital, however, the notion of trade-offs must be considered. Given that resources are scarce, devoting more resources to producing capital requires devoting fewer resources to producing goods and services for current consumption. That is, for society to invest more in capital, it must consume less and save more of its current income (the savings ratio must rise). The growth that arises from capital accumulation requires that society sacrifices consumption of goods and services in the present to enjoy higher consumption in the future.

In the 1930s, the rulers of Russia deliberately diverted resources to the production of capital goods in an attempt to try to catch up with the richer and more industrialized Western countries such as Germany, the United States and the UK. It managed to significantly expand production in core industries such as coal and steel, which in turn increased its capacity to produce other capital goods (and military equipment). The trade-off for the Russian people at the time was fewer consumer goods and a harsh life. It could be argued that while this represented significant short-term hardship for many of its people, the decision helped Russia to be in a position to fight off the Germans in World War II and emerge to be one of the planet's superpowers.

Research suggests that the correlation between growth and investment is strong. Countries that devote a large share of GDP to investment, such as China, Japan and Australia, also have a stronger average growth rate. Countries that devote a small share of GDP to investment, such as the Central African Republic, Zimbabwe and Bangladesh, tend to have low growth rates. Studies that examine a more comprehensive list of countries confirm this strong correlation between investment and growth. There is, however, a problem in interpreting these data. A correlation between two variables does not establish which variable is the cause and which is the effect. It is possible that high investment causes high growth, but it is also possible that high growth causes high investment. Perhaps, high growth and high investment are both caused by a third variable that has been omitted from the analysis. The data by themselves cannot tell us the direction of causation. Nevertheless, because capital accumulation affects productivity so clearly and directly, many economists interpret these data as showing that high investment leads to more rapid economic growth.

Diminishing Returns and the Catch-Up Effect

We have seen that increasing the saving rate will not lead to indefinite long-run growth because of diminishing returns. An increase in the saving rate leads to higher growth only for a while. As the higher saving rate allows more capital to be accumulated, the benefits from additional capital become smaller over time, and so growth slows down. In the long run, the higher saving rate leads to a higher level of productivity and income, but not to higher growth in these variables. Reaching this long run, however, can take quite a while. According to studies of international data on economic growth, increasing the saving rate can lead to substantially higher growth for a period of several decades.

The diminishing return to capital has another important implication: *ceteris paribus*, it is easier for a country to grow quickly if it starts out relatively poor. This effect of initial conditions on subsequent growth is sometimes called the **catch-up effect**. In low-income countries, workers can lack even the most rudimentary tools and, as a result, have low productivity. Small amounts of capital investment would substantially raise these workers' productivity. By contrast, workers in wealthy countries have large amounts of capital with which to work, and this partly explains their high productivity. Yet with the amount of capital per worker already so high, additional capital investment has a relatively small effect on productivity. Studies of international data on economic growth confirm this catch-up effect. Controlling for other variables, such as the percentage of GDP devoted to investment, low-income countries do tend to grow at a faster rate than wealthier countries.

catch-up effect the property whereby countries that start off poor tend to grow more rapidly than countries that start off rich

This catch-up effect can help explain variations in observations on average investment as a proportion of GDP and average growth rates over time. Since the 1970s, Japan has allocated around 10 per cent more to investment as a proportion of GDP compared to China. China, however, has grown at an average rate 1.7 times the Japanese annual average growth rate. The explanation is the catch-up effect. In 1961 Japan had GDP per person about 15 times that of China, in part because investment in China up to the end of the 1960s had been so low. With a small initial capital stock, the benefits to capital accumulation were much greater in China, and this gave the country a higher subsequent growth rate.

Investment from Abroad

The Solow model assumes a closed economy. Saving by domestic residents is not the only way for a country to invest in new capital. The other way is investment by foreigners.

Investment from abroad takes several forms. BMW might build a car factory in Portugal. A capital investment that is owned and operated by a foreign entity is called **foreign direct investment**. Alternatively, a German might buy equity in a Portuguese corporation (that is, buy a share in the ownership of the corporation). The Portuguese corporation can then use the proceeds from the equity sale to build a new factory. An investment that is financed with foreign money but operated by domestic residents is called **foreign portfolio investment**. In both cases, Germans provide the resources necessary to increase the stock of capital in Portugal. That is, German saving is being used to finance Portuguese investment.

foreign direct investment capital investment that is owned and operated by a foreign entity
foreign portfolio investment investment that is financed with foreign money but operated by domestic residents

When foreigners invest in a country, they do so because they expect to earn a return on their investment. BMW's car factory increases the Portuguese capital stock and, therefore, increases Portuguese productivity and Portuguese GDP. Yet BMW takes some of this additional income back to Germany in the form of profit. Similarly, when a German investor buys Portuguese equity, the investor has a right to a portion of the profit that the Portuguese corporation earns.

Investment from abroad, therefore, does not have the same effect on all measures of economic prosperity. Recall that GDP is the income earned within a country by both residents and non-residents, whereas GNP is the income earned by residents of a country both at home and abroad. When BMW opens its car factory in Portugal, some of the income the factory generates accrues to people who do not live in Portugal. As a result, foreign investment in Portugal raises the income of the Portuguese (measured by GNP) by less than it raises the production in Portugal (measured by GDP).

Nevertheless, investment from abroad is one way for a country to grow. Even though some of the benefits from this investment flow back to the foreign owners, this investment does increase the economy's stock of capital. This leads to higher productivity and higher wages. Moreover, investment from abroad is one way for low-income countries to learn the state of the art technologies developed and used in wealthier countries. For these reasons, many economists who advise governments in less developed economies advocate policies that encourage investment from abroad. Often this means removing restrictions that governments have imposed on foreign ownership of domestic capital.

An organization that tries to encourage the flow of capital to low-income countries is the World Bank. This international organization obtains funds from the world's advanced industrialized countries and uses these resources to make loans to less developed countries so that they can invest in roads, sewage systems, schools and other types of capital. It also offers the countries advice about how the funds might best be used. The World Bank, together with its sister organization, the International Monetary Fund (IMF), was set up after World War II. One lesson from the war was that economic distress often leads to political turmoil, international tensions and military conflict. Thus every country has an interest in promoting economic prosperity around the world. The World Bank and the IMF were set up to achieve that common goal.

Education

Education – investment in human capital – is at least as important as investment in physical capital for a country's long-run economic success. In the developed economies of Western Europe and North America, each extra year of schooling raises a worker's income by about 10 per cent on average. In less developed countries, where human capital is especially scarce, the gap between the wages of educated and uneducated workers is even larger. One way in which government policy can enhance the standard of living is to provide good schools and to encourage the population to take advantage of them.

Investment in human capital, like investment in physical capital, has an opportunity cost. When students are in school, they forego the wages they could have earned. In less developed countries, children often drop out of school at an early age, even though the benefit of additional schooling is very high, simply because their labour is needed to help support the family.

Some economists have argued that human capital is particularly important for economic growth because human capital conveys positive externalities. An educated person, for instance, might generate new ideas about how best to produce goods and services. If these ideas enter society's pool of knowledge so that everyone can use them, then the ideas are an external benefit of education. In this case, the return to schooling for society is even greater than the return for the individual. This argument would justify the large subsidies to human capital investment that we observe in the form of public education.

One problem facing some poor countries is the **brain drain** – the emigration of many of the most highly educated workers to rich countries where these workers can enjoy a higher standard of living. If human capital does have positive externalities, then this brain drain makes those people left behind poorer than they otherwise would be. This problem offers policymakers a dilemma. On the one hand, wealthier countries like those of Western Europe and North America have the best systems of higher education. It would seem natural, therefore, for low-income countries to send their best students abroad to earn higher degrees. On the other, those students who have spent time abroad may choose not to return home, and this brain drain will reduce the low-income nation's stock of human capital even further.

brain drain the emigration of many of the most highly educated workers to wealthier countries

Health and Nutrition

The term *human capital* usually refers to education, but it can also be used to describe another type of investment in people: expenditures that lead to a healthier population. Other things being equal, healthier workers are more productive. The right investments in the health of the population provide one way for a nation to increase productivity and raise living standards.

Economic historian Robert Fogel has suggested that a significant factor in long-run economic growth is improved health from better nutrition. He estimates that in Great Britain in 1780, about one in five people were so malnourished that they were incapable of manual labour. Among those who could work, insufficient intake of calories substantially reduced the work effort they could carry out. As nutrition improved, so did workers' productivity.

Fogel studies these historical trends in part by looking at the height of the population. Short stature can be an indicator of malnutrition, especially during gestation and the early years of life. Fogel finds that as nations develop economically, people eat more and the population gets taller. From 1775 to 1975, the average caloric intake in Great Britain rose by 26 per cent and the height of the average man rose by 3.6 inches (around 10 cm). Similarly, during the spectacular economic growth in the Republic of Korea from 1962 to 1995, caloric consumption rose by 44 per cent and average male height rose by 2 inches (5 cm). Research on height and body-mass index trajectories published in *The Lancet* in 2020 show that there have been gains in the mean height in a number of emerging economies, including China, where the gains in mean height of 19-year-olds was around 3.5 cm more for men and 2.3 cm for women compared to India. Of course, a person's height is determined by a combination of genetic predisposition and environment. Because the genetic makeup of a population is slow to change, such increases in average height are likely due to changes in the environment – nutrition being the obvious explanation.

Moreover, studies have found that height is an indicator of productivity. Looking at data on a large number of workers at a point in time, researchers have found that taller workers tend to earn more. Because wages reflect a worker's productivity, this finding suggests that taller workers tend to be more productive. The effect of height on wages is especially pronounced in lower-income countries, where malnutrition is a bigger risk.

Fogel won the Nobel Prize in Economics in 1993 for his work in economic history, which includes not only his studies on nutrition but also work on US slavery and the role of the railroads in the development of the US economy. In the lecture he gave when awarded the Prize, he surveyed the evidence on health and economic growth. He concluded that 'improved gross nutrition accounts for roughly 30 per cent of the growth of per capita income in Britain between 1790 and 1980'.

Today malnutrition is fortunately rare in developed nations (obesity is a more widespread problem). For people in developing nations, poor health and inadequate nutrition remain obstacles to higher productivity and improved living standards. The United Nations estimates that almost a third of the population in sub-Saharan Africa is undernourished.

The causal link between health and wealth runs in both directions. Low-income countries are poor, in part, because their populations are not healthy. Their populations are not healthy, in part, because they are poor and cannot afford adequate healthcare and nutrition. It is a vicious circle but opens up the possibility of a virtuous circle. Policies that lead to more rapid economic growth would naturally improve health outcomes, which in turn would further promote economic growth.

Property Rights, Political Stability and Good Governance

Other ways in which policymakers can foster economic growth are by protecting property rights, promoting political stability and maintaining good governance. As noted when we discussed economic interdependence, production in market economies arises from the interactions of millions of individuals and firms. When you buy a car, for instance, you are buying the output of a car dealer, a car manufacturer, a steel company, an iron ore mining company and so on. This division of production among many firms allows the economy's factors of production to be used as effectively as possible. To achieve this outcome, the economy must coordinate transactions among these firms, as well as between firms and consumers. Market prices are one way in which these transactions are coordinated.

An important prerequisite for the price system to work is an economy-wide respect for property rights. A mining company will not make the effort to mine iron ore if it expects the ore to be stolen. The company mines the ore only if it is confident that it will benefit from the ore's subsequent sale. For this reason, courts serve an important role in a market economy: they enforce property rights. Through the criminal justice system, the courts discourage direct theft. In addition, through the civil justice system, the courts ensure that buyers and sellers live up to their contracts. This is one of the reasons why institutional economists advocate research into these areas.

Although people in developed countries tend to take property rights for granted, those living in less developed or emerging countries understand that lack of property rights can be a major problem. In many countries, the system of justice does not work well. Contracts are hard to enforce, and fraud often goes unpunished. In more extreme cases, the government not only fails to enforce property rights but actually infringes upon them. To do business in some countries, firms are expected to bribe powerful government officials. Such corruption impedes the coordinating power of markets. It also discourages domestic saving and investment from abroad. The problem of corruption and bribery is extensive. Transparency International is a pressure group that exists to advance the cause of anti-corruption. Each year it publishes an index showing perceptions of corruption across the world. Countries are scored on a scale of 0–100 with 0 being highly corrupt and 100 being highly clean. Around two-thirds of the 176 countries in the ranking fall below 50.

One threat to property rights is political instability. When revolutions and coups are common, there is doubt about whether property rights will be respected in the future. A revolutionary government might confiscate the capital of some businesses, as was often true after communist revolutions. Therefore, domestic residents have less incentive to save, invest and start new businesses. At the same time, foreigners have less incentive to invest in the country. Even the threat of revolution can act to depress a nation's standard of living. It is no coincidence that countries with a strong military power, who are subject to frequent coups, are ones that are at the bottom of any standard of living league table.

Thus economic prosperity depends in part on political prosperity. A country with an efficient court system, honest government officials and a stable constitution, that is strong institutions, will enjoy a higher economic standard of living than a country with a poorly functioning court system, corrupt officials and frequent revolutions and coups. The key features of good governance include the extent to which a country is ruled by sound principles, where the rule of law, the authority of law, the absence of corruption and independent judicial processes are in existence. If these things are in place, then it is more likely that contracts and property rights can be enforced. Therefore, free markets can operate effectively to allocate scarce resources. Without good governance, many economists believe that economic development will be compromised.

Free Trade

Some of the world's poorest countries have tried to achieve more rapid economic growth by pursuing *inward-oriented policies*. These policies are aimed at raising productivity and living standards within the country by avoiding interaction with the rest of the world. This approach gets support from some domestic firms, which claim that they need protection from foreign competition to compete and grow. This is called an infant industry argument, and together with a general distrust of foreigners, has at times led policymakers in less developed countries to impose tariffs and other trade restrictions.

Many economists would support the pursuit of *outward-oriented policies* that integrate these countries into the world economy. International trade can improve the economic well-being of a country's citizens. Trade is, in some ways, a type of technology. When a country exports wheat and imports steel, the country benefits in the same way as if it had invented a technology for turning wheat into steel. A country that eliminates trade restrictions will, therefore, experience the same kind of economic growth that would occur after a major technological advance.

The adverse impact of inwards orientation becomes clear when we consider the small size of many less developed economies. The total GDP of Argentina, for instance, is about that of the southeast of England (if we include London). Imagine what would happen if the southeast were suddenly to declare that it was illegal to trade with anyone beyond the regional boundaries. Without being able to take advantage of the gains from trade, the southeast would need to produce all the goods it consumes. It would also have to produce all its own capital goods, rather than importing state of the art equipment from other cities. Living standards in the southeast would fall, and the problem would probably only get worse over time.

This is precisely what happened when Argentina pursued inward-oriented policies throughout much of the twentieth century and can also partly explain the economic problems in North Korea, which has effectively cut itself off from the rest of the world. By contrast, countries pursuing outward-oriented policies, such as the Republic of Korea, Singapore and Taiwan, have enjoyed high rates of economic growth.

The amount that a nation trades with others is determined not only by government policy but also by geography. Countries with good natural seaports find trade easier than countries without this resource. It is not a coincidence that many of the world's major cities, such as Paris, Boston, New York, Hong Kong and London, are located either next to oceans or on the banks of a major river giving easy access for seafaring trade vessels. Similarly, because landlocked countries find international trade more difficult, they tend to have lower levels of income than countries with easy access to the world's waterways.

Research and Development

As we have seen in our short look at endogenous growth theory, technological advance can come from private research by firms and individual inventors. Just as government has a role in providing a public good such as national defence, it also has a role in encouraging the research and development of new technologies. The governments in most advanced countries do this in a number of ways, for example through science research laboratories owned and funded by the government, or through a system of research grants offered to promising researchers. It may also offer tax breaks and concessions for firms engaging in R&D.

Yet another way in which government policy encourages research is through the patent system. When a person or firm invents a new product, such as a new drug, the inventor can apply for a patent. If the product is deemed truly original, the government awards the patent, which gives the inventor the exclusive right to make the product for a specified number of years. In essence, the patent gives the inventor a property right over the invention, turning their new idea from a public good into a private good. By allowing inventors to profit from their inventions – even if only temporarily – the patent system enhances the incentive for individuals and firms to engage in research.

Population Growth

Economists and other social scientists have long debated how population growth affects a society. The most direct effect is on the size of the labour force. A large population means more workers to produce goods and services. At the same time, it means more people to consume those goods and services. Beyond these obvious effects, population growth interacts with the other factors of production in ways that are less obvious and more open to debate.

FYI

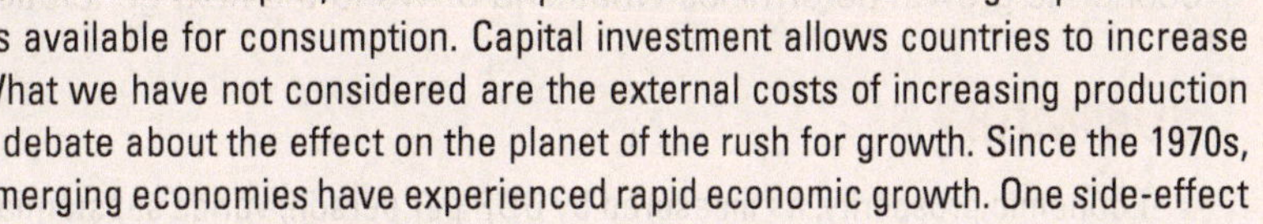

Economic Growth and Climate Change

In our discussion about economic growth in this chapter, we have implied that standards of living improve when people have more goods and services available for consumption. Capital investment allows countries to increase productivity and output per worker. What we have not considered are the external costs of increasing production in this way. There has been extensive debate about the effect on the planet of the rush for growth. Since the 1970s, many nations in what are classed as emerging economies have experienced rapid economic growth. One side-effect of that growth, however, has been an increase in emissions of greenhouse gases through, for example, the use of fossil fuels to generate energy, which has contributed to the increase in human-generated carbon emissions and the much-reported threats to standards of living from climate change.

(Continued)

One of the reasons for the lack of concerted action on reducing the impact of climate change is that there are costs involved in reducing carbon emissions and in the changes of behaviour that are deemed necessary. As with many things in economics, there are winners and losers in the changes required, and some argue that the costs fall disproportionately on poorer nations. Many of these lower-income nations point to the fact that the developed world was largely responsible for the increase in carbon emissions during their industrial development. Now that poorer nations are trying to 'catch up', they are being asked to shoulder much of the burden as they are more likely to use fossil fuels to generate energy and do not have the resources to fund greener technologies. To move from their current state to one that is at the very least carbon-neutral would require considerable investment and sacrifice.

Some commentators point to the many benefits that would flow from all nations tackling carbon emissions and implementing greener policies more generally. For example, if emissions from the use of fossil fuels were reduced, air quality would improve, which would have a positive impact on general health and would, in turn, reduce the cost burdens on health services. Similarly, changing behaviour to better diets, which would involve reducing red meat consumption and eating more plant-based foods, would also bring health and environmental benefits. A transition to trying to achieve a zero-carbon position would generate investment into a wide variety of new technologies, which would lead to new jobs and business opportunities that could benefit millions of people around the world and improve living standards.

The basis of these types of arguments is hard to question, but the reality is incredibly complex. The models used to predict climate change and its effects are becoming ever more sophisticated. The estimates of the effects on future GDP of adopting policies to tackle climate change and limit average global temperature growth below 1.5 degrees Celsius above pre-industrial levels do still vary considerably. Much like the Reverend T. Malthus, scientists today can only build models that are based on available knowledge. None of us can really know what future developments and changes will occur.

SELF TEST Describe three ways in which a government policymaker can try to raise the growth in living standards in a society. Are there any drawbacks to these policies?

CONCLUSION: THE IMPORTANCE OF LONG-RUN GROWTH

In this chapter we have discussed theories of growth and how they relate to differences in the standard of living across nations and how policymakers can endeavour to raise the standard of living through policies that promote economic growth. Policymakers who want to encourage growth in standards of living must aim to increase their nation's productive ability. They should be encouraging rapid accumulation of the factors of production and ensuring that these factors are employed as effectively as possible.

Economists differ in their views of the role of government in promoting economic growth. At the very least, government can lend support by maintaining property rights and political stability. More controversial is whether government should target and subsidize specific industries that might be especially important for technological progress. There is no doubt that these issues are among the most important in economics. The success of one generation's policymakers in learning and heeding the fundamental lessons about economic growth determines what kind of world the next generation will inherit.

SUMMARY

- Economic prosperity, as measured by GDP per person, varies substantially around the world. The average income in the world's richest countries is more than 10 times that in the world's poorest countries. Because growth rates of real GDP also vary substantially, the relative positions of countries can change dramatically over time.
- The standard of living in an economy depends, in part, on the economy's ability to produce goods and services. Productivity, in turn, depends on the amounts of physical capital, human capital, natural resources and technological knowledge available to workers.

- The Solow growth model notes that the accumulation of capital is subject to diminishing returns. In other words, the more capital an economy has, the less additional output the economy gets from an extra unit of capital. Because of diminishing returns, higher saving leads to higher growth for a period of time. Eventually it slows down as the economy approaches a higher level of capital, productivity and income. Also because of diminishing returns, the return to capital is especially high in poor countries. Other things being equal, these countries can grow faster because of the catch-up effect.
- Endogenous growth theory focuses on the importance of explaining how technology can change and offset the effects of diminishing marginal productivity. Innovation and R&D are important ways in which technology growth can arise.
- Government policies can try to influence the economy's growth rate in many ways: by encouraging saving and investment, encouraging investment from abroad, fostering education, maintaining property rights and political stability, allowing free trade, promoting the research and development of new technologies, and controlling population growth.

IN THE NEWS

Economic Growth and Productivity

One of the points of debate during the lead up to the 2024 election in the UK was the weak and sluggish growth record of the economy. However, the UK was not alone in facing problems of weak economic growth since the 2007–9 Financial Crisis. A paper published by Anna Valero and John Van Reenen in June 2024 for the Centre for Economic Performance (CEP) explored the relationship between productivity and growth to help explain the weak performance of the UK economy since 2010. The authors noted that the UK was not the only country to experience such problems. Germany, France and the US had all experienced similar problems, but the problems were worse in the UK.

In comparison with pre-Financial Crisis trends, Valero and Van Reenan found that productivity in the UK was 26 per cent lower than it would have been had the pre-Financial Crisis trend continued. A particular issue in the UK has been GDP growth per capita. The authors pointed out that the population of the UK has grown, largely as a result of a rise in net migration. While employment rates have also grown, GDP per capita grew at an average rate of 0.9 per cent from 2010, whereas in the period 1997–2010 it grew at an average rate of 1.4 per cent. The difference might not sound significant, but remember the 'rule of 70'! The key reason for the challenges the UK faces is around productivity, and productivity has been compromised because of a lack of investment in capital.

Valero and Van Reenan provide some possible explanations for this lack of investment, notably the unstable political environment over the period where austerity policies were instituted. These were followed by uncertainties created by Brexit, global challenges, including the pandemic, but also the many changes in prime ministers, and changes in direction and importance placed on different policies. To address the productivity issue, the authors suggest that there need to be reforms in key areas including the relaxing of planning barriers to help boost housing construction and infrastructure projects, and investment in public services.

©iStock/BrianAJackson

Productivity and economic growth are closely linked but in recent years raising productivity has been challenging for some countries.

The Labour government that was elected to power in July 2024 sought to focus on some of these issues by, for example, announcing ambitious plans on housebuilding, relaxation of planning rules, investment in green energy

(Continued)

programmes and in public services. One of the constraints in meeting these aims, however, is generating sufficient public revenue. The Labour government was at pains to point out the poor legacy previous governments had left. The first budget of the new government then increased taxation with the initial burden falling heavily on employers. Many pointed to this being a disincentive to innovation and investment. In addition, while the construction industry welcomed the positive mood music around house construction, it was noted that to increase building, skilled tradespeople were needed and a shortage would likely act as a significant brake on achieving the planned targets. It was also noted that while investment in infrastructure projects were important, many large-scale projects were mired in problems and red tape. Projects such as the third runway at Heathrow and a tunnel under the area around Stonehenge to improve the transport links to and from the South West have been debated for many years, and resolutions to these types of projects still look a long way away.

Critical Thinking Questions

1 Explain the relationship between productivity and economic growth. You should use appropriate diagrams to help illustrate and support your answer.
2 Assume that the average per capita income in the UK was £30,000 in 2010. Use the rule of 70 to estimate what the per capita income would be if the average annual growth rate of 1.4 per cent had continued in the years after the Financial Crisis, and compare this to the actual, assuming a post-Financial Crisis average annual growth rate of 0.9 per cent. Comment on your findings.
3 The UK is classed as a developed country and ranks in the top 10 of countries by GDP. To what extent are the problems highlighted in the article similar to those experienced by less developed countries in terms of explaining weak productivity levels?
4 Governments will often announce plans to increase investment and boost productivity. The report by Valero and Van Reenan made a number of recommendations on what the UK needs to do to improve productivity. If it were easy to do then presumably productivity levels would be higher in many parts of the world. Why is boosting investment, therefore, seemingly so difficult?
5 Consider the proposals of the Labour government outlined in the article. What do you think needs to happen or change in the UK (and other countries) to realize the ambitious aims stated of increasing productivity and growth?

Reference:

cep.lse.ac.uk/pubs/download/ea057.pdf, accessed 7 August 2025.

QUESTIONS FOR REVIEW

1 What does the level of a nation's GDP measure? What does the growth rate of GDP measure? Would you rather live in a nation with a high level of GDP and a low growth rate, or in a nation with a low level of GDP and a high growth rate? Provide the reasoning for your choice.
2 List and describe four determinants of productivity.
3 In what way is a university degree a form of capital?
4 Does a higher rate of saving lead to higher growth temporarily or indefinitely?
5 Assuming the population is stable, what effects will an increase in capital accumulation have on growth? Can a country generate sustained growth through rising capital investment?
6 What is the steady-state equilibrium?
7 Why is technological progress important in improving growth rates in any economy?
8 Why would removing a trade restriction, such as a tariff, lead to more rapid economic growth?

9 How does the rate of population growth influence the level of GDP per person?

10 Describe two ways in which the government can try to encourage advances in technological knowledge.

PROBLEMS AND APPLICATIONS

1 Most countries import substantial amounts of goods and services from other countries. Yet the chapter says that a nation can enjoy a high standard of living only if it can produce a large quantity of goods and services itself. Can you reconcile these two points?

2 List some of the key capital inputs necessary to produce each of the following:
   a. cars
   b. secondary education
   c. air travel
   d. fruit and vegetables.

3 UK income per person today is roughly four times what it was a century ago. Many other countries have also experienced significant growth over that period. What are some specific ways in which your standard of living is likely to differ from that of your great grandparents?

4 The idea of creative destruction suggests that economic growth through changes in technology can have winners and losers. In the country in which you are studying, what firms or industries have declined or disappeared as a result of new technologies? How might governments manage the effects of creative destruction on those negatively affected by the process?

5 To what extent do you think that endogenous growth theory:
   a. refutes the Solow model, or
   b. provides a further refinement to the Solow model?

6 Societies choose what share of their resources to devote to consumption and what share to devote to investment. Some of these decisions involve private spending; others involve government spending.
   a. Describe some forms of private spending that represent consumption and some forms that represent investment.
   b. Describe some forms of government spending that represent consumption and some forms that represent investment.

7 What is the opportunity cost of investing in capital? Do you think a country can 'over-invest' in capital? What is the opportunity cost of investing in human capital? Do you think a country can 'over-invest' in human capital? Explain.

8 In many developing nations, young women have lower enrolment rates in secondary schooling than young men. Describe three ways in which greater educational opportunities for young women could lead to faster economic growth in these countries.

9 Using an appropriate data source, conduct some research into the economic and political characteristics of two contrasting countries – one with a relatively high GDP per capita and one with a relatively low GDP per capita. What factors affect these differences in GDP per capita? Is there any evidence that the country with the lower GDP per capita has experienced higher growth rates in the twenty-first century? If so, why and if not, why not?

10 International data show a positive correlation between political stability and economic growth.
   a. Through what mechanism could political stability lead to strong economic growth?
   b. Through what mechanism could strong economic growth lead to political stability?

6 UNEMPLOYMENT AND THE LABOUR MARKET

Losing a job can be one of the most distressing economic events in a person's life. Most people rely on their labour earnings to maintain their standard of living, and many people get not only income from their work, but also a sense of personal accomplishment. A job loss means a lower living standard in the present, anxiety about the future and reduced self-esteem. It is not surprising, therefore, that politicians campaigning for office often speak about how their proposed policies will 'help create jobs'. Indeed, the importance of unemployment in an economy is reflected in the attention given to it by politicians. There are a number of reasons for this. Unemployment affects standards of living, and from a macroeconomic perspective, people who would like to work but cannot find a job are not contributing to the economy's production of goods and services. Although some degree of unemployment is inevitable in a complex economy with thousands of firms and millions of workers, the amount of unemployment varies substantially over time and across countries. When a country keeps its workers as fully employed as possible, it achieves a higher level of GDP than it would if it left many of its workers standing idle.

This chapter begins our study of unemployment. The problem of unemployment is usefully divided into two categories – the long-run problem and the short-run problem. In this chapter we discuss the determinants of the long-run problem – an economy's *natural rate of unemployment*. As we will see, the designation *natural* does not imply that this rate of unemployment is desirable. Neither does it imply that it is constant over time or impervious to economic policy. It merely means that this unemployment does not go away on its own, even in the long run.

As we will see, long-run unemployment does not arise from a single problem that has a single solution. Instead, it reflects a variety of related problems. As a result, there is no easy way for policymakers to reduce the economy's natural rate of unemployment and, at the same time, alleviate the hardships experienced by the unemployed.

IDENTIFYING UNEMPLOYMENT

We begin by examining more precisely what the term *unemployment* means. We consider how governments measure unemployment, what problems arise in interpreting the unemployment data, how long the typical spell of unemployment lasts and why there will always be some people unemployed.

What Is Unemployment?

Intuition might suggest that unemployment simply means someone who does not have a job. This intuition hides a number of subtleties, however. If you are in full-time education, for example, you are studying and thus are not available for full-time paid employment. What if you were not a student but were suffering from some long-term illness that meant that you were unfit for work? What if you were a parent who had made the choice to stay at home to look after children and raise a family? Again, in both these instances, although you would not have a job, we would not say that you were unemployed because you would not be available for work. These examples provide a guide that an unemployed person is not simply 'someone who does not have a job' but more accurately, 'someone who does not have a job and who is available for work'.

The notion of 'being available for work' requires further clarification. The wage rate for jobs that are unfilled is a factor in whether people choose to make themselves available for work. If too low, people may choose not to work. At another extreme, suppose you won so much money on the Euro Millions Lottery that you decided you would leave university and live off your winnings for the rest of your life. Would you be unemployed? No, because you would still be unavailable for work, no matter what wage rate you were offered. Thus being unemployed also depends upon whether you are willing to work at going wage rates.

We are now in a position to give a more precise definition of what it means to be unemployed. The number unemployed in an economy is the number of people of working age who are able and available for work at current wage rates and who do not have a job.

How Is Unemployment Measured?

There are two basic ways government agencies go about measuring the unemployment rate in the economy:

The Claimant Count One simple way is to count the number of people who, on any given day, are claiming unemployment benefit payments from the government – the so-called *claimant count*. Since a government agency is paying out the benefits, it will be relatively easy to gather data on the number of claimants. The government also has a good idea of the total labour force in employment, since it is receiving income tax payments from them. Adding to this the number of unemployment benefit claimants is a measure of the *total labour force*, and expressing the claimant count as a proportion of the labour force is a measure of the *unemployment rate*.

Unfortunately, there are a number of important drawbacks with the claimant count method. One obvious problem is that it is subject to changes in the rules the government applies for eligibility to unemployment benefit. Suppose the government gets tougher and changes the rules so that fewer people are now entitled to unemployment benefit. The claimant count will go down and so will the measured unemployment rate, even though there has been no change in the number of people with or without work. The opposite would happen if the government became more lenient and relaxed the rules so that more people became eligible.

In the UK, for example, there have been about 30 changes to the eligibility rules since the mid-1990s, all but one of which have reduced the claimant count and so reduced the unemployment rate based on this measure. The following are examples of categories of people who are excluded from the UK claimant count: anyone looking for part-time work; people who have left the workforce voluntarily for a while and now wish to return to employment (for example, those who have raised a family); and students looking for vacation work. Many – if not all – of the people in these categories would be people who do not have a job, are of working age and are able and available for work at current wage rates. Yet they would be excluded from measured unemployment in the UK using the claimant count method.

Labour Force Surveys The second, and probably more reliable, method of measuring unemployment is through the use of surveys – in other words, going out and asking people questions – based on an accepted definition of unemployment. Questions then arise as to whom to interview, how often (since surveys use up resources and are costly) and what definition of unemployment to use. Although the definition of unemployment that we developed earlier seems reasonable enough, the term 'available for work at current wage rates' may be too loose for this purpose. In the UK and many other countries, the government carries out Labour Force Surveys (LFS) based on the standardized definition of unemployment from the International Labour Office, or ILO. The ILO is the permanent secretariat of the International Labour Organization, a United Nations agency. The ILO definition of an unemployed person is someone who is without a job and who is willing to start work within the next two weeks and either has been looking for work within the past four weeks or is waiting to start a job.

The LFS is carried out quarterly throughout Europe. National statistical services collect the data which are then processed by Eurostat. The surveys are published in different languages but scrutinized by statisticians to ensure comparability between the surveys carried out in each member state. In the UK, the survey is based on a sample of about 60,000 households, and across Europe as a whole, the sample size is around 1.5 million. Based on the answers to survey questions, the government places each adult (aged 16 and older) in each surveyed household into one of three categories:

1. A person is considered employed if they spent some of the previous week working at a paid job.
2. A person is unemployed if they fit the ILO definition of an unemployed person.
3. A person who fits neither of the first two categories, such as a full-time student, homemaker or retiree, is not in the labour force (or, to use ILO terminology, is **economically inactive**). In the UK, the Office for National Statistics (ONS) defines the economically inactive as 'people not in employment who have not been seeking work within the last 4 weeks and/or are unable to start work within the next 2 weeks'.

economically inactive people who are not in employment or are unemployed due to reasons such as being in full-time education, being full-time carers or raising a family

Once the government has placed all the individuals covered by the survey in a category, it computes various statistics to summarize the state of the labour market. The **labour force** is defined as the sum of the employed and the unemployed:

$$\textit{Labour force} = \textit{Number of employed} + \textit{Number of unemployed}$$

labour force the total number of workers, including both the employed and the unemployed

The **unemployment rate** can be measured as the percentage of the labour force that is unemployed:

$$\textit{Unemployment rate} = \left(\frac{\textit{Number of unemployed}}{\textit{Labour force}}\right) \times 100$$

unemployment rate the percentage of the labour force that is unemployed measured by dividing the number of unemployed by the labour force and multiplying by 100

Unemployment rates are computed for the entire adult population and for more narrowly defined groups – men, women, youths and so on.

The same survey results are used to produce data on labour force participation. The **labour force participation rate (or economic activity rate)** measures the percentage of the total adult population of the country that is in the labour force:

$$\textit{Labour force participation rate} = \left(\frac{\textit{Labour force}}{\textit{Adult population}}\right) \times 100$$

labour force participation rate (or economic activity rate) the percentage of the adult population that is in the labour force

This statistic tells us the fraction of the population that has chosen to participate in the labour market. The labour force participation rate, like the unemployment rate, is computed both for the entire adult population and for more specific groups.

To see how these data are computed, consider the UK figures for March–May 2025. According to the *Labour Market Overview* published by the ONS, 32.531 million people were in work and 1.619 million people were unemployed. The labour force was:

$$\textit{Labour force} = 32.531 + 1.619 = 34.15$$

The unemployment rate was:

$$\text{Unemployment rate} = \left(\frac{1.619}{34.15}\right) \times 100 = 4.7\%$$

There were 9.085 million people aged between 16 and 64 classed as economically inactive.

The total population of the UK was estimated by the ONS as being 67.6 million, of which around 43.24 million were aged between 16 and 64 and classed as the adult population. The labour force participation rate, therefore, was:

$$\text{Labour force participation rate} = \left(\frac{34.15}{43.24}\right) \times 100 = 78.98\%$$

Table 6.1 shows the unemployment rate across the EU.

TABLE 6.1 **Unemployment Rates in the European Union (August 2024)**

Country	Unemployment rate (%)
Austria	5.3
Belgium	5.4
Bulgaria	4.0
Croatia	4.9
Cyprus	5.4
Czechia	2.6
Denmark	5.8
Estonia	7.9
Finland	8.3
France	7.5
Germany	3.5
Greece	9.5
Hungary	4.3
Ireland	4.3
Italy	6.2
Latvia	7.0
Lithuania	7.9
Luxembourg	5.9
Malta	3.0
Netherlands	3.7
Poland	3.7
Portugal	6.4
Romania	5.5
Slovak Republic	5.3
Slovenia	3.3
Spain	11.3
Sweden	8.4

Source: EUROSTAT

THE CAUSES OF UNEMPLOYMENT

We have defined unemployment as a situation where people of working age are out of work but able and available for work at current wage rates. The basis of this definition rests on the model of the labour market where there is a demand for workers by employers, which is a derived demand, and a supply of labour willing and able to work at different wage rates. The equilibrium wage rate is that which brings together the number of workers willing and able to work at that wage rate with the demand for labour at that wage rate. If this model were replicated at the macro level, there would be an equilibrium wage rate which would mean all those seeking work at that wage rate would be employed. At equilibrium, therefore, there is no unemployment. Changes in the supply of and demand for labour would create surpluses and shortages in the labour market, and the adjustment of the wage rate would ensure that all workers are always fully employed.

A look at statistics on the labour market, however, shows that in almost every country there are always some people who are unemployed, that is the labour markets do not clear instantaneously. We will now look at the reasons for this unemployment.

Frictional Unemployment

At any point in time in the economy there are people who are between jobs. They might have been made redundant or dismissed, are returning to work after a period of leave for travelling, seeking work after leaving university or school/college, looking for work after having time off to raise a family or wanting a career change. It takes time for workers to search for the jobs that are best suited for them. The unemployment that results from the process of matching workers and jobs is called **frictional unemployment**, and it is often thought to explain relatively short spells of unemployment.

> **frictional unemployment** unemployment that results because it takes time for workers to search for the jobs that best suit their tastes and skills

People who decide to change careers or leave one job without having another to go to immediately are making a conscious choice to become unemployed for a period. In many cases, they may have every intention of finding new work, but there will be an interim period where they are unemployed. In some cases, people may see jobs available, but feel it is not something that suits them. The job may also not be at a level they are looking for or they may feel the wage is too low. In some cases, people may choose to remain unemployed because state benefit levels are relatively generous, or tax and benefit laws are such that taking a job would leave the individual worse off. **Voluntary unemployment** refers to a situation where people choose to remain unemployed rather than take jobs which are available. This is in contrast to **involuntary unemployment** which occurs when people want work at going market wage rates but cannot find employment. Involuntary unemployment may be caused by structural reasons.

> **voluntary unemployment** where people choose to remain unemployed rather than take jobs which are available
> **involuntary unemployment** where people want work at going market wage rates but cannot find employment

Structural Unemployment

When the quantity of labour supplied exceeds the quantity demanded and the number of jobs available may be insufficient to give a job to everyone who wants one, **structural unemployment** exists. Structural unemployment can explain longer spells of unemployment.

> **structural unemployment** unemployment that results because the number of jobs available in some labour markets is insufficient to provide a job for everyone who wants one

There are a number of causes of structural unemployment and labour market theory implies that there are imperfections in the market which prevent wages adjusting to the changing demand and supply of labour. Some of these imperfections include:

Occupational and Geographic Immobility Workers who lose their jobs in one industry may find that jobs that are available require skills and experience they do not possess or are not in the immediate region where they live. To move from one occupation to another requires knowledge, skills and experience to be transferable, and this is not always the case. Where workers are unable to easily move from one occupation to another, this is referred to as **occupational immobility**.

occupational immobility where workers are unable to easily move from one occupation to another

Jobs that are available for those unemployed might be some distance away, and it may not be possible for them to easily commute to take on these jobs. In addition, the cost of commuting might mean the job becomes unviable given the wage being offered. In some cases, if jobs are available in other parts of the country, there are other very practical reasons why it is not easy for workers to move to these jobs. Differences in house prices or family commitments might mean that even though jobs are available it is not practical for workers to take these jobs. Where people are unable to take work because of the difficulties associated with moving to different regions, this is termed **geographical immobility**. It is worth noting here that one of the longer-term effects of the recent Covid-19 pandemic is a reduction in geographical immobility in some industries, where remote working has become the norm.

geographical immobility where people are unable to take work because of the difficulties associated with moving to different regions

Technological Change Changes in technology are important drivers of long-run economic growth, but such change has winners and losers. The losers are those whose knowledge, skills and experience are now redundant and as a result they have to seek new employment. The number of people working on production lines in vehicle manufacture, for example, is now substantially less than it was in the 1970s. This is largely due to the development of machines which can do the work of humans far more efficiently and more cheaply.

Structural Change in the Economy Over time structural changes affect the makeup of economies. In the UK, for example, the eighteenth and nineteenth centuries saw a shift from a predominantly agrarian economy to industrial and manufacturing. This in turn has evolved into an economy which is dominated by service industries. Structural change can be caused by competition from abroad or by changes in technology and changes in societal norms and trends. The decline in the coal mining industry in the UK, for example, is partly due to the availability of cheaper coal imports from abroad. Other factors include the increased cost of extracting coal in more marginal seams and commitments made by the government to reduce the use of carbon emissions into the atmosphere, which has resulted in the closure of coal fired power stations.

Labour Market Imperfections

We can use the model of the labour market to identify how unemployment can be caused by wages being above the market equilibrium. These are classed as imperfections in the labour market which prevent the wage rate from adjusting to equate the demand and supply of labour. It should be noted that the structural unemployment that arises from above-equilibrium wages is, in an important sense, different from the frictional unemployment that arises from the process of job search. The need for job search is not due to the failure of wages to balance labour supply and labour demand. When job search is the explanation for unemployment, workers are *searching* for the jobs that best suit their tastes and skills. By contrast, when the wage is above the equilibrium level, the quantity of labour supplied exceeds the quantity of labour demanded, and workers are unemployed because they are *waiting* for jobs to open up.

Minimum Wage Laws Minimum wage laws are a price floor applied to the labour market. Minimum wages can have an important effect on certain groups with particularly high unemployment rates. When a minimum wage law forces the wage to remain above the level that balances supply and demand, it raises the quantity of labour supplied and reduces the quantity of labour demanded compared to the equilibrium level. There is a surplus of labour. Because there are more workers willing to work than there are jobs, some workers are unemployed. It is important to note that most workers in many developed economies have wages well above the legal minimum. Minimum wage laws are binding most often for the least skilled and least experienced members of the labour force, such as teenagers. It is among these workers that minimum wage laws can offer an explanation for the existence of unemployment.

Unions and Collective Bargaining A union is a worker association that bargains with employers over wages and working conditions. **Union density** measures the proportion of the workforce that is unionized, excluding people who cannot, for legal or other reasons, be members of a union, for example members of the armed forces. Broadly speaking, this amounts to expressing the number of union members as a proportion of civilian employees plus the unemployed. According to the ONS, union density in the UK in 2023, was around 5.4 per cent, and has been steadily falling since 1995 when it stood at around 32.4 per cent. This is an even greater marked fall from the beginning of the 1980s, when it was over 50 per cent. In other European countries there is a similar trend of falling union density. In Germany, according to the most recent statistics provided by the OECD, density fell from 23.3 per cent in 1999 to 16.3 per cent in 2019. In the Netherlands the fall has been from 24.6 per cent to 15.4 per cent in 2019. In some northern European and Nordic countries, union density is still relatively high. In Denmark, for example, density in 2019 was 67 per cent, in Sweden, 65.2 per cent, and in Finland, 58.8 per cent, but these figures do represent a fall in density since 2010. One exception to the trend seems to be Iceland where density rates have been consistently at 80+ per cent. In 2020 the OECD reported the figure at 92.2 per cent.

union density a measure of the proportion of the workforce that is unionized

The Economics of Unions A union is a type of cartel. Like any cartel, a union is a group of sellers acting together in the hope of exerting their joint market power. Workers in a union act as a group when discussing their wages, benefits and working conditions with their employers. The process by which unions and firms agree on the terms of employment is called **collective bargaining**.

collective bargaining the process by which unions and firms agree on the terms of employment

When a union bargains with a firm, it asks for higher wages, better benefits and better working conditions than the firm would offer in the absence of a union. If the union and the firm do not reach agreement, the union can take various steps to put pressure on employers to come to an agreement. This includes working to rule (doing only what is agreed in the contract of employment) and, as a last resort, organizing a withdrawal of labour from the firm, called a strike. Because a strike reduces production, sales and profit, a firm facing a strike threat is likely to agree to pay higher wages than it otherwise would. Economists who study the effects of unions typically find that union workers earn more than similar workers who do not belong to unions.

When a union raises the wage above the equilibrium level, it raises the quantity of labour supplied and reduces the quantity of labour demanded, resulting in unemployment. Those workers who remain employed are better off, but those who were previously employed and are now unemployed are worse off.

The role of unions in the economy depends in part on the laws that govern union organization and collective bargaining. Normally, explicit agreements among members of a cartel are illegal. If firms that sell a common product were to agree to set a high price for that product, they would generally be held to be in breach of competition law. The government would prosecute these firms in the civil and criminal courts. In contrast, unions are given exemption from these laws in the belief that workers need greater market power as they bargain with employers.

Legislation affecting the market power of unions is a perennial topic of political debate. Members of parliaments sometimes debate *right to work laws*, which give workers in a unionized firm the right to choose whether to join the union. In the absence of such laws, unions can insist during collective bargaining that firms make union membership a requirement for employment.

Are Unions Good or Bad for the Economy? Economists disagree about whether unions are good or bad for the economy as a whole. Let us consider both sides of the debate.

Critics of unions argue that unions are merely a type of cartel. When unions raise wages above the level that would prevail in competitive markets, they reduce the quantity of labour demanded, cause some workers to be unemployed and reduce the wages in the rest of the economy. The resulting allocation of labour is, critics argue, both inefficient and inequitable. It is inefficient because high union wages reduce employment in unionized firms below the efficient, competitive level. It is inequitable because some workers benefit at the expense of other workers.

Advocates of unions contend that unions are a necessary antidote to the market power of the firms that hire workers. In some regions where one particular company is the dominant employer, if workers do not accept the wages and working conditions that the firm offers, they may have little choice but to move or stop working. In the absence of a union, therefore, the firm could use its market power to pay lower wages and offer worse working conditions than if it had to compete with other firms for the same workers. In this case, a union may balance the firm's market power and protect workers from being at the mercy of the firm owners.

Advocates also claim that unions are important for helping firms respond efficiently to workers' concerns. Whenever a worker takes a job, the worker and the firm must agree on many attributes of the job in addition to the wage: hours of work, overtime, holidays, sick leave, health benefits, promotion schedules, job security and so on. By representing workers' views on these issues, unions allow firms to provide the right mix of job attributes. In many countries, unions have now taken on additional roles in supporting workers in other areas. These include offering legal support in the event of an individual dispute at work, advice on pensions, financial services such as insurance, and support for those who have been injured or disabled at work and must retire early. Even if unions have the adverse effect of pushing wages above the equilibrium level and causing unemployment, they have the benefit of helping firms keep a happy and productive workforce.

In the end, there is no consensus among economists about whether unions are good or bad for the economy. Like many institutions, their influence is probably beneficial in some circumstances and adverse in others.

SELF TEST How might a union in the car industry affect wages and employment at Ford and Nissan plants in the UK? How might it affect wages and employment in other industries?

The Theory of Efficiency Wages The theory of efficiency wages suggests firms operate more efficiently if wages are above the equilibrium level. Therefore it may be profitable for firms to keep wages high even in the presence of a surplus of labour. The decision to keep wages above equilibrium levels may seem odd at first, given that wages are a large part of many firms' costs. Normally, we expect profit-maximizing firms to want to keep costs – and therefore wages – as low as possible. The novel insight of efficiency wage theory is that paying high wages might be profitable because they might raise the efficiency of a firm's workers.

There are several types of efficiency wage theory. Each type suggests a different explanation for why firms may want to pay high wages. Let us now consider four of these types.

Worker Health The first and simplest type of efficiency wage theory emphasizes the link between wages and worker health. Better paid workers eat a more nutritious diet, and workers who eat a better diet are healthier and more productive. A firm may find it more profitable to pay high wages and have healthy, productive workers than to pay lower wages and have less healthy, less productive workers.

This type of efficiency wage theory is of primary relevance for less developed countries where inadequate nutrition can be a common problem. Unemployment is high in the cities of many low-income African countries, for example. In these countries, firms may fear that cutting wages would, in fact, adversely influence their workers' health and productivity. In other words, concern over nutrition may explain why firms do not cut wages despite a surplus of labour.

Worker Turnover A second type of efficiency wage theory emphasizes the link between wages and worker turnover. Workers quit jobs for many reasons, for example to take jobs in other firms, to move to other parts of the country, to leave the labour force and so on. The frequency with which they quit depends on the entire set of incentives they face, including the benefits of leaving and the benefits of staying. The more a firm pays its workers, the less often its workers will choose to leave. Thus a firm can reduce turnover among its workers by paying them a high wage. Reducing turnover is important for firms because it is costly for firms to hire and train new workers. According to data reported by Talentinsight from the Chartered Institute of Personnel and Development (CIPD), the average cost of filling a vacancy is £6,125 (€7,374) rising to £19,000 (€22,875) for management vacancies. Even after they are trained, newly hired workers are not as productive as experienced workers. Firms with higher turnover, therefore, will tend to have higher production costs. Firms may find it profitable to pay wages above the equilibrium level to reduce worker turnover.

Worker Effort A third type of efficiency wage theory emphasizes the link between wages and worker effort. In many jobs, workers have some discretion over how hard to work. As a result, firms monitor the efforts of their workers, and workers caught shirking their responsibilities can be disciplined and possibly dismissed. Not all shirkers are caught immediately, because monitoring workers is costly and imperfect. A firm can respond to this problem by paying wages above the equilibrium level. High wages, it is argued, make workers more eager to keep their jobs and provide an incentive to put forward their best effort.

In the *worker effort* variant of efficiency wage theory, if the wage were at the level that balanced supply and demand, workers would have less reason to work hard because if they were fired, they could quickly find new jobs at the same wage. Therefore, firms raise wages above the equilibrium level, causing unemployment and providing an incentive for workers not to shirk their responsibilities.

Worker Quality A fourth and final type of efficiency wage theory emphasizes the link between wages and worker quality. When a firm hires new workers, it cannot perfectly gauge the quality of the applicants. By paying a high wage, the firm attracts a better pool of workers to apply for its jobs. Because people have different *reservation wages*, the lowest wage they are prepared to accept, competent workers tend to have a higher reservation wage. If the firm pays a higher wage, it has a greater chance of competent workers applying and might hope that its recruitment process can distinguish between the competent and incompetent applicants.

CRITICAL THINKING POINT The theory of efficiency wages is just that, a theory. How would you test this theory to assess its validity?

Demand-Deficient Unemployment

John Maynard Keynes' ideas on unemployment changed the nature of economics. Up until World War I, economists had largely assumed that the market mechanism would function such that unemployment would not persist. Wages would adjust to bring the demand and supply of labour into equilibrium. The post-war world began to experience significant economic shocks, the most notable of which was the Great Depression.

The effects of the stock market crash in the United States in 1929 spread across the world and many countries experienced high and persistent unemployment. According to classical economics, this should not happen. Keynes argued that the principal cause of this unemployment was due to insufficient demand in the economy. This view ran counter to a prevailing orthodoxy, which is referred to as **Say's law** after Jean Baptiste Say (1767–1832), a French economist. Say's law is succinctly expressed as 'supply creates its own demand' and is a theory that over-production in both the short run and the long run is not possible. It seems that Say was not the first to promote the idea. James Mill, the father of John Stuart Mill, and Adam Smith had both written about the idea. The theory rests on the identity of national income accounting. If output of goods and services increases and is sold, the income derived from the sale is used by recipients to purchase goods and services. Say noted: 'the mere circumstance of the creation of one product immediately opens a vent for other products'. Keynes rejected the short-run interpretation of Say's law and suggested that short-run shocks to the economy such as the stock market crash can reduce effective demand. By **effective demand**, Keynes meant the amount that people were not only willing to buy at different prices but what they can and do actually purchase. It was quite possible, Keynes argued, that demand could remain well below that sufficient to generate full employment and for unemployment to persist.

Say's law an argument that production or supply is a source of demand, that supply creates its own demand
effective demand the amount that people are not only willing to buy at different prices but what they can and do actually purchase

Summary

Since the 1930s there has been an ongoing debate in economics about the principal causes of unemployment and the extent to which these causes stem from the supply-side of the economy or the demand-side. This debate continues and was brought into sharper focus with the rise in unemployment in many European countries following the 2007–9 Financial Crisis. In essence, the debate centres on the extent to which unemployment is cyclical or structural, the latter accounting for the level of unemployment not due to changes in the economic cycle. As we build the theoretical building blocks of macroeconomics, it must be remembered that policies to cut unemployment still deeply divide opinion in the economics profession.

SELF TEST How is the unemployment rate measured? How might the unemployment rate overstate the amount of joblessness? How might it understate it?

THE NATURAL RATE OF UNEMPLOYMENT

Even when the overall economy is growing, the unemployment rate never falls to zero. Figure 6.1 shows the unemployment rate in the UK since 1971. The figure shows that the economy always has some unemployment and that the amount changes – often considerably – from year to year. The Office for Budget Responsibility (OBR) in the UK looks at what it calls the 'equilibrium unemployment rate anchor', which filters out the fluctuations in unemployment over time and arrives at an inferred rate of unemployment, which is the economy's long-run unemployment rate. This is the unemployment which exists regardless of the economic cycle and is referred to as the **natural rate of unemployment** (NRU) or the **non-accelerating inflation rate of unemployment** (NAIRU). Note, there is a difference between the two concepts. NAIRU is more of a short-term measure of the equilibrium unemployment rate and may be more volatile compared to the long-run equilibrium rate of unemployment. The deviation of unemployment from its natural rate is called **cyclical unemployment**. The NRU can be viewed as the rate of unemployment the economy gravitates to, given the number of people losing jobs over a period and the number finding work over that same period. Unemployment is a dynamic process. At any period of time, there are people losing jobs (called job separation) and people finding jobs. Suppose that every month, the rate at which people lose jobs, denoted by the Greek letter alpha (α), is 4.9 per cent, and the rate at which people find jobs, denoted by the Greek letter psi (ψ), is 65 per cent. The NRU is found by taking the job separation rate and dividing this by the sum of the job finding rate and the job separation rate:

$$NRU = \frac{\alpha}{(\psi + \alpha)} \times 100$$

In our example, the NRU is: $\left(\frac{4.9}{69.9}\right) \times 100 = 7\%$.

natural rate of unemployment the normal rate of unemployment around which the unemployment rate fluctuates
non-accelerating inflation rate of unemployment the rate of unemployment in the long run, consistent with a stable rate of inflation
cyclical unemployment the deviation of unemployment from its natural rate

FIGURE 6.1

UK Unemployment Rate Since 1971

This graph uses annual data on the unemployment rate to show the fraction of the labour force without a job, calculated by the LFS definition.

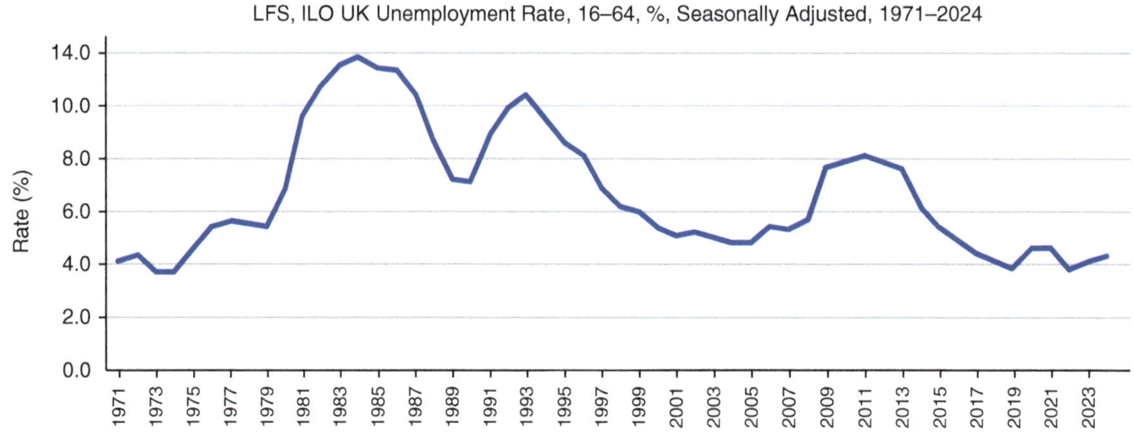

Source: Office for National Statistics

Since the 2007–9 Financial Crisis, one of the unexpected outcomes has been the steady decline in unemployment despite the prevailing economic conditions. This has occurred not only in the UK but also in the United States. In 2010, UK unemployment was around 8.0 per cent and gradually fell. It was 3.8 per cent in June 2019 before rising due to the effects of Covid-19. Estimates of the NRU were around 5.4 per cent in 2011. As unemployment continued to fall, however, the OBR revised down its estimates of the NRU and at the end of 2018, it estimated UK NRU to be 4.5 per cent. In the United States, there has been a similar downwards revision from 6.0 per cent in 2011 to 4.7 per cent in 2018.

We will discuss short-run economic fluctuations, including the year-to-year fluctuations in unemployment, later in the book. The NRU will be of particular relevance when discussing the Phillips curve. In this chapter, however, we focus on the long run and examine why there is always some unemployment in market economies and whether the theory of the NRU stands the test of time.

How Long Are the Unemployed without Work?

In judging how serious the problem of unemployment is, one question to consider is whether unemployment is typically a short-term or long-term condition. If unemployment is short term, we might conclude that it is not a big problem. Workers may require a few weeks between jobs to find the openings that best suit their tastes and skills. Yet if unemployment is long term, we might conclude that it is a serious problem. Workers unemployed for many months are more likely to suffer economic and psychological hardship.

Because the duration of unemployment can affect our view about how big a problem it is, economists have devoted much energy to studying data on the duration of unemployment spells. In this work, they have uncovered a result that is important, subtle and seemingly contradictory. That is most spells of unemployment are short, and most unemployment observed at any given time is long term.

To see how this statement can be true, consider an example. Suppose that you visited the government's unemployment office every week for a year to survey the unemployed. Each week you find that there are four unemployed workers. Three of these workers are the same individuals for the whole year, while the fourth person changes every week. Based on this experience, would you say that unemployment is typically short term or long term?

Some simple calculations help answer this question. In this example, you meet a total of 55 unemployed people: 52 of them are unemployed for one week, and three are unemployed for the full year. This means that $\frac{52}{55}$, or 95 per cent, of unemployment spells end in one week. Thus most spells of unemployment are short. Yet consider the total amount of unemployment. The three people unemployed for one year (52 weeks) make up a total of 156 weeks of unemployment. Together with the 52 people unemployed for one week, this makes 208 weeks of unemployment. In this example, $\frac{156}{208}$, or 75 per cent, of unemployment is attributable to those individuals who are unemployed for a full year. Thus most unemployment observed at any given time is long term.

This subtle conclusion implies that economists and policymakers must be careful when interpreting data on unemployment and when designing policies to help the unemployed. Most people who become unemployed will soon find jobs. Yet most of the economy's unemployment problem is attributable to the relatively few workers who are jobless for long periods of time.

Job Search

One reason why economies always experience some unemployment is job search. **Job search** is the process of matching workers with appropriate jobs. If all workers and all jobs were the same, so that all workers were equally well suited for all jobs, job search would not be a problem. Laid-off workers would quickly find new jobs that were well suited for them. Workers, of course, differ in their tastes and skills, jobs differ in their attributes, and information about job candidates and job vacancies is disseminated slowly among the many firms and households in the economy.

job search the process by which workers find appropriate jobs given their tastes and skills

Why Some Frictional Unemployment Is Inevitable

Frictional unemployment is often the result of changes in the demand for labour among different firms. When consumers decide that they prefer brand *X* to brand *Y*, the company producing brand *X* increases employment, and the other firm lays off workers. The former brand *Y* workers must now search for new jobs, and the brand *X* producer must decide which new workers to hire for the various jobs that have opened up. The result of this transition is a period of unemployment.

Similarly, because different regions of the country produce different goods, employment can rise in one region while it falls in another. Consider, for instance, a situation where the demand for diesel cars falls as consumers look to purchase greener alternatives, for example electric vehicles. The rise in demand for electric vehicles stimulates an increase in the need for charging points and this raises production and employment associated with that industry. In addition, there is a rise in demand for technicians skilled in servicing zero-emission vehicles. Changes in the composition of demand among industries or regions are called *sectoral shifts*. Because it takes time for workers to search for jobs in the new sectors, sectoral shifts temporarily cause unemployment.

Frictional unemployment is inevitable simply because the economy is always changing. Along the way, workers in declining industries find themselves out of work and searching for new jobs.

In addition to the effects of sectoral shifts on unemployment, workers will leave their jobs sometimes because they realize that the jobs are not a good match for their tastes and skills, and they wish to look for a better job. Many of these workers, especially younger ones, find new jobs at higher wages, although given the vast improvements in information technology in recent years (especially the internet) it is likely that many people search for new jobs without actually quitting their current job. Nevertheless, this churning of the labour force is normal in a well-functioning and dynamic market economy, and the result is some amount of frictional unemployment.

Public Policy and Job Search

Even if some frictional unemployment is inevitable, the precise amount is not. The faster information spreads about job openings and worker availability, the more rapidly the economy can match workers and firms. The internet, for instance, may help facilitate job search and reduce frictional unemployment. In addition, public policy may play a role. If policy can reduce the time it takes unemployed workers to find new jobs, it can reduce the economy's NRU.

Government policies try to facilitate job search in various ways. One way is through government-run employment agencies or job centres, which give out information about job vacancies. Another way is through public training schemes which aim to ease the transition of workers from declining to growing industries and to help disadvantaged groups escape poverty. Advocates of these policies believe that they make the economy operate more efficiently by keeping the labour force more fully employed and reduce the inequities inherent in a constantly changing market economy.

Critics of these policies question whether the government should get involved with the process of job search. They argue that it is better to let the private market match workers and jobs. In fact, most job searches in the economy take place without intervention by the government. Newspaper advertisements, internet job sites, headhunters and word of mouth all help spread information about job openings and job candidates. Similarly, much worker education is done privately, either through schools or through on-the-job training. These critics contend that the government is no better – and most likely worse – at disseminating the right information to the right workers and deciding what kinds of worker training would be most valuable. They claim that these decisions are best made privately by workers and employers.

Unemployment Insurance

One government policy that increases the amount of frictional unemployment, without intending to do so, is **unemployment insurance** (or, as it is called in the UK, national insurance). This policy is designed to offer workers partial protection against job loss. People who choose to quit their jobs, those that are fired for a just reason, or those who have just entered the labour force, are not eligible. Benefits are paid only to the unemployed who are laid off because their previous employers no longer need their skills.

> **unemployment insurance** a government programme that partially protects workers' incomes when they become unemployed

While unemployment insurance reduces the hardship of unemployment, it is argued that it can also increase the amount of unemployment. This explanation is based on incentives. Because unemployment benefits stop when a worker takes a new job, the unemployed, it is argued, devote less effort to job search and are more likely to turn down unattractive job offers. In addition, because unemployment insurance makes unemployment less onerous, workers are less likely to seek guarantees of job security when they negotiate with employers over the terms of employment. However, research on unemployment insurance in Europe gives a different perspective. In a paper by Konstantinos Tatsiramos (Tatsiramos, K. (2006) *Unemployment Insurance in Europe: Unemployment Duration and Subsequent Employment Stability*. Institute for the Study of Labor Discussion Paper no. 2280), the benefits to workers searching for jobs and receiving unemployment insurance is greater than the costs:

> *This paper provides evidence on the effect of unemployment benefits on unemployment and employment duration in Europe, using individual data from the European Community Household Panel for eight countries. Even if receiving benefits has a direct negative effect increasing the duration of unemployment spells, there is also a positive indirect effect of benefits on subsequent employment duration. This indirect effect is pronounced in countries with relatively generous benefit systems, and for recipients who have remained unemployed for at least six months. In terms of the magnitude of the effect, recipients remain employed on average two to four months longer than non-recipients. This represents a 10 to 20 per cent increase relative to the average employment duration, compensating for the additional time spent in unemployment.*

The findings of Tatsiramos have been supported by other similar studies, for example, Wulfgramm and Fervers (2013) (Wulfgramm, M. and Fervers, L. (2013) 'Unemployment and Subsequent Employment Stability: Does Labour Market Policy Matter?' IZA Discussion Papers 7193, Institute of Labor Economics).

A more recent study by Rotar and Krsnik (2020) (Rotar, L.J. and Krsnik, S. (2020) Analysing the Relationship Between Unemployment Benefits and Unemployment Duration. *Society and Economy*, 42(3) 280–97), however, found that benefit recipients tend to wait for their benefits to expire prior to seeking employment and so more generous benefits result in longer periods of unemployment. The effect of unemployment insurance is likely to be related to the way the scheme is designed and operated. In one US study, when unemployed workers applied to collect unemployment insurance benefits, some of them were randomly selected and each offered a $500 bonus if they found new jobs within 11 weeks. This group was then compared with a control group not offered the incentive. The average spell of unemployment for the group offered the bonus was 7 per cent shorter than the average spell for the control group. This experiment suggests that the design of the unemployment insurance system influences the effort that the unemployed devote to job search.

Even though unemployment insurance can reduce search effort and raise unemployment, we should not necessarily conclude that the policy is a bad one. The policy does achieve its primary goal of reducing the income uncertainty that workers face. In addition, when workers turn down unattractive job offers, they have the opportunity to look for jobs that better suit their tastes and skills. Some economists have argued that unemployment insurance improves the ability of the economy to match each worker with the most appropriate job.

The study of unemployment insurance shows that the unemployment rate is an imperfect measure of a nation's overall level of economic well-being. Some economists agree that eliminating unemployment insurance would reduce the amount of unemployment in the economy. Yet economists disagree on whether economic well-being would be enhanced or diminished by this change in policy.

SELF TEST How would an increase in the world price of oil affect the amount of frictional unemployment? Is this unemployment undesirable? What public policies might affect the amount of unemployment caused by this price change?

Criticisms of the Natural Rate Hypothesis

The work of John Maynard Keynes in the 1930s provided a number of challenges to the prevailing orthodoxy, specifically that the price mechanism was subject to fundamental flaws. These flaws meant that unemployment would not be short term while markets adjusted but could be persistent and long term. As Keynes' ideas were developed by economists, the apparent fundamental disagreement about how the macroeconomy works was 'resolved' through what came to be called the **neo-classical synthesis** (it is also called New Keynesian economics or Neo-Keynesianism). The term has been attributed to US Nobel Prize winning economist, Paul Samuelson. Samuelson referred to himself as a 'cafeteria Keynesian'. He was often seen as being a devotee of Keynesian ideas but saw himself picking the parts of Keynesian ideas which appealed to him and which he saw had benefit to macroeconomic analysis. The synthesis states that the reason why markets did not adjust quickly to imbalances of the supply and demand for labour was because of sticky prices and sticky wages. We will look at these ideas later in the book, but at this stage it is sufficient to say that prices and wages do not move quickly to eliminate surpluses and shortages in the market. This can result in high unemployment persisting in the short run. Appropriate use of monetary and fiscal policy could, according to the synthesis, help markets to adjust more effectively and correct imbalances. Once prices and wages have had time to adjust, full employment can be reached once again. The underlying philosophy was still *laissez-faire* capitalism – the belief that markets are the most effective way of allocating scarce resources and, where appropriate, should be left to do their work. What the synthesis did was to bring classical ideas into line with Keynes' apparent rejection of the benefits of unfettered markets. The synthesis spawned the idea of the NRU and has become a mainstay of economics teaching and philosophy since the 1970s.

neo-classical synthesis the idea that markets can be slow to adjust in the short run due to sticky prices and sticky wages but revert to long-run classical principles which could be aided by appropriate use of fiscal and monetary policies

Since the 1970s, there have been many refinements to the neo-classical synthesis. Much of Keynesian unemployment was 'involuntary' – even at prevailing wage rates, most people who are unemployed would prefer to be in work. The neo-classical synthesis explained this as a temporary situation which would eventually be resolved once prices and wages had time to adjust. It was suggested that people will not make decisions about their future economic situation (such as negotiating wage increases and considering the security of their jobs) in a vacuum, and that firms and households would build their expectations of inflation and the economy into their decision-making. This was called *rational expectations,* and again, we will deal with this in more detail later in the book.

The prevailing view of the NRU came to be that unemployment would only differ from its natural rate if expected inflation was different from actual inflation. Over time the NRU would be relatively stable. Research by Roger Farmer, a Senior Fellow at the Bank of England and Professor at the University of California, Los Angeles (UCLA), casts doubt on this stability. Average unemployment in the United States in the 1950s was around 4.5 per cent, a little higher in the 1960s, jumped to around 6.3 per cent in the 1970s, 7.3 per cent in the 1980s, around 5.7 per cent in the 1990s and about 5.6 per cent in the 2000s. Farmer suggests that the data do not match the theory and that the NRU 'is false'. Farmer goes on to explore an alternative theory, which is linked to an understanding of the trade-off between unemployment and inflation, which we will explore in later chapters.

Other economists suggest that the NRU can change over time, and there might be different reasons for this. One is the idea of **hysteresis**. The concept is 'borrowed' from physics and refers to an object which fails to return to its original state after some external shock, even when that shock subsides. Recessions, for example, can have a significant impact on both employment and unemployment. People not only lose their jobs during a recession, but those in work may come to have different views about their jobs and the degree of security they have in work. These views may persist even once the recession has gone, in what Ball and Mankiw (2002) refer to as a 'permanent scar on the economy' (Ball, L. and Mankiw N.G. (2002) 'The NAIRU in Theory and Practice'. *Journal of Economic Perspectives*, 16(4): 115–36). Other reasons for the changing NRU could be due to the changes in the structure of the labour force; the proportion of different age groups and their levels of experience, skills and productivity as a result; the developments in technologies which influence competitiveness and productivity; and the improvements in job matching – the way in which workers who are seeking employment are matched with the jobs which are available.

hysteresis the lagging effects of past economic events on future ones

The behaviour of unemployment since the 2007–9 Financial Crisis has led to further criticism of the NRU. As recession ended and unemployment began to fall, central banks looked on. Some suggested that interest rates, at historic lows in many Western countries, would have to start rising as unemployment approached its natural rate. The theory is that if unemployment falls below the natural rate, competition in the jobs market will force up wage rates, increase firms' costs and trigger inflation. In the event, as unemployment fell below the estimated natural rate, inflation did not accelerate, but unemployment has continued to fall. This might suggest that attempts to make policy based on something which does not exist are fundamentally flawed. Rather than be concerned about a natural rate, policymakers might be better placed to keep pushing unemployment ever lower. One theory related to this suggests that as unemployment continues to fall, firms will have incentives to keep labour costs under control through investment in labour-saving technologies or systems which in turn increase productivity and generate economic growth.

CASE STUDY Artificial Intelligence and the Labour Market

One of the common features of technological changes in society has been the fear of a negative impact on employment, as new technologies develop and are incorporated into firms' operations. How serious that impact will be has been widely debated. In the nineteenth century, bands of workers, called Luddites,

(Continued)

sought to stem the tide of technological change in the textile industry by smashing new machinery that threatened to replace them. As each new technology develops, there are invariably stories that emerge about how it will destroy jobs and create large-scale unemployment in its wake. The developments in artificial intelligence (AI) are no different.

There have been plenty of reports that developments in AI will lead to many jobs disappearing. Economists are in a position to strip back the hype and to provide a more objective and informed discussion on the issue. Fechner and de Montpellier, both senior economists at global financial institution ING, explored data on automation trends related to AI. They found that there was no significant link between automation and higher unemployment. However, as might be expected, they did find that different types of jobs in the economy might be affected in different ways by technological developments such as AI. They cite research by Frey and Osborne in 2013 that noted that routine-intensive jobs are more likely to be affected by AI developments.

Many fear that developments in artificial intelligence will result in jobs being lost but is the reality as bad as some say?

Overall, their study suggests that some jobs will be taken over by computerization, but that the rate at which this happens will depend on many other factors. AI may not necessarily act as a substitute to human input but may be complementary to it. Some 40 per cent of the eurozone workforce and 37 per cent of the US workforce will be affected by AI, but this does not mean that this percentage of jobs will disappear. Advanced economies are more likely to be affected than emerging economies. Labour will therefore need to adjust to the changing skills required to carry out its work as well as being mindful of the sectoral shifts that may occur. The extent of the impact will also depend on factors such as the age distribution of the population, as some economies face reductions in the working-age population in the coming years. Fechner and de Montpellier conclude by suggesting that they do not expect AI to lead to mass unemployment.

Questions:

1 Consider the trade-off between the moral judgements associated with labour and factor productivity. Where should the balance of decision-making lie in making choices between retaining labour and replacing it with technology such as AI?

2 To what extent do you think that worker reaction against the use of new technology in firm's production decisions is futile?

3 How might policymakers react to the suggestion that technology developments such as AI are more likely to impact routine-intensive jobs?

4 The impact of AI on jobs will, the authors suggest, depend on a variety of factors including the age distribution of the population, the degree of exposure of the job to AI, the extent of the substitutability and complementarity of the job, and the degree of digital competence of labour, among other things. Assess the importance of these factors in determining the size of the impact of AI developments on jobs. What other factors might influence the outcome?

References:

think.ing.com/articles/ai-will-fundamentally-transform-job-market-but-risk-of-mass-unemployment-is-low/, accessed 7 August 2025.

MARX AND THE RESERVE ARMY OF THE UNEMPLOYED

The idea of the NRU may have been developed after World War II, but the idea that there are always some people who are unemployed has been around for much longer. Karl Marx believed that unemployment was a necessary condition for capitalism to survive. Marx referred to the unemployed as the 'reserve industrial army of labour'. This reserve army consisted of different groups of people including the long-term unemployed through to those who move in and out of the labour market at different times for different reasons. Some of the people who are chronically unemployed (i.e. the long-term unemployed) may be almost unemployable for some employers. This may be because they have few skills, limited experience or a history of poor employment records, and, as such, they are only employed if there is a considerable shortage in the labour market. Equally, women who look after families are classed as part of this reserve army, because they can be brought into the labour market in times of crisis, which was the case during World Wars I and II when many women were employed on the land and in factories.

Marx suggested that capitalism could not achieve full employment, a situation where those who want work can find jobs. Under capitalism, the labour market consists of those who are willing and able to work at different wage rates (the supply of labour) and the buyers of labour (employers). Both are free to either sell or buy labour. In this labour market, workers will be moving from one job to another, and employers will, at times, shed labour as economic and technological conditions change. If full employment were a reality, those seeking work would be able to find a job quickly. This ability to move from job to job quickly would give suppliers of labour considerable power and force employers to compete with each other to hire workers, which would push up the wage rate and improve the sort of conditions that workers demand. The effect would be to erode the surplus value that capitalists get from employing labour power.

In response, capitalist employers invest further in machinery, which represents a thinly veiled threat to workers that their power can be curtailed. If wage rates were pushed up because of worker power, employers would look to replace labour with machinery and thus make existing workers unemployed. The existence of this threat of unemployment is sufficient to prevent workers from exploiting their labour power and shifts the balance to employers. Having a reserve army of the unemployed is a fundamental reminder to workers that they too could join it if they push their power too far.

The existence of a reserve army of the unemployed is also of value to capitalists in exploiting growth in economic activity. It provides a ready-made pool of potential workers that can be dipped into when output needs to be increased quickly to meet demand. If full employment existed, there would be no surplus labour and hiring additional workers to cope with increases in demand would push up costs, which would lead to lower profits and less incentive to expand. This would slow the overall growth in economic activity. A reserve army of unemployed provides a way in which capitalists can take on new workers, even those who are classed as 'unemployable', The unemployable can help employers cope with increasing output demands but provide a means of paying these workers low wages to exploit surplus value from them.

THE COST OF UNEMPLOYMENT

We mentioned at the outset of this chapter that unemployment can be one of the most distressing things to happen to anyone in their lives. Unemployment imposes costs on the individual and their family and friends. There is also a wider cost to unemployment which affects government, the taxpayer and the economy as a whole.

The Costs of Unemployment to the Individual

Loss of Earnings One of the first and perhaps most obvious costs of unemployment to an individual is the loss of earnings that results from being unemployed. Many countries provide some form of unemployment insurance as we have seen, but the sums given to the unemployed are relatively small. In most cases these are nowhere near the earnings that the individual would have earned in work. In some countries there might be other state benefits that an unemployed worker can claim, which mean that in the case of workers in low-skilled, low-paid industries the incentive to take work can be reduced. In many other cases, however, unemployment means that individuals must re-evaluate their household spending budgets. This might require households to cut back on certain luxuries like spending on leisure activities, going to the cinema, going out to eat and so on, but might also cut down on luxuries such as clothing, furniture, electrical goods, having extensions built on a house and so on. We will see shortly how this has an effect on society as a whole.

The unemployed and their families are more likely to be at risk of slipping into poverty. Remember, the definition of poverty is a household income less than 60 per cent below the median income. It is unlikely that welfare support from the state is ever going to be, on its own, sufficient to put families above this level. Therefore, unless the unemployed have savings to draw upon it is more likely that they will fall into poverty. The Trades Union Congress (TUC) in the UK estimates that around 60 per cent of working age adults in families where there is unemployment are likely to be in poverty.

In addition, some families will find that unemployment means they face problems in paying for rent or mortgages, and this can result in the loss of homes. The unemployed are more likely to have to go into debt to pay bills, and this can add to the problems highlighted in our next section.

Stress, Self-Esteem and Health Problems Being unemployed can lead to significant mental health problems. The process of becoming unemployed is stressful and can be a life-changing event for some people. Having to adjust to claiming benefits, applying for other jobs, possibly getting additional training and the chances of having repeated experiences of either not having any replies to applications or in the event of unsuccessful interviews, the feeling of rejection, is not only stressful in itself but can lead to feelings of guilt and a reduction in self-esteem. These experiences can bring on stress-related illnesses and the incidences of health problems in the unemployed can increase the longer that the unemployment continues.

Drug and Alcohol Abuse and Crime Closely linked to the self-esteem problems, the boredom that can result from being unemployed and the feeling of worthlessness that many unemployed people say they experience, is the increased potential to turn to alcohol and illegal drugs as a means of escape.

When people move from being employed and having an income to be able to afford a reasonable standard of living, to experiencing tight restrictions on incomes and spending, the feeling of social exclusion and deprivation can be acute and cause some to turn to crime as a means of maintaining what they see as a reasonable standard of living. Indeed, the correlation between crime rates and drug abuse is very high. Once people get involved with a drug or alcohol habit it becomes expensive. One way of funding this habit is to turn to crime.

Family Breakdown Families who have an experience of unemployment are more prone to break up. Divorce rates among the unemployed are higher, as the stresses of coping with adjusting to new income levels, trying to find work and so on, take their toll.

De-Skilling The longer someone is out of work the more likely it is that they will lose touch with changes in the workplace and the labour market in general. It is also more likely that they might be viewed as unemployable or not favourable candidates for employment. Changes in the workplace, in technology and in the skills needed for employment change rapidly. Those in work can take advantage of training – both off the job and on the job – to maintain their skill levels. However, the unemployed may be excluded from being able to maintain or improve their skill levels and, as a result, find it even harder to find work. This can lead to the hysteresis effect.

The implications of most of these costs to the individual are that often, society is required to help address the problems that result. This may be through government intervention to support people facing these difficulties through to additional burdens on public services like the health service, mental health services, the police and justice system and so on.

The Costs of Unemployment to Society and the Economy

The Opportunity Cost of Unemployment An individual who is willing and able to work represents a unit of productive output. If that person is unemployed the opportunity cost to society is the value of the goods and services that the individual could have produced. This 'lost output' can be considerable and represents a lower standard of living for society as a whole. If there is unemployment in society which is not simply frictional unemployment, then society will not be operating on its production possibility frontier. Instead it will operate somewhere inside it, which represents an inefficient use of resources.

The Tax and Benefits Effect People who are unemployed have lower incomes and may rely solely on government welfare payments to support their standard of living. If people lose their jobs, then they do not pay as much in income taxes. If they also reduce spending, they do not pay consumption taxes at the same level as if they were in employment. The higher the level of unemployment in a country, the greater the impact on tax revenue for the government. Not only is government revenue adversely affected, but government spending is also likely to be higher. The unemployed will claim additional benefits, and governments may also incur costs in having to deal with the social problems caused by unemployment such as drug and alcohol abuse, family breakdown and the increase in crime.

If government income is reduced through lower tax receipts and there is also a requirement to increase spending because of higher welfare spending, the pressure on government budgets can increase. It becomes more likely that the government will experience a budget deficit, a situation where its spending is higher than its revenue from taxation. If governments experience a budget deficit, then the deficit must be funded by additional borrowing. Increased government borrowing can not only cause crowding out but also puts upward pressure on interest rates, which in turn might affect investment decisions by firms. The knock-on effects can have ripples throughout the economy as our next point highlights.

The Reverse Multiplier Effect We have seen that when people experience unemployment, they cut back their spending on luxuries. They may also switch their spending to substitute goods which may be seen as inferior goods. Firms who produce these different goods may see a change in spending patterns, which can have an effect on cash flows and ultimately profits.

Goods with a relatively high income elasticity of demand are likely to be affected more significantly. If sales fall, firms earn lower incomes and may have to adjust their business to manage cash flows. This might involve cutting back on orders from suppliers, building up stocks as goods remain unsold, and, in some cases, firms may have to either lay off workers, or even make workers redundant or close down the business if it becomes insolvent. If workers are made redundant or lose their jobs in this way, this then means those workers receive lower incomes and so the process continues.

Not all firms will be affected in such an extreme way, but it is the case that in periods of high unemployment, firms may see falling profit levels. This in turn means they pay lower corporate taxes, which puts further pressure on government budgets. Some firms might see demand for their services actually increase in periods of high unemployment. If the unemployed switch spending to inferior goods, the producers of those goods might see demand rise. In the aftermath of the 2007–9 Financial Crisis and beyond, low-cost supermarkets across the UK and Europe reported seeing an increase in sales, while traditional supermarkets reported reduced sales.

The effect of unemployment, if more than simply frictional unemployment, is to produce a multiplied impact on economic activity as a whole. If there are concentrated pockets of workers losing their jobs, such as a major employer in an area, then the effect of this reverse multiplier effect can be considerable. Indeed, there are areas of the UK and Europe where the decline in industries concentrated in particular areas has led to considerable regional deprivation which has lasted for many years. Once an area is caught in the cycle of economic decline, it is extremely hard to recover.

CONCLUSION

In this chapter, we discussed the measurement of unemployment, the reasons why economies always experience some degree of unemployment and some of the costs of unemployment to society and the economy as a whole. We have seen how job search, minimum wage laws, unions, efficiency wages, and structural and technological change can all help explain why some workers do not have jobs. We have also seen that there are questions about whether the NRU is still a useful concept for policymaking.

The analysis of this chapter yields an important lesson: although the economy will always have some unemployment, its natural rate is not immutable. Many events and policies can change the amount of unemployment the economy typically experiences. As the information revolution changes the process of job search, as governments adjust the minimum wage, as workers form or quit unions, and as firms alter their reliance on efficiency wages, the NRU evolves.

Unemployment is not a simple problem with a simple solution. The costs of unemployment are significant not only to individuals but also to the economy and society, which is why so many governments around the world are highly sensitive to the problem and look to develop policies to deal with unemployment. It is worth noting that when high unemployment persists, the potential for social disorder and political upheaval is greater. It might not be surprising, therefore, that governments are keen to ensure that the problems which can arise from unemployment are given due consideration in policy formulation.

SUMMARY

- The unemployment rate is the percentage of those who would like to work who do not have jobs. Governments calculate this statistic monthly based on a survey of thousands of households.
- The unemployment rate is an imperfect measure of joblessness. Some people who call themselves unemployed may actually not want to work, and some people who would like to work have left the labour force after an unsuccessful search.
- In many advanced economies, most people who become unemployed find work within a short period of time. Nevertheless, most unemployment observed at any given time is attributable to the few people who are unemployed for long periods of time.
- One reason for unemployment is the time it takes for workers to search for jobs that best suit their tastes and skills. Unemployment insurance is a government policy that, while protecting workers' incomes, increases the amount of frictional unemployment.
- A second reason why an economy may always have some unemployment is if there is a minimum wage that exceeds the wage that would balance supply and demand for the workers who are eligible for the minimum wage. By raising the wage of unskilled and inexperienced workers above the equilibrium level, minimum wage laws raise the quantity of labour supplied and reduce the quantity demanded. The resulting surplus of labour represents unemployment.
- A third reason for unemployment is the market power of unions. When unions push the wages in unionized industries above the equilibrium level, they create a surplus of labour.
- A fourth reason for unemployment is suggested by the theory of efficiency wages. According to this theory, firms find it profitable to pay wages above the equilibrium level. High wages can improve worker health, lower worker turnover, increase worker effort and raise worker quality.
- Unemployment also occurs due to structural changes in the economy which result in firms and industries closing down while new firms and industries grow. Structural changes cause winners and losers, and it is not always easy or practical for people to find new jobs.

- John Maynard Keynes suggested, contrary to the accepted view at the time, that unemployment could remain at high levels for extended periods and that governments should use fiscal policy to help alleviate unemployment by boosting government spending.
- The neo-classical synthesis reconciled the classical view and Keynes' ideas by arguing that in the short run, markets might not adjust because of sticky prices and wages, but in the long run, classical principles hold.
- Marx argued that capitalism needed unemployment to regulate the power of workers.
- The costs of unemployment to individuals include lower incomes, loss of self-esteem, de-skilling, an increase in the possibility of mental health problems, family breakdown and crime.
- The costs of unemployment to society as a whole includes the opportunity cost of lost output, which reduces potential growth, the impact on government income and expenditure, the social costs of dealing with unemployment and its effects, the underuse of resources and the reverse multiplier effect.

IN THE NEWS

Unemployment and Hysteresis

You can be forgiven for thinking that often, in economics, we look at shocks and assume that, once the initial effect of the shock has passed, the system will revert to what it was before. Yet imagine a taut rubber band. If you pull the band out of shape, you expect it to revert back to its original shape once you release your grip on the band. However, if you subjected the band to repeated pulling, it might not revert back to its original shape. It may have become looser and, over time, it takes on a new shape. If it takes on this new shape, it is hysteresis in action.

When shocks happen to economic systems – for example a recession – unemployment is likely to rise. Once the recession has passed, will unemployment return to its former level, in other words, will it revert to the natural rate? Research suggests this is not the case. For example, if workers lose their jobs during a recession, they may lose certain skills, not have the skills to take on jobs that are or become available and, as a result, some of these workers made unemployed because of cyclical factors may remain unemployed because of structural reasons.

Research published in October 2021 by Laurence M. Ball and Joern Onken of John Hopkins University in Baltimore and University College London, respectively, throws new light on the importance of hysteresis. Increases in unemployment and increases in the natural rate of unemployment are assumed to move together in the long run. In the short run, unemployment may deviate from the natural rate but, over time, they are drawn back together. However, if hysteresis exists, then the natural rate of unemployment may end up being at a rate that is further away from the unemployment rate.

Ball and Onken looked at measures of the natural rate of unemployment in 29 OECD countries between 2002 and 2019. They assumed that shocks to aggregate demand had an impact on unemployment and they found that shocks to unemployment can have permanent effects. If an economic shock caused unemployment to rise, the increase in the unemployment rate continued to be above the natural rate of unemployment for a period of around eight years, after which the natural rate

©iStock/AndreyPopov

Workers that lose their jobs, often through no fault of their own, can find that they lose valuable skills and experience and find it harder to get new jobs.

(Continued)

was pulled to a higher level. Ball and Onken were able to quantify the effect, stating that the natural rate changed by 0.16 percentage points when unemployment deviated by one percentage point from the natural rate for one year.

The conclusion to their research notes that there was 'strong evidence of hysteresis: an innovation in actual unemployment changes the natural rate in the same direction and therefore has permanent effects'. Ball and Onken also found that the degree of hysteresis varied across different countries and that the natural rate of unemployment could be affected more strongly by decreases in unemployment compared to increases in unemployment.

Critical Thinking Questions

1 To what extent do you think that the assumption that economic shocks are 'temporary' and that economic systems will return to their pre-shock states is important in determining economic policy when dealing with issues like unemployment?

2 Economic shocks to unemployment like recessions can result in so-called 'scarring effects' on workers and affect wage rates because those who are unemployed are not part of the wage bargaining process. Why might these facts result in the post-shock natural rate of unemployment being higher than the one prior to the shock?

3 Explain how workers who are made unemployed as a result of cyclical reasons can find it hard to get back into employment for structural reasons.

4 What might be the possible policy implications of Ball and Onken's research with regard to tackling unemployment and the assumption of a natural rate of unemployment?

5 Why do you think that the natural rate of unemployment can be affected more strongly by decreases in unemployment than by increases in unemployment?

Reference:

Ball, L.M. and Onken, J. (2021) *Hysteresis in Unemployment: Evidence from OECD Estimates of the Natural Rate.* NBER Working Paper 29343, Cambridge, MA, National Bureau of Economic Research. Available at www.nber.org/papers/w29343, accessed 7 August 2025.

QUESTIONS FOR REVIEW

1 Why might a person who does not have a job not be unemployed?

2 How do national statistical offices compute the labour force, the unemployment rate and the labour force participation rate?

3 Is unemployment typically short term or long term? Explain.

4 Why is frictional unemployment inevitable? How might a government reduce the amount of frictional unemployment?

5 Why, according to Marx, does capitalism need a 'reserve army of the unemployed'?

6 What is the hysteresis effect?

7 What is the 'neo-classical synthesis'?

8 What claims do advocates of unions make to argue that unions are good for the economy?

9 Explain four ways in which a firm might increase its profits by raising the wages it pays.

10 Outline three costs of unemployment to (a) an individual and (b) to society.

PROBLEMS AND APPLICATIONS

1 Assume that in a country, of all adult people, 29,500,000 were employed, 1,120,000 were unemployed and 11,000,000 were not in the labour force. How big was the labour force? What was the labour force participation rate? What was the unemployment rate?

2 Go to the website of the UK Office for National Statistics (www.statistics.gov.uk) or Eurostat (ec.europa.eu/eurostat) or the statistics office for the country in which you are studying.
   a. What is the national unemployment rate right now?
   b. Find the unemployment rate for the demographic group that best fits a description of you (for example, based on age, sex and ethnic group). Is it higher or lower than the national average? Why do you think this is so?

3 According to a Labour Force Survey in a country, total employment increased by around 1.35 million workers between 2021 and 2026, but the number of unemployed workers increased by 350,000.
   a. How are these numbers consistent with each other?
   b. In some cases, there can be an increase in the number of people employed, but the number of unemployed people declines by a smaller amount. Why might one expect a reduction in the number of people counted as unemployed to be smaller than the increase in the number of people employed?

4 Are the following workers more likely to experience short-term or long-term unemployment? Explain.
   a. A construction worker laid off because of bad weather.
   b. A manufacturing worker who loses their job at a plant in an isolated area.
   c. A bus industry worker laid off because of competition from the railway.
   d. A short order cook (a specialist in making simple, quick meals in restaurants) who loses their job when a new restaurant opens across the street.
   e. An expert welder with little formal education who loses their job when the company installs automatic welding machinery.

5 Both Marx and Keynes criticized Say's law as being a fallacy. What do you think is the flaw in Say's argument?

6 To what extent do you think the reasons why some frictional unemployment will always exist confirms the idea of sticky wages and the neo-classical synthesis?

7 Consider an economy with two labour markets, neither of which is unionized. Now suppose a union is established in one market.
   a. Show the effect of the union on the market in which it is formed. In what sense is the quantity of labour employed in this market an inefficient quantity?
   b. Show the effect of the union on the non-unionized market. What happens to the equilibrium wage in this market?

8 Some workers in the economy are paid a flat salary and some are paid by commission. Which compensation scheme would require more monitoring by supervisors? In which case do firms have an incentive to pay more than the equilibrium level (as in the worker effort variant of efficiency wage theory)? What factors do you think determine the type of compensation firms choose?

9 Explain why changes to the structure of the population and policies to improve job matching might lead to changes in the NRU.

10 Statistics from the International Labour Organization suggest that there are around 64 million young people (those aged between 16 and 23) unemployed worldwide and that 145 million young workers live in poverty. Young people are three times more likely to be unemployed than those in other age groups, and each month out of work prior to age 23 increases the likelihood that they will experience longer periods of unemployment later in life.
   a. Why are such statistics of importance to policymakers?
   b. What specific costs might be associated with youth unemployment to young people and to society?
   c. Should policymakers devote more resources to dealing with youth unemployment compared to other groups in society? Justify your response.

PART 4 LONG-RUN MACROECONOMICS

7 SAVING, INVESTMENT AND THE FINANCIAL SYSTEM

Our analysis of long-run macroeconomic outcomes will cover three main areas: saving, investment and the financial system; the monetary system; and open market macroeconomics. We begin by looking at saving, investment and the financial system. To carry out business of virtually any sort, firms must have capital. To acquire capital, firms must have funds to finance capital investment. Funds for capital investment will often be in the form of different types of loan. The source of these loans is what households save.

The **financial system** consists of those institutions in the economy that help to match one person's saving with another person's investment. Saving and investment are key ingredients to long-run economic growth. When a country saves a large portion of its GDP, more resources are available for investment in capital, and higher capital raises a country's productivity and living standards. We have also seen that there is a proportion of income that is not spent and which is saved. At the same time there are economic actors who want to borrow to finance investments in new and growing businesses. This chapter examines how the financial system brings together savers and borrowers and explores some of the basic tools of finance.

financial system the group of institutions in the economy that help to match one person's saving with another person's investment

FINANCIAL INSTITUTIONS IN THE ECONOMY

At the broadest level, the financial system moves the economy's scarce resources from savers (people who spend less than they earn) to borrowers (people who spend more than they earn). Savers save for various reasons, for example to help put a child through university in several years, or to retire comfortably in several decades. Similarly, borrowers borrow for a variety of reasons, for example to buy a house in which to live, or to start a business with which to make a living. Many savers supply their money to the financial system with the expectation that they will get it back with interest at a later date. The expectation that the reward for saving will be the receipt of interest is not universal – Islamic finance has a very different approach. In this chapter, however, we will be focusing on what might be called 'traditional' financial institutions. Borrowers demand money from the financial system with the knowledge that they will be required to pay it back with interest at a later date.

The financial system is made up of various financial institutions that help coordinate savers and borrowers. Financial institutions can be grouped into two categories: financial markets and financial intermediaries.

Financial Markets

Financial markets are the institutions through which a person who wants to save can directly supply funds to a person who wants to borrow. Two of the most important financial markets in advanced economies are the bond market and the stock market.

financial markets financial institutions through which savers can directly provide funds to borrowers

The Bond Market When Ørsted, a Danish energy company, wants to borrow to finance a major new offshore wind farm project, it can borrow directly from the public. It does this by selling bonds. A **bond** is a certificate of indebtedness that specifies the obligations of the borrower to the holder of the bond. Put simply, a bond is an IOU. It identifies the date on which the loan will be repaid, called the *date of maturity*, and the rate of interest that will be paid periodically (called the *coupon*) until the loan matures. The buyer of a bond gives their money to Ørsted in exchange for this promise of interest and eventual repayment of the amount borrowed (the *principal*). The buyer can hold the bond until maturity or can sell the bond at an earlier date to someone else.

bond a certificate of indebtedness

There are literally millions of bonds traded in advanced economies. When large corporations or national and local governments need to borrow to finance the purchase of a new factory, a new jet fighter or a new school, they often do so by issuing bonds. The listing of the prices and interest rates on some of the most important bond issues can be found via the financial press and online. Although these bonds differ in many ways, two characteristics of bonds are most important.

The first characteristic is a bond's *term* – the length of time until the bond matures. Some bonds have short terms, such as a few months, while others have terms as long as 30 years. (The British government has even issued a bond that never matures, called a *perpetuity*. This bond pays interest forever, but the principal is never repaid.) The interest rate on a bond depends, in part, on its term. Long-term bonds are riskier than short-term bonds because holders of long-term bonds must wait longer for repayment of the principal. If a holder of a long-term bond needs their money earlier than the distant date of maturity, they have no choice but to sell the bond to someone else, perhaps at a reduced price. To compensate for this risk, long-term bonds usually (but not always) pay higher interest rates than short-term bonds.

The second important characteristic of a bond is its *credit risk*, which is the probability that the borrower will fail to pay some of the interest or principal. Such a failure to pay is called a *default*. Borrowers can (and sometimes do) default on their loans. When bond buyers perceive that the probability of default is high, they demand a higher interest rate to compensate them for this risk.

When national governments want to borrow money to finance public spending, they issue bonds. You will hear this referred to as *sovereign debt*. Some government bonds are considered a safe credit risk, such as those from Germany, for example, and tend to pay relatively low interest rates. UK government bonds have come to be referred to as *gilt-edged* bonds, or more simply as *gilts*, reflecting that, in terms of credit risk, they are 'as good as gold' (early bond certificates had a gold edge – hence the term 'gilt-edged'). In contrast, financially shaky corporations raise money by issuing *junk bonds*, which pay very high interest rates. Buyers of bonds can judge credit risk by checking with various private agencies, such as Standard & Poor's, which rate the credit risk of different bonds. Sometimes, these bonds are referred to euphemistically, but less graphically, as *below investment grade bonds*.

Bond Prices and Yield One important point to note is the relationship between a bond's price and its yield. Assume that a corporation issues a €1,000 bond over a 10-year period with a coupon of 3.5 per cent. For the duration of the 10 years, the corporation will pay the bond holder €35 a year in interest and when the bond matures the corporation will pay back the bond holder the €1,000 principal. At any time during the 10-year period the bond holder can sell the bond on the bond market. The price they get will depend on the supply and demand of those bonds on the market. The yield of the bond (in simple terms) is given by $\frac{Coupon}{Price} \times 100$. Price is quoted as a percentage of the principal.

Assume the bond holder needs to get access to cash (liquidity) quickly, so they decide to sell their bond. The price of the bond on the market is €995. The yield on this bond, therefore, is $\frac{35}{995} \times 100 = 3.52\%$. If the seller was able to sell the bond for €1,050, the yield would be $\frac{35}{1,050} \times 100 = 3.33\%$. This illustrates an important point, that there is an inverse relationship between price and yield. As bond prices rise, the yield falls and vice versa.

The reason why bond prices rise and fall on the markets is due to the demand and supply of bonds (the number of people wanting to buy bonds and the number of people wanting to sell bonds). Bond prices (and, therefore, yields) are affected by existing bonds in the market, the issue of new bonds, the likelihood of the bond issuer defaulting and interest rates on other securities. The issue of a new bond is also affected by these factors. If current interest rates are high, new issues must have a coupon which will compete and vice versa.

The Stock Market Another way for firms like Ørsted to raise funds for a major investment project is to sell stock in the company. **Stock (or share or equity)** represents ownership in a firm and is, therefore, a claim on the future profits that the firm makes. For example, if Ørsted sells a total of one million shares of stock, then each share represents ownership of $\frac{1}{1,000,000}$ of the business. A stock is also commonly referred to as a *share* or *equity*. In this book, we will use the terms 'share' and 'stock' (and 'stockholder' and 'shareholder') interchangeably.

stock (or share or equity) a claim to partial ownership and the future profits in a firm

The sale of stock to raise money is called *equity finance*, whereas the sale of bonds is called *debt finance*. Although corporations use both equity and debt finance to raise money for new investments, stocks and bonds are very different. The owner of Ørsted shares is a part owner of Ørsted. In contrast, the owner of an Ørsted bond is a creditor of the corporation. If Ørsted is very profitable, the shareholders enjoy the benefits of these profits, whereas the bondholders get only the interest on their bonds. If Ørsted runs into financial difficulty, the bondholders are paid what they are due before shareholders receive anything at all. Compared to bonds, stocks offer the holder both higher risk and potentially higher return.

As we noted just now, stocks are also called shares or equities. In the UK, bonds are also, confusingly, referred to as 'stock'. This term for government bonds has been in use in England since the late seventeenth century and is well established. To avoid confusion, however, the term is often qualified as *government stock* or *gilt-edged stock*. In general, though, despite the confusing use of language, the term *stock* refers to ownership of a firm.

Corporations can issue stock by selling shares to the public through organized stock exchanges. These first-time sales are referred to as the *primary market*. Shares that are subsequently traded among stockholders on stock exchanges are referred to as the *secondary market*. In these transactions, the corporation itself receives no money when its stock changes hands. Most of the world's countries have their own stock exchanges on which the shares of national companies trade.

The prices at which shares trade on stock exchanges are determined by the supply and demand for the stock in these companies. Because stock represents a claim to future profits in a corporation, the demand for a stock (and thus its price) reflects people's perception of the corporation's future profitability. When people become optimistic about a company's future, they raise their demand for its stock and thereby bid up the price of a share of stock. Conversely, when people come to expect a company to have little profit or even losses, the price of a share falls.

Various stock indices are available to monitor the overall level of stock prices for any particular stock market. A *stock index* is computed as an average of a group of share prices. The Dow Jones Industrial Average has been computed regularly for the New York Stock Exchange since 1896. It is now based on the prices of the shares of 30 major US companies. The Financial Times Stock Exchange (FTSE) 100 Index, is based on the top 100 companies (according to the total value of their shares) listed on the London Stock Exchange (LSE). The FTSE All-Share Index is based on all companies listed on the LSE. Indices of prices on the Frankfurt stock market, based on 30 and 100 companies respectively, are the DAX 30 and DAX 100. The NIKKEI 225 (or just plain NIKKEI Index) is based on the largest 225 companies, in terms of market value of shares, traded on the Tokyo Stock Exchange.

Because share prices reflect expected profitability, stock indices are watched closely as possible indicators of future economic conditions.

Financial Intermediaries

Financial intermediaries are financial institutions through which savers can indirectly provide funds to borrowers. The term *intermediary* reflects the role of these institutions in standing between savers and borrowers. Here we consider two of the most important financial intermediaries: banks and investment funds.

financial intermediaries financial institutions through which savers can indirectly provide funds to borrowers

Banks If the owner of a small business wants to finance an expansion of their business, they probably take a strategy quite different from a company like Ørsted. Unlike Ørsted, a small business person would find it difficult to raise funds in the bond and stock markets. Most buyers of stocks and bonds prefer to buy those issued by larger, more familiar companies. The small business person, therefore, most likely finances their business expansion with a loan from a bank.

Banks are the financial intermediaries with which people are most familiar. A primary function of banks is to take in deposits from people who want to save and use these deposits to make loans to people who want to borrow. Banks pay depositors interest on their deposits and charge borrowers slightly higher interest on their loans. The difference between these rates of interest covers the banks' costs and returns some profit to the owners of the banks.

Besides being financial intermediaries, banks play a second important role in the economy. They facilitate purchases of goods and services by allowing people to draw against their deposits, or to use debit cards to transfer money electronically from their account to the account of the person or corporation they are buying something from. In other words, banks help create a special asset that people can use as a *medium of exchange*. A medium of exchange is an item that people can easily use to engage in transactions. A bank's role in providing a medium of exchange distinguishes it from many other financial institutions. Stocks and bonds, like bank deposits, are a possible *store of value* for the wealth that people have accumulated in past saving. Access to this wealth, however, is not as easy, cheap and immediate as just swiping a debit card. For now, we ignore this second role of banks, but we will return to it when we discuss the monetary system later in the book.

Investment or Mutual Fund An **investment or mutual fund** is a vehicle that allows the public to invest in a selection, or *portfolio*, of various types of shares, bonds, or both shares and bonds. The shareholder of the fund accepts all the risk and return associated with the portfolio. If the value of the portfolio rises, the shareholder benefits. If the value of the portfolio falls, the shareholder suffers the loss.

investment or mutual fund an institution that sells shares to the public and uses the proceeds to buy a portfolio of stocks and bonds

The primary advantage of these funds is that they allow people with small amounts of money to diversify. Buyers of shares and bonds are well advised to heed the adage, 'Don't put all your eggs in one basket.' Because the value of any single stock or bond is tied to the fortunes of one company, holding a single kind of stock or bond is very risky. By contrast, people who hold a diverse portfolio of shares and bonds face less risk because they have only a small stake in each company. Investment funds make this diversification easy. With only a few hundred euros, a person can buy shares in an investment fund and, indirectly, become the part owner or creditor of hundreds of major companies. For this service, the company operating the investment fund charges shareholders a fee, usually between 0.5 and 2.0 per cent of assets each year. Closely related to investment funds are unit trusts, the difference being that when people put money into a unit trust, more 'units' or shares are issued, whereas the only way to buy into an investment fund is to buy existing shares in the fund. For this reason, unit trusts are sometimes referred to as 'open-ended'.

FYI

Key Terms in Stock Markets

When following the stock of any company, there are three key numbers to note. These numbers are reported on the financial pages of some newspapers, and they can be easily obtained online:

- **Price**. The single most important piece of information about a stock is its price. There are invariably several prices reported. The *last* price is the price at which the stock more recently traded. The *previous close* is the price of the last transaction that occurred before the stock exchange closed in its previous day of trading. A news service may also give the *high* and *low* prices over the past day of trading and, sometimes, over the past year as well. It may also report the change from the previous day's closing price.
- **Dividend**. Corporations pay out some of their profits to their shareholders; this amount is called the dividend. (Profits not paid out are called retained earnings and are used by the corporation for additional investment.) News services often report the dividend paid over the previous year for each share of stock. They sometimes report the dividend yield, which is the dividend expressed as a percentage of the stock's price.
- **Price–earnings ratio**. A corporation's earnings, or accounting profit, is the amount of revenue it receives for the sale of its products minus its costs of production as measured by its accountants. *Earnings per share* is the company's total earnings divided by the number of shares of stock outstanding. The *price–earnings ratio*, often called the P/E, is the price of a corporation's stock divided by the amount the corporation earned per share over the past year. Historically, the typical price–earnings ratio is about 15. A higher P/E indicates that a corporation's stock is expensive relative to its recent earnings; this might indicate either that people expect earnings to rise in the future or that the stock is overvalued. Conversely, a lower P/E indicates that a corporation's stock is cheap relative to its recent earnings; this might indicate either that people expect earnings to fall or that the stock is undervalued.

SELF TEST What is stock? What is a bond? How are they different? How are they similar?

Other Financial Instruments

There have been an increasing number of instruments which play a role in the financial system, many of which have become increasingly complex. In this section we will look at some of these instruments.

Collateralized Debt Obligations (CDOs) CDOs are pools of asset-backed securities which are dependent on the value of the asset that backs them up and the stream of income that flows from these assets. Essentially, CDOs work in the following way. In setting up a CDO, a manager encourages investors to buy bonds, the funds of which are used to buy pools of debt, for example mortgage debt. This debt is split and rated according to its risk of default into tranches. Low-risk tranches attract low interest rates while the riskier tranches attract higher interest rates.

Under 'normal' circumstances the payments by mortgage holders provide sufficient income each month to pay the interest to each of the tranche holders. There is a risk, of course, that some of the mortgage holders in the initial debt could default on payment, but historical data enables investors to have some idea of what this risk will be. In the event of default, some of the riskier tranches may not get paid – that is the risk they take and why they get a higher interest rate.

The development of new approaches to risk management enable these structures to be extended further into second and third 'waves' of securitized debt. Asset managers could buy particular tranches of debt (backed by mortgages ultimately) and mix them with other types of debt and sell them on to other investors. Investors in these higher risk tranches can seek ratification of the risk they are undertaking by referring to ratings agencies which examine and report on the inherent risk of the investment.

Credit Default Swaps (CDS) A **credit default swap** is a means by which bondholders can insure themselves against the risk of default.

> **credit default swap** a means by which a bondholder can insure against the risk of default

Whenever a bond is sold there is an associated risk attached to it. In the case of bonds backed by a pool of mortgage debt, such as CDOs, the risk is that the mortgage payer defaults on the payment in some way. To see how this works let us take an example.

Assume a bank has bought a bond in an asset-backed security (in reality of course it might be many bonds) worth €5 million. The bond has a principal, therefore, of €5 million. The coupon payment (the interest on the bond) is 10 per cent. The bond is backed by the stream of cash flows being paid by mortgage holders – the underlying asset to the bond. The bondholder knows that there is a risk that some mortgage holders might default and as a result the bond return might also be in default, that is it does not pay the coupon or possibly the principal. If mortgage holders all meet their obligations and pay the money back (the principal), the bank will have earned interest for as long as it held the bond. If the bond was a 10-year bond with a coupon of 10 per cent then the bondholder would have earned a 10 per cent return on the bond for 10 years (€500,000 per year for 10 years).

The bondholder can go to an insurance company (which could also be another bank or a hedge fund) and take out a policy on the risk. The bank seeking to insure the risk is referred to as the *protection buyer* and the insurance company or other financial institution, the *protection seller*. The policy will agree to restore the bondholder to their original position should the bond default. The bondholder pays the insurance company premiums over the life of the policy. Let us assume this is €100,000 a year over 10 years, and in return the insurance company would agree to pay the bondholder €5 million if the bond defaults in some way during the period of the agreement.

What the bondholder has done is to swap the risk in the bond with the insurance company. In the event of the bond defaulting, then the protection seller pays out to the protection buyer. These CDS could also be traded and in many cases the protection buyer might take out a number of such hedges against its risk. The price of a CDS is quoted in terms of basis points, where a basis point is $\frac{1}{100}$th of 1 per cent (or 0.0001 expressed as a decimal). The price quoted reflects the cost of protecting debt for a period of time. For example, the price of a CDS for Ørsted might be quoted at 255 bps, suggesting that the cost of protecting €10 million of Ørsted debt for five years would be €255,000 a year (255 × 0.0001 × 10,000,000).

If the bond was subject to default, this would trigger a payment called a *credit event*. If a credit event occurs, there are two ways in which the contract could be closed. One is through a physical settlement. In this case the protection buyer would deliver the bond to the seller who would give the buyer the value of the bond, called par. The CDS market expanded rapidly throughout the 2000s leading to multiple trading. The holder of the CDS, therefore, might not actually own the bond in question. So this method of settlement clearly does not work. The growth in the market meant that the number of contracts far outweighed the number of bonds on which they were based. To settle the claims of contract holders through physical means would not be possible. As a consequence, protection sellers undertook to settle the contract claim through cash settlement where the positions were cleared by the transfer of cash.

The protection seller must also put up some form of collateral to cover its exposure to the possible default as part of the CDS agreement. The size of the exposure in the example above would be €5 million. This would be part of the contract between the insurance seller and the buyer. The amount of the collateral required would depend on the market value of the bond and the credit rating of the protection seller. The market value of the bond can change, because the bondholder can sell their bond.

If a bond associated with a mortgage pool is deemed a higher risk, it may become more difficult to sell it, and the price would fall. At a lower price the risk involved for the protection buyer is higher, and they can exercise a call (meaning they can ask for more security known as a *collateral call*) on the protection seller to increase the collateral supplied. If, for example, the price of the bond in the example above fell to 40 cents in the euro, the insurance company would have to find 0.60 × €5,000,000 in additional collateral (€3 million). Equally, if the rating of the protection seller is downgraded, then the risk to the protection buyer also rises. In other words, the seller may not be able to meet its obligations. Once again, the protection buyer can call the seller to ask for more collateral to be provided. The insurance company would then have to find more funds to top up the collateral it has to provide to reflect the lower value of the bond.

If the seller was unable to meet its obligations, the buyer would have some protection in the form of the collateral supplied by the seller. If the bond runs its course and matures without any credit event, then the collateral is returned to the seller (who also, remember, receives premiums from the buyer).

Summary

An advanced economy contains a large variety of financial institutions. In addition to the bond market, the stock market, banks and investment funds, there are also pension funds and insurance companies. Clearly, these institutions differ in many ways, and the products they sell have become more complex in lots of cases. When analyzing the macroeconomic role of the financial system, however, it is more important to keep in mind the similarity of these institutions than the differences. These financial institutions all serve the same goal – directing the resources of savers into the hands of borrowers. We will now look at some basic tools in finance which are relevant to savers and investors. First, we discuss how to compare sums of money at different points in time. Second, we discuss how to manage risk. Third, we build on our analysis of time and risk to examine what determines the value of an asset, such as a share of stock.

PRESENT VALUE: MEASURING THE TIME VALUE OF MONEY

Imagine that someone offered to give you €100 today or €100 in 10 years. Which would you choose? The rational answer would be that getting €100 today is better, because you can always deposit the money in a bank, still have it in 10 years and earn interest on the €100 along the way. From this we can take away that money today is more valuable than the same amount of money in the future.

Now consider a harder question. Imagine that someone offered you €100 today or €200 in 10 years. Which would you choose? To answer this question, you need some way to compare sums of money from different points in time. Economists do this with a concept called *present value*. The **present value** of any future sum of money is the amount today that would need to be invested, at current interest rates, to produce that future sum. Put another way, what sum of money would you need to put into an interest-bearing account at a particular interest rate to generate the future sum? The answer to this question allows comparison of sums of money over time. If the value of a future sum expressed in today's terms is greater than the initial sum, then it is worth accepting, and vice versa.

> **present value** the amount of money today that would need to be invested using prevailing interest rates, to produce a given future amount of money

To learn how to use the concept of present value, let us work through a couple of examples.

Question: If you put €100 in a bank account today, how much will it be worth in N years? That is, what will be the **future value** of this €100? Here we are looking at the future value as the amount of money in the future that an amount of money today will yield, given prevailing interest rates.

> **future value** the amount of money in the future that an amount of money invested today will yield, given prevailing interest rates

Answer: Let us use r to denote the interest rate expressed in decimal form (an interest rate of 5 per cent means $r = 0.05$). Suppose that interest is paid annually and that the interest paid remains in the bank account to earn more interest – a process called **compounding**. Then the €100 will become:

$(1 + r) \times €100$	*after one year*
$(1 + r) \times (1 + r) \times €100$	*after two years*
$(1 + r) \times (1 + r) \times (1 + r) \times €100$	*after three years*
$(1 + r)^N \times €100$	*after N years*

For example, if we are investing at an interest rate of 5 per cent for 10 years, then the future value will be $(1.05)^{10} \times €100$, which is €163 (rounded up to the nearest whole euro. Note: we will follow this rounding up for the remainder of the chapter).

> **compounding** the accumulation of a sum of money in, say, a bank account, where the interest earned remains in the account to earn additional interest in the future

Question: Now suppose you are going to be paid €200 in N years (guaranteed risk free). What is the *present value* of this future payment at an interest rate of 5 per cent? That is, how much would you have to deposit in a bank right now at an interest rate of 5 per cent to yield €200 in N years?

Answer: To answer this question, turn the previous answer on its head. In the first question, we computed a future value from a present value by *multiplying* by the factor $(1 + r)^N$. To compute a present value from a future value, we *divide* by the factor $(1 + r)^N$. Thus, the present value of €200 in N years is $\frac{€200}{(1+r)^N}$. If we take the answer to this calculation and deposit it in a bank today, after N years it would become $(1 + r)^N \times \left[\frac{€200}{(1+r)^N}\right]$, which is €200.

If the interest rate is 5 per cent, the present value of €200 in 10 years is $\frac{€200}{(1.05)^{10}} = €123$. If €123 was deposited in a bank today, at an interest rate of 5 per cent, it would become €200 in 10 years' time.

This illustrates the general equation: if r is the interest rate, then an amount X to be received in N years has a present value of $\frac{X}{(1+r)^N}$.

Let us now return to our question: should you choose €100 today or €200 in 10 years? Our calculation tells us that the present value of €200, at an interest rate of 5 per cent, is €123. This suggests that, given the interest rate and the absence of risk, you should prefer the €200 in 10 years. The future €200 has a present value of €123, which is greater than €100. You are better off waiting for the future sum. Knowing the present value now allows us to pose the question in a slightly different way. Would you prefer €100 today or €123 today? This, of course, is a much easier question to answer assuming you are being rational. The use of present values allows us to be able to rephrase questions on future value in this way to aid decision-making.

The answer to the question is dependent on the interest rate. If the interest rate were 8 per cent, then the present value of €200 in 10 years would be $\frac{€200}{(1.08)^{10}} = €93$. In this case, you should take the €100 today (as above, if we turn the question round, would you rather have €100 today or €93 today?). Why should the interest rate matter for your choice? The answer is that the higher the interest rate, the more you can earn by depositing your money at the bank, so the more attractive getting €100 today becomes.

Applying the Concept of Present Value

The concept of present value is useful in many applications, including the decisions that companies face when evaluating investment projects. For instance, imagine that Citroën is thinking about building a new car factory to produce electric vehicles. Suppose that the factory will cost €100 million today and will yield the company €200 million in 10 years. Should Citroën undertake the project? You can see that this decision is exactly like the one we have been studying. To make its decision, the company will compare the present value of the €200 million return to the €100 million cost.

The company's decision, therefore, will depend on the interest rate. If the interest rate is 5 per cent, then the present value of the €200 million return from the factory is €123 million, and the company will choose to pay the €100 million cost. By contrast, if the interest rate is 8 per cent, then the present value of the return is only €93 million, and the company might decide to forgo the project. Thus, the concept of present value helps explain why investment declines when the interest rate rises, which we shall model later in the chapter. We must remember that the decision will also have to take account of many other factors such as risk, changing interest rates and inflation, and is thus far more complex, but the use of present value aids decision-making.

SELF TEST The interest rate is 7 per cent. What is the present value of €150 to be received in 10 years? What is the present value if the interest rate is 2 per cent and 4 per cent?

MANAGING RISK

Decision-making will always involve some element of risk. In the examples on present value, we ignored risk. Seeking to understand and take account of risk, however, is vital in any decision-making. **Risk** is the probability of something happening which results in a loss or some degree of hazard or damage. The rational response to risk is not necessarily to avoid it at any cost, but to take it into account in your decision-making. Let us consider how a person might do that.

risk the probability of something happening which results in a loss or some degree of hazard or damage

Risk Aversion

Research suggests that people tend to be **risk averse**. This means more than simply people dislike bad things happening to them. It means that they dislike bad things more than they like comparable good things. (This is also reflected in *loss aversion*. Research suggests that losing something makes people twice as miserable as gaining something makes them happy!)

risk averse exhibiting a dislike of uncertainty

For example, suppose a friend offers you the following opportunity. They flip a coin. If it comes up heads, they will pay you €1,000. If it comes up tails, you will have to pay them €1,000. Would you accept the bargain? You would not if you were risk averse, even though the probability of winning is the same as the probability of losing (50 per cent). For a risk-averse person, the pain from losing the €1,000 would exceed the gain from winning €1,000.

Economists have developed models of risk aversion using the concept of *utility*, which is a person's subjective measure of well-being or satisfaction. Every level of wealth provides a certain amount of utility, as shown by the utility function in Figure 7.1. The function exhibits the property of diminishing marginal utility: the more wealth a person has, the less utility they get from an additional euro. Thus in the figure, the utility function gets flatter as wealth increases. Because of diminishing marginal utility, the utility gained from winning €1,000 is less than from losing €1,000. As a result, people are risk averse.

FIGURE 7.1

The Utility Function

This utility function shows how utility, a subjective measure of satisfaction, depends on wealth. As wealth rises, the utility function becomes flatter, reflecting the property of diminishing marginal utility. Because of diminishing marginal utility, a €1,000 loss decreases utility by more than a €1,000 gain increases it.

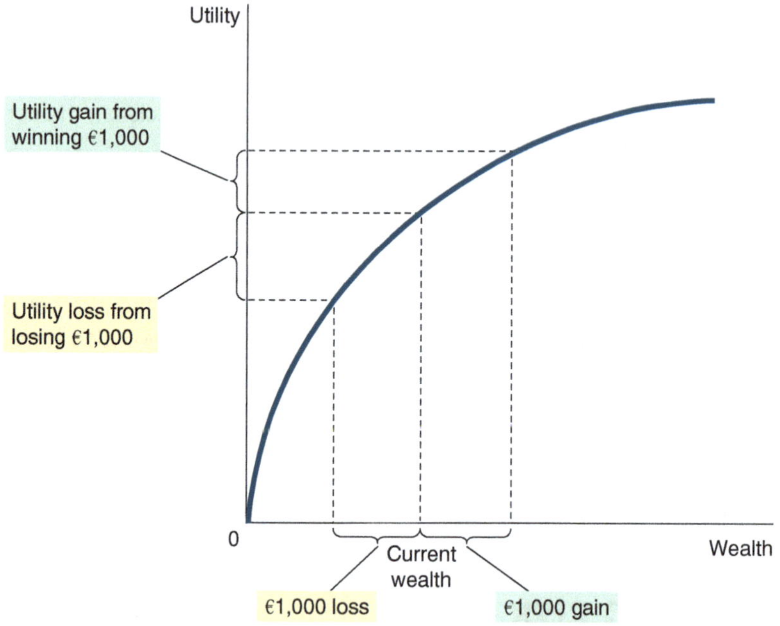

Risk aversion provides the starting point for explaining various things we observe in the economy. Let us consider three of them: insurance, diversification and the risk–return trade-off.

The Markets for Insurance

One way to deal with risk is to buy insurance. The general feature of insurance contracts, which we saw in our overview of CDS, is that a person facing a risk pays a fee to an insurance company, which in return agrees to accept all or part of the risk. There are many types of insurance. Car insurance covers the risk of you being in a car accident, fire insurance covers the risk that your house will burn down, and life assurance covers the risk that you will die and leave your family without income.

In a sense, every insurance contract is a gamble. It is possible that you will not be in a car accident or that your house will not burn down. In most years, you will pay the insurance company the premium and get nothing in return except peace of mind. Indeed, the insurance company is counting on the fact that most people will not make claims on their policies. Otherwise it could not pay out the large claims to those few who are unlucky and still stay in business.

From the standpoint of the economy as a whole, the role of insurance is not to eliminate the risks inherent in life but to spread them around more efficiently. Consider fire insurance, for instance. Owning fire insurance does not reduce the risk of losing your home in a fire. If that unlucky event occurs, the insurance company compensates you. The risk, rather than being borne by you alone, is shared among the thousands of insurance company shareholders. Because people are risk averse, it is easier for 10,000 people to bear $\frac{1}{10,000}$ of the risk than for one person to bear the entire risk themselves.

The markets for insurance suffer from two types of problems: *adverse selection* and *moral hazard.* Insurance companies are aware of these problems, and the price of insurance reflects these risks that the insurance company will face after the insurance is bought. The high price of insurance is why some people, especially those who know themselves to be low risk, decide against buying insurance and, instead, endure some of life's uncertainty on their own.

Pricing Risk

We have seen how bond issues are a means by which firms can borrow money. The buyer must have confidence that they will get their money back and also receive an appropriate reward for lending the money in the first place. There is a risk involved that the issuer will not be able to pay back the money and that risk is associated with a probability. If the issuer is very sound, then the probability of default may be close to zero, but if the issuer is extremely weak then the probability is closer to 1. We saw earlier how financial markets now deal in pools of debt (collections of different types of loans sold to an investor). As debt is pooled the outcomes become more varied. In any given pool of mortgage debt, for example, there will be some borrowers who will default and not be able to pay off their mortgages – possibly because of family bereavement or loss of their job. Other mortgage holders may look to pay off their mortgages early, some may move house and thus settle their mortgage, some will increase monthly payments or pay lump sums to help reduce the repayment period of their mortgage and so on. Assessing probabilities with such a wide range of outcomes becomes difficult.

The risk involved with such debt is therefore difficult to assess with any certainty. However, investors want to price risk as part of their decision-making so they can judge the value of an asset. If an asset is very risky, the expected returns will need to be higher and vice versa. To have an efficient market, that risk must be priced and the information on which the risk is based has to be reliable, accurate – and understood.

Let us consider an example. In your class there may be a number of students that you associate with every day. Take any one individual and we can identify a number of risks for that person. For example, there is a risk that the individual:

- fails their exams and must leave the course
- will be involved in a car crash
- will travel on an aircraft more than five times a year
- may be mugged
- may get flu.

What are the chances of these events happening? The analysis of such outcomes is what actuaries in the insurance industry do. An estimate of the probability of such events happening can be derived from analysis of data, specifically historical data. It is possible, therefore, to gather data on the average 19-year-old student coming from a particular area and with a particular background, and use this data to arrive at the probability of the event occurring. Historical data tell us, for example, that young people aged between 18 and 24 are more likely to be mugged than the elderly, despite popular perception. If we are able to identify these probabilities, then they can be priced. Securities can be issued based on the chances of these things happening. In other words, the more likely the event is to occur, the higher the price and vice versa.

While it may be possible to identify probabilities for an individual, it may be more problematic when looking at relationships between individuals. For example, if person X fails their exams, what is the probability that you will also fail your exams? If that individual gets flu, what are the chances that you also get flu? In both cases the probability might depend on your relationship with that person. If you spend a lot of time with that person, then it may be that you share similar distractions – going out every night instead of studying, skipping lectures and so on. If this were the case, then the probability of you also failing your exams and getting flu might be high, but if you have no relationship at all, then the chance of you sharing bad habits, which lead you to also failing your exams, is lower. However, given that you share some time with that person in a lecture hall or seminar room, for example, might mean that the probability of also getting flu is relatively high.

Looking at such relationships involves the concept of correlation, which is the extent to which there is any statistical relationship between two variables. If person X is involved in a car crash (and you were not in the car with them), what is the chance of you also being involved in a car crash? The chances are the correlation is very low. The probability of you both getting mugged is higher regardless of the relationship between you and so there will be a stronger correlation in this instance. The correlation is likely to become more and more unstable the more variables are introduced (number of students in this example). In the case of pools of debt, the same problems arise, and the efficiency of the information on which investors are basing their decision becomes ever more complex. Probabilities become very difficult to assess and, therefore, to price.

Actuaries have been studying these types of correlations for some years. Issuing life assurance involves a risk. Life assurance means that the event covered – the death of an individual – will occur at some point in the future (unlike insurance where the event might never happen). The job of the actuary is to provide information to the insurer on the chances of death occurring under different situations. Where information becomes available which indicates risk factors change, actuaries incorporate this into models to help insurers price the risk adequately (that is, set the premiums for the policy).

In the 1980s much work was done on studying a phenomenon known as stress cardiomyopathy. This is a condition where, in the wake of some exceptional emotional trauma, the human brain releases chemicals into the bloodstream that lead to a weakening of the heart and an increased chance of death. The condition has been referred to as a 'broken heart' because it seemed to manifest itself in particular when one partner dies soon after the death of the other. A study by Spreeuw and Wang (2008), (Spreeuw, J. and Wang, X. (2008) 'Modelling the Short-Term Dependence between Two Remaining Lifetimes'. Available at www.actuaries.org.uk/system/files/documents/pdf/Spreeuw_modelling.pdf), showed that following the death of a female partner, a man was over six times more likely to die than if their partner had not died, and women were more than twice as likely. The insurance industry takes such information and builds it into the pricing of offering joint-life policies.

Diversification of Idiosyncratic Risk

The traditional wisdom of the adage: 'Don't put all your eggs in one basket,' has been turned into a science. It goes by the name **diversification**.

> **diversification** the reduction of risk achieved by replacing a single risk with a large number of smaller unrelated risks

The market for insurance is one example of diversification. Imagine a town with 10,000 homeowners, each facing the risk of a house fire. If someone starts an insurance company and each person in town becomes both a shareholder and a policyholder of the company, they all reduce their risk through diversification. Each person now faces $\frac{1}{10,000}$ of the risk of 10,000 possible fires, rather than the entire risk of a single fire in their own home. Unless the entire town catches fire at the same time, the downside that each person faces is much smaller.

When people use their savings to buy financial assets, they can also reduce risk through diversification. A person who buys stock in a company is placing a bet on the future profitability of that company. That bet is often quite risky, because companies' fortunes are hard to predict. Microsoft evolved from a start-up by some geeky teenagers into one of the world's most valuable companies in only a few years. On the other hand, Enron, a former US energy company became insolvent with the loss of millions to investors and the jobs of workers because of fraud. It went from one of the world's most respected companies to an almost worthless one in only a few months. Fortunately, a shareholder need not tie their own fortune to that of any single company. Risk can be reduced by placing a large number of small bets, rather than a small number of large ones.

Figure 7.2 shows how the risk of a portfolio of shares depends on the number of shares in the portfolio. Risk is measured here with a statistic called *standard deviation*, which you may have learned about in a mathematics or statistics course. Standard deviation measures the volatility of a variable, that is how much the variable is likely to fluctuate. The higher the standard deviation of a portfolio's return, the more volatile and riskier it is.

FIGURE 7.2

Diversification Reduces Risk

This figure shows how the risk of a portfolio, measured here with a statistic called standard deviation (a measure of the variability about the mean), depends on the number of shares in the portfolio. The investor is assumed to put an equal percentage of their portfolio in each of the shares. Increasing the number of shares reduces the amount of risk in a stock portfolio, but it does not eliminate it.

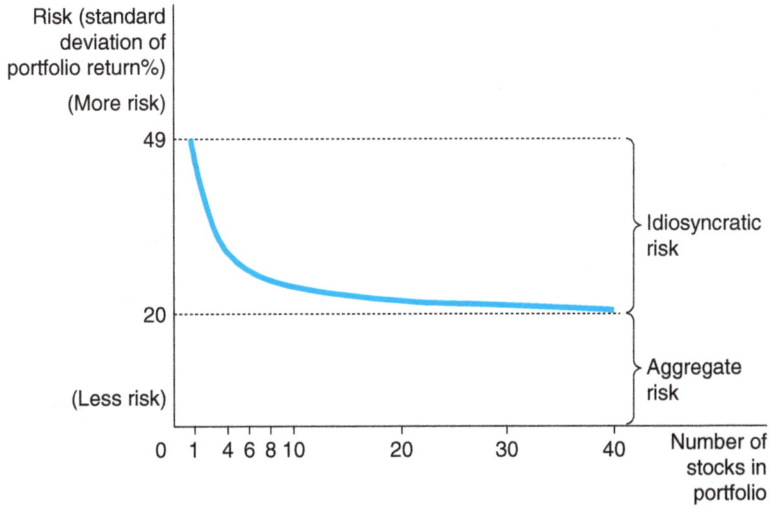

The figure shows that the risk of a stock portfolio reduces substantially as the number of shares increases. For a portfolio with a single share, the standard deviation is 49 per cent. Going from 1 share to 10 shares eliminates about half the risk. Going from 10 to 20 shares reduces the risk by another 13 per cent. As the number of shares continues to increase, risk continues to fall, although the reductions in risk after 20 or 30 shares are small.

Notice that it is impossible to eliminate all risk by increasing the number of stocks or shares in the portfolio. Diversification can eliminate **idiosyncratic risk** – the uncertainty associated with specific companies. But diversification cannot eliminate **aggregate risk** – the uncertainty associated with the entire economy, which affects all companies. For example, when the economy goes into a recession, many companies experience falling sales, reduced profit and low stock returns. Diversification reduces the risk of holding stocks, but it does not eliminate it.

idiosyncratic risk risk that affects only a single economic actor
aggregate risk risk that affects all economic actors at once

The Trade-Off between Risk and Return

There is a trade-off between risk and return which is at the heart of understanding financial decisions. Risks are inherent in holding shares, even in a diversified portfolio. Risk-averse people are willing to accept this uncertainty because they are compensated for doing so. Historically, shares have offered much higher rates of return than alternative financial assets, such as bonds and bank savings accounts. Over the past two centuries, stocks have offered an average real return of about 8 per cent per year, while short-term government bonds paid a real return of only 3 per cent per year.

When deciding how to allocate their savings, people must decide how much risk they are willing to undertake to earn the higher return. Figure 7.3 illustrates the risk-return trade-off for a person choosing to allocate their portfolio between two asset classes:

- The first asset class is a diversified group of risky stocks, with an average return of 8 per cent and a standard deviation of 20 per cent. (Note that a normal random variable stays within two standard deviations of its average about 95 per cent of the time. Thus, while actual returns are centred around 8 per cent, they typically vary from a gain of 48 per cent to a loss of 32 per cent.)

- The second asset class is a safe alternative, with a return of 3 per cent and a standard deviation of zero. The safe alternative can be either a bank savings account or a government bond.

FIGURE 7.3

The Trade-Off Between Risk and Return

When people increase the percentage of their savings that they have invested in shares, they increase the average return they can expect to earn, but they also increase the risks they face.

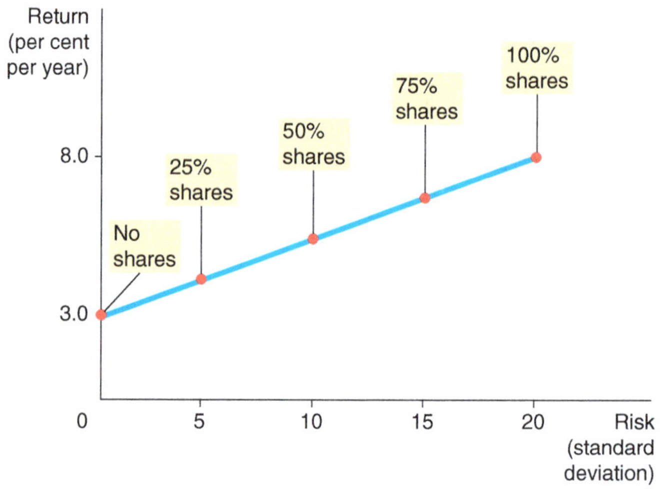

Each point in this figure represents a particular allocation of a portfolio between risky shares and the safe asset. The figure shows that the more a person puts into stocks, the greater is both the risk and the return.

Acknowledging the risk–return trade-off does not, by itself, tell us what a person should do. The choice of a particular combination of risk and return depends on a person's risk aversion, which reflects a person's own preferences. But it is important for shareholders to realize that the higher average return that they enjoy comes at the price of higher risk

SELF TEST Describe three ways that a risk-averse person might reduce the risk they face.

ASSET VALUATION

This section considers a simple question: what determines the price of a share of stock? One part of the answer is supply and demand, but that is not the end of the story. To understand share prices, we need to think more deeply about what determines a person's willingness to pay for a share of stock.

Fundamental Analysis

Let us imagine that you have decided to put 60 per cent of your savings into company shares and, to achieve diversification, you have decided to buy 20 different shares. How should you pick the 20 for your portfolio?

When you buy company shares, you are buying shares in a business. When deciding which businesses you want to own, it is natural to consider two things: the value of the business and the price at which the shares are being sold. If the price is less than the value, the stock is said to be *undervalued*. If the price is more than the value, the stock is said to be *overvalued*. If the price and the value are equal, the stock is said to be *fairly valued*. When choosing 20 stocks for your portfolio, you should prefer undervalued stocks. In these cases, you are getting a 'bargain' by paying less than the business is worth.

This is easier said than done. Learning the price is easy. You can just look it up in the newspaper or online or have it downloaded to an app on your mobile device. Determining the value of the business is the hard part. The term **fundamental analysis** refers to the detailed analysis of a company to determine its value. Many financial sector firms hire stock price analysts to conduct such fundamental analysis and offer advice about which stocks to buy.

fundamental analysis the study of a company's accounting statements and future prospects to determine its value

The value of a stock to a shareholder is what they get out of owning it, which includes the present value of the stream of dividend payments and the final sale price. Recall that *dividends* are the cash payments that a company makes to its shareholders. A company's ability to pay dividends, as well as the value of the stock when the shareholder sells their shares, depends on the company's ability to earn profits. Its profitability, in turn, depends on a large number of factors – the demand for its product, how much competition it faces, how much capital it has in place, whether its workers are unionized, how loyal its customers are, what kinds of government regulations and taxes it faces and so on. The job of fundamental analysts is to take all these factors into account to determine how much a share of stock in the company is worth.

If you want to rely on fundamental analysis to pick a stock portfolio, there are three ways to do it. One way is to do all the necessary research yourself, by reading through companies' annual reports and so forth. A second way is to rely on the advice of financial analysts. A third way is to buy into an investment fund, which has a manager (sometimes called a fund manager) who conducts fundamental analysis and makes the decision for you.

CRITICAL THINKING POINT The movement of stock prices is random and cannot be predicted, so what is the point of fundamental analysis?

SAVING AND INVESTMENT IN THE NATIONAL INCOME ACCOUNTS

Events that occur within the financial system are central to understanding developments in the overall economy. The institutions that make up this system – the bond market, the stock market, banks and investment funds – have the role of coordinating the economy's saving and investment. These in turn are important determinants of long-run growth in GDP and living standards. As a result, macroeconomists need to understand how financial markets work and how various events and policies affect them.

As a starting point for an analysis of financial markets, we discuss in this section the key macroeconomic variables that measure activity in these markets. Our emphasis here is on accounting. *Accounting* refers to how various numbers are defined and added up. A personal accountant might help an individual add up their income and expenses. A national income accountant does the same thing for the economy as a whole. The national income accounts include, in particular, GDP and the many related statistics.

Some Important Identities

The rules of national income accounting include several important identities. Recall that GDP is both total income in an economy and the total expenditure on the economy's output of goods and services. GDP (denoted as Y) is divided into four components of expenditure: consumption (C), investment (I), government purchases (G) and net exports (NX):

$$Y \equiv C + I + G + NX \qquad \textbf{(7.1)}$$

This equation is an identity because every euro of expenditure that shows up on the left-hand side also shows up in one of the four components on the right-hand side. Because of the way each of the variables is defined and measured, this equation must always hold. In general, though, we can use the usual equality sign:

$$Y = C + I + G + NX \qquad \textbf{(7.2)}$$

We will simplify our analysis by assuming that the economy we are examining is closed and does not interact with other economies, does not engage in international trade in goods and services, and does not engage in international borrowing and lending. Of course, actual economies are *open economies* – that is, they interact with other economies around the world. Assuming a closed economy is a useful simplification with which we can learn some lessons that apply to all economies.

Because a closed economy does not engage in international trade, imports and exports are exactly zero. Therefore, net exports (NX) are also zero, which leaves the identity:

$$Y = C + I + G \tag{7.3}$$

This equation states that GDP is the sum of consumption, investment and government purchases. Each unit of output sold in a closed economy is consumed, invested, or bought by the government.

To see what this identity can tell us about financial markets, if we take Y, on the left-hand side of the equation, to be GDP, we can subtract from this the things that are consumed (consumption spending and government spending). To retain the equation, we must also subtract C and G from the right-hand side, which gives:

$$Y - C - G = (C - C) + I + (G - G) \tag{7.4}$$

$$Y - C - G = I \tag{7.5}$$

What remains after paying for consumption and government purchases is called **national saving (saving)**, or just saving, and is denoted S. Recall from the circular flow of income diagram that there are withdrawals and injections from the circular flow. Saving is one of the withdrawals from the circular flow but reappears in the economy in the form of investment when savings are channelled by financial institutions.

national saving (saving) the total income in the economy that remains after paying for consumption and government purchases

Given $Y - C - G = S$ we can substitute this into equation 7.5 to get:

$$S = I \tag{7.6}$$

This equation states that saving equals investment.

To understand the meaning of national saving, it is helpful to manipulate the definition a bit more. Let T denote the amount that the government collects from households in taxes (a withdrawal from the circular flow) minus the amount it pays back to households in the form of transfer payments (such as social security payments). We can then write national saving in either of two ways:

$$S = Y - C - G \tag{7.7}$$

Or:

$$S = (Y - T - C) + (T - G) \tag{7.8}$$

Equations 7.7 and 7.8 are the same, because the two Ts in equation 7.8 cancel each other, but each reveals a different way of thinking about national saving. In particular, equation 7.8 separates national saving into two pieces: private saving ($Y - T - C$) and public saving ($T - G$).

Private saving is the amount of income that households have left after paying their taxes and paying for their consumption. In particular, because households receive income of Y, pay taxes of T and spend C on consumption, private saving is $Y - T - C$. **Public saving** is the amount of tax revenue that the government has left after paying for its spending. The government receives T in tax revenue and spends G on goods and services. If T exceeds G, the government runs a **budget surplus** because it receives more money than it spends. This surplus of $T - G$ represents public saving. If the government spends more than it receives in tax revenue, then G is larger than T. In this case, the government runs a **budget deficit**, and public saving, $T - G$, is a negative number. In this case the government must borrow money to fund spending by issuing sovereign debt in the form of bonds.

private saving the income that households have left after paying for taxes and consumption
public saving the tax revenue that the government has left after paying for its spending
budget surplus where government tax revenue is greater than spending because it receives more money than it spends
budget deficit where government tax revenue is less than spending and the government has to borrow to finance spending

Now consider how these accounting identities are related to financial markets. The equation $S = I$ reveals an important fact. For the economy as a whole, saving must be equal to investment. This fact raises some important questions: what mechanisms lie behind this identity? What coordinates those people who are deciding how much to save and those people who are deciding how much to invest? The answer is the financial system. The bond market, the stock market, banks, investment funds, and other financial markets and intermediaries, stand between the two sides of the $S = I$ equation. They take in the nation's saving and direct it to the nation's investment.

CASE STUDY Debt and Deficit

There have been two significant economic shocks in the twenty-first century. One was the 2007–9 Financial Crisis and the second was the Covid-19 pandemic that affected almost every country between 2019 and 2022. These two shocks brought the words 'debt' and 'deficit' into almost every household.

Economic shocks such as the Financial Crisis in 2007–9, the pandemic and global conflict can mean budget deficits increase but is additional borrowing a cause for concern?

Governments borrow money to finance their activities when tax revenue is insufficient to meet their needs. During Covid-19, for example, economic activity slowed considerably in many European countries, and many had to resort to borrowing to fund support packages for individuals, business and the investment in healthcare systems that were necessary. Borrowing involves two parties – the borrower (governments in this case) and the lender. A vital part of any successful financial system is the trust between both lenders and borrowers that, whatever is lent will, at some point, be paid back. In the aftermath of the 2007–9 Financial Crisis, it was not always clear whether some governments would default on borrowings. If this happens and trust breaks down, the financial system comes under severe pressure.

It is important to distinguish between government debt and a government deficit. A **government deficit** refers to a situation where a government spends more than it generates in tax revenue over a period and borrows to fund spending. For example, in June 2021, the UK government had to borrow £314.4 billion in the financial year to the end of March 2021, compared to £60.8 billion in the financial year to the end of March 2020 and £44.9 billion in the year to the end of March 2019. Expressed as a percentage of GDP, the 2021 deficit was around 15 per cent of GDP. In comparison, in 2009–10, immediately after the Financial Crisis, the deficit reached 10 per cent of GDP. The reason for this significant increase in borrowing in 2021 was the effects of the pandemic. From the peak of public sector new borrowing (PSNB) in 2020–21, the deficit has fallen with forecasts suggesting PSNB will fall to £70.6 billion in the fiscal year 2029–30.

(*Continued*)

government deficit a situation where a government spends more than it generates in tax revenue over a period
national debt the accumulation of the total debt owed by a government

The PSNB sum becomes part of the **national debt**, which is the accumulation of the total debt the government owes. In 2024, the Office for National Statistics (ONS) reported the national debt as £2.72 trillion. The national debt reported in 2020 stood at £1,875.7 billion, or £1.88 trillion. In 2021, the national debt had risen to £2,223 billion (£2.22 trillion) and is forecast to reach £3.4 trillion or £116,000 per household by 2029/30. Statistical offices also express PSNB and the national debt as a percentage of GDP. In 2019/20, PSNB as a percentage of GDP stood at 85.4 per cent rising to 96.6 per cent in 2020/21 and 98.4 per cent in 2024/25. It is forecast to ease back to 96.1 per cent by 2029/30. The national debt expressed as a percentage of GDP in quarter four of 2020 was 105.8 per cent whereas in quarter four of 2023, it was 101.3 per cent. The national debt is primarily made up of medium- and long-term bonds accounting for around 85 per cent. The remainder is made up of bills and short-term bonds, loans and currency and deposits.

This picture of increasing deficit and debt was mirrored across Europe. In 2019, 11 countries recorded budget surpluses, but all euro area countries recorded a deficit in 2020. In the second quarter of 2021, Eurostat reported that general government deficit to GDP stood at 6.3 per cent for the EU and the debt to GDP ratio stood at 98.3 per cent. Some individual countries in the EU had very high debt to GDP ratios. In Greece, for example, the debt to GDP ratio was over 207 per cent; in Italy, over 156 per cent; in Spain, 122.8 per cent; and in France, 114.6 per cent. Across the EU, the deficit has fallen since 2020. Some countries, such as Denmark, Cyprus, Ireland and Portugal, reported budget surpluses in 2023. The debt ratio in Greece had fallen to 163.9 per cent by the end of 2023.

Questions:

1 Why do you think that governments across Europe had to borrow more during the 2007–9 Financial Crisis?
2 Why might a country defaulting on its debt cause the financial system to 'come under pressure'?
3 Why do you think it is important to distinguish between government deficits and government debt?
4 To what extent do you think that governments should focus on reducing deficits in the coming years and why?

References:

commonslibrary.parliament.uk/research-briefings/sn02812/, accessed 7 August 2025.
ec.europa.eu/eurostat/web/products-euro-indicators/w/2-22102024-ap, accessed 7 August 2025.
ec.europa.eu/eurostat/statistics-explained/index.php?title=Government_finance_statistics_-_quarterly_data, accessed 7 August 2025.
www.ons.gov.uk/economy/governmentpublicsectorandtaxes/publicspending/bulletins/ukgovernmentdebtanddeficitforeurostatmaast/december2023, accessed 7 August 2025.

The Meaning of Saving and Investment

The terms *saving* and *investment* can sometimes be confusing. Most people use these terms casually and sometimes interchangeably. In contrast, the macroeconomists who put together the national income accounts use these terms carefully and distinctly.

Consider an example. Suppose that Connah earns more than he spends and deposits his unspent income in a bank or uses it to buy a bond or some stock from a corporation. Because Connah's income exceeds his consumption, he adds to the nation's saving. Connah might think of himself as 'investing' his money, but a macroeconomist would call Connah's act *saving* rather than *investment.*

In the language of macroeconomics, investment refers to the purchase of new capital, such as equipment or buildings. When Orla borrows from the bank to build herself a new house, she adds to the nation's investment. Similarly, when the O'Connell Corporation issues some new shares and uses the proceeds to build a new brass fittings factory, it also adds to the nation's investment.

Although the accounting identity $S = I$ shows that saving and investment are equal for the economy as a whole, this does not have to be true for every individual household or firm. Connah's saving can be greater than his investment, and he can deposit the excess in a bank. Orla's saving can be less than her investment, and she can borrow the shortfall from a bank. Banks and other financial institutions make these individual differences between saving and investment possible by allowing one person's saving to finance another person's investment.

SELF TEST Define private saving, public saving, national saving and investment. How are they related?

THE MARKET FOR LOANABLE FUNDS

This section will present a model of financial markets which can explain how financial markets coordinate the economy's saving and investment. The model also gives us a tool with which we can analyze various government policies that influence saving and investment.

To keep things simple, we assume that the economy has only one financial market, called the **market for loanable funds**. All savers go to this market to deposit their saving, and all borrowers go to this market to get their loans. Thus, the term *loanable funds* refers to all income that people have chosen to save and lend out, rather than use for their own consumption. In the market for loanable funds, there is one interest rate, which is both the return for saving and the cost of borrowing.

market for loanable funds the market in which those who want to save supply funds, and those who want to borrow to invest demand funds

The assumption of a single financial market, of course, is not literally true. As we have seen, the economy has many types of financial institutions. The purpose of this model is to provide a representative simplification which helps explain and predict.

Supply and Demand for Loanable Funds

The economy's market for loanable funds consists of the supply of and demand for loanable funds, and the price in this market is the interest rate. The supply of loanable funds comes from those people who have some extra income they want to save and lend out. This lending can occur directly, such as when a household buys a bond from a firm, or it can occur indirectly, such as when a household makes a deposit in a bank. The bank in turn uses the funds to make loans. In both cases, saving is the source of the supply of loanable funds.

The demand for loanable funds comes from households and firms who wish to borrow to make investments. This demand includes families taking out mortgages to buy homes, borrowing to buy a new car, and firms borrowing to buy new equipment or build factories. In each case, investment is the source of the demand for loanable funds.

The interest rate represents the amount that borrowers pay for loans and the amount that lenders receive on their saving. Because a high interest rate makes borrowing more expensive, the quantity of loanable funds demanded falls as the interest rate rises. Similarly, because a high interest rate makes saving more attractive, the quantity of loanable funds supplied rises as the interest rate rises. In other words, the demand curve for loanable funds slopes downwards, and the supply curve for loanable funds slopes upwards.

Figure 7.4 shows the interest rate that balances the supply and demand for loanable funds. In the equilibrium shown, the interest rate is 5 per cent, and the quantity of loanable funds demanded and the quantity of loanable funds supplied both equal €500 billion.

Shifts in the demand and supply of loanable funds bring about changes to the interest rate. If the interest rate was lower than the equilibrium level because of a shift in demand to the right or of supply to the left, the quantity of loanable funds supplied would be less than the quantity of loanable funds demanded.

The resulting shortage of loanable funds would encourage lenders to raise the interest rate they charge. A higher interest rate would encourage saving (thereby increasing the quantity of loanable funds supplied – a movement along the supply curve) and discourage borrowing for investment (thereby decreasing the quantity of loanable funds demanded, a movement along the demand curve). Conversely, if the demand for loanable funds shifts to the left or the supply of loanable funds shifts to the right, the quantity supplied would exceed the quantity demanded. As lenders competed for the scarce borrowers, interest rates would be driven down. In this way, the interest rate approaches the equilibrium level at which the supply and demand for loanable funds balance.

FIGURE 7.4

The Market for Loanable Funds

The model predicts that the interest rate in the economy adjusts to balance the supply and demand for loanable funds. The supply of loanable funds comes from national saving, including both private saving and public saving. The demand for loanable funds comes from firms and households that want to borrow for purposes of investment. Here the equilibrium interest rate is 5 per cent, and €500 billion of loanable funds are supplied and demanded.

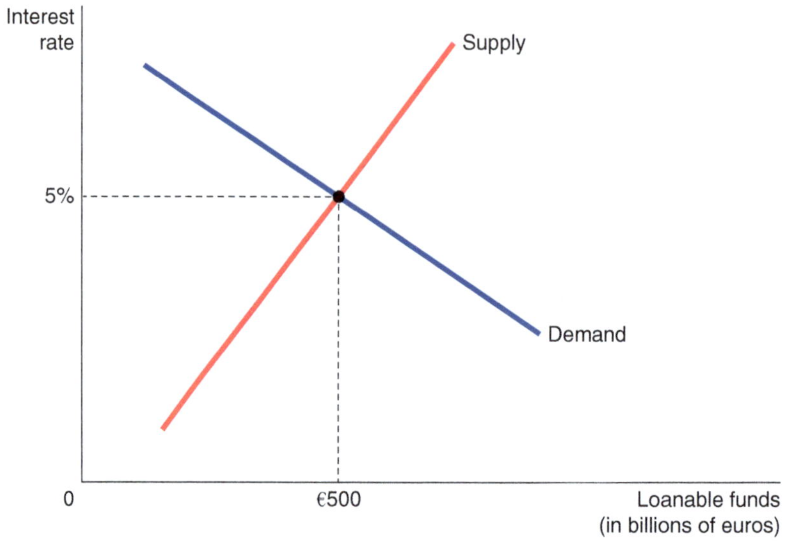

Recall that the real interest rate is the difference between the nominal interest rate and the inflation rate ($r_t = i_t - \pi_t$). The nominal interest rate is the interest rate as usually reported, that is the monetary return to saving and the cost of borrowing. Because inflation erodes the value of money over time, the real interest rate more accurately reflects the real return to saving and the cost of borrowing. Therefore, the supply and demand for loanable funds depends on the real (rather than nominal) interest rate. The equilibrium in Figure 7.4 should therefore be interpreted as determining the real interest rate in the economy. For the rest of this chapter, when you see the term *interest rate*, you should remember that we are talking about the *real interest rate*.

This model of the supply and demand for loanable funds shows that financial markets work much like other markets in the economy. The model predicts that the interest rate adjusts to balance supply and demand in the market for loanable funds. It coordinates the behaviour of people who want to save (the suppliers of loanable funds) and the behaviour of people who want to invest (the demanders of loanable funds).

We can now use this model to examine various government policies that affect the economy's saving and investment.

Policy 1: Saving Incentives

Recall that saving is an important long-run determinant of a nation's productivity. Hence if a country can raise its saving rate, the growth rate of GDP should increase (subject to the assumption of diminishing marginal productivity) and, over time, the citizens of that country should enjoy a higher standard of living.

Many economists have used the principle that people respond to incentives to suggest that the savings rates in some countries are depressed because of tax laws that discourage saving. Governments collect revenue by taxing income, including interest and dividend income. To see the effects of this policy, consider a 25-year-old who saves €1,000 and buys a 30-year bond that pays an interest rate of 9 per cent. In the absence of taxes, the €1,000 grows to €13,268 when the individual reaches age 55. Yet if that interest is taxed at a rate of, say, 33 per cent, then the after-tax interest rate is only 6 per cent. In this case, the €1,000 grows to only €5,743 after 30 years. The tax on interest income substantially reduces the future payoff from current saving and, as a result, reduces the incentive for people to save.

In response to this problem, many economists and some politicians have sometimes advocated replacing the current income tax with a consumption tax. Under a consumption tax, income that is saved would not be taxed until the saving is later spent. In essence, a consumption tax is like the VAT that European countries impose on many goods and services. VAT is an indirect tax, however, levied on a good or service at the time it is purchased by a final consumer. Consumption tax could also be a direct tax levied on an individual by calculating how much consumer expenditure they carried out over the year and taxing them on that, perhaps at higher rates as the level of consumer expenditure rises.

A more modest proposal is to expand eligibility for special savings accounts that allow people to shelter some of their saving from taxation. Let us consider the effect of such a saving incentive on the market for loanable funds, as illustrated in Figure 7.5.

FIGURE 7.5

An Increase in the Supply for Loanable Funds

A change in the tax laws to encourage more saving would shift the supply of loanable funds to the right from S_1 to S_2. As a result, the equilibrium interest rate would fall, and the lower interest rate would stimulate investment. Here the equilibrium interest rate falls from 5 per cent to 4 per cent, and the equilibrium quantity of loanable funds saved and invested rises from €500 billion to €600 billion.

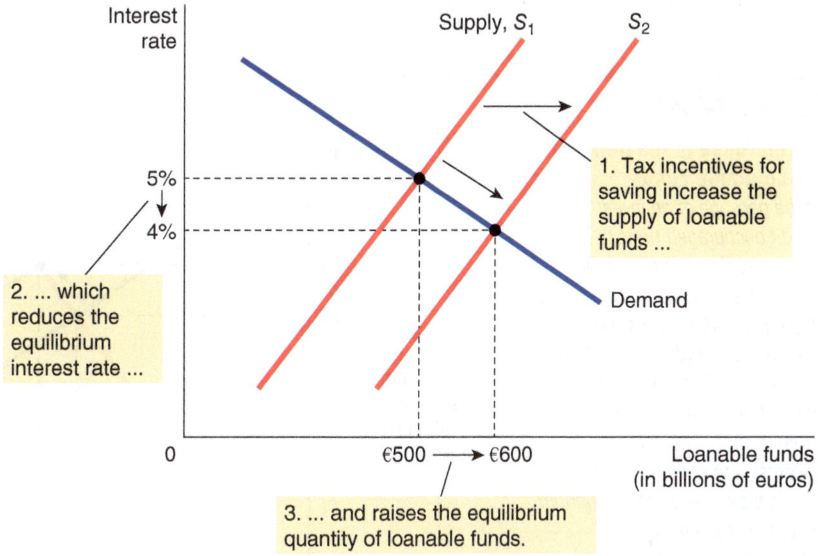

The tax change alters the incentive for households to save *at any given interest rate*. It would therefore affect the quantity of loanable funds supplied at each interest rate. The supply of loanable funds would shift. The demand for loanable funds would remain the same, because the tax change would not directly affect the amount that borrowers want to borrow at any given interest rate.

Because saving would be taxed less heavily, households would increase their saving by consuming a smaller fraction of their income. Households would use this additional saving to increase their deposits in banks or to buy more bonds. The supply of loanable funds would increase, and the supply curve would shift to the right from S_1 to S_2, as shown in Figure 7.5.

Finally, we compare the old and new equilibria. In the figure, the increased supply of loanable funds reduces the interest rate from 5 per cent to 4 per cent. The lower interest rate raises the quantity of loanable funds demanded from €500 billion to €600 billion. That is, the shift in the supply curve moves the market equilibrium along the demand curve. With a lower cost of borrowing, households and firms are motivated to borrow more to finance greater investment. Our model predicts that if a reform of the tax laws encouraged greater saving, the result would be lower interest rates and greater investment.

Although this analysis of the effects of increased saving is widely accepted among economists, there is less consensus about what kinds of tax changes should be enacted. Many economists endorse tax reform aimed at increasing saving to stimulate investment and growth. Yet others are sceptical that these tax changes would have much effect on national saving. Crucial to the outcome is the **interest elasticity of demand and supply**, which is the responsiveness of the demand and supply of loanable funds to changes in the interest rate.

Sceptics also doubt the equity of the proposed reforms. They argue that, in many cases, the benefits of the tax changes would accrue primarily to the wealthy, who are least in need of tax relief.

interest elasticity of demand and supply the responsiveness of the demand and supply of loanable funds to changes in the interest rate

Policy 2: Investment Incentives

Suppose that the government passed a tax reform aimed at making investment more attractive. In essence, this is what governments do when they institute tax allowances on investment, sometimes referred to as *investment tax credits*. These allowances give tax advantages to any firm building a new factory or buying a new piece of equipment. Let us consider the effect of such a tax reform on the market for loanable funds, as illustrated in Figure 7.6.

FIGURE 7.6

An Increase in the Demand for Loanable Funds

If the passage of an investment tax credit encouraged firms to invest more, the demand for loanable funds would increase. As a result, the equilibrium interest rate would rise, and the higher interest rate would stimulate saving. Here, when the demand curve shifts from D_1 to D_2, the equilibrium interest rate rises from 5 per cent to 6 per cent, and the equilibrium quantity of loanable funds saved and invested rises from €500 billion to €600 billion.

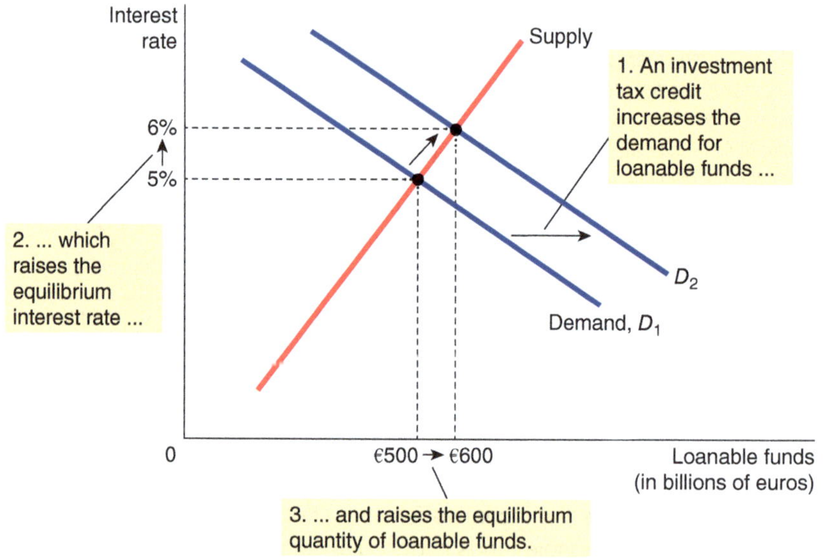

Tax allowances on investment reward firms that borrow and invest in new capital. The tax allowances alter investment at any given interest rate and thereby change the demand for loanable funds. By contrast, because the tax credit would not affect the amount that households save at any given interest rate, it would not affect the supply of loanable funds.

Because firms would have an incentive to increase investment at any interest rate, the quantity of loanable funds demanded would be higher at any given interest rate. Thus, the demand curve for loanable funds would move to the right, as shown by the shift from D_1 to D_2 in Figure 7.6.

The increased demand for loanable funds raises the interest rate from 5 per cent to 6 per cent. The higher interest rate in turn increases the quantity of loanable funds supplied from €500 billion to €600 billion, as households respond by increasing the amount they save (a movement along the supply curve). Thus, if a reform of the tax system encouraged greater investment, the result would be higher interest rates and greater saving.

Policy 3: Government Budget Deficits and Surpluses

Recall that a *budget deficit* is an excess of government spending over tax revenue. Governments finance budget deficits by borrowing in the bond market, and the accumulation of past government borrowing is called the government or national debt. A *budget surplus*, an excess of tax revenue over government spending, can be used to repay some of the government debt. If government spending exactly equals tax revenue, the government is said to have a *balanced budget*.

Imagine that the government starts with a balanced budget and then, because of a tax cut or a spending increase, starts running a budget deficit. Figure 7.7 shows what our model predicts will happen.

National saving – the source of the supply of loanable funds – is composed of private saving and public saving. A change in the government budget balance represents a change in public saving and thereby in the supply of loanable funds. Because the budget deficit does not influence the amount that households and firms want to borrow to finance investment at any given interest rate, it does not alter the demand for loanable funds.

FIGURE 7.7

The Effect of a Government Budget Deficit

When the government spends more than it receives in tax revenue, the resulting budget deficit lowers national saving. The supply of loanable funds decreases, and the equilibrium interest rate rises. Thus, when the government borrows to finance its budget deficit, it 'crowds out' households and firms who otherwise would borrow to finance investment. Here, when the supply shifts from S_1 to S_2, the equilibrium interest rate rises from 5 per cent to 6 per cent. In addition, the equilibrium quantity of loanable funds saved and invested falls from €500 billion to €300 billion.

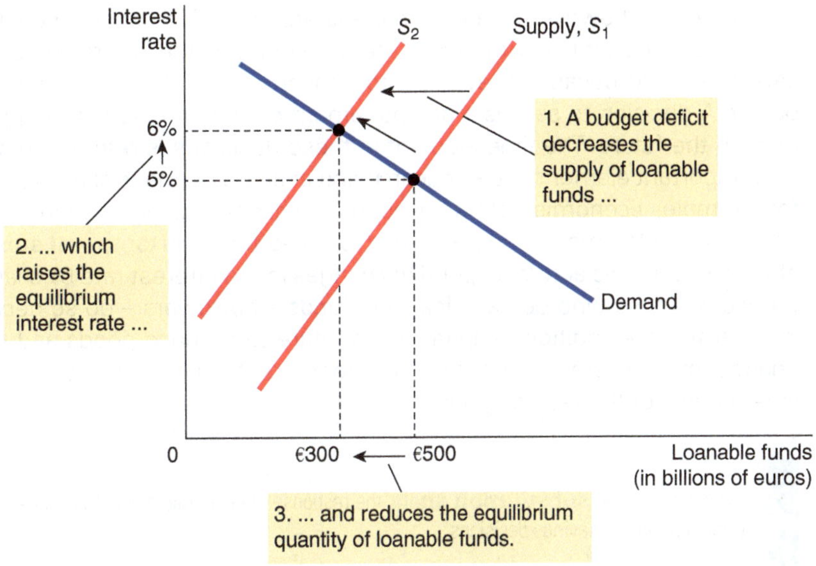

When the government runs a budget deficit, public saving is negative, and this reduces national saving. In other words, when the government borrows to finance its budget deficit, it reduces the supply of loanable funds available to finance investment by households and firms. Thus, a budget deficit shifts the supply curve for loanable funds to the left from S_1 to S_2, as shown in Figure 7.7.

In the figure, when the budget deficit reduces the supply of loanable funds, the interest rate rises from 5 per cent to 6 per cent. This higher interest rate then alters the behaviour of the households and firms that participate in the loan market. In particular, many demanders of loanable funds are discouraged by the higher interest rate (a movement along the demand curve). Fewer families buy new homes, and fewer firms choose to build new factories. The fall in investment because of government borrowing is called **crowding out** and is represented in the figure by the movement along the demand curve from a quantity of €500 billion in loanable funds to a quantity of €300 billion. That is, when the government borrows to finance its budget deficit, it crowds out private borrowers who are trying to finance investment.

crowding out a decrease in investment that results from government borrowing

Our model predicts that when the government reduces national saving by running a budget deficit, the interest rate rises and investment falls. Because investment is important for long-run economic growth, government budget deficits reduce the economy's growth rate. This analysis (and the assumptions underlying it) is the reason why many governments seek to reduce borrowing and is behind many of the austerity policies which were instituted across countries in Europe following the 2007–9 Financial Crisis.

Government budget surpluses work the opposite way to budget deficits. When government collects more in tax revenue than it spends, it saves the difference by retiring some of the outstanding government debt. This budget surplus, or public saving, contributes to national saving. Thus, a budget surplus increases the supply of loanable funds, reduces the interest rate and stimulates investment. Higher investment, in turn, means greater capital accumulation and more rapid economic growth.

Intertemporal Choice

We have seen that the financial system has the job of coordinating borrowing and lending activity. In many ways, financial markets are like other markets in the economy. The price of loanable funds – the interest rate – is governed by the forces of supply and demand, just as other prices in the economy are.

In one way, however, financial markets are special. Financial markets, unlike most other markets, serve the important role of linking the present and the future. Those who supply loanable funds – savers – do so because they want to convert some of their current income into future purchasing power. A decision to save is a postponement of consumption in the present to consumption at some point in the future. The time element in these decisions is referred to as *intertemporal choice* and is a very important element in the research and analysis of financial markets. When interest rates increase, for example, economic actors respond by changing consumption in time period t and postponing consumption to time period $t + n$. This is called the **intertemporal substitution effect** and is the rate at which economic actors respond to changes in the interest rate by changing consumption and savings decisions. Those who demand loanable funds – borrowers – do so because they want to invest today in order to have additional capital in the future to produce goods and services. Thus, well-functioning financial markets are important not only for current generations but also for future generations who will inherit many of the resulting benefits.

intertemporal substitution effect the response of economic actors to changes in the interest rate by changing consumption and savings decisions

SUMMARY

- Because savings can earn interest, a sum of money today is more valuable than the same sum of money in the future. A person can compare sums from different times using the concept of present value. The present value of any future sum is the amount that would be needed today, given prevailing interest rates, to produce that future sum.
- Because of diminishing marginal utility, most people are risk averse. Economic agents can reduce risk using insurance, through diversification, and by choosing a portfolio with lower risk and lower return.
- The value of an asset, such as a share of stock, equals the present value of the cash flows the owner of the share will receive, including the stream of dividends and the final sale price. If financial markets process available information rationally, a stock price will equal the best estimate of the value of the underlying business.
- The financial system of an advanced economy is made up of many types of financial institutions, such as the bond market, the stock market, banks and investment funds. All of these institutions act to direct the resources of households, who want to save some of their income, into the hands of households and firms who want to borrow.
- National income accounting identities reveal some important relationships among macroeconomic variables. In particular, for a closed economy, national saving must equal investment. Financial institutions are the mechanism through which the economy matches one person's saving with another person's investment.

- The interest rate is determined by the supply and demand for loanable funds. The supply of loanable funds comes from households who want to save some of their income and lend it out. The demand for loanable funds comes from households and firms who want to borrow for investment. To analyze how any policy or event affects the interest rate, we must consider how it affects the supply and demand for loanable funds.
- National saving equals private saving plus public saving. A government budget deficit represents negative public saving and, therefore, reduces national saving and the supply of loanable funds available to finance investment. When a government budget deficit crowds out investment, it reduces the growth of productivity and GDP.

IN THE NEWS

Budget Deficits, Budgets and Investment

Following the election of the Labour Party to power in the UK in 2024, there was much anticipation over the first budget presented by the Chancellor of the Exchequer, Rachel Reeves, in October of that year. Many commentators and economists recognized that the state of government finances was an issue that needed to be addressed. Equally, many also saw the need for the government to send clear signals around the challenges facing the UK economy in terms of its record on productivity and growth. The question was, how would the chancellor square the circle?

The key message from the government was around the need for investment and growth. The chancellor had stressed that she had inherited a very challenging public finance situation from the previous government, one the Conservative party was keen to deny. 'Repairing the public finances' was at the heart of the budget. To address this problem, the government announced changes to taxes with the goal of raising tax revenue. According to the Office for Budget Responsibility (OBR), budget policies aimed to increase spending by around £70 billion (or 2 per cent of GDP) each year for the next five years. This would be funded in part by an increase in tax revenues, with the burden for the increase falling mainly on employers, and through increased borrowing. The OBR forecast that there would be a 'temporary boost' to growth as a result of the policies but would 'leave GDP largely unchanged in five years'. The OBR also noted that 'the net fiscal loosening would crowd out some private investment in an economy with little spare capacity'.

©iStock/stocknshares

Government budget plans are widely scrutinized and invariably polarize opinions as to their impact on the economy and well-being.

Some critics of the budget noted that the increase in the tax burden on employers would likely increase the costs of employment and, if anything, might reduce incentives to invest rather than encourage investment. The plans to boost public spending on key areas such as the NHS and education were welcomed. Many however saw the plans as too little and the sums proposed too diluted to have any significant impact on the quality of service provision. The real-terms increase in spending on the NHS, for example, would not, it was argued, help it to move forward but would merely help it to 'stand still'. The OBR did forecast that interest rates would ease back to around 3.5 per cent by 2030. In the wake of the budget, it appeared that bond markets reacted with a degree of calm with interest rates on 10-year government bonds rising from around 4.2 per cent to about 4.45 per cent by the middle of November.

(Continued)

Critical Thinking Questions

1 In December 2024, the Consumer Prices Index (CPI) for the UK was 2.6 per cent. The Bank of England base rate was 4.75 per cent. Assume that a financial institution purchases £500 million of 10-year government bonds in January 2025 with a maturity in January 2035. What is the future value of this transaction for the institution? Explain your calculations and assumptions.

2 Using the basic information on the budget plans from October 2024 provided in the article, what predictions would you make as to the impact on the market for loanable funds and why? Use an appropriate diagram or diagrams to help illustrate your answer.

3 The OBR forecasted that the UK interest rate would fall to around 3.5 per cent by 2030. How might the model of the market for loanable funds be used to explain what might happen to the demand and/or supply of loanable funds to realize this outcome?

4 Why do you think the OBR suggested that the budget plans would involve some 'crowding out of private investment'?

5 Consider the basic proposals of the budget summarized in this article. To what extent do you think that the proposals will lead to an increase in investment and economic growth? You can use events since the budget of October 2024 to help support your argument.

References:

www.bankofengland.co.uk/monetary-policy/the-interest-rate-bank-rate, accessed 7 August 2025.
obr.uk/docs/dlm_uploads/OBR_Economic_and_fiscal_outlook_Oct_2024.pdf, accessed 7 August 2025.

QUESTIONS FOR REVIEW

1 Outline the concept of present value. The interest rate is 7 per cent. Use the concept of present value to compare €200 to be received in 10 years and €300 to be received in 20 years.

2 What benefit do people get from the market for insurance? What two problems impede the insurance company from working porfootly?

3 What is meant by the term 'fundamental analysis'?

4 What is diversification? Does a shareholder get more diversification going from 1 to 10 stocks or going from 100 to 120 stocks?

5 Why is knowledge of whether people are risk averse or risk seeking important in financial markets?

6 What is the role of the financial system? Name and describe two markets that are part of the financial system in the economy of the country in which you are studying. What is a financial intermediary? Name and describe two financial intermediaries.

7 What is national saving? What is private saving? What is public saving? How are these three variables related?

8 What is investment? How is it related to national saving?

9 Describe a change in the tax system that might increase private saving. If this policy were implemented, how would it affect the market for loanable funds?

10 What is a government budget deficit? How does it affect interest rates, investment and economic growth?

PROBLEMS AND APPLICATIONS

1 Assume the interest rate is 6 per cent. In each of the following three cases, state which you would rather receive and briefly explain why:

a. €200 today or €480 in two years?

b. €205 today or €240 in one year?

c. €1,000 in one year or €1,220 in two years?

2 A company has an investment project that would cost €10 million today and yield a payoff of €15 million in four years.
   a. Should the firm undertake the project if the interest rate is 11 per cent? 10 per cent? 9 per cent? 8 per cent?
   b. Can you work out the exact cut-off for the interest rate between profitability and non-profitability?

3 A company faces two kinds of risk. An idiosyncratic risk is that a competitor might enter its market and take some of its customers. An aggregate risk is that the economy might enter a recession, reducing sales. Which of these two risks would more likely cause the company's shareholders to demand a higher return? Why?

4 Sam has a utility function $U = w^{0.5}$, where w is her wealth in millions of euros and U is the utility she obtains from that wealth. Sam has made it through to the final stage of a game show. The host offers Sam a choice between (i) €4 million for sure, or (ii) a gamble that pays €1 million with probability 0.6, and €9 million with probability 0.4.
   a. Graph Sam's utility function. Is she risk averse? Explain.
   b. Does (i) or (ii) offer Sam a higher expected prize? Explain your reasoning with appropriate calculations. (Hint: The expected value of a random variable is the weighted average of the possible outcomes, where the probabilities are the weights.)
   c. Does (i) or (ii) offer Sam a higher expected utility? Again, show your calculations.
   d. Should Sam pick (i) or (ii)? Why?

5 For each of the following pairs, which bond would you expect to pay a higher interest rate? Explain.
   a. A bond of the UK government or a bond of an east European government.
   b. A bond that repays the principal in year 2032 or a bond that repays the principal in year 2043.
   c. A bond from Siemens or a bond from a software company operating from a business park on the outskirts of a large city.
   d. A bond issued by the national government or a bond issued by a local authority.

6 What factors might affect the decisions of economic actors to save more today for consumption in the future? Why are the decisions of economic actors today important for the welfare of economic actors in the future?

7 How might you go about pricing the risk on the following:
   a. The price of a 10-year bond from the Portuguese government
   b. The price of a 10-year bond from the German government
   c. The construction of a new oil well off the South African coast.

8 Explain the difference between saving and investment as defined by a macroeconomist. Which of the following situations represent investment? Saving? Explain.
   a. Your family takes out a mortgage and buys a new house.
   b. You use your €500 wage payment to buy stock in Volkswagen.
   c. Your flatmate earns €200 and deposits it in their account at a bank.
   d. You borrow €5,000 from a bank to buy a car to use in your pizza delivery business.

9 Suppose that Ørsted is considering the development of a new offshore wind farm in the North Sea.
   a. Assuming that Ørsted needs to borrow money in the bond market to finance the project, why would an increase in interest rates affect Ørsted's decision about whether to carry out the development?
   b. If Ørsted has enough of its own funds to finance the development of the new wind farm without borrowing, would an increase in interest rates still affect Ørsted's decision about whether to undertake the new project? Explain.

10 Suppose the government borrows €5 billion more next year than this year.
   a. Use a supply-and-demand diagram to analyze this policy. Does the interest rate rise or fall?
   b. What happens to investment? To private saving? To public saving? To national saving? Compare the size of the changes to the €5 billion of extra government borrowing.
   c. How does the elasticity of supply of loanable funds affect the size of these changes?
   d. How does the elasticity of demand for loanable funds affect the size of these changes?
   e. Suppose households believe that greater government borrowing today implies higher taxes to pay off the government debt in the future. What does this belief do to private saving and the supply of loanable funds today? Does it increase or decrease the effects discussed in parts (a) and (b)?

8 THE MONETARY SYSTEM

One of the key requirements of a capitalist system is the use of a medium of exchange or money. Prices are invariably denominated in money. The monetary system includes not only the question about what constitutes money but also involves consideration of how we price goods and services in money terms and how this changes over time. Paper and metals used as money have no intrinsic value, but their use in society is based on the trust that it will be accepted in exchange. Credit and debit cards and contactless payment systems are also widely used now, because it is accepted that money will be transferred more or less instantly from one bank account to another. The way in which we use money to attach a price to goods and services leads to questions about how and why prices change over time and the effects of such price changes.

Price rises over time can vary quite considerably. Post–World War I Germany experienced a spectacular example of a rise in the price level. The price of a newspaper rose from 0.30 marks in January 1921 to 70,000,000 marks less than two years later. Other prices rose by similar amounts. This period of significant price rises had such an adverse effect on the German economy that it is often viewed as one contributor to the rise to power of the National Socialists (Nazis) and, as a result, World War II.

The social custom of using money for transactions is extraordinarily useful in a large, complex society. Prior to the development of capitalist societies, many people relied on **barter** – the exchange of one good or service for another – to obtain the things they needed. A capitalist economy would not function if it relied on barter, primarily because trade would require the **double coincidence of wants**, which is a situation where parties to an exchange each have a good or service that the other wants.

barter the exchange of one good or service for another
double coincidence of wants a situation in exchange where two parties each have a good or service that the other wants and can thus enter into an exchange

The existence of money makes trade easier. As money flows from person to person in the economy, determined by the prices that are involved in exchange, it facilitates production and trade, thereby allowing specialization. In this chapter we begin to examine the role of money and prices in an economy. Because money is so important, we devote much effort in the rest of this book to learning how changes in the quantity of money affect various economic variables, including inflation, interest rates, production and employment. Consistent with our long-run focus, we will examine the long-run effects of changes in the quantity of money and the theory of inflation.

THE MEANING OF MONEY

Money is the set of assets in the economy that people regularly use to buy goods and services from other people. Cash is money because it can be used to buy a meal at a restaurant or a ticket to a music festival. By contrast, if you happened to own part of Meta, as Mark Zuckerberg does, you would be wealthy, but this asset is not considered a form of money. You could not buy a meal or a festival ticket with this wealth without first obtaining some cash. According to the economist's definition, money includes only those few types of wealth that are regularly accepted by sellers in exchange for goods and services.

money the set of assets in an economy that people regularly use to buy goods and services from other people

The Functions of Money

Money has three functions in the economy: it is a medium of exchange, a unit of account and a store of value. These three functions together distinguish money from other assets in the economy, such as stocks, bonds, residential property and works of art.

A Medium of Exchange When a buyer and seller enter into a transaction money acts as the **medium of exchange**, the item that buyers give to sellers when they purchase goods and services. This transfer of money from buyer to seller allows the transaction to take place. When you walk into a shop, you are confident that the shop will accept your money for the items it is selling because money is the commonly accepted medium of exchange.

medium of exchange an item that buyers give to sellers when they want to purchase goods and services

A Unit of Account In a market economy, buyers and sellers need a way in which they can measure and record transactions and draw comparisons. A **unit of account** is the measure people use to post prices and record debts. When you go shopping, you might observe that a pair of shoes is priced at €80 and a cheese sandwich at €2. Even though it would be accurate to say that the price of a pair of shoes is 40 sandwiches and the price of a sandwich is $\frac{1}{40}$ of a pair of shoes, prices are not quoted in this way. Similarly, if you take out a loan in euros or pounds from a bank, the size of your future loan repayments will be measured in euros or pounds, not in a quantity of goods and services. When we want to measure and record economic value, we use money as the unit of account.

unit of account the measure people use to post prices and record debts

A Store of Value When a seller accepts money today in exchange for a good or service, that seller can hold the money and become a buyer of another good or service at another time. A **store of value** is an item that people can use to transfer purchasing power from the present to the future. Money is not the only store of value in the economy, for a person can also transfer purchasing power from the present to the future by holding other assets. The term **wealth** is used to refer to the total of all stores of value, including both money and non-monetary assets.

store of value an item that people can use to transfer purchasing power from the present to the future
wealth the total of all stores of value, including both money and non-monetary assets

Liquidity

Economists use the term **liquidity** to describe the ease with which an asset can be converted into the economy's medium of exchange. Because money is the economy's medium of exchange, it is the most liquid asset available. Other assets vary widely in their liquidity. Most stocks and bonds can be sold easily with small cost, so they are relatively liquid assets. By contrast, selling a car or a piece of artwork requires more time and effort, so these assets are less liquid.

liquidity the ease with which an asset can be converted into the economy's medium of exchange

When people decide in what form to hold their wealth, they must balance the liquidity of each possible asset against its usefulness as a store of value. Money may be the most liquid asset, but it is far from perfect as a store of value. When prices rise, the value of money falls. In other words, when goods and services become more expensive, each euro or pound in your pocket can buy less.

The Kinds of Money

When money takes the form of a commodity with intrinsic value, it is called **commodity money**. The term *intrinsic value* means that the item would have value even if it were not used as money. One example of commodity money is gold. Gold has intrinsic value because it is used in industry and in the making of jewellery. Although today we no longer use gold as money, historically gold has been a common form of money because it is relatively easy to carry, measure and verify for impurities. When an economy uses gold as money (or uses paper money that is convertible into gold on demand), it is said to be operating under a **gold standard**.

commodity money money that takes the form of a commodity with intrinsic value
gold standard a system in which the currency is based on the value of gold and where the currency can be converted into gold on demand

Although gold has, historically, been the most common form of commodity money, other commodity monies have been used from time to time. For example, in the hyperinflation in Zimbabwe in the early 2000s, the country's people began to lose faith in the Zimbabwean dollar. People began to trade goods and services with one another, using cigarettes as the store of value, unit of account and medium of exchange.

Money without intrinsic value is called **fiat money**. A fiat is simply an order or decree, and fiat money is established as money by government decree. For example, paper euros are able to circulate as legal tender in 19 European countries because the governments of those countries have decreed that the euro is valid currency in each of their economies.

fiat money money without intrinsic value that is used as money because of government decree

Although governments are central to establishing and regulating a system of fiat money (by having a monopoly in issuing notes and coins and prosecuting counterfeiters, for example), other factors are also required for the success of such a monetary system. To a large extent, the acceptance of fiat money depends as much on expectations and social convention as on government decree. Zimbabweans preferred to accept cigarettes (or US dollars) in exchange for goods and services, because they were more confident that these alternative monies would be accepted by others in the future.

Money in the Economy

As we will see, the quantity of money circulating in the economy, called the **money stock**, has a powerful influence on many economic variables.

money stock the quantity of money circulating in the economy

In determining the money stock, the most obvious asset to include is **currency** – the paper notes and metal coins in the hands of the public. Currency is clearly the most widely accepted medium of exchange in a modern economy.

currency the paper banknotes and coins in the hands of the public

Yet currency is not the only asset you can use to buy goods and services. Most businesses also accept payment by debit card, which allows money to be transferred electronically between bank accounts.

A debit card is not really money in itself; it is the bank account on which the debit card draws which contains the money. A debit card is just a *means* of transferring money between accounts. Credit cards are not really a method of payment but a method of *deferring* payment. When you buy a meal with a credit card, the bank that issued the card pays the restaurant what it is due. In other words, you have effectively borrowed from the bank. At a later date, you will have to repay the bank (perhaps with interest). When the time comes to pay your credit card bill, you will probably do so by direct transfer from your current account. The balance in this current account is part of the economy's stock of money. Notice that credit cards are very different from debit cards, which automatically withdraw funds from a bank account to pay for items bought. A restaurateur is willing to accept payment by credit card because they get money immediately by having their bank account credited for the price of the meal, even though you do not have to pay the credit card company back immediately. Again, however, it is the underlying movement in the restaurateur's bank balance that matters.

Thus although debit cards and credit cards can each be used to settle the restaurant bill, neither of them is money – they are each a method of transferring money between bank accounts. The true movement in money occurs when bank balances change.

Wealth held in current bank accounts, therefore, is almost as convenient for buying things as wealth held as cash. Measures of the money stock include **demand deposits**, which are balances in bank accounts that depositors can access *on demand* simply by using their debit card. It is not only balances in current accounts that are part of the money stock; there are a large variety of other accounts that people hold at banks and other financial institutions. Bank depositors usually cannot use their debit cards against the balances in their savings accounts, but they can (mostly) easily transfer funds from savings into current accounts. In addition, depositors in money market funds can often use debit cards against their balances. Thus these other accounts should plausibly be counted as part of the money stock.

demand deposits balances in bank accounts that depositors can access on demand, for example by using a debit card

In a complex economy, it is, in general, not easy to draw a line between assets that can be called 'money' and assets that cannot. The coins in your pocket are clearly part of the money stock, and your smartphone clearly is not, even though you can use your smartphone for making payments in many cases, but there are many assets for which the choice is less clear. Therefore various measures of the money stock are available for advanced economies. Figure 8.1 shows the three most important measures for the euro area, in cumulative billions of euros in October 2024. M1 is a 'narrow' measure, M2, an 'intermediate' measure and M3 a 'broad' measure. Each of these measures uses a slightly different criterion for distinguishing between monetary and non-monetary assets.

In the UK, the most widely observed measures of the money stock are M0 (a narrower measure than the European M1, corresponding to notes and coins in circulation plus banks' balances held with the Bank of England) and M4 (a broad measure, similar – but not identical – to the European M3).

For our purposes in this book, we need not dwell on the differences between the various measures of money. The important point is that the money stock for an advanced economy includes not just currency but also deposits in banks and other financial institutions that can be readily accessed and used to buy goods and services.

FIGURE 8.1

Three Measures of the Money Stock for the Euro Area (Millions of Euros), October 2024

The graph shows the three measures of euro area money stock. M1 (a 'narrow' monetary aggregate that comprises currency in circulation and overnight deposits), M2 (an 'intermediate' monetary aggregate that comprises M1 plus deposits with an agreed maturity of up to two years and deposits redeemable at notice of up to three months) and M3 (a 'broad' monetary aggregate that comprises M2 plus repurchase agreements, money market fund shares and units as well as debt securities with a maturity of up to two years).

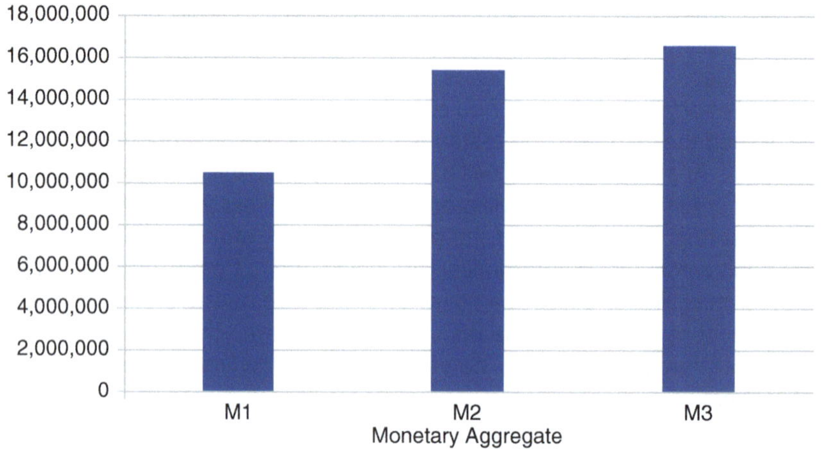

Source: European Central Bank, Frankfurt am Main, Germany

SELF TEST List and describe the three functions of money.

CASE STUDY The 'True' Austrian Money Supply

As with many aspects of economics, definitions of the money supply are open to different interpretations. The role of the money supply is going to be central to much of the analysis in the rest of this book. However, do note that if the measure of the money supply being used varies, then it is likely that the analysis and the conclusions drawn will also vary. Fortunately, economists of almost every persuasion are in agreement that currency – notes and coins – are a part of the money supply. What else should count as money and thus be part of the accepted definition is subject to different interpretations. One example is the so-called 'True' Austrian definition of the money supply put forward by the Austrian economist Ludwig von Mises in his *Theory of Money and Credit*, published in 1953. Von Mises defined the money supply as standard money plus money substitutes. Standard money he defined as notes and coins in circulation, or currency.

Money substitutes are more challenging to define, but von Mises suggested that money substitutes must be perfectly secure and immediately convertible. In other words, they must be evidence of the ownership of standard money and be a claim to money in the present. By this definition, a number of the elements of the measured money supply by central banks across the world, including the European Central Bank and the Bank of England, would not be considered as being part of the money supply and, according to economists from this school, represent a flawed measure.

The reason is that some of these elements represent the individual giving up a claim to money in the present for some promise of money in the future. For the claim to be liquidated, a further transaction has to be made sometime in the future, and as such the credit claim is not immediately convertible. For example, savings deposits at commercial banks would be included as part of M2 in many countries. Such

(*Continued*)

deposits, however, have legal terms under which they can be liquidated, for example the provision of a 30-day notice period given to the bank. As such they represent a credit claim and not a money substitute. Under the Austrian school definition, time deposits and money funds would also be classed as credit claims and thus not money substitutes.

An economist at the Mises Institute in the United States, Dr Frank Shostak, provides some clarification of the difference between a money substitute and a credit claim in an essay published in 2000 (Shostak, F. (2000) 'The Mystery of the Money Supply'. *Quarterly Journal of Austrian Economics*, 3(4):

© iStock/ronstik

What is classed as 'money' has different interpretations.

> *Once an individual places his (sic) money in a bank's warehouse he is in fact engaging in a claim transaction. In depositing his money, he never relinquishes his ownership. No one else is expected to make use of it. When Joe stores his money with a bank, he continues to have an unlimited claim against it and is entitled to take charge of it at any time. Consequently, these deposits, labelled demand deposits, are part of money.*

This must be contrasted with a credit transaction in which the lender of money relinquishes their claim over the money for the duration of the loan. Credit always involves a creditor's purchase of a future good in exchange for a present good. As a result, in a credit transaction, money is transferred from a lender to a borrower.

The debate over what is and what is not money is not simply academic; it is important for policymaking. After all, we would not use an unaccepted measure of temperature in situations where maintaining a specific level of heat or cold is required, because of the disastrous consequences that could result. If we use incorrect measures of the money supply, it follows that the consequences could be equally serious.

Questions:

1 Assume that a number of individuals hold accounts at the EconBank. Each has a stable balance of €10,000. Would this sum of money be counted as part of the money supply in most central banks? Explain.

2 Now assume that EconBank suffers a catastrophic failure and is in danger of collapse. Would economists who subscribe to the Austrian school still consider the balances to be part of the money supply? Explain.

3 To what extent do you agree with the view that deposits in a savings account which has restrictions on how and when a person can turn their savings into cash should not be classed as part of the money supply? Justify your reasoning.

THE ROLE OF CENTRAL BANKS

Whenever an economy relies on a system of fiat money – as all modern advanced economies do – many (but not all) economists believe that some agency must be responsible for regulating the system. This agency is generally known as the **central bank** – an institution designed to regulate the quantity of money made available in the economy, called the **money supply**. Two of the most important central banks in Europe are the European Central Bank and the Bank of England. Other major central banks around the world include the US Federal Reserve, the Bank of Japan and the People's Bank of China.

central bank an institution designed to regulate the quantity of money in the economy
money supply the quantity of money available in the economy

The Functions of Central Banks

Most central banks have two main functions. Macroeconomic stability is the maintenance of stable growth and prices and the avoidance of excessive and damaging swings in economic activity. The second main function is the maintenance of stability in the financial system. To achieve the first function, central banks have the power to increase or decrease the amount of currency in that economy. The set of actions taken by the central bank to affect the money supply is known as **monetary policy**.

monetary policy the set of actions taken by the central bank to affect the money supply

We will later discuss how a central bank actually changes the money supply, but it is worth noting here that an important tool the central bank can use is **open market operations**. This is the purchase and sale of non-monetary assets from and to the banking sector. For example, if the central bank decides to increase the money supply, it can do this by 'creating currency' through buying bonds in the bond market. After the purchase, the extra currency is in the hands of former bond holders (or more specifically, in their bank accounts). Thus an open market purchase of bonds by the central bank increases the money supply. Conversely, if the central bank decides to decrease the money supply, it can do this by selling bonds from its portfolio. After the sale, the currency it receives for the bonds leads to a reduction in bank accounts. Thus open market sale of bonds by the central bank decreases the money supply.

open market operations the purchase and sale of non-monetary assets from and to the banking sector by the central bank

The central bank of an economy is an important institution because changes in the money supply can profoundly affect the economy. For reasons we discuss more fully in later chapters, the central bank's policy decisions have an important influence on the economy's rate of inflation in the long run and the economy's employment and production in the short run. In particular, because of the link between the amount of money in the economy and the inflation rate, the central bank is often tasked as the guardian of price stability in a modern economy and is charged with the duty to maintain inflation at or near an inflation target. To be precise, the central bank should perhaps be thought of as the guardian of inflation stability, rather than price stability, since even with a constant, low rate of inflation, prices are, by definition, rising. If inflation is low and stable, prices might be said to be rising in a stable fashion – and, in any case, this usage is now well established, so we will follow suit.

Lender of Last Resort To maintain financial stability, central banks use their relationship with the rest of the banking system to supply liquidity, which is the cash needed to ensure transactions in the financial system are honoured. Banks have both long-term and short-term assets and also have deposits on demand which can be withdrawn at any time. At any time, therefore, banks can run short of the liquidity necessary to meet their obligations and the central bank steps in to provide the funds necessary to ensure that banks can continue to operate. This function is referred to as *lender of last resort*. In most cases, banks are not insolvent, they are simply short of funds at a particular time. The central bank can provide short-term loans to the banking system to ease the flow of funds in the system and ensure liquidity.

Many central banks are also tasked with the responsibility to monitor the banking system and supervise and regulate the system. Central banks assess banks' ability to meet different levels of financial stress and impose regulations to ensure that banks operate in a prudent manner.

THE EUROPEAN CENTRAL BANK AND THE EUROSYSTEM

The **European Central Bank (ECB)**, located in Frankfurt, Germany, was officially created on 1 June 1998 as a number of European countries had decided that they wished to enter European Monetary Union (EMU) and have the same currency – the euro – circulating among them. We will discuss the pros and cons of monetary union in a later chapter. For now, though, we just note that if a group of countries has the same currency, then it makes sense for the countries in the group to have a common monetary policy, and the ECB was set up for precisely this purpose. There were originally 11 countries making up the euro area: Austria, Belgium, Finland, France, Germany, Ireland, Italy, Luxembourg, the Netherlands, Portugal and Spain. By 2010, there were 16 countries, the new additions being Cyprus, Greece, Malta, Slovakia and Slovenia. Estonia adopted the euro in 2011, Latvia in 2014, Lithuania in 2015 and Croatia in 2023 to make the euro area, at the time of writing, consist of 20 countries.

European Central Bank (ECB) the overall central bank of the 20 countries comprising the European Monetary Union

The primary objective of the ECB is to promote price stability throughout the euro area and to design and implement monetary policy that is consistent with this objective. The ECB operates with the assistance of the national central banks in each of the euro area countries, such as the Banque de France, the Banca d'Italia, the Bank of Greece and the German Bundesbank. The network made up of the ECB together with the 20 euro area national central banks is termed the **eurosystem**.

eurosystem the system made up of the ECB plus the national central banks of each of the 20 countries comprising the European Monetary Union

The implementation of monetary policy by the ECB is under the control of the Executive Board, which comprises the President and Vice President of the ECB and four other people of high standing in the banking profession. While the Executive Board – as the name suggests – is responsible for *executing* monetary policy, the monetary policy of the ECB is actually designed by the Governing Council, which comprises the whole of the Executive Board plus the governors of the national central banks in the eurosystem (29 people in total). The Governing Council, which meets twice a month in Frankfurt, is the most important decision-making body of the ECB and decides, for example, on the level of the ECB's key interest rate, the refinancing rate. The Governing Council also decides how to interpret its duty to achieve price stability. The official definition of the ECB's monetary policy strategy is focused on 'targeting an inflation rate of 2 per cent over the medium term'.

An important feature of the ECB and of the eurosystem in general is its independence. When performing eurosystem-related tasks, neither the ECB, nor a national central bank, nor any member of their decision-making bodies is allowed to seek or take instructions from any external body, including any member governments or any EU institutions.

The President of the ECB and other members of the Executive Board are appointed for a minimum non-renewable term of office of eight years. A system of staggered appointments was used for the first Executive Board for members other than the President in order to ensure continuity. The governors of the 20 national central banks in the eurosystem are appointed for a minimum renewable term of office of five years.

THE BANK OF ENGLAND

The Bank of England was founded in 1694, although it is not the oldest European central bank (the Swedish Riksbank was founded in 1668). Arguably the most significant event in the Bank of England's more than 330-year history was when the UK government granted it independence in the setting of interest rates in 1997, which was formalized in an Act of Parliament in 1998. The important body within the Bank that makes the decision on the level at which to set the Bank's key interest rate, the repo rate, is the Monetary Policy Committee (MPC). The MPC consists of the Governor and three Deputy Governors for Monetary Policy, Financial Stability, and Markets and Banking; plus the Chief Economist at the Bank of England and four external members appointed by the Chancellor of the Exchequer (the UK finance minister). Members of the MPC serve fixed terms but can be reappointed. The MPC meets eight times a year, roughly every six weeks, and its interest rate decision is announced immediately after the meeting.

The Bank of England's mission is to 'promote the good of the people of the United Kingdom by maintaining monetary and financial stability'. The definition of price stability for the UK is given by the UK government and, in particular, the Chancellor of the Exchequer. The 1998 Bank of England Act requires that the Chancellor write to the Governor of the Bank of England once a year to specify how price stability is to be defined. Currently, the inflation target of 2 per cent is expressed in terms of an annual rate of inflation based on the CPI. If the target is missed by more than one percentage point on either side,that is if the annual rate of CPI inflation is more than 3 per cent or less than 1 per cent, the Governor of the Bank of England must write an open letter to the Chancellor explaining the reasons why inflation has increased or fallen to such an extent. It also outlines what the Bank proposes to do to ensure inflation comes back to target.

In changes made to financial regulation in the UK in June 2010, the Chancellor of the Exchequer announced that the Bank of England would have new responsibilities focusing on monetary policy and financial stability, which were confirmed in the Financial Services Bill 2012. The new system led to the Bank of England having additional responsibilities for financial stability, macroprudential supervision and oversight of microprudential supervision. These regulatory functions are overseen by three main groups, the Prudential Regulatory Authority (PRA), which is responsible for day-to-day supervision of bank safety and soundness (microprudential policy); the Financial Policy Committee (FPC), charged with 'identifying, monitoring and addressing systemic risks to the UK financial system'; and the Financial Conduct Authority (FCA), which manages protection of investors, market supervision and regulation, and the conduct of banks and financial services.

BANKS AND THE MONEY SUPPLY

Central banks play a crucial role in the monetary system. Most firms in the banking sector exist to make a profit. While there are numerous differences between financial intermediaries which make up the banking sector, we will assume they all have in common the basic function of accepting deposits and making loans. Banks must monitor their balance sheets, which consist of assets and liabilities. Most banks will earn interest on assets and pay interest on liabilities. The difference between the average interest a bank earns on its assets and the average interest rate paid on its liabilities is termed the **spread** and is a primary determinant of the profit a bank makes. We say 'most banks' because banks operating under Islamic Shariah principles do not base operations on interest (Riba) but instead share risk and reward between lenders and borrowers.

> **spread** the difference between the average interest banks earn on assets and the average interest rate paid on liabilities

A Bank's Balance Sheet

A bank's balance sheet consists of its assets and liabilities. A bank's assets might include reserves of cash, securities it holds and loans. Its liabilities include demand deposits, savings deposits, borrowings from other banks in the interbank market and, if it is a public limited company, equity capital. Its assets must equal its liabilities plus equity capital.

Banks must maintain sufficient funds to cover possible withdrawals. Some of a bank's reserves are held at the central bank, and the bank can instruct the central bank to transfer funds from its account to that of other banks in settling transactions. It is important to note that the amount of reserves does not, in itself, act as a constraint to a bank in the amount it lends.

In his book, *The End of Alchemy: Money, Banking and the Future of the Global Economy* (King, M. (2016) London: Little Brown), former Governor of the Bank of England, Mervyn King, stresses one of the major problems in banking which contributed to the 2007–9 Financial Crisis and which is of relevance to the nature of assets and liabilities in banks. King refers to the process by which banks take in deposits and make loans as 'alchemy'. He notes that banks can raise finance through taking in or creating deposits, issuing other debt instruments and increasing equity in the bank. King comments that many banks have only a relatively small proportion of loans on their balance sheets and that other types of borrowing provide a significant source of finance. Banks do not just take in deposits and make loans, he suggests. A critical feature of the 'alchemy' to which King refers is the fact that most banks have assets that are mostly long term in nature and liabilities which are short term. Part of the reason for this is that long-term assets generate greater returns. However, King notes that:

> *[t]he notion that a bank can offer safe returns on deposits that can be withdrawn at a moment's notice by using them to finance long-term illiquid risky investments is, as common sense would suggest, generally false ... The transmutation of bank deposits – money – with a safe value into illiquid risky investments is the alchemy of money and banking. Despite innumerable banking crises, belief in the alchemy persists.* (p. 104)

It is worth keeping this point in mind as we progress through the chapter and in later discussions on central bank policy and the 2007–9 Financial Crisis. Many people argue that King's words still have relevance and that lessons have not been fully learned from the Financial Crisis.

Broad measures of the money supply include bank deposits and currency. According to the Bank of England, bank deposits of various kinds account for around 97 per cent of broad money in the UK, with currency making up the other 3 per cent. Banks do not sit around waiting for customers to walk through their doors and deposit money, and then use this money to lend to other people and businesses. Banks actively find ways of making new loans. This might be in the form of granting a loan to a business for expansion or the purchase of new plant and equipment. It might be a loan to an individual to buy a car, or the granting of a mortgage to a couple seeking to buy a house. In granting a loan, the bank credits the account of the borrower with the funds. As far as the borrower is concerned, their bank statement now shows that they have 'money' to spend on whatever it is they arranged the loan for. At the point a new loan is agreed, new money is created and the money supply increases. These new loans represent assets to the bank (because the borrower will have to pay the loan plus interest to the bank) but at the same time increases liabilities by the same amount. The bank's balance sheet also expands.

The flip side of this is that when bank loans are repaid, the money supply contracts. For example, if an individual borrowed €10,000 to buy a new car, they will have to pay monthly instalments which consist of part of the capital sum (the €10,000) and some interest. If the monthly capital payment is €300, the borrower's outstanding loan shrinks by this amount, effectively reducing the money supply.

It is not only consumers and businesses borrowing and paying back loans which impact on the money supply in this way. Banks buy and sell a range of assets including bonds. The purchase of government bonds is a way in which the banking system can hold assets which are relatively liquid, as they can be sold to the central bank. Banks will also buy and sell bonds on the bond market. If a bond is purchased from a non-banking sector holder (i.e. not purchased from another bank), the funds are credited to the seller's account. This increases the money supply. Equally, if banks sell bonds to the non-banking sector, the buyer's account is debited with the sum paid and the money supply contracts.

Banks will also be involved with borrowing funds over much longer terms and with more restrictions. These loans may be highly illiquid in that they cannot easily be converted into cash. Banks can take this type of debt onto its balance sheet because it represents a form of funding which helps protect the bank from external shocks. One of the causes of the 2007–9 Financial Crisis was that the 'alchemy' which Mervyn King referred to broke down. A number of banks became heavily exposed to paying short-term obligations which pushed them to the brink of collapse. If too many of a bank's liabilities are short term, they become more unstable in the event that borrowers demand their money. Having more long-term debt helps reduce the risk. Since the Financial Crisis a number of central banks have sought to regulate on the amount of long-term debt banks hold as a way of improving security in the banking sector.

Constraints on Bank Lending While banks create money by lending, there are a number of constraints on its ability to be able to do this at will. Crucial to the constraints are monetary policy and the interest rate set by the central bank. This rate sets the basis for the structure of interest rates throughout the economy because it is the rate at which the central bank will lend to the banking system. If the central bank increases lending rates to the banking system, banks must increase the interest rate on lending to maintain spreads, and this leads to a reduction in the demand for loans. Similarly, a reduction in interest rates would be expected to stimulate the demand for loans. Exactly how much loans contract or increase in response to changes in interest rates depends on the interest elasticity of demand.

If bank lending is increasing and money growth is rising too fast, the central bank will look at the risk this poses in accelerating inflation over and above the target rate. If it is felt that the risk is too great, the central bank may increase its lending rate, which is designed to slow down the rate of growth of money through reducing lending. The 2007–9 Financial Crisis led to a slowdown in economic growth, and the threat from inflation began to subside. Central banks reduced interest rates in an attempt to encourage lending and expand the growth in money to help stimulate the economy. The fact that rates stayed so low in so many countries in the initial years after the Crisis is testament to the severity of the economic slowdown and the challenges in rebuilding confidence. Interest rates continued to remain at historically low levels largely due to the economic downturn caused by Covid-19. However, as countries began to emerge from restrictions and return to some sort of normality, supply constraints caused inflation to accelerate in a number of countries across Europe and in the UK made worse by the outbreak of conflict in Eastern Europe and the Middle East, and central banks increased interest rates to help choke off the pressure on prices. In 2024, central banks began to reduce interest rates, albeit slowly.

Banks operate in a competitive market. To generate appropriate profits, banks must be mindful of the cost of seeking out and making loans against the returns they get. The profit they make is determined, as we have seen, by the spread. This in turn is influenced by central bank monetary policy. To attract new loans, banks may have to offer rates which are lower than competitors. This, in turn, affects the profitability of its operations. If a borrower banking with First European Bank takes out a loan of €15,000 to buy a car, the funds are transferred to the seller's bank, let us call it Second European Bank, from First's reserves at the central bank. This results in a reduction in First's reserves and an increase in Second's. First now faces a situation in which it has fewer reserves and more loans in relation to its overall deposits. With fewer reserves it is in a riskier position if it needs to meet potential withdrawals or its payment obligations. Banks, therefore, cannot continue to lend indefinitely in this way. In addition, different institutions will have different cost structures, shareholder expectations of profit, not to mention the response of the public to the bank's activities. Whether it can attract new loans will be dependent on market forces and its profit requirements. Taking on more long-term debt, as outlined above, helps provide a further constraint. Long-term debt may provide the bank with more security but attracting these funds requires a higher interest rate which in turn affects banks' spread. There is a trade-off between profitable lending and security which the bank needs to make a judgement on.

The 2007–9 Financial Crisis brought risk into sharp focus. Central banks have increased the amount of regulation of the banking system in continued efforts to prevent the risk of crises developing in the future. Banks themselves also must be mindful of the risk they take in making loans that borrowers will default (termed a **credit risk**). This might mean them securing funding (referred to, inaccurately, as setting aside reserves) to absorb losses that might arise from default or wider bank sector problems, which might threaten their ability to function.

> **credit risk** the risk a bank faces in defaults on loans

Macroprudential Policy One of the criticisms of central banks during the Financial Crisis was that they did not have sufficient powers to deal with systemic risk in the banking system. **Systemic risk** refers to the risk of failure across the whole of the financial sector rather than just to one or two institutions. The risk is increased because of the interconnectedness and interdependence of the financial system. Once problems begin to occur in one area of the banking system, it cascades down to others and results in a severe economic downturn.

> **systemic risk** the risk of failure across the whole of the financial sector

In the UK, the FPC has been set up to assess the risks inherent across the financial system. It has powers to take action to prevent or reduce these risks. This is referred to as **macroprudential policy**.

macroprudential policy policies designed to limit the risk across the financial sector by focusing on improving 'prudential' standards of operation that enhance stability and reduce risk

Banks accept deposits from many people often in the form of short-term deposits. Bank customers may want to take out loans over much longer durations and so banks 'transform' many short-term deposits into a smaller number of longer-term loans. This is the 'alchemy' Mervyn King refers to. A bank's assets are all the financial, physical and intangible assets they hold or are due to be paid at some point in the future. Financial assets include loans made to households and firms, mortgages, lending to other banks and the wholesale market (transactions between large financial institutions, for example merchant banks that might be arranging for the listing of a company on the stock exchange). Other assets include cash, holdings of bonds and reserves at the central bank. Physical assets include all the property the bank owns, and intangible assets will include the brand value and reputation of the bank.

A bank's liabilities are what it owes to others. This includes all the deposits from households and firms, borrowings from other banks and wholesale markets, purchases of bonds from pension funds and insurance companies, and its share capital. If a bank makes a loan it runs the risk that the loan will not be paid back – the borrower will default. If defaults reach high levels the bank's assets fall and its liabilities increase. The other risk a bank faces is that it will be unable to meet demand for withdrawals. If withdrawals increase substantially (for example, through a bank run), the bank may have to sell off assets to raise funds and in doing so depresses the price of those assets. This is termed a **liquidity risk**. The failure of one bank can have cascade effects onto other banks and across the financial system.

liquidity risk the risk that a bank may not be able to fund demand for withdrawals

As noted above, banks face a trade-off between risk and reward. They want to lend more money to make higher profits but are constrained by the need to maintain liquidity to insulate themselves from the risk of insolvency. Banks must have sufficient sources of funding to meet their obligations. This means that if there were a sudden increase in demand for withdrawals, the bank would be in a position to secure adequate funding to be able to meet that demand. Banks do not, therefore, have a large vault where funds are stored away to use in the event of a crisis but instead must ensure that they are able to fund any such crisis event that occurs. This is the function of 'reserves'.

Banks structure their balance sheets to ensure they have a profile of assets and liabilities which enable them to respond to a rise in defaults and increased demand for withdrawals. Macroprudential regulation lays down minimum requirements banks must adhere to in structuring their balance sheets. Since share capital is the bank's 'own money' rather than money it has 'borrowed' from depositors, capital is seen as being important in being able to provide a buffer against shocks. The regulation encourages banks to take account of the risks they face, so that they themselves are capable of managing those risks rather than relying on the taxpayer to bail them out.

Another aspect of regulation is the so-called Basel Accord. This is a set of agreements by the Basel Committee on Bank Supervision, a group of central bank governors and heads of regulatory bodies which meets around four times a year to review banking supervision. The group establishes ratios of capital in the form of shareholders' equity and irredeemable and non-cumulative preference shares. The ratio of this capital in relation to the rest of the bank's assets is seen as a measure of the financial strength of a bank. It effectively acts as a cushion against financial shocks.

The so-called Basel III negotiations between 27 countries set new reserve requirements in September 2010. The new rules came into force in 2013 and were to be phased in over a period of six years (although some relaxation to the requirements on the capital reserves needed to survive a 30-day crisis was agreed in 2013 and the changes were phased in from 2015). The regulations mean that banks must maintain higher reserves to support lending – for every €50 of lending banks will have to have €3.50 of reserves compared to €1 prior to the Basel III agreement. This obviously more than triples the amount of reserves that banks will have to keep. If banks do not adhere to the new regulations, then they risk seeing the authorities placing restrictions on their activities including paying out dividends to shareholders and bonuses to staff.

THE CENTRAL BANK'S TOOLS OF MONETARY CONTROL

Central banks in many developed economies have a central function of maintaining economic stability and stable inflation. The principal way they seek to achieve these objectives is through influencing the price of money in the economy through setting interest rates. In general, a central bank has three main tools in its monetary toolbox: open market operations, the refinancing rate and reserve requirements. In addition, some central banks also use an asset purchasing facility termed quantitative easing as an integral part of its monetary policy options.

Open Market Operations

If the central bank wants to increase the money supply, it will buy bonds in the bond market. After the purchase, the extra currency is in the hands of the public in the form of a rise in account balances in banks. Thus an open market purchase of bonds by the central bank effectively increases broad money. If, on the other hand, the central bank wants to decrease broad money, it can sell bonds from its portfolio to the public. After the sale, the currency it receives for the bonds decreases account balances in banks. To be precise, the open market operations discussed in these simple examples are called **outright open market operations**, because they each involve an outright sale or purchase of non-monetary assets to or from the banking sector without a corresponding agreement to reverse the transaction at a later date.

> **outright open market operations** the outright sale or purchase of non-monetary assets to or from the banking sector by the central bank without a corresponding agreement to reverse the transaction at a later date

The Refinancing Rate

The central bank of an economy will set an interest rate at which it is willing to lend to commercial banks on a short-term basis. As we shall see, the name of this interest rate differs across central banks, although in general in this book we will follow the practice of the ECB and refer to it as the *refinancing rate*.

The way in which the central bank lends to the banking sector is through a special form of open market operations. Although outright open market operations have traditionally been used by central banks to regulate broad money, central banks more often use a slightly more sophisticated form of open market operations. This involves buying bonds or other assets from banks and at the same time agreeing to sell them back later. When it does this, the central bank has effectively made a loan and taken the bonds or other assets as collateral or security on the loan. The central bank will have a list of eligible assets that it will accept as collateral – 'safe' assets such as government bonds or assets issued by large corporations, on which the risk of default by the issuer is negligible. The interest rate that the central bank charges on the loan is the refinancing rate. Because the central bank has bought the assets, but the seller has agreed to buy them back later at an agreed price, this kind of open market operation is often called a **repurchase agreement** or 'repo' for short.

> **repurchase agreement** the sale of a non-monetary asset together with an agreement to repurchase it at a set price at a specified future date

Banks need to structure their balance sheets to ensure they can meet credit and liquidity risk. Because deposits and withdrawals at banks can fluctuate randomly, some banks may find that they have an excess of reserves one day while other banks may find that they are short of reserves. Therefore commercial banks in an economy will generally lend money to one another on a short-term basis – overnight to a couple of weeks – so that banks with excess reserves can lend them to banks that have inadequate reserves to cover their lending. This market for short-term reserves is called the **money market**. If there is a *general* shortage of liquidity in the money market (because the banks together have done a lot of lending), then the short-term interest rate at which they lend to one another will begin to rise, while it will begin to fall if there is excess liquidity among banks. The central bank closely monitors the money market and may intervene in it to affect the supply of liquidity to banks, which in turn affects their lending and hence the money supply.

money market the market in which the commercial banks lend money to one another on a short-term basis

Suppose, for example, that there is a shortage of liquidity in the market because the banks have been increasing their lending. A commercial bank may then attempt to obtain liquidity from the central bank by selling assets to the central bank and at the same time agreeing to purchase them back a short time later. In this type of open market operation, the central bank effectively lends money to the bank and takes the assets as collateral on the loan. Because the commercial bank is legally bound to repurchase the assets at a set price, this is called a *repurchase agreement*. The difference between the price the bank sells the assets to the central bank and the price at which it agrees to buy them back, expressed as an annualized percentage of the selling price, is called the repurchase or repo rate by the Bank of England and the refinancing rate by the ECB. The ECB's **refinancing rate** is thus the rate at which it will lend to the banking sector of the euro area, while the **repo rate** is the rate at which the Bank of England lends short term to the UK banking sector.

refinancing rate the interest rate at which the European Central Bank lends on a short-term basis to the euro area banking sector

repo rate the interest rate at which the Bank of England lends on a short-term basis to the UK banking sector

In the example given, the central bank added liquidity to the banking system by lending reserves to banks. This would have the effect of increasing broad money. Because the loans made through open market operations are typically very short term, with a maturity of at most two weeks, the banks are constantly having to repay the loans and borrow again, or 'refinance' the loans. If the central bank wants to mop up liquidity it can simply decide not to renew some of the loans. In practice, however, the central bank will set a reference rate of interest – the Bank of England's repo rate or the ECB's refinancing rate – and will conduct open market operations, adding to or mopping up liquidity, close to this reference rate.

In the United States the interest rate at which the Federal Reserve lends to the banking sector (corresponding to the ECB's refinancing rate or the Bank of England's repo rate) is called the **discount rate** or the federal funds rate.

discount rate the interest rate at which the Federal Reserve lends on a short-term basis to the US banking sector

Now we can see why the setting of the central bank's refinancing rate is the key instrument of monetary policy. If the central bank raises the refinancing rate, commercial banks will try to pull in their lending rather than borrow reserves from the central bank, and so the money supply will fall. If the central bank lowers the refinancing rate, banks will feel freer to lend, knowing that they will be able to borrow more cheaply from the central bank to meet their reserve requirements, and so the money supply will tend to rise.

Quantitative Easing

During the 2007–9 Financial Crisis, central banks adopted tactics to try to support the economy, one of which was an asset purchasing facility (APF) or quantitative easing (QE). The principle of QE was not new, but the scale at which it was implemented was unusual. In the UK the Bank of England cut interest rates to 0.5 per cent and in the United States, rates fell to a target of between 0 and 0.25 per cent. Having effectively exhausted the use of lowering the price of money in the economy, central banks looked at affecting the quantity of money as part of their armoury in triggering economic activity.

The process of QE involves the central bank buying assets from private sector institutions financed by the creation of broad money. Private sector institutions might include banks, pension funds and insurance companies. The type of assets purchased varies from bonds and gilt-edged stock to commercial paper (short-term promissory notes issued by companies with a maturity ranging up to 270 days but with an average of 30 days), equities and possibly toxic assets. In selling assets to the central bank, institutions will hold more money in relation to other assets and look to maintain their portfolios by using the money to buy bonds and shares of companies, which is in effect lending to firms.

An example may serve to help understand the process (we will use pounds in this example and assume the central bank is the Bank of England). Assume a pension fund has £1 billion worth of gilt-edged stock. It decides that it wants to sell £500 million worth. The Bank of England announces that it intends to purchase gilts at an auction and sets a specific date for the auction (normally a Monday and Wednesday each week for a specified period of time). The process takes place via what is called a 'reverse auction'. Rather than the buyer putting in bids for what they would be willing to pay for the item, the seller submits an electronic bid to the Bank stating what they would like to sell and at what price they would be willing to sell at. The Bank itself has a specified amount that it intends to buy at that time and the bids coming in from banks and other institutions may mean that the auction is oversubscribed (i.e. more bids to sell are received than the Bank intends to buy). As a result, the Bank is able to select which offers it will accept and at what price.

The pension fund in our example held government debt of £1 billion on its balance sheet, but following the sale of the debt to the central bank, it now has £500 million. This credit from the sale appears in its bank account, thus affecting the banking sector. The pension fund can use this £500 million to buy bonds and shares.

There will be further ripple effects in the bond market. Remember, companies use the bond market as a means of raising funds. Over a period of time these bonds will mature, and firms may issue new bonds to replace them. These new bond issues may have different coupon rates from existing ones depending on current conditions in the bond market. Assume that a company has issued a 10-year bond with a coupon, on issue, of 5 per cent. The price at which the bond sells on the market will not necessarily be the same as its par value (what it was originally issued at). The ratio of the coupon to the price gives investors the yield $\left(Yield = \frac{Coupon}{Price}\right)$. For example, if the company issues a £100 bond, with a coupon of 5 per cent, the yield will also be 5 per cent. However, if demand for this bond rises then its price may rise (to £105 for example) and as a result the yield will fall:

$$\left(\frac{5}{105} = 4.76 \text{ per cent}\right)$$

This is the inverse relationship between bond prices and yield we introduced earlier.

If the central bank intervenes to buy bonds, the supply of bonds will fall and bond prices will rise. As bond prices rise, yields fall. If our company now issues a new bond it can offer that bond at a lower coupon (there is no incentive not to buy it since buying existing bonds does not give any better return). Using the example above, if our company wanted to issue a new bond to replace the matured £100 bond, then it could offer the bond at a coupon of 4.76 per cent (or slightly higher). It would then have every chance of raising the finance. For the company it is now raising funds at 4.76 per cent rather than 5 per cent. This means that firms are now able to borrow at cheaper rates and provides an impetus for generating increased economic activity.

QE, therefore, works in a variety of ways to influence incentives. The principle of QE is relatively simple; the acid test is whether it works or not. The central bank is in a position to monitor the effects of the process as it collects data about money flows in the economy, the effect on the money supply, credit flows in corporate markets, interest rates on different types of lending (for example on mortgages), and the amount and type of lending taking place.

Digital or Cryptocurrencies

At this stage in our analysis, it is pertinent to introduce a development in the monetary system that has become increasingly important since the mid-2000s. A currency such as the euro, pound sterling, dollar and yen has the characteristics of being widely acceptable as a medium of exchange. The value of these currencies is reflected in the amount of goods and services (and other currencies) they can buy. Central banks control the issue of the currency and enact policies to try to maintain the value of the currency. A cryptocurrency has no such central bank issuer or administrator but is becoming increasingly accepted as a medium of exchange. Digital or **cryptocurrencies** are peer-to-peer networks facilitating transactions between users without an intermediary such as a bank. Cryptocurrencies can be exchanged for other currencies, goods and services.

cryptocurrencies peer-to-peer networks facilitating transactions between users without an intermediary such as a bank

Zippia Research estimates that there are over 20,000 cryptocurrencies in circulation and some 420 million users of cryptocurrencies globally. There are three cryptocurrencies that dominate the industry: Bitcoin, Ethereum and Tether. Bitcoin was developed in 2008–9. The name Satoshi Nakamoto has been attached to the creation of bitcoin. This name could be an individual or a group of people; nobody knows for sure. Bitcoins are created through mining. Mining uses software to solve mathematical problems for which a number of bitcoins are issued in exchange. This means that the issue of bitcoins has some element of self-control, since the mining process is not easy. It also helps to maintain the stability of the currency, like a central bank will seek to control a national currency through managing the quantity of the currency in circulation.

The issue of bitcoins through mining is done in a 'block' which is added to all other blocks, called a blockchain, and is then added to the network. The blockchain acts as a ledger, recording all transactions of the currency, although there is no central ledger. As of August 2018, one bitcoin was valued at around €5,458, but in early August 2025, its value was quoted around €97,800 and the market capitalization of bitcoin was around €3.2 trillion.

The development of cryptocurrencies has appeal to some people because they exist apart from government. Central banks are aware of the changes in the use of money, and some have been exploring the opportunities and risks associated with a possible introduction of a central bank digital currency (CBDC). This would be a means of purely electronic payment and be available to the general public. Commercial banks and some financial institutions can hold central bank money in digital form and make settlements using a service called the Real-Time Gross Settlement (RTGS) service, but this is not available to the general public. A CBDC would be available for general use and could be viewed as a 'digital banknote'. Because this form of currency would be issued by the central bank, one advantage would be that it would be safe and effectively regulated. The lack of regulation is something that is appealing as well as concerning about the use of cryptocurrencies. With central bank issued currency, if there is a financial crisis, the central bank invariably steps in through its role as a 'lender of last resort'. No such support is available for a cryptocurrency. Equally, cryptocurrency values can be highly volatile, which can affect the way in which they may be used to make payments. Central banks exist, in part, to maintain stability in the value of the currency.

In 2020, the Bank of England in the UK published a discussion paper looking at the possible introduction of a CBDC. A CBDC would involve the creation of (for example) a 'digital pound', an electronic version of cash. A digital currency would not be a replacement for cash. The central bank would be responsible for issuing this currency, and households and firms could use it for transactions in the same way as cash but via electronic wallets held on phones and mobile devices. These 'digital wallets' would be provided by private companies. The Bank of England has received a large number of responses to the paper and has engaged in further research and exploration of the idea.

The discussion paper and the responses highlighted five core principles that the Bank needs to take into account in its further deliberations and decision-making. The first is that a CBDC should be simple to use and be available to anyone in the UK. Second, the private sector has a role to play in the introduction of any CBDC. This, in turn, links to principle three, that consideration needs to be given to other developments in the field by the private sector and how a CBDC would compare to these alternatives. Fourth, the security of any CBDC would be of significant importance. People would want to be assured that their privacy was secured and, in addition, that any such currency would have to comply with existing laws and regulations around money laundering, the financing of terrorism and could be 'confiscated' in the event of sanctions being imposed on users. Finally, if a CBDC were introduced, it should not interfere with the Bank's primary role of ensuring monetary and financial stability. Indeed, some respondents noted that the development of a CBDC might result in new tools and policy options for central banks.

CRITICAL THINKING POINT The record of forecasting by central banks is poor and as such their control over the economy is illusory. Critically assess this view.

MONEY GROWTH AND INFLATION

Data from the ONS for 1971 show that a typical loaf of bread in the UK was priced at 9p (€0.11), a pint of milk at 5p (€0.06) and a dozen eggs at 23p (€0.28). In 2025, the prices of each of these goods were around £1.60 (€1.93), £0.85 (€1.02) and £2.60 (€3.13) respectively. The increase in price of each is 1,678 per cent for bread, 1,600 per cent for milk and 1,030 per cent for eggs. This may not come as a huge surprise. In advanced economies, most prices tend to rise over time.

In recent times there have been episodes of significant rises in the price levels in the former Yugoslavia and in Zimbabwe. Price rises in Yugoslavia ran at 5 quadrillion per cent (5 with 15 zeros after it) between October 1993 and January 1995. The Zimbabwean authorities announced that the CPI had reached 231,000,000 per cent in June 2008. The Zimbabwean central bank reported that some goods on the black market had risen by 70,000,000 per cent. Laundry soap was one of the goods that had risen by this much, but cooking oil also rose by 60,000,000 per cent and sugar by 36,000,000 per cent. Unskilled workers earned around Z$200,000,000,000 a month – at the time, equivalent to about US$10 (€9.61, £7.98). In July 2008 the Zimbabwean government issued a Z$100 billion note. If you had one, it would just about have bought you a loaf of bread. In this next section, we explore some theories of why prices rise over time and why one of the core functions of central banks is to target price stability.

WHAT IS INFLATION?

Recall that many countries use the CPI as their measure of inflation. If the index is calculated at 100 in the base year and 103 in the following year, each of these measures describes the price level. The price level is a snapshot of the weighted average of a basket of goods at a point in time. If in the subsequent year, the price level was also measured at 103, the price level would not have changed.

In our initial example, the price level changed from 100 to 103 from the base year to the following year. The rate of change in prices between these two years is 3 per cent. Inflation is an increase in the price level over a period. The rate of change in the price level reflects the speed at which prices are rising. If inflation is recorded as 3 per cent in one month, 3.5 per cent the next and 3.7 per cent the month after that, the rate at which prices are rising is getting faster or accelerating. If in the next month the inflation rate is 3.65 per cent and then 3.45 per cent the following month, prices are still rising but at a slower rate. Here inflation is not 'falling' but the rate of change is slowing or decelerating. Now assume that the inflation rate in the next four months is 3.45 per cent, again, prices are still rising but at a stable rate.

In the UK and parts of Europe in 2015, the price level actually fell. In our example, the price level might be recorded as 103 in one month and then 102 in the following month. In this case the rate of inflation would be negative at about −0.97 per cent. A negative rate of inflation is called **deflation**. Deflation is a fall in the price level over a period and occurs when the inflation rate is less than 0 per cent.

deflation a fall in the price level over a period occurring when the inflation rate is less than 0 per cent

The Classical Theory of Inflation

At the heart of the classical theory of inflation is the quantity theory of money. This theory is often called 'classical' because it was developed by some of the earliest thinkers about economic issues as far back as the sixteenth century. French lawyer, philosopher, political theorist and economist Jean Bodin (*c.*1529–96) sought to explain price rises by the increase in supply of gold and silver. Like all theories, it can be used to predict or explain phenomena, in this case why prices rise over a period.

The Level of Prices and the Value of Money

One of the reasons why inflation is such an important issue is because it is related to the value of money (the goods and services any given amount of money can be exchanged for).

The price level can be seen as a measure of the value of money. A rise in the price level means a lower value of money, because each unit of money now buys a smaller quantity of goods and services. Suppose *P* is the price level as measured by the CPI or the GDP deflator. *P* measures the number of euros needed to buy a basket of goods and services. Now turn this idea around: the quantity of goods and services that can be bought with €1 equals $\frac{1}{P}$. *P* is the price of goods and services measured in terms of money, and $\frac{1}{P}$ is the value of money measured in terms of goods and services. If *P* rises, the amount of goods and services €1 can buy falls. Thus when the overall price level rises, the value of money falls.

Money Supply, Money Demand and Monetary Equilibrium

In this analysis, we are going to assume that the central bank has total control over the money supply and that it is fixed.

The demand for money reflects how much wealth people want to hold in liquid form. Many factors influence the quantity of money demanded. The amount of cash people carry round with them, for instance, depends on how much they rely on credit cards, the use of their phone or watch to pay for the goods and services they want to buy. It also depends on whether an automatic cash dispenser is easy to find. The quantity of money demanded is also assumed to depend on the interest rate that a person could earn by using the money to buy an interest-bearing asset such as a bond rather than having it in their pocket or low interest bank account.

People hold money because it is the medium of exchange. Unlike other assets, such as bonds or stocks, cash is highly liquid in that it can be used to buy goods and services. How much people choose to hold for this purpose depends on the prices of those goods and services. The higher prices are, the more money the typical transaction requires, and the more money people will choose to hold in liquid form. A higher price level (a lower value of money) increases the quantity of money demanded.

Equilibrium in the market depends on the time horizon being considered. Later in this book we will examine the short run, and we will see that interest rates play a key role. In the long run, however, *the overall level of prices is assumed to adjust to the level at which the demand for money equals the supply.*

Figure 8.2 illustrates this idea. The horizontal axis of this graph shows the quantity of money. The left-hand vertical axis shows the value of money $\frac{1}{P}$, and the right-hand vertical axis shows the price level P. Notice that the price level axis on the right is inverted: a low price level is shown near the top of this axis, and a

FIGURE 8.2

How the Supply and Demand for Money Determine the Equilibrium Price Level

In panel (a), the horizontal axis shows the quantity of money. The left vertical axis shows the value of money, and the right vertical axis shows the price level. The supply curve for money is vertical because the quantity of money supplied is assumed to be fixed by the central bank. The demand curve for money is downwards sloping because people want to hold a larger quantity of money when each euro buys less. At the equilibrium, point A, the value of money (on the left axis) and the price level (on the right axis) have adjusted to bring the quantity of money supplied and the quantity of money demanded into balance. In panel (b), if the price level is higher at 4, the demand for money exceeds the available supply and the price level will fall back to the equilibrium at point A.

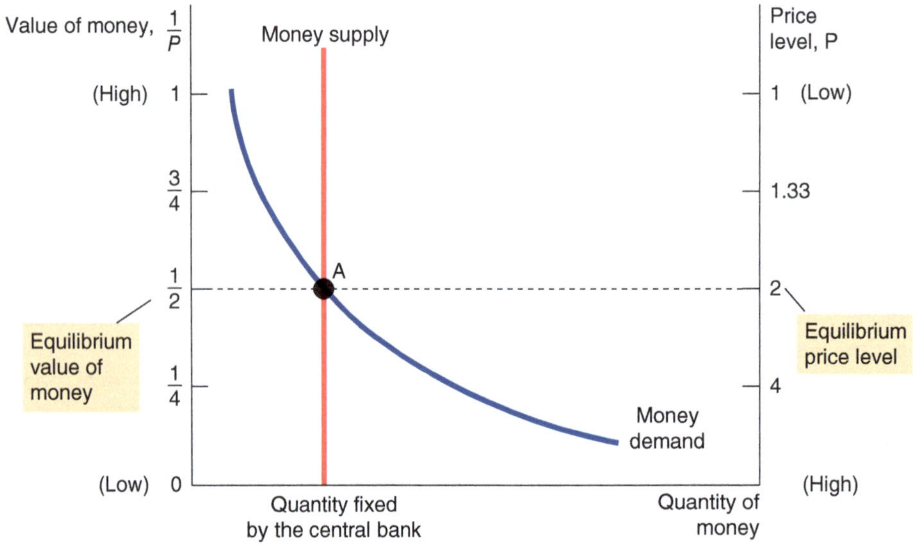

Panel (a)

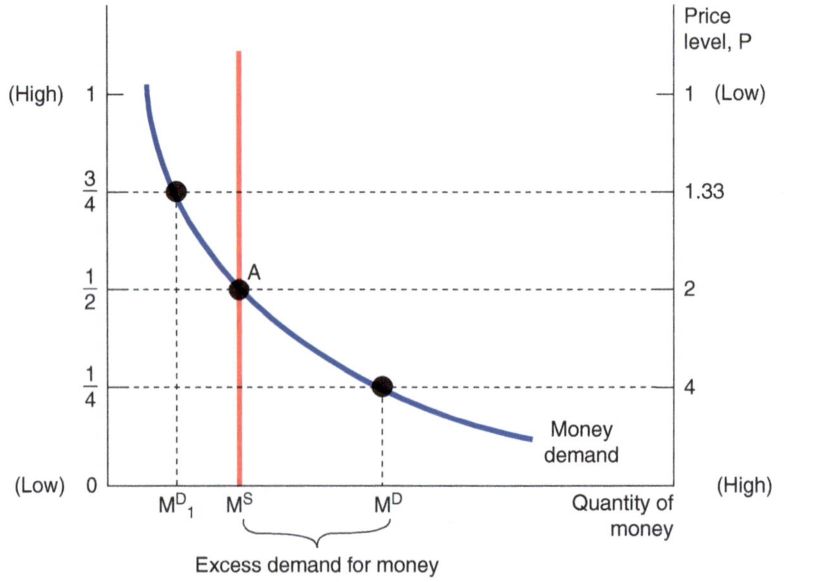

Panel (b)

high price level is shown near the bottom. This inverted axis illustrates that when the value of money is high (as shown near the top of the left axis), the price level is low (as shown near the top of the right axis).

The two curves in this figure are the supply and demand curves for money. The supply curve is vertical because of the assumption that the central bank can fix the money supply. The demand curve for money is downwards sloping, indicating that when the price level is high (and the value of money low), people demand a larger quantity of it to buy goods and services. At the equilibrium, shown in panel (a) as point A, the quantity of money demanded balances the quantity of money supplied. This equilibrium of money supply and money demand determines the value of money and the price level.

If the price level is above the equilibrium level, for example at 4 in panel (b), people will want to hold M^D to pay for goods and services, but the money supply is fixed at M^S resulting in an excess demand for money at this price level. The price level must fall to balance supply and demand. If the price level is below the equilibrium level at 1.33 in panel (b), people will want to hold M^D_1 but the supply of money is fixed at M^S, and the price level must rise to balance supply and demand. At the equilibrium price level, the quantity of money that people want to hold exactly balances the quantity of money supplied by the central bank.

CRITICAL THINKING POINT In the past 10 years the way in which people use 'money' has changed. Consider how the use of money has changed and how such changes might affect the model of monetary equilibrium presented here.

The Effects of a Monetary Injection

Starting with an assumption of equilibrium, now assume that the central bank doubles the supply of money through purchases of government bonds from the public in open market operations.

Figure 8.3 shows that the monetary injection shifts the supply curve to the right from M^S_1 to M^S_2, and the equilibrium moves from point A to point B. As a result, the value of money (shown on the left axis) decreases from $\frac{1}{2}$ to $\frac{1}{4}$, and the equilibrium price level (shown on the right axis) increases from 2 to 4.

FIGURE 8.3

An Increase in the Money Supply

When the central bank increases the supply of money, the money supply curve shifts from M^S_1 to M^S_2. The value of money (on the left axis) and the price level (on the right axis) adjust to bring supply and demand back into balance. The equilibrium moves from point A to point B. Thus when an increase in the money supply makes euros more plentiful, the price level increases, making each euro less valuable.

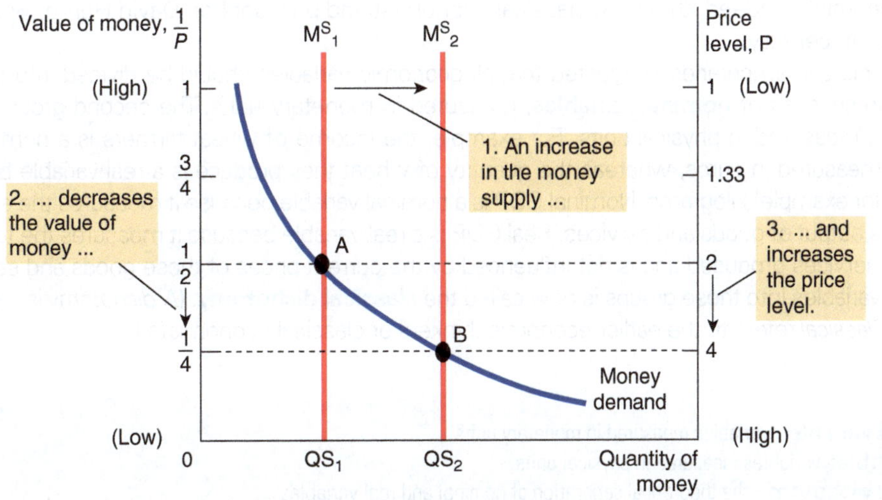

In other words, when an increase in the money supply makes euros more plentiful, the result is an increase in the price level that makes each euro less valuable.

This explanation of how the price level is determined and why it might change over time is called the **quantity theory of money**. According to the quantity theory, the quantity of money available in the economy determines the value of money, and growth in the quantity of money is the primary cause of inflation.

quantity theory of money a theory asserting that the quantity of money available determines the price level and that the growth rate in the quantity of money available determines the inflation rate

A Brief Look at the Adjustment Process

To get a complete understanding of the adjustment process we must look at short-run fluctuations in the economy, which we examine later in this book. Recall that our analysis at this point is of the long-run position.

The immediate effect of a monetary injection is to create an excess supply of money. Before the injection, the economy was in equilibrium (point A in Figure 8.3). After the monetary injection, the supply of money is greater than the demand at the prevailing price level (2) and people have more euros in their pockets than they need to buy goods and services.

People try to get rid of this excess supply of money in various ways. They might buy goods and services with their excess holdings of money. Or they might use this excess money to make loans to others by buying bonds or by depositing the money in a bank savings account. These loans allow other people to buy goods and services. In either case, the injection of money increases the demand for goods and services.

The economy's ability to supply goods and services, however, has not changed. The economy's output of goods and services is determined by the available labour, physical capital, human capital, natural resources and technological knowledge. None of these is altered by the injection of money.

Thus the greater demand for goods and services causes the prices of goods and services to increase. The increase in the price level, in turn, increases the quantity of money demanded because people are using more euros for every transaction. Eventually, the economy reaches a new equilibrium (point B in Figure 8.3), at which the quantity of money demanded again equals the quantity of money supplied.

The Classical Dichotomy and Monetary Neutrality

The quantity theory predicts that changes in the money supply lead to changes in the average level of prices of goods and services. Whether changes in the money supply affect other important macroeconomic variables, such as production, employment, real wages and real interest rates, is a question that has long intrigued economists. Indeed, the great classical economist and philosopher, David Hume, wrote about it in the eighteenth century.

Hume and his contemporaries suggested that all economic variables should be divided into two groups. The first group consists of **nominal variables**, measured in monetary units. The second group consists of **real variables**, measured in physical units. For example, the income of wheat farmers is a nominal variable because it is measured in euros, whereas the quantity of wheat they produce is a real variable because it is measured in (for example) kilograms. Nominal GDP is a nominal variable because it measures the euro value of the economy's output of goods and services. Real GDP is a real variable because it measures the total quantity of goods and services produced and is not influenced by the current prices of those goods and services. This separation of variables into these groups is now called the **classical dichotomy**. (A *dichotomy* is a division into two groups. *Classical* refers to the earlier economic thinkers or classical economists.)

nominal variables variables measured in monetary units
real variables variables measured in physical units
classical dichotomy the theoretical separation of nominal and real variables

Relative Prices Prices in the economy are normally quoted in terms of money and are therefore nominal variables. For instance, when we say that the price of wheat is €2 a kilo or that the price of barley is €1 a kilo, both prices are nominal variables, because we are referring to the number of units of a currency which have to be given up to acquire the good or service. We could represent this in the following way:

$$P_{\text{Wheat}} = \frac{€2}{\text{Wheat}}$$

$$P_{\text{Barley}} = \frac{€1}{\text{Barley}}$$

The price of wheat equals €2 per unit of wheat and the price of barley equals €1 per unit of barley.

The **relative price** is defined in terms of the nominal price of one good divided by the nominal price of another. In our example, the relative price of wheat in terms of barley is given by:

$$\text{Relative price of wheat} = \frac{\frac{€2}{\text{Wheat}}}{\frac{€1}{\text{Barley}}}$$

This can be simplified as follows:

$$\text{Relative price of wheat} = \frac{\frac{€2}{\text{Wheat}}}{\frac{€1}{\text{Barley}}} \times \frac{\frac{\text{Barley}}{€1}}{\frac{\text{Barley}}{€1}}$$

Cancelling through results in:

$$\text{Relative price of wheat} = \frac{2_{\text{Wheat}}}{1_{\text{Barley}}}$$

relative price price expressed in terms of how much of one good must be given up in purchasing another

The real value of a good is what other goods have been sacrificed in purchasing the good. This is the opportunity cost. In our example, to buy a kilo of wheat we sacrifice two kilos of barley. Similarly, the relative price of barley is given by $\frac{€1}{€2}$ which cancels through to give $\frac{1}{2}$. To buy a kilo of barley, we must sacrifice half a kilo of wheat. Relative prices are not expressed in terms of money and so relative prices are real variables.

Real Wages The concept of relative prices has several important applications, and in particular for wages. Imagine that a consumer only ever buys bananas, and that the price of a banana is €2. If the consumer's wage is €10 per hour, then the consumer can buy five bananas with their wage. Ten euros per hour is the nominal wage rate measured in money terms. The **real wage** rate is given by the ratio of the wage rate to

real wage the money wage adjusted for inflation, measured by the ratio of the wage rate to price $\frac{W}{P}$

the price of bananas, $\frac{W}{P}$. In this example the real wage rate is the number of bananas the consumer can buy with their wage, $\frac{10}{2} = 5$ bananas per hour. To be able to afford five bananas the consumer must work for an hour. If the wage rate and prices change, then the real wage rate gives a more accurate reflection of how the consumer has been affected. If the wage rate increases to €12 per hour and the price of bananas rises to €3, the real wage is now $\frac{12}{3}$ = 4 bananas per hour. We can say that the worker is now worse off, since they can now only buy four bananas for every hour they work, rather than five. The real wage (the money wage adjusted for inflation) is a real variable because it measures the rate at which the economy exchanges goods and services for each unit of labour. Similarly, the real interest rate (the nominal interest rate adjusted for inflation) is a real variable because it measures the rate at which the economy exchanges goods and services produced today for goods and services produced in the future.

Monetary Neutrality Hume suggested that the classical dichotomy is useful in analyzing the economy because different forces influence real and nominal variables. In particular, he argued that nominal variables are heavily influenced by developments in the economy's monetary system, whereas the monetary system is largely irrelevant for understanding the determinants of important real variables.

Notice that Hume's idea was implicit in our earlier discussions of the real economy in the long run. To date, we have examined how real GDP, saving, investment, real interest rates and unemployment are determined without any mention of the existence of money. As explained in that analysis, the economy's production of goods and services depends on productivity and factor supplies. The real interest rate adjusts to balance the supply and demand for loanable funds. The real wage adjusts to balance the supply and demand for labour. Finally, unemployment results when the real wage is for some reason kept above its equilibrium level. These important conclusions have nothing to do with the quantity of money supplied.

Changes in the supply of money, according to Hume, affect nominal variables but not real variables. When the central bank doubles the money supply, the price level doubles, the euro wage doubles, and all other euro values double. Real variables, such as production, employment, real wages and real interest rates, are unchanged. This irrelevance of monetary changes for real variables is called **monetary neutrality**.

> **monetary neutrality** the proposition that changes in the money supply do not affect real variables

An analogy sheds light on the meaning of monetary neutrality. Recall that, as the unit of account, money is the benchmark used to measure economic transactions. If the central bank doubles the money supply, all prices double, and the value of the unit of account falls by half. A similar change would occur if an EU directive reduced the definition of the metre from 100 to 50 centimetres. As a result of the new unit of measurement, all *measured* distances (nominal variables) would double, but the *actual* distances (real variables) would remain the same. The euro, like the metre, is merely a unit of measurement, so a change in its value should not have important real effects.

Is this conclusion of monetary neutrality a realistic description of the world in which we live? The answer is, not completely. A change in the length of the metre from 100 to 50 centimetres would not matter much in the long run. In the short run it would certainly lead to confusion and various mistakes. Similarly, many economists today believe that over short periods of time – within the span of a year or two – there is reason to think that monetary changes do have important effects on real variables. Hume himself doubted that monetary neutrality would apply in the short run.

Many economists accept Hume's conclusion as a description of the economy *in the long run*. Over the course of a decade or more, for instance, monetary changes have important effects on nominal variables (such as the price level) but only negligible effects on real variables (such as real GDP). When studying long-run changes in the economy, many economists believe that the neutrality of money offers a reasonable approximation of how the world works.

Velocity and the Quantity Equation

We can obtain another perspective on the quantity theory of money by considering the following question: how many times per year is the typical €1 coin used to pay for a newly produced good or service? The answer to this question is given by a variable called the **velocity of money**. The velocity of money refers to the rate at which money changes hands as it moves around the economy.

velocity of money the rate at which money changes hands

To calculate the velocity of money, we divide the nominal value of output (nominal GDP) by the quantity of money. If P is the price level (the GDP deflator), Y the quantity of output (real GDP) and M the quantity of money, then velocity is:

$$V = \frac{(P \times Y)}{M}$$

To see why this makes sense, imagine a simple economy that produces only pizza. Suppose that the economy produces 100 pizzas in a year, that a pizza sells for €10, and that the quantity of money in the economy is €50, made up of 50 €1 coins. Then the velocity of money is:

$$V = \frac{(€10 \times 100)}{€50}$$

$$V = 20$$

In this economy, people spend a total of €1,000 per year on pizza. For this €1,000 of spending to take place with only €50 of money, each euro coin must be spent (that is, change hands) on average 20 times per year.

With slight algebraic rearrangement, this equation can be rewritten as:

$$M \times V = P \times Y$$

This equation states that the quantity of money *(M)* times the velocity of money *(V)* equals the price of output *(P)* times the amount of output *(Y)*. It is called the **quantity equation** because it relates the quantity of money *(M)* to the nominal value of output $(P \times Y)$. The quantity equation (which is an identity or a truism) shows that an increase in the quantity of money in an economy must be reflected in one of the other three variables: the price level must rise; the quantity of output must rise, or the velocity of money must fall.

quantity equation the equation $(M \times V = P \times Y)$, which relates the quantity of money, the velocity of money and the currency value of the economy's output of goods and services

This equation is called the *equation of exchange* and was formulated by a US economist, Irving Fisher (1867–1947). The equation of exchange provides a means of linking changes in the money supply with the price level. It is assumed that the velocity of money is relatively stable over time. As a result, when the central bank changes the quantity of money *(M)*, it causes proportionate changes in the nominal value of output $(P \times Y)$. The economy's output of goods and services *(Y)* is primarily determined by factor supplies (labour, physical capital, human capital and natural resources) and the available production technology. In particular, because money is neutral, money does not affect output. With output *(Y)* determined by factor supplies and technology, when the central bank alters the money supply *(M)* and induces proportional changes in the nominal value of output $(P \times Y)$, these changes are reflected in changes in the price level *(P)*. Therefore when the central bank increases the money supply rapidly, the result is a high rate of inflation.

The Austrian School on the Velocity of Circulation

The quantity theory of money makes an important assumption, that the velocity of circulation of money *(V)* is stable over time. How accurate is such an assumption? One part of the answer might be to consider what is meant by 'stable' and over what time period we are looking. Stable does not mean constant, but what degree of volatility is acceptable to describe V as 'stable'?

Is the argument about the stability of V actually relevant? While many economists do place some value in the quantity theory, there are some who cast doubt on it. They do so because of the velocity of circulation, which they believe is a fallacy. Their argument is as follows.

When individuals make market transactions they pay through the value of the goods and services they produce themselves. A university lecturer, in reality, pays for the food they consume with the value of the lecture services they produce. Money is merely the means to facilitate the exchange. The number of times a €10 note changes hands has nothing to do with the lecturer's ability to fund their desired purchase of food. Instead, it is determined by the lecturer's ability to provide teaching services. What happens, so the argument goes, is that the lecturer is exchanging their services for money which then enables them to make transactions. The food retailer is exchanging the services they provide for money and uses it to buy the goods and services they need. In making these transactions both parties are assigning a value to the transactions they make in relation to their own particular well-being. The Austrian school argues that it is individuals' actions that determine the prices of goods and services and not the speed at which money changes hands. V cannot, therefore, say anything about the average price level or the average purchasing power of money. V is simply the value of transactions, the price multiplied by output, divided by the money stock $V = P\left(\frac{Y}{M}\right)$. As such it is a truism which is not helpful. V cannot be defined independently of the rest of the equation. It needs P, Y and M to give it any meaning, and as such V in itself cannot be a causal factor of anything. This implies that if M is rising, then if V was declining it cannot offset the growth in the price level.

The Austrian school links V to the demand for money. If V is unstable, does that also mean that the demand for money is unstable? This statement is seen as being absurd – if individuals change their decisions to hold more or less money over time as a result of changes in their personal circumstances, why would this be an issue? Their view would be that over time the demand for money changes, in the same way that over time the demand for any good or service changes. It would be absurd to expect the demand for fish to be stable over time, so why should we treat the demand for money in any different way?

The Austrian school does not deny a link between the money supply and prices, but questions the quantity theory (or the equation of exchange) as being an accurate way of looking at the economy. In doing so, they argue, false conclusions may be drawn.

The Inflation Tax

Government spending, for example building roads, paying salaries to police officers, or giving transfer payments to the those on lower income or retired from work, necessitates raising funds. The majority of the funding will come through levying taxes, such as income and sales taxes, and the rest through borrowing from the public by selling government bonds. Governments can also pay for spending by simply 'printing' the money it needs.

When the government raises revenue by printing money, it is said to levy an **inflation tax**. When the government prints money, the price level rises and the value of money falls (assuming wages are constant). If governments print money, it acts like a tax on everyone who holds money. It is even, roughly speaking, a progressive tax since the richer you are, the more money you are likely to hold and therefore the more the inflation tax will affect you.

> **inflation tax** the revenue the government raises by creating money

The importance of the inflation tax can be seen in cases of extreme inflation termed **hyperinflation**. Hyperinflation is a period of extreme and accelerating increase in the price level and typically occurs in a period where the monthly rate of inflation exceeds 50 per cent. During the hyperinflations in Germany in

> **hyperinflation** a period of extreme and accelerating increase in the price level where the monthly rate exceeds 50 per cent

the 1920s, various Latin American countries during the 1970s and 1980s, and in Yugoslavia and Zimbabwe more recently, the inflation tax would have been quite considerable.

Nearly all hyperinflations follow the same pattern. The government has high spending, limited ability to borrow and inadequate tax revenue (perhaps because the level of income in the economy is low, or there is widespread tax evasion or a poorly developed tax system, or a combination of all these factors) and, as a result, it turns to the printing press to pay for its spending. The massive increases in the quantity of money lead to accelerating inflation. The inflation ends when the government institutes fiscal reforms – such as cuts in government spending – that eliminate the need for the inflation tax, or in some cases abandons the currency completely and introduces a new currency.

As the economist John Maynard Keynes once pointed out, the temptation to just print money to pay for government spending through the inflation tax may be hard for a government to resist:

> *The burden of the tax is well spread, cannot be evaded, costs nothing to collect, and falls, in a rough sort of way, in proportion to the wealth of the victim. No wonder its superficial advantages have attracted ministers of finance.*

Of course, Keynes also recognized the great damage that high inflation can do to an economy, which is why he referred to the advantages of an inflation tax as 'superficial'.

The Fisher Effect

An important application of the principle of monetary neutrality concerns the effect of money on interest rates. Interest rates are important variables for macroeconomists to understand, because they link the economy of the present and the economy of the future through their effects on saving and investment.

To understand the relationship between money, inflation and interest rates, recall the distinction between the nominal interest rate and the real interest rate given by the formula $r_t = i_t - \pi_t$. For example, if a bank posts a nominal interest rate of 7 per cent per year and the inflation rate is 3 per cent per year, then the real value of deposits grows by 4 per cent per year. We can rewrite the equation to show that the nominal interest rate is the sum of the real interest rate and the inflation rate:

$$i_t = r_t + \pi_t$$

This way of looking at the nominal interest rate is useful because different economic forces determine each of the two terms on the right-hand side of this equation. Recall that the supply and demand for loanable funds determines the real interest rate. According to the quantity theory of money, growth in the money supply determines the inflation rate.

In the long run, over which money is neutral, a change in money growth should not affect the *real* interest rate. For the real interest rate not to be affected, the nominal interest rate must adjust one for one to changes in the inflation rate. Thus when the central bank increases the rate of money growth, the result is both a higher inflation rate and a higher nominal interest rate. This adjustment of the nominal interest rate to the inflation rate is called the **Fisher effect**.

Fisher effect the one-for-one adjustment of the nominal interest rate to the inflation rate

Keep in mind that our analysis of the Fisher effect has maintained a long-run perspective. The Fisher effect does not hold in the short run to the extent that inflation is unanticipated. A nominal interest rate is a payment on a loan, and it is typically set when the loan is first made. If inflation catches the borrower and lender by surprise, the nominal interest rate they set will fail to reflect the rise in prices. To be precise, the Fisher effect states that the nominal interest rate adjusts to expected inflation. Expected inflation moves with actual inflation in the long run, but not necessarily in the short run. The Fisher effect is crucial for understanding changes over time in the nominal interest rate.

THE COSTS OF INFLATION

Inflation is closely watched and widely discussed, because prices rising at too fast a rate can pose a number of problems.

Uncertainty and Planning

If inflation is not low and stable, then firms and households can find that planning for the future can be challenging. Returns on investment for firms, for example, can be difficult to estimate in a volatile inflationary environment. This can cause firms to delay decisions on investment. This, in turn, can affect prospects for economic growth in general. For households, especially when faced with longer-term financial decisions such as purchasing a house, the effects of inflation and how central banks might respond in terms of interest rates, can impact on mortgage payments. Again, this may cause some households to postpone such decisions or face uncertainties around what their payment obligations might be in the future. This is why many central banks target low and stable inflation rates.

A Fall in Purchasing Power? The Inflation Fallacy

We have seen that when prices rise, the value of money falls because people now need more money to buy any given set of goods and services. However, further investigation reveals that this is dependent on certain assumptions.

When prices rise, buyers of goods and services pay more for what they buy. At the same time, however, sellers of goods and services get more for what they sell. Because most people earn their incomes by selling their services, such as their labour, inflation in incomes must be taken into account. *Inflation does not, in itself, reduce people's real purchasing power*. The reason behind the so-called inflation fallacy lies in the principle of monetary neutrality. A worker who receives an annual rise of 10 per cent in their salary tends to view that rise as a reward for their own talent and effort. When an inflation rate of 6 per cent reduces the real value of that pay rise to only 4 per cent, the worker might feel that they have been cheated of what is rightfully their due. In fact, as we have discussed, real incomes are determined by real variables, such as physical capital, human capital, natural resources and the available production technology. Nominal incomes are determined by those factors and the overall price level. If the central bank were to succeed in lowering the inflation rate from 6 per cent to zero, our worker's annual rise would fall from 10 per cent to 4 per cent. They might feel less robbed by inflation, but their real income would not rise more quickly. If nominal incomes do not keep pace with rising prices, as was the case for many people in the post-Financial Crisis UK economy, then the cost of living does rise and people are worse off. Other costs of inflation show some ways in which persistent growth in the money supply does, in fact, have some effect on real variables.

SELF TEST The government of a country increases the growth rate of the money supply from 5 per cent per year to 50 per cent per year. What happens to prices? What happens to nominal interest rates? Why might the government be doing this?

Shoe Leather Costs

Because inflation erodes the real value of the money in your pocket, you can avoid the inflation tax by holding less money. One way to do this is to go to the bank more often. For example, rather than withdrawing €400 every four weeks, you might withdraw €100 once a week. By making more frequent trips to the bank, you can keep more of your wealth in your interest-bearing savings account and less in your pocket where inflation erodes its value.

The cost of reducing money holdings is called the **shoe leather cost** of inflation because making more frequent trips to the bank causes your shoes to wear out more quickly. Of course, this term is not to be taken literally. The actual cost of reducing your money holdings is not the wear and tear on your shoes, but the time and convenience you must sacrifice to keep less money on hand than you would if there were no inflation – it is in effect a transaction cost, the opportunity cost of managing your finances and banking.

shoe leather cost the resources wasted when inflation encourages people to reduce their money holdings

Shoe leather costs of inflation may seem trivial, and they are in countries experiencing only moderate inflation. This cost is magnified in countries experiencing hyperinflation, however. With a very high and accelerating inflation rate, individuals do not have the luxury of holding the local money as a store of value. Instead, they are forced to convert the domestic currency quickly into goods or into another currency, which offer a more stable store of value. The time and effort that individuals expend to reduce their money holdings are a waste of resources. If monetary authorities pursued a low inflation policy, individuals would be happy to hold the domestic currency, and they could put time and effort to more productive use.

Menu Costs

Most firms do not change the prices of their products every day. Instead, firms often announce prices and leave them unchanged for weeks, months, or even years.

Firms change prices infrequently because there are costs involved in doing so. Costs of price adjustment are called **menu costs**, a term derived from a restaurant's cost of printing a new menu. Menu costs include the cost of deciding on new prices, adjusting internal systems to coordinate the changes in prices, the cost of printing new price lists and catalogues, the cost of sending these new price lists and catalogues to dealers and customers, the cost of advertising the new prices, and even the cost of dealing with customer annoyance over price changes.

menu costs the costs of changing prices

Inflation increases the menu costs that firms must bear. In an economy with low inflation of just a few percentage points a year, annual price adjustment is an appropriate business strategy for many firms. But when high inflation makes firms' costs rise rapidly, annual price adjustment is impractical. During hyperinflations, for example, firms must change their prices daily or even more often just to keep up with all the other prices in the economy. At the height of the German hyperinflation in the 1920s, people eating in restaurants would sometimes insist on paying the bill at the beginning of the meal rather than at the end, because the price of the food would rise while they were eating!

Relative Price Variability and the Misallocation of Resources

Suppose that a fast food restaurant prints a new menu with new prices every January and then leaves its prices unchanged for the rest of the year. If there is no inflation, the restaurant's relative prices – the prices of its meals compared with other prices in the economy – would be constant over the course of the year. By contrast, if the inflation rate is 12 per cent per year, the restaurant's relative prices will automatically fall by 1 per cent each month. The restaurant's relative prices (that is, its prices compared with others in the economy) will be high in the early months of the year, just after it has printed a new menu, and low in the later months. The higher the inflation rate, the greater is this automatic variability. Thus because prices change only once in a while, inflation causes relative prices to vary more than they otherwise would.

This matters because market economies rely on relative prices to allocate scarce resources. Consumers decide what to buy by comparing the quality and prices of various goods and services. Through these decisions, they determine how the scarce factors of production are allocated among industries and firms. When inflation distorts relative prices, consumer decisions are distorted, and markets are less able to allocate resources to their best use.

Inflation-Induced Tax Distortions

Almost all taxes change incentives and cause people to alter their behaviour. Many taxes, however, become more problematic in the presence of inflation. The reason is that politicians may fail to take inflation into account when writing the tax laws. Economists who have studied the tax system conclude that inflation tends to raise the tax burden on income earned from savings.

One example of how inflation discourages saving is the tax treatment of *capital gains* – the profits made by selling an asset for more than its purchase price. Suppose that in 2017 you used some of your savings to buy stock in a company for €10 and that in 2027 you sold the stock for €50. According to the tax system, you have earned a capital gain of €40, which you must include in your income when computing how much income tax you owe. Suppose the overall price level doubled from 2017 to 2027. In this case, the €10 you invested in 2017 is equivalent (in terms of purchasing power) to €20 in 2027. When you sell your shares for €50, you have a real gain (an increase in purchasing power) of only €30. The tax system, however, does not take account of inflation and assesses your tax liability on a gain of €40. Thus inflation exaggerates the size of capital gains and inadvertently increases the tax burden on this type of income.

Another example is the tax treatment of interest income. Income tax treats the *nominal* interest earned on savings as income, even though part of the nominal interest rate merely compensates for inflation. To see the effects of this policy, consider the numerical example in Table 8.1. The table compares two economies, both of which tax interest income at a rate of 25 per cent. In economy A, inflation is zero, and the nominal and real interest rates are both 4 per cent. In this case, the 25 per cent tax on interest income reduces the real interest rate from 4 per cent to 3 per cent. In economy B, the real interest rate is again 4 per cent, but the inflation rate is 8 per cent. As a result of the Fisher effect, the nominal interest rate is 12 per cent. Because the income tax treats this entire 12 per cent interest as income, the government takes 25 per cent of it, leaving an after-tax nominal interest rate of only 9 per cent and an after-tax real interest rate of only 1 per cent. In this case, the 25 per cent tax on interest income reduces the real interest rate from 4 per cent to 1 per cent. Because the after-tax real interest rate provides the incentive to save, saving is much less attractive in the economy with inflation (economy B) than in the economy with stable prices (economy A).

TABLE 8.1 **How Inflation Raises the Tax Burden on Saving**

In the presence of zero inflation, a 25 per cent tax on interest income reduces the real interest rate from 4 per cent to 3 per cent. In the presence of 8 per cent inflation, the same tax reduces the real interest rate from 4 per cent to 1 per cent.

	Economy A (price stability) (%)	Economy B (inflation) (%)
Real interest rate	4	4
Inflation rate	0	8
Nominal interest rate (Real interest rate + Inflation rate)	4	12
Reduced interest due to 25 per cent tax (0.25 × Nominal interest rate)	1	3
After-tax nominal interest rate (0.75 × Nominal interest rate)	3	9
After-tax real interest rate (After-tax nominal interest rate – Inflation rate)	3	1

The taxes on nominal capital gains and on nominal interest income are two examples of how the tax system interacts with inflation. There are many others. Because of these inflation-induced tax changes, higher inflation tends to discourage people from saving. Recall that the economy's saving provides the resources for investment, which in turn is a key ingredient to long-run economic growth. Thus when inflation raises the tax burden on saving, it tends to depress the economy's long-run growth rate. There is, however, no consensus among economists about the size of this effect.

One solution to this problem, other than eliminating inflation, is to index the tax system. That is, the tax laws could be rewritten to take account of the effects of inflation. In the case of capital gains, for example, the tax code could adjust the purchase price using a price index and assess the tax only on the real gain.

In the case of interest income, the government could tax only real interest income by excluding that portion of the interest income that merely compensates for inflation.

In an ideal world, tax laws would be written so that inflation would not alter anyone's real tax liability. In the world in which we live, however, tax laws are far from perfect. More complete indexation would probably be desirable, but it would further complicate a tax system that many people already consider too complex.

Confusion and Inconvenience

Money is the economy's unit of account and is what we use to quote prices and record debts. The job of the central bank is a little like the job of the government department that deals with weights and measurements, i.e. to ensure the reliability of a commonly used unit of measurement. Inflation erodes the real value of the unit of account over time.

It is difficult to judge the costs of the confusion and inconvenience that arise from inflation. Earlier we discussed how the tax system incorrectly measures real incomes in the presence of inflation. Similarly, accountants incorrectly measure firms' earnings when prices are rising over time. Because inflation causes money at different times to have different real values, computing a firm's profit is more complicated in an economy with inflation. Therefore, to some extent, inflation makes investors less able to sort out successful from unsuccessful firms, which in turn impedes financial markets in their role of allocating the economy's saving to alternative types of investment.

A Special Cost of Unexpected Inflation: Arbitrary Redistributions of Wealth

So far, the costs of inflation we have discussed occur even if inflation is steady and predictable. Inflation has an additional cost, however, when it comes as a surprise. Unexpected inflation redistributes wealth among the population in a way that has nothing to do with either merit or need. These redistributions occur because many loans in the economy are specified in terms of the unit of account – money.

Consider an example. Suppose that Lars, a student, takes out a €20,000 loan at a 7 per cent interest rate from Bigbank to attend university. In 10 years the loan will have to be repaid. After his debt has compounded for 10 years at 7 per cent, Lars will owe Bigbank €40,000 (rounded). The real value of this debt will depend on inflation over the decade. If inflation has been relatively high over the period, wages and prices will have risen by a relatively large amount and Lars will be in a position to be able to pay the €40,000 debt more easily. In contrast, if the economy goes through a major deflation, then wages and prices will fall, and Lars will find the €40,000 debt a greater burden than he anticipated.

This example shows that unexpected changes in prices redistribute wealth among debtors and creditors. A high rate of inflation enriches Lars at the expense of Bigbank because it diminishes the real value of the debt. Lars can repay the loan in less valuable euros than he anticipated. Deflation enriches Bigbank at Lars' expense because it increases the real value of the debt. In this case, Lars must repay the loan in more valuable euros than he anticipated. If inflation were predictable, then Bigbank and Lars could take inflation into account when setting the nominal interest rate (recall the Fisher effect). If inflation is hard to predict, it imposes risk on Lars and Bigbank that both would prefer to avoid.

This cost of unexpected inflation is important to consider together with another fact. Inflation is especially volatile and uncertain when the average rate of inflation is high. This is seen most simply by examining the experience of different countries. Countries with low average inflation, such as Germany, tend to have stable inflation. Countries with high average inflation, such as many countries in Latin America, tend to have unstable inflation. There are no known examples of economies with high, stable inflation. This relationship between the level and volatility of inflation points to another cost of inflation. If a country pursues a high inflation monetary policy, it will have to bear not only the costs of high expected inflation but also the arbitrary redistributions of wealth associated with unexpected inflation.

The Impact on Lower Income Households and Firms

As we have seen, the CPI measures the average price change of a basket of goods. While statistical offices seek to take account of the weights of different items in the basket, inflation can have different effects on different income groups. The reporting of CPI data is often accompanied by the analysis of components of the data referred to as 'core inflation'. Core inflation looks at the changes in prices of what might be seen as essential items in consumer spending such as food and energy prices. Rises in the price of these items might be higher than other items in the basket and it can be that those on lower incomes are affected more by such inflation compared to those on higher incomes. Equally, if we look at broader inflation measures, we can note that smaller firms might be more affected by price rises in certain inputs more than larger firms.

SELF TEST List and describe six costs of inflation. Do people on fixed incomes benefit or lose out from periods of relatively high inflation?

DEFLATION

Economists generally see some inflation in the economy as being desirable (provided it is stable and manageable). The opposite of inflation is deflation where the price level actually falls. It might sound intuitive that falling prices would be a good thing, but that is not necessarily the case.

In 2014, there were concerns expressed that the UK and the eurozone might face deflation – a fall in the price level. In such a scenario, the CPI would be negative suggesting that prices, on average, had fallen. The eurozone actually experienced deflation of 0.3 per cent in the year to January 2015 and the UK CPI was −0.1 per cent in the year to April 2015 and then again in October 2015.

It is important to note the distinction between a *fall* in the price level and a *slowdown* in the rate of growth of prices. If the CPI reports inflation at 2.5 per cent in March and then 2.0 per cent in April, the rate of growth of prices has slowed down, not fallen, but if the CPI is recorded as −0.75 per cent in May, then prices have, on average, fallen.

Deflation is a relatively rare phenomenon. Most economies experience inflation at varying levels. Indeed, an inflation rate of around 2 per cent is seen as being beneficial to an economy as it encourages businesses to expand and helps create a more dynamic economy. Where deflation has occurred, it has tended not to last for very long. The deflation experienced in early 2015 in the UK, for example, was short lived. When deflation persists for some time, as it did in Japan over extensive periods in the 2000s and into the 2010s, for example, problems can arise. It is argued that one of the problems of deflation is a reluctance of consumers to spend when the expectation is that prices will be lower in the future. This argument has some logic and may apply to particular types of goods such as high-priced consumer goods – furniture, TVs and electrical goods, fridges, washing machines, dishwashers and so on. For many everyday goods like food, the likelihood of consumers deferring purchasing in the expectation that prices will be lower is less relevant. The evidence that consumers would delay purchases and thus plunge the economy into recession as consumption spending falls is not clear, especially where deflation does not persist for any length of time.

Other potential problems with deflation are related to interest rates. Interest rates in the eurozone and the UK were at historically low levels for a number of years following the 2007–9 Financial Crisis. The option for central banks to cut rates further as a means of boosting the economy was limited. Cutting rates below zero would be an incentive for savers to withdraw their deposits to prevent the value of them falling (a negative interest rate would in effect mean banks taking money out of savers deposits). If enough savers did this, then there could be pressure on banks and reduce their capacity for lending.

A period of deflation further affects borrowers and lenders. Banks' lending to business would find that the sum lent would purchase more in future when the debt is paid back if prices continued to fall, whereas firms borrowing funds would find that the burden of the debt would increase. In such a situation it might be that businesses would be more reluctant to borrow for investment resulting in a fall in aggregate demand.

One way in which businesses can reduce real wages in a period of inflation is to put a freeze on pay increases for workers. A pay freeze results in an increase in real wages which, in effect, increases the costs of businesses. If prices are falling, firms might press workers to accept a reduction in wages. If the reduction in wages was less than the rate at which prices were falling, workers would not be any worse off in real terms. However, it is extremely difficult for firms to push through pay cuts, so at the very least a pay freeze is the most likely option. If firms' costs rise, then it is possible that supply would be cut, or employees are laid off, and if either of these outcomes were to occur throughout the economy it may trigger a slowdown in economic activity. Given that all these effects could be experienced together, one of the fears of a period of persistent deflation is that the economy suffers from a downward spiral which is difficult to break.

CONCLUSION

We have discussed the causes and costs of inflation *in the long run*. The primary cause of inflation in the long run is growth in the quantity of money. When the central bank creates money in large quantities, the value of money falls quickly. To maintain stable prices, the central bank must seek to monitor the money supply and use the tools it has at its disposal to conduct monetary policy consistent with stable prices.

The costs of inflation are subtler. Are the costs, in total, large or small? All economists agree that they become huge during hyperinflation. Their size for moderate inflation – when prices rise by less than 10 per cent per year – is more open to debate.

Although we have looked at many of the most important lessons about inflation, the discussion is incomplete. When the central bank reduces the rate of money growth, prices rise less rapidly, as the quantity theory suggests. Yet as the economy makes the transition to this lower inflation rate, the change in monetary policy will have disruptive effects on production and employment. That is, even though monetary policy is neutral in the long run, it has profound effects on real variables in the short run. Later in this book we will examine the reasons for short-run monetary non-neutrality to enhance our understanding of the causes and costs of inflation.

SUMMARY

- The term *money* refers to assets that people regularly use to buy goods and services.
- Money serves three functions. As a medium of exchange, it provides the item used to make transactions. As a unit of account, it provides the way in which prices and other economic values are recorded. As a store of value, it provides a way of transferring purchasing power from the present to the future.
- Commodity money, such as gold, is money that has intrinsic value. It would be valued even if it were not used as money. Fiat money, such as paper euros or pounds, is money without intrinsic value. It would be worthless if it were not used as money.
- In an advanced economy, money takes the form of currency and various types of bank deposits, such as current accounts.
- Central banks monitor economic and price stability. They have an important role in managing broad money through variations in the price of money (interest rates).
- The European Central Bank is the overall central bank for the 20 countries participating in European Monetary Union. The eurosystem is made up of the European Central Bank plus the corresponding 20 national central banks.
- The UK central bank is the Bank of England. It was granted independence in the setting of interest rates in 1997.
- Central banks control the money supply primarily through the refinancing rate and the associated open market operations. An increase in the refinancing rate means that it is more expensive for banks to borrow from the central bank on a short-term basis if they are short of reserves to cover their lending. Therefore, they will tend to reduce their lending and the money supply will contract. Conversely, a reduction in the refinancing rate will tend to expand the money supply.
- The central bank can also use outright open market operations to affect the money supply: a purchase of government bonds and other assets from the banking sector increases the money supply, and the sale of assets decreases the money supply.

- When banks lend, they create money, but when loans are paid back, this destroys money. Central banks used quantitative easing as a means of providing a stimulus after the 2007–9 Financial Crisis through buying assets from the banking sector and expanding the money supply.
- A bank run occurs when depositors suspect that a bank may become insolvent and 'run' to the bank to withdraw their deposits. Many countries have a system of deposit insurance, and central banks are 'lenders of last resort' so bank runs can be managed more effectively. The overall level of prices in an economy adjusts to bring money supply and money demand into balance. Persistent growth in the quantity of money supplied leads to continuing inflation.
- The principle of monetary neutrality asserts that changes in the quantity of money influence nominal variables but not real variables. Many economists believe that monetary neutrality approximately describes the behaviour of the economy in the long run.
- A government can pay for some of its spending simply by printing money. When countries rely heavily on this 'inflation tax', the result can be hyperinflation.
- One application of the principle of monetary neutrality is the Fisher effect. According to the Fisher effect, when the inflation rate rises, the nominal interest rate rises by the same amount, so that the real interest rate remains the same.
- Many people think that inflation makes them poorer, because it raises the prices of the goods and services they buy. This view is a fallacy if inflation also raises nominal incomes.
- Economists have identified various costs of inflation: the uncertainty in decision-making that can be created; shoe leather costs associated with reduced money holdings; menu costs associated with more frequent adjustment of prices; increased variability of relative prices; unintended changes in tax liabilities due to non-indexation of the tax system; confusion and inconvenience resulting from a changing unit of account; arbitrary redistributions of wealth between debtors and creditors; and the potential for households and firms on low incomes to be disproportionately affected. Many of these costs are large during hyperinflation, but the size of these costs for moderate inflation is less clear.
- Deflation occurs when prices actually fall, and the effects on the economy and on incentives can be as damaging as when inflation is rising too quickly.

IN THE NEWS

How Stable and Secure are Financial Systems?

Many readers of this book will barely remember the 2007–9 Financial Crisis. The effects of this major financial crisis are still being felt in the mid-2020s. Have lessons been learned and are financial systems more stable and secure than they were back in 2007? In the UK, the Bank of England conducts a regular review of the strength and stability of the financial system and publishes a report. In November 2024, the report noted a number of issues facing not just the UK financial system but financial systems in general.

Key concerns focused on geopolitical tensions, the tendency for some countries to seek to reduce cooperation on trade, the challenge of increases in cyberattacks and the levels of government debt. This latter challenge has important implications for global interest rates. While some Western economies were seeing pressure on interest rates easing, the cost of servicing government debt had increased, notably in the UK and the United States following elections in 2024 in both countries. Similarly, some households in the UK faced challenges in restructuring debt, in particular mortgage debt, at higher interest rates.

The report noted that the prices of assets such as shares had risen and could be interpreted as a sign of confidence of steady global growth and inflation being contained. However, the report did note that when such asset prices rise, there is always a risk of some price correction that could impact on firm and household borrowing costs such that it would then affect growth.

(*Continued*)

©iStock/EyeEm Mobile GmbH

The stability and security of financial systems is vital to us all, but are central banks best placed to ensure such stability and security?

As part of its assessment of risks to the financial system, the Bank of England conducts 'stress tests' to estimate how effectively the financial system could respond to and cope with financial and economic shocks. Part of the tests look at how much capital is held by the banking system. It also looks at whether the amount held is sufficient to cope with unexpected losses triggered by different stress events. Overall, the Bank's report concluded that the UK banking system 'is in a strong position to support households and businesses, even if economic, financial and business conditions were to be substantially worse than expected'.

Critical Thinking Questions

1. The world has changed since 2007–9. What would you suggest are the main changes that have taken place that impact on a country's monetary system and what might be the nature of these effects?
2. To what extent do you think that central banks are able to control and manage the potential for systematic failures in a country's monetary system?
3. Consider some of the geopolitical pressures that currently exist. How might these pressures impact global inflation and growth prospects, and who do you think is most likely to be affected by changes in these prospects?
4. Consider the point made about government and households having to restructure debt. How might the performance of inflation in a country like the UK affect governments and households in this respect?
5. To what extent would you agree with the view that central banks should focus on achieving monetary stability rather than regulating the financial system?

References:

www.bankofengland.co.uk/financial-stability-report/2024/november-2024, accessed 7 August 2025.

QUESTIONS FOR REVIEW

1. What distinguishes money from other assets in the economy?
2. What are demand deposits, and why should they be included in the stock of money?
3. If the central bank wants to increase the money supply with outright open market operations, what does it do?
4. How do banks make profit and what considerations must banks give to the trade-off between security and profit?
5. What is the refinancing rate? What happens to the money supply when the European Central Bank raises its refinancing rate?
6. What is the difference between the price level and inflation? Explain how an increase in the price level affects the real value of money.
7. Explain the difference between nominal and real variables and give two examples of each. According to the principle of monetary neutrality, which variables are affected by changes in the quantity of money?
8. According to the Fisher effect, how does an increase in the inflation rate affect the real interest rate and the nominal interest rate?

9 If inflation is less than expected, who benefits – debtors or creditors? Explain.

10 Why is deflation a potentially damaging phenomenon?

PROBLEMS AND APPLICATIONS

1 What characteristics of an asset make it useful as a medium of exchange? As a store of value?

2 Should central banks place as much emphasis on financial stability as on price stability? Justify your answer.

3 How might changes in the behaviour of households and firms in the way they use money and the nature of 'money' impact central bank control of the financial system?

4 In what way can central banks attempt to control the broad money stock in an economy? What limitations does a central bank face in this task?

5 Why must banks have a portfolio of assets and liabilities on its balance sheet to enable them to manage risk? If banks commit to a large proportion of short-term lending, how might this affect its long-term security?

6 Suppose that this year's money supply is €500 billion, nominal GDP is €10 trillion and real GDP is €5 trillion.
   a. What is the price level? What is the velocity of money?
   b. Suppose that velocity is constant and the economy's output of goods and services rises by 5 per cent each year. What will happen to nominal GDP and the price level next year if the central bank keeps the money supply constant?
   c. What money supply should the central bank set next year if it wants to keep the price level stable?
   d. What money supply should the central bank set next year if it wants inflation of 10 per cent?

7 Suppose that changes in bank regulations expand the availability of credit cards so that people need to hold less cash.
   a. How does this event affect the demand for money?
   b. If the central bank does not respond to this event, what will happen to the price level?
   c. If the central bank wants to keep the price level stable, what should it do?

8 The economist John Maynard Keynes wrote:

> *Lenin is said to have declared that the best way to destroy the capitalist system was to debauch the currency. By a continuing process of inflation, governments can confiscate, secretly and unobserved, an important part of the wealth of their citizens.*

Critique Lenin's assertion.

9 Let us consider the effects of inflation in an economy composed only of two people: Michael, a bean farmer, and Dorothy, a rice farmer. Michael and Dorothy both always consume equal amounts of rice and beans. In year 2022, the price of beans was €1, and the price of rice was €3.
   a. Suppose that in 2027 the price of beans was €2 and the price of rice was €6. What was inflation? Was Michael better off, worse off or unaffected by the changes in prices? What about Dorothy?
   b. Now suppose that in 2027 the price of beans was €2 and the price of rice was €4. What was inflation? Was Michael better off, worse off or unaffected by the changes in prices? What about Dorothy?
   c. Finally, suppose that in 2027 the price of beans was €2 and the price of rice was €1.50. What was inflation? Was Michael better off, worse off or unaffected by the changes in prices? What about Dorothy?
   d. What matters more to Michael and Dorothy – the overall inflation rate or the relative price of rice and beans?

10 Explain whether the following statements are true, false or uncertain.
   a. 'Inflation hurts borrowers and helps lenders, because borrowers must pay a higher rate of interest.'
   b. 'If prices change in a way that leaves the overall price level unchanged, then no one is made better or worse off.'
   c. 'Inflation does not reduce the purchasing power of most workers.'

9 OPEN-ECONOMY MACROECONOMICS

So far in our development of macroeconomics, we have largely assumed a closed economy. This assumption allows us to explore unemployment and the causes of inflation without the added complexity of the effects of international trade. In an open economy, however, new macroeconomic issues arise. This chapter provides an introduction to open-economy macroeconomics. We begin by discussing the key macroeconomic variables that describe an open economy's interactions in world markets – exports, imports, the trade balance and exchange rates. Thereafter, we will develop a model to explain how these variables are determined and how they are affected by various government policies.

THE INTERNATIONAL FLOWS OF GOODS AND CAPITAL

An open economy interacts with other economies in two ways: it buys and sells goods and services in world product markets, and it buys and sells capital assets such as stocks and bonds in world financial markets.

The Flow of Goods and Services: Exports, Imports and Net Exports

Exports are domestically produced goods and services that are sold abroad, and imports are foreign-produced goods and services that are purchased by the domestic economy. When Lloyd's of London insures a building in Munich, it is paid an insurance premium for this service by the owner of the building. The sale of the insurance service provided by Lloyd's is an export for the UK and an import for Germany. When Volvo, the Swedish car manufacturer, makes a car and sells it to a Swiss resident, the sale is an import for Switzerland and an export for Sweden.

The net exports (NX) of any country are the value of its exports (X) minus the value of its imports (M). This is written: $NX = X - M$. The sale of insurance services abroad by Lloyd's raises UK net exports, and the Volvo sale reduces Swiss net exports. Because net exports tell us whether a country is, in total, a seller or a buyer in world markets for goods and services, net exports are also called the **trade balance**. If net exports are positive, exports are greater than imports, indicating that the country sells more goods and services abroad than it buys from other countries. In this case, the country is said to run a **trade surplus**. If net exports are negative, exports are less than imports, indicating that the country sells fewer goods and services abroad than it buys from other countries. In this case, the country is said to run a **trade deficit**. If net exports are zero, its exports and imports are exactly equal, and the country is said to have **balanced trade**.

trade balance the value of a nation's exports minus the value of its imports; also called net exports
trade surplus an excess of exports over imports
trade deficit an excess of imports over exports
balanced trade a situation in which exports equal imports

There are many factors that might influence a country's exports, imports and net exports, including:

- The tastes of consumers for domestic and foreign goods.
- The prices of goods at home and abroad.
- The exchange rates at which people can use domestic currency to buy foreign currencies.
- The need by firms for raw materials and resources for use in production.
- The incomes of consumers at home and abroad.
- The cost of transporting goods from country to country.
- The policies of the government towards international trade.

As these variables change over time, so does the amount of international trade.

The Flow of Financial Resources: Net Capital Outflow

Economic agents buy and sell goods and services across international markets but also participate in world financial markets. A UK resident with £50,000, for example, could use this money to buy a car from BMW in the goods market, but could instead use the money to buy stock in the German BMW corporation. The first transaction would represent a flow of goods, whereas the second would represent a flow of capital.

The term **net capital outflow** refers to the purchase of foreign assets by domestic residents minus the purchase of domestic assets by foreigners. (It is sometimes called *net foreign investment*.)

Net capital outflow = Purchase of foreign assets by domestic residents –
Purchase of domestic assets by foreigners

net capital outflow the purchase of foreign assets by domestic residents minus the purchase of domestic assets by foreigners

When a UK resident buys shares in BMW, the purchase raises UK net capital outflow. When a Japanese resident buys a bond issued by the UK government, the purchase reduces UK net capital outflow.

Recall that the flow of capital abroad takes two forms. If the French car manufacturer Renault opens a factory in Romania, that is an example of *foreign direct investment*. Alternatively, if a French citizen buys shares in a Romanian company, this is an example of *foreign portfolio investment*. In the first case, the French owner is actively managing the investment, whereas in the second case the French owner has a more passive role. In both cases, French residents are buying assets located in another country, so both purchases increase French net capital outflow.

These are some of the more important variables that influence net capital outflow:

- The real interest rates being paid on foreign assets.
- The real interest rates being paid on domestic assets.
- The perceived economic and political risks of holding assets abroad.
- The government policies that affect foreign ownership of domestic assets.

For example, consider German investors deciding whether to buy Turkish government bonds or German government bonds. To make this decision, German investors compare the real interest rates offered on the two bonds. The higher a bond's real interest rate, the more attractive it is. While making this comparison, however, German investors must also take into account the risk that one of these governments might default on its debt, as well as any restrictions that the Turkish government has imposed, or might impose in the future, on foreign investors in Türkiye.

The Equality of Net Exports and Net Capital Outflow

Net exports and net capital outflow each measure a type of imbalance in the goods and financial markets:

- Net exports measure an imbalance between a country's exports and its imports in the goods market.
- Net capital outflow measures an imbalance between the amount of foreign assets bought by domestic residents and the amount of domestic assets bought by foreigners.

An important but subtle fact of accounting states that, for an economy as a whole, these two imbalances must offset each other. That is, net capital outflow (*NCO*) always equals net exports (*NX*):

$$NCO = NX$$

This equation is an identity in that every transaction that affects one side of this equation must also affect the other side by exactly the same amount. To see why, consider an example. Suppose that BP sells some aircraft fuel to a Japanese airline, which represents an export for the UK. The UK company (BP) gives aircraft fuel to a Japanese company, and the Japanese company gives yen to a UK company. Two things have occurred simultaneously. The UK has sold to a foreigner some of its output in the goods market (the fuel), and this sale increases UK net exports. In addition, the UK has acquired some foreign assets (the yen), and this acquisition increases UK net capital outflow.

Although BP most probably will not hold on to the yen it has acquired in this sale, any subsequent transaction will preserve the equality of net exports and net capital outflow. For example, BP may exchange its yen for pounds with a UK investment fund that wants the yen to buy shares in Sony Corporation, the Japanese maker of consumer electronics. In this case, BP's net export of aircraft fuel equals the investment fund's net capital outflow in Sony shares. Hence, *NX* and *NCO* rise by an equal amount.

Alternatively, BP may exchange its yen for pounds with another UK company that wants to buy computers from Toshiba, the Japanese computer maker. In this case, UK imports (of computers) exactly offset UK exports (of aircraft fuel). The sales by BP and Toshiba together affect neither UK net exports nor UK net capital outflow. That is, *NX* and *NCO* are the same as they were before these transactions took place.

The equality of net exports and net capital outflow follows from the fact that every international transaction is an exchange. When a seller country transfers a good or service to a buyer country, the buyer country gives up some asset to pay for this good or service. The value of that asset equals the value of the good or service sold. When we add everything up, the net value of goods and services sold by a country (*NX*) must equal the net value of assets acquired (*NCO*). The international flow of goods and services and the international flow of capital are two sides of the same coin.

Saving and Investment, and Their Relationship to the International Flows

A nation's saving and investment are crucial to its long-run economic growth. Let us therefore consider how these variables are related to the international flows of goods and capital as measured by net exports and net capital outflow. We can do this most easily with the help of some simple mathematics.

The economy's gross domestic product (*Y*) as measured by the expenditure method is divided among four components: consumption (*C*), investment (*I*), government purchases (*G*) and net exports (*NX*). We write this as:

$$Y = C + I + G + NX$$

National saving is the income of the nation that is left after paying for current consumption and government purchases. National saving (*S*) equals $Y - C - G$. If we rearrange the above equation to reflect this fact, we obtain:

$$Y - C - G = I + NX$$

$$S = I + NX$$

Because $NX = NCO$, we can write this equation as:

$$S = I + NCO$$

Saving = Domestic investment + Net capital outflow

This equation shows that a nation's saving must equal its domestic investment plus its net capital outflow. In other words, when Italian citizens, for example, save a euro of their income for the future, that euro can be used to finance accumulation of domestic capital or it can be used to finance the purchase of capital abroad. In a closed economy, net capital outflow is zero, so saving equals investment. In contrast, an open economy has two uses for its saving: domestic investment and net capital outflow.

We can view the financial system as standing between the two sides of this equation. For example, suppose the Singh family decides to save some of its income for retirement. This decision contributes to national saving, the left-hand side of our equation. If the Singhs deposit their saving in an investment fund, the fund may use some of the deposit to buy shares issued by BP, which uses the proceeds to build a solar and battery storage facility in Scotland. In addition, the investment fund may use some of the Singh's deposit to buy shares issued by Toyota, which uses the proceeds to build a factory in Osaka. These transactions show up on the right-hand side of the equation. From the standpoint of UK accounting, the BP expenditure on the new facility is domestic investment, and the purchase of Toyota stock by a UK resident is net capital outflow. Thus, all saving in the UK economy shows up as investment in the UK economy or as UK net capital outflow.

Table 9.1 summarizes the three possibilities for an open economy: a country with a trade deficit, a country with balanced trade and a country with a trade surplus.

TABLE 9.1 **International Flows of Goods and Capital: Summary**

This table shows the three possible outcomes for an open economy.

Trade deficit	Balanced trade	Trade surplus
Exports < Imports	Exports = Imports	Exports > Imports
Net exports < 0	Net exports = 0	Net exports > 0
Y < C + I + G	Y = C + I + G	Y > C + I + G
Saving < Investment	Saving = Investment	Saving > Investment
Net capital outflow < 0	Net capital outflow = 0	Net capital outflow > 0

A Trade Surplus A trade surplus means that the value of exports exceeds the value of imports. Because net exports are exports minus imports, net exports are greater than zero. As a result, income from export sales must be greater than domestic spending on imports. But if income is more than spending, then saving must be more than investment. Because the country is saving more than it is investing, it must be sending some of its saving abroad. That is, the net capital outflow must be greater than zero.

A Trade Deficit A trade deficit means that the value of exports is less than the value of imports. Because net exports are exports minus imports, net exports are negative. Thus income from exports must be less than domestic spending on imports. If income is less than domestic spending, then saving must be less than investment. Net capital outflow must be negative.

A Trade Balance A country with balanced trade is between these cases. Exports equal imports, so net exports are zero. Income from export sales equals domestic spending on imports and saving equals investment. Net capital outflow equals zero.

SELF TEST Define net exports and net capital outflow. Explain how they are related.
A Swiss resident buys shares in an Indian company and the company purchases plant and equipment from a German manufacturer. Explain the effects on the accounts of the countries involved.

FYI

The Balance of Payments

The record of the flows of money as part of the transactions of international trade is presented in the balance of payments. The **balance of payments** is the official account of international payments for the import and export of goods, services and capital.

> **balance of payments** the official account of international payments for the import and export of goods, services and capital

The balance of payments consists of three elements:

The Current Account

The current account of the balance of payments records the flows of money which represent payments for goods and services transacted between the domestic economy and foreign economies. There will be the import and export of physical goods such as cars, steel, coal, clothing, food, oil and so on, and the value of the flows of funds for the import and export of services such as insurance, banking, tourism and leisure. The trade in physical goods is sometimes referred to as the visible trade balance and the trade in services is referred to as the invisible trade balance. Together, the difference between the value of imports and exports of visible and invisible items is recorded in the balance of trade.

The current account of the balance of payments also includes net income flows, that is the difference between flows of income such as wages and investment income between the domestic economy and foreigners. Net current transfers record secondary income flows such as transfers between governments or between governments and international bodies such as the European Union.

The Financial Account

The financial account records the flows of funds between the domestic economy and foreigners for investment. For example, if Nissan, a Japanese company, expands its car manufacturing facility in Sunderland in the UK, this would be recorded as a credit (a plus) on the financial account for the UK. Funds also flow between countries in payment for bonds, stocks and other financial instruments. These are classed as portfolio investment. The financial account will also include speculative money flows which occur as traders move funds from one country to another in search of returns. For example, if there is a hint that the US central bank, the Federal Reserve, is going to increase interest rates in the United States and interest rates elsewhere remain constant, traders may sell pounds and euros and buy dollars to invest in dollar-denominated assets which attract higher interest rates. These flows of funds in response to changes in interest rates or exchange rates are sometimes called 'hot money flows'.

The Capital Account

The capital account records the transfer of funds for the purchase and sale of non-financial assets such as land, the movement of funds for aid for capital works, the forgiveness of debt and the sale of embassies.

In theory, the balance of payments must balance. The balance of trade, however, does not have to balance. It is also very difficult to collect fully accurate data and as a result there is usually a balancing item which takes into account the fact that there will be statistical discrepancies.

Factors Affecting the Balance of Payments

The trade between countries can be affected by a range of factors. Key among these are interest rates, exchange rates, government policies, productivity levels in different countries, the difference in inflation rates, and levels of consumer spending in different countries on imports and exports. Some countries will have to import raw materials and foodstuffs because they do not have the resources to produce those goods. Others might have very strong export sales, for example, Germany. The state of the economy in the country in comparison to its trading partners can also affect the balance of payments. If a country is going through a contraction in economic activity, this can mean that spending on imports goes down. If a foreign country is experiencing an upturn in economic activity, this might lead to increased export sales for the domestic economy.

THE PRICES FOR INTERNATIONAL TRANSACTIONS: REAL AND NOMINAL EXCHANGE RATES

Different countries use different currencies. In trading internationally, firms will need to acquire these different currencies to complete transactions. This creates a demand and supply of currencies traded on foreign exchange markets.

Nominal Exchange Rates

The **nominal exchange rate** or more simply, *the exchange rate*, is the rate at which one currency exchanges for that of another. This rate is determined by the interaction of the demand and supply of the currency on foreign exchange markets.

nominal exchange rate the rate at which a person can trade the currency of one country for the currency of another

If you go to a bank, you might see a posted exchange rate of 165 yen per euro (¥165 = €1). If you give the bank 1 euro, it will give you 165 Japanese yen. If you give the bank 165 Japanese yen, it will give you 1 euro. (In fact, the bank will post slightly different prices for buying and selling yen. The difference gives the bank some profit for offering this service. For our purposes here, we can ignore these differences.)

An exchange rate can always be expressed in two ways. If the exchange rate is 165 yen per euro, it is also $\frac{1}{165} = 0.006$ euro per yen. If a euro is worth £0.85, a pound is worth $\frac{1}{0.85} = £1.18$. This can be a source of confusion, and there is no real hard and fast convention that people use. For example, it is customary to quote the US dollar–pound exchange rate as dollars per pound, e.g. £1 = $1.50, if 1 pound exchanges for 1.50 dollars. On the other hand, the pound–euro exchange rate can be quoted either way, as pounds per euro or euros per pound. In this book we shall, for the most part, think of the exchange rate as being the quantity of foreign currency that exchanges for one unit of domestic currency, or the foreign price of a unit of domestic currency. For example, if we are thinking of the UK as the domestic economy and the United States as the foreign economy, then the exchange rate is $1.50 per pound. If we are thinking of, say, Germany as the domestic economy, then we could express the exchange rate as dollars per euro, e.g. $1.08 dollars per euro.

In summary:

- To convert pounds into (e.g.) euros – *multiply* the sterling amount by the euro rate.
- To convert euros into pounds – *divide* the euro amount by the pound rate.

For example:
To convert £5.70 to € at a rate of £1 = €1.18, multiply 5.70 × 1.18 = €6.73.
To convert €3.45 to £ at the same rate, divide 3.45 by 1.18 = £2.92 (figures are rounded up).

Appreciation and Depreciation of Currencies

If the exchange rate changes so that a euro buys more of another currency, that change is called an **appreciation** of the euro. If the exchange rate changes so that a euro buys less of another currency, that change is called a **depreciation** of the euro. For example, when the exchange rate rises from 165 to 167 yen per euro, the euro is said to appreciate (a larger amount of yen is received in return for every euro). At the same time, because a Japanese yen now buys less of the European currency, the yen is said to depreciate (more yen has to be given up to buy one euro). When the exchange rate falls from 165 to 163 yen per euro, the euro is said to depreciate, and the yen is said to appreciate.

appreciation an increase in the value of a currency as measured by the amount of foreign currency it can buy
depreciation a decrease in the value of a currency as measured by the amount of foreign currency it can buy

At times you may have heard the media report that the pound or the euro is either 'strong' or 'weak'. These descriptions usually refer to recent changes in the nominal exchange rate. When a currency appreciates, it is said to *strengthen* because it can buy more foreign currency. Similarly, when a currency depreciates, it is said to *weaken*. If an individual gets more of the foreign currency in exchange for the same amount of the domestic currency, the domestic currency is stronger. If an individual must give up more of the domestic currency to get the same amount of the foreign currency, then the domestic currency is weaker.

The movement of currencies is important because of the effect it has on imports and exports. For example, a rise in the value of the pound against the dollar means that each pound buys more dollars. For example, if the pound appreciated from £1 = $1.50 to £1 = $1.55, UK firms buying goods from the United States would have to give up fewer pounds to get the same amount of dollars to buy the goods, which makes import prices appear cheaper. The flip side is that US buyers of UK goods will have to give up more dollars to acquire the same amount of pounds and so UK exports will appear to be more expensive.

If the pound depreciates in value, each pound now buys less of the foreign currency. In this case, UK exports appear cheaper to foreign buyers as they now get more pounds for every unit of their currency, but importers will find their costs rising as they must give up more pounds to get the same amount of the foreign currency.

In summary:

- A depreciation in a currency – import prices dearer, export prices cheaper.
- An appreciation in a currency – import prices cheaper, exports dearer.

Exchange Rate Indexes For any currency, there are many nominal exchange rates. The euro can be used to buy US dollars, Japanese yen, British pounds, Mexican pesos, and so on. When economists study changes in the exchange rate, they often use indices that measure the average change in many exchange rates. Just as the CPI turns the many prices in the economy into a single measure of the price level, an exchange rate index turns these many exchange rates into a single measure of the international value of the currency. When economists talk about the euro or the pound appreciating or depreciating, they are often referring to an exchange rate index that takes into account many individual exchange rates.

Real Exchange Rates

The **real exchange rate** is the rate at which a person can trade the goods and services of one country for the goods and services of another. For example, suppose that you go shopping and find that a kilo of Swiss cheese is twice as expensive as a kilo of English cheddar cheese. We would then say that the real exchange rate is a $\frac{1}{2}$ kilo of Swiss cheese per kilo of English cheese.

real exchange rate the rate at which the goods and services of one country trade for the goods and services of another

Real and nominal exchange rates are closely related. To see how, consider an example. Suppose that a kilo of British wheat sells for £1 and a kilo of European wheat sells for €3. What is the real exchange rate between British and European wheat? To answer this question, we must first use the nominal exchange rate to convert the prices into a common currency. If the nominal exchange rate is €2 per pound, then a price for British wheat of £1 per kilo is equivalent to €2 per kilo. European wheat, however, sells for €3 a kilo, so British wheat is only $\frac{2}{3}$ as expensive as European wheat. The real exchange rate is $\frac{2}{3}$ of a kilo of European wheat per kilo of British wheat.

We can summarize this calculation for the real exchange rate with the following equation, where we are measuring the exchange rate as the amount of foreign currency needed to buy one unit of domestic currency:

$$\text{Real exchange rate} = \frac{(\text{Nominal exchange rate} \times \text{Domestic price})}{\text{Foreign price}}$$

Using the numbers in our example, the equation applies as follows:

$$\textit{Real exchange rate} = \frac{\text{€2 per pound} \times \text{€1 per kilo of UK wheat}}{\text{€3 per kilo of European wheat}}$$

$$= \frac{\text{€2 per kilo of UK wheat}}{\text{€3 per kilo of European wheat}}$$

$$= \frac{2}{3} \text{ kilo of European wheat per kilo of UK wheat}$$

Thus, the real exchange rate depends on the nominal exchange rate and on the prices of goods in the two countries measured in the local currencies.

The real exchange rate is a key determinant of how much a country exports and imports. For example, when a British bread company is deciding whether to buy British or European wheat to make into flour and use in making its bread, it will ask which wheat is cheaper. The real exchange rate gives the answer. As another example, imagine that you are deciding whether to take a holiday in the Dordogne, France, or in Cancun, Mexico. You might ask your travel agent the price of a hotel room in the Dordogne (measured in euros), the price of a hotel room in Cancun (measured in pesos) and the exchange rate between pesos and euros. If you decide where to go on holiday by comparing costs, you are basing your decision on the real exchange rate.

When studying an economy as a whole, macroeconomists focus on overall prices rather than the prices of individual items. That is, to measure the real exchange rate, they use price indices, such as the CPI. By using a price index for a UK or European basket (P), a price index for a foreign basket (P^*), and the nominal exchange rate between the UK pound or euro and foreign currencies (e = *foreign currency per pound or euro)*, we can compute the overall real exchange rate between the UK or Europe and other countries as follows:

$$\textit{Real exchange rate} = \frac{(e \times P)}{P^*}$$

This real exchange rate measures the price of a basket of goods and services available domestically relative to a basket of goods and services available abroad.

A country's real exchange rate is a key determinant of its net exports of goods and services. A depreciation (fall) in the real exchange rate of the euro means that EU goods have become cheaper relative to foreign goods. This change encourages consumers both at home and abroad to buy more EU goods and fewer goods from other countries. As a result, EU exports rise and EU imports fall, and both of these changes raise EU net exports. Conversely, an appreciation (rise) in the euro real exchange rate means that EU goods have become more expensive compared to foreign goods, so EU net exports fall.

It is important to remember that while we are talking about the prices of exports and imports changing, the domestic price for these goods and services may not change. For example, a French wine producer may have wine for sale priced at €10 per bottle. If the exchange rate between the euro and the UK pound is £1 = €1.47 then a UK buyer of wine will have to give up $\frac{€10}{1.47}$ = £6.80 to buy a bottle of wine. If the UK exchange rate appreciates to £1 = €1.50, then the UK buyer must now give up $\frac{€10}{1.5}$ = £6.66 to buy the bottle of wine. The euro price of the wine has not changed, but to the UK buyer the price has fallen. Equally, if the pound exchange rate depreciated from £1 = €1.47 to £1 = €1.45, then the UK buyer would now have to give up $\frac{€10}{1.45}$ = £6.90 to buy the wine. Again, the euro price of the wine has not changed but the price to the UK buyer has risen because the exchange rate between the pound and the euro has changed.

SELF TEST Define the nominal exchange rate and the real exchange rate and explain how they are related. If the nominal exchange rate goes from 160 to 170 yen per euro, has the euro appreciated or depreciated? How would this affect European importers of goods from Japan and European exporters of goods to Japan?

A FIRST THEORY OF EXCHANGE RATE DETERMINATION: PURCHASING POWER PARITY

Exchange rates vary substantially over time. In 1970, one UK pound could buy $2.40, but in 1985 the pound was only worth about half this amount of dollars (the exchange rate was about $1.25). In March 2008 one pound could buy over $2 but by August 2025 the rate stood at around £1= $1.33. Over this 50-year period, the pound first almost halved in value from $2.40 to $1.25, and then increased by over 50 per cent from $1.25 to over $2.00 and then fell back down to $1.33.

Economists have developed many models to explain how exchange rates are determined, each emphasizing just some of the many forces at work. Here we develop the simplest theory of exchange rates, called **purchasing power parity** (PPP). This theory states that a unit of any given currency should be able to buy the same quantity of goods in all countries. Some economists believe that PPP describes the forces that determine exchange rates *in the long run.*

purchasing power parity a theory of exchange rates whereby a unit of any given currency should be able to buy the same quantity of goods in all countries

The Basic Logic of PPP

The theory of PPP is based on a principle called the *law of one price.* This law asserts that a good must sell for the same price in all locations, otherwise there would be opportunities for profit left unexploited. For example, suppose that coffee beans sold for less in Munich than in Frankfurt. A person could buy coffee beans in Munich for, say, €4 a kilo and then sell them in Frankfurt for €5 a kilo, making a profit of €1 per kilo from the difference in price. The process of taking advantage of differences in prices in different markets is called *arbitrage.* In our example, as the coffee buyer took advantage of the arbitrage opportunity, it would increase the demand for coffee in Munich and increase the supply in Frankfurt. The price of coffee would rise in Munich (in response to greater demand) and fall in Frankfurt (in response to greater supply). This process would continue until, eventually, the prices were the same in the two markets.

Now consider how the law of one price applies to the international marketplace. If a euro (or any other currency) could buy more coffee beans in Germany than in Japan, international traders could profit by buying coffee beans in Germany and selling them in Japan. This export of coffee beans from Germany to Japan would drive up the German price and drive down the Japanese price. Conversely, if a euro could buy more coffee beans in Japan than in Germany, traders could buy beans in Japan and sell them in Germany. This import of coffee beans into Germany from Japan would drive down the German price and drive up the Japanese price. In the end, the law of one price suggests that a euro must buy the same amount of coffee beans in all countries.

This logic is behind the theory of PPP, which states that a currency must have the same purchasing power in all countries. That is, a euro must buy the same quantity of goods in Germany and Japan, and a Japanese yen must buy the same quantity of goods in Japan as in Germany. Indeed, the name of this theory describes it well. *Parity* means equality, and *purchasing power* refers to the value of money. *Purchasing power parity* states that a unit of all currencies must have the same real value in every country.

Implications of PPP

The theory of PPP tells us that the nominal exchange rate between the currencies of two countries depends on the price levels in those countries. If a euro buys the same quantity of goods in Germany (where prices are measured in euros) as in Japan (where prices are measured in yen), then the number of yen per euro must reflect the prices of goods in Germany and Japan. For example, if a kilo of coffee is priced at ¥500 in Japan and €5 in Germany, then the nominal exchange rate must be ¥100 yen per euro

$\left(\frac{¥500}{€5} = ¥100 \text{ per } €\right)$, otherwise the purchasing power of the euro would not be the same in the two countries.

To see more fully how this works, it is helpful to use a little mathematics. Think of Germany as the home or domestic economy. Suppose that P is the price of a basket of goods in Germany (measured in euros), P^* is the price of a basket of goods in Japan (measured in yen) and e is the nominal exchange rate (the number of yen needed to buy one euro).

Now consider the quantity of goods a euro can buy at home (in Germany) and abroad. At home, the price level is P, so the purchasing power of €1 at home is $\frac{1}{P}$. Abroad, a euro can be exchanged into e units of foreign currency, which in turn have purchasing power $\frac{e}{P^*}$. For the purchasing power of a euro to be the same in the two countries, it must be the case that:

$$\frac{1}{P} = \frac{e}{P^*}$$

With rearrangement, this equation becomes:

$$1 = \frac{eP}{P^*}$$

Notice that the left-hand side of this equation is a constant, and the right-hand side is the real exchange rate. Thus, if the purchasing power of the euro is always the same at home and abroad, then the real exchange rate – the relative price of domestic and foreign goods – cannot change.

To see the implication of this analysis for the nominal exchange rate, we can rearrange the last equation to solve for the nominal exchange rate:

$$e = \frac{P^*}{P}$$

In other words, the nominal exchange rate equals the ratio of the foreign price level (measured in units of the foreign currency) to the domestic price level (measured in units of the domestic currency). According to the theory of PPP, the nominal exchange rate between the currencies of two countries must reflect the different price levels in those countries.

A key implication of this theory is that nominal exchange rates change when price levels change. Because the nominal exchange rate depends on price levels, it also depends on the money supply and money demand in each country. When a central bank in any country increases the money supply and causes the price level to rise, it also causes that country's currency to depreciate relative to other currencies in the world. In other words, when the central bank 'prints' large quantities of money, that money loses value both in terms of the goods and services it can buy and in terms of the amount of other currencies it can buy.

Referring back to the beginning of this section, why did the UK pound lose value compared to the US dollar between 1970 and 1985? A good deal of the answer relates to differences in inflation between the two countries. Between 1970 and 1985, the United States pursued, on average, a less inflationary monetary policy than the UK. Average price inflation in the UK over these 15 years was very high – about 10.5 per cent a year, while in the United States it was only about 6.5 per cent a year on average. This meant that between 1970 and 1985 the UK price level rose an average of 4 percentage points a year faster than the US price level. As UK prices rose relative to US prices, the value of the pound fell relative to the dollar.

Whether the UK pound or the US dollar buy more or fewer euros 20 years from now than they do today depends on whether the ECB oversees more or less inflation in Europe than the Bank of England does in the UK or the Federal Reserve does in the United States.

FYI

Purchasing Power Standard (PPS)

If you look at statistics produced by Eurostat, the EU's statistical office, you are likely to see data expressed in *purchasing power standard (PPS)*. This is an extension of the PPP idea but applied to the EU. PPS is an artificial currency which expresses the purchasing power of the EU 27, against the euro. In theory, therefore, one PPS would buy the same amount of goods in each EU country and so 1 PPS = €1. In reality, there will be price differences between European countries, so different amounts of euros will be needed to buy the same goods and services in different countries. PPS takes account of these differences. The PPS is found by taking any national economic aggregate, such as GDP, for example, and dividing by its PPP.

PPPs can be seen as the exchange rate of the PPS against the euro and allows for more accurate comparisons between data from different EU countries. The PPS for the EU as a whole would be 100. If GDP per capita was expressed in PPS, then any figure above 100 would show GDP per capita in that country above the EU average and any figure below 100 would indicate GDP per capita below the EU average.

Limitations of PPP

PPP provides a simple model of how exchange rates are determined. For understanding many economic phenomena, the theory works well. In particular, it can explain many long-term trends, such as the examples discussed earlier. It can also explain the major changes in exchange rates that occur during hyperinflations. Yet the theory of PPP is not completely accurate. Exchange rates do not always move to ensure that a euro has the same real value in all countries all the time. There are two reasons why the theory of PPP does not always hold in practice.

The first is that many goods are not easily traded. Imagine, for instance, that haircuts are more expensive in Paris than in New York. International travellers might avoid getting their haircuts in Paris, and some haircutters might move from New York to Paris. Yet such arbitrage would probably be too limited to eliminate the differences in prices. Thus, the deviation from PPP might persist, and a euro (or dollar) would continue to buy less of a haircut in Paris than in New York.

The second reason is that even tradable goods are not always perfect substitutes when they are produced in different countries. For example, some consumers prefer German cars, and others prefer Japanese cars. Moreover, consumer tastes can change over time. If German cars suddenly become more popular, the increase in demand will drive up the price of German cars compared to Japanese cars. Despite this difference in prices in the two markets, there might be no opportunity for profitable arbitrage, because consumers do not view the two cars as equivalent.

Thus both because some goods are not tradable and because some tradable goods are not perfect substitutes with their foreign counterparts, PPP is not a perfect theory of exchange rate determination. For these reasons, real exchange rates fluctuate over time. Nonetheless, the theory of PPP does provide a useful first step in understanding exchange rates. The basic logic is persuasive in that as the real exchange rate drifts from the level predicted by PPP, people have greater incentive to move goods across national borders. Even if the forces of PPP do not completely fix the real exchange rate, they provide a reason to expect that changes in the real exchange rate are most often small or temporary. As a result, large and persistent movements in nominal exchange rates typically reflect changes in price levels at home and abroad.

EXCHANGE RATE REGIMES

The purchasing power parity theory of exchange rates assumes that the prices of currencies move in relation to changes in demand and supply for currencies. In turn, these are driven by the demand and supply of goods and services traded internationally, and by differences in interest rates in different countries. However, a number of countries intervene in foreign exchange markets to 'manage' their currency in some way or another and so there are different types of exchange rate regime. In this next section we will provide a brief overview of these regimes.

Floating Exchange Rates

A floating exchange rate is one where the value of a currency changes in response to changes in demand and supply for the domestic currency in relation to other currencies. Changes in the value of the currency reflect the changes in demand and supply of that currency on foreign exchange markets. For example, if there is an increase in the demand for UK goods and services from abroad and demand for imports remains stable, then foreign buyers will be seeking to buy UK pounds on the foreign exchange market. This will increase the demand for pounds and lead to an appreciation of the pound. Demand for pounds might also increase because of investment in the UK by foreigners, for example if firms from foreign countries build new factories in the UK or if investment funds from abroad seek to buy UK assets to take advantage of favourable interest rates compared to those they can get on assets denominated in other currencies.

Equally, if the demand for UK imports rises but demand for exports is stable, the UK buyers of goods and services from abroad will be seeking to sell pounds to buy foreign currencies to pay for those imports and the supply of pounds increases. The value of the pound will fall in relation to how many units of a foreign currency each pound can buy.

One of the major disadvantages with floating exchange rates is the uncertainty faced by firms that engage in international trade. Firms that purchase inputs into the production process from abroad, for example, do not necessarily know what prices they must pay for their inputs and hence what the margins are going to be for their final product. If the exchange rate appreciates against other currencies, importers must exchange more currency to buy inputs from abroad and this increases their costs. Their ability to absorb this increase in costs will depend on a variety of factors. Indeed, some may find they have to either accept lower margins or pass on the increased prices to customers. This may result in demand for their product falling. The amount by which demand falls and the impact on revenue will depend on the price elasticity of demand for their product.

To manage these uncertainties, some firms may take advantage of forward exchange markets where they can take out contracts for delivery of a currency at some point in the future at a price agreed today. This can help with managing the uncertainty but it also introduces its own risks. For example, assume the current exchange rate between the UK pound and the US dollar is £1 = $1.30. A firm agrees on a contract to buy X US dollars at a rate of $1.32 for delivery in six months' time. In doing so it has some certainty of the price it has to pay and can build this into its planning. However, if in six months' time the pound has depreciated against the dollar and stands at £1 = $1.28, then the UK firm is paying more for its dollars through its forward contract than the current price. In reality, the forward exchange market is very sophisticated and many firms, mainly larger ones, can employ specialist traders to manage their forward exchange activities to minimize the risks involved.

Fixed Exchange Rates

Under a fixed exchange rate system, a country links the value of its currency to that of another currency. This is also referred to as 'pegging' the currency. Often, the currency it is pegged to is chosen because it is seen as being relatively stable and strong, such as the US dollar. Some countries may fix their exchange rate against a basket of currencies linked to an index of the average prices of those currencies. For example, the basket of currencies may consist of the dollar, the euro, the UK pound and the Japanese yen, and each may be weighted, so the dollar might account for 40 per cent of the total basket, the euro 25 per cent, the pound 15 per cent and the yen 20 per cent. The idea here is that there is likely to be less volatility with a basket of currencies compared to just one currency.

Once the currency or basket of currencies has been chosen, a rate against which the currency is fixed is decided. For example, a number of countries in the Gulf Cooperation Council (GCC) peg their currencies to the US dollar. The United Arab Emirates (UAE) dirham (AED) is pegged to the dollar at a rate of $1 = AED3.673 (to three decimal places). A fixed exchange rate does not mean that the value of the UAE dirham does not change, but the central bank will actively intervene on the foreign exchange market to engage in open market operations to maintain the rate as close to the peg as possible. One of the reasons for a country like the UAE to peg its currency to the US dollar is that oil is priced in US dollars and, since oil plays an important role in the UAE economy, it makes sense for the UAE to use the dollar as the peg. If demand for the dirham rises and there is upward pressure on the price of the dirham, traders at the central bank will sell dirham to maintain the price at the peg level or within a narrowly defined range around the peg. This is sometimes referred to as a semi-fixed exchange rate or a managed exchange rate.

By maintaining the value of a currency against another, a country can benefit in several ways. There is a greater degree of certainty around the value of the exchange rate, and this can avoid fluctuations in the value of the pegged currency, which helps firms and investors. By pegging to a currency that is relatively stable, a country can maintain a greater degree of discipline around inflation. Without such a discipline, there can be incentives to allow the value of a currency to depreciate in the hope that it boosts exports. This, however, will push up import costs, which can lead to inflationary pressures building. If firms know that the currency will not be allowed to depreciate as a means of boosting exports, they must focus on cutting their own costs and improving productivity and efficiency to compete on world markets. If, on the other hand, a currency experiences a significant appreciation, exporters will find that their goods and services are less competitive on world markets. Demand for exports will therefore fall while demand for imports will rise because it appears that imported goods and services are now cheaper. This could cause the country's balance of payments on current account to deteriorate.

While there are advantages to fixed exchange rates, there are also disadvantages. One arises in relation to the rate at which the currency is fixed. If the fixed rate does not adequately reflect the economic and trading position of the country, then there can be pressures that make the rate unsustainable. If the rate is too high, exporters will find that they are uncompetitive. If the rate is too low, it can create inflationary pressures. Maintaining the value of a currency against another necessitates the country pegging its currency to have large reserves of foreign currency to trade in international markets. These reserves are not inexhaustible. If, for example, the currency value begins to reach the floor of the narrow range permitted, the central bank will have to sell reserves of its foreign currency to buy (for example) dirham to maintain the pegged rate. If the pressure on the currency continues, these reserves can run out and the country might have to use other policy options to boost foreign currency reserves, such as increasing interest rates.

This might test the credibility of the government. If global investors believe that the government is not serious enough about maintaining the peg, they could mount speculative attacks against the currency to, in effect, test the resolve of the government. For example, in the early 1990s, the UK government entered the Exchange Rate Mechanism (ERM), a precursor to the euro where countries across Europe agreed to maintain the value of their currencies within a narrow band. The UK joined the ERM at a rate of 2.95 deutschmarks to the pound, with the value of the pound being allowed to fluctuate in a band 6 per cent above and below this rate. In September 1992, the pound was under pressure from speculators who believed that it would fall below its lower rate and took positions to benefit from the anticipated fall. To prevent the pound falling below the floor, the UK government was forced to run down reserves. As they did so, traders were selling pounds on world markets at a faster rate and eventually the government was forced to raise interest rates, initially from 10 per cent to 12 per cent on the morning of Wednesday, 16 September 1992. The interest rate move had little effect and traders continued to sell pounds. The government then increased interest rates to 15 per cent later in that same day, but this also had little impact and eventually the government announced that it was leaving the ERM. Global investors had called the UK government's bluff. The necessity of maintaining relatively high interest rates in the run-up to what was called 'Black Wednesday' to protect the value of the pound in the ERM led to a recession.

The necessity of maintaining a fixed or managed exchange rate, therefore, reduces the flexibility of a country's response to broader economic problems. If, for example, a country is experiencing a slowdown in economic activity, one policy option is to cut interest rates. If it does so, however, this might have an adverse effect on the exchange rate and cause it to move away from its peg or fixed rate. The government would have to choose between maintaining the peg and experiencing a more prolonged slowdown or dealing with the slowdown but forsaking the fixed exchange rate.

Summary

There is no 'right' or 'wrong' to the type of exchange rate regime a country adopts. Each country has to decide its regime according to its own economic circumstances. In the case of a number of GCC countries, the benefits they get from pegging their currencies to the US dollar are seen as broadly beneficial, but with such a decision come obligations and limitations and these have to be recognized. The dirham has been pegged against the US dollar since 1978, so the regime is now fairly well established, and expectations are that the UAE government can maintain the peg. As we have seen, however, there are examples where the credibility of the government can be tested and the regime collapses, causing serious and long-term economic problems. Some sort of fixed or managed exchange rates are not uncommon. A report by the International Monetary Fund (IMF) published in 2024 shows that there are 38 countries that have some sort of pegging arrangement with the US dollar (which may include actually using the US dollar as their currency), 25 that peg to the euro in some way and 8 that use a composite of currencies. In addition, 13.4 per cent of members of the IMF have a hard peg, 44.8 per cent have some sort of soft peg and 32.5 per cent have a floating exchange rate regime (www.elibrary.imf.org/fileasset/downloads/AEIEA2023001-S001.pdf).

SELF TEST Since the early 2000s, Venezuela has had high inflation and Japan has had low inflation. What do you predict has happened to the number of Venezuelan bolivars a person can buy with a Japanese yen?

A MACROECONOMIC THEORY OF THE OPEN ECONOMY

Some countries experience persistent trade deficits while others have trade surpluses.

To understand what factors determine a country's trade balance and how government policies can affect it, we need a macroeconomic theory of the open economy. The preceding section introduced some of the key macroeconomic variables that describe an economy's relationship with other economies – including net exports, net capital outflow, and the real and nominal exchange rates. We will now develop a model that identifies the forces that determine these variables and shows how they are related to one another.

To develop this macroeconomic model of an open economy, we make a number of assumptions:

- We take the economy's GDP as given.
- We assume that the economy's output of goods and services, as measured by real GDP, is determined by the supplies of the factors of production and by the available production technology that turns these inputs into outputs.
- The model takes the economy's price level as given. We assume that the price level adjusts to bring the supply and demand for money into balance.

The goal of the model is to highlight the forces that determine the economy's trade balance and exchange rate. The model applies the tools of supply and demand to an open economy but involves looking simultaneously at two related markets. These are the market for loanable funds and the market for foreign currency exchange. After we develop this model of the open economy, we use it to examine how various events and policies affect the economy's trade balance and exchange rate. We shall then be able to determine the government policies that are most likely to reverse trade deficits.

SUPPLY AND DEMAND FOR LOANABLE FUNDS AND FOR FOREIGN CURRENCY EXCHANGE

The market for loanable funds coordinates the economy's saving, investment and the flow of loanable funds abroad (net capital outflow). The market for foreign currency exchange coordinates people who want to exchange a domestic currency for the currency of other countries. In this section we discuss supply and demand in each of these markets. In the next section we put these markets together to explain the overall equilibrium for an open economy.

The Market for Loanable Funds

When we first analyzed the role of the financial system, we made the simplifying assumption that the financial system consists of only one market, called the *market for loanable funds*. All savers go to this market to deposit their saving and all borrowers go to this market to get their loans. In this market, there is one interest rate, which is both the return to saving and the cost of borrowing.

To understand the market for loanable funds in an open economy, the place to start is the equation:

$$\begin{array}{ccccc} S & = & I & + & NCO \\ \text{Saving} & = & \text{Domestic investment} & + & \text{Net capital outflow} \end{array}$$

Whenever a nation saves some of its income, it can use that money to finance the purchase of domestic capital or to finance the purchase of an asset abroad. The two sides of this equation represent the two sides of the market for loanable funds. The supply of loanable funds comes from national saving (*S*). The demand for loanable funds comes from domestic investment (*I*) and net capital outflow (*NCO*). Note that the purchase of a capital asset adds to the demand for loanable funds, regardless of whether that asset is located at home or abroad. Because net capital outflow can be either positive or negative, it can either add to or subtract from the demand for loanable funds that arises from domestic investment.

The quantity of loanable funds supplied and the quantity of loanable funds demanded depend on the real interest rate. A higher real interest rate encourages people to save and, therefore, raises the quantity of loanable funds supplied. A higher interest rate also makes borrowing to finance capital projects more costly; thus it discourages investment and reduces the quantity of loanable funds demanded.

In addition to influencing national saving and domestic investment, the real interest rate in a country affects that country's net capital outflow. To see why, consider two investment funds – one in the UK and one in Germany. They are each deciding whether to buy a UK government bond or a German government bond. The investment funds would make this decision in part by comparing the real interest rates in the UK and Germany. When the UK real interest rate rises, the UK bond becomes more attractive to both investment funds. Thus an increase in the UK real interest rate discourages British people from buying foreign assets and encourages people living in other countries to buy UK assets. For both reasons, a high UK real interest rate reduces UK net capital outflow.

We represent the market for loanable funds on the familiar supply and demand diagram in Figure 9.1.

FIGURE 9.1

The Market for Loanable Funds

The interest rate in an open economy, as in a closed economy, is determined by the supply and demand for loanable funds. National saving is the source of the supply of loanable funds. Domestic investment and net capital outflow are the sources of the demand for loanable funds. At the equilibrium interest rate, the amount that people want to save exactly balances the amount that people want to borrow for the purpose of buying domestic capital and foreign assets.

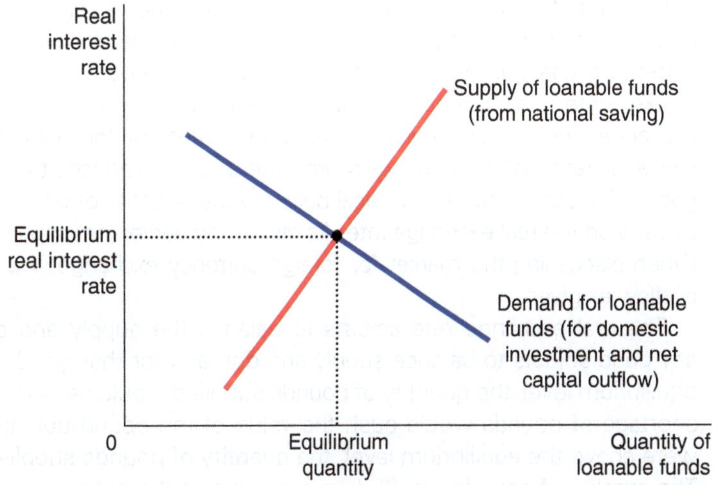

The supply curve slopes upwards because a higher interest rate increases the quantity of loanable funds supplied, and the demand curve slopes downwards because a higher interest rate decreases the quantity of loanable funds demanded. In an open economy, the demand for loanable funds comes not only from those who want loanable funds to buy domestic capital goods but also from those who want loanable funds to buy foreign assets.

The interest rate adjusts to bring the supply and demand for loanable funds into balance. If the interest rate were below the equilibrium level, the quantity of loanable funds supplied would be less than the quantity demanded. The resulting shortage of loanable funds would push the interest rate upwards. Conversely, if the interest rate were above the equilibrium level, the quantity of loanable funds supplied would exceed the quantity demanded. The surplus of loanable funds would drive the interest rate downwards. At the equilibrium interest rate, the amount that people want to save exactly balances the desired quantities of domestic investment and net capital outflow.

The Market for Foreign Currency Exchange

The second market in our model of the open economy is the market for foreign currency exchange. Let us assume that the UK is the domestic economy. Participants in this market trade UK pounds in exchange for foreign currencies. To understand the market for foreign currency exchange, we begin with another familiar equation:

$$\underset{\text{Net capital outflow}}{NCO} = \underset{\text{Net exports}}{NX}$$

This equation states that the imbalance between the purchase and sale of capital assets abroad *(NCO)* equals the imbalance between exports and imports of goods and services. For example, when the UK economy is running a trade surplus, foreigners are buying more UK goods and services than UK residents are buying foreign goods and services. What are British people doing with the foreign currency they are getting from this net sale of goods and services abroad? They must be buying foreign assets, so UK capital is flowing abroad. Conversely, if the UK is running a trade deficit, Brits are spending more on foreign goods and services than they are earning from selling abroad. Some of this spending must be financed by selling UK assets abroad, so foreign capital is flowing into the UK.

Our model of the open economy treats the two sides of this identity as representing the two sides of the market for foreign currency exchange. Net capital outflow represents the quantity of pounds supplied for the purpose of buying foreign assets. For example, when a UK investment fund wants to buy a Japanese government bond, it needs to change pounds into yen. It therefore supplies pounds in the market for foreign currency exchange. Net exports represent the quantity of pounds demanded for the purpose of buying UK net exports of goods and services. For example, when a Japanese airline wants to buy aircraft fuel produced by BP, it needs to change its yen into pounds. Consequently it demands pounds in the market for foreign currency exchange. The real exchange rate is the relative price of domestic and foreign goods and, therefore, is a key determinant of net exports. Figure 9.2 shows supply and demand in the market for foreign currency exchange. The demand curve slopes downwards for the reason we just discussed, that is a higher real exchange rate makes UK goods more expensive and reduces the quantity of pounds demanded to buy those goods. The supply curve is vertical because the quantity of pounds supplied for net capital outflow does not depend on the real exchange rate. As discussed earlier, net capital outflow depends on the real interest rate. When discussing the market for foreign currency exchange, we take the real interest rate and net capital outflow as given.

The real exchange rate adjusts to balance the supply and demand for pounds, just as the price of any good adjusts to balance supply and demand for that good. If the real exchange rate were below the equilibrium level, the quantity of pounds supplied would be less than the quantity demanded. The resulting shortage of pounds would push the value of the pound upwards. Conversely, if the real exchange rate were above the equilibrium level, the quantity of pounds supplied would exceed the quantity demanded. The surplus of pounds would drive the value of the pound downwards. At the equilibrium real exchange rate, the demand for pounds by non-UK residents arising from the UK net exports of goods and services exactly balances the supply of pounds from UK residents arising from UK net capital outflow.

At this point, it is worth noting that the division of transactions between 'supply' and 'demand' in this model is somewhat artificial. In our model, net exports are the source of the demand for pounds, and net capital outflow is the source of the supply. Thus when a UK resident imports a car made in Japan, our model treats that transaction as a decrease in the quantity of pounds demanded (because net exports fall) rather

FIGURE 9.2

The Market for Foreign Currency Exchange

The real exchange rate is determined by the supply and demand for foreign currency exchange. The supply of pounds to be exchanged into foreign currency comes from net capital outflow. Because net capital outflow does not depend on the real exchange rate, the supply curve is vertical. The demand for pounds comes from net exports. Because a lower real exchange rate stimulates net exports (and thus increases the quantity of pounds demanded to pay for these net exports), the demand curve is downwards sloping. At the equilibrium real exchange rate, the number of pounds people supply to buy foreign assets exactly balances the number of pounds people demand to buy net exports.

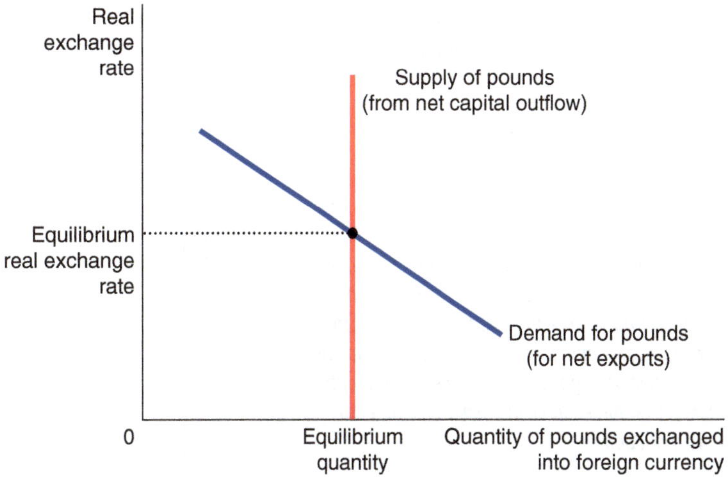

than an increase in the quantity of pounds supplied. Similarly, when a Japanese citizen buys a UK government bond, our model treats that transaction as a decrease in the quantity of pounds supplied (because net capital outflow falls) rather than an increase in the quantity of pounds demanded. This use of language may seem somewhat unnatural at first, but it will prove useful when analyzing the effects of various policies.

CRITICAL THINKING POINT To what extent do you agree with the view that the financial system has become so complex that the theory of the market for loanable funds, which was developed in the 1930s, has outlived its usefulness?

EQUILIBRIUM IN THE OPEN ECONOMY

Having considered the supply and demand in the market for loanable funds and the market for foreign currency exchange, let us now consider how these markets are related to each other.

Net Capital Outflow: The Link between the Two Markets

We have discussed how the economy coordinates four important macroeconomic variables: national saving, domestic investment, net capital outflow (*NCO*) and net exports. Keep in mind the following equations:

$$S = I + NCO$$

and

$$NCO = NX$$

In the market for loanable funds, supply comes from national saving, demand comes from domestic investment and net capital outflow, and the real interest rate balances supply and demand. In the market for foreign currency exchange, supply comes from net capital outflow, demand comes from net exports, and the real exchange rate balances supply and demand.

Net capital outflow is the variable that links these two markets. In the market for loanable funds, net capital outflow is part of demand. A person who wants to buy an asset abroad must finance this purchase by obtaining resources in the market for loanable funds. In the market for foreign currency exchange, net capital outflow is the source of supply. A person who wants to buy an asset in another country must supply pounds to exchange them for the currency of that country.

The key determinant of net capital outflow, as we have discussed, is the real interest rate. When the UK interest rate is relatively high, owning UK assets is more attractive, and UK net capital outflow is low. Figure 9.3 shows this negative relationship between the interest rate and net capital outflow. This net capital outflow curve is the link between the market for loanable funds and the market for foreign currency exchange.

FIGURE 9.3

How Net Capital Outflow Depends on the Interest Rate

Because a higher domestic real interest rate makes domestic assets more attractive, it reduces net capital outflow. Note the position of zero on the horizontal axis: net capital outflow can be positive or negative. A negative value of net capital outflow means that the economy is experiencing a net inflow of capital.

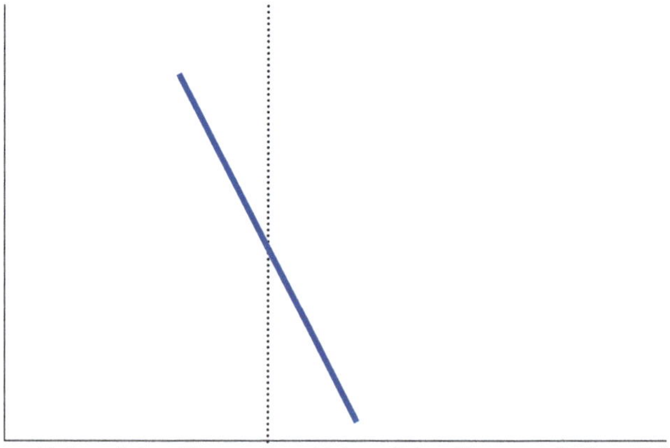

Simultaneous Equilibrium in Two Markets

We can now put all the pieces of our model together in Figure 9.4. This figure shows how the market for loanable funds and the market for foreign currency exchange jointly determine the important macroeconomic variables of an open economy.

Panel (a) of the figure shows the market for loanable funds (taken from Figure 9.1). As before, national saving is the source of the supply of loanable funds. Domestic investment and net capital outflow are the sources of the demand for loanable funds. The equilibrium real interest rate brings the quantity of loanable funds supplied and the quantity of loanable funds demanded into balance.

Panel (b) of the figure shows net capital outflow (taken from Figure 9.3). It shows how the interest rate from panel (a) determines net capital outflow. A higher interest rate at home makes domestic assets more attractive, and this in turn reduces net capital outflow. Therefore the net capital outflow curve in panel (b) slopes downwards.

Panel (c) of the figure shows the market for foreign currency exchange (taken from Figure 9.2). Because foreign assets must be purchased with foreign currency, the quantity of net capital outflow from panel (b) determines the supply of pounds to be exchanged into foreign currencies. The real exchange rate does not affect net capital outflow, so the supply curve is vertical. The demand for pounds comes from net exports. Because a depreciation of the real exchange rate increases net exports, the demand curve for foreign currency exchange slopes downwards. The equilibrium real exchange rate brings into balance the quantity of pounds supplied and the quantity of pounds demanded in the market for foreign currency exchange.

The two markets shown in Figure 9.4 determine two relative prices – the real interest rate and the real exchange rate. The real interest rate determined in panel (a) is the price of goods and services in the present relative to goods and services in the future. The real exchange rate determined in panel (c) is the price of domestic goods and services relative to foreign goods and services. These two relative prices adjust to balance supply and demand in these two markets. As they do so, they determine national saving, domestic investment, net capital outflow and net exports.

SELF TEST Describe the sources of supply and demand in the market for loanable funds and the market for foreign currency exchange. How are the two markets related?

FIGURE 9.4

The Real Equilibrium in an Open Economy

In panel (a), the supply and demand for loanable funds determine the real interest rate. In panel (b), the interest rate determines net capital outflow, which provides the supply of pounds in the market for foreign currency exchange. In panel (c), the supply and demand for pounds in the market for foreign currency exchange determine the real exchange rate.

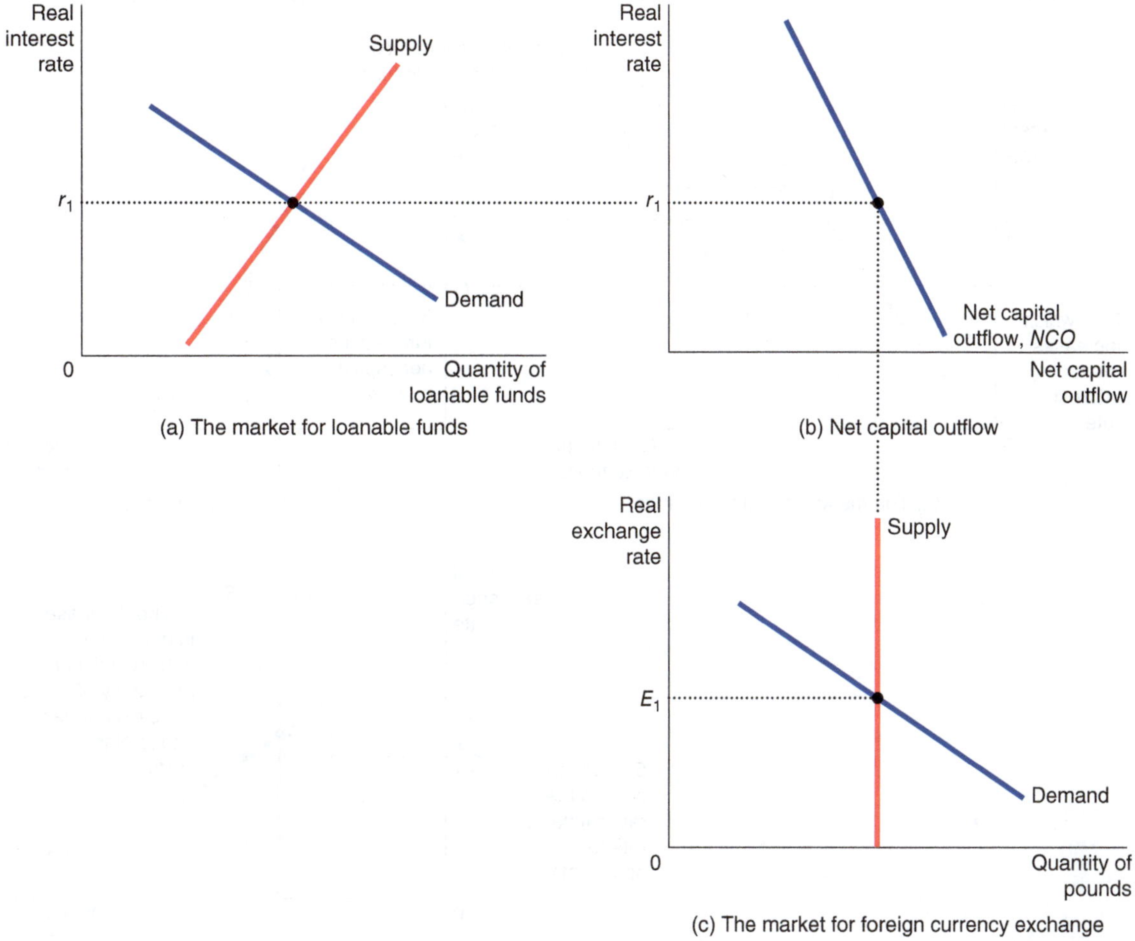

HOW POLICIES AND EVENTS AFFECT AN OPEN ECONOMY

Having developed a model to explain how key macroeconomic variables are determined in an open economy, we can now use the model to analyze how changes in policy and other events alter the economy's equilibrium. As we proceed, keep in mind that our model is just supply and demand in two markets – the market for loanable funds and the market for foreign currency exchange.

Government Budget Deficits

Assume the French government is running a budget deficit. A government budget deficit represents *negative* public saving; it reduces national saving (the sum of public and private saving). A government budget deficit, therefore, reduces the supply of loanable funds, drives up the interest rate and crowds out investment.

Because national saving is reduced, the supply curve for loanable funds shifts to the left. This is shown as the shift from S_1 to S_2 in panel (a) of Figure 9.5.

FIGURE 9.5

The Effects of a Government Budget Deficit

If the French government runs a budget deficit, it reduces the supply of loanable funds from S_1 to S_2 in panel (a). The interest rate rises from r_1 to r_2 to balance the supply and demand for loanable funds. In panel (b), the higher interest rate reduces net capital outflow. Reduced net capital outflow, in turn, reduces the supply of euros in the market for foreign currency exchange in panel (c). This fall in the supply of euros causes the real exchange rate to appreciate from E_1 to E_2. The appreciation of the exchange rate pushes the trade balance towards deficit.

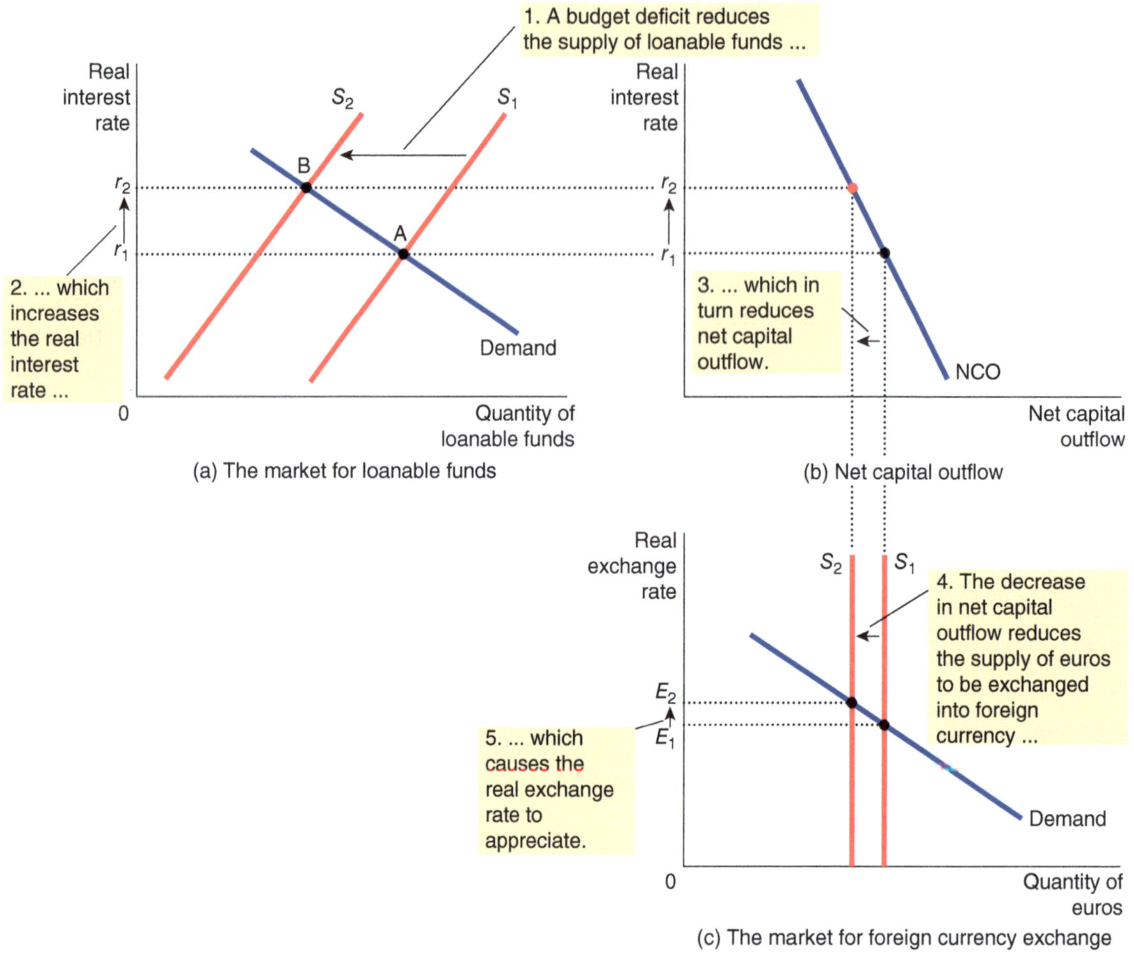

The shift in the supply curve for loanable funds leads to a rise in the interest rate from to r_1 to r_2 to balance supply and demand. Faced with a higher interest rate, borrowers in the market for loanable funds choose to borrow less. This change is represented in the figure as the movement from point A to point B along the demand curve for loanable funds. In particular, households and firms reduce their purchases of capital goods. As in a closed economy, budget deficits crowd out domestic investment.

In an open economy, however, the reduced supply of loanable funds has additional effects. Panel (b) shows that the increase in the interest rate reduces net capital outflow. This fall in net capital outflow is also part of the decrease in the quantity of loanable funds demanded in the movement from point A to point B in panel (a). Because saving kept at home now earns higher rates of return, investing abroad is less attractive, and domestic residents buy fewer foreign assets. Higher interest rates also attract foreign investors, who want to earn the higher returns on French assets. Thus, when budget deficits raise interest rates, both domestic and foreign behaviour cause French net capital outflow to fall.

Panel (c) shows how budget deficits affect the market for foreign currency exchange. Because net capital outflow is reduced, people need less foreign currency to buy foreign assets, and this induces a leftwards shift in the supply curve for euros from S_1 to S_2. The reduced supply of euros causes the real exchange rate to appreciate from E_1 to E_2. That is, the euro becomes more valuable compared to foreign currencies. This appreciation, in turn, makes French goods more expensive compared to foreign goods. Because people both at home and abroad switch their purchases away from the more expensive French goods, exports from France fall, and imports into France rise. For both reasons, French net exports fall. Hence, in an open economy, government budget deficits raise real interest rates, crowd out domestic investment, cause the currency to appreciate and push the trade balance towards deficit.

The budget deficit and trade deficit are so closely related in both theory and practice that, especially when they are both large, they are often referred to by the nickname of the *twin deficits*. We should not, however, view these twins as identical, for many factors beyond fiscal policy can influence the trade deficit.

FYI

Purchasing Power Parity as a Special Case

The model of the exchange rate developed in this section is related to the theory of PPP. According to the theory of PPP, international trade responds quickly to international price differences. If goods were cheaper in one country than in another, they would be exported from the first country and imported into the second until the price difference disappeared. In other words, the theory of PPP assumes that net exports are highly responsive to small changes in the real exchange rate. If net exports were in fact so responsive, the demand curve in Figure 9.2 would be horizontal.

Thus the theory of PPP can be viewed as a special case of the model considered here. In that special case, the demand curve for foreign currency exchange, rather than being downwards sloping, is horizontal at the level of the real exchange rate that ensures parity of purchasing power at home and abroad. That special case is a good place to start when studying exchange rates, but it is far from the end of the story.

This chapter concentrates on the more realistic case in which the demand curve for foreign currency exchange is downwards sloping. This allows for the possibility that the real exchange rate changes over time, as in fact it sometimes does in the real world.

Trade Policy

A **trade policy** is a government policy (or a policy of a body representing many governments) that directly influences the quantity of goods and services that a country or group of countries imports or exports. Trade policy takes various forms and can include tariffs, quotas and non-tariff barriers. Trade policies are common throughout the world.

trade policy a government policy that directly influences the quantity of goods and services that a country imports or exports

Let us consider the macroeconomic impact of trade policy. Suppose that the European car industry, concerned about competition from Japanese car makers, convinces the EU to impose a quota on the number of cars that can be imported from Japan into the EU. In making their case, lobbyists for the car industry assert that the trade restriction would improve the overall EU trade balance. Are they right? Our model, as illustrated in Figure 9.6, offers an answer.

The initial impact of the import restriction is, not surprisingly, on imports. Because net exports equal exports minus imports, the policy also affects net exports. Because net exports are the source of demand for euros in the market for foreign currency exchange, the policy affects the demand curve in this market.

FIGURE 9.6

The Effects of an Import Quota

When the EU imposes a quota on the import of Japanese cars, nothing happens in the market for loanable funds in panel (a) or to net capital outflow in panel (b). The only effect is a rise in net exports (exports minus imports) for any given real exchange rate. As a result, the demand for euros in the market for foreign currency exchange rises, as shown by the shift from to D_1 to D_2 in panel (c). This increase in the demand for euros causes the value of the euro to appreciate from E_1 to E_2. This appreciation of the euro tends to reduce net exports, offsetting the direct effect of the import quota on the trade balance.

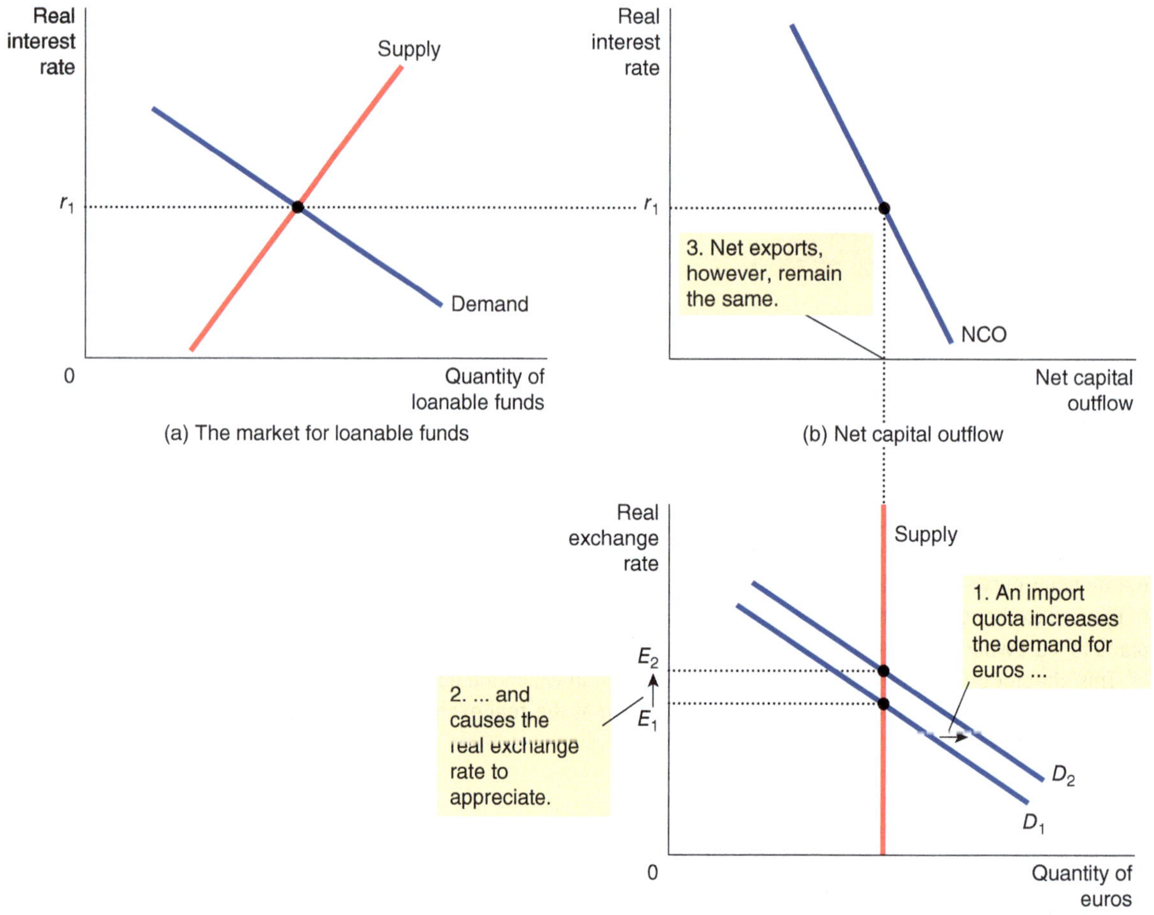

(a) The market for loanable funds

(b) Net capital outflow

(c) The market for foreign currency exchange

As the quota restricts the number of Japanese cars sold in the EU, it reduces imports at any given real exchange rate. Net exports, which equal exports minus imports, will therefore *rise* for any given real exchange rate. Because non-Europeans need euros to buy EU net exports, there is an increased demand for euros in the market for foreign currency exchange. This increase in the demand for euros is shown in panel (c) of Figure 9.6 as the shift from D_1 to D_2.

Panel (c) shows that the increase in the demand for euros causes the real exchange rate to appreciate from E_1 to E_2. Because nothing has happened in the market for loanable funds in panel (a), there is no change in the real interest rate. Because there is no change in the real interest rate, there is also no change in net capital outflow, shown in panel (b). Because there is no change in net capital outflow, there can be no change in net exports, even though the import quota has reduced imports.

The reason why net exports can stay the same while imports fall is explained by the change in the real exchange rate, that is when the euro appreciates in value in the market for foreign currency exchange, European goods become more expensive relative to non-European goods. This appreciation encourages imports and discourages exports. Both of these changes therefore work to offset the direct increase in net exports due to the import quota. In the end, an import quota reduces both imports and exports, but net exports (exports minus imports) are unchanged.

We have thus come to a surprising implication: trade policies do not affect the trade balance. That is, policies that directly influence exports or imports do not alter net exports. This conclusion seems less surprising if you recall the accounting equation:

$$NX = NCO = S - I$$

Net exports equal net capital outflow, which equals national saving minus domestic investment. Trade policies do not alter the trade balance because they do not alter national saving or domestic investment. For given levels of national saving and domestic investment, the real exchange rate adjusts to keep the trade balance the same, regardless of the trade policies the government puts in place.

Although trade policies do not affect a country's overall trade balance, these policies do affect specific firms, industries and countries. When the EU imposes an import quota on Japanese cars, European car makers have less competition from abroad and will sell more cars. At the same time, because the euro has appreciated in value, Airbus, the European aircraft maker, for example, will find it harder to compete with Boeing, the US aircraft maker. European exports of aeroplanes will fall, and European imports of aeroplanes will rise. In this case, the import quota on Japanese cars will increase net exports of cars and decrease net exports of aeroplanes. In addition, it will increase net exports from the EU to Japan and decrease net exports from the EU to the United States. The overall trade balance of the EU economy, however, stays the same.

Capital Flight

A large and sudden movement of funds out of a country is called **capital flight**. To see the implications of capital flight for an economy, we again follow our three steps for analyzing a change in equilibrium.

capital flight a large and sudden reduction in the demand for assets located in a country

Consider first which curves in our model are affected by capital flight. We will use Nigeria as an example here, because the country has experienced a considerable outflow of funds at times in the recent past. If investors around the world decide to sell some of their assets in Nigeria and use the proceeds to buy assets in other countries, this increases Nigerian net capital outflow and, therefore, affects both markets in our model. Most obviously, it affects the net capital outflow curve, and this in turn influences the supply of naira, the Nigerian currency, in the market for foreign currency exchange. In addition, because the demand for loanable funds comes from both domestic investment and net capital outflow, capital flight affects the demand curve in the market for loanable funds.

When net capital outflow increases, there is greater demand for loanable funds to finance these purchases of capital assets abroad. Thus as panel (a) of Figure 9.7 shows, the demand curve for loanable funds shifts to the right from D_1 to D_2. In addition, because net capital outflow is higher for any interest rate, the net capital outflow curve also shifts to the right from NCO_1 to NCO_2, as in panel (b).

To see the effects of capital flight on the economy, we compare the old and new equilibria. Panel (a) of Figure 9.7 shows that the increased demand for loanable funds causes the interest rate in Nigeria to rise from r_1 to r_2. Panel (b) shows that Nigerian net capital outflow increases. Although the rise in the interest rate does make Nigerian assets more attractive, this only partly offsets the impact of capital flight on net capital outflow. Panel (c) shows that the increase in net capital outflow raises the supply of naira in the market for foreign currency exchange from S_1 to S_2. That is, as people try to get out of Nigerian assets, there is a large supply of naira to be converted into other currencies such as euros and pounds. This increase in supply causes the naira to depreciate from E_1 to E_2. Thus capital flight from Nigeria increases Nigerian interest rates and decreases the value of the naira in the market for foreign currency exchange.

FIGURE 9.7

The Effects of Capital Flight

If people decide that Nigeria is a risky place to keep their savings, they will move their capital to safer havens, resulting in an increase in Nigerian net capital outflow. Consequently, the demand for loanable funds in Nigeria rises from D_1 *to* D_2*, as shown in panel (a), and this drives up the Nigerian real interest rate from* r_1 *to* r_2*. Because net capital outflow is higher for any interest rate, that curve also shifts to the right from* NCO_1 *to* NCO_2 *in panel (b). At the same time, in the market for foreign currency exchange, the supply of naira rises from* S_1 *to* S_2*, as shown in panel (c). This increase in the supply of naira causes the currency to depreciate from* E_1 *to* E_2*, so the naira becomes less valuable compared to other currencies.*

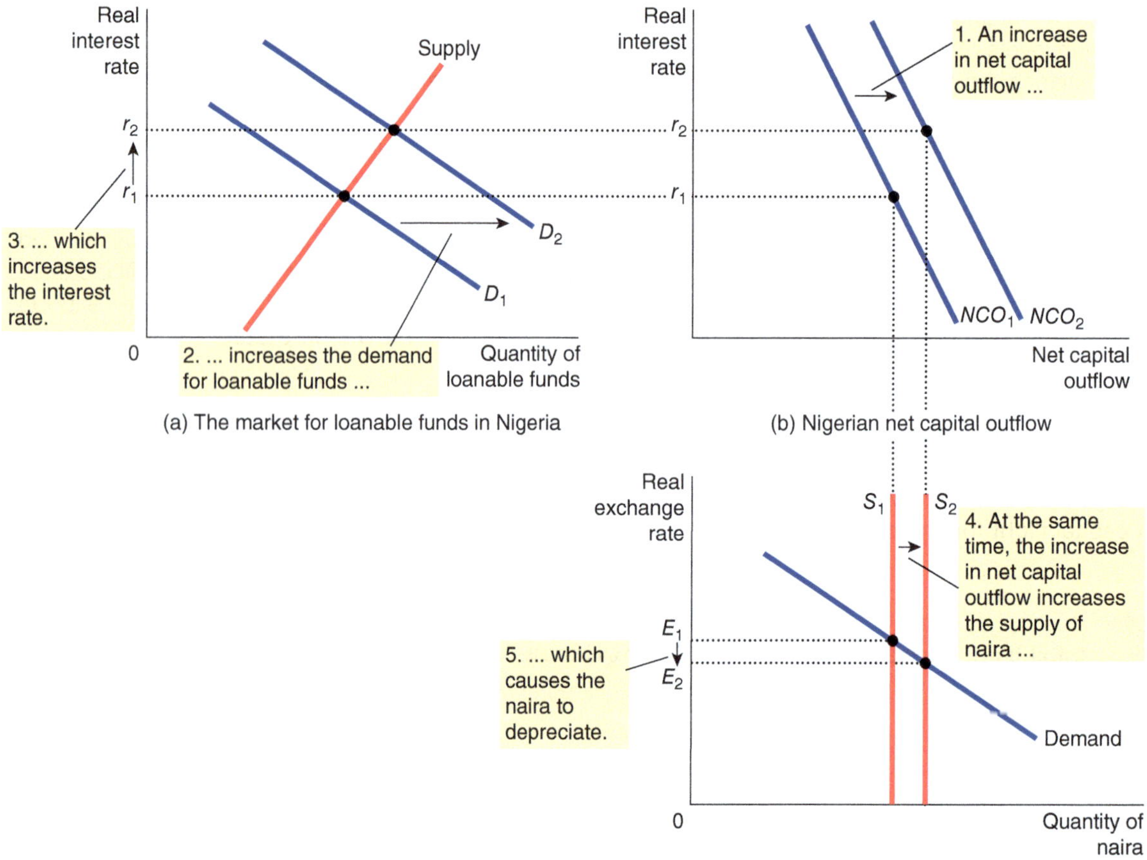

(a) The market for loanable funds in Nigeria

(b) Nigerian net capital outflow

(c) The market for foreign currency exchange

These price changes that result from capital flight influence some key macroeconomic quantities. The depreciation of the currency makes exports cheaper and imports more expensive, pushing the trade balance towards surplus. At the same time, the increase in the interest rate reduces domestic investment, which slows capital accumulation and economic growth.

Although capital flight has its largest impact on the country from which capital is fleeing, it also affects other countries. When capital flows out of Nigeria into the United States, for instance, it has the opposite effect on the US economy as it has on the Nigerian economy. In particular, the rise in Nigerian net capital outflow coincides with a fall in US net capital outflow. As the naira depreciates in value and Nigerian interest rates rise, the dollar appreciates in value and US interest rates fall. The size of this impact on the US economy is dependent on the relative size of the economy of the United States compared to that of Nigeria.

SELF TEST Suppose that Swedes decided to spend a smaller fraction of their incomes. What would be the effect on saving, investment, interest rates, the real exchange rate and the trade balance in Sweden?

CASE STUDY Politics and Open-Economy Macroeconomics

We have been discussing theoretical analysis of the impact of different policies and events using our model of an open economy in this chapter. We can use this model to analyze possible outcomes from actual events. In many cases, these actual events play out against the backdrop of politics and decisions by politicians. In 2025, Donald Trump became the 47th president of the United States after winning the election in 2024. One of the platforms he stood on during the election was trade relations with China.

According to analysts, the United States see China's economic expansion as damaging to US interests. This is partly due to the extent to which industry in China has utilized technologies developed in the United States to help boost its own industrial development. Some people in the United States believe that China has either 'copied' technologies in breach of intellectual property or has engaged in so-called 'forced technology transfers'. This is where access to markets is given in exchange for details of technologies. The growing importance of China in global trade also means that international supply chains are heavily interlinked with China. These developments are seen by the Trump administration as being detrimental to US national interests. Hence, the 'logical' step is to put pressure on China to reform its approaches to trade to consider US interests. In other words, the United States does not see China as a trade partner but as a competitor.

Ways in which the Trump administration could influence US policy in relation to China vary, but suggestions have included reducing the reliance on China in supply chains by building relationships with other countries to develop alternate supply chains. Potential candidate countries for such relationship building might also have lower labour costs, appropriate geographical location and an open stance on trade and trade development. As noted by analysts, Vietnam meets these criteria.

There are political challenges associated with the United States courting improved trade relationships with Vietnam, not least how China might respond to such a move. In addition, it is noted that while Vietnam has the potential for growth and development, it lags behind China in infrastructure, internal communication links and the size and efficiency of its ports. The Vietnamese government has indicated that it wants to encourage more firms to locate to the country, and its tax policies have been amended to encourage foreign investment. Economic growth in Vietnam has been relatively strong in recent years with forecasts suggesting rates of 6 per cent plus on average in the second half of the 2020s. However, despite this, US policymakers may find it difficult to dislodge China from global trade, and its policies will almost certainly include winners and losers.

FIGURE 9.8

Exchange Rate of US Dollar to Vietnamese Dong, 2020–2024

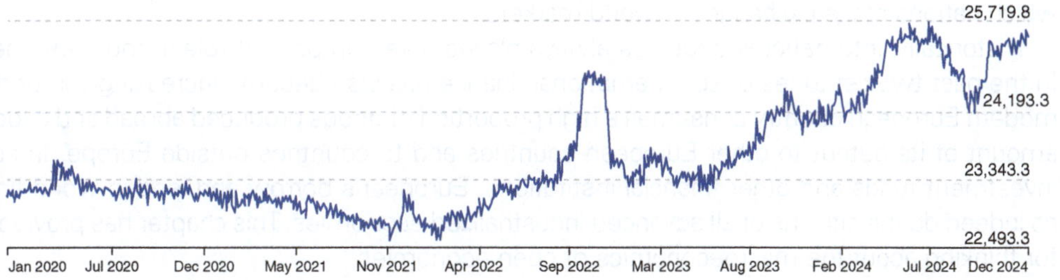

Source: Adapted from www.xe.com/en-gb/currencycharts/?from=USD&to=VND&view=5Y

(Continued)

Questions:

Should trade be seen as a competition or should we view trade as an opportunity for all to benefit?

1 Given the information you have covered to date on economists' views of trade, comment on the suggestion that the US administration is right to treat China as a competitor rather than a partner in trade.
2 How might an 'open stance on trade' affect the overall economy of a country like Vietnam?
3 Look at the information provided in Figure 9.8. How do the changes you observe influence the policy approaches of the US administration outlined in the case study?
4 Assume that the United States succeeds in its aim of reducing supply chain reliance on China and building more trade links with Vietnam through encouraging relocation of manufacturing firms from China to Vietnam. Use the two market model to help illustrate your analysis (Hint: if the policy were successful it would imply capital flight from China).

References:

www.iar-gwu.org/blog/excrw7nyavz2dx1ueg9yw6wl5u2b5d, accessed 7 August 2025.
www.xe.com/en-gb/currencycharts/?from=USD&to=VND&view=5Y, accessed 7 August 2025.

CONCLUSION

The purpose of this chapter has been to develop some basic concepts that macroeconomists use to study open economies. You should now understand why a nation's net exports must equal its net capital outflow, and why national saving must equal domestic investment plus net capital outflow. You should also understand the meaning of nominal and real exchange rates, as well as the implications and limitations of PPP as a theory of how exchange rates are determined.

The macroeconomic variables defined here offered a starting point for analyzing an open economy's interactions with the rest of the world. We developed a model that can explain what determines these variables. We then discuss how various events and policies affect a country's trade balance and the rate at which nations make exchanges in world markets.

Historically, international trade has always played a very important role in most European economies. In the past two centuries or so, international finance has also become increasingly important. The typical modern European country consumes a high proportion of goods produced abroad and exports a significant amount of its output to other European countries and to countries outside Europe. In addition, through investment funds and other financial institutions, Europeans borrow and lend in world financial markets, as indeed do the citizens of all advanced industrialized economies. This chapter has provided a basic model for thinking about the macroeconomics of open economies.

SUMMARY

- Net exports are the value of domestic goods and services sold abroad minus the value of foreign goods and services sold domestically. Net capital outflow is the acquisition of foreign assets by domestic residents minus the acquisition of domestic assets by foreigners. Because every international transaction involves an exchange of an asset for a good or service, an economy's net capital outflow always equals its net exports.

- An economy's saving can be used either to finance investment at home or to buy assets abroad. Thus national saving equals domestic investment plus net capital outflow.
- The nominal exchange rate is the relative price of the currency of two countries, and the real exchange rate is the relative price of the goods and services of two countries.
- When the nominal exchange rate changes so that each unit of domestic currency buys more foreign currency, the domestic currency is said to *appreciate* or *strengthen*. When the nominal exchange rate changes so that each unit of domestic currency buys less foreign currency, the domestic currency is said to *depreciate* or *weaken*.
- According to the theory of purchasing power parity, a unit of currency should be able to buy the same quantity of goods in all countries. This theory implies that the nominal exchange rate between the currencies of two countries should reflect the price levels in those countries. As a result, countries with relatively high inflation should have depreciating currencies, and countries with relatively low inflation should have appreciating currencies.
- To analyze the macroeconomics of open economies we look at the market for loanable funds and the market for foreign currency exchange.
- In the market for loanable funds, the interest rate adjusts to balance the supply of loanable funds (from national saving) and the demand for loanable funds (from domestic investment, and net capital outflow).
- In the market for foreign currency exchange, the real exchange rate adjusts to balance the supply of domestic currency (for net capital outflow) and the demand for domestic currency (for net exports).
- Because net capital outflow is part of the demand for loanable funds and provides the supply of domestic currency for foreign currency exchange, it is the variable that connects these two markets.
- A policy that reduces national saving, such as a government budget deficit, reduces the supply of loanable funds and drives up the interest rate. The higher interest rate reduces net capital outflow, which reduces the supply of domestic currency in the market for foreign currency exchange. The domestic currency appreciates and net exports fall.
- Although restrictive trade policies, such as tariffs or quotas on imports, are sometimes advocated as a way to alter the trade balance, they do not necessarily have that effect. A trade restriction increases net exports for a given exchange rate and, therefore, increases the demand for the domestic currency in the market for foreign currency exchange. As a result, the domestic currency appreciates in value, making domestic goods more expensive relative to foreign goods. This appreciation offsets the initial impact of the trade restriction on net exports.
- When investors change their attitudes about holding assets of a country, the ramifications for the country's economy can be profound. In particular, political instability or a lack of confidence in an economy can lead to capital flight, which tends to increase interest rates and causes the currency to depreciate.

IN THE NEWS

The Balance of Payments

The value and volume of trade between a country and its trading partners and the flows of capital and assets are monitored and reported on by most countries. In the UK, the Office for National Statistics (ONS) publishes what is known as *The Pink Book* each year which provides details of the 'Balances between inward and outward transactions, providing a net flow of transactions between UK residents and the rest of the world and reports on how that flow is funded'.

A summary of the main points in *The Pink Book* for 2024 showed the UK current account deficit, a measure of the inflow and outflow of goods and services, investment incomes and transfer payments of the UK and the rest of the world, widened in cash terms in 2023 to £53.3 billion or 2.0 per cent of nominal GDP compared to £53.1 billion or 2.1 per cent of GDP in 2022. The pattern of trade and income flows over the previous five years was heavily influenced by the Covid-19 pandemic. The ONS noted that the UK recorded the second largest current account deficit of the G7 economies in 2021, for example, with the United States recording the highest at 2.9 per cent of GDP. Germany experienced a surplus on its current account, but the surplus was the lowest since 2013 at 6.9 per cent of GDP.

(Continued)

The influence of the services sector in the UK economy has been growing for many years and *The Pink Book* noted that the UK's trade surplus in services has generally widened since the mid-2000s and in 2023 was in surplus at £172.6 billion (6.3 per cent of GDP), narrowing from £162.4 billion (6.4 per cent of GDP) in 2022.

The trade in goods has been in deficit for many years. The ONS reported that the trade deficit had narrowed from £206.5 billion (8.2 per cent of GDP) to £206.5 billion (8.2 per cent of GDP) in 2022. The main reason given was the smaller deficit in finished manufactured goods such as electrical and mechanical machinery. Overall, the value of imports of goods was £581.2 billion in 2023 and the value of exports of goods was £393.5 billion (rounded).

As we have seen in the chapter, investors look to place their funds partly on the basis of the interest rate and the returns they expect to be able to gain. *The Pink Book* reported falls in UK earnings on investment abroad. Net direct investment income fell by £27.6 billion between 2022 and 2023, largely due to earnings from direct investment abroad which fell from £161.8 billion in 2022 to £140.9 billion in 2023. *The Pink Book* also reports on the financial account which measures the 'net acquisition or net incurrence of financial assets and liabilities'. The financial account shows how the UK is financing its current account deficit. The ONS notes that there are three main types of investments which finance the UK current account deficit. Foreign direct investment or direct investment, portfolio investment and 'other'. *The Pink Book* reported that there was a net financial inflow to the UK of £48.1 billion in 2023 with financial outflows totalling £325.0 billion and financial outflows of £276.9 billion.

© iStock/thitivong

The balance of trade does not have to balance but the balance of payments must.

Critical Thinking Questions

1 Why do you think it is important for a country to record its trade flows with the rest of the world?
2 The UK trade deficit in goods has widened in the twenty-first century. What factors might have driven this trend?
3 Is the fact that the current account deficit narrowed slightly between 2022 and 2023 a cause for celebration for the the UK economy? Explain.
4 The Pink Book describes the financial account as the 'counterpart to the current and capital account'. Find out what the capital account is and explain why the financial account is described as the counterpart to the current and capital accounts.
5 Explain why the balance of payments must balance but the balance of trade need not.

Reference:

www.ons.gov.uk/economy/nationalaccounts/balanceofpayments/bulletins/unitedkingdombalanceofpaymentsthepinkbook/latest, accessed 7 August 2025.

QUESTIONS FOR REVIEW

1 Why do economists sometimes conduct analysis under assumptions of a closed economy? What do you understand by the term an 'open economy'?
2 Define net exports and net capital outflow. Explain how and why they are related.
3 Explain the relationship between saving, investment and net capital outflow.
4 If a Japanese car is priced at 500,000 yen, a similar German car is priced at €10,000, and a euro can buy ¥100, what are the nominal and real exchange rates?

5 Describe the economic logic behind the theory of purchasing power parity.

6 Describe supply and demand in the market for loanable funds and the market for foreign currency exchange. How are these markets linked?

7 What effect does a government budget deficit have on the interest rate and what effect would a budget surplus have on the exchange rate? Draw a diagram to illustrate your answer.

8 Describe the main advantages and disadvantages of fixed and floating exchange rates.

9 Suppose that a steel workers' union encourages economic actors to buy only European steel. What would this policy do to the European overall trade balance and the real exchange rate? What is the impact on the European steel industry? What is the impact on the European textile industry?

10 What effect would you expect a tariff to have on the real exchange rate? Explain using appropriate diagrams.

PROBLEMS AND APPLICATIONS

1 How would the following transactions affect UK exports, imports and net exports?
  a. A British art lecturer spends the summer touring museums in Italy.
  b. Students in Paris flock to see the latest Royal Shakespeare Company perform *King Lear* on tour.
  c. The British art lecturer buys a new Volvo.
  d. A student in Munich buys a Manchester United official team shirt (in Munich).
  e. A British citizen goes to Calais for the day to stock up on French wine.

2 Describe the difference between foreign direct investment and foreign portfolio investment. Who is more likely to engage in foreign direct investment – a corporation or an individual investor? Who is more likely to engage in foreign portfolio investment?

3 How would the following transactions affect UK net capital outflow? Also, state whether each involves direct investment or portfolio investment.
  a. A British mobile telephone company establishes an office in the Czech Republic.
  b. A US company's pension fund buys shares in BP.
  c. Toyota expands its factory in Derby, England.

4 What is happening to the Swiss real exchange rate in each of the following situations? Explain.
  a. The Swiss nominal exchange rate is unchanged, but prices rise faster in Switzerland than abroad.
  b. The Swiss nominal exchange rate is unchanged, but prices rise faster abroad than in Switzerland.
  c. The Swiss nominal exchange rate declines, and prices are unchanged in Switzerland and abroad.
  d. The Swiss nominal exchange rate declines, and prices rise faster abroad than in Switzerland.

5 A can of lemonade is priced at €0.75 in Europe and 12 pesos in Mexico. What would the peso–euro exchange rate be if purchasing power parity holds? If a monetary expansion caused all prices in Mexico to double, so that lemonade rose to 24 pesos, what would happen to the peso–euro exchange rate?

6 Germany generally runs a trade surplus. Do you think this is most related to high foreign demand for German goods, low German demand for foreign goods, a high German saving rate relative to German investment, or structural barriers against imports into Germany? Explain your answer.

7 Assume that there is a rise in the trade deficit of a country due largely to the rise in a government budget deficit. Assume also that some commentators in the popular press claim that the increased trade deficit resulted from a decline in the quality of the country's products relative to foreign products.
  a. Assume that the country's products did decline in relative quality during this period. How might this affect net exports *at any given exchange rate*?
  b. Use a three-panel diagram to show the effect of this shift in net exports on the country's real exchange rate and trade balance.
  c. Does a decline in the quality of the country's products have any effect on standards of living for its residents? (Hint: when a country's residents sell goods to non-country residents, what do they receive in return?)

8 Suppose the French suddenly develop a strong taste for British wine. Answer the following questions in words and using a diagram.
   a. What happens to the demand for pounds in the market for foreign currency exchange?
   b. What happens to the value of pounds in the market for foreign currency exchange?
   c. What happens to the quantity of UK net exports?

9 Suppose that real interest rates increase across Europe. Explain how this development will affect UK net capital outflow. Then explain how it will affect UK net exports by using a formula from the chapter and by using a diagram. What will happen to the UK real interest rate and real exchange rate?

10 Assume that saving in China has been used to finance investment into the EU. That is, the Chinese have been buying European capital assets.
   a. If the Chinese decided they no longer wanted to buy European assets, what would happen in the European market for loanable funds? In particular, what would happen to European interest rates, European saving and European investment?
   b. What would happen in the market for foreign currency exchange? In particular, what would you expect to happen to the value of the euro and the European trade balance? Explain.

PART 5 SHORT-RUN ECONOMIC FLUCTUATIONS

10 BUSINESS CYCLES

So far we have been considering long-run determinants of key economic variables. It is short-run fluctuations, however, which tend to be more obviously felt by most people. Over time, economies seem to fluctuate between periods of relative stability and instability. Economic stability sees economic growth, falling unemployment and inflation at relatively low and stable levels. Periods of instability are where economic growth declines and unemployment rises or where the economy overheats and inflation accelerates. These periods of expansion and slowdown are referred to as the **business cycle**. Measuring business cycles was pioneered by Wesley C. Mitchell and Arthur F. Burns. Their book, *Measuring Business Cycles,* published in 1946, looked at how different economic variables change as economic growth changed. Burns and Mitchell wanted to investigate why economic variables moved together in times of economic slowdown. They defined a **recession** as characterized by a period of falling incomes and rising unemployment, which technically occurs after two successive quarters of negative growth. If such a contraction in growth continues and is more severe it might be described as a **depression**.

business cycle fluctuations in economic activity such as employment and production
recession a period of declining real incomes and rising unemployment. The technical definition gives recession occurring after two successive quarters of negative economic growth
depression a severe recession

Business cycles can be analyzed through looking at periods of economic growth and identifying peaks and troughs in activity where each represent turning points. A **peak** occurs when output, employment and other variables such as retail sales or manufacturing production begin to decline together. A **trough** refers to the time when these economic variables begin to rise. Identifying when these events occur is difficult because of the complexity of the data involved and the way they are measured. In addition, some economic variables, such as employment, may not change at the same time as others and are regarded as 'lagged indicators'.

peak a point where related economic variables begin to decline
trough the point where related economic variables begin to rise

There are considerable disagreements about what causes short-run variations in economic activity. The term 'cycle' might imply that expansions and contractions are part of a regular pattern, but that is not the case. There is no specific pattern to the periods between peaks and troughs, nor to the length of the upswing and downturn in economies. The UK recession of 1920–4, for example, saw GDP fall by about 9 per cent from its peak over the first 18 months, and then take a further 27 months to get back to its pre-recession peak. In the next 12 months it rose to around 4 per cent above its pre-recession peak. In 1930–4, the length of time for the economy to recover to its pre-recession peak was around 48 months, but the economy 'only' fell to around 7 per cent below its pre-recession peak. In the 1990–3 recession, the economy took around 32 months to recover, but thereafter rose by over 8 per cent above its pre-recession peak and only fell to around 3 per cent below its pre-recession peak. The 2007–9 Financial Crisis saw the economy falling to around 6 per cent below its pre-recession peak and it was not until around 2013–14 that the economy finally reached its pre-crisis level. The Covid-19 pandemic led to a contraction of the UK economy by 10.7 per cent in 2020, the largest annual fall in real GDP for 100 years. In November 2021, the level of quarterly GDP was estimated to be 2.1 per cent below the quarter 4 level of GDP in 2019, before the pandemic took hold. Across the EU 27, GDP fell by 5.9 per cent in 2020. The reasons why short-run fluctuations occur is part of business cycle theory. The fact that different models exist reflects the disagreement among economists about the causes of short-run fluctuations.

In theory, there is no reason why business cycles occur at all. If factor resources are being employed fully, investment is sufficient to cover depreciation and labour productivity is stable, then the economy could continue to grow. However, shocks to the economy through changes in consumption and government spending can cause full employment output to be disturbed. Rigidities in markets can exacerbate the problems and cause broader volatility in the economy. This view would be a demand-side explanation to short-run fluctuations.

Other explanations include changes to productivity levels through changes in technology or the ability of workers to seek increases in real wages. Of course, events such as the 2007–9 Financial Crisis, Covid-19 and geopolitical conflicts such as those in Ukraine and the Middle East represent significant shocks to the economy and can clearly lead to contractions in economic activity. Even without such shocks, activity still fluctuates. Much debate on short-run fluctuations has centred on the role of monetary policy. As central banks increase and reduce interest rates and the money supply changes, short-run fluctuations tend to follow. Developing models which can help inform central banks' decision-making has been an important part of economic research since the late 1980s.

TREND GROWTH RATES

Most of the data we will be looking at in this chapter are classed as **time-series data**, observations on a variable over a time period and which are ordered over time. Central to the analysis of business cycles is GDP over time. Figure 10.1 shows GDP in the UK from 1960 to 2024. The value of GDP is given on the vertical axis in seasonally adjusted £m and the horizontal axis is the time period in years.

> **time-series data** observations on a variable over a time period and which are ordered over time

Figure 10.1 shows that the value of the UK economy in 1960 was around £634 billion, but by 2023 the UK economy was worth around £2.54 trillion. A trend line has been added and this shows how, over time, the GDP of the UK has risen. It also shows how actual GDP fluctuates around the trend. Graphing the GDP of other countries and indeed the EU 27 would show a similar pattern, with trend GDP rising over time but actual GDP fluctuating around this trend.

The debate over what causes short-run fluctuations also focuses attention on policy response and welfare needs. Welfare issues arise if it is assumed that the economy is deviating in some way from its equilibrium. Policy is put in place to address the welfare issues that arise. Some economists, however, believe that the economy may not be deviating from its equilibrium, but instead moves from one equilibrium point to another. If this is the case, policy is not required because there are no welfare issues arising if the economy is in equilibrium. We shall explore these differences later in the chapter.

FIGURE 10.1

GDP in the UK 1960–2024

The figure shows UK GDP, measured in seasonally adjusted millions of pounds, on the vertical axis over the period 1960–2024. A trend line has been added to show the fluctuation of actual GDP from trend GDP over time.

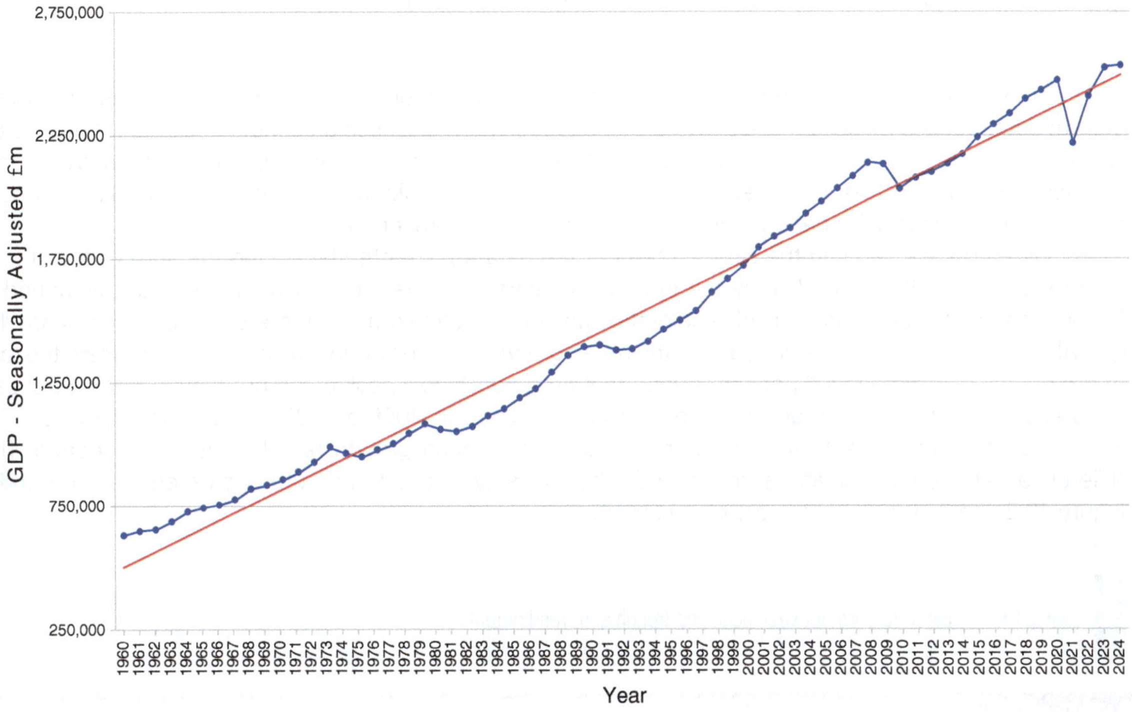

Source: Adapted from www.ons.gov.uk/economy/grossdomesticproductgdp/timeseries/abmi/qna, accessed 7 August 2025

Data Concepts

When dealing with macroeconomic variables there are a number of concepts that we will utilize over the coming chapters which need to be understood. Figure 10.2 shows the annual rate of growth of UK GDP between 1960 and 2023. It is clear from this figure that the rate of growth fluctuates over the time period. From 1962, growth accelerated and reached 5.7 per cent in 1964 before slowing down up to 1968. Thereafter growth accelerated again reaching 6.5 per cent in 1973 before the economy slumped dramatically and economic activity actual shrank in 1974 and 1975. Further recessions occurred in the early 1980s and the early 1990s. After a 15-year period of consistent growth there was a dramatic end in 2008, when the economy shrank. In 2009, the economy shrank by a further 4.2 per cent. Growth returned in 2010 but at a relatively low level before picking up in 2013 and 2014 before slowing down again in 2015. Growth slowed further in 2016 and 2017 and in 2020 there was the dramatic contraction in GDP due to the pandemic.

When economic activity is accelerating and the rate of growth is rising each year this represents a period of expansion. Depending on the rate at which real output is accelerating, it may be referred to as a *boom*.

In 2017, UK GDP grew at 2.1 per cent, and in 2018 it grew at 1.7 per cent. It is important to note that economic activity slowed down in 2018 but still continued to grow. An example serves to illustrate. Assume economic activity is measured in terms of the number of tonnes of steel produced. If output was 10 million tonnes in 2022 and 12 million tonnes in 2023, then the growth rate is 20 per cent. If output is 13.5 million tonnes in 2024, the growth rate is now 12.5 per cent. Growth has slowed compared to 2023, but the economy is still producing more steel than the year before. This is why we use the terms 'accelerating' and 'decelerating' to describe changes in the rate of growth of GDP when it is positive.

However, when real output actually shrinks then there is a **contraction** in the economy. If output of steel in 2025 is 13 million tonnes, the economy would have shrunk. Less steel is being produced compared to 2024 and growth will be −3.7 per cent.

contraction when real output is lower than the previous time period

The news media are keen to use emotive words such as 'boom', 'bust' and 'slump' when reporting growth data, but it is important to be aware of language when discussing economic growth. If expansion is considerably above trend, for example, then the term 'boom' might be appropriate, but if growth is only just above trend then that term may not be applicable. For example, does a growth rate of 0.25 per cent for the year following a 2.0 per cent growth the year before represent 'a slump'?

In Figure 10.2 we can find the simple mean of the data represented by adding the sum of the annual growth rates (148.9) and dividing by the number of years (64). The mean growth rate over this period is 2.3 per cent. In describing periods of accelerating and decelerating growth, therefore, we can compare the growth rate at a particular time period with the mean growth rate. The period from 1970 to 1973 saw the rate of growth of GDP average 4.3 per cent during that time, reaching a peak of 6.5 per cent in 1973. Between 1985 and 1988, the average growth rate was 4.5 per cent. In 2008 and 2009, GDP growth was −0.2 and −4.6 per cent respectively, considerably below the mean growth rate for the whole period. The difference between a peak and a trough in the business cycle and trend output is called the **amplitude**. Figure 10.2 shows that this can vary considerably.

amplitude the difference between peak and trough and trend output

FIGURE 10.2

UK GDP Growth Rate, 1960–2023 (%)

UK GDP fluctuates between various peaks and troughs over the period. In some cases, GDP growth is positive for a number of years and the economy is growing during that time, but in other years GDP growth is negative and the economy shrinks.

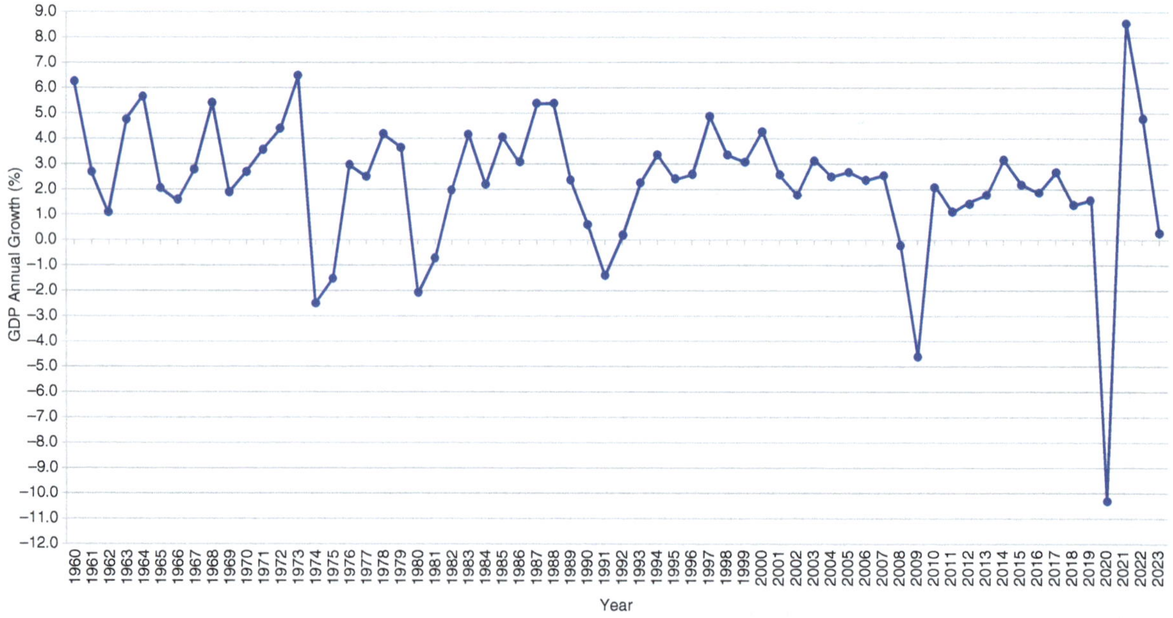

Source: www.ons.gov.uk/economy/grossdomesticproductgdp/timeseries/ihyp/pn2, accessed 7 August 2025.

SELF TEST What are the main phases of the business cycle?

Trends

An important point of disagreement about economic time-series data is the existence of trends. A **trend** is the underlying long-term movement in a data series. The trend can be upwards over time, downwards or constant. Earlier we took the mean (average) of the growth rate in UK GDP between 1960 and 2023 as being 2.3 per cent. The mean of a set of time-series data can be used as the trend.

trend the underlying long-term movement in a data series

Figure 10.1 showed UK GDP between 1960 and 2024 and a trend line was added to the data showing very clearly that the trend was upwards over the time period shown. Trends can demonstrate patterns over a period which can be described as *stationary* and *non-stationary*. **Stationary data** are time-series data that have a constant mean value over time, whereas **non-stationary data** are time-series data where the mean value can either rise or fall over time. The data in Figure 10.1 would suggest that GDP is non-stationary data rising over time. Other economic variables might exhibit the characteristic of stationary data. Unemployment, for example, tends to be more characteristic of stationary data. As with any statistical analysis, care must be taken to consider what data have been included, how the data have been constructed, what time period is involved and what test has been applied. There is often disagreement about appropriate statistical tests and measurements used in economic analysis.

stationary data time-series data that has a constant mean value over time
non-stationary data time-series data where the mean value can either rise or fall over time

The disagreement about how statistical tests are used and applied is beyond the scope of this book. However, disagreement between economists on vital issues, such as the path of business cycles and the policy options that might be applied, is derived in large part from different interpretations of the reliability and validity of different statistical methods. A trend over time has implications. For example, looking at Figure 10.1, would there be any reason to assume that the level of economic growth for the next 10 years will not continue to be positive and increasing in the UK? Non-stationary data can be assumed to have what are called **deterministic trends**. These are trends that are constant, positive or negative, independent of time for the series being analyzed and which change by a constant amount each period. GDP might deviate from trend over short-term periods, but when looked at over longer time periods will revert to the mean. In contrast, a **stochastic trend** is one where the trend variable changes by some random amount in each time period. If macroeconomic variables are analyzed assuming they exhibit a deterministic trend, for example that GDP will rise by 2.3 per cent on average, then the implication is that policy measures can be applied when GDP deviates from this average. What has caused GDP to deviate from the mean must be a transitory phenomenon (is temporary and only lasting for a short period of time). This further implies that the cause of the deviation must also be temporary and can be influenced.

deterministic trends trends that are constant, positive or negative, independent of time for the series being analyzed
stochastic trend where trend variables change by some random amount in each time period

What if the deterministic trend is illusory and we have applied an inappropriate statistical test to the time-series data we are looking at? If the data exhibit a trend that is stochastic, then policy measures might be applied that are unnecessary and possibly distorting. If the deviations are removed, the variable does not, unlike a deterministic trend, revert to the mean. Instead, the variable might move from its mean and stay away from that mean over the next time period.

The law of large numbers states that as the number of observations increases, the average of the observations is likely to be the mean of the whole population of observations. For example, if we toss a fair coin 10 times, we might observe 6 instances of heads and 4 of tails. The mean of these observations in terms of the ratio heads to tails is 6:10 or 0.6. If we toss the coin a further 90 times, we might observe 42 heads and 48 tails, a mean of 0.46. When we look at the mean of the population as a whole (100 observations) the mean is 0.48. If we toss the coin a further 10,000 times the chances are that the mean is likely to be close to 0.5. If we continued to toss the coin and observe the trend, it is likely that it would continue to be 0.5. Taking any selection of data from the total number of observations, the mean might be different, as shown above. The greater the number of observations we observe, however, the more likely it is that we will get the mean. It would not be unreasonable to assume in this particular example, that in future time periods the mean is going to continue to be 0.5.

If, however, something changes in the nature of the coin, or the friction exerted by air, the surface on which the coin lands, etc. affects the coin-tossing outcomes, then the trends (mean) we observe might be completely random for every time period we observe. Therefore, when looking at the population as a whole, the consistency of the law of large numbers is destroyed.

This summary of statistical arguments is important to bear in mind as we look at short-run variations in macroeconomic variables. The study of time-series data is complex, and it is important to take into account as we look at different schools of thought in economics. Many of the differences of opinion arise from different interpretations and use of statistics.

Procyclical and Countercyclical Movements in Macroeconomic Data

Let us assume that the GDP of a country exhibits a deterministic trend and that the trend growth over a 50-year period is 2.0 per cent. If GDP over an 18-month period is reported as 1.3 per cent, what might we expect to have happened to key macroeconomic variables? Given GDP has slowed from trend it might be expected that the number of people out of work would have risen, that inflation would have slowed, the money supply contracted and real wages would have fallen. Observations over time do show that, when economic activity slows, unemployment rises and inflation decelerates. There is some intuitive common sense in this summary. If firms are cutting back production, as a slowing of GDP implies, then they might not need as many employees. So some might be let go and, at the same time, firms may think twice about increasing prices when economic activity is slowing for fear of losing sales. They may decide to keep prices constant or even lower them to try to boost demand.

Economists often look at the movement of pairs of variables, which are called *comovements*. Typically, one of these variables is GDP. Economists will then compare another economic variable such as inflation or employment with GDP over time and see if any relationship can be determined.

Comovements may exhibit certain relationships. When a variable is above trend when GDP is above trend, the variable is said to be **procyclical**. When GDP is above trend, inflation and employment also tend to be above trend and so are classed as procyclical. Real wages and nominal interest rates are also classed as procyclical. If a variable is below trend when GDP is above trend, the variable is described as **countercyclical**. Unemployment can be classed as countercyclical because it tends to be below trend when GDP is above trend.

procyclical a variable that is above trend when GDP is above trend
countercyclical a variable that is below trend when GDP is above trend

SELF TEST Would you expect inflation to be procyclical or countercyclical in a period when economic activity is declining? What would you expect real wages to be in a period of rising economic activity?

Variables as Indicators

Economists are not fortune tellers but, in trying to understand business cycles and whether it is possible to predict changes in economic activity, they have looked at the extent to which economic variables or collections of economic variables over time give any clue to deviations from trend. Research by Mitchell and Burns in the United States in the 1930s led to an index of cyclical indicators which is now utilized by the OECD to identify potential turning points in economic activity. Figure 10.3 shows the composite leading indicators index between 2008 and 2024 for the OECD area. The arrows show turning points. For example, it is clear that the index began to decline at the start of 2008. The global recession followed. In early 2009, the index began to rise. This indicated a turning point to suggest economic activity would begin to improve.

Cyclical indicators can have three characteristics. They can be **leading indicators**, where the indicator tends to foretell future changes in economic activity. They can be a **lagging indicator**, whose changes occur after changes in economic activity have occurred. Or they can be **coincident indicators** whose changes occur at the same time as changes in economic activity. The OECD's composite leading indicators (CLI) index is classed as a leading indicator.

leading indicators indicators which can be used to foretell future changes in economic activity
lagging indicator an indicator whose changes occur after changes in economic activity have occurred
coincident indicators indicators whose changes occur at the same time as changes in economic activity

FIGURE 10.3

OECD Area Composite Leading Indicators (CLI) Index, Amplitude Adjusted, Long-Term Average = 100, Jan 2008–January 2024

The CLI index shows key turning points in the global economy since 2008.

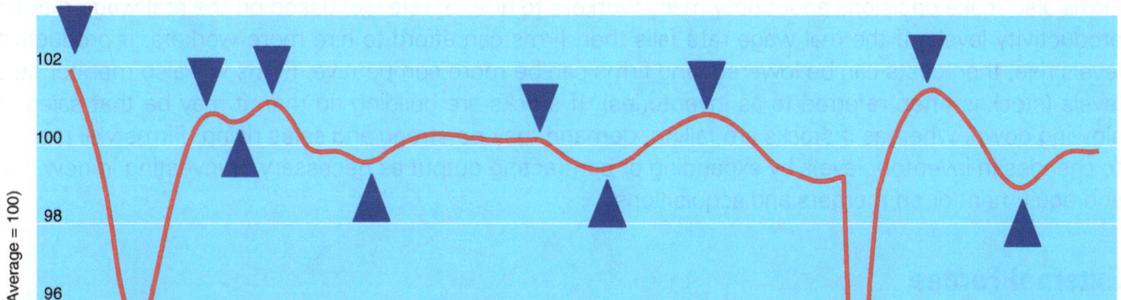

Source: OECD (2024) Composite Leading Indicator (CLI). Available at www.oecd.org/en/data/indicators/composite-leading-indicator-cli .html?oecdcontrol-b2a0dbca4d-var3=2000-05&oecdcontrol-b2a0dbca4d-var4=2024-01, accessed 7 August 2025

CAUSES OF CHANGES IN THE BUSINESS CYCLE

We know that the economy is made up of households and firms, so it is reasonable to expect that the behaviour of these two elements of the economy have a role to play in how economic activity changes.

Household Spending Decisions

Households make decisions on how much labour to supply. The amount of labour supplied depends in part on the real wage rate. The rate of growth of wages in relation to prices affects consumers' purchasing power. How consumers perceive changes in real wages is an important factor in decision-making. Households also make consumption decisions on everyday goods and services, leisure and entertainment. They also decide on whether to purchase what are sometimes called 'big-ticket' items such as durable household goods (TVs, washing machines, cars, fridge freezers, etc.) not to mention decisions on purchasing houses or flats. Purchasing decisions on these items may in themselves be cyclical. If a couple buy their first home, for example, it may be that in the next year they spend considerable amounts on furniture, decorating and household goods. It then may be several years before goods begin to wear out and need replacing or the house needs decorating again.

Households will also make decisions based on changes in interest rates, house prices and taxation. Increases in interest rates may encourage a rise in saving and a reduction in consumption. Changes in house prices affect people's wealth and the effect can lead to changes in spending, especially if people are able to borrow on the strength of the value of their property. Changes in tax rates affect different people in different ways and can have a considerable impact on behaviour.

Firms' Decision-Making

Firms make decisions about production levels – how much output to produce – based on what they think they can sell. If firms face strong demand, they are likely to increase output, may take on more workers, and buy more raw materials and semi-finished goods in order to satisfy demand. Some firms may look to expand by investing in new equipment and machinery or by acquiring new premises or even other firms. Firms also make decisions about how many workers to hire (or release) based on the real wage rate and productivity levels. If the real wage rate falls then firms can afford to hire more workers. If productivity levels rise, then costs can be lowered, and firms can be more competitive. Firms will also monitor stock levels (stock is often referred to as inventories). If stocks are building up then it may be that sales are slowing down, whereas if stocks are falling, demand may be strong and sales rising. Firms will respond to changes in inventory levels by expanding or contracting output as necessary or investing in new plant and equipment or on mergers and acquisitions.

External Forces

In an open economy, movements in exchange rates affect the competitiveness of domestic and foreign firms through changes in import and export prices. Economic activity abroad can also have an impact on countries as consumption and investment decisions by firms and consumers abroad change. The problems faced by a number of countries in the euro area since the 2007–9 Financial Crisis slowed the pace of recovery.

We must also take into account the effect of events which are often totally unpredictable such as drought, flood, tsunamis, hurricanes, extreme cold, or earthquakes, through to events such as political upheaval, war, terrorism and conflict. These can all have far-reaching effects on individual countries and the global economy. The pandemic, conflict in Ukraine and the Middle East, riots, terror incidents and extreme weather events remind us that few economies are isolated from external shocks.

Government Policy

Governments have control over a considerable amount of economic activity. They make decisions about tax rates and consider the incentive effects of such changes. Decisions about major infrastructure investment can have ripple effects throughout an economy. Government agents can also have an effect on economic activity. Central banks are independent of most governments across Western Europe, but in the UK, for example, the government sets the target for inflation. The Bank of England is responsible for setting monetary policy to meet the target the government has set. Changes in interest rates will affect both households and firms through policy decisions like quantitative easing and measures designed to help ease or restrict credit flows to business and households.

Confidence and Expectations

Households and firms not only make decisions based on current needs but also on the future. It is unlikely that an individual will make a decision to take out a loan for €25,000 to buy a car if that person believes the security of their job is in question. The news media provide information on the state of the economy, governments make pronouncements, senior finance ministers and banking officials are interviewed about their forecasts for the economy. Employees will get a sense of how the firms they work for are performing, and those in the public sector may take close note of government policy decisions. Workers may look at current inflation rates and their wages and may make judgements about inflation in the future and, therefore, what sort of wage rise they need to maintain their standard of living. Firms may also consider inflation rates and make judgements about price rises to consumers based on what they expect inflation to be in the future and how inflation in raw materials might affect their costs.

Our expectations of the future shape our decisions, and confidence of firms and households to make decisions is something that is very difficult to quantify and equally difficult to know when it changes. At what point does any individual begin to believe that stock or house prices have reached a peak? At what point does a firm take the decision to make redundancies and why does confidence begin to decline or to pick up? These are all difficult questions to answer but confidence and expectations play a significant part in swings in economic activity.

SELF TEST A country's finance minister presents the government's annual financial statement and advises that they expect GDP to contract sharply in the coming year because of adverse international economic conditions. How might such a speech influence confidence and expectations of households and firms?

BUSINESS CYCLE MODELS

Attempts to try to understand how business cycles occur have led to models which differ in the assumptions that are made. On the one hand, there are models which assume that markets clear quickly and, as a result, the welfare of economic actors (firms and households) is maximized. Consequently, there are no reasons why economic actors should change their behaviour. On the other, there are models which assume that markets do not always clear quickly and that rigidities are present, particularly with regard to prices and wages, which means that for a time, economic actors will not be maximizing welfare.

We will provide an overview of some of the main business cycle models with perspectives that consider the supply-side of the economy and the demand-side of the economy, and we will finish with dynamic stochastic general equilibrium (DSGE) models.

Supply-Side: The New Classical Model

This model is based around analysis of the supply-side of the economy and the operation of the labour market. It is assumed that the labour market clears, but that workers have imperfect information. The model highlights the importance of anticipated and unanticipated price changes. If workers correctly anticipate price changes, they can change their behaviour such that real wages and the amount of labour they supply adjust to clear the market. For example, if the price level rises, real wages then fall, and therefore firms will be encouraged to hire more labour. If the price change is anticipated, workers will recognize that real wages will fall and therefore supply less labour. As a result, the demand for labour will be greater than the supply of labour so the nominal wage will rise. However, the real wage at the new equilibrium will be constant.

If workers do not anticipate the change in prices, the real wage will fall, firms will demand more labour, but workers will continue to offer the same amount of labour hours. Therefore, the demand for labour will be in excess of the supply, which leads to a rise in nominal wages. However, this rise will be less than the price rise. The result is that output will rise but the real wage will fall. The increase in output will be above trend GDP. In this model there has been a deviation from equilibrium output because workers have incomplete information and are not aware of the impact of changes in the price level.

Aggregate Supply Shocks A further aspect of the new classical model looks at how shocks to aggregate supply can cause deviations from trend output. These shocks affect the productivity of factors of production and can be temporary, such as the effect of natural disasters, or permanent, as when new technologies are developed. The developments in computer technology since the 1990s, for example, have had a permanent impact on productivity. It is likely that developments in digital technology and network connectedness that characterize the so-called Industry 4.0 will also have a major impact on efficiency and productivity in the coming years.

If supply shocks are temporary, such as the effect of an earthquake, productivity declines and demand for labour and other factors will fall, which will also lead to a fall in output below trend GDP. It is possible to observe aspects of this argument in events which have occurred since the early 2010s. An earthquake in Northern Japan in 2011 caused extensive damage and disruption to supply chains across the globe. Firms found that component parts were in short supply and some firms had to lay off workers and suspend production until the supply chains were re-established. The global nature of business means that such natural disasters can have far-reaching effects. The policy decisions of governments to counter and control the global pandemic caused major disruption to supply chains and labour markets.

Supply-Side: The New Keynesian Model

Later in the book we will look in more detail at the contribution of John Maynard Keynes to macroeconomics. One of the main propositions that Keynes put forward was that markets do not clear as quickly as classical economists believed. The assumption is that the ability of the goods and labour market to clear are impaired by the existence of *sticky prices* and *sticky wages,* which is associated with 'New Keynesian' interpretations. In labour markets, firms enter into contractual agreements with workers and are also constrained by labour market legislation and regulation, which means that it is not always easy to adjust the labour force to changed economic circumstances. Excess demand or supply in the labour market will not be eliminated quickly by changes in wages, because of these wage rigidities, and in particular, wages tend to be sticky downwards. It becomes difficult for firms to adjust wages downwards when there is an excess supply of labour as a result of changing economic conditions, such as a change in the price level.

Sticky prices occur where there are costs to firms of changing prices – so-called menu costs. Changing economic conditions in the goods market may warrant a change in price to clear the market. However, because firms face costs in changing prices, it may be that prices are changed infrequently. In addition to the internal costs to firms of diverting labour resources to changing prices, firms will have agreements with suppliers and retailers about prices built into contracts which may not be capable of being renegotiated for some time. The existence of menu costs means that prices will be sticky and prevent markets from clearing in the short run.

Demand-Side: The New Classical Model

Recall that national expenditure or aggregate demand (AD) is composed of consumption spending, investment spending, government spending and net exports. Changes to any or all of the components of AD could cause a deviation of output from trend. Later in the book we will look at causes of shifts in AD, but in this section, we are going to trace through the effect of an assumed change in AD. An increase in AD, for example, will, *ceteris paribus*, lead to a rise in the price level. A rise in the price level reduces real wages, and firms look to employ more workers with the result that the nominal wage will rise. The rise in AD will lead to an increase in output and the price level increases. The increase in the number of workers employed causes a fall in unemployment. The New Classical interpretation rests on workers misinterpreting a rise in nominal wages as a rise in real wages. In other words, they do not fully take into account the effect on wages of the price rise, the so-called *inflation fallacy*.

The result of this is that the economy moves to a temporary equilibrium where the expectations of some economic actors are not fully incorporated because they are incorrect. However, over time, workers will begin to realize that real wages have changed and, as a result, begin to change their behaviour. As workers negotiate for wage rises that maintain their standard of living, firms' costs rise, and some firms will cut back supply. This results in the economy returning to trend output but with a higher price level once expectations have fully adjusted.

If AD falls, then the economy will enter a period of contraction with output and prices falling in the short run. The reverse process to the one outlined above will take place. Real wages rise and firms begin to cut back on output, which increases unemployment. The demand for labour will be in excess of the supply of labour and nominal wage rates will fall. Workers see the fall in nominal wages as a fall in the standard of living, but over time their expectations will adjust to take into account the fall in the price level and output will return to trend.

Cyclical Implications The analysis provided above has implications for the nature of the cyclicality of key macroeconomic variables. In the new classical model, when output is above trend, unemployment is countercyclical, and employment will be above trend and so be procyclical. Inflation will be procyclical, but real wages will be countercyclical because as output rises real wages fall.

Demand-Side: The Keynesian Model

Recall that the New Keynesian model assumes sticky prices and wages. If there is an increase in AD, then wages and prices will take time to adjust. The increase in demand will mean firms' stocks begin to decline and so they will take steps to increase output and, in so doing, increase employment. In the short run, therefore, output increases above trend, but the price level does not change because of sticky prices.

Over time, however, the economy will return to trend because firms will eventually be able to raise prices and nominal wages will also increase. The rise in nominal wages affects firms' costs, and some will begin to cut back output, which returns to trend but with a higher price level. This is the same outcome as that given in the new classical model above, but the way in which the economy has adjusted to the deviation from trend has differed. If AD is reduced, the reverse situation will apply and explains why recessions occur.

The speed with which the economy returns to trend after an AD shock will depend on the time it takes for prices and wages to adjust to the changed economic conditions. In this model, employment, real wages and inflation are procyclical, and unemployment is countercyclical.

Real Business Cycles

At the heart of the model of real business cycles is the belief that changes in technology, both positive and negative technology shocks, affect productivity regardless of the real wage rate. The model assumes that there are no market imperfections, that firms and households are profit and utility maximizing and that markets clear. Against the background of these assumptions, if there is a negative technology shock, then labour productivity falls and the demand for labour falls. Output will fall as a result and unemployment will increase. Output falls because aggregate supply (AS) falls, which creates excess demand in the economy. An excess of AD will lead to a rise in the price level. If the price level increases this affects the real interest rate. Recall that the real interest rate is the nominal interest rate minus inflation. If inflation rises and the nominal interest rate is constant, then the real interest rate will fall. A fall in the real interest rate would lead to a rise in investment by firms.

Real business cycle models suggest that technology shocks can be a major cause of short-run fluctuations in output. The causes of business cycles, therefore, are technology shocks that cause permanent shifts in AS. When AS shifts, however, the expectations of economic actors are still correct, and so there is no reason for governments or central banks to intervene and apply policy prescriptions. The real business cycle model, therefore, does not see growth over time as being a deterministic trend but a stochastic one. In real business cycle models, employment, labour productivity and real wages are procyclical.

CASE STUDY

Austrian Business Cycle Theory (ABCT)

Expectations play a key role in modern macroeconomic modelling. Decisions are made not only with the past and present in mind but also the future. People are aware that central banks control interest rates, even if they are not fully conversant with the economics of central banks. Ask yourself a question, therefore: what do you think the next interest rate move will be in your country? Then consider where you think interest rates will be in two, three and five years' time. If you think interest rates are going to rise, how far will they increase and at what point do you think they will change direction?

ABCT focuses on the role of central banks in business cycles. Assume that the central bank decides to increase interest rates. Firms considering investment projects will now consider whether the project remains viable and, at the margin, whether some projects will be shelved. This leads to a slowdown in the economy. However, firms will also know that at some point in the future interest rates will fall and investment projects will then be undertaken helping to fuel growth. The increasing and lowering of interest rates by the central bank is perceived as being 'artificial'. This is because the interest rate is not changed because of imbalances in the demand and supply of loanable funds, but because of perceptions of changes in inflation. The artificial changes in interest rates 'fool' firms and households into making decisions which generate expansions and contractions in the economy, and hence are a cause of business cycles.

Critics of the ABCT argue that firms and households are not so dumb as to be fooled by interest rate changes, at least not in the longer term, having suffered repeated cycles. Interest rates remained at historically low levels for far longer after the 2007–9 Financial Crisis than many people expected. In the first half of the 2020s, however, interest rates rose and, it could be argued, few expect them to fall to the low levels witnessed throughout most of the 2010s.

Many decisions are not made with the macroeconomy in mind. Individuals, for example, may consider future changes in interest rates when making major financial decisions on mortgages or borrowing for high-priced items such as cars. These individuals are acting in their own self-interest. Equally, firms will anticipate changes in demand when interest rates change. If rates are increased, they expect demand to fall and put plans in place to be in a position to contract output. Again, these firms are acting out of self-interest.

Economic actors respond to short-term changes in economic circumstances not long term ones. If a family can lower its mortgage payments by rescheduling its mortgage, it makes sense to do so. Equally, firms do not want to be caught out with no spare capacity when demand does increase and lose out to competitors who have prepared with more foresight. Far from being 'fooled', economic actors are fully aware of the likely future direction of interest rates, but that does not stop them from acting in a way which fuels cycles of expansion and contraction. According to some Austrian school economists, it is not economic actors that should shoulder the blame but central banks who intervene in financial markets.

© iStock/Ceri Breeze

Interest rates affect us all in some way, but is central bank control of interest rates beneficial overall or does it lead to the inevitable creation of business cycles?

(*Continued*)

Questions:

1. Why are expectations considered such an important element of macroeconomic analysis?
2. Critics of ABCT argue that economic actors cannot be 'fooled' repeatedly. To what extent are economic actors impeded by imperfect information?
3. Consider the interest rate environment in your country. What do you expect to happen to interest rates in the next five years and how might your expectations influence your decision-making over that time period?
4. To what extent do you agree with the ABCT view that central banks are complicit in the creation of business cycles?

CRITICAL THINKING POINT Real business cycle theory does not sufficiently consider the importance of rigidities and market imperfections. Supply-side shocks to an economy are not the main explanations of deviations in output and employment from trend in most developed countries. The focus should be far more on changes on the demand side. Critically assess this statement.

MACROECONOMIC MODELS OF THE ECONOMY

Economists develop models to help understand how the economy works. The economy is extremely complex, and it is unlikely that any model will fully capture every element and interaction of the macroeconomy. However, models can be valuable in providing information to policymakers and analysts to give perspectives on policy decisions, the effects of policy and the anticipated effects of changes in key variables in the model. Since the 1970s, advances in statistical and econometric techniques have been significant. This has enabled economists to build ever more sophisticated models of the economy. The process continues as existing assumptions break down, observation reveals different behaviours and outcomes, and understanding develops. This has been the case for DSGE models.

Dynamic Stochastic General Equilibrium Models

DSGE models developed from the research spawned by real business cycle models. They are now increasingly used by central banks, including the ECB, as part of the toolbox in analyzing, forecasting and making policy decisions. They are highly complex and rely on a large number of equations each seeking to explain relationships between economic variables, many of which we have covered so far. They are subject to constant revision in an attempt to improve their rigour and predictive power. Policymakers can take these models and tweak coefficients and assumptions to explore different outcomes and match these outcomes to observed reality to assess the validity and reliability of the models.

DSGE models are called dynamic because they build in intertemporal choices. The decisions of economic actors are not only based on current circumstances but anticipated future situations. These models allow for interaction between policy and actors' behaviour. The term *stochastic* means 'random'. DSGE models include random shocks to the economy which can cause fluctuations in economic activity away from trend. The final element, general equilibrium, refers to the assumption that prices, wages and interest rates adjust to changes in supply and demand in markets.

The Building Blocks of DSGE Models

While there are different DSGE models, most include three key elements: households, firms and a monetary authority (the central bank). Recent developments in DSGE models seek to include the financial sector and a government sector to help model the influence of fiscal policy. The DSGE model used by the Federal Reserve Bank of New York, for example, has eight 'agents': households, labour employing firms, competitive final goods producing firms, monopolistically competitive intermediate goods producing firms, competitive capital producing firms, capital producing entrepreneurs who rent output to intermediate goods producing firms, a representative bank and a government agent that includes a monetary authority that sets short-term interest rates and an authority that sets and collects taxes and engages in public spending. (Source: github.com/FRBNY-DSGE/DSGE.jl/blob/main/docs/DSGE_Model_Documentation_1002.pdf, accessed 25 April 2025.) For the purposes of this introduction to DSGE models, we will focus on households, firms and the monetary authority.

Households Households represent the demand side of the economy, which in turn determines GDP. The equations which define household relationships focus on the real interest rate and expectations of the future. Households are assumed to maximize their welfare subject to their budget constraint. It should be noted that the individual elements of the model are built on microeconomic foundations. The welfare-maximizing equations are increasingly being adapted to incorporate behavioural aspects of household behaviour, such as the effects of past consumption in decision-making.

We have looked at the role of interest rates in decision-making and the real interest rate plays a key role in these models. If interest rates fall, households have more of an incentive to consume rather than save, which in turn drives up demand. If interest rates rise, the opposite effects are assumed. If expectations of the future are positive, then regardless of the interest rate, demand increases and vice versa. There is, thus, a negative relationship between real interest rates and desired spending. Demand influences inflation and expectations of future inflation.

Households are also the suppliers of labour. Consumption levels are influenced by the amount of hours worked, which determines labour supply. Households trade-off work and leisure. If they want to increase consumption, then they may have to offer more hours. The wage received can either be spent or saved, and the amount of goods consumers are able to purchase is affected by inflation. The amount saved is determined by the returns available given by the real interest rate.

Demand shocks can occur if, for example, households borrow extensively to finance consumption and then pull back on consumption to pay back debt or where widespread default hits households negatively.

Firms Firms are assumed to maximize profits and operate under a production function where output is dependent on technology, capital and labour. Labour is assumed to be a key element in firms' cost structures, and the level of technology influences factor productivity. It is assumed that firms have some element of monopoly power and can set prices. Price is set on a mark-up basis over the marginal cost of production, which in turn is affected by labour costs. The extent of the mark-up is determined by the expected stream of profits that flow in the future and incorporates the importance of expectations in firms' decisions. It is further assumed that firms' desire to change price is infrequent because of menu costs.

In times of economic growth, to increase output to meet demand, firms must encourage workers to supply more labour. Workers will supply more labour if the wage rate increases but this increases firms' marginal costs and may result in an increase in price. There is a direct link, therefore, between real activity and inflationary pressures.

Supply shocks can arise in the form of changes in technology which affect productivity levels and real wages. The capital stock of firms is determined by the savings decisions of households but can also be affected by the efficiency of the financial sector. As noted earlier, the financial sector is being increasingly built into DSGE models. If the financial system is operating inefficiently, firms will find it harder to access the capital they need at the time they need it and, in addition, the price of accessing capital may increase.

Monetary Authorities The demand and supply in goods and labour markets feed into monetary policy decisions by central banks who control short-term interest rates. Interest rates are set based on the central bank's analysis of current inflation, expected future inflation and GDP (or real activity). In making their decision, it is assumed central banks operate under what is called a *Taylor rule* (which we shall cover in more detail later in the book). This links interest rates to the target inflation rate the central bank operates under, past interest rate setting and the output gap. This is the difference between current output and trend. If inflationary pressures are building, the central bank increases interest rates, which influences both household and firm decision-making. Equally, if the economy is suffering contraction (implying that inflation is decelerating), the central bank can reduce interest rates to help stimulate the economy to keep inflation at its target.

The Use and Value of DSGE Models

As noted, DSGE models can be used as part of the toolbox for monetary authorities. They can be used to help provide forecasts, to analyze the effect of different policy decisions, and to look at how outcomes can be affected by varying the policy parameters. It may even be the case the models can suggest that no policy action is needed. Research suggests that over a quarter (three months), DSGE models can be as reliable in forecasting output and inflation as purely statistical analysis but can be slightly more reliable over a year. This is not to say that policymakers rely solely on these models. They provide information which can be incorporated with statistical analyses, surveys carried out by business organizations, and the expertise and judgements of central bankers in helping to arrive at decisions. Where shocks occur, the models can help to identify the nature of the shock and allocate weights to determine the magnitude and direction of the effects. In helping to provide a clearer picture of the symptoms, the use of these models can assist in determining the appropriate policy response.

Very few economists would claim that DSGE models are perfect and that there is not a lot more scope for improvement in developing the reliability and validity of these models. What many would say is that they are better than nothing and provide an aid to decision-making. Weaknesses which have been recognized include the assumption that consumption, wages, investment and output all tend to grow at the same rate in the long run, which is not always borne out by observation of the data. The 2007–9 Financial Crisis made it clear that the role of the financial sector needs to be more fully incorporated into future modelling designs as well as a greater recognition of the role and effect of fiscal policy on the economy. These all continue to be works in progress and part of the way in which economics is evolving and developing its understanding of how the macroeconomy works.

In addition to the above, there has also been criticism of DSGE models by heterodox economists who question some of the fundamental assumptions of the models. In particular, the assumption of constrained optimization on the part of both firms and households and general equilibrium are based on neo-classical principles and methodology which, as we have seen, have been the subject of much criticism.

CONCLUSION

In this chapter we have provided some background to the more extensive analysis of short-term economic fluctuations, which we will begin to explore. We have introduced a number of key concepts which need to be borne in mind as we explore these fluctuations, not least building a familiarity with the behaviour of key macroeconomic variables over time.

We have also learned that economists have different interpretations of business cycles based on different assumptions about how the economy works, the extent to which markets clear and how economic actors behave. Models of business cycles focus on both the supply-side and demand-side of the economy, and it is likely that the answers to the questions surrounding policy decisions to help smooth out deviations in trend growth are to be found in a combination of these different models. The model of the real business cycle raises questions about whether the trends that we 'see' in time-series data, which form the basis of analysis, are actually present, and if trends do not exist, then policy measures designed to reduce deviations from trend are misguided.

SUMMARY

- Economies experience periods of changing levels of economic activity.
- Key macroeconomic data are often time-series data which can raise questions about the validity and reliability of statistical tests applied to datasets.
- Economic growth appears to follow a trend which rises over a period of time.
- Deviations from this trend are known as the business cycle.
- The business cycle has characteristic features which include peaks in economic activity, slowdown, troughs and upturns, with key turning points.

- Trends can be stationary and non-stationary. Non-stationary data can exhibit deterministic trends which change by a constant amount independent of time, or be stochastic where the trend variable changes by a random amount.
- Macroeconomic data can be viewed in pairs with one of the pairs generally GDP. The variable compared may be either procyclical or countercyclical.
- Collecting macroeconomic data can allow economists to view certain indicators as leading, coincident or lagging.
- Changes in the business cycle can be caused by changes in decision-making by households and firms, by external shocks, government policy and changes in confidence or expectations of the future.
- Business cycle models differ in the assumptions they make about the extent to which markets clear and the relationship between the supply-side and demand-side of the economy.
- Real business cycles emphasize the effects of changes in technology as causes of changes in economic activity.
- Central banks and policymakers have increasingly used sophisticated DSGE models of the economy to aid in decision-making.

IN THE NEWS

Gender and Business Cycles

In our discussion of business cycles, their causes and models used in seeking to understand them, we have alluded to the assumptions economists make that underpin the analysis. Households form a key element of business cycle models. The ONS notes that there were 28.4 million households in the UK in 2023 and that the average household size was 2.36 residents per household. In economic analysis of business cycles, how far do economists consider the nature of 'households', or do they simply assume that members of households all exhibit the same behaviour?

In an article published in 2024 for the International Monetary Fund (IMF), Diego Gomes explored the literature around the relationship between gender and business cycles. The article highlighted that taking gender into account is an important aspect of analyzing and understanding business cycles. It suggests that assumptions of gender neutrality in understanding economic fluctuations may underestimate and render inaccurate forecasts around short-term economic activity.

Some of the points raised in the report note that the employment of men is more susceptible to changes in monetary policy in advanced economies, emerging markets and developing economies. Women, on the other hand, are significantly less exposed to unemployment from business cycles in advanced economies. The unemployment rate of men increases more rapidly than that of women during economic downturns. In countries where the workforce is ageing, the sensitivity of unemployment to economic cycles can also be greater in men than women. Equally, women's incomes and hours worked are reported to be less sensitive to business cycles compared to men.

When analyzing the effects of monetary policy shocks, the experience of men and women also differs. A tightening of monetary policy can be associated with a narrowing of the gender employment gap, whereas loosening of monetary policy sees little significant effects on this measure. When considering fiscal policy, increased government spending in times of economic downturn can impact more positively on women's employment than men's. It can also result in increases in the participation rate of women in the workforce.

© iStock/AndreyPopov

Business cycles may affect women differently to men but is enough consideration built into economic models to reflect this?

(*Continued*)

What reasons might lie behind these findings? One explanation offered is that men and women play distinctive roles in the labour market. For example, men may be more likely to be employed in jobs that are more susceptible to cyclical changes, interest rate and fiscal policy shocks. It is also noted that many households may still be subject to 'traditional' views, in which the man is the 'breadwinner' while the woman provides supplementary income, referred to as the 'added worker effect'. This effect, however, may be influenced by the changing make-up of households. In the UK, for example, there are an increasing number of one-person households, accounting for around 30 per cent of all households. In addition, the historically typical composition of a household unit (one woman, one man and children) is also changing as society changes. According to Just Like Us, an LGBT+ and young people's charity, the number of same sex couple families in the UK has increased by 125 per cent since 1996 to 217,000.

Critical Thinking Questions

1 How might models of the business cycle take into account differences in behaviours and make-up of households in seeking to understand the causes and effects of business cycles?
2 To what extent do you think that the assumptions made around the analysis of business cycles limit their value?
3 What reasons might you offer to explain why women may be less exposed to unemployment in downturns than men? Why is understanding the nature and scope of such a relationship important?
4 What do you think is meant by the 'gender employment gap' and what explanations can you offer for why it seems to respond differently between men and women to changes in monetary and fiscal policy?
5 How far should changes in society and the make-up of a population be taken into account when seeking to develop our understanding of business cycles? Is delving into greater detail around this merely adding unnecessary complexity to an already complex issue?

References:

Gomes, D.B.P. (2024) Gender and Business Cycles. IMF Gender Note 2024/001, International Monetary Fund, Washington, DC.
www.justlikeus.org/wp-content/uploads/2024/06/LGBT-parents-report-2024-by-Just-Like-Us.pdf, accessed 25 April 2025.
www.ons.gov.uk/peoplepopulationandcommunity/birthsdeathsandmarriages/families/bulletins/familiesandhouseholds/2023, accessed 25 April 2025.

QUESTIONS FOR REVIEW

1 What are time-series data? Give three examples of key macroeconomic variables that are examples of time-series data.
2 What are the main stages of a typical business cycle and how long do these stages last?
3 What is the difference between a deterministic trend and a stochastic trend?
4 Would you expect the following variables to be procyclical or countercyclical if GDP was above trend? Explain.
   a. inflation
   b. unemployment
   c. employment
   d. real wages
   e. nominal interest rates
5 Unemployment is classified as a 'lagging indicator'. Explain what this means and why unemployment is classed as such.
6 Why might changes in household decision-making cause a deviation in GDP from trend?
7 What role does household and firms' confidence play in business cycles?
8 What is the role of unanticipated price changes in the new classical model of business cycles?
9 What is the key difference between real business cycle models and other business cycle models?
10 What are the principal features of DSGE models?

PROBLEMS AND APPLICATIONS

1 Refer to Figure 10.1.
   a. Estimate the amplitude of the deviations from trend over the period shown.
   b. Estimate the length of time between the beginning of the deviation from trend and the return to trend in each case.

2 In one time period, the growth rate of GDP of a country is recorded as 3.4 per cent against a trend growth rate of output of 2.8 per cent. In the next two time periods, the growth rate of GDP is recorded as 2.8 per cent and 2.0 per cent respectively. Is the country experiencing a recession? Explain.

3 Go to the national statistics office website for your country (this could be the ONS in the UK or Eurostat for the EU) and look up unemployment and inflation figures since 1994. Plot the data on a spreadsheet, graph it and identify the trend. Is the trend stationary, non-stationary, or indeterminate? Explain.

4 Is it always possible to discern a trend in any time-series data? What problems might arise if trends are apportioned to time-series data that are not really present?

5 Look up the following comovements for the country in which you are studying on an appropriate website. Explain whether the comovements are procyclical or countercyclical; GDP and:
   a. inflation
   b. employment
   c. unemployment
   d. the money supply (M1).

6 Firms experience a rise in stocks. Explain why this might have occurred and what you expect firms' response to this event might be and how this might affect output.

7 Why might household and firms' confidence and expectations change leading to deviations in output from trend? Is there any way in which changes in confidence can be measured to provide an indicator of changes in economic activity?

8 Critics of DSGE models argue that despite their complexity and sophistication, they fail to provide sufficient accuracy in forecasting to be useful. In addition, they also claim that the neo-classical foundations and assumptions upon which the models are constructed are fundamentally flawed. Why do you think these critics level such accusations against these models, and to what extent do you agree with their reservations of the value of these models in helping forecasting and policymaking?

9 To what extent do you think that workers are always fooled by the inflation fallacy?

10 Which business cycle model do you find the most compelling and why?

11 KEYNESIAN ECONOMICS AND IS–LM ANALYSIS

Neo-classical orthodoxy had held that markets, including labour markets, cleared without government involvement in both the short run and the long run. The Great Depression of the 1930s across Europe and the United States saw millions of people losing their jobs, and unemployment remained at high levels throughout the decade.

In 1936, economist John Maynard Keynes published a book entitled *The General Theory of Employment, Interest, and Money*, which attempted to explain short-run economic fluctuations in general and the Great Depression in particular. Macroeconomics as a separate path of economic research stemmed from the experiences of the Great Depression. Keynes was not the first to question classical paradigms; recall how Mitchell and Burns' work on business cycles was being carried out some several years before the Great Depression. Keynes picked up this tradition and helped create interest in the analysis of aggregate phenomena.

Keynes' primary message was that recessions and depressions can occur because of inadequate aggregate demand (AD) for goods and services. Keynes had long been a critic of classical economic theory because it could explain only the long-run effects of policies. A few years before *The General Theory*, Keynes had written the following about classical economics:

> *The long run is a misleading guide to current affairs. In the long run we are all dead. Economists set themselves too easy, too useless a task if in tempestuous seasons they can only tell us that when the storm is long past, the ocean will be flat.*

Keynes' message was aimed at policymakers as well as economists. As the world's economies suffered with high unemployment, Keynes advocated policies to increase AD, including government spending on public works. Keynes argued for the necessity of short-run interventions in the economy. In the two decades after World War II, Keynes' ideas permeated economic policy in many developed countries but, in the 1970s, accelerating inflation and rising unemployment led to policymakers turning away from Keynesian policies. The focus on monetary and supply-side policies as the main ways of controlling the economy in most developed countries in Europe in the 1980s and beyond, had largely consigned Keynesian demand management to the economic history books. However, the 2007–9 Financial Crisis and subsequent recession reignited the debate about the role of Keynesian economics in macro policy. Keynes' contribution to economic thinking is widely acknowledged and it is valuable to have some insight into Keynesian economics. This chapter will begin this process.

THE KEYNESIAN CROSS

Classical economics placed a fundamental reliance on the efficiency of markets and the assumption that they would clear. At a macro level, this meant that if the economy was in disequilibrium and unemployment existed, wages and prices would adjust to bring the economy back into equilibrium at full employment. **Full employment** is defined as a point where those people who want to work at the going market wage level are able to find a job. Any unemployment that did exist would be classed as voluntary unemployment. The experience of the Great Depression of the 1930s brought the classical assumptions under closer scrutiny. The many millions suffering from unemployment could not all be volunteering to not take jobs at the going wage rates. Some must, therefore, have been involuntarily unemployed. We have also seen that prices can be sticky, meaning markets may not always adjust to clear surpluses and shortages quickly.

full employment a point where those people who want to work at the going market wage level are able to find a job

Planned and Actual Spending

Fundamental to Keynesian analysis is the distinction between *planned* and *actual* decisions by households and firms. **Planned spending, saving or investment** refers to the desired or intended actions of firms and households. A publisher, for example, may plan to sell 10,000 copies of a textbook in the first six months of the year. An individual may plan to go on holiday to Türkiye in the summer and save up to finance the trip. A person may intend to save €1,000 over the year to put towards paying for a wedding next year.

planned spending, saving or investment the desired or intended actions of households and firms

Actual spending, saving or investment refers to the realized, *ex post* (after the event) outcome. The publisher may only sell 8,000 copies in the first six months and so has a build-up of stock (inventories) of 2,000 more than planned. The holidaymaker may fall ill and is unable to go on holiday and so their actual consumption is lower than planned (whereas actual saving is more than planned because they have not spent what they intended). The plans for saving for the wedding may be compromised by the need to spend money on repairing a house damaged by a flood.

actual spending, saving or investment the realized or *ex post* outcome resulting from actions of households and firms

Planned and actual outcomes, therefore, might be very different. Keynes suggested that there was no reason why equilibrium national income would coincide with full employment output. Wages and prices might not adjust in the short run because of sticky wages and prices. Therefore, the economy could be at a position where the level of demand in the economy was insufficient to bring about full employment. The mass unemployment of the 1930s could be alleviated, he argued, by governments intervening in the economy to manage demand to achieve the desired level of employment.

The Equilibrium of the Economy

We have seen that a country's GDP (which we will refer to as national income), is divided among four components: consumption spending, investment spending, spending by government and net exports.

Imagine a situation where, at every point, total expenditure in the economy given by $C + I + G + NX$ was exactly the same as national income. We could represent this in diagrammatic form as a 45 degree line such as the ones in panels (a) and (b) in Figure 11.1.

In panels (a) and (b), the 45 degree line connects all points where consumption spending (actual expenditure) would be equal to national income (planned expenditure). This line can be thought of as the equivalent of the capacity of the economy – the aggregate supply (AS) curve.

The $C + I + G + NX$ line is a function of income – in other words, spending depends on income. If income is higher, spending will also be higher and so the $C + I + G + NX$ line has a positive slope. The vertical intercept of the $C + I + G + NX$ line, given as E_0, is termed **autonomous spending or autonomous expenditure**. This is the component of expenditure which does not depend on income/output, government spending being a key element of this expenditure.

autonomous spending or autonomous expenditure spending which is not dependent on income/output

FIGURE 11.1

Deflationary and Inflationary Gaps

The 45 degree line shows all the points where consumption spending equals income. The vertical intercept of the expenditure line shows autonomous expenditure. The economy is in equilibrium where the expenditure line, C + I + G + NX, *cuts the 45 degree line. In panel (a) this equilibrium is lower than full employment output* (Y_f) *at* Y_1. *There is insufficient demand to maintain full employment output. The government would need to shift the expenditure line up to* $C + I + G + NX_1$ *to eliminate the deflationary gap. In panel (b) the equilibrium is higher than full employment output – the economy does not have the capacity to meet demand. In this case the government needs to shift the* C + I + G + NX *line down to* $C + I + G + NX_2$ *to eliminate the inflationary gap.*

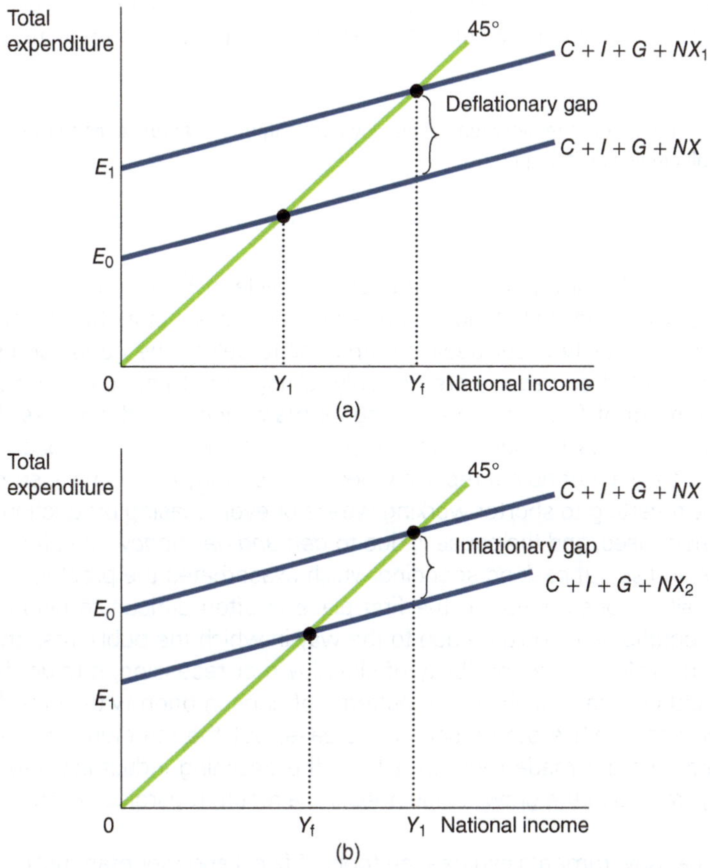

Where actual spending is equal to planned spending is the short-run equilibrium of the economy. Note that the use of the term 'equilibrium' in this context does not mean the 'best' or 'desired' equilibrium. It is simply a point where actual spending is equal to planned spending. The economy is in equilibrium where the $C + I + G + NX$ line cuts the 45 degree line. This is referred to as the *Keynesian cross.* In panel (a) in Figure 11.1 the economy is in equilibrium at a national income of Y_1. However, full employment national income is at Y_f. Actual spending of $C + I + G + NX$ in panel (a) gives an equilibrium which is less than that required for full employment output (Y_f). At the equilibrium Y_1 there is spare capacity in the economy, that is some resources are not being used to their full extent, capital may be underused and unemployment will exist. This is the equivalent to an economy being at a point inside its production possibilities frontier. The difference between full employment output, and the expenditure required to meet it, is termed the **deflationary gap** or **output gap**. Expenditure needs to rise to $C + I + G + NX_1$ to eliminate the deflationary gap, which is the vertical distance between actual spending and spending necessary to achieve full employment.

deflationary gap or **output gap** the difference between full employment output and expenditure when expenditure is less than full employment output

In panel (b) of Figure 11.1, the $C + I + G + NX$ line cuts the 45 degree line at an output level Y_1, which is higher than full employment output, Y_f. In this situation the economy does not have the capacity to meet actual spending. This will trigger inflationary pressures. The difference between full employment output and the expenditure line here is called the **inflationary gap**. Actual spending needs to be reduced to eradicate the inflationary gap and the $C + I + G + NX$ line needs to be reduced to $C + I + G + NX_2$ to bring the economy to an equilibrium where actual spending equals full employment output.

inflationary gap the difference between full employment output and actual expenditure when actual expenditure is greater than full employment output

Demand Management The deviations in the business cycle in Keynesian analysis are primarily due to demand-side factors. The principle behind Keynesian economics is, at its heart, very simple and intuitive. Downturns in economic activity occur because firms fail to sell all the goods and services they planned to sell. If customers (and of course we are not only talking about final consumers but also about other businesses as customers of firms) are not buying as many goods and services, firms will not need to produce as many and so cut back production as stocks rise. If production is cut back then firms do not need as many workers. So they either do not replace workers when they retire, make some workers redundant, or lay off workers by reverting to shorter working weeks or even ceasing production temporarily for a time period. Unemployment rises, and the cause is due to *demand deficiency*. The affected workers now see a fall in their incomes and so cut back on spending which exacerbates the problem.

The cause of a fall in consumption in the first place is often difficult to pinpoint. It could be due to confidence and expectations. It could be due to the way in which the public responds to news items (the more the news media refer to the possibility of slowdown or recession, it might become a self-fulfilling prophecy). Or it could be due to a change in patterns of consumption with some firms seeing a decline in demand for their goods while others see an increase, but the structural change causes a disruption in demand. Workers who are made redundant from the declining industries may not have the skills to move to jobs being created in the growth industries. As a result, regardless of the wage rate, they remain unemployed.

Keynes argued that governments can use the tools of fiscal and monetary policy, and in particular fiscal policy, to influence demand in the economy and reduce deflationary and inflationary gaps. Taxation is a leakage from the circular flow of income but can be manipulated by the government. Equally, government can vary its own expenditure, and the combinations of changes in tax and government spending can be used as levers to manage demand to bring the economy into equilibrium at a point nearer to full employment output. If the value of full employment output, the amount the economy is capable of producing if all existing resources are used fully (planned spending), is €1 trillion, for example, but actual spending is only €800 billion, the deflationary or output gap would be €200 billion. The government might introduce policy levers which lead to a cut in taxes and a boost to government spending to generate this additional €200 billion in spending. The use of these levers has some interesting features, which we will describe in the next section.

SELF TEST Why might actual spending differ from planned spending?
If planned spending in an economy is €500 billion but actual spending is €400 billion, is there an inflationary gap or a deflationary gap? Explain.
What might the government do in this situation to bring spending more in line with full employment output?

THE MULTIPLIER EFFECT

The $C + I + G + NX$ line is referred to as the expenditure function. Planned expenditure is dependent on the level of consumption, plus investment, plus government spending plus net exports and can be written:

$$E = C + I + G + NX$$

Actual expenditure/output (remember that expenditure is one way of measuring output – these two things are the same) will be denoted as (Y). The economy will be in equilibrium when planned expenditure is equal to actual expenditure ($E = Y$).

The positive slope of the expenditure function implies that planned spending rises as income rises. What determines the slope of the expenditure function has important policy implications. When a government makes a purchase, say it enters into a contract with a construction company for €10 billion to build a new offshore wind farm, that purchase has repercussions. The immediate impact of the higher demand from the government is to raise employment and profits at the construction company (which we shall call WindEn). WindEn, in turn, must buy resources from other contractors to carry out the job and so these suppliers also experience an increase in orders. Workers at these firms see higher earnings and the firms' owners see higher profits. They respond to this increase in income by raising their own spending on consumer goods. As a result, the government purchase from WindEn raises the demand for the products of many other firms and individuals in the economy. Because each euro spent by the government can raise the AD for goods and services by more than a euro, government purchases are said to have a **multiplier effect** on AD.

> **multiplier effect** the additional shifts in aggregate demand that result when expansionary fiscal policy increases income and thereby increases consumer spending

The multiplier effect continues even after this first round. When consumer spending rises, the firms that produce these consumer goods hire more people and experience higher profits. Higher earnings and profits stimulate consumer spending once again, and so on. Thus there is positive feedback as higher demand leads to higher income, which in turn leads to even higher demand. Once all these effects are added together, the total impact on the quantity of goods and services demanded can be much larger than the initial impulse from higher government spending.

The multiplier effect arising from the response of consumer spending can be strengthened by the response of investment to higher levels of demand. For instance, WindEn might respond to the higher demand for building services by buying more mechanized building equipment. In this case, higher government demand spurs higher demand for investment goods. This positive feedback from demand to investment is sometimes called the *investment accelerator*.

CASE STUDY **The Accelerator Principle**

The accelerator principle relates the *rate of change* of AD to the *rate of change* in investment. To produce goods, a firm needs equipment. Imagine that a machine is capable of producing 1,000 tablet computers per week. Demand for tablet computers is currently 800. A rise in demand for tablet computers of up to 200 is capable of being met without any further investment in new machinery. However, if the rate of growth of demand continues to rise, it may be necessary to invest in a new machine.

(*Continued*)

Increases in demand do not always mean that investment in productive capital is increased.

Imagine that in year 1, demand for tablet computers rises by 10 per cent to 880. The business can meet this demand through existing equipment. In year 2, demand increases by 20 per cent and is now 1,056. The existing capacity of the machine means that this demand cannot be met, but the shortage is only 56 units, so the firm decides that it might increase price rather than invest in a new machine. In year 3, demand rises by a further 25 per cent. Demand is now 1,320, but the machine is only capable of producing a maximum of 1,000 tablet computers. The firm decides to invest in a new machine. The manufacturers of the new machine will therefore see a rise in their order books as a result of the increase in demand. An increase in demand of 25 per cent has led to an 'accelerated' rise in investment of 100 per cent. Investment is a component of AD, so economists are interested in the way investment adjusts to changes in demand in the economy. As this brief example shows, the relationship between an increase in demand and an increase in investment is not a simple one.

Questions:

1. What factors might determine the ability of a firm to meet additional demand for their goods or services?
2. Think back to your microeconomics course. If a firm has spare capacity and can meet additional demand, does this imply that it is not operating efficiently? Considering your answer, how might it impact on policymaking models such as DSGE models covered in the previous chapter?
3. Apart from the increase in demand, what other factors would a firm take into consideration when investing in new capital equipment?

A Formula for the Spending Multiplier

A little algebra permits us to derive an equation for the size of the multiplier effect that arises from consumer spending. An important number in this equation is the **marginal propensity to consume**, which is the fraction of extra income that a household consumes rather than saves. For example, suppose that the marginal propensity to consume is $\frac{3}{4}$. This means that for every extra pound or euro that a household earns, the household spends $\frac{3}{4}$ of it and saves $\frac{1}{4}$. The **marginal propensity to save** (MPS) is the fraction of extra income that a household saves rather than consumes. With an MPC of $\frac{3}{4}$, when the workers and owners of WindEn earn €10 billion from the government contract, they increase their consumer spending by $\frac{3}{4} \times$ €10 billion, or €7.5 billion. (You should see from the above that $MPC + MPS = 1$. The equation for the multiplier can also be expressed in terms of the *MPS*.)

marginal propensity to consume the fraction of extra income that a household consumes rather than saves
marginal propensity to save the fraction of extra income that a household saves rather than consumes

To gauge the impact on spending of a change in government purchases, we follow the effects step by step. The process begins when the government spends €10 billion, which implies that national income (earnings and profits) also rises by this amount. This increase in income in turn raises consumer spending by $MPC \times$ €10 billion, which in turn raises the income for the workers and owners of the firms that produce the consumption goods. This second increase in income again raises consumer spending, this time by $MPC \times (MPC \times$ €10 billion). These feedback effects go on and on.

To find the total impact on the demand for goods and services, we add up all these effects:

Change in government purchases	= €10 billion
First change in consumption	= $MPC \times$ €10 billion
Second change in consumption	= $(MPC)^2 \times$ €10 billion
Third change in consumption	= $(MPC)^3 \times$ €10 billion
•	•
•	•
•	•
Total change in demand	= $(1 + MPC + MPC^2 + MPC^3 + \ldots) \times$ €10 billion

We can write the multiplier using '…' to represent a pattern of similar terms as follows:

$$\textit{Multiplier} = (1 + MPC + MPC^2 + MPC^3 + \ldots)$$

This multiplier tells us the demand for goods and services that each euro of government purchases generates.

To simplify this equation for the multiplier, recall from your school algebra that this expression is an infinite geometric series. For x between -1 and 1:

$$1 + x + x^2 + x^3 + \ldots$$

The sum of this series as the number of terms tends to infinity, is given by:

$$\frac{1}{1 - x}$$

In our case, $x = MPC$. Thus:

$$\text{Multiplier}(k) = \frac{1}{(1 - MPC)}$$

We have said that the $MPC + MPS = 1$ so the multiplier can also be expressed as:

$$\text{Multiplier}(k) = \frac{1}{(MPS)}$$

For example, if the MPC is $\frac{3}{4}$, the multiplier is $\frac{1}{\left(1-\frac{3}{4}\right)}$. In this case, the €10 billion of government spending generates €40 billion of demand for goods and services.

This equation for the multiplier shows an important conclusion, that the size of the multiplier depends on the marginal propensity to consume. While an MPC of $\frac{3}{4}$ leads to a multiplier of 4, an MPC of $\frac{1}{2}$ leads to a multiplier of only 2. Thus a larger MPC means a larger multiplier. To see why this is true, remember that the multiplier arises because higher income induces greater spending on consumption. The larger the MPC, the greater the induced effect on consumption and the larger the multiplier. The MPC determines the slope of the consumption element of the planned expenditure function.

Other Applications of the Multiplier Effect

Because of the multiplier effect, a euro of government purchases can generate more than a euro of AD. The logic of the multiplier effect, however, is not restricted to changes in government purchases. Instead, it applies to any event that alters spending on any component of planned expenditure, that is consumption, investment, government purchases or net exports.

For example, suppose that a recession overseas reduces the demand for Ireland's net exports by €1 billion. This reduced spending on Irish goods and services depresses Ireland's national income, which reduces spending by Irish consumers. If the MPC is $\frac{3}{4}$ and the multiplier is 4, then the €1 billion fall in net exports means a €4 billion contraction in output.

As another example, suppose that a stock market boom increases households' wealth and stimulates their spending on goods and services by €2 billion. This extra consumer spending increases national income, which in turn generates even more consumer spending. If the MPC is $\frac{3}{4}$ and the multiplier is 4, then the initial impulse of €2 billion in consumer spending translates into an €8 billion increase in AD.

The multiplier is an important concept in macroeconomics because it shows how the economy can amplify the impact of changes in spending. A small initial change in consumption, investment, government purchases or net exports can end up having a large effect on AD and, therefore, on the economy's production of goods and services.

Withdrawals from the Circular Flow The amount spent in each successive round of spending is termed *induced expenditure*. The multiplier showed how the eventual change in income would be determined by the size of the MPC and the MPS. The higher the MPC the greater the multiplier effect.

However, in an open economy with government, any extra €1 is not simply either spent or saved. Some of the extra income may be spent on imported goods and services or go to the government in taxation – withdrawals from the circular flow. Withdrawals (W) from the circular flow are classed as endogenous as they are directly related to changes in income. Withdrawals are saving (S), taxation (T) and imports (M).

We must also take into consideration injections into the circular flow of income. Governments receive tax revenue (a withdrawal from the circular flow), but uses it to spend on the goods and services they provide for citizens (an injection into the circular flow. Firms earn revenue from selling goods abroad (exports) which are an injection into the circular flow. In addition, firms use savings (a withdrawal) as a source of funds to borrow for investment (an injection). Injections into the circular flow are exogenous – they are not related to the level of output or income – and are investment (I), government spending (G) and export earnings (X).

The slope of the expenditure line as a whole, therefore, will be dependent on how much of each extra €1 is withdrawn. For each additional €1 of income, some will exit the circular flow of income in taxation, some through savings and some through spending on imports. The marginal propensity to taxation (MPT) is the proportion of each additional €1 of income taken in taxation by the government and the marginal propensity to import (MPM), the proportion of each additional €1 of income spent on goods from abroad. When we take into consideration the fact that each extra €1 in income is not disposable income, that is it is not all available for consumption, the multiplier effect when considering the *marginal propensity to withdraw* (MPW) will be much lower than if we were simply considering the MPC alone in any increase in income.

We can restate the equation for the multiplier (k) in an open economy with a government as:

$$K = \frac{1}{(MPS + MPT + MPM)}$$

Or:

$$K = \frac{1}{(MPW)}$$

The size of the MPW will determine the slope of the expenditure line: the steeper the slope of the expenditure line the greater the size of the multiplier, as shown in Figure 11.2.

FIGURE 11.2

The Slope of the Expenditure Line and Changes in Autonomous Expenditure

Panel (a) shows a relatively shallow expenditure line, which would mean that the marginal propensity to withdraw would be high and the value of the multiplier would be relatively low. Using the Greek letter delta (Δ) to mean 'change', the impact on national income (ΔY) of a change in government spending (ΔG) would be more limited in comparison to the effect as shown in panel (b), where the expenditure line is much steeper reflecting a higher value of the multiplier where the MPW was relatively low. In this case it takes a smaller rise in government spending to achieve the same increase in national income.

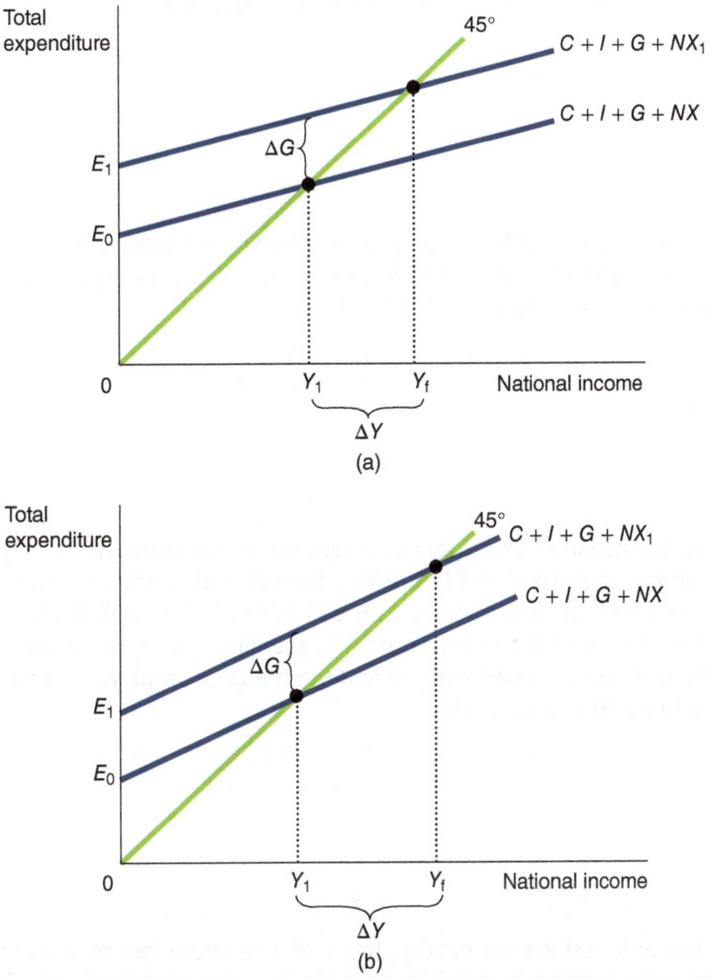

Equilibrium of Planned Withdrawals and Injections

Seeing the economy from the perspective of withdrawals and injections is helpful to understand how demand management might work. Let us start with the national income equation:

$$\text{Output} \equiv \text{Expenditure} \equiv \text{Income}$$

Recall that in a closed economy $S = I$ with savings a withdrawal and investment an injection. We can extend this analysis to state that in equilibrium, in an open economy with a government, planned withdrawals would equal planned injections:

$$\text{Planned } S + T + M = \text{Planned } I + G + X$$

At this point all the output being produced by the economy would be 'bought' by households and firms. However, if actual withdrawals are greater than planned injections, then the economy would be experiencing a deficiency in demand. For example, assume that full employment output (Y_f) is €120 billion. Withdrawals are a function of income. Assume that S, T and M have the following values:

$$S = 0.1Y$$
$$T = 0.2Y$$
$$M = 0.2Y$$

So if income increased by €1, savings would change by $0.1 \times 1 = 10$ cents and so on. Now assume that investment is €20 billion, government spending is also €20 billion and the value of exports is €10 billion. Given these figures the equilibrium level of national income would be:

$$\begin{aligned} \text{Planned } S + T + M &= \text{Planned } I + G + X \\ 0.1Y + 0.2Y + 0.2Y &= 20 + 20 + 10 \\ 0.5Y &= 50 \end{aligned}$$

This implies that:

$$Y = 100$$

This equilibrium is below the level of full employment output by €20 billion. The government could manage demand to achieve full employment output in different ways. It could increase its spending by €10 billion and through the multiplier effect see Y rise to €120 billion:

$$\begin{aligned} \text{Planned } S + T + M &= \text{Planned } I + G + X \\ 0.1Y + 0.2Y + 0.2Y &= 20 + 30 + 10 \\ 0.5Y &= 60 \end{aligned}$$

This implies that:

$$Y = 120$$

In an open economy, the government might not simply target full employment but might wish to reduce net exports. For example, assume Y_f = €120 billion, the value of exports is given as €10 billion, but the value of imports would be $0.2Y$ and so would be €24 billion (0.2×120). If the government wanted to reduce net exports to zero it might cut government spending, but change tax rates so that the MPT increases. If government spending was cut to 5 and the marginal propensity to tax raised to 0.4 then the government could achieve zero net exports:

$$\begin{aligned} \text{Planned } S + T + M &= \text{Planned } I + G + X \\ 0.1Y + 0.4Y + 0.2Y &= 20 + 5 + 10 \\ 0.7Y &= 35 \end{aligned}$$

This implies that:

$$Y = 50$$

It is clear that the policy to reduce net exports has had a severe effect on national income. One of the features of demand management is that it is possible for governments to use fiscal policy to achieve desired output levels. There will be consequences for other areas of the economy, however, which may have more long-term effects.

If government sets policy to achieve a reduction in unemployment through boosting the economy, then net exports would fall and the country would be running a trade deficit ($NX < 0$). Recall that trade influences net capital outflow and the exchange rate. Changes in the exchange rate affect the competitiveness of firms in the economy. So, even though the government might reduce unemployment, its policy causes longer-term effects which might cause it to have to alter policy to deal with these effects (such as a currency crisis), which in turn might reduce income and increase unemployment again.

THE IS AND LM CURVES

The Keynesian cross gives us a picture of the economy in short-run equilibrium. (Note, if you access a copy of Keynes' *General Theory* you might be surprised to see a complete absence of Keynesian cross diagrams. The use of these diagrams was developed by later economists to help portray Keynes' ideas.)

In equilibrium, planned expenditure equals income ($E = Y$). This equilibrium is referred to as equilibrium in the *goods market*. We have also seen how equilibrium in the money market is given by the intersection of the demand for money and the supply of money. At this point, we consider the concept of **real money balances** – what money can actually buy or the real value of money, given by the ratio of the money supply (M) to the price level P, $\frac{M}{P}$.

real money balances what money can actually buy given the ratio of the money supply to the price level $\frac{M}{P}$

The goods market and the money market are both interrelated with the linking factor being the interest rate. Following Keynes' analysis of the goods market and the money market (via the liquidity preference theory which we will look at in more detail later in the book), Nobel Prize winning economist John Hicks developed a theory that described the links between the two and showed how changes in both fiscal and monetary policy could be analyzed. The framework for this analysis is known as the IS–LM model.

IS–LM describes equilibrium in these two markets and together determines a *general equilibrium* in the economy. General equilibrium in the economy occurs at the point where the goods market and money market are both in equilibrium at a particular interest rate and level of income. The remainder of this chapter will provide an introduction to the IS–LM model. The model forms the basis of many intermediate courses in macroeconomics. Some have argued, however, that it is now outdated and fails to represent how the modern economy works, particularly since the 2007–9 Financial Crisis. We will look at an alternative representation of the model that seeks to take into account some of these objections. Regardless of the debates about the validity of the model, it does represent a useful way of understanding how the goods and money markets interact. As an exercise in analytical thinking, it is helpful in seeing the effects of monetary and fiscal policy on the macroeconomy.

IS stands for investment and saving; LM stands for liquidity and money. The link between these two markets is the rate of interest (i).

The IS Curve

The IS curve shows the relationship between the interest rate and level of income (Y) in the goods market. In Figure 11.3, panel (a) shows the Keynesian cross diagram from Figure 11.2, with equilibrium point A where the expenditure line $C + I + G + NX$, crosses the 45 degree line. Panel (b) shows the IS curve. The rate of interest is on the vertical axis and on the horizontal axis is output (national income). The equilibrium point A in panel (a) is associated with a rate of interest i_1. This is plotted as point A^* on panel (b). If interest rates fall then the expenditure line shifts upwards to the left and there will be a new equilibrium point B where the expenditure line $C + I + G + NX_1$ crosses the 45 degree line. This is plotted as B^* on panel (b), showing the equilibrium of the goods market at a lower interest rate associated with a higher level of national income. If we connect these two points we get the IS curve. The curve connects all possible points of equilibrium in the goods market associated with a particular interest rate and level of national income.

The IS curve shows an inverse relationship between the interest rate and output in that a fall in interest rates leads to a rise in income and vice versa. The rise in income will be dependent on the size of the interest rate change and the size of the multiplier. The slope of the IS curve is determined by the responsiveness of consumption and investment ($C + I$) to changes in interest rates. This is important because it leads to different outcomes. Where economists tend to disagree is the *extent* to which $C + I$ are responsive to changes in interest rates rather than any disagreement about the validity of the relationship of $C + I$ and the interest rate. The more responsive $C + I$ are, the flatter the IS curve.

FIGURE 11.3

The IS Curve

The IS curve is derived from the Keynesian cross diagram and shows all possible points of equilibrium in the goods market associated with a particular interest rate and level of income. In panel (a) initial equilibrium is where the C + I + G + NX *line crosses the 45 degree line at point* A. *This point is plotted on the IS curve as point* A*. *An increase in* C + I + G + NX *to* C + I + G + NX_1 *shows a new equilibrium point in the goods market,* B, *which is plotted on the IS curve as* B*. *These two points are connected to form the IS curve.*

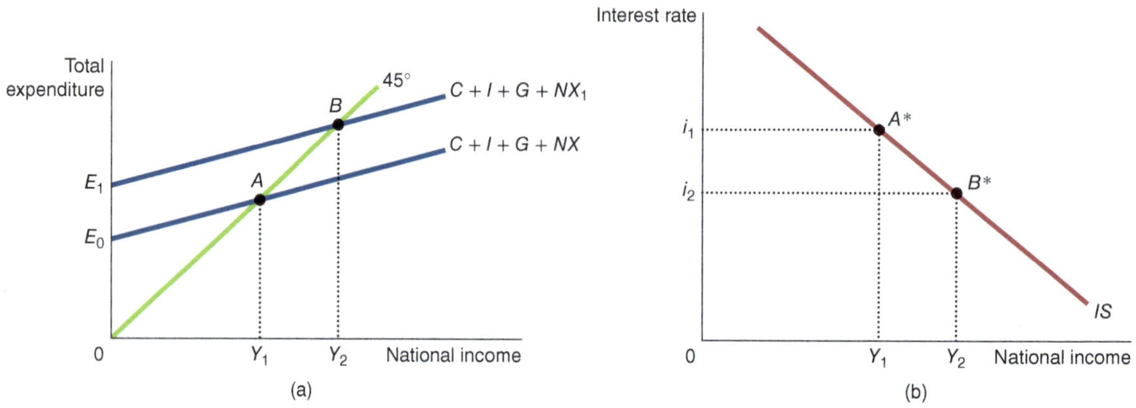

Shifts in the IS Curve Shifts in the IS curve come about as a result of changes in autonomous expenditure. If, for example, government spending rises, this occurs independent of any change in interest rates. A rise in autonomous spending would be associated with a shift in the IS curve to the right. The prevailing interest rate would now be associated with a higher level of income. Equally, if autonomous spending fell, then the IS curve would shift to the left, showing a lower level of income at the prevailing interest rate.

The LM Curve

The LM curve shows all points where the money market is in equilibrium given a combination of the rate of interest and national income. In Figure 11.4, panel (a) shows the money market with the demand for money inversely related to the interest rate. The money supply is shown as a vertical line and it is assumed that the money supply is fixed by the central bank. Equilibrium in the money market is where the demand for money (D_m) curve intersects the money supply curve (M_s), at point *A* in panel (a) at interest rate i_1, and a quantity of real money balances *M*. Panel (b) shows the LM curve with the interest rate on the vertical axis and national income on the horizontal axis. The equilibrium point, *A*, in the money market is plotted as point A^* in panel (b). Increases in income will have an effect on the demand for money and assuming the money supply is fixed, this will affect the equilibrium interest rate. Assume that national income rises; the demand for money curve in panel (a) would shift to the right to D_{m1}, indicating that the public wish to hold higher money balances at all interest rates. At the prevailing interest rate the demand for money is now higher than the supply of money and so the interest rate would rise. The new equilibrium in the money market is given as point *B* and this is plotted on the LM diagram as point B^*. If we connect the two points we get the LM curve. The LM curve plots all combinations of interest rates and national income where the money market is in equilibrium.

The LM curve has a positive slope showing that an increase in income is associated with an increase in the interest rate and vice versa. The slope of the LM curve will be dependent on the responsiveness of the demand for money to changes in interest rates. Again, the extent of this relationship is often a point of disagreement among economists.

FIGURE 11.4

The LM Curve

The LM curve shows all points where the money market is in equilibrium given a combination of the rate of interest and national income. In panel (a), the money market is in equilibrium where the demand for money (D_m) equals the supply of money (M_s) at point A. This point is plotted on the LM curve in panel (b) as point A. An increase in the demand for money causes a shift of the curve to the right to D_{m1} with a new equilibrium point of B. This is plotted on panel (b) as point B* and the points connected to form the LM curve.*

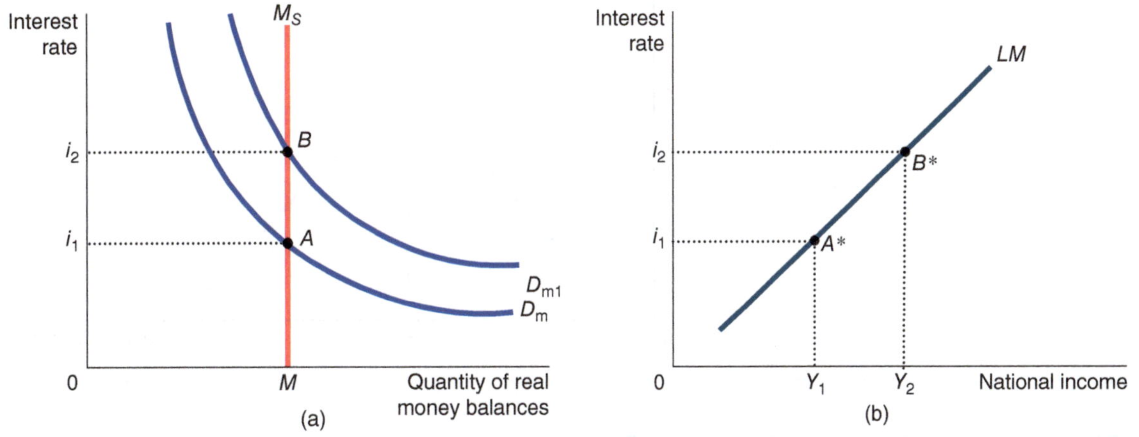

Shifts in the LM Curve The LM curve can shift if the central bank expands or contracts the money supply (we will say more about how this might happen later in the chapter). Assuming income is held constant, a rise in the money supply (for example), will cause interest rates to fall and a new equilibrium will be reached at a given level of income. This would be associated with a shift of the LM curve downwards to the right showing a new combination of income and interest rate at which the money market is in equilibrium.

GENERAL EQUILIBRIUM USING THE IS–LM MODEL

Equilibrium is found where the IS curve intersects the LM curve. Remember that any point on either curve describes a point of equilibrium in the goods market and the money market at a rate of interest and level of national income. In Figure 11.5, the point where the IS curve intersects the LM curve gives a point where both markets are in equilibrium at an interest rate i_e and a level of national income Y_e. Hence it follows that at this point planned expenditure equals actual expenditure ($E = Y$), and the demand for money equals the supply of money $D_m = M_s$.

Having established this general equilibrium, we can use the model to analyze the impact of fiscal and monetary policy changes in an attempt to stabilize the economy and how these two policies are interrelated. Further analysis of both policies will be covered later in the book but this uses our basic model of IS–LM. The detail of IS–LM analysis is beyond the scope of this book; however, the remainder of this chapter will introduce some of the key implications of the model.

The Effect of a Change in Fiscal Policy

Assume that the government chooses to increase spending to boost economic activity. This increase in autonomous expenditure shifts the IS curve to the right as shown in panel (a) of Figure 11.6. The result is that national income will rise but there will also be an increase in interest rates. A similar outcome would occur if the government chose to cut taxes as the means of boosting the economy. The result of either policy would be dependent on the MPW and the size of the multiplier. The opposite would occur if the government chose to cut spending or increase taxes – national income and interest rates would both fall.

FIGURE 11.5

General Equilibrium

Equilibrium in the economy is found where the IS curve intersects with the LM curve. At this point both the goods market and the money market are in equilibrium at a particular interest rate, i_e, and level of national income, Y_e.

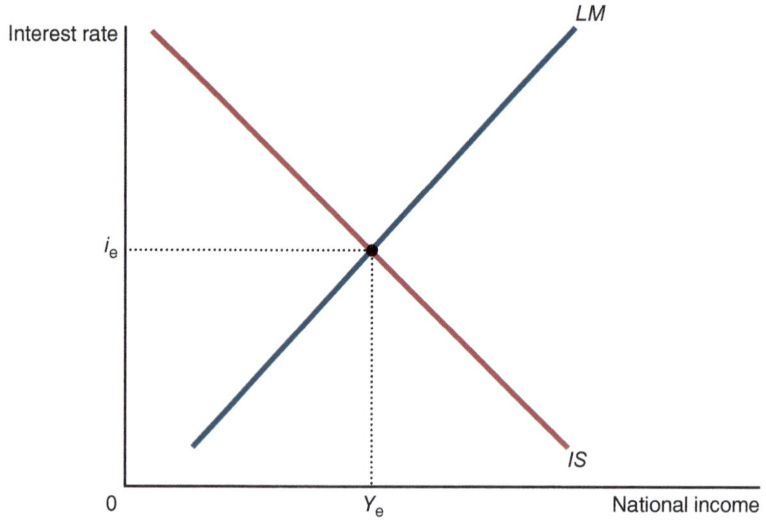

The Effect of a Change in Monetary Policy

If the central bank decided to expand the money supply the LM curve would shift to the right to LM_1 as shown in panel (b) of Figure 11.6. The new equilibrium would lead to a lower interest rate and a higher level of national income. The reverse outcome would occur if the central bank tightened monetary policy by reducing the money supply.

FIGURE 11.6

The Effects of Fiscal and Monetary Policy

In panel (a), a rise in government spending shifts the IS curve to the right resulting in a new equilibrium with a higher interest rate and level of national income. In panel (b), an increase in the money supply would shift the LM curve to the right and a new equilibrium would result in a lower interest rate and higher level of national income.

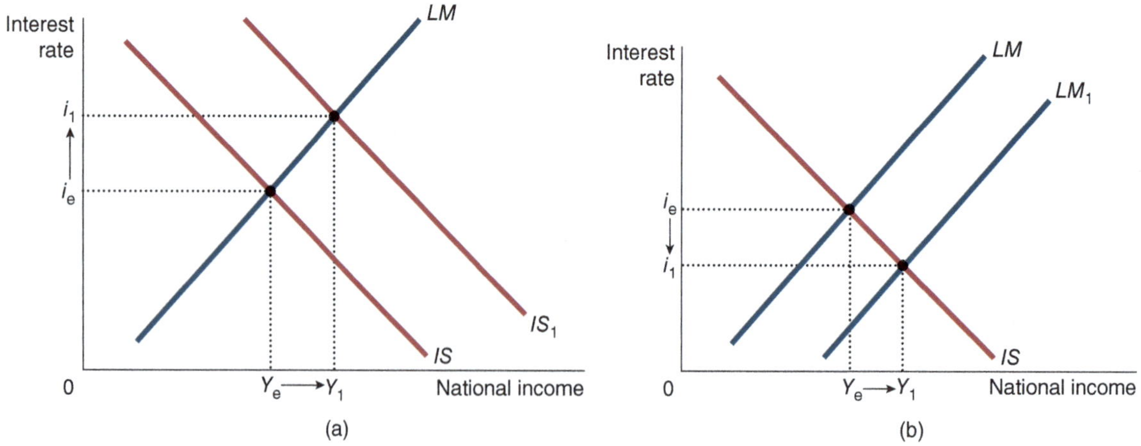

Fiscal and Monetary Policy Interactions In reality, central banks do not act totally in isolation of government, even if they are independent. Central banks will be aware of what governments are doing. The Bank of England and the ECB have a responsibility to maintain price stability, and this may be reflected in the form of a target for inflation. Central banks will be monitoring the effect of fiscal policy changes on the economy and how these changes might affect inflationary pressures. These inflationary pressures can be influenced by the central bank's control over short-term interest rates through the rate at which it lends to the financial system. Governments may wish to implement fiscal policy with the aim of influencing unemployment, for example. Such a policy may have effects on inflationary pressures which the central bank wants to nullify.

Let us assume that the government reduces taxation to encourage more people to take jobs in the economy or to increase spending through consumers having more disposable income. The IS curve would shift to the right, as shown in Figure 11.7, and national income and interest rates would rise. If the central bank wants to keep interest rates constant, it must expand the money supply. By doing so, the LM curve shifts to the right to LM_1, national income would rise further than if the central bank had not acted, to Y_2, and the interest rate will remain at its initial level. If the bank had not altered the money supply, then the effects of the reduction in tax would have been partially offset by a rise in interest rates, which would have curbed spending.

FIGURE 11.7

Maintaining Interest Rates Constant Following a Shift in the *IS* Curve

A shift in the IS curve to the right would, without central bank action, lead to a rise in the interest rate and in national income. If the central bank wants to maintain the interest rate, it must increase the money supply and shift the LM curve to the right. The result would be to maintain the interest rate at i_e, but the increase in national income would be greater than if the central bank had not acted.

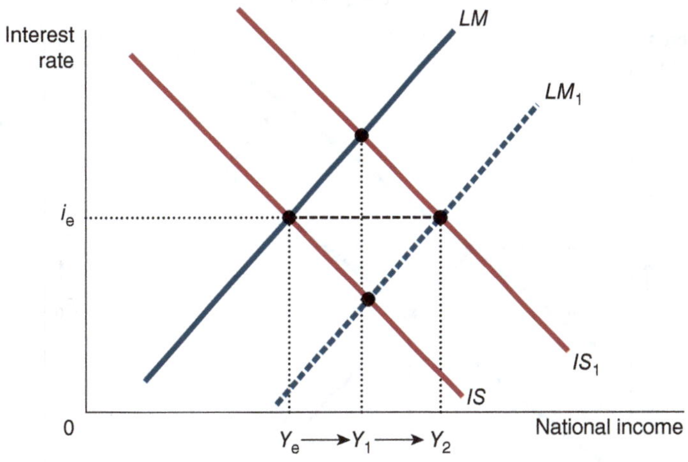

If the government had increased taxes, then the IS curve would shift to the left and both national income and interest rates would fall. If the central bank wants to keep interest rates constant it must reduce the money supply, and the result would be that the fall in national income would be compounded. If the central bank wanted to avoid this outcome, it could expand the money supply and interest rates would fall. This would help to offset the shift in the IS curve and reduce the impact on national income.

FROM IS–LM TO AGGREGATE DEMAND

It is a short step from using this model to the AD and AS model that we will use to analyze changes in the economy later in the book. Remember that the supply of real money balances is given by $\frac{M}{P}$. Assume the average price of a unit of output in the economy is €10 and the money supply is €100. The supply of real money balances is $\frac{100}{10} = 10$, that is at the current price level the supply of money in the economy can buy 10 units of output. If the average price of a unit of output in the economy rises to €20 and the money supply is constant, real money balances will fall to 5 units $\left(\frac{100}{20} = 5\right)$. This fall in the supply of real money balances shifts the LM curve to the left, as shown in panel (a) of Figure 11.8. The result is that interest rates rise and national income falls. There is, therefore, an inverse relationship between the price level and national income. The AD curve is derived by plotting the relationship between national income and the price level, as shown in panel (b) of Figure 11.8. The AD curve slopes downwards from left to right because of the inverse relationship between the price level and national income.

FIGURE 11.8

Deriving the Aggregate Demand Curve

In panel (a) a rise in the price level reduces real money balances and shifts the LM curve to the left to LM_1. This leads to a rise in the equilibrium interest rate to i_1 and a fall in national income from Y_0 to Y_1. The inverse relationship between the price level and national income is plotted in panel (b). A rise in the price level from P_0 to P_1 leads to a fall in national income from Y_0 to Y_1. The aggregate demand curve slopes downwards from left to right.

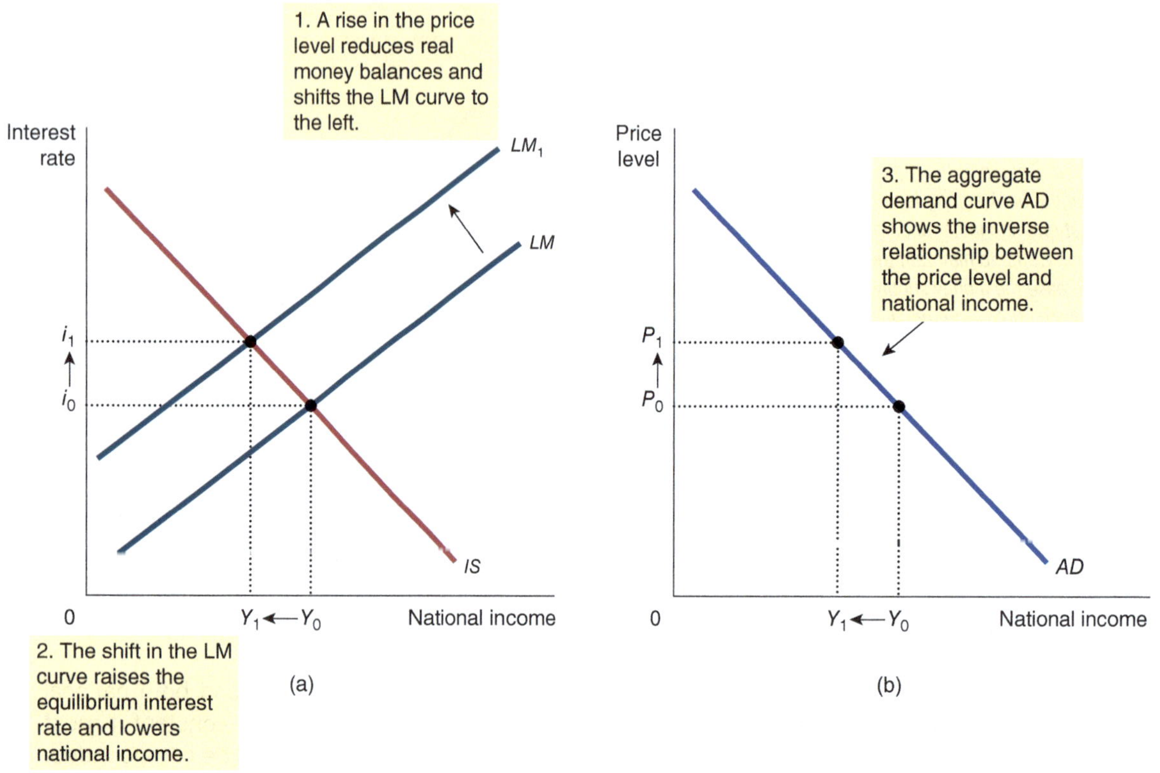

Shifts in the Aggregate Demand Curve If we assume the price level remains constant, a change in national income in the IS–LM model will result in a shift in the AD curve. Changes in both fiscal and monetary policy, assuming a given constant price level, will cause the AD curve to shift. If the government imposes an austerity package which seeks to cut government spending and raise taxes at a given price level, the IS curve will shift to the left and national income will fall. At the given price level, AD in the economy will now be less and the AD curve will shift to the left as shown in panel (a) of Figure 11.9.

If the central bank expands the money supply (possibly through a programme of asset purchasing or quantitative easing), the LM curve will shift to the right and national income will rise. At the given price level, the AD curve will shift to the right showing a higher level of national income at the given price level as shown in panel (b) of Figure 11.9.

A loosening of fiscal policy (increased government spending and/or lower taxes) and a reduction in the money supply (a tightening of monetary policy) will have the opposite effects from those described in Figure 11.9.

FIGURE 11.9

Shifts in the Aggregate Demand Curve as a Result of Monetary and Fiscal Policy

Panel (a) represents a situation where the government tightens fiscal policy, which shifts the IS curve to the left and reduces national income. At a given price level, the AD curve shifts to the left and a lower level of national income is associated with the given price level. Panel (b) represents a situation where the central bank loosens monetary policy, which causes the LM curve to shift to the right and lowers the interest rate. At the given price level, the AD curve shifts to the right with a higher level of national income.

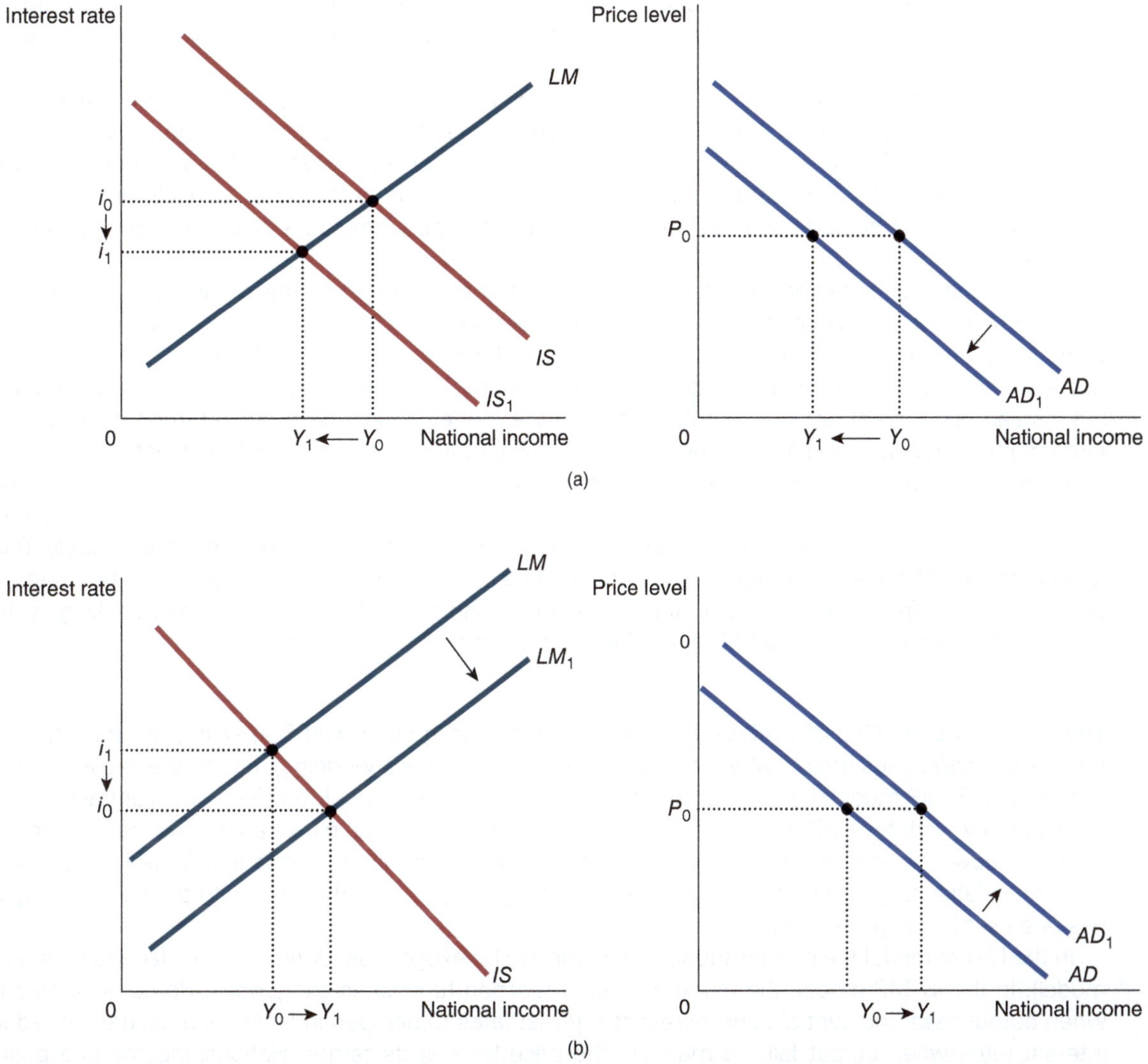

Criticisms of IS–LM, and the Romer Model

This short introduction to IS–LM analysis and the effect of changes in fiscal and monetary policy helps to highlight a number of important issues that you may start to consider as your study of economics moves to the next level. The effects of changes in fiscal and monetary policy are dependent on a number of factors related to the slope of the IS and LM curves, their relative position and how far each shifts in response to changes in policy. It is entirely possible that a change in fiscal policy can be countered by a change in monetary policy that leaves national income unchanged. The potential outcomes are many, and economists try to pinpoint more accurately what changes in policy will mean for the economy as a whole. This means conducting research to quantify such changes. The outcome of such research will be dependent on the value of variables that economists input into their models and on the relative strength of factors affecting the variables in the model.

One example of how the model has developed is the role which microeconomic analysis plays in understanding the macroeconomy. We saw an example of how microeconomic understanding feeds into macroeconomics in our look at DSGE models. Some economists argue that microeconomic principles cannot be divorced from the macroeconomy. We have seen how changing economic conditions may lead to wages and prices adjusting at different rates and markets being slow to clear as a result. If national income falls, for example, the assumption might be that prices and wages in the economy would also fall to help bring markets back into equilibrium. Sticky wages and prices may lag behind the reduction in economic activity as firms may be forced into trying to maintain cash flow rather than seeking to expand market share. As prices are sticky, sales fall and firms cut back output, which further impacts on economic activity.

Professor Mankiw was one of the economists who helped to reconcile the idea of sticky prices and menu costs with rational behaviour in his paper, 'Small Menu Costs and Large Business Cycles: A Macroeconomic Model of Monopoly', published in *The Quarterly Journal of Economics* in 1985. The debate over IS–LM has continued and has generated large amounts of valuable and interesting research which has helped build our understanding of the economy as a whole. It still has its critics, however.

Indeed, one such disagreement focuses on a central assumption of the model itself. Some higher education institutions have questioned the value of teaching IS–LM at all, because they argue that the world is now a very different place from the one Hicks knew back in the 1930s when he first developed Keynes' ideas. One of the major criticisms is that central banks no longer control the money supply, but instead set interest rates. Attempts to control the money supply have proved to be difficult and so targeting the interest rate is seen as being a more viable option to achieving policy objectives.

We have seen how central banks set interest rates through open market operations. If the central bank wishes to reduce interest rates, its traders will be instructed to buy bonds. Banks and financial institutions who sell these bonds will receive funds in return which will effectively expand the money supply. This in turn shifts the LM curve to the right and interest rates fall. If the central bank increases interest rates, the opposite occurs. Traders will be instructed to sell bonds and thus take funds out of the banking system, reducing the money supply. The LM curve shifts to the left and interest rates rise.

The IS–MP Model One of Professor Mankiw's close colleagues, David Romer (indeed they are more than simply colleagues given that each was best man at the other's wedding), has suggested an approach termed the IS–MP model, which attempts to build on the IS–LM model to reflect how central banks and the economy work today. The assumption in the model is that central banks adjust the money supply as outlined above to generate the interest rate that they want. The interest rate is adjusted in accordance with the inflation target that the central bank is working with or, as is the case with the Bank of England, has been set by the government.

In the IS–LM model the money supply is assumed to be exogenous (determined by factors outside the model). In the IS–MP model, the monetary policy reaction function is exogenous. Romer assumes that when output rises, the central bank increases interest rates to dampen inflationary pressures. It reduces interest rates when output falls to maintain the price level at its target. National income is a positive function of the interest rate, therefore. Romer plots this upwards sloping relationship as the MP curve. The MP function is assumed to be exogenous, but in reality both the money supply and the MP function can and do change in response to economic activity and events.

The MP function takes into account the fact that central banks now target inflation and set interest rates to achieve this goal. This is in contrast to simply assuming government (or a central bank) sets the money supply and that interest rates adjust to balance this supply of money with the demand for money. Crucially, Romer suggests that changes in inflation can cause a shift in the MP curve. If the central bank increases interest rates, the money supply will fall, which will affect the price level and expectations on inflation. Equally, if the central bank cuts interest rates the money supply will rise and expectations on inflation will also change as a result.

It is at this point where the microeconomic element of the analysis takes on some importance. Expectations of price changes may not match the reality because of the extent of price stickiness. If we assume that prices are completely sticky (that is, the price level is fixed), they will not change when the money supply changes. Expectations on inflation will, therefore, be zero. If the money supply rises then the supply of real money balances, $\frac{M}{P}$, also rises and is greater than the demand for real money balances. As the money market is now out of equilibrium, we might expect the interest rate to fall, but it could also be that the level of income could rise, or a combination of the two might occur. There will be a movement along the IS curve and a fall in interest rates will be accompanied by a rise in national income. This implies that the central bank can directly control the real interest rate by adjusting money supply appropriately to achieve the interest rate it desires.

If prices adjusted instantaneously then a change in the money supply would not affect the supply of real money balances because the ratio $\frac{M}{P}$ would hold as before at the rate of interest and level of income; in other words, the money market would remain in equilibrium. There would be no movement along the IS curve and the central bank would not be able to affect the real interest rate.

In reality, prices are not fixed, but the speed with which prices adjust to changes in economic conditions will vary. Some will adjust relatively quickly, others will take much longer and will be sticky. These sticky prices will influence the ratio of the money supply to the price level (the supply of real money balances). There may therefore be some expectations of inflation which will exist in the economy because M will rise by a greater proportion than P. An increase in the money supply will raise expected inflation and vice versa. If prices are sticky, then an increase in the nominal money supply will cause the money market to move out of equilibrium. Expected inflation, however, will affect the real interest rate. The nominal interest rate may have to be higher as a result.

The extent to which prices are sticky, therefore, has an important influence on the way in which a central bank can influence the interest rate to achieve its inflation targets. Such an analysis raises interesting questions when interest rates are reduced as was the case in response to the 2007–9 Financial Crisis and the subsequent recession. The UK, Europe and the United States saw their central banks reducing interest rates to historically low levels. To reduce interest rates, the central bank instructs its traders to buy bonds and the money supply will rise. Increases in the money supply may be associated with an increase in the price level. Indeed, some economists expressed alarm at the scale of quantitative easing conducted by central banks and predicted accelerating inflation. In times where economic activity is restrained, however, expectations of inflation may remain subdued and the money market may remain out of equilibrium as a result. The reason is that at these low interest rates people are willing to hold a greater amount of real money balances without any change in interest rate or output – after all, the interest rate cannot fall much further. This is the *liquidity trap* and may imply that monetary policy can have little effect on stimulating economic growth.

SELF TEST Draw diagrams to show the effect on interest rates and the level of national income of: (a) a decision by the government to raise taxes to cut a public deficit; and (b) a decision by a central bank to increase interest rates.

CRITICAL THINKING POINT Some economics departments at universities do not cover IS–LM anymore as it is seen as being outdated. Given what you have read so far, and taking into account the view of your own institution, do you think the model still has relevance and should be taught?

Keynesianism Post Crisis

The 2007–9 Financial Crisis reignited the debate about the value of Keynesian demand management policies. A number of countries introduced fiscal stimulus packages in the wake of the Financial Crisis. This led to questions about the benefits of such packages and even whether they amount to a stimulus. In late 2008 the EU announced a fiscal stimulus package of €200 billion. In the UK the Chancellor of the Exchequer had to admit that government borrowing might reach £175 billion, and be 79 per cent of GDP in 2013–14 (in the latter part of 2012 it stood at 73 per cent of GDP). In the United States the package was reported to be $800 billion. Meanwhile, China was reported to be injecting $585 billion and Japan $275 billion. Critics argued that such packages were not enough to bridge the output gap that had widened in most economies. In the United States, for example, the gap between potential and actual GDP was estimated by some economists at around $2 trillion. Other criticisms of fiscal stimulus packages suggested that they were not really what they seemed to be. If they were, then they would not bring the benefits that were claimed for them because of crowding out.

For example, in a study of the EU stimulus package in February 2009, David Saha and Jakob von Weizsäcker said, 'It should be recognized that the likely real impact on aggregate demand in the near future may well be more limited than suggested by the headline figures' (aei.pitt.edu/10549/1/UPDATED-SIZE-OF-STIMULUS-FINAL.pdf). In their analysis of the fiscal stimulus in Italy, announced as €80 billion, Saha and Weizsäcker conclude that the stimulus was not a stimulus at all, but a fiscal tightening amounting to €0.3 billion. In parts of Europe there were concerns that any major fiscal stimulus package would put pressure on the public debt and affect the stability of the euro, around which so much of the future prosperity of the EU lies.

One of the concerns about any fiscal stimulus is the extent to which it creates real wealth. Governments may spend more money, but on what? If the money is spent on public works, such as the building of new schools, hospitals, roads and so on, then surely this would boost AD? To an extent it would, but how is this additional spending to be financed? To raise the money governments will either tax their citizens more or increase borrowing. Additional spending on the construction of a new road may put money into the pockets of construction companies and its workers. However, to fund this the government must tax other wealth producers, thus offsetting some of the benefits of the stimulus. If the spending goes on additional benefits for those who become unemployed, then critics argue that the government is not contributing to wealth creation. These individuals may be supported in times of hardship and may spend their benefits on food and other goods, but they are not actually generating any wealth in return for the benefits they receive. Indeed, Keynes himself acknowledged that there were limitations to stimulus packages. In an article in *The Times* newspaper in the UK in 1937, a year after *The General Theory* was published, he wrote:

> *But I believe that we are approaching, or have reached, the point where there is not much advantage in applying a further general stimulus at the centre … It follows that the later stages of recovery require a different technique. To remedy the condition of the distressed areas ad hoc measures are necessary. The Jarrow marchers were, so to speak, theoretically correct … We are in more need today of a rightly distributed demand than of a greater aggregate demand.*

Structural changes in the economy might require more long-term investment if improvements in unemployment prospects and growth are to be achieved.

If governments must borrow more, then crowding out may emerge. In this scenario, the government is competing with the private sector for funds. Since the supply of loanable funds is finite, if governments take more of these funds it is argued that there will be less available for the private sector. If it is also assumed that the private sector uses such investment funds more efficiently than the public sector, then not only do fiscal stimulus packages crowd out private investment, they divert investment funds to less productive uses.

Krugman and Crowding In While this view is accepted by some economists, there are those that suggest that extraordinary times call for extraordinary action. One such proponent of this view was Paul Krugman. Krugman consistently argued that the depth of the 2007–9 Financial Crisis and global recession was such that a fiscal stimulus was necessary to get out of a liquidity trap and would lead to 'crowding in'. A liquidity trap occurs when monetary policy is insufficient to generate the economic stimulus necessary to get out of recession. In the United States and the UK, for example, interest rates were lowered by the Fed and the Bank of England to near zero. The Bank of Japan's key interest rate stood at 0.1 per cent in August 2009 while the ECB had rates at 1 per cent.

Krugman argued that private investment is a function of the state of the economy and, given the depth of the global recession, investment had plummeted. Investment, therefore, in this situation, was more responsive to product demand than to the rate of interest. If governments applied appropriate fiscal stimuli, this would improve the state of the economy and thus encourage private sector investment. As private sector investment increases, this improves productive potential and helps bring economies out of recession. Far from crowding out, Krugman argued, the fiscal stimulus would lead to crowding in.

Critics of this view suggest that increased government spending would crowd out private investment to an extent. Any fiscal stimulus must therefore take into account the loss of the benefits of that private investment in assessing the success of such a policy. The success of a stimulus package in putting economies on a sounder footing and bringing benefits to future generations would be highly dependent on the type of spending carried out by governments worldwide. Spending on new schools and transport infrastructure may improve the future productive potential of the economy and tackle the structural problems that exist in some economies as referred to above.

However, the issues of rent seeking and logrolling have to be taken into consideration. Rent seeking occurs where decisions are made leading to resource allocation that maximizes the benefit to the decision-maker at the expense of another party or parties. Logrolling is where decisions may be made on resource allocation to projects that have less importance, in return for the support of the interested party in other decision-making areas. In both cases, it is argued that resource allocation is not as efficient as that carried out by the private sector. This must therefore be taken into consideration in assessing the benefits of public sector spending as a result of any stimulus package.

CONCLUSION

There continues to be debate on Keynesian approaches in macroeconomics in addition to the debate on the value and relevance of the IS–LM model. What is not in much doubt is that an understanding of the relationship between the goods market and the money market is a useful way of developing a broader understanding of analyzing the economy as a whole. This short introduction to such analysis provides some pointers to the IS–LM model and to some of the issues that economists are debating. Depending on the university that you attend, a greater or lesser emphasis may be placed on the IS–LM model. Having some awareness of the model does help to develop a focus on the important connections between the money supply, interest rates and economic activity.

SUMMARY

- Keynes developed *The General Theory* as a response to the mass unemployment which existed in the 1930s.
- He advocated governments intervene to boost demand through influencing aggregate demand.
- The Keynesian cross diagram shows how the economy can be in equilibrium when $E = Y$.
- This equilibrium may not be sufficient to deliver full employment output, and so the government can attempt to boost demand to help achieve full employment.
- John Hicks developed Keynes' ideas in the form of the IS–LM model, which shows general equilibrium in the economy.
- The IS (investment–saving) curve shows all points of equilibrium in the goods market at a particular interest rate and level of national income.
- The LM (liquidity–money supply) curve shows points where the money market is in equilibrium at particular rates of interest and level of national income.
- General equilibrium occurs where the IS curve intersects the LM curve. At this interest rate and level of national income, both the goods market and money market are in equilibrium.
- Fiscal policy and monetary policy can cause shifts in the IS and LM curves bringing about new equilibrium positions. The outcome will depend on a variety of factors including the response of consumption and investment to changes in interest rates and the public's response to holding monetary balances as a result of a change in interest rates.
- There have been criticisms that the IS–LM model does not represent the way monetary policy is conducted in modern economies.
- Economists have developed new models to incorporate the changes in policy.

IN THE NEWS

To Keynes or not to Keynes...

The theory around Keynesian economics is broadly accepted. Governments can intervene in economies to seek to influence broader economic outcomes, to try to boost output through public spending. However, adopting essentially Keynesian economic policy is much more contentious. At its heart, Keynesian economic policy implies increased public spending and tends to be associated with an increase in public debt and a widening budget deficit. Part of the discussion around whether to adopt Keynesian policies is centred around belief systems.

Across Europe and in the UK, there seems to have been a leaning towards rejecting Keynesian principles in recent years. Few politicians would disagree with the view that central banks should manipulate interest rates to try to influence economic outcomes, but more seem to be less certain about governments manipulating budgets to secure economic outcomes. In the UK, for example, the Chancellor of the Exchequer's first budget after the Labour party secured its general election win in 2024 focused on correcting the state of the public finances and aiming to move the budget deficit into a surplus. Across Europe, political leaders are also focused on trimming back the fiscal expansion that was used in response to the effects of the pandemic. Part of the sentiment against Keynesianism, some argue, is a misguided belief that an economy should be run like a household where spending has to be matched by income. It is also framed by the fundamental belief that, somehow, spending by governments is less efficient and effective than that of the private sector. For example, it is widely accepted that across Europe and the UK investment is needed to develop green energy. What is the most effective way of achieving this? Is it through public or private spending?

If we want to view the issues from an objective basis then we might reasonably ask what the evidence is on which these belief systems are based? A Chicago Booth European experts panel published in 2019 revealed some interesting points. Two points raised were:

1. When the economy is operating below its potential, larger fiscal deficits are likely to increase demand and output.
2. When the economy is operating below its potential and monetary policy is at the effective lower bound, fiscal policy should prioritize increasing output over decreasing public debt.

In response to the first point, 35 per cent strongly agreed and 50 per cent agreed. For the second point, 17 per cent strongly agreed and 45 per cent agreed. The so-called experts, therefore, seem to be expressing views different from those of some politicians.

Comments around the questions and the responses were also interesting. In response to the first point, for example, Sir Christopher Pissarides noted: 'Old fashioned Keynesianism works!' What does Pissarides know? Well, he is a Nobel Prize winner and secured the prize for the analysis of search frictions in labour markets. The work he and fellow prize winner, Dale Mortenson, were honoured for has also been applied to other markets. Despite the broad agreement around the value of basic Keynesian ideas, there were a number of comments that were caveats to the opinions offered. Some noted that their response very much depended on things such as how big the deficit might be, whether the questions referred to the short run or long run, and what the borrowing rate would be for governments. Perhaps one such comment encapsulates

© iStock/pkawasaki

What is the best way of achieving particular economic goals such as net-zero targets? Government intervention or leave it to the market?

(Continued)

the issue perfectly. Peter Neary, Professor of Economics at the University of Oxford, who sadly died in 2021, observed, 'Agree, but this is more a political/moral judgment than a scientifically grounded view. And depends on circumstances, especially size of deficit.'

Critical Thinking Questions

1 Why is consideration of belief systems important in considering analysis of economic policy?
2 Some press comments noted that the UK Chancellor of the Exchequer, Rachel Reeves, who studied politics, philosophy and economics at the University of Oxford, had aligned herself to Keynesian principles in the years prior to taking office. In her first budget, however, she was 'unashamedly anti-Keynesian'. Why do you think political leaders might change their policy choices when actually taking up office?
3 Using the models outlined in this chapter, assume that a government commits to a policy of investing in green energy systems as part of its goal of achieving net zero targets and phasing out carbon-based energy provision. What are the arguments for the government using public spending to achieve this objective. What are the arguments for it being financed by the private sector via incentives provided by the government? Which do you think would achieve the stated outcome more effectively and what does your answer depend on?
4 Given the results of the experts' panel on the two points posed, why do you think politicians across Europe seem to be leaning more against Keynesian policies?
5 Is it meaningful to ask questions on views of Keynesian policy without a considerable number of caveats built into the questions? To what extent do you agree with the comment expressed by Peter Neary? Should politicians be guided by evidence rather than belief systems?

References:

www.euractiv.com/section/economy-jobs/opinion/the-brief-the-keynesian-times-are-over/, accessed 7 August 2025.
www.kentclarkcenter.org/surveys/european-fiscal-and-monetary-policy/, accessed 7 August 2025.

QUESTIONS FOR REVIEW

1 Distinguish between planned expenditure and actual expenditure.
2 Draw a Keynesian cross diagram to show the effects of a rise in autonomous expenditure on an economy operating below full employment output.
3 What is meant by the terms: *inflationary gap* and *deflationary gap*?
4 What is the marginal propensity to consume?
5 Why does the $MPC + MPS = 1$?
6 What is the multiplier? Can the multiplier be negative as well as positive? Explain.
7 Explain how the marginal propensity to withdraw affects the outcome of a rise in autonomous expenditure.
8 Use diagrams to describe how the IS and LM curves are derived.
9 Using the IS–LM model, explain the effect on the economy of a reduction in autonomous expenditure resulting from a cut in public spending by the government.
10 A central bank wishes to reduce inflationary expectations by increasing interest rates. Use the IS–MP model to analyze the effect on the economy of such a move.

PROBLEMS AND APPLICATIONS

1 What, according to Keynes, was the main reason why recessions and depressions occurred? As a result of identifying this key reason, what did Keynes suggest was an appropriate policy repose?

2 Explain, using an appropriate diagram, how a deflationary gap can occur and how this gap can be eliminated.

3 Suppose economists observe that an increase in government spending of €10 billion raises the total demand for goods and services by €30 billion.
   a. If these economists ignore the possibility of crowding out, what would they estimate the *MPC* to be?
   b. Now suppose economists allow for crowding out. Would their new estimate of the *MPC* be larger or smaller than their initial one? Explain your answer.

4 Suppose the government reduces taxes by €2 billion, that there is no crowding out and that the *MPC* is 0.75.
   a. What is the initial effect of the tax reduction on AD?
   b. What additional effects follow this initial effect? What is the total effect of the tax cut on AD?
   c. How does the total effect of this €2 billion tax cut compare to the total effect of a €2 billion increase in government purchases? Why?

5 Assume the economy is in equilibrium. Analyze the effect of a cut in autonomous expenditure on economic activity and the level of unemployment. You should use a diagram to help illustrate your answer.

6 What does the *IS* curve show? What does the *LM* curve show?

7 What determines the slope of the *IS* curve? What determines the slope of the *LM* curve? In relation to your answer to these questions, explain why these determinants can be a source of disagreement among economists.

8 Use the *IS–LM* model to explain the following:
   a. The government institutes significant cuts in public expenditure.
   b. The central bank institutes an asset purchasing facility (quantitative easing) which expands the money supply by €300 billion.
   c. The central bank fears that inflationary pressures are rising and increases interest rates.
   d. The government increases taxation to try to reduce a large budget deficit.

9 Assume that a period of deflation leads to a rise in the supply of real money balances. Explain the effect of this change on the economy using the *IS–LM* model and then what effect it would have on AD and why.

10 Do you think that Keynes' ideas still have some relevance today? Explain.

12 AGGREGATE DEMAND AND AGGREGATE SUPPLY

Although there remains some debate among economists about how to analyze short-run fluctuations, in this chapter we will look at the *model of aggregate demand (AD) and aggregate supply (AS)*, which is widely used among economists to analyze the short-run effects of various events and policies.

THREE KEY FACTS ABOUT ECONOMIC FLUCTUATIONS

Short-run fluctuations in economic activity occur in all countries and at numerous times throughout history. As a starting point for understanding these year-to-year fluctuations, let us remind ourselves of some of their most important properties.

Fact 1: Economic Fluctuations Are Irregular and Unpredictable

Economic fluctuations correspond to changes in business conditions. When real GDP grows rapidly, business is good. During such periods of economic expansion, firms find that customers are plentiful and that profits are growing. On the other hand, when real GDP falls, some firms experience declining sales and dwindling profits. Recall that economic fluctuations are not at all regular, and they are almost impossible to predict with much accuracy.

Fact 2: Most Macroeconomic Quantities Fluctuate Together

Real GDP is the variable that is most commonly used to monitor short-run changes in the economy. Real GDP measures the value of all final goods and services produced within a given period of time. It also measures the total income (adjusted for inflation) of everyone in the economy.

It turns out, however, that for monitoring short-run fluctuations, it does not really matter which measure of economic activity you look at. Most macroeconomic variables that measure some type of income, spending, or production, fluctuate closely together. When real GDP falls in a recession, so does personal income, corporate profits, consumer spending, investment spending, industrial production, retail sales, home sales, car sales and so on. Because recessions are economy-wide phenomena, they show up in many sources of macroeconomic data.

Although many macroeconomic variables fluctuate together, they fluctuate by different amounts. In particular, investment spending varies greatly over the business cycle. When economic conditions deteriorate, much of the decline is attributable to reductions in spending on new factories, housing and inventories. If we look historically at investment in the UK, for example, referred to as gross fixed capital formation (GFCF) and including business as well as public sector investment, it fell sharply in 2020, the year of the pandemic. It recovered subsequently to reach pre-pandemic levels by early 2022 and then rose by almost 4 per cent between quarter three 2023 and quarter three 2024.

Fact 3: As Output Falls, Unemployment Rises

Changes in the economy's output of goods and services are strongly correlated with changes in the economy's utilization of its labour force. In other words, when real GDP declines, the rate of unemployment rises. The negative relationship between unemployment and real GDP is referred to as **Okun's law** after the Yale economist who published his observations in the 1960s. Okun noted that to keep the unemployment rate steady, real GDP needs to grow at or close to its potential. If the unemployment rate is to be reduced, real GDP must grow above potential. Being more specific, to reduce the unemployment rate by 1 per cent in a year, real GDP must rise by around 2 per cent more than potential GDP over the year.

Okun's law a 'law' which is based on observations that to keep the unemployment rate steady, real GDP needs to grow at or close to its potential

Okun's findings are hardly surprising. When firms choose to produce a smaller quantity of goods and services, they lay off workers, expanding the pool of unemployed. However, there is generally a time lag between any downturn in economic activity and a rise in unemployment and vice versa. Even when positive growth resumes, therefore, unemployment is likely to continue to rise for some time afterwards, which is why unemployment is referred to as a 'lagged indicator'.

EXPLAINING SHORT-RUN ECONOMIC FLUCTUATIONS

Describing the patterns that economies experience as they fluctuate over time is easy. Explaining what causes these fluctuations is more difficult, and the theory of economic fluctuations remains controversial. We are now going to develop a model used to explain short-run fluctuations in economic activity.

How the Short Run Differs from the Long Run

In previous chapters we developed theories to explain what determines most important macroeconomic variables in the long run. We have looked at the level and growth of productivity and real GDP. We have explained how the financial system works and how the real interest rate adjusts to balance saving and investment. We have looked at why there is always some unemployment in the economy and explained the monetary system and how changes in the money supply affect the price level, the inflation rate and the nominal interest rate. We then extended this analysis to open economies in order to explain the trade balance and the exchange rate.

All of this previous analysis was based on two related ideas: the *classical dichotomy* and *monetary neutrality*. Recall that the classical dichotomy is the separation of variables into real variables (those that measure quantities or relative prices) and nominal variables (those measured in terms of money). According to classical macroeconomic theory, changes in the money supply affect nominal variables but not real variables. As a result of this monetary neutrality, we were able to examine the determinants of real variables (real GDP, the real interest rate and unemployment) without introducing nominal variables (the money supply and the price level).

Do these assumptions of classical macroeconomic theory apply to the world in which we live? The answer to this question is of central importance to understanding how the economy works. Many economists believe that classical theory describes the world in the long run but not in the short run. Beyond a period of several years, changes in the money supply affect prices and other nominal variables but do not affect real GDP, unemployment or other real variables. When studying year-to-year changes in the economy, however, the assumption of monetary neutrality is no longer appropriate. Many economists believe that, in the short run, real and nominal variables are highly intertwined. In particular, changes in the money supply can temporarily push output away from its long-run trend.

To understand the economy in the short run, therefore, we need a new model. To build this new model, we rely on many of the tools we have developed in previous chapters but must abandon the classical dichotomy and the neutrality of money.

The Basic Model of Economic Fluctuations

Our model of short-run economic fluctuations focuses on the behaviour of two variables. The first variable is the economy's output of goods and services, as measured by real GDP. The second variable is the overall price level, an average of prices of all goods and services in an economy as measured by the CPI or the GDP deflator. Output is a real variable, whereas the price level is a nominal variable. Hence by focusing on the relationship between these two variables, we are highlighting the breakdown of the classical dichotomy.

We analyze fluctuations in the economy as a whole with the **model of aggregate demand and aggregate supply**, which is illustrated in Figure 12.1. On the vertical axis is the overall price level in the economy. On the horizontal axis is the overall quantity of goods and services. The **aggregate demand curve** shows the quantity of goods and services that households, firms and the government want to buy at each price level. The **aggregate supply curve** shows the quantity of goods and services that firms produce and sell at each price level. According to this model, the price level and the quantity of output adjust to bring AD and AS into balance.

model of aggregate demand and aggregate supply the model that some economists use to explain short-run fluctuations in economic activity around its long-run trend
aggregate demand curve a curve that shows the quantity of goods and services that households, firms and the government want to buy at each price level
aggregate supply curve a curve that shows the quantity of goods and services that firms choose to produce and sell at each price level

FIGURE 12.1

Aggregate Demand and Aggregate Supply
Economists use the model of AD and AS to analyze economic fluctuations. On the vertical axis is the overall level of prices. On the horizontal axis is the economy's total output of goods and services. Output and the price level adjust to the point at which the AS and AD curves intersect.

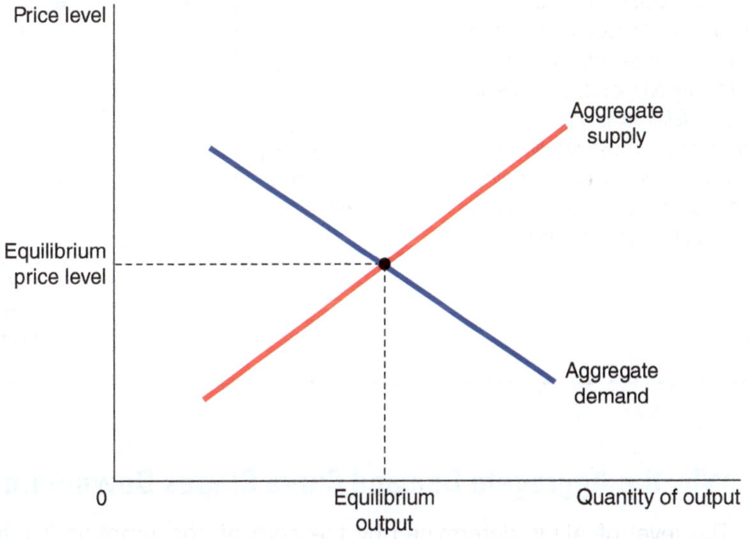

It may be tempting to view the model of AD and AS as nothing more than a large version of the model of market demand and market supply. In fact, this model is quite different. When we consider demand and supply in a particular market for a good, such as streaming TV, the behaviour of buyers and sellers depends on the ability of resources to move from one market to another. When the price of streaming services rises, the quantity demanded falls because buyers will use their incomes to buy products or services other than streaming services. Similarly, a higher price of streaming services raises the quantity supplied. This is because firms that produce these services can increase production by hiring workers away from other parts of the economy. This *microeconomic* substitution from one market to another is impossible when we are analyzing the economy as a whole. After all, the quantity that our model is trying to explain – real GDP – measures the total quantity produced in all of the economy's markets. To understand why the AD curve is downwards sloping and why the AS curve is upwards sloping, we need a *macroeconomic* theory. Developing such a theory is our next task.

SELF TEST How does the economy's behaviour in the short run differ from its behaviour in the long run? Draw the model of AD and AS. What variables are on the two axes?

THE AGGREGATE DEMAND CURVE

The AD curve tells us the quantity of all goods and services demanded in the economy at any given price level. As Figure 12.2 illustrates, the AD curve is downwards sloping reflecting the inverse relationship between the price level and national income. This means that, *ceteris paribus*, a fall in the economy's overall level of prices (from, say, P_1 to P_2) tends to raise the quantity of goods and services demanded (from Y_1 to Y_2).

FIGURE 12.2

The Aggregate Demand Curve

A fall in the price level from P_1 to P_2 increases the quantity of goods and services demanded from Y_1 to Y_2. There are three reasons for this negative relationship. As the price level falls, real wealth rises, interest rates fall and the exchange rate depreciates. These effects stimulate spending on consumption, investment and net exports. Increased spending on these components of output means a larger quantity of goods and services demanded.

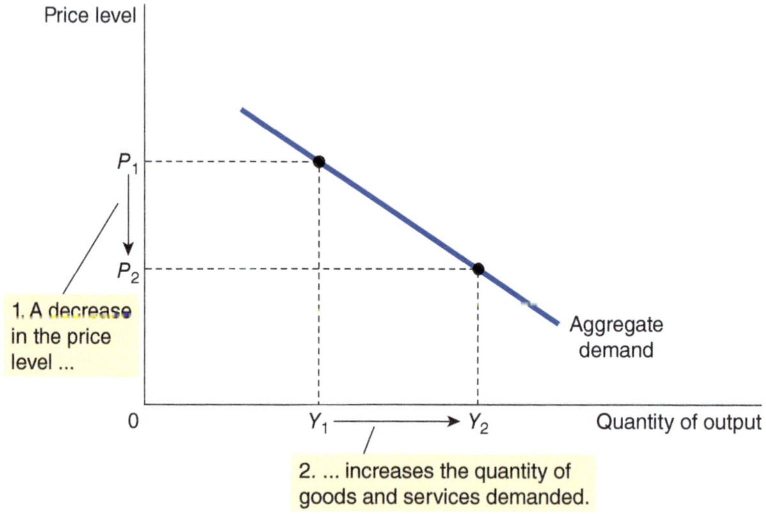

Why the Aggregate Demand Curve Slopes Downwards

The level of AD is determined by the sum of consumption (*C*), investment (*I*), government purchases (*G*) and net exports (*NX*). For now, we assume that government spending is fixed by policy. The other three components of spending depend on economic conditions and, in particular, on the price level. To understand the downwards slope of the AD curve, we must examine how the price level affects the quantity of goods and services demanded for consumption, investment and net exports.

The Price Level and Consumption: The Wealth Effect Consider the money that you hold as cash, and your bank account. The nominal value of this money is fixed, but its real value is not. When prices fall, this money is more valuable because it can be used to buy more goods and services. Thus a decrease in the price level makes consumers wealthier, which in turn encourages them to spend more. The increase in consumer spending means a larger quantity of goods and services demanded.

The Price Level and Investment: The Interest Rate Effect The price level is one determinant of the quantity of money demanded. The lower the price level, the less money households need to hold to buy the goods and services they want. When the price level falls, therefore, households try to reduce their holdings of money by lending some of it out, which in turn increases the supply of real money balances. For instance, a household might use its excess money to buy interest-bearing bonds. Or it might deposit its excess money in an interest-bearing savings account, and the bank would use these funds to make more loans. In either case, as households try to convert some of their money into interest-bearing assets, they drive down interest rates. Lower interest rates, in turn, encourage borrowing by firms that want to invest in new factories and equipment, and by households who want to invest in new housing. Thus a lower price level reduces the interest rate, encourages greater spending on investment goods, and thereby increases the quantity of goods and services demanded.

The Price Level and Net Exports: The Exchange Rate Effect As we have just discussed, a lower price level lowers the interest rate. In response, some investors will seek higher returns by investing abroad. For instance, as the interest rate on European government bonds falls, an investment fund might sell European government bonds to buy US government bonds. As the investment fund tries to convert its euros into dollars to buy the US bonds, it increases the supply of euros in the market for foreign currency exchange. The increased supply of euros causes the euro to depreciate relative to other currencies. Because each euro buys fewer units of foreign currencies, non-European goods (that is, imports) become more expensive to European residents. However, exporters find that foreign buyers get more euros for each unit of their currency. This change in the real exchange rate (the relative price of domestic and foreign goods) increases European exports of goods and services, and decreases European imports of goods and services. Net exports, which equal exports minus imports, also increase. Thus when a fall in the European price level causes European interest rates to fall, the real value of the euro falls, and this depreciation stimulates European net exports and thereby increases the quantity of goods and services demanded in the European economy.

Summary

There are, therefore, three distinct but related reasons why a fall in the price level increases the quantity of goods and services demanded:

- Consumers are wealthier, which stimulates the demand for consumption goods.
- Interest rates fall, which stimulates the demand for investment goods.
- The exchange rate depreciates, which stimulates the demand for net exports.

For all three reasons, the AD curve slopes downwards. This is reflected in Figure 12.2.

The AD is determined *ceteris paribus*. We have considered how a change in the price level affects the demand for goods and services, holding the amount of money in the economy constant. The AD curve is drawn for a given quantity of money.

Why the Aggregate Demand Curve Might Shift

Recall that changes in monetary and fiscal policy can cause a shift in the LM and IS curves and, at a given price level, a shift in AD. We are going to explore shifts in the AD curve in more detail here. The downwards slope of the AD curve shows that a fall in the price level raises the overall quantity of goods and services demanded. Many other factors, however, affect the quantity of goods and services demanded at a given price level. When one of these other factors changes, the AD curve shifts.

Shifts Arising from Consumption Suppose people suddenly become more concerned about saving for retirement and, as a result, reduce their current consumption. Because the quantity of goods and services demanded at any price level is lower, the AD curve shifts to the left. Conversely, imagine that a stock market boom makes people wealthier and less concerned about saving. The resulting increase in consumer spending means a greater quantity of goods and services demanded at any given price level, so the AD curve shifts to the right.

Thus any event that changes how much people want to consume at a given price level shifts the AD curve. One policy variable that has this effect is the level of taxation. When the government cuts taxes, it encourages people to spend more, so the AD curve shifts to the right. When the government raises taxes, people cut back on their spending and the AD curve shifts to the left.

Shifts Arising from Investment Any event that changes how much firms want to invest at a given price level also shifts the AD curve. For instance, imagine that the developments in Industry 4.0 improve efficiencies in industry due to digital connectiveness and, as a result, demand for these types of technology by firms in general increases. Because the quantity of goods and services demanded at any price level is higher, the AD curve shifts to the right. Conversely, if firms become pessimistic about future business conditions, they may cut back on investment spending, shifting the AD curve to the left.

Tax policy can also influence AD through investment. An investment tax credit (a tax rebate tied to a firm's investment spending) increases the quantity of investment goods that firms demand at any given interest rate. It therefore shifts the AD curve to the right. The repeal of an investment tax credit reduces investment and shifts the AD curve to the left.

Another policy variable that can influence investment and AD is the money supply. An increase in the money supply lowers the interest rate in the short run (the LM curve shifts to the right). This makes borrowing less costly, which stimulates investment spending and thereby shifts the AD curve to the right at a given price level. Conversely, a decrease in the money supply shifts the LM curve to the left and raises the interest rate. This discourages investment spending and thereby shifts the AD curve to the left at the given price level. Many economists believe that changes in monetary policy have been an important source of shifts in AD in most developed economies at some points in their history.

Shifts Arising from Government Purchases The most direct way that policymakers shift the AD curve is through government purchases. For example, suppose the government decides to reduce purchases of new weapons systems. Because the quantity of goods and services demanded at any price level is lower, the AD curve shifts to the left. Conversely, if the government starts building more motorways, the result is a greater quantity of goods and services demanded at any price level, and the AD curve shifts to the right.

Shifts Arising from Net Exports Any event that changes net exports for a given price level also shifts AD. For instance, when the United States experiences a recession, it buys fewer goods from Europe. This reduces European net exports and shifts the AD curve for the European economy to the left. When the United States recovers from its recession, it starts buying European goods again, shifting the AD curve to the right.

Net exports sometimes change because of movements in the exchange rate. Suppose, for instance, that international speculators bid up the value of the euro in the market for foreign currency exchange. This appreciation of the euro would make goods produced in the euro area more expensive compared to foreign goods, which would depress net exports and shift the AD curve to the left. Conversely, a depreciation of the euro stimulates net exports and shifts the euro area AD curve to the right.

SELF TEST Explain the three reasons why the AD curve slopes downwards. Give an example of an event that would shift the AD curve. Which way would this event shift the curve?

THE AGGREGATE SUPPLY CURVE

The AS curve tells us the total quantity of goods and services that firms produce and sell at any given price level. Unlike the AD curve, which is always downwards sloping, the AS curve shows a relationship that depends crucially on the time horizon being examined. In the long run, the AS curve is vertical, whereas in the short run the AS curve is upwards sloping. To understand short-run economic fluctuations and how the short-run behaviour of the economy deviates from its long-run behaviour, we need to examine both the long-run AS curve and the short-run AS curve.

Why the Aggregate Supply Curve is Vertical in the Long Run

In the long run, an economy's production of goods and services (its real GDP) depends on its supplies of labour, capital and natural resources, and on the available technology used to turn these factors of production into goods and services. Because the price level does not affect these long-run determinants of real GDP, the long-run AS curve is vertical, as in Figure 12.3. In other words, in the long run, the economy's labour, capital, natural resources and technology determine the total quantity of goods and services supplied, and this quantity supplied is the same regardless of what the price level happens to be.

FIGURE 12.3

The Long-Run Aggregate Supply Curve

In the long run, the quantity of output supplied depends on the economy's quantities of labour, capital and natural resources and on the technology for turning these inputs into output. The quantity supplied does not depend on the overall price level. As a result, the long-run AS curve is vertical at the natural rate of output.

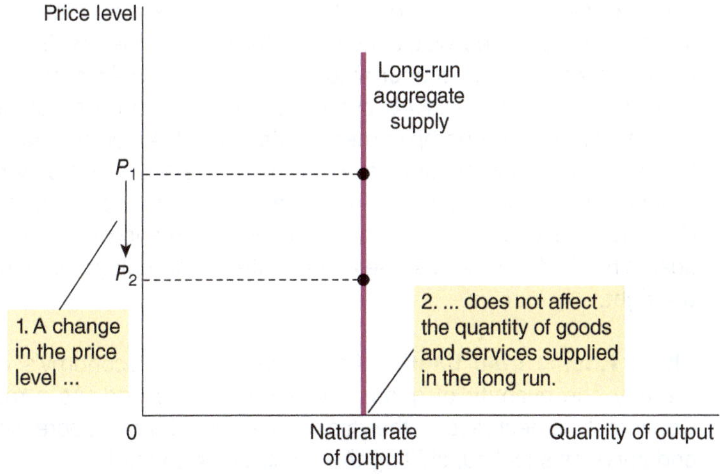

The vertical long-run AS curve is, in essence, just an application of the classical dichotomy and monetary neutrality. As we have already discussed, classical macroeconomic theory is based on the assumption that real variables do not depend on nominal variables. The long-run AS curve is consistent with this idea, because it implies that the quantity of output (a real variable) does not depend on the level of prices (a nominal variable). As noted earlier, many economists believe that this principle works well when studying the economy over a period of many years, but not when studying year-to-year changes. Thus the AS curve is vertical only in the long run.

You might wonder how supply curves for specific goods and services can be upwards sloping if the long-run AS curve is vertical. The reason is that the supply of specific goods and services depends on *relative prices*, that is the prices of those goods and services compared to other prices in the economy. For example, when the price of streaming services rises, holding other prices in the economy constant, there is an incentive for suppliers of these services to increase their production by taking labour and other inputs away from the production of other goods, such as mobile phones or laptop computers. By contrast, the economy's overall production of goods and services is limited by its labour, capital, natural resources and technology. Thus when all prices in the economy rise together, there is no change in the overall quantity of goods and services supplied because relative prices and thus incentives have not changed.

Why the Long-Run AS Curve Might Shift

The position of the long-run AS (LRAS) curve shows the quantity of goods and services predicted by classical macroeconomic theory. This level of production is sometimes called *potential output* or *full employment output*. To be more accurate, we call it the **natural rate of output** because it shows what the economy produces when unemployment is at its natural, or normal, rate. The natural rate of output is the level of production towards which the economy gravitates in the long run.

natural rate of output the output level in an economy when all existing factors of production (land, labour, capital and technology resources) are fully utilized and where unemployment is at its natural rate

Any change in the economy that alters the natural rate of output shifts the LRAS curve. Because output in the classical model depends on labour, capital, natural resources and technological knowledge, we can categorize shifts in the LRAS curve as arising from these sources.

Shifts Arising from Labour Imagine that an economy experiences an increase in immigration from abroad and that these people found work. Because there is a greater number of workers, the quantity of goods and services supplied would increase. As a result, the LRAS curve would shift to the right. Conversely, if many workers left the economy to go abroad, the LRAS curve would shift to the left.

The position of the LRAS curve also depends on the natural rate of unemployment. Any change in the natural rate of unemployment shifts the LRAS curve. For example, if a government were to raise the minimum wage substantially, the natural rate of unemployment would rise, and the economy would produce a smaller quantity of goods and services. As a result, the LRAS curve would shift to the left. Conversely, if a reform of the unemployment insurance system were to encourage unemployed workers to search harder for new jobs, the natural rate of unemployment would fall and the LRAS curve would shift to the right.

Shifts Arising from Capital An increase in the economy's capital stock increases productivity and, thereby, the quantity of goods and services supplied. As a result, the LRAS curve shifts to the right. Conversely, a decrease in the economy's capital stock decreases productivity and the quantity of goods and services supplied, shifting the LRAS curve to the left.

Notice that the same logic applies regardless of whether we are discussing physical capital or human capital. An increase either in the number of machines or in the number of university degrees will raise the economy's ability to produce goods and services. Thus either would shift the LRAS curve to the right.

Shifts Arising from Natural Resources An economy's production depends on its natural resources, including its land, minerals and weather. A discovery of a new mineral deposit shifts the LRAS curve to the right. A change in weather patterns that makes farming more difficult shifts the LRAS curve to the left.

In many countries, important natural resources are imported from abroad. A change in the availability of these resources can also shift the AS curve. Events occurring in the world oil market, in particular, have historically been an important source of shifts in AS.

Shifts Arising from Technological Knowledge Perhaps the most important reason that the economy today produces more than it did a generation ago is that our technological knowledge has advanced. The invention of the computer, for instance, has allowed us to produce more goods and services from any given amounts of labour, capital and natural resources. As a result, it has shifted the LRAS curve to the right.

Although not literally technological, there are many other events that act like changes in technology. The opening up of international trade has effects similar to inventing new production processes, so it also shifts the LRAS curve to the right. Conversely, if the government passed new regulations preventing firms from using some production methods, perhaps because they were too dangerous for workers, the result would be a leftwards shift in the LRAS curve.

Summary

The LRAS curve reflects the classical model of the economy. Any policy or event that raised real GDP can now be viewed as increasing the quantity of goods and services supplied and shifting the LRAS curve to the right. Any policy or event that lowered real GDP can now be viewed as decreasing the quantity of goods and services supplied and shifting the LRAS curve to the left.

A New Way to Depict Long-Run Growth and Inflation

Having introduced the economy's AD curve and the LRAS curve, we now have a new way to describe the economy's long-run trends. Figure 12.4 illustrates the changes that occur in the economy from decade to decade. Notice that both curves are shifting. Although there are many forces that govern the economy in the long run and can, in principle, cause such shifts, the two most important in practice are technology and monetary policy. Technological progress enhances the economy's ability to produce goods and services, and this continually shifts the LRAS curve to the right. At the same time, because the central bank increases the money supply over time, the AD curve also shifts to the right. As the figure illustrates, the result is trend growth in output (as shown by increasing *Y*) and continuing inflation (as shown by increasing *P*). This is just another way of representing the classical analysis of growth and inflation we conducted earlier in the book.

FIGURE 12.4

Long-Run Growth and Inflation in the Model of Aggregate Demand and Aggregate Supply

As the economy becomes better able to produce goods and services over time, primarily because of technological progress, the LRAS curve shifts to the right. At the same time, as the central bank increases the money supply, the AD curve also shifts to the right. In this figure, output grows from Y_{2007} *to* Y_{2017} *and then to* Y_{2027}*, and the price level rises from* P_{2007} *to* P_{2017} *and then to* P_{2027}*. Thus the model of AD and AS offers a new way to describe the classical analysis of growth and inflation.*

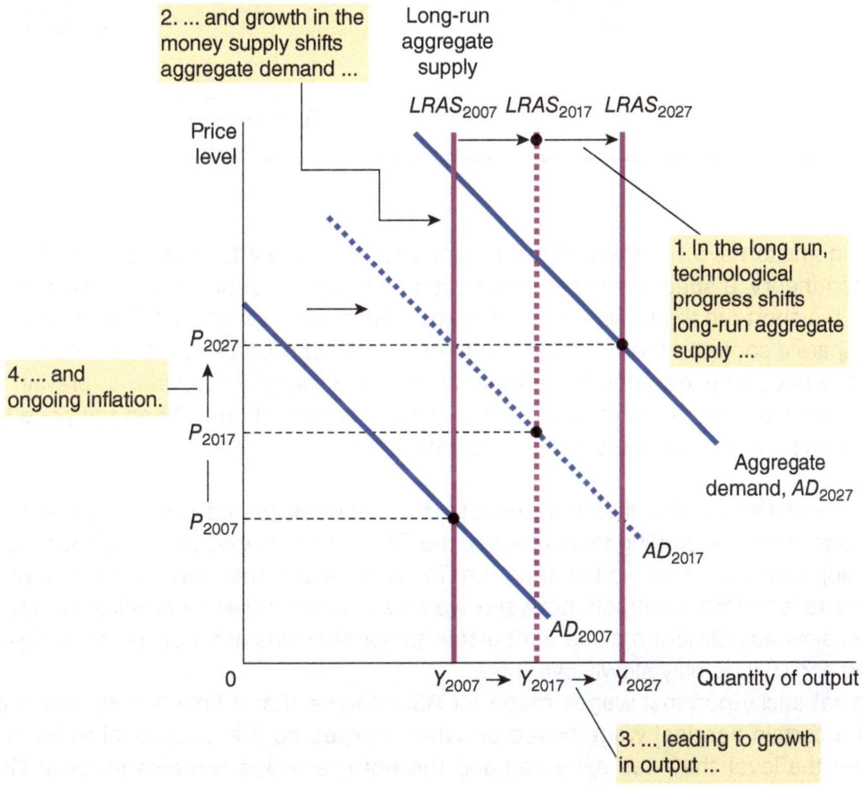

The purpose of developing the model of AD and AS, however, is not to dress our long-run conclusions in new clothing. Instead, it is to provide a framework for short-run analysis, as we will see in a moment. As we develop the short-run model, we keep the analysis simple by not showing the continuing growth and inflation depicted in Figure 12.4. It is worth remembering that long-run trends provide the background for short-run fluctuations. Short-run fluctuations in output and the price level should be viewed as deviations from the continuing long-run trends.

Why the AS Curve Slopes Upwards in the Short Run

We now come to the key difference between the economy in the short run and in the long run, that is the behaviour of AS. As we have already discussed, the LRAS curve is vertical. By contrast, in the short run, the AS curve is upwards sloping, as shown in Figure 12.5. That is, over a period of a year or two, an increase in the overall level of prices in the economy tends to raise the quantity of goods and services supplied, and a decrease in the level of prices tends to reduce the quantity of goods and services supplied.

FIGURE 12.5

The Short-Run AS Curve

In the short run, a fall in the price level from P_1 to P_2 reduces the quantity of output supplied from Y_1 to Y_2. This positive relationship could be due to sticky wages, sticky prices or misperceptions. Over time, wages, prices and perceptions adjust, so this positive relationship is only temporary.

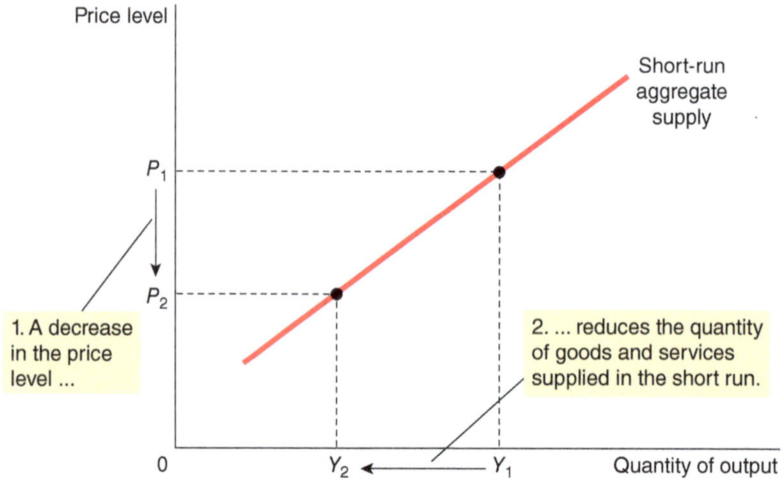

Macroeconomists have proposed three theories for the upwards slope of the short-run AS (SRAS) curve. In each theory, a specific market imperfection causes the supply-side of the economy to behave differently in the short run than it does in the long run. Although each of the following theories will differ in detail, they share a common theme: the quantity of output supplied deviates from its long-run or 'natural' level when the price level deviates from the price level that people *expected* to prevail. When the price level rises above the expected level, output rises above its natural rate. When the price level falls below the expected level, output falls below its natural rate.

The Sticky Wage Theory The first and simplest explanation of the upwards slope of the SRAS curve is the sticky wage theory. According to this theory, the SRAS curve slopes upwards because nominal wages are slow to adjust or are 'sticky' in the short run. To some extent, the slow adjustment of nominal wages is attributable to long-term contracts between workers and firms that fix nominal wages for a period. In addition, this slow adjustment may be attributable to social norms and notions of fairness that influence wage-setting and change only slowly over time.

To see what sticky nominal wages mean for AS, imagine that a firm has agreed in advance to pay its workers a certain nominal wage based on what it expected the price level to be. If the price level P falls below the level that was expected and the nominal wage remains stuck at W, then the real wage, $\frac{W}{P}$, rises above the level the firm planned to pay. Because wages are a large part of a firm's production costs, a higher real wage means that the firm's real costs have risen. The firm responds to these higher costs by hiring less labour and producing a smaller quantity of goods and services. In other words, because wages do not adjust immediately to the price level, a lower price level makes employment and production less profitable. Therefore, firms reduce the quantity of goods and services they supply.

The Sticky Price Theory The sticky price theory emphasizes that the prices of some goods and services also adjust sluggishly in response to changing economic conditions. This slow adjustment of prices occurs in part because of the *menu costs* to adjusting prices. These menu costs include the cost of printing and distributing price lists, changing prices in online environments or mail order catalogues and the time required to change price tags. As a result of these costs, prices as well as wages may be sticky in the short run.

To see the implications of sticky prices for AS, suppose that each firm in the economy announces its prices in advance based on the economic conditions it expects to prevail. Then, after prices are announced, the economy experiences an unexpected contraction in the money supply, which will reduce the overall price level in the long run. Although some firms reduce their prices immediately in response to changing economic conditions, other firms may not want to incur additional menu costs and, therefore, may temporarily lag behind. Because these lagging firms have prices that are too high, their sales decline. Declining sales, in turn, cause these firms to cut back on production and employment. In other words, because not all prices adjust instantly to changing conditions, an unexpected fall in the price level leaves some firms with higher than desired prices. These higher than desired prices depress sales and induce firms to reduce the quantity of goods and services they produce.

The Misperceptions Theory A third approach to the SRAS curve is the misperceptions theory. According to this theory, changes in the overall price level can temporarily mislead suppliers about what is happening in the individual markets in which they sell their output. As a result of these short-run misperceptions, suppliers respond to changes in the level of prices, and this response leads to an upwards sloping AS curve.

To see how this might work, suppose the overall price level falls below the level that people expected. When suppliers see the prices of their products fall, they may mistakenly believe that their *relative* prices have fallen. For example, wheat farmers may notice a fall in the price of wheat before they notice a fall in the prices of the many items they buy as consumers. They may infer from this observation that the reward to producing wheat is temporarily low, and they may respond by reducing the quantity of wheat they supply. Similarly, workers may notice a fall in their nominal wages before they notice a fall in the prices of the goods they buy. They may infer that the reward to working is temporarily low and respond by reducing the quantity of labour they supply. In both cases, a lower price level causes misperceptions about relative prices. These misperceptions induce suppliers to respond to the lower price level by decreasing the quantity of goods and services supplied.

Summary

There are three explanations for the upwards slope of the SRAS curve:

- sticky wages
- sticky prices
- misperceptions.

Economists debate which of these theories is correct, and it is very possible each contains an element of truth. For our purposes in this book, the similarities of the theories are more important than the differences. All three theories suggest that output deviates from its natural rate when the price level deviates from the price level that people expected. We can express this mathematically as follows:

$$Q = NRQ + a(APL - EPL)$$

where Q = Quantity of output supplied, NRQ = Natural rate of output, APL = Actual price level, EPL = Expected price level and a is a number that determines how much output responds to unexpected changes in the price level.

Notice that each of the three theories of SRAS emphasizes a problem that is likely to be only temporary. Whether the upwards slope of the AS curve is attributable to sticky wages, sticky prices or misperceptions, these conditions will not persist forever. Eventually, as people adjust their expectations, nominal wages adjust, prices become unstuck and misperceptions are corrected. In other words, the expected and actual price levels are equal in the long run, and the AS curve is vertical rather than upwards sloping.

Why the SRAS Curve Might Shift

The SRAS curve tells us the quantity of goods and services supplied in the short run for any given level of prices. We can think of this curve as similar to the LRAS curve but made upwards sloping by the presence of sticky wages, sticky prices and misperceptions. Thus, when thinking about what shifts the SRAS curve, we must consider all those variables that shift the LRAS curve plus a new variable, the expected price level, that influences sticky wages, sticky prices and misperceptions.

As we discussed earlier, shifts in the LRAS curve normally arise from changes in labour, capital, natural resources or technological knowledge. These same variables shift the SRAS curve. For example, when an increase in the economy's capital stock increases productivity, both the LRAS and SRAS curves shift to the right. When an increase in the minimum wage raises the natural rate of unemployment, both the LRAS and SRAS curves shift to the left.

The important new variable that affects the position of the SRAS curve is people's expectation of the price level. As we have discussed, the quantity of goods and services supplied depends, in the short run, on sticky wages, sticky prices and misperceptions. Yet wages, prices and perceptions are set on the basis of expectations of the price level. When expectations change, therefore, the SRAS curve shifts.

To make this idea more concrete, let us consider a specific theory of AS: the sticky wage theory. According to this theory, when workers and firms expect the price level to be high, they are more likely to negotiate high nominal wages. High wages raise firms' costs and, for any given actual price level, reduce the quantity of goods and services that firms supply. Thus, when the expected price level rises, wages are higher, costs increase and firms supply a smaller quantity of goods and services at any given actual price level. Thus the SRAS curve shifts to the left. Conversely, when the expected price level falls, wages are lower, costs decline, firms increase production at any given price level, and the SRAS curve shifts to the right.

A similar logic applies in each theory of AS. The general lesson is the following:

- An increase in the expected price level reduces the quantity of goods and services supplied and shifts the SRAS curve to the left.
- A decrease in the expected price level raises the quantity of goods and services supplied and shifts the SRAS curve to the right.

As we will see in the next section, this influence of expectations on the position of the SRAS curve plays a key role in reconciling the economy's behaviour in the short run with its behaviour in the long run. In the short run, expectations are fixed and the economy finds itself at the intersection of the AD curve and the SRAS curve. In the long run, expectations adjust and the SRAS curve shifts. This shift ensures that the economy eventually finds itself at the intersection of the AD curve and the LRAS curve.

SELF TEST Explain why the LRAS curve is vertical. Explain three theories for why the SRAS curve is upwards sloping. How believable do you find each of these three theories?

TWO CAUSES OF ECONOMIC FLUCTUATIONS

Our model of AD and AS provides the tools to analyze two basic causes of short-run fluctuations. To keep things simple, we assume the economy begins in long-run equilibrium, as shown in Figure 12.6. Equilibrium output and the price level are determined by the intersection of the AD curve and the LRAS curve, shown as point A in the figure. At this point, output is at its natural rate. The SRAS curve passes through this point as well, indicating that wages, prices and perceptions have fully adjusted to this long-run equilibrium. That is, when an economy is in its long-run equilibrium, wages, prices and perceptions must have adjusted so that the intersection of AD with SRAS is the same as the intersection of AD with LRAS.

FIGURE 12.6

The Long-Run Equilibrium

The long-run equilibrium of the economy is found where the AD curve crosses the LRAS curve (point A). When the economy reaches this long-run equilibrium, wages, prices and perceptions will have adjusted so that the SRAS curve crosses this point as well.

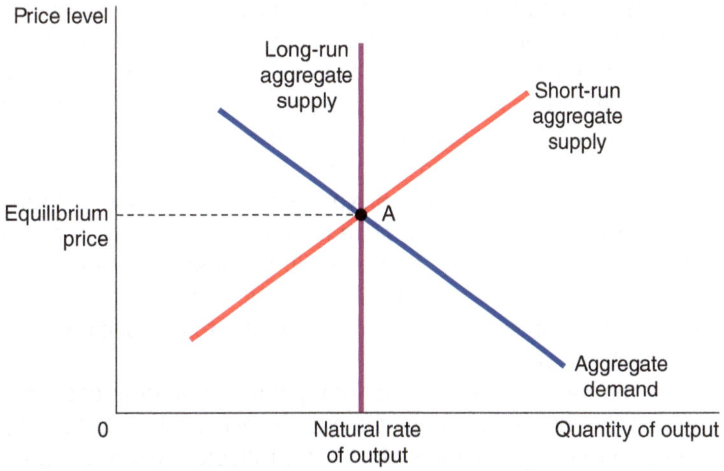

The Effects of a Shift in Aggregate Demand

Suppose that for some reason a wave of pessimism suddenly overtakes the economy. The cause might be a government scandal, a crash on the stock market or the outbreak of conflict in an important economic region. Because of this event, many economic agents lose confidence in the future and alter their plans. Households cut back on their spending and delay major purchases, and firms put off buying new equipment. This reduces the AD for goods and services. That is, for any given price level, households and firms now want to buy a smaller quantity of goods and services. As Figure 12.7 shows, the AD curve shifts to the left from AD_1 to AD_2.

In the short run, the economy moves along the initial SRAS curve AS_1, going from point A to point B. As the economy moves from point A to point B, output falls from Y_1 to Y_2, and the price level falls from P_1 to P_2. The falling level of output indicates that the economy is in a recession. Although not shown in the figure, firms respond to lower sales and production by reducing employment. Thus the pessimism that caused the shift in AD is, to some extent, self-fulfilling. Pessimism about the future leads to falling incomes and rising unemployment.

FIGURE 12.7

Contraction in Aggregate Demand

A fall in AD, which might be due to a wave of pessimism in the economy, is represented with a leftward shift in the AD curve from AD_1 to AD_2. The economy moves from point A to point B. Output falls from Y_1 to Y_2, and the price level falls from P_1 to P_2. Over time, as wages, prices and perceptions adjust, the SRAS curve shifts to the right from AS_1 to AS_2, and the economy reaches point C, where the new AD curve crosses the LRAS curve. The price level falls to P_3, and output returns to its natural rate, Y_1.

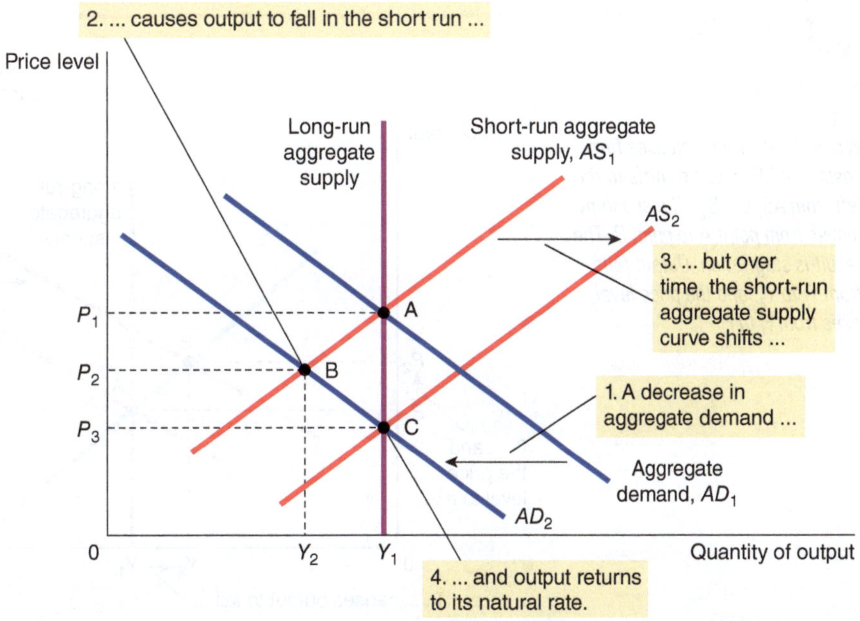

The short-run problem of recession prompts policymakers to take action and one option is to increase AD. As we noted earlier, an increase in government spending or an increase in the money supply would increase the quantity of goods and services demanded at any price and shift the AD curve to the right. If policymakers can act with sufficient speed and precision, they can offset the initial shift in AD, return the AD curve back to AD_1 and bring the economy back to point A. We will discuss in more detail the ways in which monetary and fiscal policy influence AD, as well as some of the practical difficulties in using these policy instruments later in the book.

Even without action by policymakers, the recession will remedy itself over a period of time. Because of the reduction in AD, the price level falls. Eventually, expectations catch up with this new reality, and the expected price level falls as well. Because the fall in the expected price level alters wages, prices and perceptions, it shifts the SRAS curve to the right from AS_1 to AS_2 in Figure 12.7. This adjustment of expectations allows the economy over time to approach point C, where the new AD curve (AD_2) crosses the LRAS curve.

In the new long-run equilibrium, point C, output is back to its natural rate. Even though the wave of pessimism has reduced AD, the price level has fallen sufficiently (to P_3) to offset the shift in the AD curve. Thus, in the long run, the shift in AD is reflected fully in the price level and not at all in the level of output. In other words, the long-run effect of a shift in AD is a nominal change (the price level is lower) but not a real change (output is the same).

To sum up, this story about shifts in AD has two important lessons:

- In the short run, shifts in AD cause fluctuations in the economy's output of goods and services.
- In the long run, shifts in AD affect the overall price level but do not affect output.

The Effects of a Shift in Aggregate Supply

Imagine once again an economy in its long-run equilibrium. Now suppose that suddenly some firms experience an increase in their costs of production. For example, strong demand from Asia might drive up commodity prices which are used in the production of a wide variety of goods.

For any given price level, firms now want to supply a smaller quantity of goods and services. Thus, as Figure 12.8 shows, the SRAS curve shifts to the left from AS_1 to AS_2. (Depending on the event, the LRAS curve might also shift. To keep things simple, however, we will assume that it does not.)

FIGURE 12.8

An Adverse Shift in Aggregate Supply

When some event increases firms' costs, the SRAS curve shifts to the left from AS_1 to AS_2. The economy moves from point A to point B. The result is stagflation. Output falls from Y_1 to Y_2, and the price level rises from P_1 to P_2.

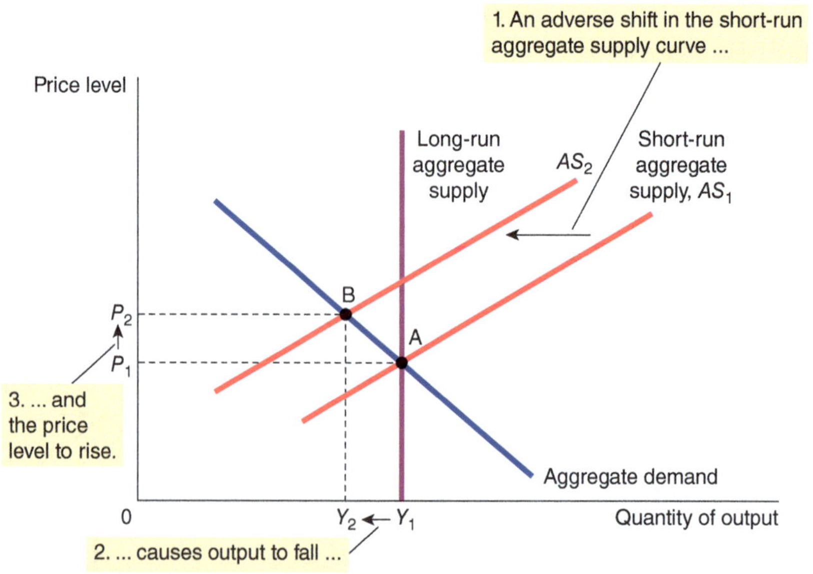

In the short run, the economy moves along the existing AD curve, going from point A to point B. The output of the economy falls from Y_1 to Y_2 and the price level rises from P_1 to P_2. Because the economy is experiencing both *stagnation* (falling output) and *inflation* (rising prices), such an event is called **stagflation**.

stagflation a period of falling output and rising prices

Faced with stagflation there are no easy choices for policymakers. One possibility is to do nothing. In this case, the output of goods and services remains depressed at Y_2 for a while. Eventually, however, the recession will remedy itself as wages, prices and perceptions adjust to raise production costs. A period of low output and high unemployment, for instance, puts downwards pressure on workers' wages. Lower wages, in turn, increase the quantity of output supplied. Over time, as the SRAS curve shifts back towards AS_1, the price level falls, and the quantity of output approaches its natural rate. In the long run, the economy returns to point A, where the AD curve crosses the LRAS curve. This is the view that those who believe free markets are the most efficient way of allocating scarce resources might adopt.

Alternatively, policymakers who control monetary and fiscal policy might attempt to offset some of the effects of the shift in the SRAS curve by shifting the AD curve. This possibility is shown in Figure 12.9. In this case, changes in policy shift the AD curve to the right from AD_1 to AD_2, exactly enough to prevent the shift in AS from affecting output. The economy moves directly from point A to point B. Output remains at its natural rate, and the price level rises from P_1 to P_3. In this case, policymakers are said to *accommodate* the shift in AS because they allow the increase in costs to permanently affect the level of prices. This intervention by policymakers would be seen as being desirable by supporters of Keynesian policy.

FIGURE 12.9

Adverse Shift in Aggregate Supply

Faced with an adverse shift in AS from AS_1 to AS_2, policymakers who can influence AD might try to shift the AD curve to the right from AD_1 to AD_2. The economy would move from point A to point B. This policy would prevent the supply shift from reducing output in the short run, but the price level would permanently rise from P_1 to P_3.

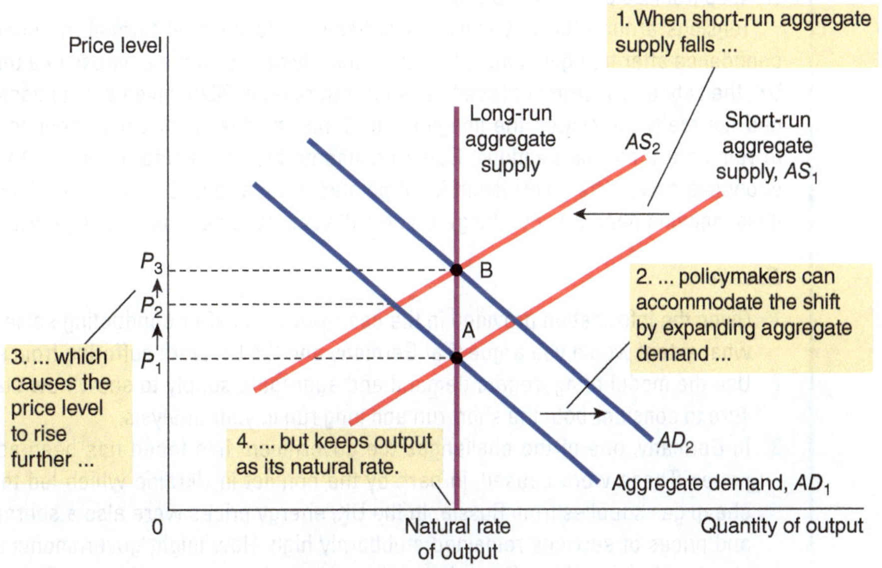

These different views on policy form a key aspect of the debate between economists about action in the face of short-run fluctuations in economic activity.

To sum up, this story about shifts in AS has two important lessons:

- Shifts in AS can cause stagflation, which is a combination of recession (falling output) and inflation (rising prices).
- Policymakers who can influence AD cannot offset both of these adverse effects simultaneously.

CASE STUDY Policy Challenges

© iStock/Nikolaev

Much of our information on the economy is supplied by the media but is the media too focused on the short run?

Reading textbook explanations of theories associated with macroeconomy can make the challenges of policymakers in influencing economic outcomes sound relatively simple. Of course the reality is not like that. If a government wants to boost growth then it can adopt policies to shift the aggregate demand curve to the right. At the same time it must recognize that doing so without increasing productive capacity and productivity could result in inflationary pressures.

In Europe and the UK, politicians are experiencing the challenges of seeking to counter sluggish or zero growth and inflation that remain stubbornly above target. Germany has experienced stagflation-like conditions with negative growth in the first half of 2024, although it avoided technical recession in the third quarter of the year. Its economy was only slightly larger than it was prior to the pandemic. The CPI has been heading upwards since 2020 although at more moderate levels since highs of almost 9 per cent in 2023. In the UK, growth stalled in the second half of 2024 and the economy shrank in October, according to data published by the Office for National Statistics (ONS). Inflation, meanwhile, accelerated a little in the second half of 2024 standing at 2.6 per cent in November 2024, up from 2.3 per cent in October.

Tensions around the economy in Germany led to political turmoil. Its chancellor lost a vote of no confidence after trying to lead with only a minority following the collapse of a three-party coalition. In the UK, the Labour government faced calls for it to reset in 2025, given perceptions that its focus on growth had not really captivated the imagination. Concerns over measures announced in the budget seemed to reinforce these perceptions. Some commentators suggested, however, that 2025 would see better economic news. The government itself pointed out that addressing the problems of an economy which it claimed had been run into the ground for 10 years was not going to be possible in just a few months.

Questions:

1. Given the information provided in the case study and after conducting some of your own research, to what extent would you argue that Germany and the UK were suffering from stagflation?
2. Use the model of aggregate demand and aggregate supply to show how stagflation could occur. Be sure to consider both the short run and long run in your analysis.
3. In Germany, one of the challenges the government has faced has been adjusting to higher energy prices. These were caused, in part, by the conflict in Ukraine which led to a reduction in relatively cheap gas supplies from Russia. In the UK, energy prices were also a source of inflationary pressure and prices of services remained stubbornly high. How might governments respond to such external shocks when seeking to formulate policy targeted at growth? Use your knowledge of the components of aggregate demand and supply as part of your answer.
4. To what extent do you agree with the view that the media is too focused on the short run when reporting macroeconomic issues and needs to pay more attention to the long run?

References:

www.cityam.com/uk-economy-at-risk-of-stagflation-as-growth-stalls-under-labour/, accessed 7 August 2025.
www.ons.gov.uk/economy/inflationandpriceindices/bulletins/consumerpriceinflation/november2024, accessed 7 August 2025.
think.ing.com/snaps/german-gdp-q3-24/, accessed 7 August 2025.

SELF TEST Suppose that the election of a popular prime minister suddenly increases people's confidence in the future. Use the model of AD and AS to analyze the effect on the economy.

NEW KEYNESIAN ECONOMICS

Recall that Keynesian economics developed in response to the depression of the 1930s, when the assumptions of classical economics that markets would clear appeared to be failing. Keynesian ideas were the mainstay for economic policy across the developed world in the post-war era. There was something of a consensus among economists at the time that our understanding of the macroeconomy was considerable. The latter part of the 1960s began to reveal some flaws in that assumption as global conditions changed. The breakdown of fixed exchange rates in the late 1960s and the oil crisis in the early 1970s presented macroeconomists with significant challenges in explaining the economic conditions that existed in some countries, stagflation in particular.

Economics came to be classified as a debate between Keynesians, on the one hand, who pointed to markets not clearing quickly, and the neo or new classicists, on the other, who re-emphasized the efficiency of markets. The latter argued that microeconomics provided a foundation for understanding macroeconomics.

Out of this debate emerged a group referred to as 'New Keynesians'. New Keynesian economics placed an emphasis on providing sound microeconomic principles to underpin Keynesian macroeconomics. Specifically, New Keynesians sought to explain how price and wage stickiness had its foundation in the microeconomic analysis of labour markets and price-setting by firms.

Features of New Keynesian Economics

New Keynesians would argue that short-run fluctuations in economic output violate the classical dichotomy, as outlined earlier in this chapter. Changes in nominal variables like the money supply do have an influence on output and employment – real variables – in the short run. In addition, they would argue that to develop an understanding of changes in economic activity, an understanding of the imperfections in the economy is necessary. These include that firms operate under imperfect competition, that consumers and firms are subject to imperfect information and that there are built-in rigidities in the economy which hinder the movement of prices and wages, as we have noted.

Can we conclude from this that the economists classed as New Keynesians are supporters of demand management, but with some reservations? The answer to this is 'no'. The splitting of economics into different schools of thought has been convenient for the mass media to present disagreements between economists in relatively simple terms. The reality is that there is probably more agreement in economics than most members of the public would imagine. A difference in some base assumptions and a difference in the relative size of parameters in models is largely the reason why economists disagree. Many economists would subscribe to the view that changes in the money supply affect AD (a so-called 'monetarist' view). They would also agree that price rigidities in the macroeconomy exist because of imperfections in the microeconomy. Some New Keynesian economists would, equally, not be in support of policy intervention to correct short-term fluctuations in the economy by attempting to manipulate AD. The main reason is that they would argue the effects of such policy interventions take time to work through the economy, by which time economic conditions have changed. Therefore, the policy would not be as effective as anticipated. Changes in interest rates, for example, are estimated to take around 18 months to work through the economy. Tax changes might be received in different ways by different people. Also, it is never certain enough to predict how people will react to a tax cut or a tax increase in any precise quantifiable way to make such a policy option a clear-cut choice. Equally, policies to increase government spending on infrastructure projects, for example, often take many years to have any effect even if such projects are 'shovel ready', meaning they can be put into operation quickly.

New Keynesian economics reminds us that the complexities of the economy perhaps deserve a more discerning look at the detail behind what economists are actually saying, how much they agree, and why they agree, as much as why they might disagree and the extent of such disagreements.

CRITICAL THINKING POINT 'New Keynesian economics is alive and well. The New Keynesian model has proved to be quite flexible, with a growing number of extensions being developed by researchers in order to incorporate new assumptions or account for new phenomena. Indeed, it is hard to think of an alternative macroeconomic paradigm that would do away with the two defining features of the New Keynesian model: nominal rigidities and monetary non-neutralities.' (Source: Galí, J. (2018) 'The State of New Keynesian Economics: A Partial Assessment'. *Journal of Economic Perspectives*, 32(3): 87–112. Available at pubs.aeaweb.org/doi/pdfplus/10.1257/jep.32.3.87, accessed 7 August 2025.)

Critically assess this view. Galí is noted as a key figure in New Keynesian economics. Does this cast doubt on the analysis provided in the article and in the conclusion quoted above?

SUMMARY

- All societies experience short-run economic fluctuations around long-run trends. These fluctuations are irregular and largely unpredictable. When recessions do occur, real GDP and other measures of income, spending and production fall, and unemployment rises.
- We can analyze short-run economic fluctuations using the model of AD and AS. According to this model, the output of goods and services and the overall level of prices adjust to balance AD and AS.
- The AD curve slopes downwards for three reasons. First, a lower price level raises the real value of households' money holdings, which stimulates consumer spending. Second, a lower price level reduces the quantity of money households demand; as households try to convert money into interest-bearing assets, interest rates fall, which stimulates investment spending. Third, as a lower price level reduces interest rates, the local currency depreciates in the market for foreign currency exchange, stimulating net exports.
- Any event or policy that raises consumption, investment, government purchases or net exports at a given price level increases AD. Any event or policy that reduces consumption, investment, government purchases or net exports at a given price level decreases AD.
- The LRAS curve is vertical. In the long run, the quantity of goods and services supplied depends on the economy's labour, capital, natural resources and technology, but not on the overall level of prices.
- Three theories have been proposed to explain the upwards slope of the SRAS curve. According to the sticky wage theory, an unexpected fall in the price level temporarily raises real wages, which induces firms to reduce employment and production. According to the sticky price theory, an unexpected fall in the price level leaves some firms with prices that are temporarily too high, which reduces their sales and causes them to cut back production. According to the misperceptions theory, an unexpected fall in the price level leads suppliers to mistakenly believe that their relative prices have fallen, which induces them to reduce production. All three theories imply that output deviates from its natural rate when the price level deviates from the price level that people expected.
- Events that alter the economy's ability to produce output, such as changes in labour, capital, natural resources or technology, shift the SRAS curve (and may shift the LRAS curve as well). In addition, the position of the SRAS curve depends on the expected price level.
- One possible cause of economic fluctuations is a shift in AD. When the AD curve shifts to the left, for instance, output and prices fall in the short run. Over time, as a change in the expected price level causes wages, prices and perceptions to adjust, the SRAS curve shifts to the right, and the economy returns to its natural rate of output at a new, lower price level.
- A second possible cause of economic fluctuations is a shift in AS. When the AS curve shifts to the left, the short-run effect is falling output and rising prices, a combination called stagflation. Over time, as wages, prices and perceptions adjust, the price level falls back to its original level and output recovers.
- New Keynesian economics represents a research tradition that questions the classical dichotomy and recognizes imperfections in the economy as key elements in explaining short-run deviations from trend.

IN THE NEWS

The Drive for Growth

One of the disadvantages of textbooks is that articles based on news reports can become dated very quickly, so that by the time readers look at them the information can be inaccurate. However, this can be turned into a positive as it allows for reflection on how economists forecast and how accurate those forecasts turn out to be.

© iStock/Mongkol Onnuan

By the time you read this, will government promises on growth begin to be realized?

In the UK, government economic policy is underpinned by 'independent and authoritative analysis' provided by a body set up in 2010 called the Office for Budget Responsibility (OBR). The OBR produces detailed five-year forecasts for the economy and public finances twice a year. Its economic and fiscal outlook published in October 2024 was set against the backdrop of the first budget presented by the Labour government which had gained power in July 2024.

The OBR's report noted that the budget planned to increase government spending by around £70 billion (€84.3 billion) a year up to 2029. This would result in the size of the state being at 44 per cent of UK GDP compared to 39 per cent prior to the pandemic. This spending was to be funded by tax rises of around £36 billion and the remainder through borrowing. The OBR forecast that UK GDP in 2025 would grow by around 2 per cent before easing back to 1.5 per cent in 2026 and 1.3 per cent in the remaining years of the forecast. It also forecast that inflation would accelerate to 2.6 per cent in 2025 and then ease back to target.

The OBR noted that its forecast were set against various risks, notably around what might happen to productivity, net migration, inactivity in the labour market and the path of interest rates. Forecasts are based on known factors. While risks and error margins are often built into forecasting, as we have seen in our brief coverage of DSGE models, shocks such as the conflict in Ukraine and the Middle East, the policies adopted by the new administration in the United States, how Europe performs, policies adopted by China, and so on, could all conspire to blow the forecasts off course.

Critical Thinking Questions

1 Why do you think that having a body such as the OBR is seen as important in economic policymaking?
2 Use aggregate demand and aggregate supply diagrams to show what effects the key elements of the UK government's budget measures might be expected to have on output and price level. Ensure that your assumptions are stated and clarified as part of your analysis.
3 Why do you think the OBR noted that risks to the forecast depended, in part, on what happens to productivity, inactivity and net migration? Consider how these might influence the outcomes of the analysis provided in your answer to Question 2.
4 In the last 10 years, the world has witnessed a number of external shocks, including the pandemic, conflict, extreme weather events, geopolitical tensions and so on. If forecasts are so prone to external shocks, and assuming that many shocks are not predictable, then what value can forecasts provide?
5 Consider the forecasts provided in this article and do some research to find out what actually happened in 2025 and 2026. Has the government's aim of driving growth been partly realized? How close were the forecasts made by the OBR to the actual outcome? What factors might have affected the difference between the two? Use appropriate diagrams and other content from the book to help enrich your answer.

Reference:

obr.uk/docs/dlm_uploads/OBR_Economic_and_fiscal_outlook_Oct_2024.pdf, accessed 7 August 2025.

QUESTIONS FOR REVIEW

1 What do you understand by the term 'economic activity'?
2 What is the official definition of a recession?
3 Name two macroeconomic variables that decline when the economy goes into a recession. Name one macroeconomic variable that rises during a recession.
4 Draw a diagram with AD, SRAS and LRAS. Be careful to label the axes correctly.
5 List and explain the three reasons why the AD curve is downwards sloping.
6 Explain why the LRAS curve is vertical.
7 List and explain the three theories for why the SRAS curve is upwards sloping.
8 What might shift the AD curve to the left? Use the model of AD and AS to trace through the effects of such a shift.
9 What might shift the AS curve to the left? Use the model of AD and AS to trace through the effects of such a shift.
10 What outcomes are possible if AD and AS are both shifting? Use the model of AD and AS to outline some of these possible outcomes.

PROBLEMS AND APPLICATIONS

1 Why do you think that investment is more variable over the business cycle than consumer spending? Which category of consumer spending do you think would be most volatile: durable goods (such as furniture and car purchases), non-durable goods (such as food and clothing) or services (such as haircuts and medical care)? Why?
2 Suppose that the economy is in a long-run equilibrium. Use a diagram to illustrate the state of the economy showing AD, SRAS and LRAS.
   a. Now suppose that commodity prices are falling, which suggest a downturn in the economy and a fall in AD. Use your diagram to show what happens to output and the price level in the short run. What happens to the unemployment rate?
   b. Use the sticky wage theory of AS to explain what will happen to output and the price level in the long run (assuming there is no change in policy). What role does the expected price level play in this adjustment? Illustrate your analysis with a graph.
3 Explain whether each of the following events will increase, decrease or have no effect on LRAS.
   a. A country experiences a wave of immigration.
   b. A government raises the minimum wage above the national average wage level.
   c. A war leads to the destruction of a large number of factories.
4 Consider Figure 12.7. How does the unemployment rate at points B and C compare to the unemployment rate at point A? Under the sticky wage explanation of the SRAS curve, how does the real wage at points B and C compare to the real wage at point A?
5 Explain why the following statements are false.
   a. 'The AD curve slopes downwards because it is the horizontal sum of the demand curves for individual goods'.
   b. 'The LRAS curve is vertical because economic forces do not affect LRAS'.
   c. 'If firms adjusted their prices every day, then the SRAS curve would be horizontal'.
   d. 'Whenever the economy enters a recession, its LRAS curve shifts to the left'.
6 For each of the three theories for the upwards slope of the SRAS curve, carefully explain the following.
   a. How the economy recovers from a recession and returns to its long-run equilibrium without any policy intervention.
   b. What determines the speed of the recovery?
7 Suppose the central bank expands QE and, as a result, expectations of a rise in the price level increase. What will happen to output and the price level in the short run? Compare this result to the outcome if the central bank expanded QE but the public did not change its expectation of the price level.

8 Suppose workers and firms suddenly believe that inflation will be quite high over the coming year. Suppose also that the economy begins in long-run equilibrium, and the AD curve does not shift.

a. What happens to nominal wages? What happens to real wages?

b. Using an AD/AS diagram, show the effect of the change in expectations on both the short-run and long-run levels of prices and output.

c. Were the expectations of high inflation accurate? Explain.

9 Explain whether each of the following events shifts the SRAS curve, the AD curve, both, or neither. For each event that does shift a curve, use a diagram to illustrate the effect on the economy.

a. Households decide to save a larger share of their income.

b. Cattle farmers suffer a prolonged period of foot and mouth disease which cuts average cattle herd sizes by 80 per cent.

c. Increased job opportunities overseas cause many people to leave the country.

10 Suppose that firms become very optimistic about future business conditions and invest heavily in new capital equipment.

a. Use an AD/AS diagram to show the short-run effect of this optimism on the economy. Label the new levels of prices and real output. Explain, in words, why the aggregate quantity of output supplied changes.

b. Now use the diagram from part (a) to show the new long-run equilibrium of the economy. (For now, assume there is no change in the LRAS curve.) Explain, in words, why the aggregate quantity of output demanded changes between the short run and the long run.

c. How might the investment boom affect the LRAS curve? Explain.

13 THE INFLUENCE OF MONETARY AND FISCAL POLICY ON AGGREGATE DEMAND

We are now going to examine in more detail how the tools of monetary and fiscal policy influence the position of the aggregate demand (AD) curve. We have previously discussed the long-run effects of these policies. We have seen how fiscal policy affects saving, investment and long-run economic growth. We have also seen how central bank activity influences the money supply, and how the money supply affects the price level in the long run. We now see how these policy tools can shift the AD curve and, in doing so, affect short-run economic fluctuations.

Recall that many factors influence AD besides monetary and fiscal policy. In particular, desired spending by households and firms determines the overall demand for goods and services. When desired spending changes, AD shifts. If policymakers do not respond, such shifts in AD cause short-run fluctuations in output and employment. As a result, monetary and fiscal policymakers sometimes use the policy levers at their disposal to try to offset these shifts in AD and thereby stabilize the economy. Here we discuss the theory behind these policy actions and some of the difficulties that arise in using this theory in practice.

HOW MONETARY POLICY INFLUENCES AGGREGATE DEMAND

The AD curve shows the total quantity of goods and services demanded in the economy for any price level. Recall that the AD curve slopes downwards for three reasons:

- **The wealth effect.** A lower price level raises the real value of households' money holdings, and higher real wealth stimulates consumer spending.
- **The interest rate effect.** A lower price level lowers the interest rate as people try to lend out their excess money holdings, and the lower interest rate stimulates investment spending.
- **The exchange rate effect.** When a lower price level lowers the interest rate, investors move some of their funds overseas and cause the domestic currency to depreciate relative to foreign currencies. This depreciation makes domestic goods cheaper compared to foreign goods and, therefore, stimulates spending on net exports.

These three effects should not be viewed as alternative theories. Instead, they occur simultaneously to increase the quantity of goods and services demanded when the price level falls and to decrease it when the price level rises.

Although all three effects work together in explaining the downwards slope of the AD curve, they are not of equal importance. Because money holdings are a small part of household wealth, the wealth effect is the least important of the three. Whether or not the exchange rate effect is important depends upon the degree of openness of the economy. The UK and most other European economies have relatively open economies in the sense that imports and exports represent a much larger fraction of total GDP. This means that the exchange rate effect can be significant. However, the exchange rate effect is probably secondary to the interest rate effect, even in relatively open economies, for two reasons. First, the interest rate effect impacts immediately upon the whole economy, affecting consumers, homebuyers and firms across the board. The loss of competitiveness that is part of the exchange rate effect impacts only upon traded goods, and affects mainly firms producing tradable goods and consumers buying tradable goods. Second, many of the countries of Europe have a common currency – the euro – which they share with many of their major trading partners, so that the exchange rate effect is muted.

To understand how policy influences AD, therefore, we shall examine the interest rate effect in more detail. Here we develop a theory of how the interest rate is determined, called the **theory of liquidity preference**, which was originally developed by John Maynard Keynes in the 1930s. After we develop this theory, we use it to understand the downwards slope of the AD curve and how monetary policy shifts this curve. By shedding new light on the AD curve, the theory of liquidity preference expands our understanding of short-run economic fluctuations.

theory of liquidity preference Keynes' theory that the interest rate adjusts to bring money supply and money demand into balance

The Theory of Liquidity Preference

In his classic book, *The General Theory of Employment, Interest, and Money*, John Maynard Keynes proposed the theory of liquidity preference to explain what factors determine the economy's interest rate. The theory is, in essence, just an application of supply and demand. According to Keynes, the interest rate adjusts to balance the supply and demand for money. We introduced some elements of the theories covered here as part of the IS–LM model.

Recall the distinction between the *nominal interest rate* (the interest rate as usually reported) and the *real interest rate* (the interest rate corrected for the effects of inflation). Which interest rate are we now trying to explain? The answer is both. In the analysis that follows, we hold constant the expected rate of inflation. (This assumption is reasonable for studying the economy in the short run, as we are now doing.) Thus, when the nominal interest rate rises or falls, the real interest rate that people expect to earn rises or falls as well. For the rest of this chapter, when we refer to changes in the interest rate, you should envision the real and nominal interest rates moving in the same direction.

Let us now develop the theory of liquidity preference by considering the supply and demand for money and how each depends on the interest rate.

Money Supply The first element of the theory of liquidity preference is the supply of money. As we have previously noted, the money supply is assumed to be controlled by the central bank, such as the Bank of England, the European Central Bank or the US Federal Reserve. The central bank can alter the money supply through the purchase and sale of government bonds in outright open market operations. When the central bank buys government bonds, the money it pays for the bonds is typically deposited in banks, and this money is added to bank reserves. When the central bank sells government bonds, the money it receives for the bonds is withdrawn from the banking system and bank reserves fall. In addition to these open market operations, the central bank can alter the money supply by changing the refinancing rate (the interest rate at which banks can borrow reserves from the central bank).

These details of monetary control are important for the implementation of central bank policy, but they are not crucial in this chapter. Our goal here is to examine how changes in the money supply affect the AD for goods and services. For this purpose, we can ignore the details of how central bank policy is implemented and assume that the central bank controls the money supply directly. In other words, the quantity of money supplied in the economy is fixed at whatever level the central bank decides to set it.

Because the quantity of money supplied is fixed by central bank policy, it does not depend on other economic variables. In particular, it does not depend on the interest rate. Once the central bank has made its policy decision, the quantity of money supplied is the same, regardless of the prevailing interest rate. We represent a fixed money supply with a vertical supply curve in Figure 13.1.

What is important to keep in mind as we discuss the liquidity preference theory is that central banks interact with the banking system through setting overnight rates. This sets the tone for the structure of interest rates throughout the economy. However, the spread of interest rates between the overnight rate and other interest rates is not directly controlled by central banks. It is these interest rates that are influenced by liquidity preference.

FIGURE 13.1

Equilibrium in the Money Market

According to the theory of liquidity preference, the interest rate adjusts to bring the quantity of money supplied and the quantity of money demanded into balance. If the interest rate is above the equilibrium level (such as at r_1), the quantity of money people want to hold (M_1^d) is less than the quantity the central bank has created. This surplus of money puts downwards pressure on the interest rate. Conversely, if the interest rate is below the equilibrium level (such as at r_2), the quantity of money people want to hold (M_2^d) is greater than the quantity the central bank has created. This shortage of money then puts upwards pressure on the interest rate. Thus, the forces of supply and demand in the market for money push the interest rate towards the equilibrium interest rate, at which people are content holding the quantity of money the central bank has created.

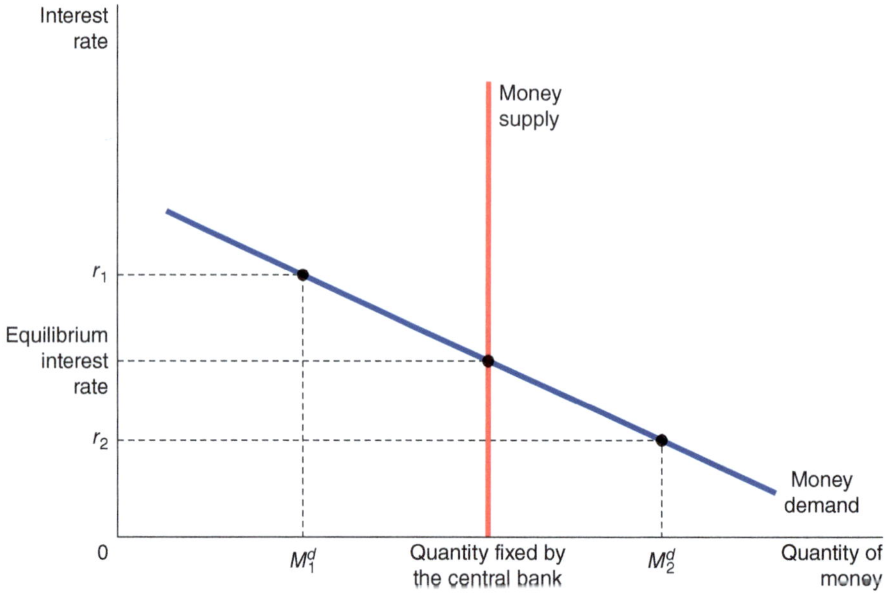

Demand for Money The second element of the theory of liquidity preference is the demand for money. As a starting point for understanding money demand, recall that any asset's *liquidity* refers to the ease with which that asset is converted into the economy's medium of exchange. Money is the economy's medium of exchange, so it is by definition the most liquid asset available. The liquidity of money explains the demand for it. People choose to hold money instead of other assets that offer higher rates of return because money can be used to buy goods and services.

Although many factors determine the quantity of money demanded, the one emphasized by the theory of liquidity preference is the interest rate. The reason is that the interest rate is the opportunity cost of holding money. That is, when you hold wealth as cash in your pocket, instead of as an interest-bearing bond or bank account, you forgo the benefits of the interest you could have earned (the opportunity cost). An increase in the interest rate raises the opportunity cost of holding money. There is an incentive, therefore, for people to exchange cash holdings for interest-bearing deposits and this, as a result, reduces the quantity of money demanded. A decrease in the interest rate reduces the opportunity cost of holding money. The cost of the benefits forgone are not as high, so there is more incentive to hold money as cash and, as a result, the quantity demanded increases. Thus, as shown in Figure 13.1, the money demand curve slopes downwards.

Equilibrium in the Money Market According to the theory of liquidity preference, the interest rate adjusts to balance the supply and demand for money. There is one interest rate, called the *equilibrium* *interest rate*, at which the quantity of money demanded exactly balances the quantity of money supplied. If the interest rate is at any other level, people will try to adjust their portfolios of assets and, as a result, drive the interest rate towards the equilibrium.

For example, suppose the interest rate is above the equilibrium level, such as r_1 in Figure 13.1. In this case, the quantity of money that people want to hold, (M_1^d), is less than the quantity of money that the central bank has supplied. Those people who are holding the surplus of money will try to get rid of it by buying interest-bearing bonds or by depositing it in an interest-bearing bank account. Because bond issuers and banks prefer to pay lower interest rates, they respond to this surplus of money by lowering the interest rates they offer. As the interest rate falls, people become more willing to hold money until, at the equilibrium interest rate, people are happy to hold exactly the amount of money the central bank has supplied.

Conversely, at interest rates below the equilibrium level, such as r_2 in Figure 13.1, the quantity of money that people want to hold, (M_2^d), is greater than the quantity of money that the central bank has supplied. As a result, people try to increase their holdings of money by reducing their holdings of bonds and other interest-bearing assets. As people cut back on their holdings of bonds, bond issuers find that they have to offer higher interest rates to attract buyers. Thus, the interest rate rises and approaches the equilibrium level.

The Downwards Slope of the Aggregate Demand Curve

Having seen how the theory of liquidity preference explains the economy's equilibrium interest rate, we now consider its implications for the AD for goods and services. As a warm-up exercise, we begin by using the theory to re-examine a topic we have already covered, that is the interest rate effect and the downwards slope of the AD curve. In particular, suppose that the overall level of prices in the economy rises. What happens to the interest rate that balances the supply and demand for money, and how does that change affect the quantity of goods and services demanded?

Recall that the price level is one determinant of the quantity of money demanded. At higher prices, more money is exchanged every time a good or service is sold. As a result, people will choose to hold a larger quantity of money. That is, a higher price level increases the quantity of money demanded for any given interest rate. Thus, an increase in the price level from P_1 to P_2 shifts the money demand curve to the right from MD_1 to MD_2, as shown in panel (a) of Figure 13.2.

FIGURE 13.2

The Money Market and the Slope of the Aggregate Demand Curve

An increase in the price level from P_1 to P_2 shifts the money demand curve to the right, as in panel (a). This increase in money demand causes the interest rate to rise from r_1 to r_2. Because the interest rate is the cost of borrowing, the increase in the interest rate reduces the quantity of goods and services demanded from Y_1 to Y_2. This negative relationship between the price level and quantity demanded is represented with a downwards sloping AD curve, as in panel (b).

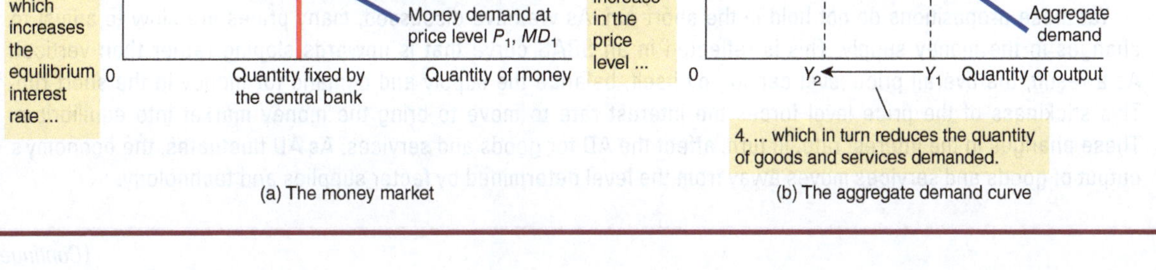

Notice how this shift in money demand affects the equilibrium in the money market. For a fixed money supply, the interest rate must rise to balance money supply and money demand. The higher price level has increased the amount of money people want to hold and has shifted the money demand curve to the right. Yet the quantity of money supplied is unchanged, so the interest rate must rise from r_1 to r_2 to discourage the additional demand.

This increase in the interest rate has ramifications not only for the money market but also for the quantity of goods and services demanded, as shown in panel (b) of Figure 13.2. At a higher interest rate, the cost of borrowing and the return to saving are greater. Fewer households choose to borrow to buy a new house, and those who do buy smaller houses, so the demand for residential investment falls. Fewer firms choose to borrow to build new factories and buy new equipment, so business investment falls. Thus, when the price level rises from P_1 to P_2, increasing money demand from MD_1 to MD_2 and raising the interest rate from r_1 to r_2, the quantity of goods and services demanded falls from Y_1 to Y_2.

This analysis of the interest rate effect can be summarized in three steps:

1. A higher price level raises money demand.
2. Higher money demand leads to a higher interest rate.
3. A higher interest rate reduces the quantity of goods and services demanded.

Of course, the same logic works in reverse as well. A lower price level reduces money demand, which leads to a lower interest rate, and this in turn increases the quantity of goods and services demanded. The end result of this analysis is a negative relationship between the price level and the quantity of goods and services demanded, which is illustrated with a downwards sloping AD curve. This is the same conclusion we reached when looking at the effect of a shift in the LM curve.

FYI

Interest Rates in the Long Run and the Short Run

At this point, we should pause and reflect on a seemingly awkward embarrassment of riches. It might appear as if we now have two theories for how interest rates are determined. One states that the interest rate adjusts to balance the supply of, and demand for, loanable funds (that is, national saving and desired investment). By contrast, we just established here that the interest rate adjusts to balance the supply and demand for money.

To reconcile these two theories, we must again consider the differences between the long-run and short-run behaviour of the economy. Three macroeconomic variables are of central importance: the economy's output of goods and services, the interest rate and the price level. According to the classical macroeconomic theory, these variables are determined as follows:

1. *Output* is determined by the supplies of capital, or the supplies of labour and the available production technology for turning capital and labour into output (the natural rate of output).
2. For any given level of output, the *interest rate* adjusts to balance the supply and demand for loanable funds.
3. The *price level* adjusts to balance the supply and demand for money. Changes in the supply of money lead to proportionate changes in the price level.

These are three of the essential propositions of classical economic theory. Many economists believe that these propositions do a good job of describing how the economy works *in the long run*.

Yet these propositions do not hold in the short run. As we have discussed, many prices are slow to adjust to changes in the money supply. This is reflected in an SRAS curve that is upwards sloping rather than vertical. As a result, the overall price level cannot, by itself, balance the supply and demand for money in the short run. This stickiness of the price level forces the interest rate to move to bring the money market into equilibrium. These changes in the interest rate, in turn, affect the AD for goods and services. As AD fluctuates, the economy's output of goods and services moves away from the level determined by factor supplies and technology.

(*Continued*)

For issues concerning the short run, then, it is best to think about the economy as follows:

1. The *price level* is stuck at some level (based on previously formed expectations) and, in the short run, is relatively unresponsive to changing economic conditions.
2. For any given price level, the *interest rate* adjusts to balance the supply and demand for money.
3. The level of *output* responds to the AD for goods and services, which is in part determined by the interest rate that balances the money market.

Notice that this precisely reverses the order of analysis used to study the economy in the long run.

Thus, the different theories of the interest rate are useful for different purposes. When thinking about the long-run determinants of interest rates, it is best to keep in mind the loanable funds theory. This approach highlights the importance of an economy's saving propensities and investment opportunities. By contrast, when thinking about the short-run determinants of interest rates, it is best to keep in mind the liquidity preference theory. This theory highlights the importance of monetary policy.

Changes in the Money Supply

So far, we have used the theory of liquidity preference to explain more fully how the total quantity demanded of goods and services in the economy changes as the price level changes. That is, we have examined movements along the downwards sloping AD curve. The theory also sheds light, however, on some of the other events that alter the quantity of goods and services demanded. Whenever the quantity of goods and services demanded changes *for a given price level*, the AD curve shifts.

One important variable that shifts the AD curve is monetary policy. To see how monetary policy affects the economy in the short run, suppose that the central bank increases the money supply by buying government bonds in open market operations. (Why the central bank might do this will become clear later after we understand the effects of such a move.)

As panel (a) of Figure 13.3 shows, an increase in the money supply shifts the money supply curve to the right from MS_1 to MS_2.

FIGURE 13.3

A Monetary Injection

In panel (a), an increase in the money supply from MS_1 *to* MS_2 *reduces the equilibrium interest rate from* r_1 *to* r_2. *Because the interest rate is the cost of borrowing, the fall in the interest rate raises the quantity of goods and services demanded at a given price level from* Y_1 *to* Y_2. *Thus, in panel (b), the AD curve shifts to the right from* AD_1 *to* AD_2.

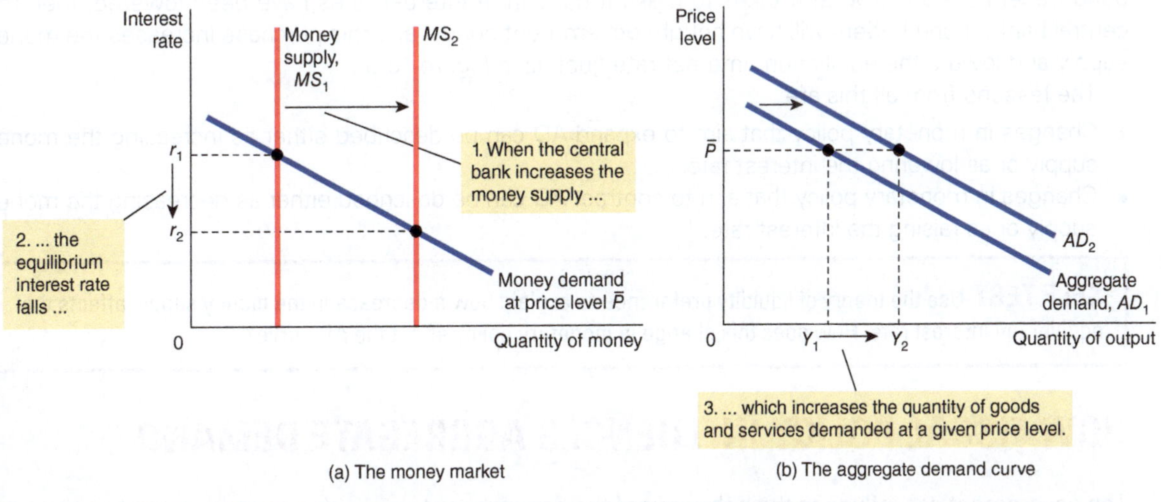

Because the money demand curve has not changed, the interest rate falls from r_1 to r_2 to balance money supply and money demand. That is, the interest rate must fall to induce people to hold the additional money that the central bank has created.

Once again, the interest rate influences the quantity of goods and services demanded, as shown in panel (b) of Figure 13.3. The lower interest rate reduces the cost of borrowing and the return to saving. Households buy more and larger houses, stimulating the demand for residential investment. Firms spend more on new factories and new equipment, stimulating business investment. As a result, the quantity of goods and services demanded at a given price level $\overline{P}$ rises from Y_1 to Y_2. Of course, there is nothing special about $\overline{P}$. The monetary injection raises the quantity of goods and services demanded at every price level. Thus, the entire AD curve shifts to the right.

To sum up, when the central bank increases the money supply, it leads to a fall in the interest rate and increases the quantity of goods and services demanded for any given price level, shifting the AD curve to the right. Conversely, when the central bank contracts the money supply, the interest rate rises to bring the money market into equilibrium and reduces the quantity of goods and services demanded for any given price level, shifting the AD curve to the left.

We explored the same principle as part of the introduction to the IS–LM model. In that case a loosening of monetary policy causes the LM curve to shift to the right, and at the given price level, the AD curve shifts to the right (and vice versa).

The Role of Interest Rates

Our discussion so far in this chapter has treated the money supply as the central bank's policy instrument. When the central bank buys government bonds in open market operations, it increases the money supply and expands AD. When the central bank sells government bonds in open market operations, it decreases the money supply and contracts AD.

More reflective of current central bank policy is to treat the interest rate, rather than the money supply, as its policy instrument. The central bank's decision to set interest rates rather than target a certain level (or rate of growth) of the money supply does not fundamentally alter our analysis of monetary policy. The theory of liquidity preference illustrates an important principle. Monetary policy can be described either in terms of the money supply or in terms of the interest rate. When the central bank sets a target for the refinancing rate of, say, *x* per cent, the central bank's bond traders are told: 'Conduct whatever open market operations are necessary to ensure that the equilibrium interest rate equals *x* per cent.' In other words, when the central bank sets a target for the interest rate, it commits itself to adjusting the money supply to make the equilibrium in the money market hit that target.

As a result, changes in monetary policy can be viewed either in terms of a changing target for the interest rate or in terms of a change in the money supply. Recall that when you read that the central bank has lowered interest rates, you should understand that this occurs only because the central bank's bond traders are doing what it takes to make it happen. If interest rates have been lowered, then the central bank's bond traders will have bought government bonds, and this purchase increases the money supply and lowers the equilibrium interest rate (just as in Figure 13.3).

The lessons from all this are:

- Changes in monetary policy that aim to expand AD can be described either as increasing the money supply or as lowering the interest rate.
- Changes in monetary policy that aim to contract AD can be described either as decreasing the money supply or as raising the interest rate.

SELF TEST Use the theory of liquidity preference to explain how a decrease in the money supply affects the equilibrium interest rate. How does this change in monetary policy affect the AD curve?

HOW FISCAL POLICY INFLUENCES AGGREGATE DEMAND

The government can influence the behaviour of the economy not only with monetary policy but also with fiscal policy. Fiscal policy refers to the government's choices regarding the overall level of government spending or taxes. We have examined how fiscal policy influences saving, investment and growth in the long run. In the short run, however, the primary effect of fiscal policy is on the AD for goods and services.

Changes in Government Purchases

Recall that changes in autonomous spending can have an effect on the level of spending in the economy which is greater than the initial injection. The multiplier effect means that AD will shift by a larger amount than the increase in government spending. However, the crowding-out effect suggests that the shift in AD could be *smaller* than the initial injection. While an increase in government purchases stimulates the AD for goods and services, it also causes the interest rate to rise. A higher interest rate reduces investment spending and chokes off AD. The reduction in AD that results when a fiscal expansion raises the interest rate is called the crowding-out effect.

To see why the crowding-out effect occurs, let us consider what happens in the money market using an example where the government invests in wind farms using the WindEn example from earlier in the book. This increase in demand raises the incomes of the workers and owners of this firm (and, because of the multiplier effect, of other firms as well). As incomes rise, households plan to buy more goods and services and, as a result, choose to hold more of their wealth in liquid form. That is, the increase in income caused by the fiscal expansion raises the demand for money.

The effect of the increase in money demand is shown in panel (a) of Figure 13.4. Because the central bank has not changed the money supply, the vertical supply curve remains the same. When the higher level of income shifts the money demand curve to the right from MD_1 to MD_2, the interest rate must rise from r_1 to r_2 to keep supply and demand in balance.

FIGURE 13.4

The Crowding-Out Effect

Panel (a) shows the money market. When the government increases its purchases of goods and services, the resulting increase in income raises the demand for money from MD_1 *to* MD_2*, and this causes the equilibrium interest rate to rise from* r_1 *to* r_2*. Panel (b) shows the effects on AD. The initial impact of the increase in government purchases shifts the AD curve from* AD_1 *to* AD_2*. Yet, because the interest rate is the cost of borrowing, the increase in the interest rate tends to reduce the quantity of goods and services demanded, particularly for investment goods. This crowding out of investment partially offsets the impact of the fiscal expansion on AD. In the end, the AD curve shifts only to* AD_3*.*

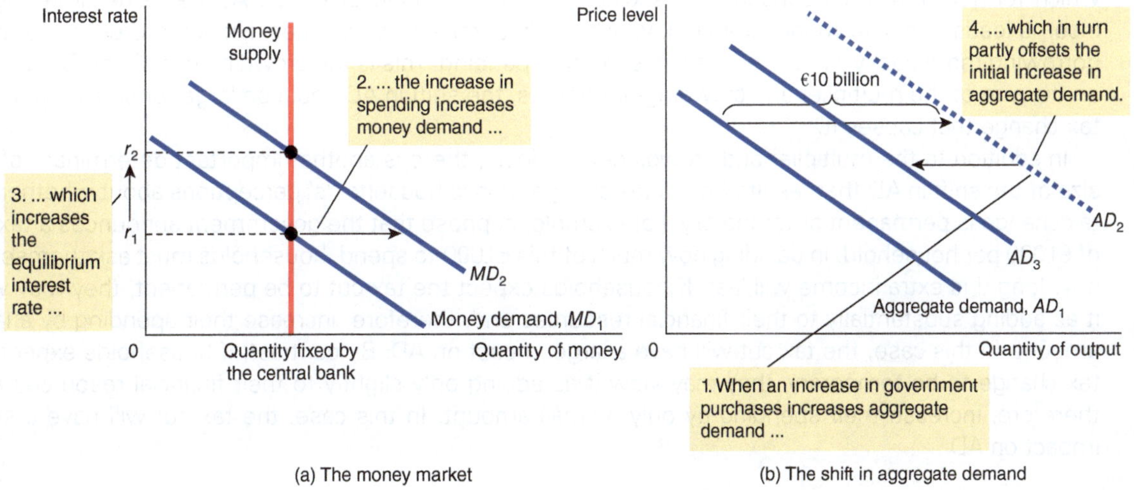

The increase in the interest rate, in turn, reduces the quantity of goods and services demanded. In particular, because borrowing is more expensive, the demand for residential and business investment goods declines. That is, as the increase in government purchases increases the demand for goods and services, it may also crowd out investment. This crowding-out effect partially offsets the impact of government purchases on AD, as illustrated in panel (b) of Figure 13.4. The initial impact of the increase in government purchases is to shift the AD curve from AD_1 to AD_2, but once crowding out takes place, the AD curve drops back to AD_3.

To sum up, when the government increases its purchases by €10 billion, the AD for goods and services could rise by more or less than €10 billion, depending on whether the multiplier effect or the crowding-out effect is larger.

CRITICAL THINKING POINT The challenge of reducing carbon emissions and encouraging the use and adoption of low-carbon technologies is considerable and will almost certainly require significant public investment. Public investment, however, will crowd out private investment leading to a less efficient outcome.

Such a view is inconsistent with the evidence. Research by Deleidi *et al.* suggests public investment in this context could 'have a positive but also consistently the largest effect on private investment flow relative to feed-in tariffs, taxes, and renewable portfolio standards in general, and for wind and solar technologies separately'. Use the link to the research and comment on the nature of the research conducted and whether the results could be generalized to other examples of public investment.

(Source: Deleidi, M., Mazzucato, M. and Semieniuk, G. (2019) 'Neither Crowding In Nor Out: Public Direct Investment Mobilising Private Investment into Renewable Electricity Projects'. *UCL Institute for Innovation and Public Purpose, Working Paper Series* (IIPP WP 2019-10). Available at www.ucl.ac.uk/bartlett/sites/bartlett/files/final_neither_crowding_in_nor_out_deleidi_mazzucato_semieniuk_web.pdf, accessed 7 August 2025)

Changes in Taxes

The other important instrument of fiscal policy, besides the level of government purchases, is the level of taxation. When the government cuts personal income taxes or increases allowances, for instance, it increases households' take-home pay. Households will save some of this additional income, but they will also spend some of it on consumer goods. Because it increases consumer spending, the tax cut shifts the AD curve to the right. Similarly, a tax increase depresses consumer spending and shifts the AD curve to the left.

The size of the shift in AD resulting from a tax change is also affected by the multiplier and crowding-out effects. When the government cuts taxes and stimulates consumer spending, earnings and profits rise, which further stimulates consumer spending. This is the multiplier effect. At the same time, higher income leads to higher money demand, which tends to raise interest rates. Higher interest rates make borrowing more costly, which reduces investment spending. This is the crowding-out effect. Depending on the size of the multiplier and crowding-out effects, the shift in AD could be larger or smaller than the tax change that causes it.

In addition to the multiplier and crowding-out effects, there is another important determinant of the size of the shift in AD that results from a tax change. This is households' perceptions about whether the tax change is permanent or temporary. For example, suppose that the government announces a tax cut of €1,000 per household. In deciding how much of this €1,000 to spend, households must ask themselves how long this extra income will last. If households expect the tax cut to be permanent, they may view it as adding substantially to their financial resources and, therefore, increase their spending by a large amount. In this case, the tax cut will have a large impact on AD. By contrast, if households expect the tax change to be temporary, they may view it as adding only slightly to their financial resources and, therefore, increase their spending by only a small amount. In this case, the tax cut will have a small impact on AD.

SELF TEST Suppose that the government reduces spending on motorway construction by €1 billion. Which way does the AD curve shift? Explain why the shift might be larger than €1 billion. Explain why the shift might be smaller than €1 billion.

CASE STUDY Fiscal Multipliers

The theory seems intuitive enough. If government spends money on a major infrastructure project it is logical that the income received will be spent and feed through to other parts of the economy. As a result, this would lead to a rise in national income that is a multiple of the initial injection. Most economists would not disagree with this base analysis. Where they do disagree, however, is on the size of the multiplier effect and therefore whether this is the best way to smooth out short-term fluctuations in economic activity. There has been a considerable amount of research into the size of fiscal or government expenditure multipliers, which is the change in output that arises as a result of a change in government expenditure.

Does the size of the fiscal multiplier matter? The difference in the estimates of the size of the fiscal multiplier, according to two leading macroeconomists, is revealing. Robert Barro, a Harvard Professor, wrote in 2009 that the size of the fiscal multiplier in peacetime was close to zero. Christine Romer, a Professor of Economics at the University of California, Berkeley and a former Chair of Economic Advisors to President Obama, suggested that the multiplier was nearer to 1.6. When the US government passed a stimulus package of US$787 billion (€692 billion) in 2009, the difference in the number of jobs created of these two estimates of the multiplier effects would be around 3.75 million according to three economists, Mendoza, Vegh and Ilzetzki, in an IMF working paper.

What the research does seem to show is that the size of the fiscal multiplier is dependent on a wide range of factors. The fiscal multiplier might be different in developed and developing countries. It might also depend on whether the government spending 'shock' is anticipated or unanticipated, how open the economy is, the exchange rate regime used by the country (whether exchange rates are fixed against other currencies, managed, or allowed to float freely in response to market conditions), whether the economy is experiencing a financial or debt crisis and the time preferences of the population of a country. Time preferences refer to how people react to the fiscal stimulus. If a government cuts taxes or increases spending, what proportion of the increase in income would be spent and what proportion saved? Also, to what extent would people build into their decision-making the expectation that a 'windfall' now, will 'inevitably' lead to tax rises in the future? The idea that people will save most of any increase in government spending because they expect to have to pay higher taxes in the future is called Ricardian Equivalence and was initially developed by David Ricardo in the nineteenth century. It has subsequently been refined somewhat by Robert Barro. The size of the fiscal multiplier will depend in part, therefore, on the extent to which consumers are Ricardian in their response.

A discussion paper written by Gilberto Marcheggiano and David Miles (Bank of England External MPC Discussion Paper no. 39, January 2013) noted that 'Empirical studies … face great challenges in measuring multipliers because of the difficulties of identifying exogenous fiscal shocks and controlling for other factors that might affect output responses.' They further note that studies on the size of fiscal multipliers include estimates between 1.2 and 1.8 and in other cases, 0.8 to 1.5.

© iStock/mahout

Investment in large-scale infrastructure projects creates ripple effects throughout the economy but how large are these effects?

In October 2024, the Institute for Government in the UK published a paper on how the Office for Budget Responsibility (OBR) estimates fiscal multipliers. It noted how the OBR uses different fiscal multipliers in its analysis, each associated with different types of spending and how it affects real GDP. In addition, it calculates a multiplier associated with a permanent tax cut. The tax multiplier is assumed to be 0.3 in year one, tapering off to zero by year five.

(Continued)

The multiplier for annually managed expenditure covering spending on things like pensions and benefits is assumed to be 0.6 in year one falling to zero over a five-year period. Capital departmental expenditure limits include spending on infrastructure, which will produce a lasting asset for the public sector, and has a multiplier of 1 in year one, falling to 0.5 in year two. Resource departmental expenditure limits cover day-to-day spending on things like salaries and has a multiplier of 0.9 in year one, falling to 0.7 in year two. The paper notes that the demand effect tapers to zero by the fifth year, because it is assumed that potential GDP remains unchanged and that actual GDP cannot exceed potential output for long periods of time. If this were the case, it is assumed that inflationary pressures would build and that the Bank of England would raise interest rates. Subsequently, real wage rates would rise. Both developments would then dampen economic activity, forcing the economy back towards potential output.

Questions:

1 How do you think the size of the fiscal multiplier would vary when a government announced an increase in spending of €50 billion to be spent on infrastructure projects compared to a cut in income taxes which would put an equivalent amount into people's pockets?
2 Why do you think that Barro and Romer have such different views of the size of the fiscal multiplier?
3 The size of the fiscal multiplier will depend on Ricardian Equivalence. To what extent do you think people adjust their spending decisions in response to expectations of future tax changes?
4 If it is difficult to empirically arrive at a reliable and accurate measure of the size of fiscal multipliers, does this mean that policymakers should avoid resorting to the use of fiscal policy as a means of stimulating an economy? Justify your answer.

References:

www.instituteforgovernment.org.uk/sites/default/files/2024-10/Fiscal-modifiers-obr-demand.pdf, accessed 7 August 2025.
www imf.org/external/pubs/ft/wp/2011/wp1152.pdf, accessed 7 August 2025.

USING POLICY TO STABILIZE THE ECONOMY

We have seen how monetary and fiscal policy can affect the economy's AD for goods and services. These theoretical insights raise some important policy questions. Should policymakers use these instruments to control AD and stabilize the economy? If so, when? If not, why not?

The Case for an Active Stabilization Policy

Government spending is one determinant of the position of the AD curve. When the government cuts spending, AD will fall, which will depress production and employment in the short run. If the central bank wants to prevent this adverse effect of the fiscal policy, it can act to expand AD by increasing the money supply. A monetary expansion would reduce interest rates, stimulate investment spending and expand AD. If monetary policy responds appropriately, the combined changes in monetary and fiscal policy could leave the AD for goods and services unaffected.

This analysis is exactly the sort followed by the members of the policy-setting committees of central banks like the Bank of England and the European Central Bank. They know that monetary policy is an important determinant of AD. They also know that there are other important determinants as well, including fiscal policy set by the government, and so they will watch debates over fiscal policy with a keen eye.

This response of monetary policy to the change in fiscal policy is an example of a more general phenomenon, which is the use of policy instruments to stabilize AD and, as a result, production and employment. We have seen how the Great Depression in the 1930s spawned a belief that governments should act to manage AD in the wake of the research which followed Keynes' *General Theory*. As a result, economic stabilization has been seen as an explicit or implicit goal of government macroeconomic policy in European and North American economies following World War II. In the UK, for example, this view was embodied in a government White Paper, published in 1944, which explicitly stated, 'The Government accepts as one of its primary aims and responsibilities the maintenance of a high and stable level of employment after the War.' In the United States, similar sentiments were embodied in the Employment Act of 1946. This explicit recognition by governments of a responsibility to stabilize the economy has two implications. The first, more modest, implication is that the government should avoid being a cause of economic fluctuations itself. Thus, many economists advise against large and sudden changes in monetary and fiscal policy, for such changes are likely to cause fluctuations in AD. Moreover, when large changes do occur, it is important that monetary and fiscal policymakers be aware of, and respond to, the other's actions.

The second, more ambitious, implication of this explicit admission of responsibility – and one that was especially dominant in the first 30 years after the end of World War II – was that the government should respond to changes in the private economy to stabilize AD. To put the reasons for the pursuit of active stabilization policies into context, it is important to note that politicians remembered the problems of the Great Depression before the war and were keen to avoid a recurrence. This was not only because of the misery involved for millions of people but also because of the political effects of economic depression which were associated with a rise in extremism. Poverty was directly linked with the rise of extremism and political instability. As the war ended, therefore, they wanted to look forward to a better world in which governments could help avoid these problems. The adoption of Keynesian demand management policies seemed to offer some promise that full employment could be achieved.

Keynes (and his many followers) argued that AD fluctuates because of largely irrational waves of pessimism and optimism. He used the term 'animal spirits' to refer to these arbitrary changes in attitude. When pessimism reigns, households reduce consumption spending and firms reduce investment spending. The result is reduced AD, lower production and higher unemployment. Conversely, when optimism reigns, households and firms increase spending. The result is higher AD, higher production and inflationary pressure. Notice that these changes in attitude are, to some extent, self-fulfilling.

In principle, the government can adjust its monetary and fiscal policy in response to these waves of optimism and pessimism and, thereby, stabilize the economy. For example, when people are excessively pessimistic, the central bank can expand the money supply to lower interest rates and expand AD. When they are excessively optimistic, it can contract the money supply to raise interest rates and dampen AD.

The Case Against an Active Stabilization Policy

Some economists argue that the government should avoid active use of monetary and fiscal policy to stabilize the economy. They claim that these policy instruments should be set to achieve long-run goals, such as rapid economic growth and low inflation, and that the economy should be left to deal with short-run fluctuations on its own. Although these economists may admit that monetary and fiscal policy can stabilize the economy in theory, they doubt whether it can do so in practice.

The primary argument against active monetary and fiscal policy is that the effects of these policies may be, to a large extent, uncertain both in terms of magnitude and timing. As we have seen, monetary policy works by changing interest rates. This can have strong and rapid effects on consumer spending if (as in the UK) a large number of people are buying their house with a mortgage loan on which the interest rate can vary according to market interest rates. Quite simply, if interest rates go up, then mortgage payments go up and people have less money to spend. Yet if people have mortgages on which the interest rate is fixed for one or more years ahead, then the interest rate change will only affect mortgage payments with a very long lag. If many people live in rented accommodation (as is the case in some of the countries of continental Europe), then a rise in interest rates will have no strong effects through this channel at all. In all cases, however, the interest rate rise will still clearly affect consumer spending, because buying goods on credit (for example, with a credit card) will be more expensive. The net effect on consumer spending may, therefore, be hard to predict, especially in terms of its timing.

Monetary policy can also affect AD through its influence on investment spending. Many firms make investment plans far in advance. Thus, many economists believe that it takes at least six months for changes in monetary policy to have much effect on output and employment. Most central banks readily admit that changes in interest rates can take up to 18 months to work their way through the economy. Moreover, once these effects occur, they can last for several years.

Critics of stabilization policy argue that because of these uncertain lags, the central bank should not try to fine tune the economy. They claim that the central bank often reacts too late to changing economic conditions and, as a result, ends up being a cause of, rather than a cure for, economic fluctuations. These critics advocate a passive monetary policy, such as slow and steady growth in the money supply.

Fiscal policy may also work with a lag. Of course, the impact of a change in government spending is felt as soon as the change takes place and cuts in direct and indirect taxation can feed through into the economy quickly. However, considerable time may pass between the decision to adopt a government spending programme and its implementation. In the UK, for example, the government has often tended to undershoot on its planned spending, partly because of problems in attracting sufficient extra staff into key public services such as transport, education and health. At the same time, announcements about changes to income taxes (both personal and corporate) tend to occur months (and sometimes years) before implementation. In the intervening time period, households and businesses factor in the impending changes into their behaviour and so the effects are uncertain.

These lags in monetary and fiscal policy are a problem in part because economic forecasting is so imprecise. If forecasters could accurately predict the condition of the economy a year in advance, then monetary and fiscal policymakers could look ahead when making policy decisions. In this case, policymakers could stabilize the economy despite the lags they face. Decisions are made, in part, on the basis of existing statistical data which are fed into models. That data can be inaccurate and subject to revision, as we have seen. Without accurate and up to date information, the outcome from modelling can vary considerably. In practice, however, major recessions and depressions arrive without much advance warning. The best policymakers can do at any time is to respond to economic changes as they occur.

Automatic Stabilizers

Economists – both advocates and critics of stabilization policy – agree that the lags in implementation render policy less useful as a tool for short-run stabilization. The economy would be more stable, therefore, if policymakers could find a way to avoid some of these lags. In fact, they have **automatic stabilizers**, changes in fiscal policy that stimulate AD when the economy goes into a recession without policymakers having to take any deliberate action.

automatic stabilizers changes in fiscal policy that stimulate AD when the economy goes into a recession, without policymakers having to take any deliberate action

The most important automatic stabilizer is the tax system. When the economy goes into a recession, the amount of taxes collected by the government falls automatically because almost all taxes are closely tied to economic activity and because in many countries, income taxes are progressive. This means that as economic activity increases, an increasing proportion of income is paid in tax and vice versa. Income tax depends on households' incomes and corporation tax depends on firms' profits. Because incomes and profits both fall in a recession, the government's tax revenue falls as well. Taxes are a withdrawal from the circular flow which has the effect of dampening the level of AD. If tax revenues are lower, it means that consumers have more disposable income to spend on consumption and businesses on investment. If economic activity increases, then tax revenues will rise. These automatic tax changes either stimulate or dampen AD and, thereby, reduce the magnitude of economic fluctuations.

Government spending also acts as an automatic stabilizer. In particular, when the economy goes into a recession and workers are laid off, more people apply for state unemployment benefits, welfare benefits and other forms of income support. Extra spending on benefits and the welfare system helps to provide a cushion against too large a fall in economic activity. This increase in government spending stimulates AD at exactly the time when it is insufficient to maintain full employment. However, it must be taken into consideration that to finance this additional spending (at a time when tax revenue is falling) governments may have to borrow. This additional borrowing can put upwards pressure on interest rates and dampen the overall effect.

Automatic stabilizers are generally not sufficiently strong to prevent recessions completely. Nevertheless, without these automatic stabilizers, output and employment would probably be more volatile than they are. For this reason, many economists would not favour a policy of always running a balanced budget, as some politicians have proposed. When the economy goes into a recession, taxes fall, government spending rises and the government's budget moves towards deficit. If the government faced a strict balanced budget rule, it would be forced to look for ways to raise taxes or cut spending in a recession. In other words, a strict **balanced budget** rule would eliminate the automatic stabilizers inherent in the current system of taxes and government spending and would, in effect, be an 'automatic destabilizer'.

balanced budget where the total sum of money received by a government in tax revenue and interest is equal to the amount it spends, including on any debt interest owing

SELF TEST Suppose a wave of negative 'animal spirits' overruns the economy, and people become pessimistic about the future. What happens to AD? If the central bank wants to stabilize AD, how should it alter the money supply? If it does this, what happens to the interest rate? Why might the central bank choose not to respond in this way?

CONCLUSION

Before policymakers make any change in policy, they need to consider all the effects of their decisions. Earlier in the book we examined classical models of the economy, which describe the long-run effects of monetary and fiscal policy. There we saw how fiscal policy influences saving, investment and long-run growth, and how monetary policy influences the price level and the inflation rate.

In this chapter we examined the short-run effects of monetary and fiscal policy. We saw how these policy instruments can change the AD for goods and services and, thereby, alter the economy's production and employment in the short run. When the government reduces spending to balance the budget, it needs to consider both the long-run effects on saving and growth and the short-run effects on AD and employment. When the central bank reduces the growth rate of the money supply, it must take into account the long-run effect on inflation as well as the short-run effect on production. We will move on to discuss the transition between the short run and the long run more fully, and we will see that policymakers often face a trade-off between long-run and short-run goals.

SUMMARY

- In developing a theory of short-run economic fluctuations, Keynes proposed the theory of liquidity preference to explain the determinants of the interest rate. According to this theory, the interest rate adjusts to balance the supply and demand for money.
- An increase in the price level raises money demand and increases the interest rate that brings the money market into equilibrium. Because the interest rate represents the cost of borrowing, a higher interest rate reduces investment and, thereby, the quantity of goods and services demanded. The downwards sloping AD curve expresses this negative relationship between the price level and the quantity demanded.
- Policymakers can influence AD with monetary policy. An increase in the money supply reduces the equilibrium interest rate for any given price level. Because a lower interest rate stimulates investment spending, the AD curve shifts to the right. Conversely, a decrease in the money supply raises the equilibrium interest rate for any given price level and shifts the AD curve to the left.
- Policymakers can also influence AD with fiscal policy. An increase in government purchases or a cut in taxes shifts the AD curve to the right. A decrease in government purchases or an increase in taxes shifts the AD curve to the left.
- When the government alters spending or taxes, the resulting shift in AD can be larger or smaller than the fiscal change. The multiplier effect tends to amplify the effects of fiscal policy on AD. The crowding-out effect tends to dampen the effects of fiscal policy on AD.

- Because monetary and fiscal policy can influence AD, the government sometimes uses these policy instruments to stabilize the economy. Economists disagree about how active the government should be in this effort. According to advocates of active stabilization policy, changes in attitudes by households and firms shift AD. If the government does not respond, the result is undesirable and unnecessary fluctuations in output and employment.
- According to critics of an active stabilization policy, monetary and fiscal policy work with such long lags that attempts at stabilizing the economy often end up being destabilizing.

IN THE NEWS

Monetary Policy Challenges

As we have noted, the key indicators associated with macroeconomics are all interrelated. Policymakers try to monitor all the key indicators and variables and to build these into models to help make forecasts and aid policy decisions.

Setting monetary policy can be particularly challenging. In theory, we know that many central banks seek to target a relatively low and stable rate of inflation, typically around 2 per cent. If inflationary pressures develop we expect central banks to raise interest rates to choke off the inflationary pressure. The reverse is adopted if the economy is sluggish and inflation is below target. In the latter part of the 2020s we saw inflation rates in the UK, Europe and the United States well above the 2 per cent target. Sure enough, the Bank of England, European Central Bank (ECB) and the Federal Reserve (Fed) all increased interest rates. As inflation began to slow, interest rates began to fall. In November 2024, the Bank of England cut interest rates to 4.75 per cent, 0.75 percentage points lower than the peak of 5.5 per cent reached in late 2023 and into 2024. In Europe, the ECB cut its main interest rate by 0.25 per cent to 3.0 per cent, the fourth time it had reduced rates since the summer of 2024. In the United States, the Fed cut its key interest rates to a range of 4.25–4.50 per cent at its December 2024 meeting, again from a high of a range between 5.25 and 5.50 per cent in July 2023.

The cuts in interest rates might have been expected in response to a slowdown in the rate of growth of prices, but in the UK inflation accelerated slightly from 2.3 per cent in November to 2.6 per cent in December 2024, with the Bank of England forecasting inflation peaking at 2.8 per cent into 2025 before coming back to target. The OBR had forecast inflation peaking at 2.6 per cent at the time of the UK Budget in October 2024. In the United States, inflation at the end of 2024 was 2.7 per cent, somewhat higher than its target. In the EU, inflation had sped up slightly from 2.2 per cent in November 2024 to 2.4 per cent in December of that year.

Were central banks right to have cut interest rates given the inflation situation? Of course, policy decisions are not made on the basis of what macroeconomic data is today but what the trends might be for the future. We can assume, therefore, that the monetary policy committees on the three central banks would be expecting inflationary pressures to be easing. However, some economists have questioned this assumption. In the UK, for example, some economists were concerned that above inflation wage increases awarded to public sector workers with no corresponding increase in productivity would have inflationary consequences. In addition, they pointed to an expansion in the money supply, as measured by M4, as signs that inflation might accelerate rather than ease.

© iStock/Dimitrios Karamitros

Monetary policy is not an exact science and is dependent on many interrelated factors and influences.

(*Continued*)

One of the problems facing the EU and the UK has been around the sluggish growth in GDP. The monetary policy committees might have had one eye on trying to help boost growth by making its interest rate decisions and the other on weighing the risk around the existing inflationary pressures. Some economists suggested that global supply pressures were likely to be weak and this would have a moderating effect on inflationary pressures.

Critical Thinking Questions

1 Assume that the central bank wishes to maintain a stable supply of money and the equilibrium rate of interest is 5.75 per cent. Using the theory of liquidity preference, what might have been the cause of reductions in interest rates in the UK, Europe and the United States? Use appropriate diagrams to help illustrate your answer.

2 Analyze the likely effect on aggregate demand of the fall in the rate of interest. Again, use appropriate diagrams to help illustrate your answer.

3 What would you expect to happen to the money supply as a result of the reduction in interest rates, and how might this impact aggregate demand and the price level? What effect does this also have on the quantity of output, and what might the extent of the effect depend on?

4 Now assume that governments in both the UK and EU wish to boost the quantity of output to counter the sluggish growth they have been experiencing. How might this policy compromise the goal of the Bank of England and the ECB in managing the rate of inflation target at around 2 per cent? Use appropriate diagrams to illustrate your answer.

5 'Further reductions in interest rates will not result in increased growth in the UK or the EU and risks setting off another inflationary spiral.' Critically analyze and evaluate this statement.

References:

blogs.lse.ac.uk/businessreview/2025/01/07/the-challenges-for-uk-interest-rates-and-inflation-in-2025/, accessed 7 August 2025.
commonslibrary.parliament.uk/research-briefings/sn02802/, accessed 7 August 2025.
ec.europa.eu/eurostat/statistics-explained/index.php?title=Inflation_in_the_euro_area, accessed 7 August 2025.

QUESTIONS FOR REVIEW

1 What are the three ways in which monetary policy affects AD?

2 What is the theory of liquidity preference?

3 How does the theory of liquidity preference help explain the downwards slope of the AD curve?

4 Use the theory of liquidity preference to explain how a decrease in the money supply affects the AD curve.

5 The government spends €500 million improving canals for trade and leisure use. Explain why AD might increase by more than €500 million. Explain why AD might increase by less than €500 million.

6 If governments commit to demand management policies to maintain the economy as near to full employment output as possible, what effect do you think this may have on expectations and economic actors' responses to government policy initiatives?

7 Suppose that survey measures of consumer confidence indicate a wave of pessimism is sweeping the country. If policymakers do nothing, what will happen to aggregate AD? What should the government do if it wants to stabilize AD? If the government does nothing, should the central bank stabilize AD? If so, how?

8 How might a government use taxation as a tool in expansionary fiscal policy?

9 Outline the arguments for and against an active stabilization policy.

10 Give an example of a government policy that acts as an automatic stabilizer. Explain why this policy has this effect.

PROBLEMS AND APPLICATIONS

1 Explain how each of the following developments would affect the supply of money, the demand for money and the interest rate. Illustrate your answers with diagrams.
   a. The central bank's bond traders buy bonds in open market operations.
   b. An increase in credit card availability reduces the cash people hold.
   c. Households decide to hold more money to use for holiday shopping.
   d. A wave of optimism boosts business investment and expands AD.
   e. A significant fall in oil prices shifts the SRAS curve to the right.

2 Suppose banks install automatic teller machines on every street corner and, by making cash readily available, reduce the amount of money people want to hold.
   a. Assume the central bank does not change the money supply. According to the theory of liquidity preference, what happens to the interest rate? What happens to AD?
   b. If the central bank wants to stabilize AD, how should it respond?

3 The economy is in a recession with high unemployment and low output.
   a. Use a graph of AD and AS to illustrate the current situation. Include the AD curve, the SRAS curve and the LRAS curve.
   b. Identify an open market operation that would restore the economy to its natural rate.
   c. Use a graph of the money market to illustrate the effect of this open market operation. Show the resulting change in the interest rate.
   d. Use a graph similar to the one in part (a) to show the effect of the open market operation on output and the price level. Explain in words why the policy has the effect that you have shown in the graph.

4 This chapter explains that expansionary monetary policy reduces the interest rate and thus stimulates demand for investment goods. Explain how such a policy also stimulates the demand for net exports.

5 Suppose government spending increases. Would the effect on AD be larger if the central bank took no action in response, or if the central bank were committed to maintaining a fixed interest rate? Explain.

6 In which of the following circumstances is expansionary fiscal policy more likely to lead to a short-run increase in investment? Explain.
   a. When the investment accelerator is large, or when it is small?
   b. When the interest sensitivity of investment is large, or when it is small?

7 Assume the economy is in a recession. Explain how each of the following policies would affect consumption and investment. In each case, indicate any direct effects, any effects resulting from changes in total output, any effects resulting from changes in the interest rate and the overall effect. If there are conflicting effects making the answer ambiguous, say so.
   a. An increase in government spending.
   b. A reduction in taxes.
   c. An expansion of the money supply.

8 For various reasons, fiscal policy changes automatically when output and employment fluctuate.
   a. Explain why tax revenue changes when the economy goes into a recession.
   b. Explain why government spending changes when the economy goes into a recession.
   c. If the government were to operate under a strict balanced budget rule, what would it have to do in a recession? Would this make the recession more or less severe?

9 Assume that a law has been proposed that would make price stability the sole goal of monetary policy. Suppose such a law were passed.
   a. How would the central bank respond to an event that contracted AD?
   b. How would the central bank respond to an event that caused an adverse shift in SRAS?
   c. In each case, is there another monetary policy option that would lead to greater stability in output?

10 An economy is operating with a negative output gap of €400 billion. The government of this economy wants to close this output gap. The central bank agrees to adjust the money supply to hold the interest rate constant so there is no crowding out. The MPC is 0.8, and the price level is fixed in the short run. In what direction and by how much would government spending need to change to close the output gap? Explain your thinking.

14 THE SHORT-RUN TRADE-OFF BETWEEN INFLATION AND UNEMPLOYMENT

Recall the long-run determinants of unemployment and inflation. The natural rate of unemployment depends on various features of the labour market, such as minimum wage laws, the market power of unions, the role of efficiency wages and the effectiveness of job search. The inflation rate depends primarily on growth in the money supply, which, it is assumed, a nation's central bank controls. In the long run, therefore, inflation and unemployment are largely unrelated problems. In the short run the situation is very different. The relationship between inflation and unemployment is a topic that has attracted the attention of some of the most important economists from the 1970s onwards. It still occupies attention and particularly so since the mid-2000s onwards. During this time many countries have experienced periods of inflation at relatively low and stable levels but unemployment at rates below the estimated natural rate of unemployment. This has then been followed by periods where inflation has been accelerating but unemployment has remained relatively low. The best way to understand this relationship is to see how thinking about it has evolved over time.

THE RELATIONSHIP BETWEEN INFLATION AND UNEMPLOYMENT

David Hume

Studies on the relationship between unemployment and inflation are not a new phenomenon. In the early part of the nineteenth century, the convertibility of currency into gold was suspended during the Napoleonic Wars and the period was marred by accelerating inflation. At the same time, many small banks collapsed, which resulted in a reduction in the money supply. The consequence was a serious economic decline which caused considerable hardship as unemployment rose. This was not the first time that economic decline had caused problems. The Scottish philosopher, historian and economist, David Hume, wrote on the issue in 1752. In an essay entitled *Of Money*, Hume suggested that if the money supply is increased when an economy is below full employment, spending will increase, which in turn creates economic expansion. Firms take on more workers as a result and unemployment falls. However, the demand for labour pushes up wage costs, and firms pass on these additional costs onto consumers in the form of higher prices. Hume established a link between changes in the money supply and output and hinted at an inverse link between inflation and unemployment.

Tinbergen and Klein

The first Nobel Prize in Economics winner, Jan Tinbergen, carried out econometric studies of links between inflation and unemployment in the late 1930s, which focused on the demand for labour, wage rates and prices. The resulting model implied a trade-off between wage increases and disequilibrium in the labour market. Tinbergen's work was followed up by the 1980 Nobel Prize winner, Lawrence Klein, in work at the Cowles Commission for Research in Economics at the University of Chicago in the 1940s and 1950s. Klein's work was part of an intellectual tradition carried on by Friedman and Phelps, whom we will come to later. In building a model of the US economy, Klein suggested that workers' wage demands would be informed in part by inflation and by expected inflation, but that these demands would also take into account prevailing unemployment. The work of the Cowles Commission established a relationship between wage inflation and output gaps.

Arthur Brown

The links between the rate of increase in wages and inflation is part of a short-run cause of inflation referred to as **cost-push inflation**. Cost-push inflation occurs where firms face higher costs and pass these on in the form of higher prices. Wages are one of the most important costs facing firms. Workers may demand higher wages, fuelled in part either by a recognition that there is excess demand in the labour market and/or because of expected higher inflation. If firms accommodate higher wages, they may pass them on to consumers as higher prices. This is particularly likely if firms believe that demand is likely to continue to be strong. As inflation accelerates, workers demand higher wages in the next round and a *wage–price spiral* develops.

cost-push inflation a short-run cause of accelerating inflation due to higher input costs of firms which are passed on as higher consumer prices

We have noted that the long-run cause of inflation can be explained by the quantity theory of money, but short-run causes may go deeper than simply a rise in the money supply. Arthur Brown was an economist who wanted to understand the causes of inflation in more detail. Brown had spent the war years as a civil servant and then joined James Meade, the 1977 Nobel Prize winner, in the economic section of the Cabinet Office before becoming Professor of Economics at the University of Leeds. In 1955, he published a book entitled *The Great Inflation, 1939–51*. The book contained charts showing changes in wage rates on the vertical axis and unemployment on the horizontal axis. In an obituary published in *The Guardian* in 2003, one of Brown's students, Professor Tony Thirlwall (from the University of Kent), noted that, 'He precisely anticipated the Phillips curve, which plots the inverse relation between wage and price inflation and the rate of unemployment.' (Source: www.theguardian.com/news/2003/mar/12/guardianobituaries.obituaries.)

Indeed, there are some who argue that the Phillips curve should more accurately be referred to as the 'Brown curve'.

THE PHILLIPS CURVE

In 1958, a New Zealand economist working at the London School of Economics, A.W. Phillips, published an article in the British journal *Economica* that would make him famous. The article was entitled 'The Relationship between Unemployment and the Rate of Change of Money Wages in the UK, 1861–1957'. In it, Phillips showed a negative correlation between the rate of unemployment and the rate of inflation. That is, Phillips showed that years with low unemployment tend to have high inflation, and years with high unemployment tend to have low inflation. (It should be noted that Phillips examined inflation in nominal wages rather than inflation in prices, but for our purposes that distinction is not important. These two measures of inflation usually move together because of the relationship between wage inflation and the excess demand for labour.) George Akerlof, in his Nobel Prize lecture in 2001, referred to the Phillips curve as, 'probably the single most important macroeconomic relationship'.

Origins of the Phillips Curve

The circumstances surrounding the publication of the paper which made Phillips famous are interesting. In 1957, Phillips was being supported as a candidate for the Tooke Chair of Economic Theory at the London School of Economics (LSE), but at that time he had only a limited publication record. Despite this, those who knew him, including James Meade, regarded him highly and there has been a suggestion that the paper published in *Economica* was 'a rushed job'. Indeed, Phillips himself said as much and noted that his analysis of the data from 1861–1913 was 'a good weekend's work'. Allan G. Sleeman, in a paper published in the *Journal of Economic Perspectives* in 2011, argues that the paper was pushed for publication as a means of providing support for the position at the LSE and not necessarily submitted by Phillips himself, but by his supporters. Regardless of the circumstances surrounding the publication, the paper investigated the relationship between the rate of change in money wages and unemployment in the UK. The paper looked at two time periods, data between 1861 and 1913, and from 1913 to 1957. The first set of data seemed to imply a relationship between the rate of change of money wages (in per cent per year) which was drawn on the vertical axis, and unemployment (as a percentage) on the horizontal axis. The second period was one characterized by a great deal of upheaval, both economic and political. It seems that Phillips was not satisfied that the relationship was as strong in the second period as the first. Indeed, he did not make any claim that he had discovered a stable relationship. He referred to the paper as a 'crude attempt', and while other economists became fascinated with the seed which Phillips had planted, he himself moved on to other topics.

The paper spawned much further research with economists such as Richard Lipsey, Paul Samuelson and Robert Solow replicating Phillips' model and applying different techniques to assess its validity. The Phillips curve was introduced to the wider public after being included in Paul Samuelson's fifth edition of his undergraduate textbook *Economics* in the early 1960s, and in Lipsey's *An Introduction to Positive Economics*, published in 1963. Both books were used widely in undergraduate teaching on both sides of the Atlantic.

Samuelson and Solow Although Phillips' discovery was based on data for the UK, researchers quickly extended his finding to other countries. Two years after Phillips published his article, Samuelson and Robert Solow published an article in the *American Economic Review* called 'Analytics of Anti-inflation Policy' in which they showed a similar negative correlation between inflation and unemployment in data for the United States. They reasoned that this correlation arose because low unemployment was associated with high AD, which in turn puts upwards pressure on wages and prices throughout the economy. In other words an inflationary gap, where AD is greater than trend output, leads to an increase in prices in the short run. Samuelson and Solow dubbed the negative association between inflation and unemployment the **Phillips curve**. Figure 14.1 shows an example of a Phillips curve like the one found by Samuelson and Solow.

Phillips curve a curve that shows the short-run trade-off between inflation and unemployment

FIGURE 14.1

The Phillips Curve

The Phillips curve illustrates a negative association between the inflation rate and the unemployment rate. At point A, inflation is low and unemployment is high. At point B, inflation is high and unemployment is low.

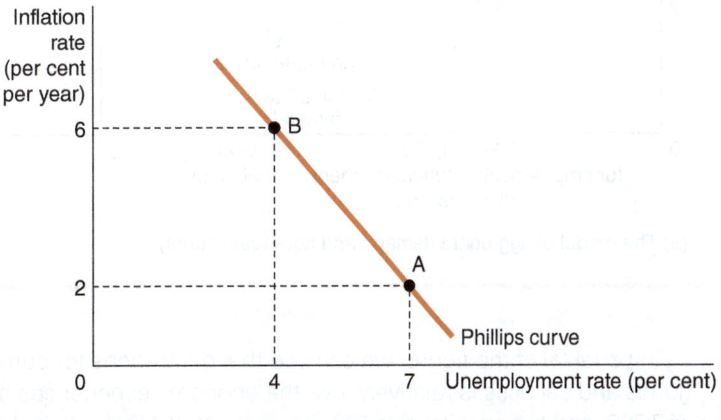

Samuelson and Solow were interested in the Phillips curve because they believed that it held important lessons for policymakers. In particular, they suggested that the Phillips curve offers policymakers a menu of possible economic outcomes. By altering monetary and fiscal policy to influence AD, policymakers could choose any point on this curve. Point A offers high unemployment and low inflation. Point B offers low unemployment and high inflation. Policymakers might prefer both low inflation and low unemployment, but the historical data as summarized by the Phillips curve indicates that this combination is not possible. According to Samuelson and Solow, policymakers face a trade-off between inflation and unemployment, and the Phillips curve illustrates that trade-off.

Aggregate Demand, Aggregate Supply and the Phillips Curve

The model of AD and AS provides an explanation for the menu of possible outcomes described by the Phillips curve. The Phillips curve simply shows the combinations of inflation and unemployment that arise in the short run as shifts in the AD curve move the economy along the SRAS. Recall that an increase in the AD for goods and services leads, in the short run, to a larger output of goods and services and a higher price level. Larger output means greater employment and, thus, a lower rate of unemployment. In addition, whatever the previous year's price level happens to be, the higher the price level in the current year, the higher the rate of inflation. Thus, shifts in AD push inflation and unemployment in opposite directions in the short run.

To see more fully how this works, let us consider an example. To keep the numbers simple, imagine that the price level (as measured, for instance, by the Consumer Prices Index) equals 100 in the year 2026. Figure 14.2 shows two possible outcomes that might occur in 2027. Panel (a) shows the two outcomes using the model of AD and AS. Panel (b) illustrates the same two outcomes using the Phillips curve.

FIGURE 14.2

How the Phillips Curve Is Related to the Model of Aggregate Demand and Aggregate Supply

Panel (a) shows the model of AD and AS. If AD is low, the economy is at point A; output is low (7,500), and the price level is low (102). If AD is high, the economy is at point B; output is high (8,000), and the price level is high (106). Panel (b) shows the implications for the Phillips curve. Point A, which arises when AD is low, has high unemployment (7 per cent) and low inflation (2 per cent). Point B, which arises when AD is high, has low unemployment (4 per cent) and high inflation (6 per cent).

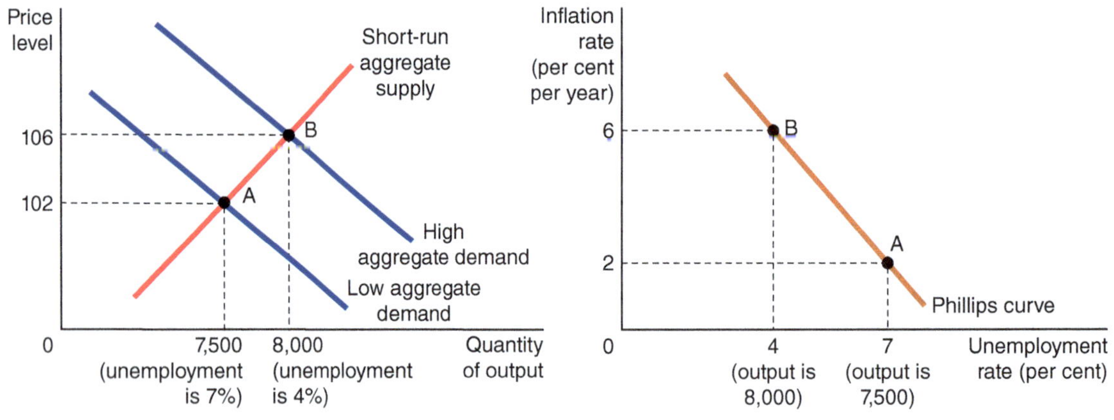

(a) The model of aggregate demand and aggregate supply

(b) The Phillips curve

In panel (a) of the figure, we can see the implications for output and the price level in 2027. If the AD for goods and services is relatively low, the economy experiences outcome A. The economy produces output of 7,500, and the price level is 102. By contrast, if AD is relatively high, the economy experiences outcome B with output at 8,000, and the price level is 106. Thus, higher AD moves the economy to an equilibrium with higher output and a higher price level.

In panel (b) of the figure, we can see what these two possible outcomes mean for unemployment and inflation. Because firms need more workers when they produce a greater output of goods and services, unemployment is lower in outcome B than in outcome A. In this example, when output rises from 7,500 to 8,000, unemployment falls from 7 per cent to 4 per cent. Moreover, because the price level is higher at outcome B than at outcome A, the inflation rate (the percentage change in the price level from the previous year) is also higher. In particular, since the price level was 100 in year 2026, outcome A has an inflation rate of 2 per cent, and outcome B has an inflation rate of 6 per cent. Thus, we can compare the two possible outcomes for the economy either in terms of output and the price level (using the model of AD and AS), or in terms of unemployment and inflation (using the Phillips curve).

As we have seen, monetary and fiscal policy can shift the AD curve. Therefore, monetary and fiscal policy can move the economy along the Phillips curve. Increases in the money supply, increases in government spending, or cuts in taxes expand AD and move the economy to a point on the Phillips curve with lower unemployment and higher inflation. Decreases in the money supply, cuts in government spending, or increases in taxes contract AD and move the economy to a point on the Phillips curve with lower inflation and higher unemployment. In this sense, the Phillips curve offers policymakers a trade-off between combinations of inflation and unemployment.

SELF TEST Draw the Phillips curve. Use the model of AD and AS to show how policy can move the economy from a point on this curve with high inflation to a point with low inflation.

SHIFTS IN THE PHILLIPS CURVE: THE ROLE OF EXPECTATIONS

The value of the Phillips curve as a basis for policy decisions is dependent on the extent to which the relationship between wage growth and, by extension, inflation and unemployment, is stable over time. Research continued into the Phillips curve relationship throughout the 1960s.

The Long-Run Phillips Curve

In 1968, Milton Friedman published a paper in the *American Economic Review*, based on an address he had recently given as president of the American Economic Association. The paper, entitled 'The Role of Monetary Policy', contained sections on 'What Monetary Policy Can Do' and 'What Monetary Policy Cannot Do'. Friedman argued that one thing monetary policy cannot do, other than for only a short time, is pick a combination of inflation and unemployment on the Phillips curve. At about the same time, another economist, Edmund Phelps, also published a paper denying the existence of a long-run trade-off between inflation and unemployment.

Friedman and Phelps based their conclusions on classical principles of macroeconomics. Recall that classical theory points to growth in the money supply as the primary determinant of inflation. Classical theory also states that monetary growth does not have real effects. It merely alters all prices and nominal incomes proportionately. In particular, monetary growth does not influence those factors that determine the economy's unemployment rate, such as the market power of unions, the role of efficiency wages, or the process of job search. Friedman and Phelps concluded that there is no reason to think the rate of inflation would, *in the long run*, be related to the rate of unemployment.

Here, in his own words, is Friedman's view about what the central bank can hope to accomplish in the long run:

> *The monetary authority controls nominal quantities – directly, the quantity of its own liabilities [currency plus bank reserves]. In principle, it can use this control to peg a nominal quantity – an exchange rate, the price level, the nominal level of national income, the quantity of money by one definition or another – or to peg the change in a nominal quantity – the rate of inflation or deflation, the rate of growth or decline in nominal national income, the rate of growth of the quantity of money. It cannot use its control over nominal quantities to peg a real quantity – the real rate of interest, the rate of unemployment, the level of real national income, the real quantity of money, the rate of growth of real national income, or the rate of growth of the real quantity of money.*

These views have important implications for the Phillips curve. In particular, they imply that monetary policymakers face a long-run Phillips curve that is vertical, as in Figure 14.3. If the central bank increases the money supply slowly, the inflation rate is low and the economy finds itself at point A. If the central bank increases the money supply quickly, the inflation rate is high and the economy finds itself at point B. In either case, the unemployment rate tends towards its natural rate. The vertical long-run Phillips curve illustrates the conclusion that unemployment does not depend on money growth and inflation in the long run.

FIGURE 14.3

The Long-Run Phillips Curve

Friedman and Phelps argued that there is no trade-off between inflation and unemployment in the long run. Growth in the money supply determines the inflation rate. Regardless of the inflation rate, the unemployment rate gravitates towards its natural rate. As a result, the long-run Phillips curve is vertical.

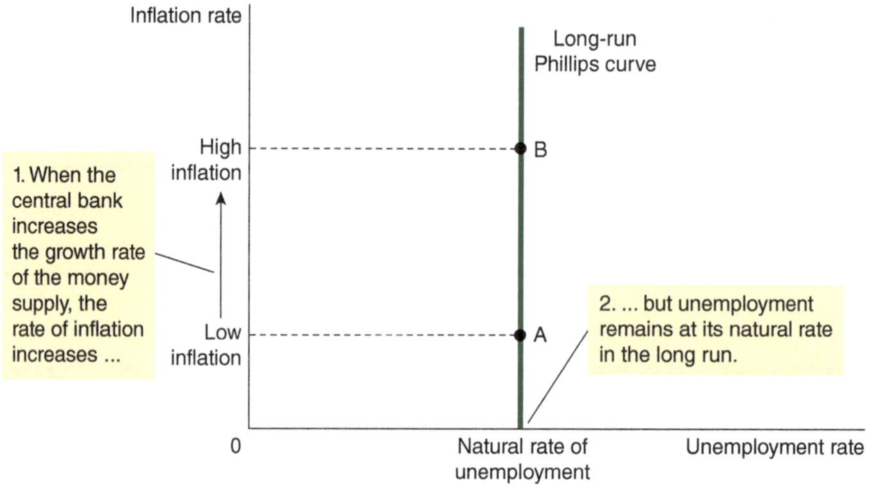

The vertical long-run Phillips curve is, in essence, one expression of the classical idea of monetary neutrality. As you may recall, we expressed this idea with a vertical LRAS curve. Indeed, as Figure 14.4 illustrates, the vertical long-run Phillips curve and the vertical LRAS curve are two sides of the same coin. In panel (a) of this figure, an increase in the money supply shifts the AD curve to the right from AD_1 to AD_2. As a result of this shift, the long-run equilibrium moves from point A to point B.

FIGURE 14.4

How the Long-Run Phillips Curve is Related to the Model of Aggregate Demand and Aggregate Supply

Panel (a) shows-the model of AD and AS with a vertical AS curve. When expansionary monetary policy shifts the AD curve to the right from AD_1 to AD_2, the equilibrium moves from point A to point B. The price level rises from P_1 to P_2, while output remains the same. Panel (b) shows the long-run Phillips curve, which is vertical at the natural rate of unemployment. Expansionary monetary policy moves the economy from lower inflation (point A) to higher inflation (point B) without changing the rate of unemployment.

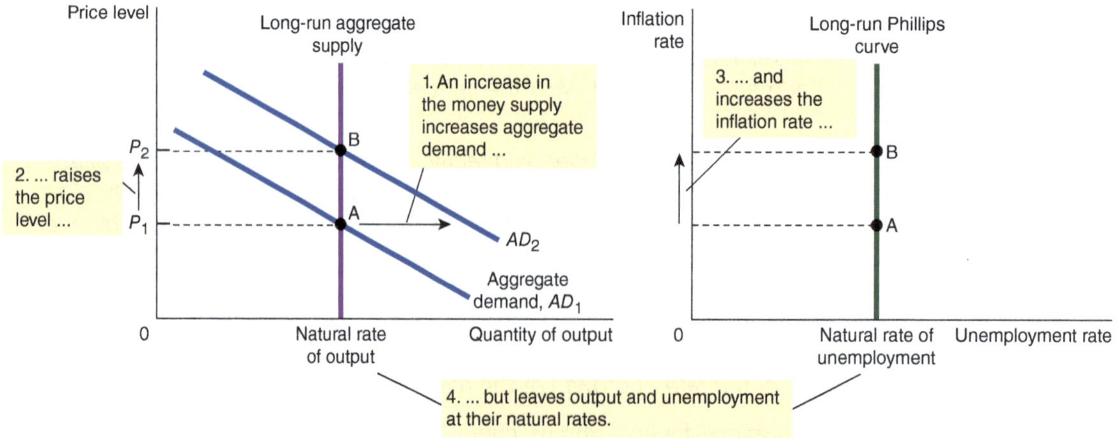

(a) The model of aggregate demand and aggregate supply

(b) The Phillips curve

The price level rises from P_1 to P_2, but because the AS curve is vertical, output remains the same. In panel (b), more rapid growth in the money supply raises the inflation rate by moving the economy from point A to point B. Because the Phillips curve is vertical, the rate of unemployment is the same at these two points. Thus, the vertical LRAS curve and the vertical long-run Phillips curve both imply that monetary policy influences nominal variables (the price level and the inflation rate) but not real variables (output and unemployment). Regardless of the monetary policy pursued by the central bank, output and unemployment are, in the long run, at their natural rates.

The Natural Rate of Unemployment Friedman and Phelps used the adjective 'natural' to describe the unemployment rate towards which the economy tends to gravitate in the long run. As we have seen, the natural rate of unemployment is not necessarily the socially desirable rate of unemployment. Neither is the natural rate of unemployment constant over time. This unemployment is 'natural' because it is beyond the influence of monetary policy.

Although the conclusion of Friedman and Phelps was that monetary policy cannot influence the natural rate of unemployment, other types of policy can. To reduce the natural rate of unemployment, policymakers could look to policies that improve the functioning of the labour market, for example minimum wage laws, collective bargaining laws, unemployment insurance and job training schemes. A policy change that reduced the natural rate of unemployment would shift the long-run Phillips curve to the left. In addition, because lower unemployment means more workers are producing goods and services, the quantity of goods and services supplied would be larger at any given price level and the LRAS would shift to the right. The economy could then enjoy lower unemployment and higher output for any given rate of money growth and inflation. We will look at some of these policies designed to affect the supply side of the economy later in the book.

Reconciling Theory and Evidence

Friedman and Phelps' conclusion was based on an appeal to *theory*. In contrast, the negative correlation between inflation and unemployment documented by Phillips, Samuelson and Solow was based on *data*. Why should anyone believe that policymakers faced a vertical Phillips curve when the world seemed to offer a downwards sloping one? Should the findings of Phillips, Samuelson and Solow not lead us to reject the classical conclusion of monetary neutrality?

Friedman and Phelps were well aware of these questions. They offered a way to reconcile classical macroeconomic theory with the finding of a downwards sloping Phillips curve in data from the UK and the United States. They argued that policymakers can pursue expansionary monetary policy to achieve lower unemployment for a while (that is, in the short run), but eventually unemployment returns to its natural rate, and more expansionary monetary policy leads only to higher inflation.

Friedman and Phelps reasoned that the SRAS curve is upwards sloping, indicating that an increase in the price level raises the quantity of goods and services that firms supply. In contrast, the LRAS curve is vertical, indicating that the price level does not influence quantity supplied in the long run. We have presented three theories to explain the upwards slope of the SRAS curve: sticky wages, sticky prices and misperceptions about relative prices. Because wages, prices and perceptions adjust to changing economic conditions over time, the positive relationship between the price level and quantity supplied applies in the short run but not in the long run. Friedman and Phelps applied this same logic to the Phillips curve. Just as the AS curve slopes upwards only in the short run, the trade-off between inflation and unemployment holds only in the short run. Just as the LRAS curve is vertical, the long-run Phillips curve is also vertical.

To help explain the short-run and long-run relationship between inflation and unemployment, Friedman and Phelps focused on *expected inflation*. Expected inflation measures how much people expect the overall price level to change. The expected price level affects the wages and prices that people set and the perceptions of relative prices that they form. As a result, expected inflation is one factor that determines the position of the SRAS curve. In the short run, the central bank can take expected inflation (and thus the SRAS curve) as already determined. When the money supply changes, the AD curve shifts and the economy moves along a given SRAS curve. In the short run, therefore, monetary changes lead to unexpected fluctuations in output, prices, unemployment and inflation. In this way, Friedman and Phelps explained the Phillips curve that Phillips, Samuelson and Solow had documented.

Yet the central bank's ability to create unexpected inflation by increasing the money supply exists only in the short run. In the long run, people come to expect whatever inflation rate the central bank chooses to produce. Because wages, prices and perceptions will eventually adjust to the inflation rate, the LRAS curve is vertical. In this case, changes in AD, such as those due to changes in the money supply, do not affect the economy's output of goods and services. Thus, Friedman and Phelps concluded that unemployment returns to its natural rate in the long run.

The Short-Run Phillips Curve

The analysis of Friedman and Phelps can be summarized in the following equation (which is another expression of the AS equation we presented earlier in the book):

$$\text{Unemployment rate} = \text{NRU} - a(\text{Actual inflation} - \text{Expected inflation})$$

This equation relates the unemployment rate to the natural rate of unemployment (NRU), actual inflation and expected inflation. In the short run, expected inflation is given. As a result, higher actual inflation is associated with lower unemployment. (How much unemployment responds to unexpected inflation is determined by the size of *a*, a number that in turn depends on the slope of the SRAS curve.) In the long run, however, people come to expect whatever inflation the central bank produces (or specifies as the target rate). Thus, actual inflation equals expected inflation, and unemployment is at its natural rate.

This equation implies there is no stable short-run Phillips curve. Each short-run Phillips curve reflects a particular expected rate of inflation. To be precise, if you graph the equation, you will find that the short-run Phillips curve intersects the long-run Phillips curve at the expected rate of inflation. Whenever expected inflation changes, the short-run Phillips curve shifts.

According to Friedman and Phelps, it is dangerous to view the Phillips curve as a menu of options available to policymakers. To see why, imagine an economy at its NRU with low inflation and low expected inflation, shown in Figure 14.5 as point A. Now suppose that policymakers try to take advantage of the trade-off between inflation and unemployment by using monetary or fiscal policy to expand AD. In the short run when expected inflation is given, the economy goes from point A to point B.

FIGURE 14.5

How Expected Inflation Shifts the Short-Run Phillips Curve

The higher the expected rate of inflation, the higher the short-run trade-off between inflation and unemployment. At point A, expected inflation and actual inflation are both low, and unemployment is at its natural rate. If the central bank pursues an expansionary monetary policy, the economy moves from point A to point B in the short run. At point B, expected inflation is still low, but actual inflation is high. Unemployment is below its natural rate. In the long run, expected inflation rises, and the economy moves to point C. At point C, expected inflation and actual inflation are both high, and unemployment is back to its natural rate.

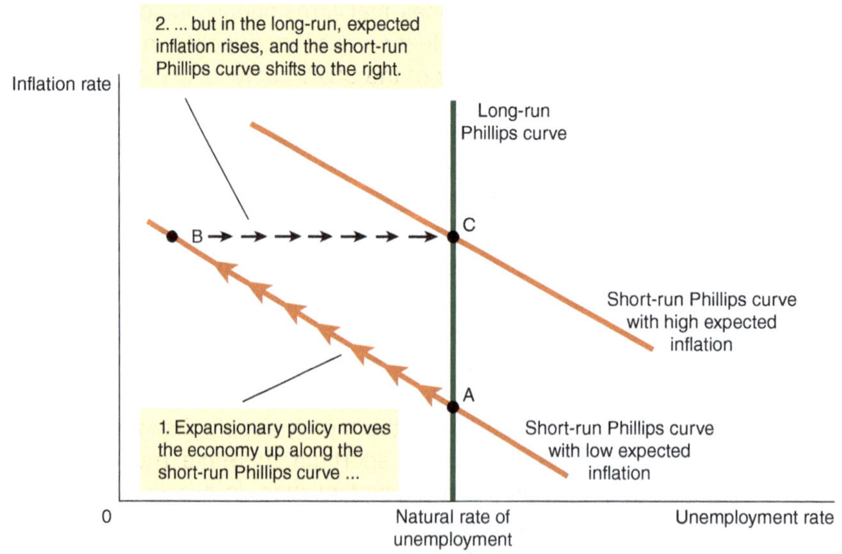

Unemployment falls below its natural rate, and inflation rises above expected inflation. Over time, people get used to this higher inflation rate, and they raise their expectations of inflation. When expected inflation rises, firms and workers start taking higher inflation into account when setting wages and prices. The short-run Phillips curve then shifts to the right, as shown in the figure. The economy ends up at point C, with higher inflation than at point A but with the same level of unemployment.

Thus, Friedman and Phelps concluded that policymakers do face a trade-off between inflation and unemployment, but only a temporary one. If policymakers use this trade-off, they lose it.

The Unemployment–Inflation Trade-Off

Friedman and Phelps made a bold prediction in 1968. If policymakers try to take advantage of the Phillips curve by choosing higher inflation to reduce unemployment, they will succeed at reducing unemployment only temporarily. This view, that unemployment eventually returns to its natural rate regardless of the rate of inflation, is called the **natural rate hypothesis**.

natural rate hypothesis the claim that unemployment eventually returns to its normal, or natural, rate, regardless of the rate of inflation

To some economists at the time, it seemed ridiculous to claim that the Phillips curve would break down once policymakers tried to use it. Research suggested, however, that this was exactly what happened in both the UK and the United States. Beginning in the late 1960s, the UK government, for example, followed policies that expanded the AD for goods and services. On top of this, the UK and many other developed economies in the late 1960s and early 1970s, experienced an increase in AD due to US involvement in the Vietnam War. This increased US government spending (on the military), boosted US AD and so boosted net exports from other countries to the United States. In addition, in 1971, as a result of the relaxation of certain controls on bank lending, the UK experienced a major expansion in the money supply. In the following year, the government announced an extraordinarily expansionary fiscal policy, in terms of extra spending and tax reduction. The economy began to seriously overheat, and inflation started to rise. But, as Friedman and Phelps had predicted, unemployment did not stay low.

As we have seen, many governments in the Western world adopted Keynesian policies as the basis for managing the economy. In the 20 years after the war, fiscal policy was dominant. In times of rising unemployment fiscal policy was loosened and tightened when inflation began to speed up. The government could pull its fiscal levers of tax and public spending to 'fine tune' the economy. The unusual circumstances of post-war reconstruction across Europe and the United States meant that inflation did not seem to present a major problem.

Some economists argued that the focus on fiscal policy meant that households formed expectations not only about inflation but also about government policy. In the UK, many large industries were in public ownership including the railways, coal, electricity, water, airports and airlines, telecommunications and steel. In addition, trade unions enjoyed considerable power in many industries. Workers came to expect, it was argued, increases in real wages each year and that this would be accommodated by monetary expansion. In addition, the government would respond by loosening fiscal policy if the economy slowed down. This, it was argued, led to a fall in productivity and increased inflationary pressures as the government and industry accommodated wage increases. In the aggregate, UK industry became sluggish, lacked flexibility and lost competitiveness.

These conditions led to rising inflation and an inability of the government to reduce unemployment below the natural rate. After the oil crisis and miners' strike of the early 1970s and the fiscal boom produced by the government, stagflation took hold and the UK seemed to lurch from 'boom to bust'. Eventually the government was forced to borrow money from the IMF in 1976. In a famous speech to the Labour Party Conference in the same year, the then Prime Minister, James Callaghan, echoed Friedman and Phelps' theory to the nation when he said:

We used to think that you could spend your way out of a recession and increase employment by cutting taxes and boosting government spending. I tell you in all candour that that option no longer

exists, and in so far as it ever did exist, it only worked on each occasion since the war by injecting a bigger dose of inflation into the economy. And each time that happened, the average level of unemployment has risen. Higher inflation followed by higher unemployment. That is the history of the last 20 years.

This effectively led to a move away from Keynesian policies and a shift in emphasis on monetary policy in the UK, while in the United States a similar focus on the money supply was also pursued. The focus of policy on the use of monetary and supply-side policies was seen as the way of keeping inflation under control and lowering the natural rate of unemployment. Throughout the 1980s, the UK and US governments trumpeted the benefits of supply-side policies. These looked at ways of expanding the productive capacity of the economy to shift the AS curve to the right. Such policies stressed the importance of enterprise, reducing business regulation, improving incentives through cutting taxes and benefits, reducing trade union power, and investing in education and training to improve the workings and flexibility of the labour market in the long run.

Supply-side policies take some time to have an effect, but structural economic reforms by the UK government throughout the 1990s led to a leftwards shift in the Phillips curve. What caused this favourable shift in the short-run Phillips curve? Part of the answer lies in a low level of expected inflation. The policy of inflation targeting since 1992, combined with the independence of the Bank of England in 1997, created a credible policy framework in which workers and firms knew that interest rates would be raised if the economy began to overheat, and they tended to moderate their wage claims and price-setting accordingly. Since the Bank of England now sets interest rates independently, people also know that there is no way in which politicians can use expansionary monetary policy for political reasons, such as to gain popularity before an election. This led to a period of relatively stable economic conditions in the UK with economic growth, low inflation and relatively low levels of unemployment right up until around 2008 when the Financial Crisis began to unfold.

In contrast, many European countries suffered relatively high levels of unemployment despite the European Central Bank having independence in the setting of monetary policy. Why was this? One argument that has been put forward to explain high European unemployment in the twenty-first century, and which seems to have some credibility, centres on the level of labour market regulation. As we pointed out above, the 1980s in the UK were characterized both by a weakening of the power of the trade unions and by a reduction in business regulation in general, and in labour market regulation in particular. While, for example, this had the effect of reducing job security for many people by making it easier for employers to terminate contracts, it also had the effect of making labour markets much more flexible. Thus, somewhat paradoxically perhaps, if it is harder to fire someone, firms will think hard before taking on new labour and unemployment may actually rise. Similarly, the minimum wage is typically set at a much higher level (relative to the average wage) in European countries like France and Germany, which again is a reason why the natural rate of unemployment might be higher in those countries.

Data on the history of UK inflation and unemployment from the early 1970s shows very little evidence of the simple negative relationship between these two variables that Phillips had originally observed. In particular, as inflation remained high in the early 1970s, people's expectations of inflation caught up with reality, and the unemployment rate rose along with inflation. By the mid-1970s, policymakers had concluded that Friedman and Phelps had appeared to have been correct in that there is no trade-off between inflation and unemployment in the long run.

SELF TEST Draw the short-run Phillips curve and the long-run Phillips curve. Explain why they are different.

THE LONG-RUN VERTICAL PHILLIPS CURVE AS AN ARGUMENT FOR CENTRAL BANK INDEPENDENCE

The question over whether monetary policy should be in the hands of an elected government or an unelected central banker rests in part on accountability. Most developed economies have opted to give central banks operational independence over monetary policy.

To see why, suppose the economy is at a point with the natural rate of unemployment and a low level of inflation. If a government is in charge of monetary policy, it can direct the central bank to change interest rates or the money supply. Now imagine that this government was facing a general election in two years' time. There is every temptation to provide a short-term stimulus by reducing interest rates and expanding the money supply so that the economy moves along the short-run Phillips curve. This stimulus might be a vote winner, but once the election has been fought people's expectations of inflation catch up with actual inflation. The short-run Phillips curve will shift up and the economy will return to its natural rate of unemployment, but now with a higher level of inflation. In the long run the economy is in a worse state than if monetary policy had remained neutral.

This story implies a cynical view of politics, and most governments would strenuously deny that they would carry out such policies just to get re-elected. More importantly, however, the story also implies that people (workers and managers of firms) are easily duped. Why? Because everyone will know that the government has a strong incentive to pursue an expansionary monetary policy just before an election. In fact, firms and workers may begin raising prices and wages before the election in anticipation of the expansionary monetary policy. This is an interesting result and one worth stressing. If people believe that the government is about to pursue an expansionary monetary policy, then inflationary expectations will increase. Inflation will rise but unemployment will not fall. In essence, the economy jumps immediately to the new long-run equilibrium.

Credibility of policy is a crucial factor in macroeconomics. The importance of expectations is such that if control of monetary policy is given to the central bank and a clear mandate is given about its role, expectations adjust to the policy. It is then more likely that inflation will be stable. The central bank's incentives are different from those of an elected government. Provided its actions are credible, the economy ends up with unemployment no different from that if a government was in control of monetary policy, but with a lower level of inflation.

There are also potential benefits to governments of having an independent central bank in charge of monetary policy. If the government controlled monetary policy it might reason that firms and workers may factor the government's temptation into their price and wage setting. In this instance the economy would jump to the long-run equilibrium just before the election.

This situation is an example of a *Nash equilibrium*. Remember that a Nash equilibrium is a situation in which economic actors interacting with one another each choose their best strategy given the strategies that all the other actors have chosen. Here, firms and workers know that if they do not raise inflationary expectations before an election, the government will most likely pursue an expansionary monetary policy. But they will lose out because their prices and wages will be lower in real terms. As a result, they raise inflationary expectations and the short-run Phillips curve shifts up, moving the economy to a long-run equilibrium with higher inflation and the natural rate of unemployment. Does the government still have the same temptation to inflate at this new equilibrium? Possibly, but there will certainly be some point on the vertical, long-run Phillips curve where inflation is already so high that the government will not want to risk pushing it higher, even if it means a short-run reduction in unemployment. If firms and workers can guess roughly what this level of inflation is, they will set their wages and prices so that the economy will jump straight to that point. If, at this point, the government has no temptation to inflate the economy to gain popularity, and if firms and workers know this so that they have no incentive to change their price and wage setting behaviour, then we will have reached the Nash equilibrium.

Another way of thinking about this is to say that the Nash equilibrium represents the *time consistent policy*. A time consistent policy is simply one which a government does not have a temptation to renege on at some point in time and will usually represent a Nash equilibrium.

This new point may represent time consistency in economic policy. However, it is actually worse than the original position for the government's electoral chances, since inflation is higher and unemployment is still at the natural rate. Hence the best thing to do to maximize the chances of re-election is for the government to make the central bank independent, in the sense of handing over control of monetary policy. This is provided of course that the central bank sees its role as the guardian of price stability. In other words, provided that the central bank is 'conservative' with respect to price stability.

It is a testimony to the power of macroeconomic theory that this argument has persuaded many governments around the world to grant independence to their central bank in the conduct of monetary policy. The European Central Bank, for example, has been independent since its inception in 1998, and the

Bank of England was granted independence in 1997. The European Central Bank both designs its monetary policy (for example, decides what level of inflation in the euro area to aim for) and implements it. The Bank of England, on the other hand, has independence in the implementation of monetary policy but its inflation target is set by the UK Chancellor of the Exchequer.

SHIFTS IN THE PHILLIPS CURVE: THE ROLE OF SUPPLY SHOCKS

Friedman and Phelps had suggested in 1968 that changes in expected inflation shift the short-run Phillips curve. Indeed, the experience of the early 1970s convinced many economists that Friedman and Phelps were right. Within a few years, however, the economics profession would turn its attention to a different source of shifts in the short-run Phillips curve: shocks to AS.

Conflict between Israel and its Arab neighbours triggered a series of oil price shocks as Arab oil producers used their market power to exert political pressure on Western governments who supported Israel. In 1974, the Organization of Petroleum Exporting Countries (OPEC) also began to exert its power as a cartel to increase its members' profits. The countries of OPEC, such as Saudi Arabia, Kuwait and Iraq, restricted the amount of crude oil they pumped and sold on world markets. This reduction in supply caused the price of oil to almost double over a few years in the 1970s.

A large increase in the world price of oil is an example of a supply shock. A **supply shock** is an event that directly affects firms' costs of production and thus the prices they charge. It shifts the economy's AS curve and, as a result, the Phillips curve. Oil is a constituent part of so many production processes that increases in its price have far-reaching effects. For example, when an oil price increase raises the cost of producing petrol, heating oil, tyres, plastic products, distribution and many other products, it reduces the quantity of goods and services supplied at any given price level. As panel (a) of Figure 14.6 shows, this reduction in supply is represented by the leftwards shift in the AS curve from AS_1 to AS_2. The price level rises from P_1 to P_2, output falls from Y_1 to Y_2 and the economy experiences stagflation.

supply shock an event that directly alters firms' costs and prices, shifting the economy's AS curve and thus the Phillips curve

FIGURE 14.6

An Adverse Shock to Aggregate Supply

Panel (a) shows the model of AD and AS. When the AS curve shifts to the left from AS_1 to AS_2, the equilibrium moves from point A to point B. Output falls from Y_1 to Y_2, and the price level rises from P_1 to P_2. Panel (b) shows the short-run trade-off between inflation and unemployment. The adverse shift in AS moves the economy from a point with lower unemployment and lower inflation (point A) to a point with higher unemployment and higher inflation (point B). The short-run Phillips curve shifts to the right from PC_1 to PC_2. Policymakers now face a worse trade-off between inflation and unemployment.

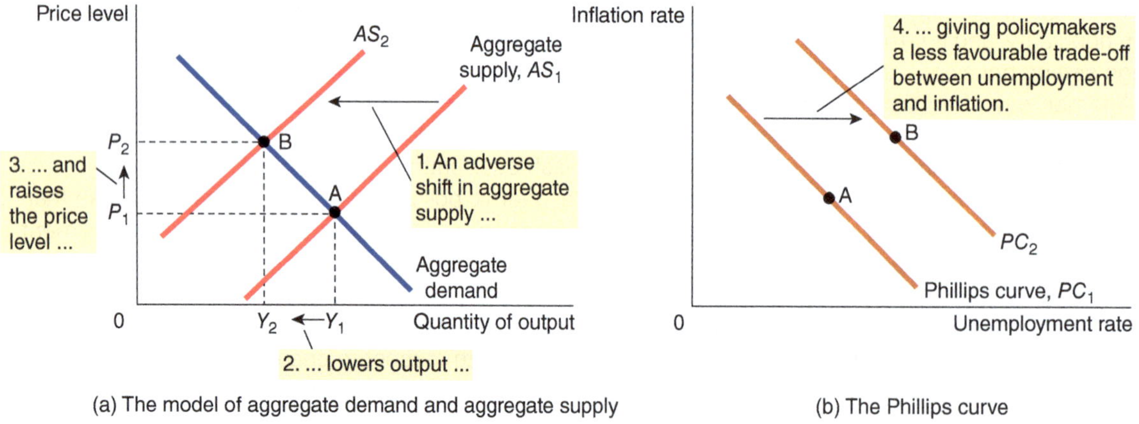

This shift in AS is associated with a similar shift in the short-run Phillips curve, shown in panel (b). Because firms need fewer workers to produce the smaller output, employment falls and unemployment rises. Because the price level is higher, the inflation rate – the percentage change in the price level from the previous year – is also higher. Thus, the shift in AS leads to higher unemployment and higher inflation. The short-run trade-off between inflation and unemployment shifts to the right from PC_1 to PC_2.

Confronted with an adverse shift in AS, policymakers face a difficult choice between fighting inflation and fighting unemployment. If they contract AD to fight inflation, they will raise unemployment further. If they expand AD to fight unemployment, they will raise inflation further. In other words, policymakers face a less favourable trade-off between inflation and unemployment than they did before the shift in AS. They must live with a higher rate of inflation for a given rate of unemployment, a higher rate of unemployment for a given rate of inflation, or some combination of higher unemployment and higher inflation.

An important question is whether this adverse shift in the Phillips curve is temporary or permanent. The answer depends on how people adjust their expectations of inflation. If people view the rise in inflation due to the supply shock as a temporary aberration, expected inflation does not change and the Phillips curve will soon revert to its former position. If people believe the shock will lead to a new era of higher inflation, then expected inflation rises and the Phillips curve remains at its new, less desirable position.

SELF TEST Give an example of a favourable shock to AS. Use the model of AD and AS to explain the effects of such a shock. How does it affect the Phillips curve?

THE COST OF REDUCING INFLATION

In the first half of the 2020s, a number of governments faced the challenge of high inflation. In Lebanon, for example, inflation in 2020 was 84.9 per cent, according to the World Bank, in Nigeria it was 11.4 per cent and in Türkiye almost 79 per cent. In the UK, the CPI reached 11.1 per cent and across the EU, 10.6 per cent in October 2022. If the Phillips curve trade-off holds, then governments seeking to reduce inflation must accept higher rates of unemployment because economic growth will be reduced. Economists have attempted to quantify the effects of **disinflation**, the reduction in the rate of inflation.

disinflation the reduction in the rate of inflation

The Sacrifice Ratio

To reduce the inflation rate, the central bank must pursue contractionary monetary policy. Figure 14.7 shows some of the effects of such a decision. When the central bank slows the rate at which the money supply is growing, it contracts AD. The fall in AD, in turn, reduces the quantity of goods and services that firms produce, and this fall in production leads to a fall in employment. The economy begins at point A in the figure and moves along the short-run Phillips curve to point B, which has lower inflation and higher unemployment. Over time, as people come to understand that prices are rising more slowly, expected inflation falls and the short-run Phillips curve shifts downwards. The economy moves from point B to point C. Inflation is lower and unemployment is back at its natural rate.

Thus, if a nation wants to reduce inflation, it must endure a period of high unemployment and low output. In Figure 14.7, this cost is represented by the movement of the economy through point B as it travels from point A to point C. The size of this cost depends on the slope of the Phillips curve and how quickly expectations of inflation adjust to the new monetary policy.

FIGURE 14.7

Disinflationary Monetary Policy in the Short Run and Long Run

When the central bank pursues contractionary monetary policy to reduce inflation, the economy moves along a short-run Phillips curve from point A to point B. Over time, expected inflation falls and the short-run Phillips curve shifts downwards. When the economy reaches point C, unemployment is back at its natural rate.

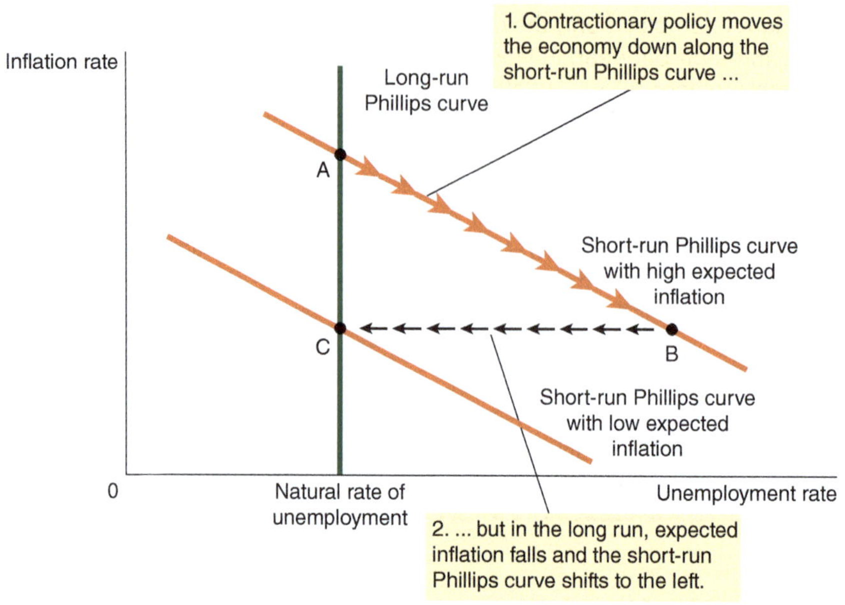

Many studies have examined the data on inflation and unemployment to estimate the cost of reducing inflation. The findings of these studies are often summarized in a statistic called the **sacrifice ratio**. The sacrifice ratio is the number of percentage points of annual output lost in the process of reducing inflation by 1 percentage point given by the equation:

$$\text{Sacrifice ratio} = \frac{\text{Euro cost of loss of production}}{\text{Percentage change in inflation}}$$

A typical estimate of the sacrifice ratio is around three to five. That is, for each percentage point that inflation is reduced, 3 to 5 per cent of annual output must be sacrificed in the transition.

> **sacrifice ratio** the number of percentage points of annual output lost in the process of reducing inflation by 1 percentage point

According to studies of the Phillips curve and the cost of disinflation, this sacrifice could be paid in various ways. Assume that inflation was running at 10 per cent and a government wanted to reduce it to 5 per cent. If each percentage point reduction in inflation would cost 3 per cent of annual output, then the cost would be 15 per cent of annual output lost in a year. Such an outcome would be extremely harsh. Another option would be to spread out the cost over several years. If the reduction in inflation took place over five years, for instance, then output would have to average only 3 per cent below trend during that period to add up to a sacrifice of 15 per cent. An even more gradual approach would be to reduce inflation slowly over a decade. Whatever path was chosen, however, reducing inflation would not be easy.

Rational Expectations and the Possibility of Costless Disinflation

As policymakers in the early 1980s wrestled with high inflation and considered the costs of reducing inflation, a group of economics professors was leading an intellectual revolution that would challenge the conventional wisdom on the sacrifice ratio. This group included such prominent economists as Robert Lucas, Thomas Sargent and Robert Barro. Their revolution was based on a new approach to economic theory and policy called **rational expectations**.

rational expectations the theory according to which people optimally use all the information they have, including information about government policies, when forecasting the future

The rational expectations model came to supplant the **adaptive expectations** model, which was the idea that individuals and organizations base their expectations of inflation in the future on past actual inflation rates. Critics of the adaptive expectations model argued that individuals take into account more information when forming their judgement than simply past inflation rates. The rational expectations model accounted for this available information. According to the theory of rational expectations, therefore, people optimally use all the information they have, including information about government policies, when forecasting the future.

adaptive expectations a model which states that individuals and organizations base their expectations of inflation in the future on past actual inflation rates

This new approach has had profound implications for many areas of macroeconomics, but none is more important than its application to the trade-off between inflation and unemployment. As Friedman and Phelps had emphasized, expected inflation is an important variable that explains why there is a trade-off between inflation and unemployment in the short run but not in the long run. How quickly the short-run trade-off disappears depends on how quickly expectations adjust. Proponents of rational expectations built on the Friedman–Phelps analysis argue that when economic policies change, people adjust their expectations of inflation accordingly. Studies of inflation and unemployment that tried to estimate the sacrifice ratio had failed to take account of the direct effect of the policy regime on expectations. As a result, estimates of the sacrifice ratio were, according to the rational expectations theorists, unreliable guides for policy.

In a 1982 paper entitled 'The End of Four Big Inflations' (one of which was the UK inflation of the late 1970s and early 1980s), Thomas Sargent described this new view as follows:

> *An alternative 'rational expectations' view denies that there is any inherent momentum to the present process of inflation. This view maintains that firms and workers have now come to expect high rates of inflation in the future and that they strike inflationary bargains in light of these expectations. However, it is held that people expect high rates of inflation in the future precisely because the government's current and prospective monetary and fiscal policies warrant those expectations . . . An implication of this view is that inflation can be stopped much more quickly than advocates of the 'momentum' view have indicated, and that their estimates of the length of time and the costs of stopping inflation in terms of forgone output are erroneous. This is not to say that it would be easy to eradicate inflation. On the contrary, it would require more than a few temporary restrictive fiscal and monetary actions. It would require a change in the policy regime . . . How costly such a move would be in terms of forgone output and how long it would be in taking effect would depend partly on how resolute and evident the government's commitment was.*

According to Sargent, the sacrifice ratio could be much smaller than suggested by previous estimates. Indeed, in the most extreme case, it could be zero. If the government made a credible commitment to a policy of low inflation, people would be rational enough to lower their expectations of inflation immediately. The short-run Phillips curve would shift downwards, and the economy would reach low inflation quickly without the cost of temporarily high unemployment and low output. The credibility of government policy is thus of prime importance.

SELF TEST What is the sacrifice ratio? How might an improvement in a government's credibility of its commitment to reduce inflation affect the sacrifice ratio?

FYI

Wage Curve Theory

We have said that Phillips' research looked at the relationship between the rate of growth of wages and unemployment. The relationship of the wage rate to unemployment takes us a small step towards linking the level of inflation with unemployment. The rate of growth in wages is a factor that influences the overall level of prices in the economy. Wages represent a cost to employers. Other things being equal, if they rise then employers might well seek to raise prices to cover the increased cost. If this happens throughout the economy on an aggregate level, wage growth leads to inflation. If the rate of growth of wages slows down, we might expect the labour market to be looser. In other words, the demand for labour in relation to the supply of labour would be falling. Under normal market conditions, we would expect the wage rate to start to fall. In reality, this translates to the slowing down in the rate of growth of wages.

Further research into the Phillips curve led to the development of the so-called expectations augmented Phillips curve, captured in the following equation:

$$\Delta p_t = E_t \Delta p_t + 1 + (NR_t - RU_t)$$

This says that the change in the inflation rate in a time period (Δp_t) is equal to expected inflation in a time period ($E_t \Delta p_t + 1$) and the natural rate of unemployment minus the national unemployment rate (RU_t). This helped to explain what seemed to be happening in many Western economies in the 1970s. Households were *anticipating* inflation in the future and basing their behaviour and decision-making on those expectations. Therefore, the Phillips curve was shifting. This helped to explain how higher inflation might also be experienced at the same time as higher unemployment, so-called 'stagflation'.

There have, however, been a number of economists who have questioned the existence of the Phillips curve. One economist did pose that very question. David Blanchflower has worked at several institutions, including the University of Surrey and Warwick University in the UK. He is a former member of the Bank of England's Monetary Policy Committee and works at Dartmouth College in New Hampshire in the United States.

Remember that the assumption of the Phillips curve is that there is a relationship between the rate of growth of wages and unemployment. When unemployment rises, the *rate of growth of wages* falls and vice versa. This makes intuitive sense, since if there is a large pool of unemployed workers, employed workers will be hesitant to push for higher wage claims for fear of joining the ranks of the unemployed.

Blanchflower has been quoted as suggesting that as a result of his work, 'the Phillips curve is wrong, it's as fundamental as that'. The following is a summary of his analysis in support of this view.

The traditional Phillips curve relates the rate of growth of wages with the level of unemployment. Within this relationship, a higher level of unemployment is associated with a lower level of the rate of growth of wages. Conversely, if unemployment rates were low, the rate of growth of wages would be higher. Such a relationship is given as a macroeconomic one rather than microeconomic, that is it holds for the economy as a whole. If the level of unemployment increases, therefore, it suggests there will be excess supply in the labour market. In such cases, the labour market will adjust and the rate of growth of wages will fall to eliminate the excess supply.

Blanchflower and his colleague, Andrew Oswald, spent time researching links between unemployment and wage rates at a *microeconomic level* and found that the relationship between unemployment and wages might be different depending on the region that was being investigated. Their research looked at the *level of pay* rather than the rate of growth of wages. They argued that the *level* of pay was negatively related to the level of unemployment rather than the rate of growth in pay.

According to this argument, a worker in Region A, which has a high level of unemployment, would earn lower wages than an equivalent worker in Region B with lower levels of unemployment. Blanchflower and Oswald's research

(*Continued*)

casts doubt upon the standard explanation, in both regional economics and labour economics, that the wage rate in an area is positively linked to the level of unemployment in an area. In other words, the higher the level of unemployment, the higher the wage level needed to persuade someone to work in that area and vice versa.

Their work would tend to call into question some of the basic laws of economics, particularly those related to something like the minimum wage. The conventional wisdom might be that if the minimum wage was introduced into an economy, the higher wage levels would be associated with a rise in unemployment. Blanchflower and Oswald's analysis suggests that this may not be the case, and that in some areas there might even be a rise in the level of employment associated with a rise in wage levels.

Figure 14.8 highlights the traditional view of the effect of the imposition of a minimum wage (*MW*) set above the market wage level (W_1) on the level of unemployment. The minimum wage causes a fall in the quantity of labour demanded and an increase in the quantity supplied of labour (a movement along the *D* and *S* curves for labour). The result is an increase in the amount of unemployment, shown by the distance $Q_3 - Q_2$.

FIGURE 14.8

The Traditional Explanation of the Effect of a Minimum Wage Set above the Equilibrium Wage Level

If the minimum wage (MW) is above the equilibrium level (W_1), then unemployment is the difference between Q_3 and Q_2.

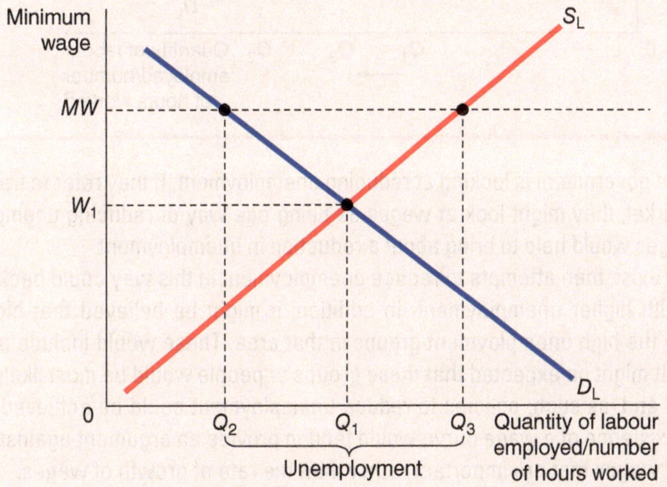

To understand this, it is important to refer back to the basic model of the labour market shown in Figure 14.9. If the demand for labour, for example, rose as indicated by a shift in the demand for labour curve to the right (D_L to D_{L1}), then there would be an excess demand for labour shown by the distance $Q_2 - Q_1$. Wage rates would rise in response to this shortage of labour and as the shortage is competed away, more people would end up being employed (Q_3) at higher wage rates (W_2). A rise in wage rates, therefore, is positively correlated with a fall in unemployment and vice versa.

Blanchflower and Oswald's research was based around millions of observations. They identified the existence of wage curves in 16 countries, and since the publication of their research in 1994 a number of other researchers have confirmed their findings. Blanchflower and Oswald suggested that their wage curve would have an elasticity of −0.1. What this refers to is the responsiveness of rates of pay to changes in unemployment. An elasticity of −0.1, therefore, would suggest that if we took two regions within an economy, Region A and Region B, and if unemployment was 2 per cent in Region B but 4 per cent in Region A, we would expect wages to be around 10 per cent lower in Region A than in Region B. This suggests some sort of causal relationship stemming from the level of unemployment in an area feeding through to the level of wages in that area, rather than the other way around.

The suggestion that there is a relationship between the rate of growth of wages (and by implication, inflation) and unemployment, as we saw in the early part of this chapter, has implications for policymakers. This is based in part on the idea that controlling the rate of growth in wages (and hence inflation) is an important step in controlling unemployment. If, however, Blanchflower and Oswald's research on wage curves is correct, it changes the emphasis of policymaking at both a macro and micro level.

(*Continued*)

FIGURE 14.9

A Microeconomic Model of the Labour Market

A shift in the labour demand curve creates unemployment of the difference between Q_3 and Q_2.

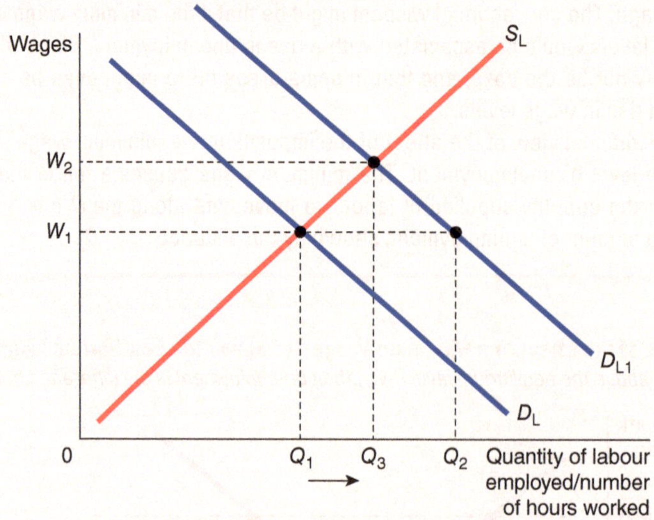

Let us assume that the government is looking at reducing unemployment. If they refer to traditional macroeconomic models of the labour market, they might look at wages as being one way of reducing unemployment in that area. In other words, a fall in wages would help to bring about a reduction in unemployment.

If a wage curve does exist, then attempts to reduce unemployment in this way could backfire, since falling wages would be associated with higher unemployment. In addition, it might be believed that high unemployment might affect most dramatically the high unemployment groups in that area. These would include people with low levels of education, for example. It might be expected that these groups of people would be most likely to take on jobs that are created at lower wages and, as such, policies to reduce unemployment could be achieved without a major impact on inflation. Again, the existence of a wage curve would tend to provide an argument against doing this. This is partly because it is the *level* of wages that are important rather than the rate of growth of wages.

CRITICAL THINKING POINT In 2018, the Chair of the Federal Reserve, Jerome Powell, was quoted as saying: '[The] persistent shortfall in inflation from our target has led some to question the traditional relationship between inflation and the unemployment rate, also known as the Phillips curve. [...] My view is that the data continue to show a relationship between the overall state of the labor market and the change in inflation over time. That connection has weakened over the past couple of decades, but it still persists, and I believe it continues to be meaningful for monetary policy.'

How far does the 'connection' have to weaken before it becomes meaningless for monetary policy? (Source: Powell, J.H. (2018) 'The Outlook for the U.S. Economy.' Speech given at the Economics Club of Chicago (April 6). Available at www.cato.org/cato-journal/winter-2020/phillips-curve-poor-guide-monetary-policy#references, accessed 7 August 2025)

INFLATION TARGETING

In many countries of the world today, including the UK and the euro area, the framework of monetary policy involves setting targets for inflation to be achieved over the medium term of two years or so, and then adjusting interest rates to achieve this objective. Inflation targeting arose partly because attempts to control the money supply in the 1980s proved extremely difficult. Governments announced targets for the growth in the money supply, and invariably these targets were missed. Explicit money supply targeting was abandoned in favour of a target for inflation.

In the case of the Bank of England, the inflation target is set by the Chancellor of the Exchequer and is currently 2.0 per cent. The ECB, Sweden's Riksbank and Norway's Norges Bank all also have inflation targets of 2 per cent; and the Swiss National Bank (SNB) has a target of 'less than 2 per cent per annum'.

Central banks are tasked with using the tools at their disposal, including interest rates and quantitative easing, to guide inflation to the target. Central banks use models such as dynamic stochastic general equilibrium (DSGE) models to forecast inflation and adjust policy in the light of expected differences between forecast inflation and the target. The framework under which monetary policy is conducted could be carried out by applying rules. Indeed, Milton Friedman advocated the use of such rules to help central banks stick to publicly announced measures by which the money supply would increase each year. Such rules would be 'simple, predictable, and credible', and prevent central banks from making bad decisions which might have damaging economic effects. Ben Bernanke, former chair of the US Federal Reserve, however, preferred to have a broader framework which he termed 'constrained discretion'. **Constrained discretion** involves the recognition of a clear goal (or target) but allows policymakers the freedom to respond to economic, financial and political shocks using all the data available and their collective judgement. The use of constrained discretion allows for inflation to not always be at target, but to be achieved over a period, typically defined as the medium term of two to three years. The primacy of stable prices is also important in a successful inflation-targeting regime. If central banks lose sight of the focus of setting policy to achieve stable prices by, for example, setting policy to focus on unemployment, exchange rates or wages, then credibility will be lost.

constrained discretion a monetary policy framework which acknowledges a clear goal (or target) but allows policymakers the freedom to respond to economic, financial and political shocks using all the data available and their collective judgement

Types of Targeting

The level of the money supply and the exchange rate can be thought of as intermediate targets of monetary policy. That is to say, they may be targeted in order to achieve certain other policy objectives, such as real GDP growth, employment and inflation. An important principle we have learnt in our study of monetary policy is that many economists believe that in the long run, monetary policy cannot affect the real side of the economy, that is real GDP and employment. In the long run, the only final target of monetary policy can be the inflation rate. Therefore, targeting the money supply or the exchange rate as a framework for monetary policy means that we are targeting those variables because it is felt that they will ultimately affect the rate of price inflation. Also, since neither the money supply nor the exchange rate is directly controllable, they cannot be instruments of monetary policy. In other words, the central bank cannot just set the level of the money supply it wants. It must attempt to bring about that level by open market operations and other means. Similarly, it cannot just set the level of the exchange rate it wants. It must try to bring about that level by setting interest rates and other means. Hence the money supply and the exchange rate should really be viewed as intermediate targets that the central bank may aim for, because it is believed that they will ultimately affect the final target of inflation. So why not just target the inflation rate? Interest rates (or at least some interest rates) are under the control of central banks, so they are definitely an instrument of monetary policy. We know that raising interest rates reduces AD and so dampens inflation. Monetary authorities could just raise interest rates whenever inflation rose above a level that was considered desirable, say 2 per cent. This would be a crude form of inflation targeting.

There are two problems with this crude inflation targeting. First, changing (or not changing) interest rates today will not affect inflation today, rather it will only affect inflation in the future, since it takes time for the policy to have an effect on the economy. Second, there may be other factors that would affect inflation in the future. Suppose, for example, that inflation was at its target of 2 per cent per year. The central bank, therefore, decides not to change interest rates, since it is achieving its inflation target. However, suppose there was, at the same time, a wave of very high wage settlements in the economy, above any increases in labour productivity. Over the next six months to a year, this is expected to lead to a rise in price inflation in the economy as workers spend more and as firms pass on some of the wage increases in the form of higher prices. Should the central bank wait for the inflation to arrive, or should it act now by raising interest rates in anticipation of the inflationary pressures coming from higher wages? It can be argued that the better policy is to target not today's inflation, as it is already too late to have any effect on that, but future inflation. Of course, no one knows with certainty what future inflation is going to be, therefore a policy of inflation targeting generally involves targeting the forecast rate of inflation.

The success of the central bank in achieving its target over the medium term is dependent in large part on its ability to accurately forecast inflation up to two years ahead. In the interests of transparency and credibility, the Bank of England publishes detailed analyses of its forecasts, and these are closely scrutinized. In the case of the Bank of England, if actual inflation does fall outside a range of plus or minus 1 per cent of the target, the Governor of the Bank of England is required to write a formal, public letter to the Chancellor of the Exchequer, explaining why inflation is out of the target range, what measures are being taken to get it back on course, and when it is expected to be back on target.

The Taylor Rule

Constrained discretion allows policymakers some leeway in making policy in response to economic, financial and political shocks to the economy. In addition to models, survey data and judgement, there may be some use of 'rules' in deciding monetary policy. In 1993 John Taylor, an economist at Stanford University in the United States, spent some time observing the behaviour of the Federal Reserve's Federal Open Market Committee (FOMC). Taylor's observations led him to put forward what has become known as the *Taylor rule*, which has been an influential idea since it was published. For many economists, focus has centred on the extent to which the rule is followed in interest rate decision-making around the world, if at all. John Taylor was observing the US economy and the work of the FOMC. Inflation in the United States had come under a far greater degree of control in the 1980s when the FOMC was headed by Paul Volcker. Part of Taylor's conclusion was that the FOMC had reacted more aggressively to inflation than had occurred before 1979. His observations led to the notion of the interest rate setting body 'leaning into the wind' when it came to inflation. By this he meant being willing to raise rates more significantly in response to an inflation threat (when the economy was deemed to be overheating, for example), and reducing interest rates if there was a slowdown in the economy along with a threat of recession, than had been the case prior to 1979.

Taylor suggested that the pattern of FOMC behaviour with regard to interest rates during the period 1979–92 could be expressed as an equation – the 'rule'. This equation, given below, has been simplified, but in essence captures the main flavour of his original work:

$$r = p + 0.5y + 0.5(p - 2) + 2$$

where r = the short-term interest rate in percentage terms per annum; p = the rate of inflation over the previous four quarters measured as the GDP deflator; and y = the difference between real GDP and potential output (the 'output gap').

Taylor made a number of assumptions about the US economy in this equation. He assumed that there was a target level of inflation, which he put at 2 per cent. He also made an assumption that the equilibrium real interest rate was also 2 per cent. The equation offers a rule or guide to policymakers about what the level of interest rates should be if there is a target for inflation of 2 per cent. In effect, interest rates can be set in response to the deviation of inflation from the target and the deviation of real output from potential output. It suggests that the response to inflation or output being off target should be met with a more aggressive response to monetary policy. This is the so-called leaning into the wind.

Suppose, for example, that the output gap was zero – that actual GDP was at its potential level – but that inflation was currently 5 per cent, 3 per cent above the assumed target level of 2 per cent. Then the Taylor rule would suggest that the central bank should aim to set the short-term interest rate at 8.5 per cent, corresponding to a real rate of interest of 8.5 − 5 = 3.5 per cent. If, however, GDP was, say, 2 per cent below its potential level, so that there was an output gap of −2 per cent, then the Taylor rule would suggest setting the nominal interest rate a little lower, at 7.5 per cent.

Studies have shown that a number of countries seem to have patterns of interest rates that follow the Taylor rule relatively closely. In reality, Taylor and other researchers appreciated that decision-makers could not stick rigidly to such a rule, because sometimes circumstances might dictate the need to apply discretion. Taylor argued that while a rule gave a guideline to policymakers, it also implied that any deviation from the rule had to be explained through a coherent and well-argued case, and that such a discipline was helpful to overall monetary policy decisions.

Nominal GDP Targeting

Inflation targeting has been the subject of some debate and criticism in the aftermath of the 2007–9 Financial Crisis. The typical expectation of post-recession macroeconomic variables is for a gradual recovery, growth beginning to pick up and, as it does, inflationary pressures slowly building. As the output gap narrows, the labour market becomes tighter as demand for labour rises, unemployment falls and wage growth begins to accelerate. Central banks following an inflation target will monitor these developments and adjust monetary policy as appropriate, to guide inflation to target. As unemployment falls and inflation accelerates (the expected Phillips curve relationship), interest rates will be gradually increased, moderating the expansion in output and keeping the economy relatively stable.

The experience of some countries, notably the UK and the United States, was somewhat different. The unemployment rate fell well below its estimated natural rate, GDP had been positive but sluggish, and inflation did not accelerate as might have been expected, especially given the size of quantitative easing. The Bank of England's repo rate remained at 0.5 per cent from 2009 to 2016 when it was reduced to 0.25 per cent following the referendum on the UK's membership of the EU. In November 2017 it was raised back to 0.5 per cent and in August 2018 to 0.75 per cent. Bank rate was reduced to 0.1 per cent in response to the Covid-19 pandemic and remained at this level until December 2021 when rates rose to 0.25 per cent. The Bank of England's asset purchasing facility (QE) stood at £435bn in January 2019. This was expanded considerably in response to the pandemic and in November 2021 stood at £895 billion. The Bank of England itself stated that, 'The objective of quantitative easing is to boost the money supply through large-scale asset purchases and, in so doing, to bring about a level of nominal demand consistent with meeting the inflation target in the medium term' (Source: Bank of England Market Operations Guide January 2025. Available at www.bankofengland.co.uk/markets/bank-of-england-market-operations-guide accessed 7 August 2025).

Given this economic situation, critics argued that the Bank of England had 'unofficially' departed from inflation targeting. Some economists argued that the relationship between inflation and unemployment had broken down, with inflation and unemployment moving in the same direction. The Bank of England pointed out that its primary remit from the UK Chancellor is to maintain price stability. It also noted, however, that it is also expected to support the government's policy for growth and employment. Critics argue that the two targets are compromised if inflation targeting is used.

Another option which has been suggested by some economists as a preferable way to conduct monetary policy would be to target nominal GDP (NGDP). NGDP is the total expenditure in the economy calculated by multiplying output by the price at which that output is sold. If NGDP rises, this will be due to a rise in prices, a rise in output or a combination of the two. If prices rise by 2 per cent and output increases by 1 per cent, NGDP rises by 3 per cent.

NGDP targeting would mean that a central bank would use the tools at its disposal to target a particular growth rate of NGDP. If NGDP fell below trend, as happened in the recession following the 2007–9 Financial Crisis, the central bank would expand the money supply through a combination of interest rate changes and open market operations. The consequence of this might be inflation accelerating beyond any notional target for a period, but the benefit would be that unemployment would not fall as much as would be the case under inflation targeting. If NGDP accelerated beyond trend, the central bank would tighten monetary policy and, as a result, inflation might be under 'target' for a period.

Proponents of NGDP targeting claim that it would not mitigate against all external shocks (such as the rapid fall in oil prices experienced in 2014–15). It would, however, result in a more stable economy without the swings in unemployment, which can be so damaging to people and the economy as a whole. Part of the reason for this claim is that the decision to make people redundant in the midst of a recession tends to be delayed (unemployment, remember is a lagging indicator) and an assumption that wages are sticky. If spending in the economy falls, wages do not adjust downwards, and firms find themselves having to pay wages to workers whose skills are not being exploited to the full. If wages do not fall, then the ultimate option facing firms is to let workers go. Under NGDP targeting, when spending falls, the central bank would expand the money supply to stimulate the economy, even if this meant that inflation gathered pace. Such a policy implies that the perceived costs of inflation in the short to medium term are less than the costs of higher unemployment which may be experienced under an inflation targeting policy.

The experience of the UK, the United States and Europe in recent years has seen the behaviour of inflation, growth and unemployment not following the patterns that economists expect. The global Covid-19 pandemic and the conflicts in Ukraine and Gaza have further muddied the waters. Economists are asking what might explain the change in the relationship between inflation and unemployment since the Financial Crisis. Without a clear understanding of central bank policy, markets find it difficult to forecast, plan and make decisions, which in itself can lead to instability.

NGDP targeting is not a new idea. The 1977 Nobel Prize winner, James Meade (who supported Phillips' promotion at the LSE in the 1950s), made reference to the idea in his Prize lecture. Other economists, including Martin Weale, a former member of the Monetary Policy Committee (MPC), and Sir Charles Bean, former Deputy Governor of the Bank of England and now Professor of Economics at the LSE, have both also explored the idea at different times in their career.

Whether NGDP would have been a better policy option in the wake of the 2007–9 Financial Crisis is, like much in economics, open to debate. Much depends on the period of time over which we consider economic variables such as growth, inflation and unemployment. Supporters of inflation targeting would argue that the policy in most developed countries is not so rigid as to ignore the wider economic environment. Therefore, inflation above or below target can be accommodated by inflation targeting provided the target is maintained in the medium term. The CPI in the UK, for example, fluctuated over the period from 2015 to 2024 as highlighted in Figure 14.10, but the average over this period has been just over 2.0 per cent. If the 'medium term' is defined as a period of three to four years, then between quarter one of 2015 and quarter four of 2018, the CPI averaged 1.52 per cent. Between quarter one of 2019 and quarter four of 2022, the average was 3.29 per cent. The average between quarter one of 2023 and quarter three of 2024 was 5.3 per cent.

FIGURE 14.10

UK CPI, 2015–2024
CPI (Rate %)

The chart shows that CPI has fluctuated over the period from highs of around 9.4 per cent to lows of 0.0 per cent. The average over the period is 2.77 per cent.

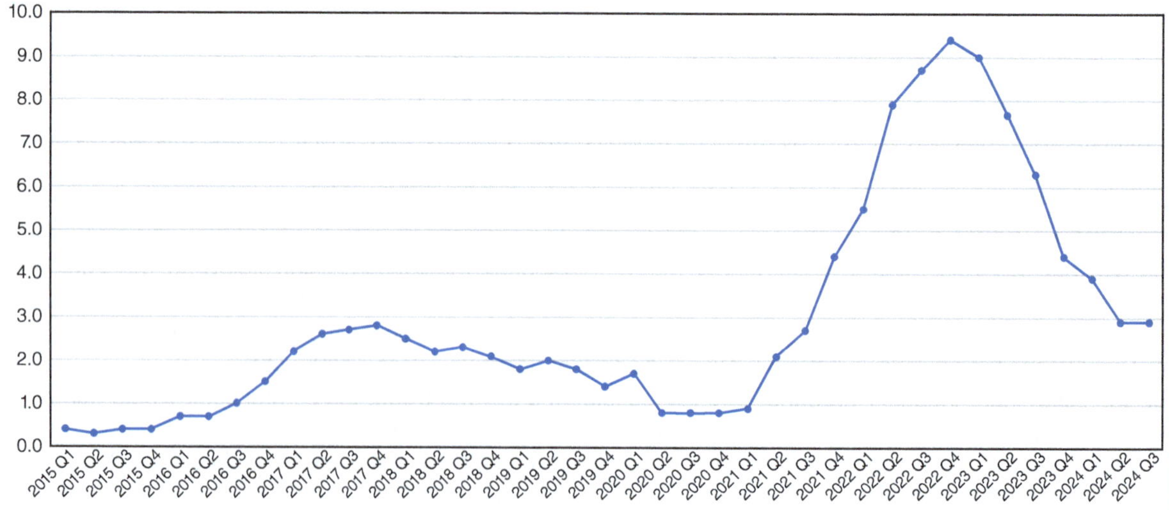

In a speech to the Institute for Economic Affairs (IEA) in February 2013, Sir Charles Bean argued that the Bank had sufficient flexibility to accommodate shocks and to allow inflation to deviate from target. He also argued that given the availability and reliability of data on which to make decisions, the risk inherent in inflation targeting was lower than that of NGDP targeting.

REFLECTING ON THE PHILLIPS CURVE

It is not easy to fully appreciate the extent to which Phillips' 'weekend work' has influenced macroeconomic thinking since the 1960s. Some of the best minds in economics have debated the fundamental notion behind the Phillips curve, that there is a short-run trade-off between inflation and unemployment. In the early years after the Samuelson–Solow paper, then Federal Reserve chair, William McChesney Martin, cast doubt on the suggestion that policymakers had at their disposal a 'menu' of options. One of Martin's criticisms was that focusing just on either an inflation or an unemployment target missed what he described as 'collateral, and perhaps deleterious, side effects on other objectives' (Speech to the Joint Economic Committee of the US Congress, February 1963).

The 1970s witnessed high and accelerating rates of inflation triggered by supply-side shocks. This seemed to confirm what some economists and policymakers had thought, that there was no trade-off between inflation and unemployment. Economists turned their attention to other areas of research, notably the money supply and monetary policy. In the 1990s, however, interest in the Phillips curve was revived and the development of DSGE models incorporated Phillips curve-like relationships. In particular, New Keynesians sought to incorporate the role of expectations in a New Keynesian Phillips curve, which not only took into account expectations of current inflation but also future inflation and how this would impact on firms' marginal cost. This has implications for mark-up pricing, a method where a certain percentage of mark-up is added to the cost of a product to arrive at the selling price, which in turn affects inflation.

The focus on providing a regime which targets inflation and maintains credibility stemmed in part from the success of countries like Switzerland and Germany in maintaining stable, low rates of inflation. By the 2000s, the majority of developed countries had moved to inflation targeting. What this did was herald a shift away from targeting monetary aggregates and focused attention on the role of central banks in the economy. Central banks act to change interest rates when it is forecast that inflation will begin to deviate from target. In so doing, there is an element of monetary discipline built into the actions of the monetary authorities which renders a focus on monetary aggregates redundant. This is one reason why there is criticism in some quarters of the retention of the teaching of the IS–LM model in some undergraduate programmes. Central banks do not 'control' the money supply directly in 'modern' economies.

The New Keynesian Phillips curve links the output gap and inflationary pressures in the economy. Models can provide some estimation of the expected size of the output gap. This in turn helps form expectations of future inflation. There is debate over cause and effect. Is inflation a symptom of an overheating economy or does an overheating economy cause inflation? If central banks take steps to moderate inflation by changing interest rates, the impact on other areas of the economy is not costless. In other words, costless disinflation is a fallacy. The New Keynesian Phillips curve assumes that inflation leads measures of the output gap, but critics argue that the evidence suggests this is not the case. One of the challenges facing economists in understanding the cause and effect is the role of lags in models. Policy actions do not lead to instantaneous changes in inflation, unemployment or growth. Each of these may be subject to different time lags, and this has implications for the outcomes of models used and for the importance of monetary aggregates. If growth in the money supply precedes inflation rather than the other way around, this implies money aggregates may be important in forecasting future inflation. Central banks have a difficult task in juggling the many different variables involved in complex models, getting the direction of cause and effect, and judging the length and importance of time lags in making policy.

The 2007–9 Financial Crisis provided further evidence of the difficulties in identifying cause and effect. One of the agreed causes of the crisis was the extent to which credit had ballooned in many economies, that is economic actors were borrowing extensively. Was such a demand for credit borne out of the fear that interest rates were about to rise and thus borrowing rose substantially in advance? Or was it due to confidence that economies were perceived as strong and would continue to grow in the foreseeable future? The policy response of central banks would need to be different in each case. This is one of the reasons why financial markets are being incorporated into DSGE models as a way of making the models more robust and reflective of the workings of modern economies.

The Flat Phillips Curve?

We have already hinted that the macroeconomy has not 'behaved' in a way that economists would have expected since the 2007–9 Financial Crisis. Unemployment fell below the 'natural rate' in many countries. When this happened, it was expected that wage growth would begin to rise as the labour market continued to tighten. As wage growth accelerates, firms' costs increase, consumption rises and inflation begins to accelerate. This did not happen. Inflation remained below target for a number of years in the United States and the UK following the Financial Crisis, and was relatively stable around target across Europe. This may be partly because wage growth did not accelerate as unemployment fell (and employment rose).

In a speech to the Oxford Economics Society in November 2017, then Deputy Governor for Financial Stability at the Bank of England, and one of the members of the MPC, Sir Jon Cunliffe, questioned whether the Phillips curve was 'lower, flat or hiding?' Cunliffe noted that the unemployment rate was at levels last seen in 1975. At that time, however, average wages rose by 24 per cent, whereas in 2017, average weekly earnings grew by only 2.2 per cent. Cunliffe continued by noting that this was the rate of wage growth in 2011, when unemployment was above 8 per cent. The relationship between inflation and unemployment had 'apparently disappeared'. Cunliffe told his audience that he had no 'answers to the puzzle' but did offer some 'candidate explanations'.

Measures of the Labour Market The labour market is a very different place from the one Phillips and his contemporaries knew. The development of the gig economy, the increased participation rate of women in the labour force, zero hours contracts and the growth of part-time and self-employment mean that wage structures might be very different from those which existed in the 1990s or earlier. It could be the case that the way unemployment is measured, and in particular the capacity of the labour market, is being 'undermeasured'. Cunliffe noted that many people who are employed in part-time jobs, the gig economy and so on, would like to work more. Measuring this might give a better indication of the spare capacity in the labour market and its ability to absorb more workers without wage rates accelerating. Cunliffe is not the first to have raised this as a possible factor. Lena Komileva, chief economist at G+ Economics, has also cited the changing work environment and work practices as factors which may explain why the Phillips curve is flatter.

A Shift of the Phillips Curve Downwards A shift downwards of the Phillips curve is associated with lower levels of unemployment and weaker upwards pressure on wages. Cunliffe noted that the natural rate of unemployment could be lower than estimated, and inflation expectations could also be relatively stable. Thus pressure on wages to rise is equally subdued. Estimates of the natural rate of unemployment could be lower because search and match is more efficient, resulting in lower frictional unemployment. This might also be supported by improvements in education where the labour force is better educated and better able as a result to find new jobs quickly. The number of people having undergraduate degrees in many developed countries has risen as a proportion of the labour force, so there could be some basis for this explanation.

The Slope of the Phillips Curve We have looked at Phillips curves that are downwards sloping from left to right and noted that the long-run Phillips curve is vertical. The downwards slope of the Phillips curve relates the sensitivity of inflation to changes in unemployment, inflation being the dependent variable. The steeper the curve the more sensitive inflation is to changes in unemployment, hence the suggestion that as unemployment falls, the effect on inflation is greater as tight labour markets force up wage costs. As we have seen, however, since the Financial Crisis, the sensitivity of wage costs to unemployment seems to be very low, which would imply a flatter Phillips curve. If the Phillips curve still exists, then it may have become flatter since the Financial Crisis, and Cunliffe suggests that workers' appetite for risk may have changed. The Financial Crisis was so serious that many workers may feel far more insecure than prior to the Crisis. Cunliffe suggests this insecurity may have changed workers' perceptions about the strength of their bargaining power in negotiations over pay, and this may have also been influenced by the effects of the pandemic, which might help explain the lack of growth of wages and a flatter Phillips curve. In addition, the rise of the gig economy, zero hours contracts and globalization has further changed the labour market. Firms build identical plants across the globe and can relatively easily switch production to different plants. Workers know this, and it contributes to their weaker bargaining position and increased insecurity.

The Phillips Curve Has Disappeared The final possibility is that the Phillips curve, as Blanchflower suggested, is simply wrong or doesn't exist anymore. Most economists would agree that the Phillips curve has had to be adapted and reinterpreted in the decades since Phillips' paper. Over that time changes in the labour market and the macroeconomy have necessitated research into the data, and a recognition that the relationship and the factors underlying inflation and unemployment have changed. In addition, as we have seen, it has been suggested that the idea of a natural rate of unemployment does not exist. Rather than there being one equilibrium long-run unemployment rate, there might exist multiple equilibria in the labour market. Cunliffe argues, however, that further empirical and research evidence is necessary before the Phillips curve is consigned to the economics dustbin, and it still has a valuable role to play in macroeconomic policy.

CASE STUDY Key Macroeconomic Data

We have seen how, in the years following the 2007–9 Financial Crisis, the behaviour of inflation and unemployment did not seem to follow economists' expectations. Unemployment across Europe and the UK fell but inflation remained subdued. Then we had the pandemic and conflict in Ukraine which presented significant external shocks and, in particular, disrupted global supply chains. As economies emerged from pandemic restrictions, inflation began to accelerate. As might have been expected, unemployment did spike during the pandemic. In the UK, for example, the unemployment rate reached 5.3 per cent in the fourth quarter of 2020 but then fell and was at 3.6 per cent in the third quarter of 2022. From that point it hovered at around 4 per cent to the start of 2025. This pattern of unemployment was mirrored across the EU with a peak around 7.6 per cent in 2020 falling to around 5.9 per cent at the start of 2025.

The Bank of England and the ECB increased interest rates in response to the acceleration of inflation and rates of inflation did slow. An important question that has to be asked of this particular episode is what the acceleration of inflation was caused by. Was it due to pressures in the labour market that translated through to prices? In the five years before the pandemic, average pay growth hovered around the 2.5 per cent range. Following the pandemic, the rate of growth of wages averaged just over 6 per cent. Was this the cause of the acceleration of inflation or was it a consequence of it? Economists have noted that supply chain constraints pushed goods prices and energy prices much higher and this had a contributory effect on inflation in the UK and Europe. Total consumer spending in the UK, for example, increased by just over 15 per cent between 2020 and 2023. The rate of economic growth in the UK over that period averaged 0.85 per cent, but the figures are somewhat skewed by the dramatic slowdown in the economy in 2020 and the subsequent recovery period. Growth in the latter part of 2024, however, did seem to stall.

Questions:

1 Given the information in the case study, to what extent would you agree that there is a Phillips curve type relationship between unemployment and inflation?

2 If the main cause of inflation is due to supply chain constraints and conflict, does this render policy decisions based on a Phillips curve analysis redundant?

How far are changes in microeconomic markets such as the labour market a driver of wider macroeconomic variables?

(*Continued*)

3 The pandemic and the conflict in Ukraine are examples of significant economic shocks. Are these shocks so specific and unusual that they should not be factored into the debate about the Phillips curve? Or is it the case that while they are 'of their time' they are not really any different from economic shocks that have occurred since the 1970s?

4 To what extent do you agree with the view that the Bank of England and ECB should not have increased interest rates as far as they did and that this is the main reason why economic growth is so sluggish in the UK and across Europe?

References:

ec.europa.eu/eurostat/statistics-explained/index.php?title=Unemployment_statistics, accessed 7 August 2025.

www.imf.org/en/Blogs/Articles/2024/10/16/global-inflationary-episode-offers-lessons-for-monetary-policy, accessed 7 August 2025.

www.ons.gov.uk/employmentandlabourmarket/peoplenotinwork/unemployment/timeseries/mgsx/lms, accessed 7 August 2025.

www.ons.gov.uk/employmentandlabourmarket/peopleinwork/earningsandworkinghours/timeseries/kac3/lms, accessed 7 August 2025.

www.ons.gov.uk/economy/nationalaccounts/satelliteaccounts/datasets/consumertrendschainedvolumemeasureseasonallyadjusted, accessed 7 August 2025.

www.ons.gov.uk/economy/grossdomesticproductgdp/timeseries/ihyp/pn2, accessed 7 August 2025.

CONCLUSION

This chapter has examined how economists' thinking about inflation and unemployment has evolved over time. It is difficult to underestimate the importance of the Phillips curve in macroeconomic policymaking. We have discussed the ideas of many of the best economists of the twentieth century: from the Phillips curve of Phillips, Samuelson and Solow, to the natural rate hypothesis of Friedman and Phelps, to the rational expectations theory of Lucas, Sargent and Barro. Six of this group have already won Nobel prizes for their work in economics. Our discussion has been based around the UK economy, but the principles apply across other economies too. The UK is a convenient case study in the changing interpretation and application of economic theory.

SUMMARY

- The Phillips curve describes a negative relationship between inflation and unemployment. By expanding AD, policymakers can choose a point on the Phillips curve with higher inflation and lower unemployment. By contracting AD, policymakers can choose a point on the Phillips curve with lower inflation and higher unemployment.
- Many economists now subscribe to the view that the trade-off between inflation and unemployment described by the Phillips curve holds only in the short run. In the long run, expected inflation adjusts to changes in actual inflation, and the short-run Phillips curve shifts. As a result, the long-run Phillips curve is vertical at the natural rate of unemployment.
- The short-run Phillips curve also shifts because of shocks to AS. An adverse supply shock, such as the increase in world oil prices during the 1970s, gives policymakers a less favourable trade-off between inflation and unemployment. That is, after an adverse supply shock, policymakers must accept a higher rate of inflation for any given rate of unemployment, or a higher rate of unemployment for any given rate of inflation.
- When the central bank contracts growth in the money supply to reduce inflation, it moves the economy along the short-run Phillips curve, which results in temporarily high unemployment. The cost of disinflation depends on how quickly expectations of inflation fall. Some economists argue that a credible commitment to low inflation can reduce the cost of disinflation by inducing a quick adjustment of expectations.
- Credibility in maintaining low inflation has been a driver behind many countries granting independence to central banks to conduct monetary policy with the primary aim of maintaining price stability.

- An alternative to inflation targeting is NGDP targeting which would allow for monetary policy to expand and contract in response to changes in nominal GDP. This might mean that inflation is higher or lower that a desired 'target', as monetary policy responds to shocks in the economy but would lead to a more stable economy.
- Since the 2007–9 Financial Crisis, the trade-off between inflation and unemployment seems to have changed prompting further research into the Phillips curve and whether it even exists anymore.

IN THE NEWS

The Phillips Curve Myth?

Throughout this chapter we have presented a historical story, one of ongoing research into the relationship between inflation and unemployment. We have seen how central banks incorporate this relationship into models to provide data on which policy decisions are based. We have also seen how some economists and central bankers have questioned the shape and existence of the Phillips curve given events since the mid-2000s. Other commentators have also posed questions around the Phillips curve. One such commentator is Vipin Bharathan, a contributory journalist for the *Forbes Magazine*, a US publication focusing on business, finance, investment and technology.

In the article, Bharathan argues that the Phillips curve is a myth and that policy decisions need to be based on more accurate data than is currently used by many central banks. The developments around Industry 4.0 and, in particular, the use of blockchain technology might, he argues, provide a step forward in this respect.

Bharathan notes that the Phillips curve was 'created from pre-WWI data for the UK', and suggests that economics as a discipline is prone to using theories and models that have gained traction but which are flawed or based on outdated data. The relationship between inflation and unemployment, he notes, is too complex and the Phillips curve is too gross a simplification. He argues that this simplistic theory is being accepted as 'real' and that policy decisions are being made based on it, 'Bad models plus bad data yield results once in a while, similar to a broken clock that is right twice a day.'

There are suggestions by some economists that for the United States (and by association other economies such as the UK and Europe) to bring the inflation experienced in the early 2020s under control, a significant period of unemployment must be endured. In a speech in London in 2022, for example, Lawrence Summers, former US Treasury Secretary, was quoted as saying, 'We need five years of unemployment above 5 per cent to contain inflation – in other words, we need two years of 7.5 per cent unemployment or five years of 6 per cent unemployment or one year of 10 per cent unemployment.' Is this what has happened to bring inflation down?

It is also noted that the story of how the Phillips curve became part of the mainstream in macroeconomics can be questioned. Bharathan cites Fellow of Balliol College Oxford, James Forder, who wrote a reassessment of the historical development of the Phillips curve in a book published in 2014.

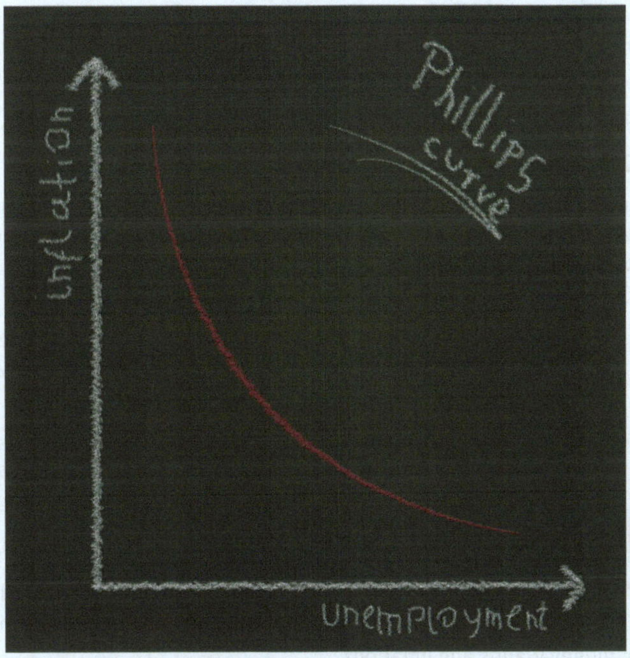

© iStock/MattZ90

Is the Phillips curve real or is it just a myth?

(*Continued*)

The book is presented as Forder showing that, 'the myth of the Phillips curve as a choice between inflation and labour costs was created by an anti-labour cost sentiment among economists'.

The article then goes on to note that the inflation experienced in many countries in the early 2020s was caused by events such as the pandemic and the conflicts in Ukraine and the Middle East, and as such constitutes unexpected inflation. If these are the causes of the most recent inflation event, then, Bharathan argues central banks are 'helpless to control it'. If the Phillips curve is based on a theory that links the rate of growth of wages and labour costs to output, then if wage inflation is not the cause, why use a theory that assumes this as the basis for policy? Several features of economies that have changed in recent years are not incorporated into the Phillips curve, it is argued. For example, the effect of immigration on productivity and labour costs, globalization, innovation and increases in productivity are not adequately represented in the research around the Phillips curve.

The article continues its critique of the Phillips curve and of the role of central banks and touches upon the argument that central banks should be abolished and policy determined by algorithm perhaps based on some rule like the Taylor rule. It also notes how data collected and used by central banks can often be inaccurate and lack currency. The use of AI in policymaking along with blockchain technology might help improve the accuracy of data and, in turn, improve the quality of decision-making. Decisions on monetary policy should be made more frequently than is currently the case in some countries. The Federal Open Markets Committee meets nine times a year and the Bank of England's MPC meets around eight times a year.

All in all, the article presents a damning indictment on economics as a profession, its underlying biases and its inability to look at its models with sufficient criticality.

Critical Thinking Questions

1 How can we judge articles such as the one referred to when assessing our understanding of theories like the Phillips curve? What other information would you wish to gather to help judge the article?
2 Comment on the quote provided by Summers. What do you think Summers was basing this analysis on and how accurate do you think his comments are in the light of what you have read about the sacrifice ratio in this chapter?
3 Why is it important for a discipline like economics to reflect on its history and how we have come to know what we know about topics such as the relationship between inflation and unemployment?
4 Why do you think Bharathan argues that central banks are 'helpless to control' the type of inflation that occurred in the early 2020s?
5 The article raises some important and fundamental questions. Is the Phillips curve a myth? Has the theory been distorted to suit the agendas of economists with particular views and biases? Should central banks be abolished and replaced by AI? What are your views on these topics and how might you critically assess such questions?

References:

finance.yahoo.com/news/5-years-6-unemployment-1-114324347.html?guccounter=1, accessed 7 August 2025.
www.forbes.com/sites/vipinbharathan/2024/09/17/puncturing-the-phillips-curve-myth/, accessed 7 August 2025.
www.jamesforder.uk/about-me, accessed 7 August 2025.

QUESTIONS FOR REVIEW

1 Phillips originally looked at the rate of change in money wages rather than inflation, but the Phillips curve has come to be associated with the trade-off between inflation and unemployment. What is the relationship between the rate of change of money wages and inflation?
2 Explain why, in the short run, there might be a trade-off between inflation and unemployment.
3 Draw the short-run trade-off between inflation and unemployment. How might the central bank move the economy from one point on this curve to another?

4 Draw the long-run trade-off between inflation and unemployment. Explain how the short-run and long-run trade-offs are related.

5 Why do economists place such importance on the role of expectations in macroeconomic policy?

6 What is so 'natural' about the natural rate of unemployment? Why might the natural rate of unemployment differ across countries?

7 Explain how expected inflation might cause a shift in the short-run Phillips curve.

8 Suppose a drought destroys farm crops and drives up the price of food. What is the effect on the short-run trade-off between inflation and unemployment?

9 What reasons are put forward for keeping central banks independent in setting monetary policy?

10 What are the main differences between inflation targeting and NGDP targeting?

PROBLEMS AND APPLICATIONS

1 Suppose the natural rate of unemployment is 6 per cent. On one graph, draw two Phillips curves that can be used to describe the four situations listed here. Label the point that shows the position of the economy in each case.
   a. Actual inflation is 5 per cent and expected inflation is 3 per cent.
   b. Actual inflation is 3 per cent and expected inflation is 5 per cent.
   c. Actual inflation is 5 per cent and expected inflation is 5 per cent.
   d. Actual inflation is 3 per cent and expected inflation is 3 per cent.

2 Illustrate the effects of the following developments on both the short-run and long-run Phillips curves. Give the economic reasoning underlying your answers.
   a. A rise in the natural rate of unemployment.
   b. A decline in the price of imported oil.
   c. A rise in government spending.
   d. A decline in expected inflation.

3 Suppose that a fall in consumer spending causes a recession.
   a. Illustrate the changes in the economy using both an AD/AS diagram and a Phillips curve diagram. What happens to inflation and unemployment in the short run?
   b. Now suppose that over time expected inflation changes in the same direction that actual inflation changes. What happens to the position of the short-run Phillips curve? After the recession is over, does the economy face a better or worse set of inflation–unemployment combinations?

4 Suppose the economy is in a long-run equilibrium.
   a. Draw the economy's short-run and long-run Phillips curves.
   b. Suppose a wave of business pessimism reduces AD. Show the effect of this shock on your diagram from part (a). If the central bank undertakes expansionary monetary policy, can it return the economy to its original inflation rate and original unemployment rate?
   c. Now suppose the economy is back in long-run equilibrium, and then the price of imported oil rises. Show the effect of this shock with a new diagram like that in part (a). If the central bank undertakes expansionary monetary policy, can it return the economy to its original inflation rate and original unemployment rate? If the central bank undertakes contractionary monetary policy, can it return the economy to its original inflation rate and original unemployment rate? Explain why this situation differs from that in part (b).

5 Suppose the central bank believed that the natural rate of unemployment was 6 per cent when the actual natural rate was 5.5 per cent. If the central bank based its policy decisions on its belief, what would happen to the economy?

6 Suppose the central bank announced that it would pursue contractionary monetary policy to reduce the inflation rate. Would the following conditions make the ensuing recession more or less severe? Explain.
   a. Wage contracts have short durations.
   b. There is little confidence in the central bank's determination to reduce inflation.
   c. Expectations of inflation adjust quickly to actual inflation.

7 Some economists believe that the short-run Phillips curve is relatively steep and shifts quickly in response to changes in the economy. Would these economists be more or less likely to favour contractionary policy to reduce inflation than economists who had the opposite views?

8 Imagine an economy in which all wages are set in three-year contracts. In this world, the central bank announces a disinflationary change in monetary policy to begin immediately. Everyone in the economy believes the central bank's announcement. Would this disinflation be costless? Why or why not? What might the central bank do to reduce the cost of disinflation?

9 Given the unpopularity of inflation, why do elected leaders not always support efforts to reduce inflation? Economists believe that countries can reduce the cost of disinflation by letting their central banks make decisions about monetary policy without interference from politicians. Why might this be so?

10 Some economists have proposed that central banks should use the following rule for choosing their target interest rate (r):

$$r = 2 + p + \tfrac{1}{2}\frac{(y - y^*)}{y^*} + \tfrac{1}{2}(p - p^*)$$

where:

p is the average of the inflation rate over the past year

y is real GDP as recently measured

y^* is an estimate of the natural rate of output

p^* is the central bank's target rate of inflation which is given as 2 per cent.

a. Explain the logic that might lie behind this rule for setting interest rates. Would you support the use of this rule?
b. Some economists advocate such a rule for monetary policy but believe p and y should be the forecasts of future values of inflation and output. What are the advantages of using forecasts instead of actual values? What are the disadvantages?

15 SUPPLY-SIDE POLICIES

The focus of policy in the post-war era was firmly on managing aggregate demand. In the late 1960s and into the 1970s demand management came to be questioned and some economists switched their focus to the capacity of the economy – aggregate supply. In particular, economists began looking at the effects of (often) frequent changes in taxes which was a feature of demand management on the supply-side of the economy.

We have seen that in the long run the AS curve is vertical, but in the short run it slopes upwards from left to right. Shifting the AS curve to the right would increase the capacity of the economy and increase national income (and thus lower unemployment) but reduce pressure on prices. A concentration on the supply-side of the economy could, therefore, help to bring about sustainable economic growth, higher growth, lower unemployment, and stable or even lower inflation. Supply-side policies focus on ways of influencing the factors which affect AS. If AS represents the quantity of goods and services that firms choose to produce at different price levels, then looking at what influences firms' behaviour is an important starting point.

SHIFTS IN THE AGGREGATE SUPPLY CURVE

There is a range of factors which can cause the AS curve to shift, as we have seen. We summarized these as changes in labour, physical or human capital, the availability of natural resources, changes in technology and expectations of the price level. This summary provides us with the bare bones on which to explore in more detail how shifts in the AS curve might arise.

So far, we have looked at the AS curve in the short run as being upwards sloping and in the long run as vertical. The vertical long-run AS curve makes intuitive sense if you think about AS in terms of the capacity of the economy. Imagine that every individual in an economy who wanted to work at the going wage rate could find work (that is, there was full employment). In addition, every firm was producing at its maximum capacity and there were no machines or capital lying idle. Then the economy would be producing at its maximum capacity, which we will refer to as full employment output (Y_f).

We have explored the analysis that in the short run the AS curve can shift causing temporary deviations from this full employment output. Eventually, however, once changes in prices, wages and misperceptions work through the economy, output returns to its long-run equilibrium. Changes in AD can cause fluctuations in economic activity, and fiscal and monetary policy can be implemented to manage demand and attempt to stabilize fluctuations. However, if policies are put in place to boost AD, for example, the effects might depend on the extent of the output gap that exists and the flexibility of the economy to respond to the increase in AD. The extent to which unemployment is reduced and how far the price level changes, will be affected by the flexibility of the economy.

Figure 15.1 shows a different shaped AS curve from those we have looked at so far. At the full employment level of output, the AS curve is vertical. Between Y_1 and Y_f, however, the AS curve becomes increasingly steep, whereas between Y_2 and Y_1 the AS curve is almost horizontal. This is referred to as the New Keynesian AS curve.

FIGURE 15.1

The New Keynesian Aggregate Supply Curve

The New Keynesian aggregate supply curve is vertical at full employment output Y_f. At low levels of national income, the AS curve is virtually horizontal, reflecting the fact that there is considerable spare capacity in the economy. As national income rises, however, the ability of firms to expand output becomes more difficult and so the AS curve becomes gradually steeper until it becomes vertical at full employment output.

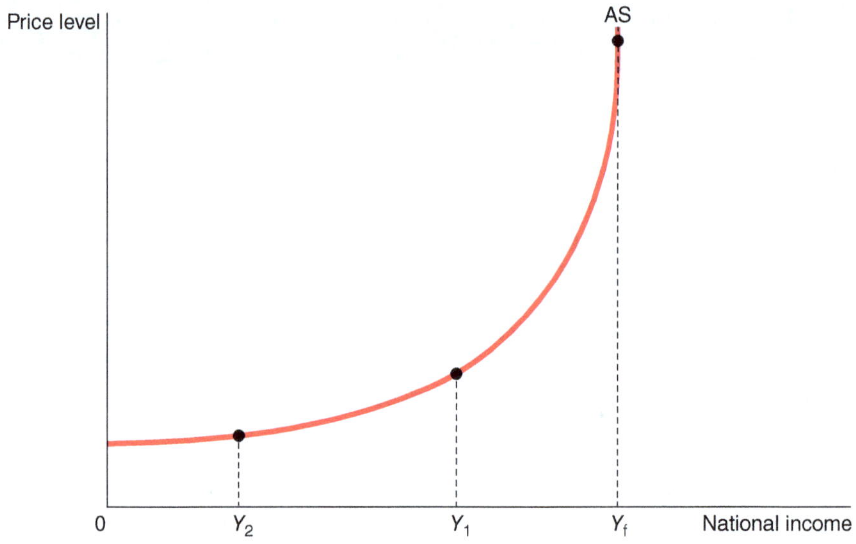

Between the origin and Y_2 there is a considerable amount of spare capacity in the economy, but that spare capacity begins to diminish the closer to full employment output at Y_f. This has implications for the effect on national income and the price level if AD shifts, as shown in Figure 15.2. If the economy starts out at Y_1 with the price level P_1, there is considerable spare capacity in the economy and the output gap is large. If fiscal and/or monetary policy shifts the AD curve to the right, the increase in national income rises by a relatively large amount from Y_1 to Y_2. The increase in the price level is only small, suggesting that the Phillips curve is relatively shallow and the trade-off between the reduction in unemployment and the rise in the price level is favourable. If policy continues to push AD to the right, the trade-off changes and the increase in national income begins to get smaller the nearer to full employment output, while the rise in the price level increases at a faster rate.

Why does the trade-off become less favourable over time? The reason is that as AD increases, the pressure on society's scarce resources becomes greater. If AD increased from AD_3 to AD_4, for example, firms would be looking to expand output to meet the increased demand and would look to buy more factor inputs. As the demand for these factor inputs rises, the price of them increases. Certain types of labour might become scarce more quickly than others, and wage rates in these industries might rise sharply as a result. The demand for skilled labour in the construction industry, for example, might rise, but the supply of people with these skills tends to be inelastic in the short run. It takes time to train skilled bricklayers, plumbers, plasterers and electricians. Those who have these skills will find they are in demand and they can sell their labour for higher wages as a result. Firms that pay the higher wages see their costs increase. With demand rising, however, they feel they can pass on these higher costs to the consumer in the form of higher prices and so inflation begins to accelerate. The closer the economy comes to full employment output, the greater will be the production bottlenecks that arise as resources become scarcer. So the effect on prices will be greater, but the ability of the economy to grow further will decline.

FIGURE 15.2

The Aggregate Supply Curve and Production Bottlenecks

Increases in AD, when there is considerable spare capacity in the economy, can lead to relatively large increases in national income with only relatively small rises in the price level. If AD keeps increasing, resource constraints will eventually mean that national income will only rise by relatively small amounts, but the pressure on resources will cause the price level to rise more quickly.

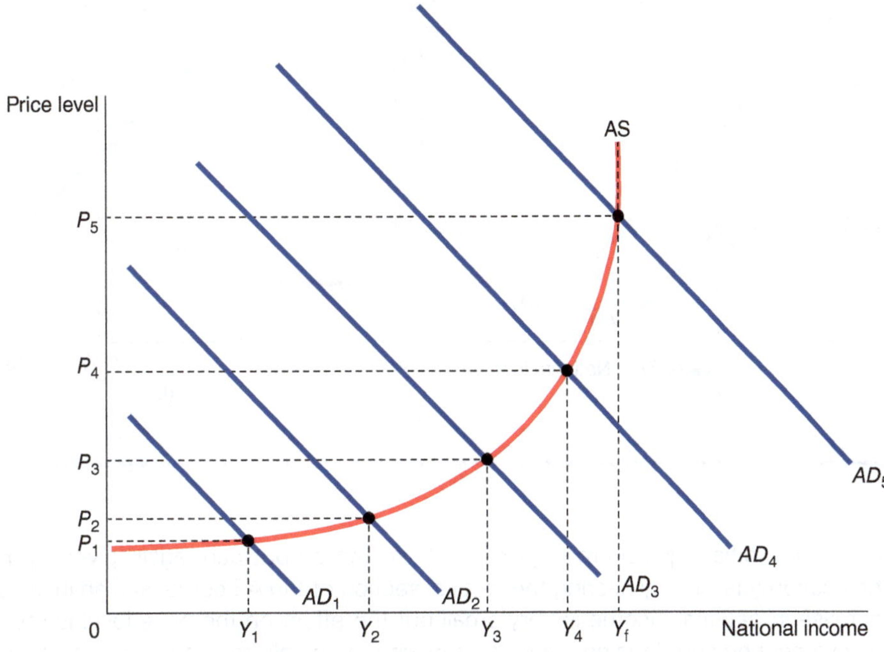

The Importance of the Output Gap

The supply-side focus arises because of the difficulty of policymakers knowing what the size of the output gap is at any particular moment in time, that is where the economy is on the AS curve. The output gap can be calculated in two ways. The first is to subtract actual output from potential output where potential output is based on the assumption that markets are perfectly competitive. The second is to subtract actual output from natural output where natural output assumes imperfect competition and rigidities in prices and wages. We have seen how monetary and fiscal policy operate side by side, even if governments are not deliberately trying to influence AD. Changes in tax rates, tax allowances and government spending decisions will have effects on the level of AD, while changes in monetary policy affect investment decisions and the exchange rate and, as a result, net exports. If the net effect of monetary and fiscal policy is to boost AD, the size of the output gap will have an effect on the resulting changes in the price level and national income.

This is illustrated in Figure 15.3. Assume the economy in panel (a) is in equilibrium at Y_1. The output gap is given by the distance between full employment output and actual output $Y_f - Y_1$. An increase in AD to AD_2 would lead to a rise in national income to Y_2, and a rise in the price level to P_2. The output gap narrows but the economy is beginning to experience some bottlenecks in production and, as a result, the increase in national income has come at a price of accelerating inflation. Any further increases in AD would mean the economy is in danger of overheating – where supply-side constraints mean that the pressure on prices increases.

FIGURE 15.3

The Effect of the Size of the Output Gap

Panel (a) shows the effect on national income and the price level of a rise in aggregate demand where the output gap is relatively large. In contrast, if the economy is in an initial equilibrium when the output gap is small, as in panel (b), then a rise in AD will have a much larger effect on the price level.

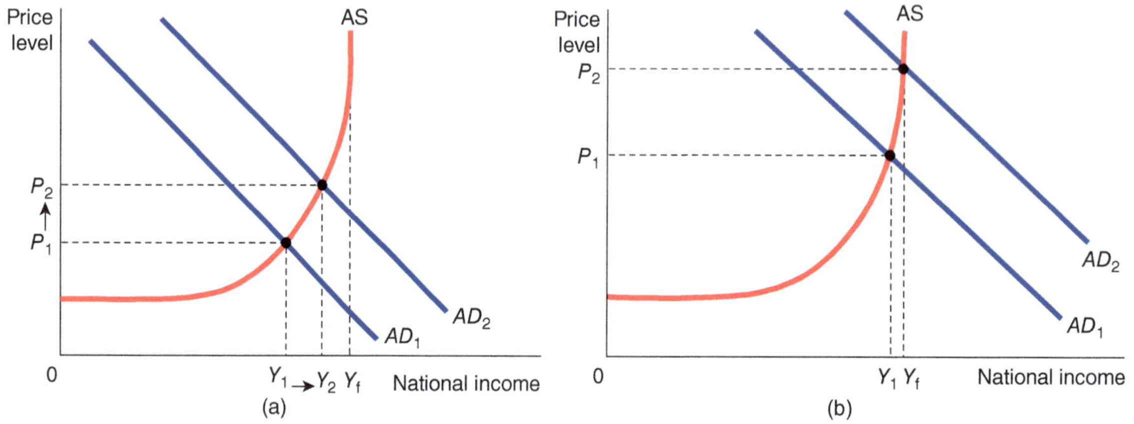

In panel (b), the initial equilibrium is given by Y_1 so the output gap, again given by $Y_f - Y_1$, is much smaller. The economy is already nearing the vertical section of the AS curve, and an increase in AD means that the increase in national income is very small but the effect on the price level is much stronger. The economy is overheating and does not have the capacity to be able to cope with the rise in AD and so the main effect feeds through to prices.

The size of the output gap is simple in theory but much more difficult, in reality, to estimate. The models used vary and the size of the various parameters that modellers input into the equations can lead to widely differing results. If policymakers base decisions on an estimated output gap that is incorrect, the effects of policy can be different from those anticipated. It is for this reason that supply-siders argue that a focus on increasing the productive capacity of the economy needs to be an important element of the policy mix.

Sustainable Growth

Supply-side economists suggest that if policy is concentrated on increasing the capacity of the economy, then in the long run it is possible to increase national income but keep the price level more stable. This is illustrated in Figure 15.4.

Assume society faces an initial AS curve, AS_1, and AD curve, AD_1. The initial equilibrium is at point A with a price level of P_1 and national income at Y_1. An increase in AD to AD_2 would, given the initial AS curve, see the economy begin to experience more significant production bottlenecks, and as a result the price level would start to accelerate. If supply-side policies succeeded in shifting the AS curve to the right to AS_2, this would give a new full employment output capacity at Y_{f2} compared to Y_{f1}. The increase in AD to AD_2 would now result in a rise in national income to Y_2 from Y_1, but the increase in the price level would be relatively small, rising from P_1 to P_2. Many economists would argue that a little inflation in an economy is a good thing as it acts as an incentive to firms to produce and expand. By shifting AS to the right, the economy could increase standards of living and reduce unemployment but keep prices stable (where price stability is defined as having an inflation rate which was deemed acceptable, that is the target inflation rate). This would represent sustained economic growth.

FIGURE 15.4

Sustained Economic Growth

If supply-side policies are successful in shifting the AS curve from AS_1 to AS_2, an increase in AD from AD_1 to AD_2 results in a relatively large increase in national income from Y_1 to Y_2 but with only a modest increase in the price level from P_1 to P_2. The new AS curve is associated with an increased capacity of the economy shown by the increase in full employment output from Y_{f1} to Y_{f2}.

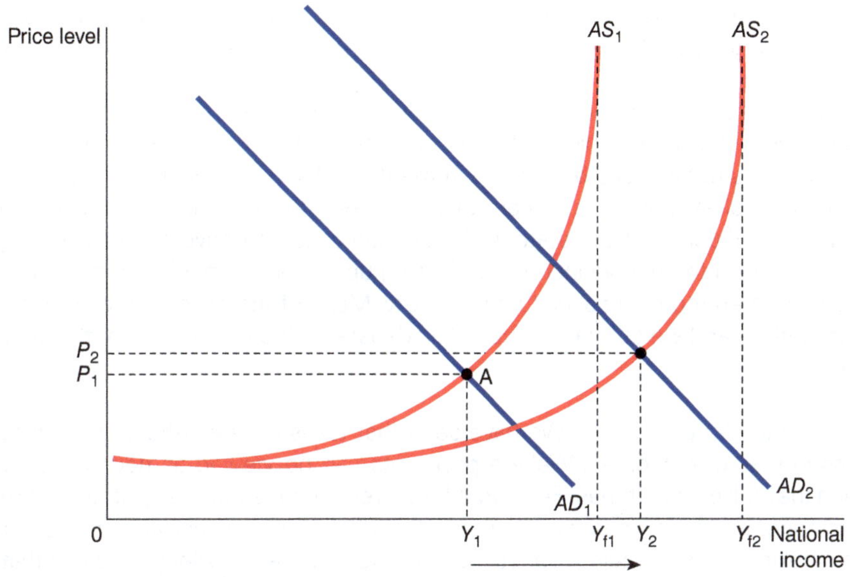

SELF TEST What are the factors which can cause a shift in the AS curve to the right? What is meant by the term 'production bottlenecks'?

TYPES OF SUPPLY-SIDE POLICIES

Supply-side economists tend to be associated with a fundamental belief in the power of markets and the private sector to allocate resources efficiently – at least more efficiently than might be the case with public sector provision. Give these assumptions, policies addressing the extent to which the working of markets can be improved will ensure more efficient allocation of resources. These policies are classed as **market-orientated supply-side policies**. If governments are going to intervene in the economy then supply-siders believe that the focus should be on investing in resources that improve the working of the economy such as developing infrastructure, improving research and development, and investing in education. These policies are referred to as **interventionist supply-side policies**. We will now look at the policies which come under these broad classifications in more detail.

market-orientated supply-side policies policies designed to free up markets to improve resource allocation through more effective price signals

interventionist supply-side policies policies focused on improving the working of markets through investing in infrastructure, education, and research and development

Market-Orientated Supply-Side Policies

The intention of market-orientated supply-side policies is to help markets work more efficiently by improving the effectiveness of price signals to improve resource allocation. Underpinning these policies is a philosophical belief that markets are the most effective way of allocating resources. The use of Keynesian demand management policies had led to governments becoming more and more involved in the economy, with a number of industries or firms run by the state on behalf of the people as a whole. Many governments increasingly built up the welfare state to support those in need and, of course, all this government spending meant taxes tended to be raised to pay for the increase in the services provided by the state.

Supply-side policies came to the fore in the 1980s, when governments in the developed world were trying to cope with stagflation. This section is not intended to be a history lesson, but there will be references to policies put in place by the governments in the United States and the UK to highlight key issues arising in supply-side policies. A core of what was referred to as the 'supply-side revolution' was on rolling back the influence of the state in the economy, cutting government spending, reforming the tax and benefit system to improve incentives, freeing up the labour market to make it more flexible and encouraging a more entrepreneurial culture in society. Many of the policies implemented were designed to improve incentives and are still part of the public debate on the relative role of the state and the market in the economy.

Reform of Tax and Welfare Policy We have seen that taxes have an effect on incentives and can lead to distortions in market outcomes. Welfare payments can be viewed as negative taxes, giving people support when they fall on hard times. Few would disagree with the necessity of taxing firms, products and individuals to generate tax revenue for government, and to influence behaviour in desired directions, such as reducing smoking or encouraging reductions in waste. If we acknowledge the fact that taxes – positive and negative – distort market outcomes, then the debate shifts to the level of taxation.

In many countries in Europe and in the United States, income and corporate taxes were relatively high in the 1970s and 1980s. In the UK, for example, the basic rate of income tax was 33 per cent in 1978. There were also higher rates associated with higher levels of income, with the top tax rate being 98 per cent on unearned income and 83 per cent on earned income. Corporation tax in the UK in 1978 was 53 per cent for larger companies and 42 per cent for small companies. In the United States, income tax rates ranged from 14 per cent to 70 per cent and corporate tax rates were near 50 per cent. Corporate taxes in Germany in 1981 were around 56 per cent, in Norway just over 50 per cent, 48 per cent in the Netherlands, and in Sweden almost 58 per cent. Table 15.1 shows the top rates of income tax in a selection of nine European countries for 1979, 1995 and 2024.

TABLE 15.1 **Top Rates of Income Tax in Nine European Countries, 1979–2024**

Country	Top income tax rate 1979 (%)	Top income tax rate 1995 (%)	Top income tax rate 2024 (%)
Belgium	76.3	55.0	53.5
Denmark	66.0	63.5	55.9
Germany	56.0	53.0	47.5
Ireland	60.0	48.0	48.0
Netherlands	72.0	60.0	49.5
Norway	75.4	13.7	39.6
Portugal	80.0	40.0	53.0
Sweden	86.5	30.0	52.3
UK	83.0	40.0	45.0

Source: OECD/Trading Economics/Tax Foundation Europe

Supply-siders argued that high rates of income and corporate taxes were acting as a disincentive to individuals and to businesses. We need here to remind ourselves of the distinction between average and marginal tax rates. Remember that marginal tax rates refer to the amount of tax taken on every extra euro or pound of earnings. In the UK, some people faced a marginal tax rate (at relatively high levels of earnings) of 83 per cent. The government would leave the individual with just 17 pence from every extra pound earned. Supply-siders argued that such high rates of tax acted as a significant disincentive to work and be entrepreneurial if the rewards from hard work were subject to such rates.

Cutting both income and corporate taxes, therefore, could lead to the incentive for people to take work and work harder (more hours) if the rewards were greater. Income tax rates, it was argued, altered the trade-off between work and leisure. Higher tax rates reduce the opportunity cost of leisure and so people will opt to reduce work and take more leisure. If tax rates are lowered and people get to keep more of the income they earn, the effect is like an increase in wages. The income effect works in the opposite direction from the substitution effect, and labour supply increases.

High corporate and income taxes also act as an incentive for firms and individuals to engage in tax avoidance (which is legal) or tax evasion (which is illegal). Higher tax rates, it is argued, encourage firms and individuals to find ways in which their tax liability can be reduced, which may include putting money into offshore 'tax havens' and firms spending money on tax deductible assets which may not have any major impact on productivity (like investing in plusher office suites, buying luxury company cars, locating conferences at more luxurious venues and so on). Also included is channelling income into offshore companies which then return the money in the form of 'loans' on which there is no income tax. Such schemes are not illegal, but some would claim that they are morally wrong.

Tax evasion is illegal and refers to attempts by firms and individuals to avoid declaring income which is subject to taxation. This might be in the form of traders accepting cash for work carried out which is then not declared as income, through to more sophisticated money laundering schemes. His Majesty's Revenue and Customs (HMRC), the body responsible for collecting taxes for the UK government, estimated the tax gap, the difference between total tax liabilities and tax collected in the tax year 2022–3, to be 4.8 per cent. The total tax liability was assumed to be £823.8 billion and so the amount of tax not collected for various reasons was £39.8 billion. Organizations like the Tax Justice Network estimate that countries are missing out on around half a trillion dollars (£406 billion, €485 billion) in tax per annum through the underpayment of tax by the very wealthy and multinational corporations. Around half of this sum is accounted for by only Australia, Canada, Israel, Japan, New Zealand, South Korea, the UK and the United States.

Supply-siders argue that reducing tax rates can change incentives to work and incentives to avoid or evade paying taxes. Cutting tax rates can, therefore, mean that tax revenues actually increase. An example serves to illustrate. Assume that the top rate of income tax in a country is 80 per cent and that this rate applies to the whole of an individual's income (in reality most income tax regimes are progressive and stepped so that those on lower incomes pay a lower rate compared to those on higher rates). An individual earning €500,000 would have to pay €400,000 in tax and gets to keep the remaining €100,000. If the government reduced the tax rate to 60 per cent, the individual faces the incentive that they get to keep more of every €1 of earnings, which acts as a powerful incentive to work harder. The individual works harder in the next year and earns €750,000, on which they pay tax of €450,000 and keep €300,000. The individual has more of an incentive to work harder because they get to keep more of their earnings and the government generates more in overall tax revenue.

Income and corporate tax rates fell in many countries across Europe in the 1980s and into the 1990s. In addition to reducing actual tax rates, governments can also change tax allowances relating to the amount of income earned before having to pay tax. In the UK, for example, in 2010, the amount earned before paying tax stood at £6,500, but in 2024 stood at £12,570. Changing tax rates also has an effect on those who are looking for work. If tax rates are high or tax allowances are low, it can be the case that the incentive for people to go into work and come off benefits is also low. Assume, for example, an individual is receiving €10,000 a year in various benefits but pays no income tax. A job becomes available which pays €12,000. If the worker takes the job but then becomes liable for tax at a rate of (say) 25 per cent on all their earnings, they will receive an after-tax income of €9,000. There is no incentive for the person to take the job, to come off benefits and pay income tax. If the tax rate were reduced to (say) 10 per cent, the person would receive an after-tax income of €10,800 and so there would be more of an incentive to take the job and come off benefits. Not only would the government be better off by not having to pay this individual benefits, it would be receiving €1,200 in tax revenue, a net benefit to the government of €11,200. In addition, by getting a job, the individual is now not subject to the same issues and problems we outlined as the costs of unemployment to individuals earlier in the book, which reduces the social externalities associated with unemployment.

This approach is also linked with reform of the welfare system to provide incentives to individuals to get off benefits and into work. By making access to benefits subject to more rigorous tests and/or reducing welfare payments, individuals are forced to reassess their position. They may not become so reliant on the welfare state and look to find ways to support themselves. This means they must be more flexible in taking jobs which they may otherwise have shunned because they did not match their expectations, wage demands or qualifications.

The combined effects of these policies mean that the labour market is more efficient, with fewer people being voluntarily unemployed. In addition, those in work are prepared to work harder and be more productive, and enterprise and initiative are thereby rewarded.

The analysis so far is fairly intuitive, but the reality depends on a number of factors, not least the elasticity of supply of labour. If the elasticity of supply of labour is relatively low, then any increase in wages through tax cuts or changes in allowances will only have a limited effect on the increase in the supply of labour (often measured in labour hours). If the elasticity of supply of labour was 0.1, for example, a rise in the wage rate of 5 per cent would only lead to an increase in labour supply of 0.5 per cent. The long-run elasticity of supply of labour, however, might be larger than those in the short run because workers have time to adjust their behaviour. Research by Nobel Prize winning economist Edward Prescott in 2002, suggested that there was a considerable difference between the elasticities of labour supply in France and the United States, which were largely due to differences in the tax systems between the two countries.

CASE STUDY The Laffer Curve and Supply-Side Economics

One day in 1974, rumour has it that the US economist, Arthur Laffer, sat in a Washington restaurant with some prominent journalists and politicians. He picked up a napkin and drew a figure on it to show how tax rates affect tax revenue. The illustration looked like that shown in the image included in this case study. Laffer suggested that the United States was on the downwards sloping side of this curve. Tax rates were so high, he argued, that reducing them would actually raise tax revenue.

Most economists were sceptical of Laffer's suggestion. The idea that a cut in tax rates could raise tax revenue was correct as a matter of economic theory, but there was more doubt about whether it would do so in practice. There was little evidence for Laffer's view that tax rates – in the United States or elsewhere – had in fact reached such extreme levels.

Nevertheless, the thinking underlying the **Laffer curve** (as it became known) became very influential in policy circles during the 1980s, particularly in the United States during the years of President Ronald Reagan's administration and in the UK during Prime Minister Margaret Thatcher's government. Tax rates – particularly income tax rates – were cut aggressively in both countries during the 1980s.

Laffer curve the relationship between tax rates and tax revenue

In the UK, for example, under Prime Minister Thatcher the top rate of income tax was cut from 83 per cent to 60 per cent in 1980 and then again to 40 per cent in 1988. Economists have, however, found it hard to trace any strong incentive effects of these tax cuts leading to increases in total tax revenue as the Laffer curve would suggest. A study by the UK's Institute for Fiscal Studies (IFS), for example, concluded that at most about 3 per cent of the increase in tax revenue between 1980 and 1986 could be attributed to the 1980 income tax cut.

In the United States, President Reagan also cut taxes aggressively, but the result was less tax revenue, not more. Revenue from personal income taxes in the United States (per person, adjusted for inflation) fell by 9 per cent from 1980 to 1984, even though average income (per person, adjusted for inflation) grew by 4 per cent over this period. The tax cut, together with policymakers' unwillingness to restrain spending, began a long period during which the US government spent more than it collected in taxes. Throughout Reagan's two terms in office, and for many years thereafter, the US government ran large budget deficits.

(*Continued*)

Laffer's argument is not completely without merit. Although an overall cut in tax rates normally reduces revenue, some taxpayers, at some times, may be on the wrong side of the Laffer curve. The idea that cutting taxes can raise revenue may be correct if applied to those taxpayers facing the highest tax rates, but most people face lower marginal rates. Where the *typical* worker is on the top end of the Laffer curve, it may be more appropriate. In Sweden in the early 1980s, for instance, the typical worker faced a marginal tax rate of about 80 per cent. Such a high tax rate provides a substantial disincentive to work. Studies have suggested that Sweden would indeed have raised more tax revenue if it had lowered its tax rates.

Policymakers disagree about these issues, in part because they disagree about the size of the relevant elasticities. The more elastic supply and demand are in any market, the more taxes in that market distort behaviour, and the more likely it is that a tax cut will raise tax revenue. There is no debate, however, about the general lesson. How much revenue the government gains or loses from a tax change cannot be computed just by looking at tax rates. It also depends on how the tax change affects people's behaviour.

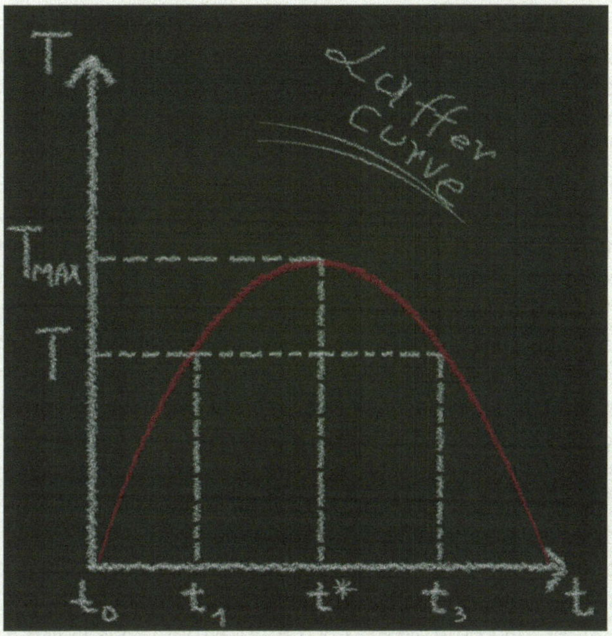

© iStock/MattZ91

The Laffer curve – what evidence is there for this theory?

Questions:

1 Laffer notes that the curve named after him relates tax rates and total tax revenue and acknowledges that the idea has been around for centuries. He quotes the Arab sociologist, philosopher and historian Ibn Khaldun, who noted, 'At the beginning of dynasties, tax rates are low and revenues are high and at the end of dynasties, tax rates are high and revenues low.' What do you think can be inferred from this statement?

2 Look at the image included in this case study, which depicts a typical Laffer curve. Over the range of the Laffer curve between the horizontal intercepts, there are two tax rates that give the same tax revenue. Choose a point where tax revenue is the same for two different tax rates and explain which rate you would recommend governments adopt and why.

3 Laffer notes that there are two effects that drive the shape of the curve. The arithmetic effect results in additional revenue per unit of currency of the tax base. The economic effect occurs when an increase in tax rates reduces incentives and causes the tax base to shrink, resulting in lower revenues. Looking at the image included in this case study, which range of tax rates do you think would result in the arithmetic effect and which in the economic effect? Can you arrive at any conclusions about the relationship between the two effects?

4 Can the Laffer curve ever tell a government what the optimum tax rate is for the country? Explain.

Reference:

www.youtube.com/watch?v=FCk2-QVqCck, accessed 6 August 2025.

SELF TEST Consider the respective size of the income and substitution effects on the supply of labour curve as a result of a cut in higher rate taxes. Under what circumstances would a cut in tax rates actually lead to a backwards bending supply curve of labour?

Flexible Labour Markets In addition to changing the tax and benefits system, supply-siders argue for more flexibility in labour markets. There are different aspects to this policy which include reducing the power of trade unions and improving market signals to both employers and workers. We have seen how trade unions can raise wages above market rates. The more powerful the trade unions, the higher they can push wages above market rates. In the 1970s and into the 1980s, the power of trade unions in the UK was substantial. Days lost to strikes averaged 12.8 million per year in the 1970s. The UK government, in the early 1980s, argued that trade unions exercised too much power and passed a series of new laws which reduced their power considerably. The result was that trade unions had to adapt and evolve. The number of people belonging to trade unions and the number of days lost to strikes fell sharply in the latter part of the 1980s and beyond. Many more people now negotiate pay levels with employers individually or at a local level rather than through unions. As a result, supply-siders would argue that wage rates more accurately reflect market conditions.

More flexible labour markets also relate to the ease with which employers can respond to market conditions by adjusting the labour force. This is sometimes referred to as the ability to 'hire and fire'. The more flexible the labour market, the fewer rigidities that would exist.

Flexible labour markets might include the use of short-term contracts. Workers have more flexible working arrangements, so that workers with the right skills are attracted to work, and employers are able to shed workers more easily when the economy is contracting. The rise of the so-called 'gig economy' has further raised the debate about flexible labour markets. The development of the internet and smartphone technology have promoted communication and connectivity in many different ways. Firms in delivery and transport, in particular, have been able to exploit this technology to improve services to customers, but they need highly flexible workers. Traditional contracts of work where employees are recruited on a wage or salary and have various legal employment rights such as paid holidays, sick pay and pension contributions, are not suitable for some of the firms utilizing connectivity technologies as part of their business. The workers needed in these types of business are more like self-employed contractors of the firm rather than employees. Each employment task is like a mini contract between firm and worker. This has resulted in the term 'gig economy'. This refers to a labour market in which workers do not have permanent jobs but instead have a relationship with a firm which is characterized by short-term contracts, freelance work or zero hours contracts.

For firms, the use of workers on these terms can mean greater flexibility for adjusting to changes in demand and can help control labour costs. For workers, there is a degree of independence and flexibility which can be appealing.

As with many issues in economics, flexible labour markets and developments like the gig economy have some downsides which must be balanced against the benefits to firms and workers, and has been the subject of increasing debate. Governments have been considering the issues and looking at the extent to which employment law needs to be changed to take account of the developments in the labour market.

Labour markets can also be made more flexible by improving market information for both employers and employees, so that those people looking for work can be matched with those seeking employment. Many governments provide so-called 'job centres' through which employers can advertise jobs and those looking for work can attend to get advice, be put in touch with prospective employers and be given help with improving their CVs, interview skills, job application techniques and so on.

Reducing Government Spending If governments wish to increase spending, they borrow more, raise taxes or do a combination of the two. We have seen how any fiscal expansion can be moderated by the crowding-out effect. It follows that if governments were able to reduce spending and borrow less, the opposite effect would occur, sometimes referred to as 'crowding in'. Cutting back the amount that governments borrow was a feature of the post 2007–9 Financial Crisis austerity programmes which many countries chose to implement. In more recent times the UK government, for example, outlined plans to reduce government borrowing in its budget of 2024, from £4.5 billion in 2024–5 to £2.1 billion in 2029–30. If borrowing can be scaled back, interest rates will fall, and this has an effect on firms' decisions to invest.

In addition to the crowding-in argument, there is a fundamental philosophical belief among supply-siders that government spending is not likely to be as efficient as the equivalent spending by the private sector. If government, therefore, steps back from its involvement in the economy and leaves resource allocation more to the private sector, the funds will be used more productively and more efficiently, which will improve the productive capacity of the economy.

In practice, many governments find it extremely difficult to cut back spending. The effects on government services and those who use them can be considerable. The sort of people who are most affected are often those on low income and the most vulnerable in society such as older people, those with mental illnesses, children and those who require social and/or health care. The political decisions which must be made when government spending is cut back are extremely difficult. Few governments can be so sure of the mandate they receive from the electorate to make the sorts of decisions which would lead to a substantial fall in government spending when so many people are likely to be affected in an adverse way. Closing hospitals, schools, social care programmes, homes for older people and those with mental illnesses might save considerable sums of money, but these represent electoral suicide.

Privatization and Deregulation One of the major changes in the economy of the UK since the late 1980s has been *privatization*, the move to transfer public ownership of assets to the private sector and the increase in the role of private sector firms in providing government services. Privatization has also been a feature of other European countries, including Austria, Denmark, Finland, France, Germany, Ireland, Italy, the Netherlands and Spain.

In the post-war era in the UK, many industries were state-owned, including coal, the railways, the utilities (water, gas and electricity), steel and telecommunications. In addition, a number of firms were taken into state ownership, including some in the motor, aviation and engineering industries. During the 1980s and 1990s, many of these industries and firms were sold and became private sector entities. In addition, other services such as refuse collection, cleaning and catering services were opened up to provision by private sector organizations.

Once again, the philosophical underpinning of privatization in all its forms is the belief that the private sector, driven by providing high quality services and the profit motive, is more likely to provide the services required by the public at lower cost. Operations would also be at higher productivity levels and be undertaken more efficiently than if provision was in the public sector. It was also argued that transferring assets to the private sector would help increase competition with the resulting benefits of lower prices and increased choice.

There is much debate as to the extent to which the benefits which were at the heart of the justification for privatization have been realized. The privatization of natural monopolies such as water, gas and electricity has created a complex system which many consumers have difficulty understanding. Despite regulatory bodies being set up to monitor the activities of these now private monopolies, there is some suspicion that the existence of monopoly power has reduced consumer surplus and led to deadweight losses. However, some studies have suggested that privatization has delivered better services, improved products, lower prices and more choice more efficiently for the public. It is also the case that there has been some criticism of some privatized industries, notably the rail and water industries in the UK. In some cases, rail franchises have been taken back into public ownership because of reported failures in the provision of efficient services.

In addition to privatization programmes, many governments looked to pass legislation which cut back on the regulations that were argued to impede the efficient working of financial and goods markets. Deregulation has succeeded in removing some of these imperfections in the market. For example, in transport, local bus routes have been deregulated to prevent local monopolies, which has resulted in more choice and lower prices for consumers. In financial markets, there has been an explosion of new products and much greater freedom for individuals and firms to be able to access credit. While this did have some impact on the global economy in the 1990s and into the 2000s, many have argued that deregulation went too far, and that appropriate checks and balances were not in place to prevent the 2007–9 Financial Crisis.

CRITICAL THINKING POINT Comment on the assumptions that underlie market-orientated supply-side policies. How might economists test the accuracy of these assumptions?

SELF TEST Why do policies to improve the flexibility of labour markets have to balance the rights of employers and employees?

Interventionist Supply-Side Policies

Recall that the creation of knowledge is a public good, that firms free ride on knowledge created by others and as a result devote too few resources to creating new knowledge. The investment in infrastructure such as communications networks, roads, rail, ports and airports is vital to the effectiveness of an economy. However, the sums needed to be invested in this sort of infrastructure and the risk involved are often extremely high. In addition, the opportunity to make adequate profit by private firms is not always easy, obvious or, in some cases, desirable. For example, the development of new motorway systems or airport expansion raises concerns among environmentalists and local people who are affected by the negative externalities. The planning process can often take many years and be extremely expensive in addition to the actual cost of construction. The result is that governments often take the lead in the provision of such infrastructure, albeit using private firms as noted above. Interventionist supply-side policies refer to the ways in which governments seek to encourage investment in education, training, research and development, and infrastructure and location of firms to help the economy work more effectively and efficiently.

Infrastructure Investment Governments will often take the lead in providing funds for infrastructure projects which have been identified as having long-term beneficial effects on the economy and will help to improve capacity. The sort of projects that governments support are invariably identified as being important in helping businesses to be more efficient, cutting costs and waste, and improving supply chains. Improvements to roads, rail, ports and airports help firms to distribute goods more efficiently. Improvements to communications networks help to make service industries more efficient. Developments to energy and water supplies through the building of new power stations or improvements to supply networks can also help firms secure their energy needs and reduce costs if these networks operate more efficiently.

Investment in Education and Training The school and higher education system in an economy is a source of improvements in the quality of future human capital. While many would not see education as purely a means of producing future workers, the sort of skills which school and university leavers possess influence their ability to secure work and their productivity levels. As we have seen, productivity is a key factor in improving economic growth and standards of living.

The sort of education system that a country has will, therefore, be important and a number of countries have invested in trying to improve standards. The difficulty comes in defining what appropriate standards are for individuals and for wider society. Some countries place a heavy emphasis on improving maths and science skills, because these are crucial in helping to create new knowledge and innovation in industry. Governments might provide grants or allowances to help boost interest in maths, science and engineering degrees. Maths and physics graduates may be given incentives to put their skills to use in teaching in schools where there tends to be a paucity of highly qualified individuals in these subject areas.

Governments may also help to support training. Firms may be reluctant to invest too many resources into training workers because of the lack of control they have over what workers do with the training they receive. On the one hand, a better trained workforce is beneficial to a firm because it makes workers more productive. On the other, it also makes workers more marketable and there is a risk that the worker moves on to a better job and another firm will benefit from the investment in training made by the initial firm. By providing help and support for training, governments may help to overcome this free rider problem.

Research and Development R&D is essential to the long-term improvement of knowledge creation, the development of new products and new processes. R&D is, however, expensive and unless the results can be protected in some way, the knowledge created becomes a public good. This is one of the reasons why many governments invest in supporting and funding R&D. Research bodies can be set up which receive requests for funding from firms and higher education institutions, sometimes in partnership. These bodies then decide on the allocation of funds based on the perceived value and importance of the research being proposed. Governments may also provide tax credits, tax relief or grants to help support R&D in smaller firms.

Regional or Industrial Policies In a number of European countries, economies are unevenly balanced. There are regions which are poorer than others. Firms will often gravitate to where the markets are biggest or where there are natural advantages such as ports, good infrastructure links and so on. Some regions are poor because they used to be the centre of industries that have declined. The decline of industries such as shipbuilding, iron and steel, the motor industry and the coal industry, for example, has not been matched by new industries springing up to absorb the jobs lost. As a result, a negative multiplier process can take hold, which means the region may stay economically undeveloped for long periods. Governments may seek to reverse such economic imbalance by locating some of its own activities in these regions, providing investment grants, premises at reduced rents, employment subsidies and other measures to encourage firms to locate in these areas and develop jobs. The intention is that, in encouraging investment in these areas, a positive regional multiplier effect will take hold.

SELF TEST Why is investing in the right sort of education and training considered important to the success of interventionist policies?

CONCLUSION

Supply-side policies have an intuitive feel to them. One of the main problems, however, is that shifting the AS curve to the right is a long-term process. Investing in education, training and R&D, for example, can boost the quality of human capital, but the benefits to the economy may not be felt for many years. Market-orientated policies may sound impressive and laudable, but the evidence to support the effectiveness of such policies is not overwhelming. It is perhaps safe to say that policies to improve the efficiency of markets and the capacity of the economy must be carried out hand in hand with other policies and not be seen as being an either/or policy option to fiscal and monetary policy. Indeed, the differences between fiscal, monetary and supply-side policies are sometimes difficult to disentangle. If a government announces it is investing billions in a high-speed rail network, does this represent a fiscal boost or is it purely focused on improving the supply-side of the economy?

SUMMARY

- Supply-side policies became a focus of many governments in the 1980s and into the 1990s.
- Supply-side policies are designed to shift the AS curve to the right.
- Shifting the AS curve to the right can lead to sustained economic growth which increases national income but keeps prices stable, countering the production bottlenecks that can occur if the focus is on increasing AD through fiscal or monetary policy.
- Supply-side policies can take two main forms: market-orientated policies or interventionist policies.
- Market-orientated policies are designed to free up markets so that they allocate resources more effectively and efficiently.
- Interventionist policies are designed to improve the working of the market and require government intervention to overcome the public good element of the investment in infrastructure, education, training, and research and development.

IN THE NEWS

Nonsense Output Gaps

As we have seen, supply-side policies aim to target the ability of an economy to produce goods and services to shift the aggregate supply curve to the right over time. A focus on such policies has implications across a wide range of economic variables. One important element associated with the supply-side of the economy that governments or other bodies such as the European Commission, IMF and OECD address is potential and actual growth. The difference between the two is the output gap. Potential output can be estimated by looking at the labour supply in a country and how this will change in future years, the capital stock and factor productivity. It is noted that potential output can only be estimated, whereas current output can be more accurately measured.

The estimates are based on assumptions the estimating body uses and these can be subject to considerable uncertainty. Using past data and trends to extrapolate the future can be subject to inaccuracy rendering the estimate inaccurate. In a report entitled 'Better Forecasts', the Institute for Government in the UK noted that the Office for Budget Responsibility (OBR) has revised its forecasts of the size of the output gap numerous times since 2009 and, it adds, on each occasion it has been 'repeatedly over-optimistic about the prospects for potential output growth'. However, this report also notes that the OBR has been reluctant to make links between policy announcements by government and how these might affect potential output growth unless it adheres to four 'tests'. These are significance of the policy measure, the extent to which the measure will have lasting impact on productive potential, whether it is additional to existing policies and not a continuation, and whether it is evidence-based in relation to the policy's effectiveness.

Given these uncertainties and caveats, some commentators have argued that the consensus of the economics profession on output gaps is 'nonsense'. Robin Brooks, Greg Basile and Jonathan Fortun, economists at the Institute for International Finance, posed a series of questions around the validity and reliability of calculations of the output gap. Some have pointed out that such questioning is not new. They argue that policy decisions such as those around the supply-side of the economy must have some benchmark against which to judge the effectiveness or effects of the policy. As with many things in economics, the argument might not be about the basic principles of the topic, in this case that improving productivity, efficiency of markets, infrastructure, etc. does boost the capacity of the economy. Rather it may be about how far it does so and thus, in turn, may be influenced by the size and nature of the policy intervention.

A problem arises if the benchmark against which any policy can be judged is inaccurate. If, therefore, estimates of the output gap are flawed or subject to inaccuracies, regardless of how conceptually sound they are, then the whole issue becomes nonsense. Depending on what and who you read on this issue, there will be different perspectives. Some suggest that these different perspectives are dependent on the belief systems and political philosophies that are held. Bill Mitchell, Chair in Economics and Director of the Centre of Full Employment and Equity (CofFEE), an official research centre at the University of Newcastle in New South Wales. Australia, notes for example that, 'The concept of biased estimates of output gaps and so-called "full employment unemployment rates" goes to the heart of the way the neoliberal economists, who dominate

© iStock/SweetBunFactory

Estimates of potential output can be extremely difficult, so how useful is it in formulating economic policy?

(Continued)

policymaking units in government and places like the IMF, the OECD and the European Commission, create technical smokescreens to justify their dirty work.'

Critical Thinking Questions

1 Why is an estimate of potential output and the output gap important in decisions on policies to improve the supply-side of an economy?

2 Why can potential output only ever be an 'estimate' and to what extent do you think this presents a problem to policymakers?

3 Why do you think that a body like the OBR is 'reluctant to make links between policy announcements by government and how these might affect potential output growth', and how far do the four tests appear to be useful for decisions on whether to include policy measures in any such estimate of potential output growth?

4 What do you understand by the term 'neo-liberal economists' and why do you think it matters that we apply such labels in discussions on economic policymaking?

5 'Conceptually, the idea of output gaps and supply-side policies is not at question. What is at question is whether policy can be made based on inaccurate estimations of such concepts. It is like deciding what clothes to wear based only on the use of a broken thermometer that does not tell you the true temperature.' Critically evaluate this statement.

References:

billmitchell.org/blog/?p=41671, accessed 6 August 2025.
cgt.columbia.edu/news/tooze-output-gap-nonsense/, accessed 6 August 2025.
www.bruegel.org/blog-post/campaign-against-nonsense-output-gaps, accessed 6 August 2025.
www.instituteforgovernment.org.uk/sites/default/files/2024-10/OBR-supply-policy-forecasting.pdf, accessed 6 August 2025.

QUESTIONS FOR REVIEW

1 What is meant by 'sustainable economic growth'?

2 Explain the shape of the New Keynesian AS curve.

3 What are the two ways in which the output gap can be calculated and what is the difference between them?

4 What is the relevance of the size of the output gap in policymaking?

5 Using an AS/AD diagram, show how a rise in AD could lead to a rise in national income but with no change in the price level.

6 What are the two main types of supply-side policy and what is the difference between them?

7 Why do supply-siders emphasize the importance of marginal tax rates in relation to incentives?

8 What is the Laffer curve?

9 Why do flexible labour markets improve the efficiency and capacity of the economy?

10 Why is it necessary for governments to invest in education, training, and research and development?

PROBLEMS AND APPLICATIONS

1 Using the New Keynesian AS curve, explain why, when the output gap is very large, the AS curve has an almost horizontal slope.

2 Why might governments find it difficult to accurately measure the size of the output gap?

3 Assume that a government is successful in shifting the AS curve to the right. Show what happens to the Phillips curve in such a situation.

4 What sort of trade-offs do governments face if a decision was being considered to reduce the level of welfare benefits as part of a market-orientated supply-side policy?

5 Governments that have implemented major cuts in higher rates of income tax have been accused of giving more money to the wealthy at the expense of the less well off. Construct an argument to counter such an accusation.

6 What sort of assumptions underlie the policy that cuts in income taxes would increase the supply of labour hours offered in an economy? How reliable do you think these assumptions might be?

7 What are the potential costs and benefits of policies designed to improve the flexibility of labour markets?

8 Why do governments find it difficult to reduce spending?

9 A government announces a decision to increase investment in spending on higher education with the intention of increasing the participation rate in higher education by young people, to 45 per cent (that is, that 45 per cent of school leavers would choose to go to university).
   a. Does it matter what sort of degrees these young people do at university?
   b. To what extent is the proportion of young people going on to university an important factor in improving the quality of human capital?
   c. What else might the government need to put in place to ensure that the policy is a longer-term success (hint: will there be appropriate jobs for young people when they graduate)?

10 How would a government be able to tell whether a policy of increasing private sector involvement in public sector services provision actually leads to a more efficient outcome compared to having those same services provided by the public sector?

PART 6 INTERNATIONAL MACROECONOMICS

16 ECONOMIC SHOCKS

History is full of examples of economic shocks that have had considerable and often long-lasting impacts on economies both nationally and globally. Shocks have been caused by crises such as the crash in the price of tulip bulbs in the 1630s, the South Sea Bubble in the early 1700s, which left thousands of investors ruined, the Great Depression in the late 1920s and early 1930s, the OPEC oil price shock of the 1970s, the Asian crisis in the late 1990s, the 2007–9 Financial Crisis, the economic shocks of the Covid-19 global pandemic and conflict in Eastern Europe and the Middle East. In addition to these periodic crises, there are also changes in technologies that give rise to new challenges and new opportunities, resulting in some firms and industries disappearing and considerable structural change.

Economic shocks can often originate in financial markets. The South Sea Bubble and the Great Depression were both examples of such crises. Economic shocks can also originate outside of financial markets. The oil price shock of the 1970s was political in origin. Economic shocks tend to be unexpected. When they arise their effects can be immediate, which was the case when the Covid-19 pandemic hit in 2019–20 and restrictions imposed by governments to contain the spread of the pandemic had an immediate impact on economies (recall that we have defined the economy as the amount of exchange that takes place). In other cases, their effects can be widespread but may occur over many years. This is the case when there are revolutions in the way technology allows firms to operate in different ways. Regardless of the cause, the shock affects the way the economy works as a whole. Sometimes, these effects will impact on particular industries but have a ripple effect throughout the rest of the economy. For example, globalization and the developments in technology have changed the way consumers are able to acquire goods and services and this has had a negative impact on some firms and industries and a positive effect on others. Patterns of change in macroeconomic variables can arise as a result, for example changes in patterns of employment or unemployment, in inflation and in economic growth.

In this chapter we will look at some of the more recent economic shocks and how these have impacted firms, governments and individuals. It is always difficult to forecast the future, but one thing is almost certain. There will be more economic shocks and economists will investigate, seek to understand and analyze and learn from these to help cope with the inevitable challenges that will arise.

THE 2007–9 FINANCIAL CRISIS

The 2007–9 Financial Crisis led to a widespread and deep global recession. The 1990s and early 2000s saw relatively benign economic conditions in much of Europe, the UK and the United States, characterized by a period of relatively low inflation, high employment, low unemployment and stable growth. Such was the relative stability experienced that the period was termed **The Great Moderation** (in the UK, it was termed 'The Great Stability').

> **The Great Moderation** the period of economic stability characterized by relatively low inflation, high employment, low unemployment and stable and persistent growth

Causes of the Crisis

One of the causes could perhaps be seen as an unintended consequence. In the UK and the United States, deregulation began in the 1980s. It was set against the belief that excessive regulation limited the ability of the economy's supply side to operate efficiently. A series of legislation dramatically changed the banking and financial landscape. Rules and regulations surrounding the activities of banks and building societies were abolished or relaxed. One of the consequences of deregulation in financial market was that access to mortgages now became easier for millions of people.

The Sub-prime Market In the United States, extending mortgage opportunities to those not traditionally seen as being part of the market (the **sub-prime market**) expanded rapidly in the early 2000s.

> **sub-prime market** individuals not traditionally seen as being part of the financial markets because of their high credit risk

The growth of sub-prime mortgages began to take an increasing share of the total mortgage market in the United States. Sub-prime loans accounted for around 35 per cent of all mortgages issued in the United States in 2004. In the United States, the S&P/Case-Schiller National Home Price Index increased from 100 in 2000 to around 190 in 2006. Increased borrowing in the UK also rose, not just for mortgages but for consumer purchases. In the UK, the average house price rose from around £30,000 in 1983 (€35,745) to almost £200,000 (€238,000) in 2007.

The Rise in Defaults

In financial markets, the growth in sub-prime and other lending was further developed through packaging mortgage-backed securities into pools of debt and selling them on, a process known as **securitization**. As we saw earlier in the book, this packaging of debt through collateralized debt obligations (CDOs) was 'insured' through credit default swaps (CDS).

> **securitization** the packaging of mortgage-backed securities into pools of debt and selling them on

In 2006–7, the prevailing concern among central banks was the development of inflationary pressure which was met with successive increases in interest rates. As interest rates rose, borrowers, especially those on sub-prime mortgages in the United States, began to feel the pressure, and reports of the number of defaults on sub-prime loans began to rise.

Once mortgage defaults began to rise to alarming numbers, the number of financial institutions affected, and their exposure, became clearer. The whole edifice was based on the expectation that the underlying assets would continue to generate an income stream over time. In other words, the very large majority of mortgage holders would continue to pay their monthly mortgage repayments.

As the sub-prime market collapsed, the exposure of banks and financial institutions to bad debt started to become more obvious and a number of banks reported significant write-downs and losses. Confidence in the banking system, so important to its functioning, began to fall. Banks were not sure of their own exposure to these bad debts (referred to as toxic debt) and so were also unsure about the extent of other banks' exposure. Interbank lending began to become much tighter as banks were unwilling to lend to each other. They also faced the task of trying to shore up their own balance sheets. Accessing credit was, therefore, far more expensive and limited in nature, and the higher price of borrowing was passed onto the consumer: individuals and businesses. When business loans are less easy to obtain or more expensive, businesses find it difficult to manage their cash flow and insolvency can result. A number of banks in the United States and in other countries, including the UK, Iceland and Germany, experienced problems. Some were rescued by being acquired and others were propped up by significant government intervention.

Banking Collapse The issue of moral hazard might be the reason why one of the most spectacular banking collapses in recent times occurred on 15 September 2008. The US investment bank Lehman Brothers had been a bank at the forefront of the sub-prime and CDS market. It had built its business on leveraging, that is borrowing heavily to finance its activities. Over the weekend of 13 and 14 September 2008, last ditch talks were convened to try to find a way of rescuing Lehman Brothers in the same way that Bear Stearns and Merrill Lynch had been rescued. However, the debts at Lehman and the extent of their exposure to sub-prime and CDS were too great. Lehman Brothers filed for Chapter 11 bankruptcy protection on 15 September.

The collapse of Lehman led to further strains within the financial system. Many banks were now exposed and in danger of failing themselves as they had to meet payment obligations and did not have the funds available in reserves to do so. Banks that were struggling to meet their obligations attempted to raise funds in the interbank money markets, which were almost at a standstill. Banks around the world found themselves in this difficult situation and had to take more assets back onto their balance sheets. This meant they had to reinstate sufficient reserves to support these liabilities and this further reduced their willingness to lend. Instead, the focus shifted to restoring balance sheets by taking in deposits but not lending. The collapse of Lehman was seen as a spectacular event because it showed that central banks were not prepared to step in to help any bank that got into trouble.

The Path to Global Recession

The problems in financial markets began to be felt in the real economy fairly quickly. Interest rates had been rising up to the middle of 2008 in an attempt to curb demand in the United States, the UK and Europe, and those increases had started to feed through via the interest rate transmission mechanism.

It was, however, the effect of the tight credit market that exacerbated the depth of the downturn in many countries. One by one, countries in the developed world saw economic growth falling. A major cause of the downturn was due to the problems businesses had in accessing funds from banks. Businesses, especially small businesses, rely on cash flow for their survival. Many need flexibility and understanding from their banks when faced with shocks to their cash flow, and tight credit markets meant that many businesses found banks unwilling to lend and extend overdrafts. Even if a bank was prepared to lend, the interest rate attached to the loan was often prohibitive. Faced with cash flow problems and an inability to get the finance to support them, many smaller businesses began to close.

Larger businesses were not immune to the problems. As global production fell, unemployment rose. In the United States, the unemployment rate rose from 6.2 per cent in August 2008 to 9.7 per cent a year later. In the UK, in the three months to June 2008, it was 5.3 per cent increasing to 7.9 per cent a year later. Across the EU, unemployment was in excess of 10 per cent.

The banking crisis and the credit squeeze triggered the subsequent recession which was deep and widespread. Given the relative calm of the global economy during The Great Moderation, questions were asked as to why the global economy had got into such a state. Some of the blame was laid at the door of economists and, in particular, those economists who had placed faith in models and theories to explain the economy and financial markets which now seemed to have failed. Central to the questions being asked was the efficient markets hypothesis.

The Efficient Markets Hypothesis

A diversified portfolio of shares or assets is one way of reducing the risk of investing. 'Expert' fund managers can be employed to conduct the fundamental analysis required to maximize returns. There is another way to choose shares for a portfolio: pick them randomly by, for instance, putting the stock pages of the *Financial Times* on a notice board and throwing darts at the page. This may sound crazy, but there is reason to believe that it will not lead you too far astray. That reason is called the **efficient markets hypothesis (EMH)**.

> **efficient markets hypothesis (EMH)** the theory that asset prices reflect all publicly available information about the value of an asset

To understand the EMH, the starting point is that stock markets contain a large number of buyers and sellers and that the market has sufficient liquidity to enable stock to be bought and sold at any time. Buyers and sellers in the market monitor news stories and conduct fundamental analysis to try to determine stock values. The second feature of the EMH is that the equilibrium of supply and demand sets the market price. This means that, at the market price, the number of shares being offered for sale exactly equals the number of shares that people want to buy. In other words, at the market price, the number of people who think the share is overvalued exactly balances the number of people who think it is undervalued. As judged by the typical person in the market, all shares are fairly valued all the time.

According to this theory, the stock market is **informationally efficient**. It reflects all available information about the value of the asset. Share prices change when information changes. When good news about a company's prospects become public, both the value and the stock price rise. When a company's prospects deteriorate, both the value and price fall. At any moment in time, the market price is the best guess of the company's value based on available information.

> **informationally efficient** reflecting all available information in a rational way

The Random Walk One implication of the EMH is that stock prices should follow a **random walk**. This means that changes in stock prices are impossible to predict from available information. If, based on publicly available information, a person could correctly predict that a stock price would rise by 10 per cent tomorrow, the stock market must be failing to incorporate that information today. According to this theory, the only thing that can move stock prices is news that changes the market's perception of the company's value. But news must be unpredictable – otherwise, it would not really be news. For the same reason, changes in stock prices should be unpredictable.

> **random walk** the path of a variable whose changes are impossible to predict

If the EMH is correct, then there is little point in spending many hours studying the business pages to decide which shares to add to your portfolio. If prices reflect all available information, no stock is a better buy than any other. The best you can do is buy a diversified portfolio.

Efficient Markets Hypothesis: A Cause of the 2007–9 Financial Crisis?

The assumption of efficient markets and the belief that markets self-correct and revert to reflect true market value was the basis of the regulatory framework that underpinned the financial system in most major centres of the world prior to the 2007–9 Financial Crisis.

The EMH implies there is no predictability in stock prices, which means that no one investor can gain any benefit through exploiting predictability. There has been considerable research into the EMH following the Financial Crisis, which suggests that there may be some predictability in stock prices depending on certain circumstances. Analysts studying these patterns (or more realistically, computers programmed to identify such patterns) mean that any element of predictability can be exploited by those in the market. However, if this information becomes freely available and widely known, then it will be built into decision-making and the opportunity for profiting from the predictability disappears or becomes so small as to not be worthwhile exploiting.

Herd Mentality Much of the reasoning behind the EMH is based on the assumption of rational behaviour. The question raised in the wake of the Financial Crisis was the extent to which behaviour in financial markets was rational. That may not be the case. Rather than looking at information, analyzing it rationally and basing decisions on the data available, herd mentality can take over and lead to people responding to others' behaviour.

Herd mentality can manifest itself when markets are rising as they were in the period before the Crisis. If house prices have been rising for 20 years, why should they not continue to rise over the next 20 years? Participants in the market may not be expert analysts, but rather ordinary households making decisions with imperfect knowledge. People taking on mortgages or buying second homes may not have looked at other relevant data such as the growth in credit and changes in real wages, which may have an impact on longer-term property prices. People jump into the market having heard of the returns that can be made and, as more people join in, decision-making becomes further based on mimicking others' behaviour rather than on fundamental analysis. There is an old adage that says that if something sounds too good to be true, it probably is. There is a subtle difference between valuing an asset based on fundamental analysis – the present value of future dividends – and valuing it based on the emulation of others' behaviour and an assumption that prices will rise indefinitely. When the price gets detached from the fundamentals and starts to be contingent only on what everyone in the market expects everyone else will think, a so-called asset bubble starts to form. If these speculative bubbles do exist, it suggests that markets react to what Alan Greenspan called 'irrational exuberance' and what Keynes referred to as 'animal spirits'. In speculative bubbles, asset prices rise because of an expectation of what others think the asset will be worth in the future. Keynes believed that, given the fact most investors will sell shares they own at some point in the future, it is not unreasonable to have some concern about others' valuation of that asset. Such views could lead to irrational waves of optimism and pessimism. The EMH is based on an assumption that there are a sufficient number of people in the market who act rationally to counter the few that do not.

SELF TEST Why is the phrase 'all publicly available information' important in the EMH?

Asset Price Bubbles

There is much debate about whether asset price bubbles ever exist and, if they do, what should be done about them. The EMH would suggest that large swings in asset prices are the result of major changes in information about fundamentals. Proponents of the EMH view argue that bubbles can only exist if driven by irrational behaviour or rigidities in the market, which prevent prices from adjusting quickly. These market rigidities might exist if the market is small, for example.

The challenge for the authorities (central banks and government) is to be able to tell when a bubble is occurring and, if it is, whether and when to take action. A decision to intervene and take policy action to 'burst' the bubble would have to depend on whether the authorities believe that the bubble is going to get out of hand and cause damage to the wider economy if it bursts. It could be that the bubble bursts of its own accord and the market self-corrects. Research into major bubbles suggests different levels of effect on the economy.

The potential danger is that bubbles affect the real economy through a wealth effect, which fuels consumer spending and encourages firms to make decisions based on changes in their balance sheets as a result of changing asset values. The increase in house prices in the United States and the UK did fuel additional borrowing and further consumer spending, which led to an acceleration of inflation that prompted central banks to increase interest rates. If central banks intervene too early and attempt to burst the bubble, would the effect on the wider economy be more damaging than the aftermath of the bubble bursting of its own accord? These are unknowns and require judgement on behalf of central bankers. The challenges are made more difficult with globalization, as it is much easier for money to move between economic centres around the global economy.

The person who developed the model of the EMH, Eugene Fama, faced considerable criticism following the Crisis. However, in 2013, he was awarded the Nobel Prize for Economics for his work on capital asset pricing. In his Nobel Prize lecture, Fama addressed the issue of asset price bubbles and defended his position. However, the issue continues to generate fierce debate and differences of opinion.

Fama argues that, to date, no credible alternative has been put forward. Proponents of the behavioural approach argue that there is much evidence of 'animal spirits', 'irrational exuberance' or 'herd mentality'. Perhaps it is safe to conclude that there is much life in the debate and it provides interesting avenues for further research.

CRITICAL THINKING POINT In defending his position, Fama has pointed out a concept referred to as 'ex-post selection bias'. Ex-post means 'after the event' in that it is easy to highlight a few people who predict bubbles. Do these few people have better access to information than thousands of others in being able to make such predictions? Where does your position lie on the idea of asset bubbles and what reasons and evidence would you use to support your position?

Minsky's Financial Instability Hypothesis

One theory that was revitalized following the debate around the EMH was the financial instability hypothesis developed by Hyman Minsky (1919–96). Minsky was Professor of Economics at Washington University in St Louis in the United States and began writing on financial instability in the 1950s. Minsky was a keen student of business cycles. He rejected the classical assumption that the invisible hand would result in equilibrium as well as the Keynesian idea of demand management. Minsky saw capitalism as fundamentally flawed and considered financial crises a natural feature of such a system.

Minsky's financial instability hypothesis began with an assumption that a capitalist economy has capital assets and a sophisticated financial system. Firms in capitalist systems buy resources, which represent future income streams or profit. Part of the spending on resources includes investment in capital which is facilitated by financial institutions. The financial system is complicated by the fact that households can access credit to buy consumer goods and invest in shares and other financial assets. Governments are also heavily involved in the financial system, borrowing for their own use and, in some cases, stepping in to bailout financial institutions and firms.

The emphasis on the way the capitalist system works is central to the instability hypothesis and in particular the link between expected profits and investment. The question Minsky posed was what role debt had in this system. He accepted that financial institutions are profit-making bodies and that profits can be increased through innovation. There are different ways in which financial institutions can operate. One way is to take in deposits, re-lend and hedge against the risk involved, specifically the risk of default. This might be viewed as 'traditional banking'.

A second way is through speculative financing. Here, the obligations an institution has are met by the income streams it receives, although these income streams are insufficient to pay off the principal. In this case, new debt is issued to enable the institution to meet its principal obligations.

Finally, there are 'Ponzi' units. The term comes from an Italian, Charles Ponzi, who developed a money-making venture in the United States in the 1920s. He relied on attracting new investors to the scheme, whose money was used to pay existing investors and hence maintain the venture. Ponzi schemes are illegal across much of the developed world. Ponzi units share some of the characteristics of a Ponzi scheme in that the income streams from activities are insufficient to pay the principal and the interest due on debts. Ponzi units finance their obligations through further borrowing or selling assets. The risk to debt holders of such an approach is considerably higher than hedge financing.

If hedge financing is the main way in which financial institutions operate, then the economy is more like a self-equilibrating system. If speculative, however, and Ponzi finance begins to account for a larger proportion, then the economy is more likely to be what Minsky called a 'deviation amplification system'. Where financial systems are strong and appropriate regulation is in place, innovation may be limited and the economy will be experiencing a 'period of tranquillity'. This stability, however, encourages risk-taking and innovation (for example, more speculative and Ponzi financing), pushing the economy towards instability and a speculative frenzy, which we have seen termed 'irrational exuberance', 'herd mentality', 'animal spirits' and asset bubbles. The situation can be exacerbated by the authorities failing to intervene, partly because they are caught in the belief that the situation is under control and partly because of regulatory capture. **Regulatory capture** refers to a situation where regulatory agencies become unduly influenced and dominated by the industries they are supposed to be regulating.

> **regulatory capture** a situation where regulatory agencies become unduly influenced and dominated by the industries they are supposed to be regulating

Minsky's hypothesis has three main aspects:

1. Economies can have stable financing systems but also unstable ones.
2. During periods of relative stability and prosperity, the economy will transition to increasing instability as innovation and risk-taking increase.
3. Business cycles are not caused by external shocks alone but are made worse by the internal dynamics of a capitalist system.

Minsky argued that financial markets create their own internal forces, which generate periods of asset inflation and credit expansion. This is followed by contractions in credit and asset deflation. Financial markets are not self-optimizing or stable, and far from allocating resources efficiently, the outcomes may be sub-optimal.

Minsky suggested that some of these internal forces relate to the lack of supply of assets which drive demand in those markets. For example, the lack of supply of housing drives demand for housing and forces prices upwards. Changing asset prices (such as houses) act as a driver for demand for those assets. If house prices are rising quickly there is an incentive for buyers to get into the market quickly to avoid having to pay higher prices and to benefit from rising prices once they have purchased. This fuels demand further and so drives price up higher.

The story of the 2007–9 Financial Crisis resonates remarkably closely with the Minsky hypothesis. It is not surprising, therefore, that his ideas were seen as being 'ahead of their time' and worth reviving and exploring.

THE SOVEREIGN DEBT CRISIS

Sovereign debt refers to bonds issued by national governments to finance expenditure. One of the consequences of the 2007–9 Financial Crisis was the focus on the problems faced by a number of countries in Europe in managing debt. Recall that budget deficits are the difference between the amount of tax revenue and government spending. Deficits are financed by government borrowing and, as borrowing increases, the overall debt rises. Governments must manage this debt by ensuring that they have enough funds to be able to pay back government bonds when they reach maturity and also to pay the interest on the bonds which are outstanding. Lending to governments has invariably been seen as relatively risk-free. In the wake of the Financial Crisis it became clear that for some governments, this was not the case.

> **sovereign debt** the bonds issued by national governments to finance expenditure

The macroeconomic shock created by the Financial Crisis led to a global slowdown in economic activity. When countries experience a prolonged period of economic slowdown, tax revenues decline and spending on welfare support increases. While automatic stabilizers moderate the effects, in a severe recessionary period these automatic stabilizers can be diluted. In this environment, governments need to increase borrowing, but the reduced confidence of markets in their ability to meet debt obligations means that some countries can be brought to the verge of bankruptcy. In other words, they cannot raise enough funds to meet debt and everyday public spending obligations.

The Greek Debt Crisis

The country that has come to epitomize the sovereign debt crisis is Greece. In 2009, Greece announced that its deficit would reach almost 13 per cent of GDP, double the amount it forecast a year previously. In early 2010 the country's debt was reported as €300 billion, more than the value of its GDP, and it found that it was becoming increasingly difficult to meet its debt obligations.

In February and March 2010, the Greek government tried to take a stance on public spending, proposing major cuts in jobs, pensions, wages and services. Greek workers took to the streets in protest. It became a real possibility that Greece would default and be forced to leave the euro, and markets started to look to other EU governments to organize a bailout. The financial markets were nervous that the problems in Greece would spread to other high-debt countries (the so-called 'contagion effect') and there were fears that the crisis could tip Europe back into recession.

The Development of the Crisis

A number of countries had relied on borrowing internationally, including Ireland, Spain and Portugal, and were particularly affected by the so-called 'credit crunch'. As banks in these countries teetered on the brink of collapse, they looked to national governments for support. If governments allowed these banks to fail then the effect on the population as a whole, not to mention the wider banking sector in Europe, would likely be significant. To help support their banking systems, governments had to borrow money – but few of these governments had the fiscal flexibility to do so without increasing borrowing.

Bailouts The first part of the Greek bailout was negotiated in late April into May 2010. In November 2010, Ireland's government also had to seek support and in May 2011, Portugal followed suit. In June 2011, Greece needed a second bailout, which was eventually agreed in March 2012. On 13 July 2015, an agreement was reached on a third bailout. In June 2012, Spain had to seek help and in March 2013, the banking system in Cyprus was on the verge of collapse. Banks closed for almost two weeks while the Cypriot government negotiated with the EU and IMF causing widespread problems for many ordinary people seeking to make everyday purchases. Cypriot banks were subject to considerable restructuring and when they reopened in March 2013, there were significant limitations on the amount of money that could be withdrawn. Capital controls on money leaving Cyprus were also imposed. After reforms, the IMF approved a bailout fund of €280 million and set an end to the IMF funding in 2016, reflecting the progress the country made post-crisis.

The European Financial Stability Fund (EFSF) and the European Stability Mechanism (ESM) The discussions over the first Greek bailout led European finance ministers to establish the European Financial Stability Fund (EFSF) in May 2010 to provide support for countries that face default. The EFSF raised funds by issuing bonds and other financial instruments through capital markets. The money raised was lent to countries seeking assistance on the understanding that reforms were put in place. The establishment of the EFSF was designed to be a temporary measure pending the establishment of a more permanent means of supporting countries in financial difficulties. The permanent replacement for the EFSF, the European Stability Mechanism (ESM), began operations in October 2012. Like the EFSF, the ESM raises funds on the capital markets and works with the IMF in dealing with member states who request assistance. The ESM will only provide support if the member state seeking help agrees to implement fiscal adjustment and structural reform. Structural reform refers to changes in the labour and capital markets designed to help improve the efficiency of the economy. One of the elements of ESM support is a consideration of the situation of the member country and the overall stability of the euro area. If it is considered that the financial stability of the euro area is under threat, then the ESM can provide support.

THE DEBATE OVER BUDGETS

The sovereign debt crisis led to a number of countries adopting austerity programmes, including significant public spending cuts, tax rises and structural reforms. The practical implications of this policy are more complex. People of the country where austerity programmes are implemented are likely to be severely affected. The effects of such policies being adopted during a period of weak economic activity are likely to be that national income will decline and unemployment will rise.

Structural and Cyclical Deficits

The focus on public sector deficits raises questions about the difference between cyclical and structural deficits. A **cyclical deficit** occurs when government spending and income are disrupted by the 'normal' economic cycle. In times of strong economic growth, government revenue from taxes will rise and spending on welfare and benefits will fall, resulting in public finances moving into surplus (or the deficit shrinks appreciably). In times of economic slowdown, the opposite occurs and the size of the budget deficit will rise (or the surplus shrink). A **structural deficit** refers to a situation where the deficit is not dependent on movements in the economic cycle but is due to a government 'living beyond its means' that is spending what it has not got.

> **cyclical deficit** a situation when government spending and income are disrupted by the deviations in the 'normal' economic cycle
> **structural deficit** a situation where the deficit is due to a government 'living beyond its means' that is spending persistently more than its income

Economists are divided in their views about the nature and importance of structural deficits. What follows is a summary of the arguments on both sides.

Argument 1: Policymakers Need to Eradicate Structural Deficits The existence of a structural deficit implies that the public finances will be even worse when entering a recession. It will necessitate an increase in the levels of borrowing which are unsustainable in the long term. As a result of the size of these deficits, the risk of default by governments on their debt is greater. Increasingly they will find it difficult to service their debt and the cost of so doing will rise. This also creates uncertainty in financial markets and threatens the survival of the currency. As a result, fiscal consolidation is essential to reduce long-term interest rate and currency instability and to help promote economic growth. This fiscal consolidation should primarily be in the form of cuts in public spending rather than increases in taxes, as these may damage employment and investment.

Argument 2: The Idea of a Structural Deficit is a Myth The idea that government deficits are structural is unhelpful. The assumption is that governments must borrow more because of the gap between income and expenditure. How certain can we be though that the only reason governments are borrowing money is simply due to the changes to public finances wrought by a recession? The whole notion of a structural deficit assumes that it is the amount governments borrow when the economy is operating at its trend level. This implies that to measure it we need to know how far the economy is operating below trend – the output gap.

The problem is that there is considerable disagreement on the size of the output gap. It is accepted that a recession will destroy some potential output, but how much is open to some interpretation. A number of studies have attempted to quantify the impact of economic downturns on the output gap and the outcomes vary significantly. The size of the output gap is important because it has a direct effect on the cyclical component of the deficit. The larger the output gap the larger will be the cyclical component and the smaller the structural. This in turn affects any estimates of the size of borrowing when the economy does return to trend, in other words the size of the structural deficit.

Any calculations on the deficit would also be subject to assumptions about the sensitivity of taxes and spending to changes in GDP. How does tax revenue rise in relation to changes in GDP? This will depend in part on assumptions about the number of people who are able to find work as the economy expands. It also depends on the extent to which potential output has been destroyed. How do changes in government spending vary in relation to changes in GDP? How many people will get off benefits, and what effect will short-term fiscal stimulus measures have on spending? As an increasing number of assumptions are made, calculations of the size of the structural deficit could be very different. Which one should be used as the basis for policy decisions? In the light of this analysis, is it useful to think of the idea of a structural deficit at all?

Fiscal Consolidation

The extent to which budget deficits should be a cause for concern is a persistent macroeconomic debate. Whether a government should seek to balance budgets is a source of debate among economists. Our study of financial markets showed how budget deficits affect saving, investment and interest rates. But how big a problem are budget deficits?

Argument 1: The Government Should Balance Its Budget When a government fails to balance its budget, it must borrow money by issuing bonds to make up the shortfall. The most direct effect of high and rising government debt is to place a burden on future generations of taxpayers. When these debts and accumulated interest come due, future taxpayers will face a difficult choice. They can pay higher taxes, enjoy less government spending or both to make resources available to pay off the debt and accumulated interest. Or they can delay the day of reckoning and put the government into even deeper debt by borrowing once again to pay off the old debt and interest.

In addition to this direct effect, budget deficits also have various macroeconomic effects. Because budget deficits represent *negative* public saving, they lower national saving (the sum of private and public saving). Reduced national saving causes real interest rates to rise and investment to fall. Over time, reduced investment leads to a smaller stock of capital. A lower capital stock reduces labour productivity, real wages and the economy's production of goods and services. Thus, when the government increases its debt, future generations are born into an economy with lower incomes as well as higher taxes.

There are, nevertheless, situations in which running a budget deficit is justifiable. Throughout history, the most common cause of increased government debt is war. Military conflict raises government spending temporarily and can be financed by borrowing. If governments had to rely on taxes, high tax rates would greatly distort the incentives faced by those who are taxed. High tax rates would be unfair to current generations of taxpayers who are already making sacrifices to fight the war.

Similarly, it is reasonable to allow a budget deficit during a temporary downturn in economic activity or during economic shocks such as the Covid-19 pandemic, which necessitated large injections of fiscal support to firms and workers because of the restrictions imposed to try to control the spread of the virus. If the government tried to balance its budget during a recession, it would have to raise taxes or cut spending at a time of high unemployment. Such a policy would tend to depress AD at precisely the time it needed to be stimulated and, therefore, would tend to increase the magnitude of economic fluctuations. When the economy goes into recovery, however, the opposite is true. Then, tax receipts grow as the level of economic activity rises and transfer payments tend to fall. The government should therefore be able to run a budget surplus and use the money to pay off the debt incurred by the budget deficit it ran during the recession.

Wars or significant events such as Covid-19 aside, over the course of the business cycle, there is no excuse for not balancing the budget. If the government runs a deficit when the economy is in a recession, it should run a comparable surplus when the economy recovers, so that on average the budget balances. Compared to the alternative of ongoing budget deficits, a balanced budget, or at least a budget that is balanced over the economic cycle, means greater national saving, investment and economic growth. It means that future university graduates will enter a more prosperous economy.

Argument 2: The Government Should Not Balance its Budget The problem of government debt is often exaggerated. Although government debt does represent a tax burden on younger generations, it is often not large compared with the average person's lifetime income. The case for balancing the government budget is made by confusing the economics of a single person or household with that of a whole economy. Economies, unlike people, do not have finite lives. In some sense, they live forever, so there is never any reason to clear the debt completely.

Critics of budget deficits sometimes assert that government debt cannot continue to rise forever, as it would, in fact, have consequences. Just as a bank evaluating a loan application compares a person's debts to their income, we should judge the burden of the government debt relative to the size of the nation's income. Population growth and technological progress cause the total income of the economy to grow over time. As a result, the nation's ability to pay interest on government debt grows over time as well. The focus should not be on looking at the total amount of debt but at the ratio of debt to income. As long as this is not increasing, then the level of debt is sustainable. In other words, as long as the level of government debt grows more slowly than the nation's income, there is nothing to prevent government debt from growing forever.

Moreover, it is misleading to view the effects of budget deficits in isolation. The budget deficit is just one piece of a large picture of how the government chooses to raise and spend money. In making these decisions over fiscal policy, policymakers affect different generations of taxpayers in many ways.

The government's budget deficit or surplus should be considered together with these other policies. For example, suppose the government reduces the budget deficit by cutting spending on public investments, such as education. Does this policy make younger generations better off? The government debt will be smaller when they enter the labour force, which means a smaller tax burden. Yet if they are less well educated than they could be, their productivity and incomes will be lower. Many estimates of the return on schooling (the increase in a worker's wage that results from an additional year in school) find that it is quite large. Reducing the budget deficit rather than funding more education spending could, all things considered, make future generations worse off. A distinction has to be made between borrowing to finance investment, which helps boost the future productive capacity of the economy, and borrowing to finance current government expenditure (on things such as wages for public sector workers).

The qualification that the government budget on current expenditure will be balanced on average over the economic cycle allows for the effect of automatic stabilizers such as the increase in welfare expenditure and reduction in tax revenue that automatically occur in a recession (the opposite in a boom). These then help flatten out economic fluctuations. Allowing a budget deficit on investment expenditure is sensible because, although it leads to rising public debt, it also leads to further growth opportunities through spending on education, roads and so on. Just asserting that the government should balance its budget, irrespective of the economic cycle and irrespective of what kind of expenditures it is making, is overly simplistic.

Austerity or Growth?

The arguments outlined above crystallize the debate over the nature and importance of government budgets and austerity policies. While there might be general agreement that countries do need to get more control over debt and their deficits, austerity policies adopted after the 2007–9 Financial Crisis were, some argued, counterproductive.

The Argument for Austerity Countries must take steps to get public finances under control. If attempts are made to increase borrowing to spend out of recession the effect will be increased inflation, higher borrowing costs and further uncertainty across the whole of Europe. There is also a moral dimension to the necessity for austerity. It is not fair to expect the taxpayers of countries that have maintained a sound fiscal stance and abided by the rules to pay for the lax behaviour of governments in other countries.

In the short to medium term, the effects of austerity are considerable, but the long-term benefits of sounder finances, improved structural reforms and a stronger banking sector are that all countries in Europe will be more competitive. They would then be in a position to benefit from stronger and more sustained economic growth in the future.

The Argument for Growth The main cause of Europe's problems stemmed from the financial system not from government debt. Austerity at a time of economic slowdown will affect economies considerably. It will be further exacerbated by the lack of credit in economies caused by banks seeking to recapitalize and rebuild their balance sheets. Without an adequate supply of credit, consumer spending and business investment will decline and lead to a prolonged and damaging period of economic depression. If output declines, tax revenues will fall and government spending on benefits will rise and, far from alleviating the debt crisis, will merely force governments to borrow more. The only way to solve the debt crisis is to get economies growing again. Governments need to adopt Keynesian style stimulus spending. Stronger economic growth will lead to increased tax revenues, and if unemployment falls, government spending on welfare support drops, reducing the need to borrow.

MODERN MONETARY THEORY

The Office for National Statistics (ONS) reports that public sector net borrowing in the UK in 2007 was around £41.6 billion. This rose to £159.8 billion in 2009 as a result of the Financial Crisis. Government borrowing then gradually fell to £47.3 billion in 2019. In January 2020, the government recorded negative borrowing of –£9.9 billion. Then Covid-19 hit the country. In 2020, the ONS reported government borrowing at almost £273 billion. In April 2020 alone, borrowing was £49.2 billion. Across the EU, the deficit was recorded as €76.5 billion in 2019 but €922.5 billion in 2020. This pattern of increasing public sector deficits was reflected across many countries around the world.

As news reports began to highlight the extent of the increase in borrowing and the widening of budget deficits, there were also comments made about how such large sums of money would be paid for in the future. So the debate about budget deficits and austerity was raised once again and continues to be a point of debate and disagreement.

For countries like the UK and the United States, the issues around budget deficits are different from those of the EU for one very good reason. They are sovereign nations that have the sole legal authority to issue their currencies, that is they can issue the pound and dollar respectively. Modern Monetary Theory (MMT) is based around an understanding of this crucial fact.

A Currency Issuing Government is not Like a Household

MMT theorists make the point that governments that issue their own currency are not like a household or a firm. If a household wishes to spend more, it either must earn more income or borrow money. MMT theorists note that there is a prevailing view that if governments want to spend more, then, yes, they can borrow more. At some point, however, the spending has to be financed by higher taxes. Often it is believed that governments must raise funds before they spend, much like households and firms have to do. MMT theorists, however, argue that this view misunderstands the nature of sovereign nations that issue their own currency.

Governments that have the monopoly on issuing their own currency do not have to receive money in the form of tax revenues to spend it. They can simply spend pounds or dollars because they have the monopoly over currency issue. This is the reason why governments like the UK can increase spending when faced with economic shocks like the 2007–9 Financial Crisis and Covid-19. The UK government did not have to increase taxes in 2007 to pay for the financial support programmes that it put in place to support the financial system, firms and individuals. Neither did it have to put up taxes in early 2020 to pay for the support measures it put in place in response to the pandemic.

Instead, the UK government issued bonds. As we have seen, a bond is an IOU, issued by the government in this case. The buyer of the bond lends the government money and in return the government agrees to pay a coupon (the interest rate) and invariably promises to pay back the loan at some point in the future. Lenders are willing to buy bonds from governments like the UK and the United States because they are deemed safe and the likelihood of default is extremely small. The buyers of these bonds tend to be large institutional investors such as pension funds, insurance companies, investment funds and banks, who buy them as part of their overall investment portfolio.

Let us use an example to highlight how the transactions work. Assume that a government announces plans to invest in a major infrastructure project to the value of £75 billion. Bonds are issued to the value of £75 billion and, as institutional investors take up these bonds, the UK government instructs its bank, the Bank of England, to debit the accounts of the purchaser and credit its own account. Individual firms involved in the planning and construction of the infrastructure project put in a claim to the government for the various costs they incur and the government instructs the Bank of England to credit the accounts of these firms and debit its own account. The transactions are all carried out through computer keystrokes in effect. No actual cash changes hands. The government is not instructing the Bank of England to order the printing of more notes or minting of more coins. These are simply electronic transactions that alter the balance sheets of the institutional investors, banks and firms taking advantage of the new project. The balance sheet of the Bank of England will just reflect the transaction as it will now show an increase in liabilities to the tune of £75 billion but also an increase in assets of £75 billion from the receipts of the sale of the bonds.

There is no reason why this process could not continue indefinitely. In theory, the government could spend to fund anything it wants. If, for example, it wanted to expand programmes to end child poverty, invest in new housing or in green energy solutions, or increase spending on education, welfare programmes, health services and social care, it could.

Macroeconomic Accounting

The logic behind this lies in a basic understanding of accounting. A key accounting principle is that every financial asset has an equal and opposite financial liability. For example, assume an insurance company buys a UK government bond. The Bank of England receives a credit on its account for the total sum the insurance company has chosen to spend on the bonds it has purchased. This credit represents an asset on its balance sheet. However, in selling the bonds, the Bank of England has also created a liability. It is liable to repay the value of the bonds bought by the insurance company at some point in the future. We can also look at this in another way. The insurance company, in buying the bonds, has acquired an asset (ownership of the bond) and the Bank of England has an equal but opposite financial liability. Looking at it in this way highlights the difference between two macroeconomic sectors: the public sector represented by the domestic government and the private sector represented by the insurance company. The transaction merely represents a transfer between these two sectors. A domestic government deficit is reflected in a domestic private surplus. But of course, it is not only domestic private investors that will purchase UK government bonds. Foreign entities will also purchase UK government bonds and UK entities will buy bonds from foreign governments. This gives us a third sector, the foreign sector. In the same way that in our exploration of national income accounting, income equals expenditure equals the value of output, in the aggregate, all these must balance each other out and we get the simple equation:

$$\text{Domestic private balance} + \text{Domestic government balance} + \text{Foreign balance} = 0$$

This equation is derived from the work of distinguished British economist, Wynne Godley, and is explained in more detail by L Randall Wray, one of the leading thinkers in MMT. Wray is a professor of economics at the University of Missouri, in Kansas City in the United States, and a former student of Hyman Minsky. Wray notes that this basic identity highlights the fact that if one of the three sectors runs a surplus, then at least one must be running a deficit. Equally, if the government domestic balance is in deficit, then either or both of the domestic private balance and the foreign balance must be in surplus.

The Need for Taxation

Wray and other proponents of MMT note that in theory, a government with a monopoly over the issue of its currency can never become insolvent. However, if this is the case, then why do we have taxes to raise revenue for the government? Modern monetary theorists provide three main reasons why taxation is important:

1. A government with monopoly power to issue its currency requires that currency to be legitimized through its citizens paying taxes. In effect, UK residents must earn the pounds that the UK government issues to pay their taxes to the government. The UK government (for example) does not allow UK taxes to be paid in any other currency. Workers are exchanging their labour skills for the currency, and they need this currency to fulfil their legal obligations to the government to pay their taxes.
2. The second reason why taxes are important is to help balance out government spending. If government spent whatever it liked, this could trigger serious inflation because the country may not have the resource capabilities to satisfy all the spending desires. In other words, governments that issue sovereign currencies must be aware of the real productive capacity of the economy, that is the level of aggregate supply. By imposing taxes, government can remove spending power from its citizens, and this can help to moderate inflationary pressures.
3. Taxes are also important, as we have seen, for wealth distribution purposes or to encourage incentives. To combat the challenges of climate change, for example, governments can use taxes as a means of penalizing undesirable behaviour (for example, the manufacture and purchase of diesel vehicles) and reward desirable behaviour (such as the manufacture and purchase of zero-emissions vehicles).

Looking at government finances in this way can seem counterintuitive. Indeed, some advocates of MMT agree that it took them some time to think differently about the situation. Stephanie Kelton, a professor of economics and public policy at Stony Brook University in New York, is one of these people. In her book *The Deficit Myth* (2020, John Murray Publishers) Kelton notes that it can seem obvious that governments tax individuals and firms to raise money to enable them to finance their expenditures. When tax revenue is insufficient to finance spending, the government then must 'collect' money from buyers of bonds to pay for its spending plans. However, she notes that this scenario can be viewed from a different angle. Governments with a monopoly over the issue of its currency do not need individuals or firms to provide it with its own currency as it can secure its own currency easily itself. Equally, when tax revenues are insufficient to finance spending, the government does not need to borrow. What it is actually doing, Kelton argues, is offering investors a different kind of money, one that pays some interest. The money must be there in the first place for investors to hand over to the government in exchange for these IOUs. Kelton notes that when individuals take out a mortgage to buy a house, they do not go to a bank or building society with a large quantity of money and then ask to borrow the money. Mortgages and other loans are taken out by households because they do not have the money available to make the purchase of the house or car or whatever else it is that households borrow money for. The difference is that governments do have the money because they issue their currency; governments thus spend by first supplying the currency that can be used to buy bonds (and pay taxes).

Critics of Modern Monetary Theory

In this section we have presented the very basics of MMT. As with many other economic theories covered in this book, we do not have the space to explain all its elements in detail, but suffice to say there is an increasing body of literature covering this area. Equally, as with any economic theory, there are critics who point to limitations in the theory or suggest that it is plain 'wrong'. One of the main criticisms relates to the link between increasing government spending and the risk of inflation. However, proponents of MMT do recognize that unfettered spending can cause inflation, put pressure on exchange rates, 'crowd out' private spending and possibly create perverse incentives, hence the comment earlier around recognizing the productive capacity of the economy and its resources. Wray notes that, 'Just because a government can afford to spend does not mean it ought to spend.' What Wray means is that we should not be looking at government spending from the perspective of whether a government can afford to spend money. That is not the issue, because governments that have a monopoly on the issue of its currency and can force people to pay taxes in that currency can always afford to spend. Instead, setting government budgets can be a useful discipline to help manage and evaluate government spending projects to ensure that the spending does provide some valuable benefit to society as a whole and/or the economy.

Sovereign Currency Issuers One important point to note with regard to MMT is that it relates to countries that have a monopoly in the issue of their currencies. It does not apply, for example, to the countries of the euro area that have relinquished their right to issue currency. The members of the euro area are currency users rather than currency issuers. The right to issue currency is carried out by the European Central Bank (ECB) on behalf of the euro area members. This is one of the reasons why the problems in Greece became so serious. The Greek government, as a currency user rather than a currency issuer, faced constraints in its spending in the same way that households and firms do. Equally, countries that peg their currency to another currency or a basket of currencies such as some countries in the Middle East face constraints on their spending. In the case of countries that peg their exchange rate, they can be forced to default.

Summary

In this section we have given a brief taster of a theory that is garnering much interest in economics. The interest in MMT seems to have gained more momentum as a result of the often eyewatering amounts of borrowing that some governments undertook to provide the support necessary to maintain economies during the pandemic. Debate continues in relation to the management of public finances. MMT provides a different way of thinking about government spending and deficits which does not automatically imply that austerity policies must be instituted to pay for the spending.

SELF TEST Why do proponents of MMT argue that sovereign currency issuers should not be viewed in the same way as households or firms when managing their income and expenditure?

GLOBALIZATION

Economic shocks are not always immediate and obvious. They can be the result of gradual changes in the way in which economies work and how firms must change their operations over time and adapt to new economic realities. One example of this type of shock has been globalization. The term **globalization** refers to the growth of interdependence among world economies usually seen as resulting from the removal of many international regulations affecting financial flows. In one respect, this means that it is becoming easier for firms to conduct business across national boundaries and to engage in trade around the world. This clearly opens up major opportunities but also presents difficulties and challenges that have to be recognized and managed, not least the ethical and cultural issues of carrying out business in a global market.

globalization the growth of interdependence among world economies usually seen as resulting from the removal of many international regulations affecting financial flows

Doing business globally means that a firm can get its product and brand positioned anywhere in the world. It is highly likely that regardless of where you are in the world, for example, you will be able to find a store that sells Coca-Cola. Many businesses have expanded their reach by setting up operations in different countries but are headquartered in their country of origin. These types of organizations are referred to as **multinationals** or multinational corporations (MNCs). These firms have developed, and seek to exploit, a global brand presence. It is not only firms in product markets who have such a global presence; other markets, such as commodity and financial markets, could be argued to be even more global.

multinationals organizations characterized by having operations in a number of countries although their main headquarters will be in one country – normally the country in which the firm originally developed

The Reasons for Globalization

The development of global markets is mainly due to technological change, particularly the internet, but also transport and other forms of communication. Firms have been able to exploit the developments in these technologies to increase efficiency, gain scale economies and produce and communicate 365 days of the year. The main reasons for globalization can be summarized as follows:

Transport and Logistics The developments in low-cost transport systems and improvements in infrastructure in many countries around the world mean that component parts can travel across the globe many times as part of a production process before being assembled into a final product. Crucially, the cost of producing in this way has not increased at the same rate as the productivity benefits. As a result unit costs are kept low, which means that firms are able to offer consumers high-quality products at relatively low and competitive prices.

In particular, the advancements in containerization as a means of transporting goods enables firms to move far more goods per hour and with much lower levels of labour than was the case in the 1970s. Containers come in standardized sizes and can be loaded in very large quantities onto ships and then at the port onto freight trains and lorries to be delivered to factories, warehouses and distribution hubs. A paper published in 2013 by Bernhofen *et al.* on 'Estimating the Effects of the Container Revolution in International Trade' (papers.ssrn.com/sol3/papers.cfm?abstract_id=2228625) suggested that containerization had increased bilateral trade (the trade of goods between two countries) between developed countries in the northern hemisphere by some 700 per cent in the period between 1966 and 1990.

For developments in technologies like containerization to be commercially viable, there must be appropriate infrastructure available. Investment in port facilities to handle the size of ships that carry containers is essential. Once containers arrive in port, there need to be road and rail systems available for the onward journey of cargo to distribution hubs, warehouses and finally retail outlets. The importance of having this infrastructure is highlighted by the fact that countries that have developed ports to cope with the demands of containerization are most likely to see the economic benefits of increased trade. For poorer countries, the inability to invest in this sort of infrastructure holds them back in their development.

Capital Mobility Trade requires a medium of exchange. Countries will have different regulations and laws associated with their currencies and, if these make it harder to engage in international trade, the benefits are going to be fewer. Since the 1970s, many countries have relaxed currency laws and regulation, which has meant that capital is able to flow more freely between countries. This has increased the ability of firms to invest in developing operations in other countries and to move funds around to maximize returns. In so doing, the benefits of international trade are shared across more countries.

The Expansion of Global Credit Markets The complexity of financial markets has increased, partly because of the development of new products designed to boost access to credit for businesses across the globe. Firms looking to borrow funds for investment and expansion can increasingly look at global financial markets and access cheaper credit. Products developed to help firms insure their debt more effectively have also improved the creditworthiness of global businesses, which means they can benefit from financial economies of scale.

The Collapse of the Soviet Bloc and Emerging Markets A significant proportion of the world's countries operated under a different economic system until the early part of the 1990s. Social, political and economic change in Eastern Europe led to countries gaining independence, embracing the market economy and opening up their borders to trade. It is not only the former Soviet Bloc countries that have increased trade with the rest of the world. Many countries in South America, Africa and Asia, some of which are classed as emerging economies, have seen their share of trade as a percentage of national income increase. The ratio of exports plus imports to national income is called **trade openness**. The extent to which trade openness leads to wider economic benefits for the countries involved is debated. Some empirical research suggests a causal link between increased trade openness and improved economic growth. Of course, the extent to which all citizens share in the improved economic growth must be investigated if broader conclusions on the benefits are to be drawn.

trade openness the ratio of exports plus imports to gross domestic product

The Growth of Multinational Companies Sometimes, statistics can tell a story with far more clarity than words. The World Trade Organization (WTO) notes that the top 500 multinational corporations account for almost 70 per cent of global trade. If the turnovers of MNCs were compared to the GDP of countries, then 51 of the 100 largest economies of the world would be corporations. (Source: archive.globalpolicy.org/socecon/tncs/top200.htm) These statistics highlight the importance of MNCs in global trade and the way in which they have contributed to the growth in trade across borders since the 1970s.

THE COSTS AND BENEFITS OF GLOBALIZATION

Economic theory predicts that trade can benefit everyone. However, as with many things in economics, this is highly dependent on a number of assumptions. Globalization has brought benefits to billions of people, but the extent to which everyone can share these benefits is still open to question.

The Benefits of Globalization

Choice and Price The opportunity to expand sales globally means that many businesses can invest in production systems that result in economies of scale. The lower unit costs can be passed on to consumers in the form of lower prices. In addition, consumers have access to a much wider choice of goods and services and, assuming the principle of 'more is preferred to less', this improves standards of living.

Shareholder Value Businesses can exploit global markets to source cheaper factor inputs, which not only lowers unit cost but improves the flexibility of firms to improve their competitiveness around the world. The wider access to markets means firms can increase revenues and, with lower unit costs, improve profitability.

Inward Investment As businesses expand in different countries, investment can create a multiplier effect, which not only improves the living standards of local people but also generates opportunities for local businesses to expand as suppliers and in turn increases employment. Inward investment also means that technologies and knowledge are more widely shared, which is also likely to bring economic benefits.

The Costs of Globalization

It is not clear just how far the benefits of globalization outlined above extend. The World Bank reports that despite trade liberalization, the number of people living on less than US$2.15 per day stands at around 700 million or 8.5 per cent of the global population. The WTO notes that low and middle-income countries managed to increase their share of global exports in 2022 by 15 percentage points from 17 per cent in 1995. Despite some improvements in these figures, we need to be mindful of the costs of globalization.

The Power of Multinationals The statistic noting that 51 of the top 100 'economies' are a corporation is an indicator of the size and global reach of MNCs. The power that these corporations can wield has been highlighted as a cause for concern, as it might manifest itself in pressure on governments to make decisions on investment and planning that may not be in the best interests of the majority of citizens. The desire to secure inward investment might be transitory, with MNCs capable of switching investments from country to country seeking out the most favourable returns. Knowledge of this may lead to some governments relaxing the regulatory environment, which may not always improve the welfare of the population as a whole. MNCs are also criticized for driving down wages and for using suppliers who exploit workers to maintain lucrative contracts. The pay and conditions of workers in factories in developing and emerging countries are often publicized. Most MNCs claim, however, that they have rigorous and robust codes of practice in place that seek to minimize such exploitation. Consumers also have a role to play here. Many consumers are willing to buy goods at low prices without necessarily considering the pay and conditions of the workers who make these products.

Some arguments suggest that inward investment by MNCs can help to create employment and increase standards of living. The size of such an effect will depend on the nature of the business and the number and type of people employed. If the MNC is capital-intensive, the effect on job creation might be relatively small. It also depends on the number of local people employed and how many high-skilled workers the MNC brings in from its own ranks. If MNCs are producing goods that are also produced in the domestic economy, the competition they bring in might be too great for local firms, leading to them closing down and putting domestic labour out of work. The dynamics of inward investment by MNCs is complex and the relative costs and benefits must be considered on a case-by-case basis.

Standardization One feature of global business is the increase in standardization. Wherever you go in the world, the customer experience of many products is very similar. Whether it be a McDonald's burger, Windows operating system, Apple's iPad, Coca-Cola, Head and Shoulders shampoo, Colgate toothpaste or BMW cars, regardless of where you are in the world, these are highly standardized products. In one respect, this can be a good thing in that quality can be assured and all customers get the same experience, but standardization also results in a lack of product diversity and sets up barriers to entry for domestic businesses to compete effectively.

Climate Change Proponents of the view that human-made increases in carbon dioxide emissions are resulting in changes in the climate argue that globalization is contributing to the problem. Globalization could be devastating for some countries, whereas other countries might well benefit through improved technology to mitigate the worst effects. Attempts at agreement between global leaders to reduce carbon emissions have been extremely difficult to secure. This is partly because developing countries seeking to improve living standards for their populations through economic growth are being asked by wealthier nations to cut their carbon emissions, compromising their attempts at growth. Many developing nations take the view that the extent of the problem has been caused by the wealthier nations' profligacy since the 1920s. Developing nations want to see the developed world take far more responsibility for their historical actions and have much greater involvement in solving the problem.

Interdependence The 2007–9 Financial Crisis highlighted the extent to which financial institutions around the world are highly interdependent. The expansion of global credit and the reduction in the barriers to flows of capital across borders mean that more than ever before, shocks that occur in one country can very quickly affect businesses across the globe and exacerbate the effects of the shock.

In product markets, there are similar problems. Many businesses rely on complex logistics and supply chains for their production processes. So, if problems arise in one country, this can affect global production. An earthquake in Japan, for example, could have a significant effect on car manufacturers and component suppliers in European countries. Covid-19 highlighted the extent to which global economies are highly interdependent, as it caused major disruption to global supply chains.

Inequality and Equity The benefits of trade are not shared equally between all citizens in a country and between countries. Trade between countries in the northern hemisphere and many countries in the southern hemisphere tends to favour the wealthier northern countries. Also, within countries, a relatively small number of people will become ever wealthier, while the majority remain in relative poverty. When the gap between those on the highest incomes and those on the lowest incomes increases and poverty persists, there is unrest and the potential for civil and political turmoil and terrorism. Impoverished people may see that they are not sharing in wealth creation. In some cases, they see no other option but to resort to violence to advance their cause or simply to survive. The problems of piracy off the coast of Somalia and the supply of heroin from Afghanistan exist in part because those involved have few alternatives to make a living. Despite the risks involved, the alternative is not sufficiently rewarding to encourage them to do anything else.

The Wider Implications of Globalization

There are wider social and environmental implications of globalization in addition to those outlined above, not least the potential damage to eco-systems, the increasing use of non-renewable resources and damage to Indigenous cultures. Firms are increasingly aware of these potential difficulties and make considerable attempts to demonstrate transparency in their actions and accountability. Many large firms produce social and environmental accountability reports, which aim to highlight how they are managing their operations to limit the negative effects of their activities on stakeholders.

Cultural and Religious Sensitivities

Cultural and religious differences present challenges to businesses trading abroad. There are many examples of different cultural sensitivities that need to be taken into account, such as how to greet people, how the use of colour can have different meanings in different parts of the world, and how certain gestures and body language can be interpreted very differently throughout the world. For example, showing the soles of the feet is considered highly offensive in many Muslim countries. In parts of Asia, touching the head is not polite because the head is believed to house the soul. In Islamic and Hindu cultures, the use of the left hand for social interaction is considered insulting. Having hands in pockets or sitting cross-legged is considered disrespectful in Türkiye, while making eye contact is expected in the West and in some Arabic cultures, but not in Japan, parts of Africa, the Caribbean and parts of Latin America. For firms seeking to do business in different parts of the world, it is imperative to understand, appreciate, respect and follow local cultures and sensitivities if they are to trade successfully.

CASE STUDY Responding to Energy Price Shocks

In February 2022, Russia launched what it called a 'special military operation' in Ukraine. Western media and governments referred to the action as 'an invasion'. The effects of the conflict contributed to a spike in energy prices that affected firms and households across Europe and the UK. Following the outbreak of the conflict, gas prices across Europe rose by 115 per cent and electricity prices by 237 per cent by the summer of 2022. Fetzer *et al.* carried out some research in 2024 to understand how firms responded to this energy price shock.

They discovered that firms adopted five main responses to the shock. As might be expected, the average response from firms was to pass on the increased costs to customers in the form of higher prices, although smaller firms tended to be more likely to adopt this approach. Larger firms were better able to absorb some of the cost increases and invest in capital improvements. Many firms sought to build cash reserves and increase debt levels. Most, it appeared, avoided shedding staff or declaring insolvency. Small and large firms seemed to make operational adjustments, in particular adopting remote working, which helps to reduce internal costs and shifts the burden onto employees at home. How firms responded was found to be highly individual and dependent on their size and the industry they operated in. Construction firms, it was found, tended to invest in capital while smaller firms in the hospitality industry tended to increase stocks. Despite the significance of the energy price rise, Fetzer *et al.* found that confidence among small businesses remained relatively high with most not seeing the shock as a threat to survival although, of course, some firms will have exited markets.

The conclusion of the report's authors is that governments can respond to future shocks of this sort by targeting firm size and industry needs. This implies more tailored support for businesses that takes into account how such shocks affect different firms in different industries. The sort of policies used to help support firms responding to energy price shocks is likely to be different from that needed when adjusting to changing market conditions.

© iStock/Fahroni

Energy price shocks present challenges to firms in deciding how far to pass on increased costs to consumers.

Questions:

1. What factors might firms consider in deciding the extent to which they are able to pass on higher energy costs to consumers in the form of higher prices? (Hint: consider who 'consumers' actually are in this context and the differences in how we might define 'firms').
2. What effect on the economy do you think might result if firms respond to such a shock by building cash reserves and increasing debt? What might the extent of the effects depend on?
3. Operational decisions such as encouraging remote working may have been a legacy of the pandemic where remote working became far more the norm. Such an operational decision may result in helping to manage costs but can also come with disadvantages. What do you think these disadvantages might be, how significant are they, and what do they depend on?
4. What lessons might be gained from the type of research carried out by Fetzer *et al.* for governments seeking to support firms when facing external shocks?

References:

cepr.org/voxeu/columns/navigating-economic-shocks-how-firms-adapted-energy-crisis, accessed 6 August 2025.
cepr.org/voxeu/columns/impact-war-ukraine-energy-prices-consequences-firms-financial-performance, accessed 6 August 2025.

SELF TEST How might economists estimate the relative costs and benefits of globalization to arrive at a judgement about whether it has been a 'good' thing or not?

THE GIG ECONOMY

The development of the internet, digitalization and advances in smartphone technology have promoted communication and connectivity in many different ways and allowed innovation and entrepreneurship to generate new ways of doing business. In some cases, these developments in technology represent a significant challenge to existing business models and force existing firms to have to adapt their model or risk having to exit the market. Many of these businesses are not necessarily completely new. Many of the developments that utilize connectivity technologies are based on traditional businesses but take them in different directions and improve the customer experience. For example, the growth of online retailing and the deregulation of markets have enabled parcel delivery firms to expand and improve the speed and efficiency of their services. Customers can not only receive their parcels quickly, they can also track their progress. This includes from when the parcels are despatched by the retailer to when they arrive in the delivery firm's warehouse. From there they can track when they are on the road, the anticipated time slot for delivery and who is delivering their package. Once delivered, the customer can be informed of what time it was received, who signed for it (if required) and where it was left if no one was in.

Firms that offer these types of services need highly flexible workers. Traditional contracts of work where employees are recruited on a wage or salary and have various legal employment rights such as paid holidays, sick pay and pension contributions are not suitable for some of the firms utilizing connectivity technologies as part of their business. The workers needed in these types of businesses are more like self-employed contractors of the firm rather than employees. Each employment task is like a mini-contract between firm and worker and has resulted in the term '**gig economy**'. This refers to a labour market in which workers do not have permanent jobs but instead have a relationship with a firm that is characterized by short-term or zero-hour contracts or freelance work. The term 'gig' comes from the music industry where musicians provide a single performance. It is reputed to have derived from the word 'engagement' in relation to jazz musicians in the United States in the 1920s.

gig economy a labour market in which workers have short-term, freelance or zero-hours contracts with employers and where workers are more akin to being self-employed than employed

For firms, the use of workers on these terms can mean greater flexibility of adjusting to changes in demand and can help control labour costs. For workers, there is a degree of independence and flexibility that can be appealing. However, as with many issues in economics, the gig economy has some downsides which must be balanced against the benefits to firms and workers and have been the subject of increasing debate. Governments have been considering the issues and looking at the extent to which employment law needs to be changed to take account of the developments in the labour market.

The Nature of the Gig Economy

The basic premise of workers in the gig economy is that they are self-employed or independent contractors. Workers who are self-employed do not have the same employment rights as those who are classed as 'employed'. Employed workers in many European countries are entitled to paid holidays, to being paid the national minimum or living wage of the country they are working in, to being paid when off work through illness and to receiving the country's statutory redundancy pay. In addition, employed workers are protected against unfair dismissal. Workers in the gig economy have no such rights. Instead, they receive a payment for work carried out for the 'contractor'. They are then responsible for paying their income tax, any other employment taxes, such as National Insurance Contributions in the UK, and for making their own arrangements for their pension and any other financial protection they choose to take out.

The Benefits to Workers One of the reported benefits of working in the gig economy for individuals is the flexibility it affords. Workers are free to work as much or as little as they choose and to work when it is convenient for them. Workers have the freedom and incentives that other self-employed people have who are running their own businesses. For gig economy workers, however, the fact that they are working for contactors means they are not bearing all of the risks of running a business in the way that the contractor is.

The types of work in the gig economy include work such as the delivery of fast foods, meals, parcels and packages; so-called 'ride-hailing' drivers (as distinct from a taxi); work doing household chores and maintenance; video production; property renting right through to software development. Firms like Uber, Airbnb, TaskRabbit, Deliveroo, 90 Seconds, LiquidTalent and Evri are all part of the gig economy.

The Benefits to Firms Firms using workers in the gig economy can manage their workflows and their costs more effectively. Not only do they not have the full costs of employment, they also have the flexibility to hire workers to carry out tasks as and when they need them. As a result they can increase productivity. Because they are employing workers for particular tasks, such as carrying a passenger from one location to another, they can pay according to the task rather than the hour. This can mean that they can legally pay workers less than the minimum wage in the country concerned, which is invariably expressed as an amount per hour.

The estimates of the numbers working in the gig economy varies, but a report by the Chartered Institute for Personnel and Development published in 2023, notes that there were around 464,000 people working in the gig economy in the UK, representing 1.4 per cent of total employment. Only 20 per cent of these people see it as their main source of income. The ONS does not produce figures for employment in the gig economy, because it notes there are widely differing definitions of what constitutes a 'gig-economy worker'.

The Debate over the Gig Economy

The disadvantages to workers have been at the centre of the debate about the gig economy. Are these workers really self-employed? Should they be eligible for the same sort of employment rights that employed workers have? Are firms using the gig economy as a means of exploiting workers and paying low wages?

In October 2016, two UK-based Uber drivers argued at an employment tribunal that they should not be classed as self-employed but as employed workers. They won their case. Uber appealed against the decision, but it was upheld by an Employment Appeal Tribunal in 2017. Uber then took the case to the Court of Appeal, which also upheld the ruling and then to the Supreme Court. In February 2021, the Supreme Court also upheld the decision, leaving Uber no further legal recourse given the Supreme Court is the highest legal court in Britain. The original tribunal noted, 'The notion that Uber in London is a mosaic of 30,000 small businesses linked by a common "platform" is to our mind faintly ridiculous.' The ruling meant that Uber, and potentially many other companies like it, might have to change its business model. Trade unions in the UK welcomed the decision saying it represented greater protection for workers in this type of employment. Uber pointed to the flexibility and independence of decision-making that its drivers have in organizing their own time and work commitments. Reports at the time of the decision seemed to suggest that Uber drivers themselves were split on whether the decision was a good thing or not. To meet the additional employment rights, Uber would have to charge customers more and this could affect the business model and ultimately mean fewer jobs. Supporters of the judgement pointed to the control that Uber had over their lives in terms of what drives they do, when they do them and, as such, they were more employed than self-employed.

The UK government commissioned a report on the issues, which was published in July 2017. The report was titled: *Good Work: The Taylor Review of Modern Working Practices*. Matthew Taylor was a former political strategist for Tony Blair and at the time of writing is chief executive of the NHS Confederation. The report noted that work was essential to well-being and happiness but that it was also important that the terms under which people work are fair and help people to progress.

The report made seven recommendations. One of the main ones was that workers should be classed not as independent contractors but as 'dependent contractors'. The report noted that there was a distinction between these two terms and that the law needed to be clearer about distinguishing between those who are genuinely self-employed and those who are dependent contractors. This, it noted, would ensure that the flexibility that is at the heart of the benefits to both firms and workers are maintained but that workers can be treated fairly. The current state of affairs tended to be a 'one-sided flexibility' and firms needed stronger incentives to treat workers fairly. Dependent workers would not be employees but also not self-employed, and should be entitled to sick pay and paid holidays. Taylor's report concluded that regulation was not necessarily the way to achieve 'better work', but responsible corporate governance and good management were also key.

The report was greeted in different ways, with trade unions welcoming the recommendations while some employment lawyers commented that the new definition of dependent contractor would merely complicate an already complex legal framework. In the United States, it has been suggested that transactions in the gig economy could be subject to a small tax which would be earmarked to help provide additional benefits for workers. This, it is argued, maintains the flexibility for firms and workers while at the same time providing benefits for workers. By supporting workers in this way, the gig economy could continue to expand and be successful.

Zero-hours Contracts

Workers on zero-hours contracts and workers in the gig economy are often spoken of in the same breath, but there is a difference. As firms have sought greater labour flexibility to help manage demand and reduce costs, the offer of zero-hours contracts helps manage these elements of the labour market. A worker employed on a zero-hours contract is offered work as and when the firm has a need. The worker can be called upon to carry out that work under the terms of the contract, but they do have the right to turn down the work. There is no compulsion for the firm to offer work under the contract. In addition, the firm must pay at least the national minimum or living wage and workers under zero-hours contracts are entitled to paid annual leave.

For workers, zero-hours contracts give them some flexibility because they cannot be prevented from seeking work with another employer. The fact that they can turn down work if it is not convenient provides further flexibility, although it may be the case that workers feel pressured to accept hours when offered.

In 2000, the number of workers on zero-hours contracts in the UK, according to the Labour Force Survey from the ONS, was just over 225,000, representing 0.8 per cent of people in employment. This had risen to just over 900,000 (2.8 per cent) by 2016 and hit a high of just over one million in the three months to June 2020 (3.0 per cent). In the three months to March 2025 it was 1.170 million, representing 3.4 per cent of people in employment in the UK (not seasonally adjusted).

DIGITIZATION AND INDUSTRY 4.0

Throughout history, society has been impacted by technological change. Sometimes, this technological change might seem to have been primitive such as when humans first discovered how to create metal implements. At other times, the technological change has been more significant, for example during the Industrial Revolution. What we are living through at the moment is a period of considerable technological change, which has been called Industry 4.0 (I4.0). This is likely to have a considerable impact on the way in which firms operate and is already manifesting itself in the way in which firms are planning for the future.

What is Industry 4.0?

I4.0 in many respects represents a natural development from advances in computer technologies since the 1970s. There are few businesses these days that do not make some use of computer technology in one way or another. I4.0 takes this technology to a different level. The foundation of the development of computer technology is the digitization of information. Many firms have been able to use this process to change their business model, and new firms have taken advantage of digitization to create new business opportunities. Many of the social networks that so many people now use and rely on could reasonably be included in the process of digitization. The next phase in this development – and what really characterizes I4.0 – is the linking together of all these technologies to create new opportunities and to drive networking and communication.

We can see examples of these developments in the form of the so-called 'Industrial Internet of Things' (IIoT). Here, physical things, including people, can be connected to the internet and data shared between these things to improve communication, understanding, decision-making, choices, manging processes and even daily life. On a simple level, some domestic fridges can be connected to the internet and help the householder manage the stock in the fridge. Usage of products from the fridge can trigger orders from retailers to ensure that the household does not run out of those products.

The IIoT is also bringing massive change to the agricultural sector. Farmers can utilize sensors in and around their fields that communicate with onboard computers in tractors and can help in the management of depth of tilling of the soil, seed sowing, harvesting information, irrigation and many other elements of the growing and harvesting process.

Other aspects of I4.0 include developments in cloud computing, data analysis, augmented reality, AI and machine learning.

Augmented Reality Augmented reality gives people a means of experiencing the physical world through different sensory means. One example is the developments in GPS technology. GPS allows people to not only see a map of where they are going on their car display screens but to actually see a visual representation of the area they are travelling in. GPS is more than just a map with routes, road names, junctions and so on. The driver sees a 3D visual representation of where they are driving, along with the directions they are advised to travel to get to their destination. This technology can be applied to a wide range of manufacturing applications helping users to, for example, identify where faults may lie in equipment and helping pinpoint problems more quickly and efficiently.

Big Data Many computer systems are capable of collecting and generating massive amounts of data. Big data refers to the analysis of this data to find patterns, trends and other useful information which firms can then use to their advantage in some way. It might manifest itself in completely different ways of understanding customer behaviour and tailoring offers and advertising to customers, but it can also be utilized in manufacturing to help improve processes and systems and reduce costs and increase efficiencies. Big data has a major role to play in supply chains, helping to improve the efficiency and speed with which firms are able to get goods and services to their customers.

Artificial Intelligence and Machine Learning The digital connectedness that characterizes much of I4.0 also provides the opportunity for technologies to work together and for machines to process information and learn from that information. In doing so, machines can then put this new learning into action to provide more functionality, improve processes and make decisions. In effect, machines can emulate some elements of human intelligence and do tasks that humans do.

Many people experience AI in the home through the use of smart speakers and other devices, including 'smart assistants' like Apple's Siri, Amazon's Alexa, Microsoft's Cortana and Google's Gemini. Firms are using AI as a means of communicating with customers more effectively. Chatbots, for example, can be used to engage with consumers answering simple questions 24/7. In industry more broadly, AI is increasingly being used for predictive analytics, which can help to reduce equipment and machine malfunctions or breakdowns, improve performance and assist in maintenance and repair, forecasting and scheduling, and workforce training.

Blockchain Blockchain is a form of database which differs from standard databases in that it stores information in blocks that are linked. Firms are increasingly using blockchain technology as a means of facilitating and recording transactions. The transactions are recorded on a network of computers throughout the world and not just on a firm's own computer network. The risks associated with network breakdown, downtime, human error or interference and so on are reduced and so this represents a safer way of recording and storing data. Each transaction is processed and stored as blocks and then linked together. This provides a record of all transactions, which are viewable but not editable. These transactions can be financial, relate to legal documentation or inventory. They may also occur in the energy industry where those who have surplus energy can feed it into the grid and those who need energy can purchase it. They can also be in the housing market, where rental and property purchase transactions can be made via blockchain technology, and in advertising, where customer targeting can be more focused and effective.

The Implications of Industry 4.0

As with other parts of this chapter, we have only been able to provide a very brief overview of I4.0. Many of the technological developments that can be classed as being part of I4.0 are not necessarily new. AI, for example, has been worked on for many years (Alan Turing was one of the early proponents of AI through his work on code breaking during World War II). The way in which these technologies are now being applied to a wide range of industries, however, is truly revolutionizing the way in which these technologies can influence productivity and efficiency and generate new and more effective products and services. To this extent, I4.0 represents a 'shock' and as with any economic shock, there will be winners who adapt and adopt the technologies quickly and effectively, and losers, who will see their existing business models become redundant. Firms will have to think carefully about hiring staff, about the skills they need, about training and development of staff and about the purpose and function of their business. I4.0 offers tremendous opportunities but also challenges. One major challenge is ensuring the security of these connected systems and so cyber security is set to be a growth area in the future.

SUMMARY

- Economic shocks have occurred throughout history.
- The 2007–9 Financial Crisis led to one of the worst economic downturns since the Great Depression in the 1920s and 1930s.
- The causes of the Financial Crisis lay in the increased exposure to risk in the financial system and the increase in debt taken on by households and the financial system.
- A number of economic theories and approaches came under severe criticism following the Financial Crisis. In particular, the EMH came under attack for ignoring behavioural effects which were seen as being at the heart of asset bubbles.
- Other approaches and theories saw a revival of interest, including Keynesian demand management and Minsky's financial instability hypothesis.
- The sovereign debt crisis developed as a result of the 2007–9 Financial Crisis. A number of countries had to seek financial assistance from the EU and the IMF. The ESM represents a permanent mechanism to help support countries in financial difficulties.
- An ongoing debate has developed about the management of public finances and the need to promote growth.
- Modern Monetary Theory provides an alternative lens through which to view government spending and budget deficits.
- Economic shocks can also be caused by developments in international trade such as the increasing interdependence among world economies that characterizes globalization.
- Developments in technology have led to shocks to economies through new business models being developed, which challenge existing ones and bring new ways of thinking and working to economic activity.
- The gig economy and I4.0 are examples of how technology and developments in technology are providing new opportunities and threats to the way organizations operate.

IN THE NEWS

AI and Productivity

One of the general assumptions around technology developments is that it will be associated with improvements in productivity. The rapid development of I4.0 technologies has been linked with improvements in productivity, and in particular AI has been touted as a potential source of rapid improvements in productivity over time. What evidence is there to support such assumptions?

A study by Czarnitzki *et al.*, published in *the Journal of Economic Behavior and Organization* in 2023, sought to provide some evidence to estimate likely productivity effects. The study was based on a sample of firms in Germany using data generated by the Community Innovation Survey (CIS) of the European Commission.

They noted that the literature highlighted how different applications such as autonomous vehicles (robots), voice recognition, speech/text generating systems, predictive maintenance or trained neural networks to optimize business energy consumption could be associated with improved productivity. However, they also noted that there exists some scepticism as to whether AI might produce the sort of productivity benefits that proponents claim. Even when AI technologies are adopted, it may be up to three years before the benefits to productivity are experienced.

The authors utilized a version of the production function that we introduced earlier in the book and added in AI as an additional input. Applying the data to the production function and taking account of various other factors as part of their analysis, they found that the use of AI technologies, 'has a positive and significant impact on firm productivity', and that AI had 'significantly increase[d] both sales and value-added'. One concern that has been raised in relation to the adoption of AI technologies is the impact on labour, the so-called 'displacement effect'. To counter this, Czarnitzki *et al.* note that governments may need to adopt policies around education and the use of the tax system. In part, government needs to play a role not only in supporting labour but also in supporting firms in encouraging the adoption of AI technologies through improving skills, investing in appropriate infrastructure and privacy regulation. Overall, the authors observe that a relatively small number of firms utilize AI technologies and more need to be aware of the benefits of AI.

© iStock/Galeanu Mihai

The benefits of technologies such as AI may not be felt or realized for many years as firms and households develop their understanding of its use and implications.

Critical Thinking Questions

1. Why is it important to use evidence on issues such as the potential benefits of technologies such as AI on productivity?
2. Why might there be a time lag before the benefits of adopting AI technology are realized by firms?
3. What do you think is meant by the term 'displacement effect' and why should policymakers be concerned by this effect?
4. This research suggests that there are productivity benefits from adopting AI technologies. If this is the case, why are more firms not utilizing AI in their production processes? What might be the limitations of this particular research?
5. Critically assess the policy options open to governments in supporting firms in the adoption and use of AI technologies. Should firms see AI technology as a 'shock'?

(Continued)

Reference:

Czarnitzki, D., Fernández, G.P. and Rammer, C. (2023) 'Artificial Intelligence and Firm-level Productivity'. *Journal of Economic Behavior & Organization,* 211(July): 188–205. Available at www.sciencedirect.com/science/article/pii/S0167268123001531, accessed 6 August 2025.

QUESTIONS FOR REVIEW

1 Outline the main causes of the 2007–9 Financial Crisis.
2 What is meant by the term 'efficient markets hypothesis'?
3 What are the main features of Minsky's financial instability hypothesis?
4 Why did governments such as those in Greece, Spain, Ireland, Portugal and Italy experience such a rise in deficits and debt in the wake of the Financial Crisis?
5 What are the main arguments for and against the implementation of austerity programmes in countries which have experienced sovereign debt problems?
6 Outline the main features of modern monetary theory.
7 What is globalization and in what way does it represent a 'shock' to economies?
8 What are the main costs and benefits of globalization?
9 How do developments such as the gig economy present challenges to existing business models?
10 What are the main features of Industry 4.0?

PROBLEMS AND APPLICATIONS

1 As the 2007–9 Financial Crisis developed, newspapers often carried lurid headlines about the extent to which house prices were falling, for example 'House Prices Fall 50 Per Cent'. Economists might view these headlines from a more critical perspective.
   a. What does 'House Prices Fall 50 Per Cent' actually mean? (This might sound a strange question, but think about it from a homeowner's perspective.)
   b. Is the price of a house and its value the same thing? Explain.
   c. Is the value of a house only relevant to those who are actually buying and selling a property? Explain.
   d. A homeowner bought a house in 2003 for €320,000 and in 2006 it was valued at €550,000. They had to sell the property at the height of the Financial Crisis due to a job relocation. The price they received was €380,000. How much did the homeowner lose (if anything)? Explain your answer.
2 Consider some of the implications of the assumption of rational behaviour in a market for an asset such as bonds. What might you expect to see happening in such a market in response to new information?
3 'I suspect that the end result will not be an abandonment of the belief of many in the profession that the stock market is remarkably efficient in its utilization of information. Periods such as 1999 where "bubbles" seem to have existed, at least in certain sectors of the market, are fortunately the exception rather than the rule. Moreover, whatever patterns or irrationalities in the pricing of individual stocks that have been discovered in a search of historical experience, are unlikely to persist and will not provide investors with a method to obtain extraordinary returns. If any $100 bills are lying around the stock exchanges of the world, they will not be there for long.' (Malkiel, B.G. (2003) *The Efficient Markets Hypothesis and its Critics.* CEPS Working Paper no 91.) To what extent would you agree with this assessment of the value of the EMH?
4 To what extent do you think that Minsky's financial instability hypothesis is the most accurate theory to explain the 2007–9 Financial Crisis?
5 Governments across Europe instituted austerity measures in an attempt to cut budget deficits, which ballooned after the Financial Crisis. Were they right to do this when economic recovery was so weak?

6 Suppose the government cuts taxes and increases spending, raising the budget deficit to 12 per cent of GDP. If nominal GDP is rising 7 per cent per year, are such budget deficits sustainable forever? Explain. If budget deficits of this size are maintained for 20 years, what is likely to happen to your taxes and your children's taxes in the future? Can you do something today to offset this future effect?

7 'Modern monetary theory presents a completely different way of viewing government spending and budget deficits. Never again should we be constrained by the view that governments must raise funds before they can spend on worthwhile productive activities which can resolve many of the significant economic and social problems many countries face.' To what extent do you agree with this statement?

8 To what extent would you agree with the view that globalization brings more benefits than costs to the world economy?

9 Comment on the view that there should be greater regulation of the gig economy to ensure that workers are better protected and their rights secured.

10 Consider the following three questions:
   a. In what way does I4.0 represent an economic shock?
   b. How does I4.0 differ from shocks to the global economy such as financial crises?
   c. How do you see the way in which firms and economies will respond to this shock and who might be the winners and losers?

17 THE EUROPEAN UNION

For around 70 years, the project to bring European countries closer together and develop both economic and political integration has been a feature of global history. The EU has been successful in maintaining peaceful relations between nations that have a history of conflict between them. Many would also argue that it has been successful in developing the economies of member states despite the ups and downs of the economic and political landscape.

The EU does, however, face challenges that are potentially more damaging and complex than any it has had to face before. Dissatisfaction and disillusionment with the European project have surfaced in a number of countries with the rise of so-called 'populist' political groups demanding priorities be given to national rather than European needs. Migration from countries in Africa and parts of the Middle East have placed significant strains on EU finances, institutions and the tolerance of the people of the EU. The desire of EU leaders to push for greater political and economic integration and to 'complete the single market' is at odds with some national priorities. The euro has survived over 25 years but has not been without its problems. All these headwinds are challenging enough on their own without the fact that the referendum in the UK in 2016 resulted in a vote for the country to leave the EU. The UK formally left the EU in January 2021. The issue created division and rancour not only in the UK but across Europe, with lasting repercussions for the UK and the rest of the EU. In this chapter we will look at the central issue of the euro and common currencies as well as some of the issues facing the EU in the second half of the 2020s.

COMMON CURRENCY AREAS

A **common currency area** is a geographical area throughout which a single currency circulates as the medium of exchange. Another term for a common currency area is a *currency union*. A closely related phenomenon is a *monetary union*. Strictly speaking, this is a group of countries that has adopted permanently and irrevocably fixed exchange rates among its various currencies. Nevertheless, the terms common currency area, currency union and monetary union are often used more or less interchangeably, and in this chapter, we will follow this practice.

common currency area a geographical area throughout which a single currency circulates as the medium of exchange

Usually we speak of common currency areas when the people of a number of economies, generally corresponding to different nation states, take a decision to adopt a common currency as their medium of exchange, as was the case with European Monetary Union (EMU) in the 1990s, when a number of European nations decided to give up their national currencies and use a common currency called the *euro*. The creation of the euro was a bold move. Many economists were sceptical that it would work. Milton Friedman, writing in 1997, noted that Europe was not conducive to a common currency. He contrasted Europe with the United States and commented that Europe did not have a common language, that it had different customs and loyalties and that the movement of goods, capital and labour was not as free as in the United States. Regulation was greater and there were more rigidities in wages and prices. Friedman suggested that in such circumstances, shocks to different economies could be handled more effectively by managing the individual nation's exchange rate. He concluded that the 'drive for the euro has been motivated by politics not economics'.

However, two years later, Friedman wrote that he was less pessimistic about the prospects for the euro than he had been because countries in Europe had demonstrated more discipline than he had anticipated, and inflation rates and interest rates, among other economic variables, had converged to a greater extent and more rapidly than he had expected. However, he was sceptical of the chances of survival of the euro and, in 2004, noted that it could collapse in a few years due to the differences building up between the then 12 nations of the euro zone.

Some of the differences that Friedman referred to exist today and, in some respects, were there already at the birth of the euro. Some of the northern European states are suspicious of their southern neighbours, who they view as being profligate and free riders on the discipline shown by the governments in the north. Many of the southern states saw benefits in joining the euro as they could buy into the price stability that Germany in particular had enjoyed (recall that the ECB was based on the Bundesbank).

The euro has survived. It has certainly been through some challenging times, but it did survive its first real test when the 2007–9 Financial Crisis occurred and the resulting sovereign debt crisis which almost brought it to its knees. Yet despite the fact that the euro has survived, it must be remembered that it is a relatively young currency. The transfer of monetary sovereignty to the ECB and the giving up of the ability to manipulate exchange rates to cope with asymmetric shocks means that different countries face different problems that require different policy options. The absence of the option to devalue the currency to make exports more competitive means that the adjustment to asymmetric shocks tends to be through real wages. The Greeks found this out in the post-Crisis period and continue to face considerable economic challenges.

THE EURO

At the time of writing there are 20 countries that have joined **European Economic and Monetary Union**, or EMU. (Note that 'EMU' stands for 'Economic and Monetary Union', not European Monetary Union, as is often supposed.) The countries that currently form the euro area are Austria, Belgium, Croatia, Cyprus, Estonia, Finland, France, Germany, Greece, Ireland, Italy, Latvia, Lithuania, Luxembourg, Malta, the Netherlands, Portugal, Slovakia, Slovenia and Spain. The move towards a single European currency has a very long history. The main landmarks in its formation started in 1992 with the Maastricht Treaty (formally known as the Treaty on European Union), which laid down (among other things) various criteria for being eligible to join the proposed currency union. To participate in the new currency, member states had to meet strict criteria such as a government budget deficit of less than 3 per cent of GDP, a government debt-to-GDP ratio of less than 60 per cent, combined with low inflation and interest rates close to the EU average. The Maastricht Treaty also laid down a timetable for the introduction of the new single currency and rules concerning the setting up of a European central bank. The ECB came into existence in June 1998 and forms, together with the national central banks of the countries making up the common currency area, the European System of Central Banks (ESCB). The ESCB is responsible for ensuing price stability and implementing the single European monetary policy.

> **European Economic and Monetary Union** the European currency union that has adopted the euro as its common currency

The euro officially came into existence on 1 January 1999, when 12 countries adopted it (although Greece did not join the EMU until 1 January 2001). On this date, exchange rates between the old national currencies of euro area countries were irrevocably locked and a few days later the financial markets began to trade the euro against other currencies such as the US dollar, as well as securities denominated in euros.

The period from the beginning of 1999 until the beginning of 2002 was a transitional phase, with national currencies still circulating within the euro area countries, and prices in shops displayed in both euros and local currency. On 1 January 2002 the first euro notes and coins came into circulation and, within a few months, the switch to the euro as the single medium of exchange was complete throughout the euro area.

The formation of the EMU was driven in part by political reasons but there were perceived economic benefits as well. In particular, there was a belief that having a common European currency would help 'complete the single market' for European goods, services and factors of production, which had been an ongoing project for much of the post-war period.

The Single European Market

Following the devastation of two World Wars in the first half of the twentieth century, some of the major European countries (in particular France and Germany) expressed a desire to make further wars impossible between them through a process of strong economic integration. It was hoped that this would lead to greater social and political harmony. This led to the development of the European Economic Community (EEC) – now referred to as the **European Union**, or EU. The official website of the European Union defines the EU as 'a family of democratic European countries, committed to working together for peace and prosperity'.

European Union a group of democratic European countries committed to working together for peace and prosperity

Initially the EU consisted of just six countries: Belgium, Germany, France, Italy, Luxembourg and the Netherlands. In 1973, Denmark, Ireland and the UK joined. Greece joined in 1981, Spain and Portugal in 1986, and Austria, Finland and Sweden in 1995. In 2004 the biggest ever enlargement took place with 10 new countries joining. Croatia became a member state in July 2013 and at the time of writing there are nine 'candidate countries' seeking membership. These are Albania, Bosnia and Herzegovina, Georgia, Moldova, Montenegro, North Macedonia, Serbia, Türkiye and Ukraine. Kosovo is classed as a 'potential candidate'.

The creation of the **Single European Market** was a major political and economic development. In the Single European Market, labour, capital, goods and services could move freely. It was argued that as member states got rid of obstacles to trade between themselves, companies would start to enjoy economies of scale as they expanded their market across Europe. At the same time, inefficient firms would be exposed to more cross-border competition, either forcing them out of business or forcing them to improve efficiency. The aim was to provide businesses with an environment of fair competition in which economies of scale could be reaped and a strong consumer base developed to enable expansion into global markets. Households could take advantage of lower prices, greater choice of goods and services, and work opportunities across a wide area, while the economy in general would benefit from the enhanced economic growth.

Single European Market a (still not complete) EU-wide market throughout which labour, capital, goods and services can move freely

Early steps towards the creation of the Single European Market included the abolition of internal EU tariff and quota barriers in 1968 and a movement towards greater harmonization in areas such as indirect taxation, industrial regulation and EU-wide policies towards agriculture and fisheries.

Nevertheless, it proved difficult to make progress on the more intangible barriers to free movement of goods, services, capital and labour. For example, even though internal tariffs and quotas had been abolished in the EU, local tax systems and technical regulations on goods and services still differed from country to country so that it was in practice often difficult to export from one country to another. Thus, a car produced in France might have to satisfy a certain set of emission and safety requirements in one European country and another set of requirements in another EU country. Or a qualified engineer might find that their qualifications obtained in Italy were not recognized in Germany. The result was that during the 1970s and early 1980s, growth in the EU member states began to lag seriously behind that of international competitors, especially the United States and Japan. Therefore, in 1985, a discussion document was produced by the European Commission that subsequently led to a European Act of Parliament, the 1986 Single European Act. This identified some 300 measures that would have to be addressed to complete the Single European Market and set 31 December 1992 as the deadline for completion. The creation of the Single European Market was to be brought about by EU Directives telling the governments of member states what changes needed to be put into effect to achieve four goals:

1. The free movement of goods, services, labour and capital between EU member states.
2. The approximation of relevant laws, regulations and administrative provisions between member states.
3. A common, EU-wide competition policy, administered by the European Commission.
4. A system of common external tariffs implemented against countries that are not members of the EU.

The Single European Market is still far from complete. In particular, there are still strong differences in national fiscal systems, while academic and professional qualifications are not easily transferable and labour mobility across EU countries is generally low. Some of the reasons for this are hard to overcome. Language barriers and relative levels of economic development hamper the movement of factors. Member states continue to compete with one another economically, at times seeking their own national interest rather than the greater good of the EU.

Nevertheless, the years between 1985 and 1992 did see some important steps in the development of the Single European Market and the resulting achievements were not negligible. The European Commission estimates that the Single European Market helped create 2.5 million new jobs and generated €800 billion in additional wealth in the 10 years or so following 1993.

The creation of a single European currency was seen as a final step towards 'completing the market', which meant two things: (i) getting rid of the transaction costs from intra-EU trade that resulted from different national currencies (and which acted much as a tariff) and (ii) removing the uncertainty and swings in national competitiveness among members caused by exchange rate movements. Before EMU, most EU countries participated in the Exchange Rate Mechanism (ERM), which was a system designed to limit the variability of exchange rates between members' currencies. However, the ERM failed to reduce volatility in the exchange rate and, in any case, had no effect on the transaction costs arising from bank charges associated with changing currencies when engaging in intra-EU trade.

THE BENEFITS AND COSTS OF A COMMON CURRENCY

Benefits of a Single Currency

Elimination of Transaction Costs One obvious and direct benefit of a common currency is that it makes trade easier between members and, in particular, reduces the transaction costs involved in trade between members of the common currency area. When a German company imports French wine, it no longer pays a charge to a bank for converting German marks into French francs with which to pay the wine producer; it can just pay in euros. Of course, the banking sector loses out on the commission it charged for converting currencies, but the reduction in transaction costs is a net gain. This is because paying a cost to convert currencies is in fact a deadweight loss in the sense that companies pay the transaction cost but get nothing tangible in return.

Reduction in Price Discrimination It is sometimes argued that a second, albeit indirect, gain to the members of a common currency area results from the reduction in price discrimination that should ensue when there is a single currency. If goods are priced in a single currency it is much harder to disguise price differences across countries. As we have discussed, price discrimination involves a deadweight loss to society. This argument assumes that the transparency in prices will lead to arbitrage in goods across the common currency area. People will buy goods where they are cheaper (tending to raise their price in that location) and reduce their demand for goods where they are more expensive (tending to reduce the price in that location).

Overall, however, EMU seems unlikely to bring an end to price discrimination across euro area countries. For items like groceries, having a single currency is unlikely to be much of an impetus to price convergence across the common currency area because of the large transaction costs (mainly related to travelling) involved in arbitrage relative to the prices of the goods themselves. To take advantage of price differences, cross-border shopping can take place, if it is relatively easy and convenient. Doing so across the whole of the EU, however, means that the effects are necessarily more limited. Big ticket items like household appliances and electronic goods, where the transaction costs may be lower as a percentage of the price of the good in question, are also unlikely to be arbitraged heavily across national borders by consumers because of their durable nature and the need for confidence in after-sales service. In addition, the fact that different countries in the EU still have different plugs and power systems also reduces the overall impact.

Reduction in Foreign Exchange Rate Variability A third argument in favour of a common currency relates to the reduction in exchange rate variability and uncertainty that results from having a single currency. Exchange rates can fluctuate substantially on a day-to-day basis. Before EMU, when a German supermarket imported wine from France to be delivered, say, three months later, it had to worry about how much a French franc would be worth in terms of German marks at that point and, therefore, what the total cost of the wine would be in marks. This uncertainty might deter the supermarket company from importing wine and instead lead it to concentrate on selling German wines, thereby foregoing the gains from trade and reducing economic welfare. The supermarket could have eliminated the uncertainty by getting a bank to agree to sell the francs at an agreed rate against marks to be delivered three months later (an example of a forward foreign exchange contract). However, the bank would charge for this service, which would be equivalent to a tariff on imported wine, and this again would represent a deadweight loss to society.

The reduction in uncertainty arising from the removal of exchange rate fluctuations can also have a positive effect on investment in the economy. For example, companies that export a large amount of their output to other euro area countries can plan for the future with less risk. Less uncertainty concerning the receipts from a company's exports means that investment projects such as building new factories appear less risky. An increase in investment will benefit the whole economy because it is likely to lead to higher economic growth.

Costs of a Single Currency

The major cost to an economy when joining a common currency area relates to the fact that it gives up its national currency. It is therefore giving up its freedom to set its own monetary policy and the possibility of macroeconomic adjustment coming about through movements in the external value of its currency. Monetary policy is decided by the ECB. This is a potential problem. Suppose, for example, that there is a shift in consumer preferences across the common currency area away from goods and services produced in one country (Germany, say) and towards goods and services produced in another country (France, say). This situation is depicted in Figure 17.1, which shows a leftwards shift in the German AD curve and a rightwards shift in the French AD curve. What should policymakers in France and Germany do about this? One answer to this is nothing. In the long run, each economy will return to its natural rate of output. In Germany, this will occur as the price level falls and wages, prices and perceptions adjust. As unemployment rises in Germany, wages eventually begin to fall. Lower wages reduce firms' costs and so, for any given price level, the amount supplied will be higher. In other words, the German SRAS curve will shift to the right until eventually it intersects with the AD curve at the natural rate of output. The opposite happens in France, with the SRAS curve shifting to the left. The adjustment to the new equilibrium levels of output is also shown in Figure 17.1.

Note that, if Germany and France had maintained their own currencies and a flexible foreign exchange rate, the short-term fluctuations in AD would be alleviated by a movement in the exchange rate. In other words, as the demand for French goods rises, and falls for German goods, the demand for French francs increases and the demand for German marks depresses. This makes the value of francs rise in terms of marks in the foreign currency exchange market. French goods thus become more expensive to German residents since they must now pay more marks for a given number of French francs. Similarly, German goods become less expensive to French residents. Therefore, French net exports fall, leading to a fall in AD. This is shown in Figure 17.2, where the French AD curve shifts back to the left until equilibrium is again established at the natural rate of output. Conversely – and also shown in Figure 17.2 – German net exports rise and the German AD curve shifts to the right until equilibrium is again achieved in Germany.

FIGURE 17.1

A Shift in Consumer Preferences Away from German Goods Towards French Goods

The German fall in AD leads to a fall in output from Y_1^G to Y_2^G, and a fall in the price level from P_1^G to P_2^G. The increase in French AD raises output from Y_1^F to Y_2^F. Over time, however, wages and prices will adjust, so that German and French output return to their natural levels, Y_1^G and Y_1^F, with lower prices in Germany, at P_3^G, and higher prices in France, at P_3^F.

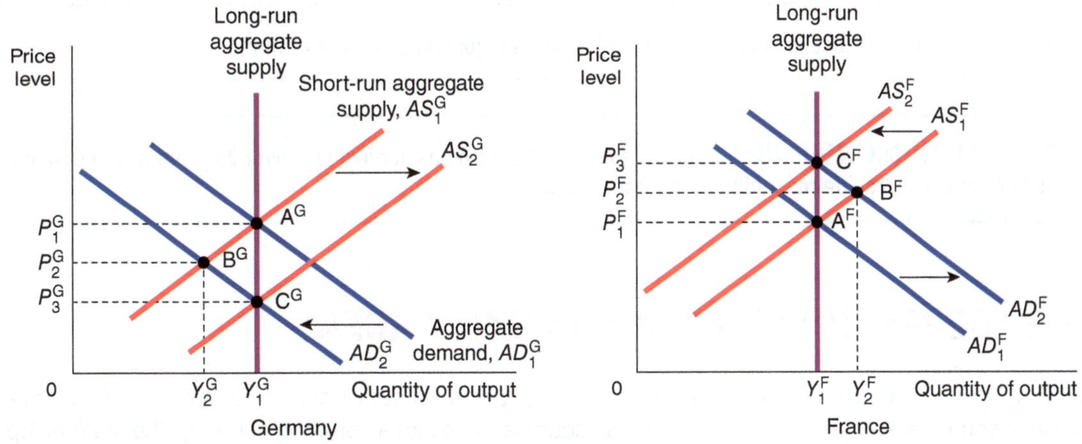

FIGURE 17.2

A Shift in Consumer Preferences with Flexible Exchange Rates

Until prices have had time to adjust, the fall in German AD leads to a fall in output from Y_1^G to Y_3^G. However, because this is due to a fall in net foreign demand, the value of the German currency falls, making German goods cheaper abroad. This raises net exports and restores AD. The converse happens in France in that the increase in net foreign demand raises the external value of the French currency, making French goods more expensive abroad and choking off AD to its former level.

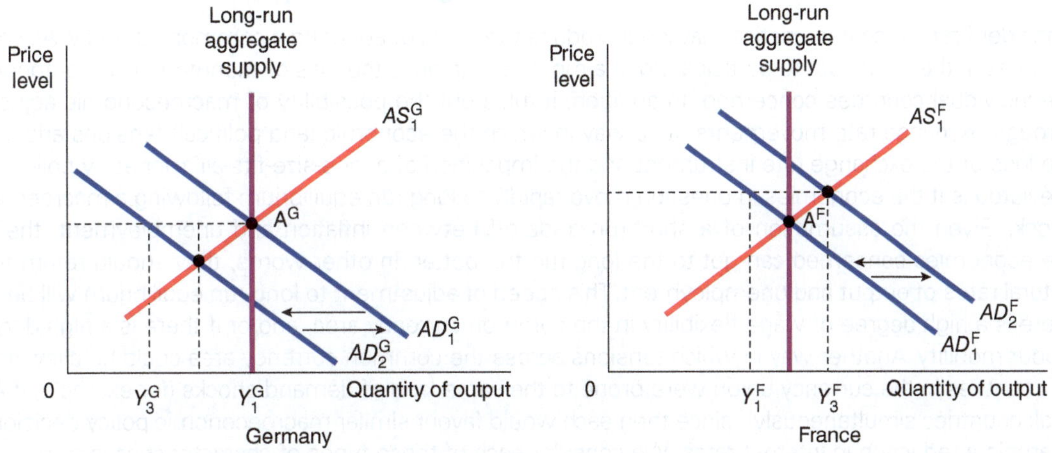

In a currency union, however, this automatic adjustment mechanism is not available, since, of course, France and Germany have the same currency (the euro). The best that can be done is to wait for wages and prices to adjust in France and Germany so that AS shifts in each country, as in Figure 17.1. The resulting fluctuations in output and unemployment in each country will tend to create tensions within the monetary union, as unemployment rises in Germany and inflation rises in France. German policymakers, dismayed at the rise in unemployment, will favour a cut in interest rates to boost AD in their country, while their French counterparts, worried about rising inflation, will be calling for an increase in interest rates to curtail French AD. The ECB will not be able to keep both countries happy. Most likely, it will set interest rates higher than the German desired level and lower than the French desired level.

The ECB pursues an inflation targeting strategy, and the inflation rate it targets is based upon a CPI constructed as an average across the euro area. If a country's inflation rate (or expected inflation rate) is below the euro area average, the ECB's monetary policy will be too tight for that country. If it is above the average, the ECB's monetary policy will be too loose for it. All that is possible is a 'one-size-fits-all' monetary policy. It is for this reason that entry to the euro area is restricted to those countries that can meet the criteria where inflation and interest rates are close to the EU average.

SELF TEST List and discuss the key costs and benefits of joining a currency union.

CRITICAL THINKING POINT Does the fact that the euro has survived for over 25 years now mean that it is here to stay? Provide reasoning for your argument.

THE THEORY OF OPTIMUM CURRENCY AREAS

Optimum currency area (OCA) theory attempts to set down a set of criteria for a group of countries that would in some sense make it 'optimal' for those countries to adopt a common currency. The qualifier 'optimal' here refers to the ability of each of the countries to limit the costs of monetary union and enhance the benefits. It is generally used loosely, since there is no way of ensuring whether it is indeed optimal for a group of countries to form a currency union. More often than not, countries will fulfil some but not all of the OCA criteria.

optimum currency area a group of countries for which it is optimal to adopt a common currency and form a currency union

Characteristics that Reduce the Costs of a Single Currency

Consider first the characteristics that would reduce the costs of adopting a common currency. As we have discussed, the main cost to participating in a monetary union is the loss of monetary policy autonomy for the individual countries concerned. In addition, it rules out the possibility of macroeconomic adjustment through exchange rate movements. One way in which the economic (and political) tensions arising from the loss of the exchange rate instrument and the imposition of a 'one-size-fits-all' monetary policy will be alleviated is if the economies in question move rapidly to long-run equilibrium following a macroeconomic shock. Given the assumption of a short-run trade-off between inflation and unemployment, the faster the economies concerned can get to the long run the better. In other words, they should return to their natural rates of output and unemployment. This speed of adjustment to long-run equilibrium will be high if there is a high degree of wage flexibility in the common currency area, and/or if there is a high degree of labour mobility. Another way in which tensions across the common currency area could be alleviated is if all countries in the currency union were prone to the same kind of demand shocks (for example, if AD fell in all countries simultaneously), since then each would favour similar macroeconomic policy decisions, for example a reduction in interest rates. We consider each of these types of characteristics in turn.

Real Wage Flexibility Suppose there is a high degree of wage flexibility in each of the member countries, so that wages respond strongly to rises and falls in unemployment. This means that the adjustment to long-run equilibrium, as shown in Figure 17.1, occurs very quickly. In our example, the shift in AD in Germany leads to falling wages, so that firms make more profit for any given level of prices, the AS curve shifts to the right and Germany returns to the natural rate of output. If wages are very flexible, this adjustment may be very rapid, so that the short run is very short indeed. Similarly for France, the rightwards shift in AD leads to rapidly rising wages. As firms find it less profitable to produce any given level of output, the supply curve shifts leftwards and a new long-run equilibrium is established at the natural rate of output. Hence, by compressing the short run, tensions across the monetary union are ironed out very quickly.

Note that it is the real wage that is of importance here: it is real wages that must adjust to affect the AS curve by making it more (or less) profitable for firms to produce a given level of output at any given level of prices.

Labour Mobility Alternatively, suppose that labour is highly mobile between the member countries of the currency union, such that unemployed workers in Germany can simply migrate to France and find a job. Again, the macroeconomic imbalance is alleviated, since unemployment in Germany will fall as many of the unemployed have left the country. In addition, inflationary wage pressures in France decline as the labour force expands with the migrants from Germany. Therefore, labour mobility may in some measure cushion a currency union from **asymmetric shocks**, a situation where changes in AD and/or supply differ from one country to another.

asymmetric shocks a situation where changes in aggregate demand and/or supply differ from one country to another

Capital Mobility Sometimes economists argue that capital mobility can compensate for the loss of monetary autonomy and the absence of exchange rate adjustment among the members of a common currency area. A distinction should be made here between physical capital (plant and machinery) and financial capital (bonds, company shares and bank loans). In terms of cushioning a currency union from asymmetric shocks, movements in physical capital can help by expanding productive capacity in countries experiencing a boom, as firms in other member countries build factories there. However, given the long lags involved in the installation of plant and equipment, physical capital mobility is likely to be helpful mainly for narrowing persistent regional disparities rather than offsetting short-term shocks.

The mobility of *financial* capital may be more useful in cushioning economies from short-term output shocks. For example, residents of a country experiencing a recession may wish to borrow money from the residents of a country experiencing a boom to overcome their short-term difficulties. In our two-country example, German residents would effectively borrow money from French residents to make up for their temporary fall in income. Clearly, this would require that German residents can easily borrow from French residents through the capital markets, as financial capital mobility will be highest between countries whose capital markets are highly integrated with one another. For example, if a bank has branches in more than one country of a currency union, then borrowing and lending between growth and recession countries will be more or less automatic. Residents in the growth country increase the money they are holding in the bank as their income goes up and residents of the country in recession increase their overdrafts (or reduce their money holdings) as their income goes down.

We can relate this discussion back to the notion of permanent income and to the market for loanable funds. Recall that a family's ability to buy goods and services depends largely on its permanent income, which is its normal or average income, since people tend to borrow and lend to smooth out transitory variations in income. Now, when an AD shock adversely affects the German economy, some German households will see their transitory income fall and will want to borrow to increase income back up to the permanent or normal level. Since many German households are now doing this at the same time, if borrowing is restricted to German financial markets, interest rates will likely rise and borrowing will generally become more difficult. If the market for loanable funds is restricted to the domestic market, then we might expect the supply of loanable funds to decrease in a recession and the demand to increase, raising interest rates. The resulting rise in interest rates may even make the recession worse by reducing investment.

On the other hand, in France, the economic boom means that many households are experiencing income levels above their permanent or average level and so will tend to increase their saving. If the German households can borrow from the French households – if the market for loanable funds covers both France and Germany – they can both consume at a level consistent with their normal or average levels of income with less of an effect on interest rates. There will be an increase in the supply of loanable funds because French residents are saving more. This will partly or even wholly offset the increase in the demand for loanable funds arising from German residents who want to borrow more. When the German economy comes out of recession and goes into recovery, German households can then repay the loans.

Of course, although we have discussed only bank loans, there are other forms of financial capital, such as bonds and company shares. The principle of the recessionary economy being able to obtain funds from the booming economy remains the same, however. In effect, therefore, financial capital market integration across countries allows households to insure one another against asymmetric shocks so that the variability of consumption over the economic cycle can be reduced.

Symmetric Macroeconomic Shocks In describing the costs of belonging to a monetary union, we have used the example of a positive demand shock in one country and a simultaneous negative demand shock in another. A similar analysis would have followed if we had simply allowed either a positive or a negative demand shock in one country and no shock at all in the other country. The central point was that the demand shock was asymmetric in the sense that it impacted differently on different members of the currency union, requiring different short-run policy responses. Clearly, if the shock were symmetric there would be no problem. If, for example, AD rose simultaneously in all member countries, increasing expected future inflation, then a policy of raising interest rates would be welcomed by all members of the monetary union. This would be the case if the economic cycles of each of the member countries were synchronized in the sense that they enter recession as well as the recovery phase of the cycle around the same time. In this scenario, disagreements about the best interest rate policy are less likely to occur.

Characteristics that Increase the Benefits of a Single Currency

High Degree of Trade Integration The greater the amount of trade that takes place between a group of countries, that is the greater the degree of trade integration, the more they will benefit from adopting a common currency. One of the principal and most direct benefits of a currency union is the reduction in transaction costs that are incurred in trade transactions where there is a constant need to switch one national currency into another on the foreign currency exchange market. Clearly, therefore, the greater the amount of international trade that is carried out between member countries, the greater the reduction in transaction costs that having a common currency entails.

The reduction in exchange rate volatility – another benefit of a currency union – will also be greater, the greater the degree of intra-union trade. This is because more firms will benefit from knowing with certainty exactly the revenue generated from their sales to other currency union members, rather than having to bear the uncertainty associated with exchange rate fluctuations.

SELF TEST What is meant by an optimum currency area? List and discuss the key characteristics of an optimum currency area.

IS EUROPE AN OPTIMUM CURRENCY AREA?

Having determined what characteristics of a group of countries would strengthen the benefits of a single currency and reduce the costs, we can take a closer look to see whether Europe – and in particular the group of 20 countries that comprise the euro area – forms an optimum currency area.

Trade Integration

The degree of trade integration can be assessed by looking at imports from and exports to other EU countries expressed as a percentage of GDP. The degree of trade integration across Europe is quite variable. The EU produces a 'scorecard' that monitors and reports on the progress on trade integration. In the most recent scorecard available at the time of writing, it was noted that trade integration in the EU had more than doubled since 1993. Trade integration for the initial 12 countries stood at 11.4 per cent of GDP but has risen to 26.3 per cent for the EU 27 in 2022.

Trade integration is measured through eight indicators, which look at levels and change. There are four main categories in both EU trade integration in goods and services and openness to imports of goods and services. The European Commission notes that priorities for the future include increasing trade integration in services, the recognition of qualifications and structural reforms that can help remove barriers to new technologies and business models across the EU.

Some economists argue that some of the criteria for an optimum currency area – such as a high degree of trade integration – may be endogenous. This means being a member of a currency union may enhance the degree of trade done between members of the union, precisely because of the decline in transaction costs in carrying out such trade.

Overall, many – if not all – European countries have gained a great deal from the reduction in transaction costs in international trade as a result of the single currency. In 2014, for example, the Single Euro Payments Area (SEPA) became operational in all euro area countries. SEPA has been designed to facilitate euro transfers, direct debits and payments between member states. A report on the economic benefits of the euro published in 2021 suggests that harmonization of the European payments system under SEPA has resulted in an annual benefit of €22 billion due to increased price convergence and process efficiency (Brans, P., Clemens, U., Kattami, C. and Meyermans, E. (2021) The Economic Benefits of the Euro. *Quarterly Report on the Euro Area*, 20(1): 47–61).

Some estimates put the overall gains at about 0.25–0.5 per cent of euro area GDP. This may not sound massive but remember that transaction costs are a deadweight loss. Moreover, the gains are not one-off. They accrue continuously as long as the single currency persists, since they would have to be paid in the absence of the currency union. They therefore become cumulative. In addition, if the degree of euro area trade integration rises over time as a result of the single currency, as some economists have suggested, then the implicit gain from not having to pay transaction costs also rises over time.

The other, indirect benefit of a single currency when there is a high degree of trade integration comes from the reduction in uncertainty associated with doing away with the volatility in the exchange rates between members' national currencies (since those currencies are replaced with a common currency). These gains are hard to quantify, but they certainly exist for the euro area.

Real Wage Flexibility

A great deal of research has been done on real wage flexibility in Europe and virtually all of it concludes that continental European labour markets are among the most rigid in the world, although the degree of real wage growth flexibility tends to be greater in central and eastern Europe (Rusinova, D., Lipatov, V. and Heinz, F.F. (2015) 'How Flexible Are Real Wages in EU Countries? A Panel Investigation'. *Journal of Macroeconomics*, 43(1): 140–54). In contrast, the UK labour market, at least since the 1980s, has become one of the most flexible. One reason for this is the fact that all EU countries have minimum wage laws (although the UK also has a minimum wage), but perhaps a more important reason is the high degree of collective wage bargaining that is common in continental Europe, that is wage agreements that cover a large number of workers. Figures on the degree of unionization of the labour force are quite deceptive in this sense. For example, in the early 2000s, in the UK, Italy and Germany about 30 per cent of the workforce belonged to a trade union, while in France the figure was around 10 per cent (this has since fallen to around 8 per cent). Continental European unions, however, often have collective bargaining and other workplace rights that UK trade unionists can only envy. The power of unions and the inflexibility of the labour market is something that has been a concern in France for some time and in 2013, an agreement was reached between the government and unions on reforms to the country's complex and strict labour laws. The agreement was greeted with mixed responses with some saying it did not go far enough and others suggesting the agreement marked the end of workers' rights in France.

The introduction of the single European currency may also have had a negative effect on European wage flexibility, since many European collective wage agreements between workers and a firm in one country will also often extend to the firm's workforce in other European countries. A single currency therefore highlights wage and price differences across countries. To return again to our example of a negative demand shock in Germany and a positive shock in France, a company with employees in both countries would find it hard to reduce real wages in Germany while raising them in France.

Furthermore, European labour law is generally much more restrictive in many continental European countries than it is in the UK or the United States. The level of payroll taxes is higher, so that reducing or increasing the workforce can become very costly to firms. This means that even if there are movements in the real wage, firms are slow to expand or contract their output in response and shifts in AS are slow to come about.

On the whole, therefore, adjustment to asymmetric shocks through real wage movements is unlikely to be significant in the euro area.

Labour Mobility

Labour is notoriously immobile across European countries, at least if we rule out migration from the newer, eastern members of the EU such as Poland, Romania and Bulgaria, and consider just the 20 euro area countries or these plus Denmark and Sweden. A report published in 2023 showed that there were 10 million people between 20 and 64 living in another member state representing 4.9 per cent of the total workforce. Some 50 per cent of all movers of working age came from Romania, Poland and Italy (*Intra-EU Labour Mobility at a Glance*, Publications Office of the European Union). In part this relatively low number of movers may perhaps be attributed to differences in language, culture and other social institutions across Europe that make it difficult for workers to migrate. However, it seems that European workers are very loath to move location even within their own countries. Indeed, the degree of labour mobility as measured by the percentage of the workforce that moves geographical location over any given period is much lower within any particular European country than it is within the United States, and is even lower between the euro area countries. Europe therefore scores very low on this optimum currency area criterion.

Financial Capital Mobility

The EU defines financial integration as 'the extent to which financial services are available under the same rules and conditions across the region. A well-integrated financial system implies that assets with the same risk-return characteristics have the same prices, irrespective of the country in which they are traded. This contributes to the uniform transmission of the ECB's monetary policy across the euro area' (*www.ecb.europa.eu/home/search/financial_integration/html/index.en.html*). Prior to the introduction of the euro, financial integration among euro area countries was relatively low, in both the wholesale and retail capital markets. However, following the introduction of the euro, integration of the wholesale financial markets increased dramatically. In particular, a liquid euro money market with single interbank market interest rates was established so that a bank in, say, Luxembourg can now borrow euros just as easily and at the same rate of interest from another bank in Frankfurt as it can from a bank located in the same street in Luxembourg. In the government bond market, the degree of market integration is also high, shown by the fact that the interest rates on government bonds of the different euro area countries are very similar and tend to move very closely together. Overall, the euro area financial system now encompasses a wider range of financial intermediaries, including fintech companies. **Fintech** is short for financial technologies. It refers to technologies that are primarily used in the financial services industry and includes mobile payments, transferring money, loans, fund raising and asset management. It is of increasing relevance in financial markets and more and more businesses are making use of fintech services.

fintech financial technologies used in the financial services industry, including mobile payments, transferring money, loans, fund raising and asset management

On the other hand, the integration of retail market products, such as loans to households and small and medium-sized enterprises, is lagging behind compared with the wholesale market products. This becomes evident from persistent cross-country differences in bank lending rates and the rather limited cross-border retail banking activity. Indeed, national banking sectors have remained largely segregated with only marginal cross-border penetration.

Symmetric Demand Shocks

The economic cycle across the countries of the euro area appears to be positively correlated, in the sense that the timing of strong growth and downturns is very close. The problem is not so much that the turning points do not coincide, but that certain countries' growth rates differ. For example, between 2005 and 2007, Ireland's and Greece's growth rates outstripped the performance of the euro area as a whole, but then they both had considerable problems as a result of the 2007–9 Financial Crisis. Ireland recovered and its GDP growth was recorded by Eurostat at 5.9 per cent in 2020, whereas the rate for Greece was −9.8 per cent and for Spain −10.8 per cent. Ireland was the only EU country to record a positive growth rate of GDP in 2020. It can be argued that monetary policy between 2008 and 2014 for the euro area as a whole did not match the needs of the Greek and Irish economies over that same period. It also did not match the respective needs of the Greek, Spanish and Irish economies in the early 2020s. Figure 17.3 shows growth rates of GDP in 2023 and highlights the differences between member states.

FIGURE 17.3

Growth Rates of Real GDP in the EU 27, 2023

The figure highlights differences in growth rates between members of the EU 27.

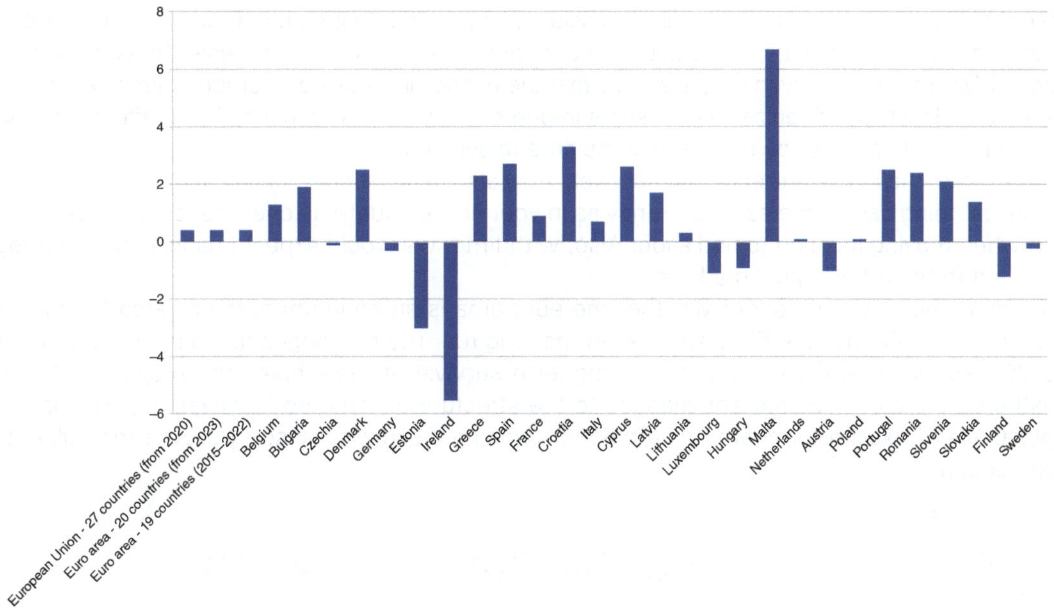

Source: ec.europa.eu/eurostat/databrowser/view/tec00115/default/table?lang=en

Overall, therefore, the evidence is a little mixed. On the whole though it suggests that the problem of asymmetric demand shocks is not a great one for the current member countries of the EMU. The fact that there is no strong evidence of asymmetric demand shocks at the aggregate level, however, does not rule out the possibility that there may be asymmetric shocks at other levels in the economy. In fact, researchers have found that many of the shocks that impact upon European countries asymmetrically tend to be specific to a region or to an industry rather than to a country as a whole. As an example, there are differences in economic effects between the northern and southern parts of Italy. However, this problem is not made worse by joining a monetary union, since a country that experiences, say, a negative shock to one of its industries or regions would not be able to deal with this using monetary or exchange rate policy without generating imbalances in its other regions or industries. The idea of a two-speed EU to cater for the countries that have experienced debt crisis problems since the Financial Crisis – Portugal, Ireland, Italy, Greece and Spain – has highlighted that there are some countries that seem better able to weather economic storms than others.

Germany, France, the Netherlands, Denmark and Sweden all recovered from the Financial Crisis more quickly, even if the strength of their recovery was muted. Economists have noted that the degree of integration of the euro area and the EU as a whole does impact on the ability of countries to recover from economic shocks. If EU countries rely on each other for export-led growth, then if a group of these countries faces considerable fiscal difficulties and implements austerity measures, the level of demand in these economies falls. This would then affect demand in the other economies, thus dragging down growth in all the euro area countries and the EU as a whole.

Summary: Is Europe an Optimum Currency Area?

As in many policy debates in economics, there is no clear-cut answer to this question. Certainly, many European countries have a high degree of intra-union trade and economic cycles that are more or less synchronized. However, labour mobility and wage flexibility (and labour market flexibility in general) are low in Europe. While the euro has increased financial market integration in the euro area's wholesale financial markets, the retail markets remain highly segregated at the national level.

Therefore, if very strong differences in the economic cycle were to emerge across the euro area, the lack of independent monetary and exchange rate policy would be acutely felt. For that reason, many economists argue that Europe – meaning the current euro area – is not an optimum currency area. Nevertheless, as we have noted in our discussion, it is possible that some of the optimum currency area criteria may be endogenous. In particular, the single currency is likely to generate even greater trade among EMU members. Given this, it is likely that the economic cycles of member currencies will become even more closely synchronized as AD shifts in one country have stronger spillover effects in other euro area countries. This may, however, take some time to synchronize.

Over time, the single currency, if it survives, may also raise labour mobility across Europe in the long run, since being paid in the same currency as in your home country is one less issue to come to terms with when moving location to find a job. Also, with time, we would expect financial market integration to spread to the retail capital markets.

Perhaps the only true test of whether the euro area is an optimum currency area (or can become one) is to see whether the EMU survives in the long run. The challenges faced by the euro area since the 2007–9 Financial Crisis did put the long-term survival of the whole euro project in doubt but it weathered the storm. Significant changes to the structure of the euro however, in particular financial regulation and fiscal reform, are the subject of ongoing discussion. Fiscal policy is the subject of our next section.

FISCAL POLICY AND COMMON CURRENCY AREAS

Our discussion so far has centred on the loss of autonomy in monetary policy that is entailed in adopting a single currency among a group of countries. However, it is obvious that there is nothing in the adoption of a common currency that implies that members of the currency union should not still retain independence in fiscal policy. For instance, in our example of an asymmetric demand shock that expands demand in France and contracts AD in Germany, the French government could reduce government spending to offset the demand shock. The German government for its part could expand government spending. In fact, even if France and Germany did not make up an optimal currency area, because wages are sticky and labour mobility low between the countries, national fiscal policy could, in principle, still be used to ameliorate the loss of monetary policy autonomy.

Fiscal Federalism

Suppose that a currency union has a common fiscal policy in the sense of having a single, common fiscal budget covering tax and spending decisions across the common currency area. This means that fiscal policy in the currency union works much as fiscal policy in a single national economy. A surplus of government tax revenue over government spending in one region could be used to pay for a budget deficit in another region. Return again to our example of an asymmetric demand shock that expands AD in France and contracts AD in Germany. Remember that there are automatic stabilizers built into the fiscal policy of an economy that stimulate AD when the economy goes into recession without policymakers having to take any deliberate action. In particular, since almost all taxes are closely related to the level of economic activity in the economy, tax revenue will automatically decline in Germany as a result of the AD shock that shifts it into recession. At the same time, transfer payments in the form of unemployment benefit and other social security benefits will also rise in Germany. The opposite will be true in France, where the automatic stabilizers will be operating in reverse as transfer payments fall and tax receipts rise with the level of economic activity. These changes will tend to expand AD in Germany and contract it in France, to some extent offsetting the asymmetric demand shock.

If the governments of France and Germany have a common budget, then the increased net government revenue in France can be used to offset the reduction in net government revenue in Germany. If the resulting movements in the aggregate are not enough to offset the demand shock, then the French and German governments may even go further and decide to increase government expenditure further in Germany and pay for it by reducing spending, and perhaps raising taxes in France.

This kind of arrangement – a fiscal system for a group of countries involving a common fiscal budget and a system of taxes and fiscal transfers across countries – is known as **fiscal federalism**. The problem with it is that the taxpayers of one country (here France) may not be happy with having to pay for government spending and transfer payments in another country (in this example, Germany).

fiscal federalism a fiscal system for a group of countries involving a common fiscal budget and a system of taxes and fiscal transfers across countries

National Fiscal Policies in a Currency Union: The Free Rider Problem

Assume that for political reasons, fiscal federalism is not an option open to the currency union. We still need to explore the possibility of individual members of the union using fiscal policy to offset asymmetric macroeconomic shocks that cannot be dealt with by a common monetary policy. In particular, in our example, what is wrong with Germany running a big government budget deficit in order to counteract the fall in AD and borrowing heavily to finance the deficit? One answer may lie in the effect of a rise in the debt of a member country on other members of the currency union.

Whenever a government raises its levels of debt to very high levels, there is the possibility that the government may default on the debt (which, as we have seen, was a concern following the Financial Crisis). Where a country is not a member of a currency union and controls its own monetary policy, it can engineer a surprise inflation by a sudden increase in the money supply, so that the real value of the debt shrinks. When there is a sharp rise in the price level, this will usually be accompanied by a sharp fall in the foreign currency value of the domestic currency. This means that valued in foreign currency, the stock of government debt will now be worth far less. Thus, the government has in effect defaulted on a large portion of its debt by reducing its value both internally and externally.

If a country no longer enjoys monetary policy autonomy and is not able to devalue the external value of its currency since it uses a common currency, then the only other way of reneging on its debts is through an outright default (for example, stopping interest payments or failing to honour capital repayments when they fall due). Generally, the financial markets are good at disciplining governments that run up large debts, by charging them high rates of interest on the debt that the government issues. After all, if you thought there was even a slight possibility that you might not get your money back if you lent it, you would want to be paid a higher rate of interest in order to compensate for that risk. It is rarely impossible for a country to borrow money on international markets, but if interest rates are higher than about 7 per cent, then the cost of servicing the debt becomes unsustainable in the longer term, particularly if economic growth is as weak as it was in Greece, for example. If the cost of borrowing is consistently above 7 per cent, then it is likely that governments will be in even more trouble and become more likely to default.

In the case of a monetary union, therefore, this means that excessive debt issuance by one member country will tend to force up interest rates throughout the whole of the common currency area. Although the ECB controls very short-term interest rates in the euro area through its refinancing operations, it does not control longer-term interest rates such as those paid on 10-year or 20-year government bonds. Hence, fiscal profligacy by a government in the euro area will tend to push up the cost of borrowing for all members of the currency union.

However, interest rates may not be raised enough to discipline properly the high-borrowing government. This is because the markets feel that the other members of the monetary union would not allow the country concerned to default. If it threatened to do so, the other members would probably rush in and buy up its government debt and bail out the country concerned. If the markets believe in this possibility, then the debt will not be seen as risky as it otherwise would be. Therefore, the interest rates charged to the debtor country on its debt will not be as high as they otherwise might be. The intervention by the ECB, EU finance ministers and the IMF to bail out the economies of Ireland, Greece and other countries following the 2007–9 Financial Crisis was a case in point as ministers struggled to keep the EMU together.

The net effect is for a government to pay interest rates on its large stock of debt that are lower because of the implicit belief that it will be bailed out if it has problems servicing the debt. All other members of the currency union would thus pay higher interest rates on their government debt, because the government has flooded the financial markets with euro-denominated government bonds. In essence, this is an example of the free rider problem. The government is therefore enjoying the benefits of a fiscal expansion without paying the full costs.

In addition, if that government is using the proceeds of its borrowing to fund a strong fiscal expansion, this may undo or work against the anti-inflationary monetary policy of the ECB by stoking up AD throughout the whole of the euro area.

To circumvent some of these problems, the currency union members can enter into a 'no bailout' agreement that states that member countries cannot expect other members to come to their rescue if their debt levels become unsustainable. In fact, exactly such a 'no bailout' agreement exists among members of EMU. Unfortunately, however, it has become clear that the 'no bailout' clause is not credible. The attempts by members to support profligate countries throughout the sovereign debt crisis confirmed this. If an EMU member were to default on its debt, this would have strong repercussions throughout the euro area. It would potentially lead to the financial markets losing confidence in debt issued by other members and to strong selling of the euro in the foreign currency exchange market. To avoid this, EMU members acted to bail out member countries threatening to default on their debt.

For these reasons, the members of the currency union may wish to impose rules on one another concerning the conduct of national fiscal policies to avoid fiscal profligacy by any one member. At the outset of the EMU, a set of fiscal rules was indeed drawn up and agreed to by EMU members. This set of rules was known as the Stability and Growth Pact (SGP). The SGP was a set of formal rules by which members of the EMU were supposed to be bound in their conduct of national fiscal policy. Its main components were as follows:

- Members should aim to achieve balanced budgets.
- Members with a budget deficit of more than 3 per cent of GDP would be subject to fines that may reach as high as 0.5 per cent of GDP unless the country experiences exceptional circumstances (such as a natural disaster or a pandemic) or a very sharp recession in which GDP declines by 2 per cent or more in a single year.

In practice, the SGP proved to be something of a toothless watchdog. As the euro area experienced sluggish growth in the early years of the EMU, several member countries – and in particular France and Germany, two of the largest member countries – found themselves in breach of the SGP excessive deficit criteria. However, both France and Germany managed to persuade other EMU members not to impose fines and, in 2004, the European Commission drew up guidelines for softening the SGP. These guidelines included considering more widely the sustainability of countries' public finances on an individual basis, paying more attention to overall debt burdens and to long-term liabilities such as pensions, rather than to a single year's deficit. The consequences of the 2007–9 Financial Crisis made the limitation of the SGP even more clear.

THE FISCAL COMPACT

The problems with the debt crisis faced by a number of European countries in the wake of the 2007–9 Financial Crisis and the attempts to keep the euro area together led to the negotiation of a treaty that came into force on 1 January 2013. This has become known as the fiscal compact, but its full title is the *Treaty on Stability, Coordination and Governance in the Economic and Monetary Union.* The intention of the fiscal compact is to:

> *[s]trengthen the economic pillar of the Economic and Monetary Union by adopting a set of rules intended to foster budgetary discipline through a fiscal compact, to strengthen the coordination of economic policies and to improve the governance of the euro area, thereby supporting the achievement of the European Union's objectives for sustainable growth, employment, competitiveness, and social cohesion.*

The treaty echoes some of the features of the SGP in that it requires the budgets of participating member states to be in balance or in surplus and that the structural deficit must not exceed 0.5 per cent of the country's nominal GDP.

Each member country has a minimum benchmark figure for long-term sustainability, which is reviewed annually. Deviation from the balanced budget rule is allowed in exceptional circumstances, such as a severe economic downturn. However, if a member state deviates from the rule, an automatic correction mechanism, which must be built into the country's legal system, is triggered. Participant countries were expected to have this legal mechanism enshrined into EU law by 1 January 2018. Member states are also subject to a budgetary and economic partnership programme, which outlines detailed structural reforms that have to be put into place if the deficit rules are breached and detail how the country intends to remedy its deficit problems.

Imposing greater fiscal discipline might sound sensible to prevent governments from profligacy and reduce the free rider problem. The consequences, however, are essentially simple. If debt is too high, the government concerned must cut spending and raise taxes. If governments are seeking to balance budgets, account must be taken of the effect on the other aspects of the economy. This is why the fiscal compact has been referred to as 'institutionalized austerity'.

Recall that savings of households and firms is denoted as S and that in equilibrium, savings equals investment ($S = I$) in a closed economy. If governments have a balanced budget, then tax receipts (T) equal government spending (G), that is $T = G$. The external current account is given by net exports (NX). If there is an imbalance in private savings and/or government budgets, this shows up in net capital outflow. Recall that the link between the market for loanable funds and the market for foreign currency exchange is $S = I + NX$. This can be rearranged to give $S - I = NX$. Rearranging the national accounting equation gives $(S - I) + (T - G) = NX$, where $T - G$ is the government deficit. If the government is to balance its budget, the sum of the other elements of the economy must also balance. However, bringing these other aspects into balance is not easy. If the government is forced to cut spending and increase taxes, national income will fall, *ceteris paribus*. An increase in taxes will have the effect of reducing private saving. If saving falls, then interest rates rise, investment may decline and the net result is a rise in unemployment. In addition, over time, the reduced investment leads to a lower stock of capital. A lower capital stock reduces labour productivity, real wages and the economy's production of goods and services. The political ramifications of bringing the budget into balance could be severe for governments and lead to political instability, which further undermines market confidence.

The fiscal compact has been subject to considerable disagreement, debate and revision in the European Parliament. One of the criticisms is that the rules around it are seen to be too complex. A key challenge is the extent to which any of the main tenets of the treaty can be legally enforced. Violations of the rules could be taken to the Court of Justice for the European Union, but this has not been tested as yet. A review and revision of the new SGP was begun in early 2020 but suspended as Covid-19 took hold. Many governments had to expand their spending significantly to manage the crisis, measures that are allowed by the treaty, but bringing closer harmonization of fiscal policies across the EU is still some way off.

CASE STUDY The Impact of the Conflict in Ukraine

©iStock/Serhii Ivashchuk

The conflict in Ukraine has forced a number of European countries to reconsider spending decisions on defence and, as a result, put pressure on fiscal rules.

The geopolitical tensions that have intensified following the conflict in Ukraine have raised important issues in the EU regarding the fiscal rules its members subscribe to. The conflict has drawn attention on defence spending. Countries close to the border with Ukraine and Russia have been warning of the need to strengthen defences. The contribution of European nations to the funding of NATO has been highlighted with the re-election of US President Donald Trump, who expressed concerns that too many European countries were 'free riding' on the United States.

The fiscal rules dictate that debt be kept at or below 60 per cent of GDP and that deficits are kept below 3 per cent of GDP in the medium term. A number of countries face challenges in meeting these rules. The situation has been exacerbated by the renewed focus on defence. Poland, for example, intends to increase spending on defence, increasing the percentage spend in relation to GDP from the 2.5 per cent it committed in 2022 to 5 per cent in 2025. If countries do commit to spending more on defence, and this results in them breaching fiscal rules, should they be subject to punishment? Or, should the rules be bent to allow countries to respond to the changed circumstances?

Some analysts are not sure that this would be wise. They point to the lengthy negotiations that went into reframing the agreement and the fact that it has not been in place sufficiently long to justify amending it so soon. Why have a set of rules and then seek to break or bend them? It defeats the object of having rules. They also note that it would entail deciding what would be permitted under investment in military spending and how EU authorities would exercise control over this. Then there is the problem of the extent to which the EU should exercise control over something that is inherently national in nature and which citizens of member states would see as unnecessary interference. One possible alternative to allowing nations to 'bend the rules' might be to look at defence spending from the perspective of it being an EU-wide public good with positive externalities for all members. Could the EU, therefore, agree to a common funding of defence projects that would satisfy these economic principles?

Questions:

1. How does the changing situation across Europe, highlighted in the first paragraph of the case study, reflect the impact of economic shocks considered earlier?
2. How do countries typically finance spending on defence and how might this contribute to a breach in the fiscal rules which they have signed up to as part of the fiscal compact?
3. Given the situation facing a number of EU countries as a result of the conflict in Ukraine, to what extent do you agree that the fiscal rules should be relaxed or even dropped to enable countries to focus more on building defences?
4. How might a Europe-wide funding programme for boosting defence operate and what challenges might exist in implementing such an initiative?

Reference:

www.bruegel.org/analysis/should-european-unions-fiscal-rules-bend-accommodate-defence-transition, accessed 6 August 2025.

THE FUTURE OF THE EUROPEAN UNION

There are a number of challenges facing the EU as it enters its seventh decade of existence. What follows is a brief summary of some of these challenges.

Populism

The austerity policies that a number of governments in the EU adopted, sometimes under pressure from wealthier and more stable members, have had a severe impact on millions of people. It is perhaps not surprising that people look to apportion blame for the difficult situation they find themselves in to politicians, and EU politicians in particular. Greeks did not necessarily see their own government as being the cause of their problems but instead saw their government being held to ransom by the German government.

Not all governments had to impose austerity policies to the same extent as Greece, but even in some of the wealthier countries that make up the EU, and countries where growth has been reasonable and unemployment relatively low, populism has gained some traction. In Italy, corruption, problems with the banking system and increasing government debt have led to dissatisfaction with the mainstream political parties. In the Netherlands, Austria and France, right-wing politicians gained seats following elections. In 2024, there were problems in France and Germany where votes of no confidence saw collapses in government amid internal tensions.

Populism can be defined as an attempt by groups to appeal to the 'ordinary' people who are 'cast aside' by the political elite and marginalized in society. Populist groups may form themselves into political parties, presenting themselves as a 'champion of the people'. In so doing, the policies they put forward are reflective of what may be classed as the 'popular' will of the people. Populism in parts of Europe has been associated with the growth of right-wing groups, though this is not necessarily always characteristic of populism.

The Migrant Problem Some of the reason for the rise in votes for populist parties has been the increase in migration into the EU. Data from Eurostat notes that the number of migrants entering the EU since 2013 has increased sharply from about 1.5 million in 2013 to over 2 million a year up to 2021 and then 5.1 million in 2022.

A large proportion of the migrants entering the EU has been from countries experiencing conflict or severe economic problems. Sympathy for these migrants has been widespread, but equally the sheer number of people has placed pressure on resources in countries policing, monitoring, processing and accepting migrants. The publicity surrounding the number of migrants arriving in Europe and the economic impact of caring for them has created divisions within member states. There are those who wish to find ways of accommodating and integrating migrants, and others who feel resources are already stretched and the influx of migrants is putting too much pressure on economies.

The response of Europe to the migrant crisis has been fragmented. Some countries have sought to put up physical barriers to prevent migrants entering their countries. Some have advocated returning migrants to their country of origin unless there is very good evidence that doing so would result in human rights abuses. Others have sought to tackle the organized criminal gangs that are behind some of the trafficking of migrants, while others have been more welcoming of migrants.

Greece and Italy faced some of the most immediate challenges of migrants arriving on their shores. These countries felt that they were bearing the brunt of the migrant problem and not getting much assistance from other EU countries. Germany did open its doors to receiving migrants, but the number entering Germany created significant tensions. One of the reactions to the migrant problem has been the opportunity for right-wing political groups to take advantage of the mistrust and anger about the influx of people, which has fuelled some populist sentiment.

One of the challenges that faces the EU in dealing with the migrant problem is the existence of the **Schengen area**, so named because the agreement to establish the area was signed in the village of Schengen in Luxembourg in 1985. The EU Commission describes the Schengen area thus:

> *The border-free Schengen Area guarantees free movement to more than 425 million EU citizens, along with non-EU nationals living in the EU or visiting the EU as tourists, exchange students or for business purposes (anyone legally present in the EU). Free movement of persons enables every EU citizen to travel, work and live in an EU country without special formalities. Schengen underpins this freedom by enabling*

citizens to move around the Schengen Area without being subject to border checks. (Source: home-affairs.ec.europa.eu/policies/schengen-borders-and-visa/schengen-area_en, accessed 6 August 2025)

Freedom of movement is one of the fundamental tenets of the single market. Tensions around the influx of migrants have led to some disagreement among EU members and in June 2024, new rules were adopted to strengthen the EU's external borders.

Schengen area 29 countries, including Iceland, Liechtenstein, Switzerland and Norway, who have agreed to allow free movement between their countries with no passport and border controls

While the migrant crisis has not been the only reason for the rise in populist support, it has been a contributory factor. Populists have gained political power in a number of EU countries. In Croatia, Finland, Italy, the Netherlands and Sweden, far right parties have direct involvement in coalition governments of different kinds. In Portugal and Slovakia, far right groups performed well in national elections. It would be too simplistic to say that the rise in populism is attributable to any one factor. In many countries the reasons for populist support are complex. However, what is less in doubt is that these political forces are asking questions about the EU and whether it is still fit for purpose and meeting the disparate needs of its citizens.

SELF TEST As an economist, how would you judge whether migration was a 'good' thing or not?

The EU Post-Brexit

On 23 June 2016, the UK went to the polls to vote in a referendum. The question they voted on was simple. Should the United Kingdom remain a member of the European Union or leave the European Union? Voters were given two options, one to tick a box saying, 'Remain a member of the European Union' and the second saying, 'Leave the European Union'. The result of the referendum was 17,410,742 votes cast to leave the EU (51.9 per cent) and 16,141,241 votes in favour of remaining in the EU (48.1 per cent). In Wales and England, the majority voted to leave the EU, while in Scotland and Northern Ireland, the majority voted to remain.

Over the next four years, extensive negotiations and bitter disagreements ensued in the UK itself and between the UK and Europe. On 1 January 2021, the UK formally left the EU. As Brexit becomes a reality, there have been tensions, for example over fishing rights between France and the UK, and over the Northern Ireland border. Firms across the UK and Europe have had to get used to new rules and regulations regarding trade between the UK and Europe.

One of the questions that arose at the time of the Brexit negotiations was what effect it would have on the future of the EU as a whole. Would dissatisfaction with the EU surface in other countries and would the union eventually fall apart? Politicians and policymakers in the EU are aware of the challenges and tensions that exist and understand they need to manage some delicate balances if the EU is to continue and be strengthened in the future.

The European Commission regularly conducts a review of attitudes to the EU, which it publishes as a 'Eurobarometer'. At the time of writing, the most recent publication of this barometer published in the autumn of 2024 showed that 51 per cent of Europeans 'tend to trust the EU', the highest since 2007. Some 69 per cent felt the EU was a place of security and stability, and 81 per cent supported the euro.

Security and defence was seen as a priority for 33 per cent of respondents, perhaps not surprising given the conflict on the EU's eastern borders, and 44 per cent cited peace and stability as having the largest positive impact on their lives in the short term.

SUMMARY

- A common currency area (aka currency union or monetary union) is a geographical area through which one currency circulates and is accepted as the medium of exchange.
- The formation of a common currency area can bring significant benefits to the members of the currency union, particularly if there is already a high degree of international trade among them (that is, a high level of trade

integration). This is primarily because of the reductions in transaction costs in trade and the reduction in exchange rate uncertainty.

- There are, however, costs of joining a currency union, namely the loss of independent monetary policy and also of the exchange rate as a means of macroeconomic adjustment. Given a long-run vertical supply curve, the loss of monetary policy and the lack of exchange rate adjustment affect mainly short-run macroeconomic adjustments.
- These adjustment costs will be lower the greater the degree of real wage flexibility, labour mobility and capital market integration across the currency union, and also the less the members of the currency union suffer from asymmetric demand shocks.
- A group of countries with a high level of trade integration, high labour mobility and real wage flexibility, and a high level of capital market integration that does not suffer asymmetric demand shocks across the different members of the group, is termed an optimum currency area (OCA). An OCA is most likely to benefit from currency union.
- It is possible that a group of countries may become an OCA after forming a currency union. Having a common currency may enhance further trade integration, thereby helping to synchronize members' economic cycles. It may also help foster increased labour mobility and capital market integration.
- Real wage flexibility and labour mobility in the euro area both appear to be relatively low. While the introduction of the euro has led to a high degree of euro area financial market integration at the wholesale level, retail financial markets remain nationally segregated. Overall, therefore, the euro area is probably not at present an optimum currency area, although it may eventually become one.
- The problems of adjustment within a currency union that is not an OCA may be alleviated by fiscal federalism. This is a common fiscal budget and a system of taxes and fiscal transfers across member countries. In practice, however, fiscal federalism may be difficult to implement for political reasons.
- The national fiscal policies of the countries making up a currency union may be subject to a free rider problem. This is where one country issues a large amount of government debt and pays a lower interest rate on it than it might otherwise have paid. It leads to other member countries having to pay higher interest rates as well. It is for this reason that a currency union may wish to impose rules on the national fiscal policies of its members.
- Populism has grown partly due to the migrant crisis, which the EU has had to cope with, but it is by no means restricted to that problem. It is a complex and multifaceted aspect of change across the EU.

IN THE NEWS

The Economic Effects of Brexit

The UK leaving the EU has been one of the major discussion points regarding the EU. At the time of the referendum and after, there was fierce debate about the relative merits or consequences of the move. Research by economists at the National Institute of Economic and Social Research (NIESR) outlined some of the headline effects for the UK.

Considering the trends in the UK economy after 2010, had these trends been maintained, the authors estimate that real income and private consumption per head of the UK population could have been 8–9 per cent and 11–12 per cent higher, respectively. They also note that there has been a decline in UK trade with the EU, a reduction in productivity and a fall in willingness to invest in the UK. One of the assumptions made around the modelling which led to these outcomes was that when the result of the referendum became known, economic actors would have anticipated these shocks. Therefore, expectations play a role in the economic outcomes of Brexit.

In the immediate aftermath of the referendum result, the UK government and the EU spent time in detailed discussions on their post-Brexit relationship. The EU–UK Trade and Cooperation Agreement (TCU) was signed at the end of 2020. The authors assume, however, that expectations had been formed even before this agreement was finalized. In the three years following the transition period during which the TCU was being negotiated, the authors

(Continued)

estimate that UK real GDP was between 2 and 3 per cent lower than if the UK had remained a member of the EU. This equates to a loss of around £850 per head of the UK population.

The researchers suggest that the negative impacts will continue into the next decade and equate to around 5 to 6 per cent of GDP by 2035, which is £2,300 per head of the population. The key factors influencing this outcome relate to a decline in the UK's terms of trade with the EU and a fall in productivity. The terms of trade refer to the ratio of the average of a country's real export prices in relation to import prices. As a result of Brexit, the average price of imports has risen in relation to the average increase in the price of exports. This means that consumers face higher import prices, and earnings from exports buy less resulting in a decline in living standards.

© iStock/Panorama Images

It may be over ten years since the Brexit vote but the effects are still working their way through economies.

Critical Thinking Questions

1 The research cited focuses on the UK, but do you think the EU is also worse off as a result of the UK leaving the union? Explain.
2 Why might you need to know more about the NIESR to arrive at a balanced assessment of this research and its findings?
3 What information would you want to know about the methodology behind the findings of the research to assess the validity and reliability of the research?
4 How appropriate do you think it is to have assumed that consumers and businesses 'perfectly anticipated the shocks of Brexit'? Explain.
5 Do the findings of this research suggest the UK was wrong to leave the EU? Provide clear reasonings and support for the argument you give.

Reference:

niesr.ac.uk/publications/revisiting-effect-brexit?type=global-economic-outlook-topical-feature, accessed 6 August 2025.

QUESTIONS FOR REVIEW

1 Why did Milton Friedman cast doubt on the likely success of the project to launch a single currency across Europe?
2 What are the main advantages of forming a currency union? What are the main disadvantages?
3 What are the main characteristics that reduce the costs of a common currency?
4 How would an asymmetric supply-side shock to a country that was a member of a currency union affect the country and the other members of the currency union?
5 What is an optimum currency area? List the criteria that an OCA must satisfy.
6 What is fiscal federalism? How might the problems of macroeconomic adjustment in a currency union be alleviated by fiscal federalism?
7 What do you understand by the term 'populism' in the context of the EU?
8 What are the main reasons for the growth in support for populist political groups across Europe?
9 How does the announcement of a strengthening of the rules to secure external borders of the Schengen area highlight the challenges from migration faced by the EU?
10 Why has the migrant crisis increased pressure on EU governments and increased the tensions between members of the EU?

PROBLEMS AND APPLICATIONS

1 Consider two countries that trade heavily with one another – Cornsylvania and Techoland. The national currency of Cornsylvania is the cob, while the Techoland national currency is the byte. The output of Cornsylvania is mainly agricultural, while the output of Techoland is mainly high-technology electronic goods. Suppose that each economy is in a long-run macroeconomic equilibrium.
   a. Use diagrams showing AD, SRAS and LRAS to illustrate the state of each economy.
   b. Now suppose that there is an increase in demand for electronic goods in both countries, and a simultaneous decline in demand for agricultural goods. Use your diagrams to show what happens to output and the price level in the short run in each country. What happens to the unemployment rate in each country?
   c. Show, using your diagrams, how each country could use monetary policy to reduce the short-run fluctuation in output.
   d. Show, using your diagrams, how movements in the cob–byte exchange rate could reduce short-run fluctuations in output in each country.

2 Suppose Techoland and Cornsylvania form a currency union and adopt the electrocarrot as their common currency. Now suppose again that there is an increase in demand for electronic goods in both countries, and a simultaneous decline in demand for agricultural goods. As president of the central bank for the currency union, would you raise or lower the electrocarrot interest rate, or keep it the same? Explain. (Hint: you are charged with maintaining low and stable inflation across the electrocarrot area.)

3 Suppose that Techoland and Cornsylvania decide to engage in fiscal federalism and adopt a common fiscal budget.
   a. Show, again using the AD/AS model, how fiscal policy can be used to alleviate the short-run fluctuations generated by the asymmetric demand shock.
   b. Given the typical lags in the implementation of fiscal policy, would you advise the use of federal fiscal policy to alleviate short-run macroeconomic fluctuations? (Hint: distinguish between automatic stabilizers and discretionary fiscal policy.)

4 The United States can be thought of as a non-trivial currency union since, although it is a single country, it encompasses many states that have economies comparable in size to those of some European countries. Given that the United States has had a single currency for 230 years, it may be thought of as a successful currency union. Yet many of the US states produce very different products and services, so that they are likely to be impacted by different kinds of macroeconomic shocks (expansionary and recessionary) over time. For example, Texas produces oil, while Kansas produces agricultural goods. How do you explain the long-term success of the US currency union given this diversity? Are there any lessons or predictions for Europe that can be drawn from the US experience?

5 Explain, giving reasons, whether the following statements are true or false.
   a. 'A high degree of trade among a group of countries implies that there would be benefits from them adopting a common currency and forming a currency union.'
   b. 'A high degree of trade among a group of countries implies that they should definitely adopt a common currency and form a currency union.'

6 Do you think that the free rider problem associated with national fiscal policies in a currency union is likely to be a problem in actual practice? Justify your answer.

7 If the interest rate on Spanish government debt is rising while that of Germany is falling:
   a. What does this tell you about the view of the markets on the two countries?
   b. If the interest rate is rising, what is happening to the price of bonds for the two countries? Explain.

8 Members of the euro zone have forsaken monetary independence. This means they are not able to manipulate their currency to help manage asymmetric shocks. How does currency manipulation help in the case of asymmetric shocks and is such a policy a long-term solution to overcoming a country's economic problems?

9 For a common currency area to work effectively it is argued that on joining, member states need to be at a similar stage in the economic cycle. Why do you think this is the case?

10 Populist movements have been said to reflect 'the will of the people'. Economists such as Kenneth Arrow and theories like the 'median voter theorem' along with the ideas of French political economist the Marquis de Condorcet, suggest the idea of the 'will of the people' is a myth. Do some research into these ideas and discuss whether the 'will of the people' is indeed a myth.

18 SUSTAINABILITY ECONOMICS

It is difficult to imagine anyone being unaware of the issue of global warming or climate change (the two phrases are often used interchangeably but are not the same thing), issues around the availability of water, and biodiversity and the environment in general. The conventional wisdom is that economic growth (powered by human activity) has led to the creation of negative externalities that have resulted in average temperatures rising around the globe. Global warming, in turn, leads to changes in the climate and more instances of extreme weather events, which together will result in widespread and disastrous consequences. Human-generated carbon dioxide emissions have been cited as the main reason for these changes, and continued human activity without changes to the way we do things will result in increasingly harmful effects on the environment, the loss of biodiversity and the extinction of species.

Governments, firms and individuals around the world must find ways to cut carbon emissions and to approach the way we live, work and produce in different ways to help mitigate the damage we are inflicting on the planet. It is argued that only drastic and lasting cuts in carbon emissions can forestall the impending disaster.

SUSTAINABILITY

The transformation process is at the heart of almost every business. Firms take scarce resources and convert them into goods and services that are then sold to different customers. Some of these customers are individuals, some are other businesses and some are other organizations such as charities, non-governmental organizations and governments. Resources are scarce, and some resources are scarcer than others. When many resources are used up, they are no longer available for use elsewhere and in many cases, these resources are not renewable. Future generations, therefore, may find that what we take for granted today may not be available in the future. The planet might be a very different place for them because of the actions of businesses both in the past and today.

Sustainability refers to the capacity of economic activity to produce goods and services for current use that does not compromise the ability of future generations to also meet their economic needs. Recognizing that economic activity has a wider cost than simply the factor inputs that go into producing output is fundamental to the concept of externalities we discussed earlier in the book. The idea that production can have both benefits and costs to a third party (or parties) that are not accounted for in production decisions is not new. It has been around since the nineteenth century, when Henry Sidgwick (1838–1900), an English philosopher and economist in the utilitarian tradition, considered the notion of 'spillover costs and benefits'. Developments in the theory of externalities enabled firms to begin to produce reports that took into consideration the external costs and benefits of their immediate actions. However, it is still difficult for businesses to determine how sustainable they are. This is because of the limitations of fully understanding the overall impact of their actions on the environment, on eco-systems, on natural resources, on climate and biodiversity and of being able to accurately estimate its costs and benefits.

sustainability the capacity of economic activity to produce goods and services for current use that does not compromise the ability of future generations to also meet their economic needs

Key Questions About Sustainability

Perhaps the first thing to say on sustainability is that it is an extremely complex topic. It is also highly subjective. It arouses passions on both sides of the debate. Therefore, one of the important things to remember when looking at sustainability is to approach it from an economist's perspective. That is, we must seek out the facts, understand the issues, focus on the evidence, try to quantify the costs and benefits and, as a result, adopt a positive rather than normative stance on the issue. In other words, we must approach the issue thinking like an economist. As with any issue where there is plenty of misinformation, disinformation, hearsay and speculation, the economist's job is to work with others to understand the issues more effectively and to present policy options that are based on objectivity.

A number of key questions have to be considered when looking at sustainability. In this chapter we are providing a taster of some of them. Many of you reading this may begin to pursue a more detailed study of the topic in later courses.

Some of these questions that need to be considered include the following:

1. How do we balance the need for economic activity to satisfy the wants and needs of today and to positively impact on standards of living with the wants and needs of future generations?
2. How do we measure these intertemporal choices? For example, to reduce the level of emissions of greenhouse gases (GHGs), which will limit the effects of climate change, we will need to adopt behavioural changes today that involve a cost and enable future generations to receive benefits. How do we value the costs of choices made today with benefits that might accrue in 20, 50 or even 100 years' time?
3. Efficiency means reducing waste to a minimum, but how do we define efficiency in the context of sustainability? To get global change that improves sustainability, there must be a collective understanding of what we are trying to achieve and a definition of efficiency that we can all work towards.
4. Who should be responsible for designing and implementing the changes that will need to be made to improve sustainability and who should bear the cost? Should it be governments and, if so, which governments bear the most responsibility? Should it be those that contributed to the increase in GHG emissions over the last 200 years of rapid industrialization? Should it be those that are seeking to 'catch-up' now and who are trying to help take millions out of poverty but are using technologies that are not sustainable according to the definition we have provided? Should firms take the leading role or is it the responsibility of all of us, as dwellers on planet Earth, to change our behaviour?

The answers to these questions are not easy and there are considerable disagreements over them, but they have to be confronted if sustainability is to become more than just a buzzword.

Changes in Approach to Sustainability

Recognizing that firms' activities have a wider impact on society and the environment is not new. The increased awareness of the public about the extent to which business activity has an impact is perhaps more recent. Developments in news media, expansion of social media and improvements in education have combined to bring to the fore the issues facing the planet and its future. As expectations on businesses in relation to their 'environmental footprint' increase, many have started to produce environmental and social responsibility reports in addition to the more traditional finance and accounting reports.

Many of these reports seem to be keen on demonstrating how organizations are seeking to cut costs by using resources more efficiently and reducing the environmental footprint of their operations. Some firms face accusations over their attempts at corporate social responsibility, with people considering them mere marketing exercises, sometimes referred to as '**greenwashing**'. Yet, ultimately, these firms are judged by traditional measures of success, which are based on their ability to generate returns on investment and make profits. It is in their interest to find ways of cutting costs, but cutting costs and having a deep commitment to sustainability are different things.

greenwashing the suggestion or implication that a product or service is sustainable, environmentally friendly, eco-friendly or 'green' that may be misleading or false

One effect of the reports is to encourage firms to think more carefully about their costs and indeed what they consider as costs. Do firms simply value the costs they immediately incur in production, or should external costs (and benefits) be considered? If so, how far should this process continue? If external costs and benefits are to be factored in, then how are they to be accurately valued? Many firms operate in relatively mature markets where growth is not easy. Expanding globally is one option as a means of increasing revenue and profit, and looking at the whole value chain might provide opportunities for improving profits, returns and efficiencies. The **value chain** refers to all the processes that a firm is involved with which add value. These processes are not simply the transformation process of factor inputs into output, but the goodwill the firm generates, its marketing activities, its brand development and recognition, customer services and back-office activities.

value chain all the processes that a firm is involved with which add value

As firms delve further into their value chains, some seek to understand more fully the relationship between their operations and broader aspects of the environment and ecosystems. For example, food production depends on growing basic ingredients such as cereals, vegetables and fruit, which are then used in other food products. A successful harvest can be dependent on insects and animals pollinating plants. Food production firms will need to take into account the value of the positive externalities provided by insects and animals in food production costs.

The Intergovernmental Science-Policy Platform on Biodiversity and Ecosystem Services (IPBES), in a report published in 2019, estimates that 75 per cent of global food production by volume is dependent on insect and animal pollination. This 'service' provided by insects and animals, therefore, has a value that firms can account for. The question is, how can these elements of the value chain be priced? The IPBES estimates the market value linked to pollinators at between US$235 billion and US$577 billion (in 2015 US dollars, €229bn–€562 billion). Considering the value of this positive externality, it is logical that firms should look to find ways in which they can protect pollinators.

Similar arguments apply to other aspects of sustainability, particularly regarding the use of non-renewable resources, energy, forests, wetlands, rivers, oceans and so on. These factors all contribute in different ways to global production of goods and services. This means they are part of firms' value chains, and it is now more widely recognized that they have an economic value, which perhaps was not fully appreciated in the past.

Incorporating and understanding the costs and benefits associated with sustainable production, therefore, become an economic proposition and one that is vital in generating profits not just in the present but also in the future. More firms are recognizing that profit can be equated with minimizing their impact on the environment. This is increasingly becoming a driver in the way firms are planning future output and investment programmes. Sustainability is becoming associated with longer-term survival.

Socially Responsible Investing To plan for future production, account for external costs and benefits and ensure longer-term profitable survival, firms need to invest. There is a trade-off associated with the short-term adjustment processes, which may result in higher costs and lower profits, with long-term survival, competitive advantage and profits in the future. Investment in innovation and value chain analysis require funding. Another external benefit that firms are taking advantage of through sustainability is in securing investment funds.

Socially responsible investing refers to individuals and firms with funds to invest making decisions based on the ethical and sustainable credentials of the investment. Businesses that outsource operations to firms that employ child labour are involved in gambling, pay low wages, supply arms and weapons. Businesses that cannot show that they are taking sustainability seriously may all not be chosen for investment. The sums of money involved are significant. The Forum for Sustainable and Responsible Investment reports that funds devoted to socially responsible investment in the United States alone was in excess of US$52.4 trillion in 2024 (compared to US$17.1 trillion in 2020).

socially responsible investing investment decisions that take into account sustainability, ethical and governance factors

Sustainability, therefore, has evolved to become something that firms see as having real long-term economic value. Understanding and pricing the whole value chain, including the external costs and benefits, can help firms develop longer-term profitability and resilience.

SELF TEST How might firms adjust their production processes to improve their sustainability?

Definitions of Efficiency

Economics focuses on how we make use of scarce resources that have competing uses. It could be argued that 'waste' is one of the things that economists most dislike. Waste implies extravagance, having no purpose or value, or being unusable in some way. Waste can be the by-product of production, but it can also be inherent in production processes. The elimination of waste, or at the very least the reduction and minimization of waste, might be argued to be central to economics. Efficiency implies that waste is reduced to a minimum or eliminated. In long-run equilibrium, under conditions of perfect competition, firms produce at the lowest point on their average cost curve. This is referred to as *productive efficiency*. At this point, output is maximized using the minimum amount of inputs. Finding the optimum combination of factor inputs to produce a given output is referred to as *technical efficiency*. However, there is little benefit in a firm producing according to these definitions of efficiency if consumers do not place a value on what is being produced. In other words, goods and services are produced and distributed according to consumer wants and needs, which are reflected by the price they are willing to pay. *Allocative efficiency* occurs where the value placed on a unit of output measure by the marginal utility gained in consuming that output is equal to the marginal cost of producing that unit of output.

We have also seen that firms can produce efficiently but may not take into consideration the external costs and benefits of their production decisions. *Social efficiency*, therefore, occurs where the private and social costs and benefits of production are equal to the private and social benefits of consumption.

CASE STUDY **Agriculture and Methane**

The United Nations Environment Programme, in a report published in 2024, noted that emissions from manure and gastroenteric releases account for almost a third of human-caused methane emissions. Methane is said to be 80 times more potent than carbon as a greenhouse gas over a 20-year period. Producers of meat and rice (paddy fields are also a source of methane emission) may not take into account the damage to the environment that methane output imposes. The price of meat and rice, therefore, may not reflect the social costs of producing them. There will, as a result, be overconsumption of meat and rice. The socially efficient output level would be lower. Therefore, encouraging farmers to find ways of making methane 'useful' in some way and reducing its environmental impact, along with an encouragement to consumers to reduce their meat and rice consumption, would result in a more socially efficient outcome. This

©iStock/Tiphanie May

The levels of methane produced by agriculture, livestock agriculture in particular, has been a source of concern in relation to sustainability. Can technology help provide ways to reduce methane emissions?

(*Continued*)

sounds simple in theory but in practice raises many questions. If farmers reduce output of meat and rice, what happens to their livelihoods? Should governments (by which we really mean the taxpayer) compensate farmers for reducing meat and rice output and/or finding ways to invest in making methane 'useful' rather than simply a 'waste' product (according to our definition above)? What are the ethical issues around persuading consumers to reduce meat and rice consumption? What right have governments or any other body or organization to tell individuals what they should and should not eat? Are individuals sufficiently informed about the external costs and benefits of consumption to make appropriate and informed choices? These are all challenges that highlight the difficulties of confronting issues of sustainability.

Technology can assist in the task of reducing methane emissions. For example, farmers can use more nutritious feed so that meat production becomes more 'efficient'. Different types of feed might be used to help reduce methane production by livestock, and improved management of manure might also help. Methane could be 'harvested' to produce biogas. The flooding of rice fields could be managed more effectively to reduce methane output. These might all be ways in which methane generation could be managed more efficiently and contribute to reaching the 1.5 degree Celsius target of the Paris Agreement (a legally binding international treaty on climate change).

Questions:

1 Use a supply and demand diagram to show how the output of meat could be socially inefficient.
2 Consider some of the questions posed in the case study around dealing with the issue of reducing methane emissions. What are some of the practical and ethical issues associated with these questions that would arise?
3 If farmers are encouraged to use more nutritious feed for their animals and this reduces methane generation, what type of efficiency would this represent? Explain.
4 To what extent do you think methane is a 'waste' product as defined in this chapter? (Hint: consider ways in which methane might be used for other purposes such as that suggested in the case study.) Consider the costs and benefits associated with such approaches.

CLIMATE CHANGE

Climate change has become one of the most important challenges facing humankind. The basic premise is that human activity since the early 1800s has resulted in a significant increase in emissions, which act as 'greenhouse gases' and are resulting in a rise in average global temperatures. An increase in the average global temperature could have long-lasting and far-reaching catastrophic effects, including an increase in the prevalence of extreme weather events. Extreme weather events have always happened, but climate change is, arguably, increasing their frequency and severity. These extreme weather events are highly damaging to property, to human life and to the eco-systems on which so much life depends.

To combat climate change, discussions have been ongoing for a number of years on ways in which damaging emissions can be reduced, production methods changed to make them more environmentally friendly and human behaviour adjusted to reduce the impact of our activities on the environment. Commentators emphasize the scale of the challenge that faces us all and of the difficulties in getting global agreement on ways in which we can address the problems we all face. These challenges are at the very heart of economics – the study of how scarce resources are used to meet competing wants and needs.

The Stern Review

An early foray into the economics of climate change was the *Stern Review on Climate Change*, published in 2006. This 700-page report was one of the first in-depth studies of the economics of climate change, and it drew a number of conclusions:

1. The evidence to support climate change is 'now overwhelming'.
2. 'The benefits of strong and early action far outweigh the economic costs of not action.'

3. 'Hundreds of millions of people could suffer.'
4. 'Overall costs and risks of climate change will be equivalent to losing at least 5 per cent of GDP each year now and forever.'
5. 'If a wider range of risks and impacts is taken into account, the damage could rise to 20 per cent of GDP and more.'
6. The cost of action 'can be limited to 1 per cent of global GDP each year'.
7. If no action is taken, greenhouse gas in the atmosphere 'could reach double its pre-industrial level as early as 2035'.
8. This will lead to global average temperatures rising by between 2 and 5 degrees centigrade.
9. Stabilization of carbon dioxide at current levels requires emissions to be cut by 25 per cent by 2050 – 'and perhaps much more'.
10. 'Emissions can be cut through increased energy efficiency, changes in demand and through adoption of clean power, heat and transport technologies.'
11. Climate change 'is the greatest market failure the world has ever seen'. The Stern Review notes a number of other points:

> *If the Greenland and West Antarctic ice sheets begin to melt irreversibly, the world would be committed to substantial increases in sea level in the range 5–12 m over a timescale of centuries to millennia. The immediate effect would be a potential doubling of the rate of sea level rise 1–3 mm per year from Greenland and as high as 5 mm per year from the West Antarctic Ice Sheet (WAIS). For illustration, if these higher rates were reached by the end of this century, the upper range of global sea-level rise projections would exceed 1 m by 2100. Both of these ice sheets are already showing signs of vulnerability with ice sheet discharge accelerating over large areas, but the thresholds at which large scale changes are triggered remain uncertain. (p. 21)*

Questions Raised by the Stern Review If we assume that the science on climate change is certain, then a number of questions arise. First, what are the costs of not doing anything? Second, what are the costs of doing something now compared to the benefits that will be gained. Crucially, how do we measure the value of these costs and benefits and when do we measure them?

Cost–benefit analysis is an important part of the way economists think about the world and about problems. If we are able to place a value on the costs of a particular decision in relation to the benefits, then we have the basis for an informed decision. For example, if the costs of climate change were estimated at 5 per cent of global GDP every year for the next 50 years, then we have some base information on which to make a decision. If, as a result of immediate action now, those costs could be reduced to 1 per cent of global GDP every year for the next 50 years, then this would provide some way of identifying the benefits derived from immediate action.

However, the economist would be asking what the costs of achieving those benefits might be. If the value of the costs of achieving the benefits is much less than the value of the benefits (let us assume that the cost of achieving the benefits is 0.0025 per cent of global GDP), then there may be a clear mandate for introducing immediate changes. But what if the costs are 3.75 per cent of global GDP? Would the mandate be as convincing? What if the cost were 3.95 per cent of global GDP?

Clearly, if the cost of achieving the benefit were higher than 4 per cent of global GDP, it would be logical to suggest that the costs outweighed the benefits. As a result we might think again about taking immediate action. There are considerable difficulties of measuring costs and benefits and these difficulties increase the more we look into the future, because there are so many uncertainties and variables that could affect the valuation.

SELF TEST How important do you think a review like that carried out by Stern is to economics in making a contribution to issues like climate change?

Valuing Costs and Benefits The Stern Review presents an argument for dealing with climate change based, in part, on 'intertemporal equity'. This basically looks at how we might value the benefits or costs experienced by people now compared to the costs and benefits affecting people at some future point in time. In economics, such a consideration is one factor in decision-making.

In carrying out such an analysis we must take into account the value of the welfare of people today compared to the value of the welfare of future generations. Earlier in the book we looked at measuring the time value of money using present value (PV). This is a means of discounting the fact that a sum money in the future is not worth as much as that same sum today. Recall that PV is given by:

$$PV = x/(1+r)^n$$

where r = the discount rate, x = the amount to be received in n years and n = number of years.

Stern spends some time outlining the assumptions made in the analysis. The discount value applied to the analysis is, therefore, an important factor in the validity and reliability of the argument presented. Reliability in scientific studies refers to whether the results of any 'experiment' or study can be replicated and found to produce the same or similar results. Validity refers to the extent to which the results of any experiment/modelling can be generalized to other contexts.

The discount rate applied by the Stern Review is an important factor in its argument relating to the welfare of future generations and thus the sacrifice that the current generation needs to make to generate those future benefits. A low discount rate implies that the sacrifice made today needs to be greater to generate the required benefits in the future. Stern states, 'The argument in the chapter and in the appendix and that of many other economists and philosophers who have examined these long-run ethical issues, is that "pure time discounting" is relevant only to account for the exogenous possibility of extinction. From this perspective it should be small.'

Clearly an assumption of a low discount rate leads to a conclusion that the sacrifices necessary to be made today to ensure the welfare of future generations is relatively high. If a different discount rate were used, then a different conclusion might be drawn. This is one example of how assumptions of variables might affect an argument being put forward. There are numerous references used in the text to support points being made. As an economist we might expect such evidence will be used to support claims and assertions. However, economists would also ask what evidence was not used, which might add a different slant to the argument. For that we must rely on other researchers who provide comment on research like the Stern Review or who offer counter arguments.

The Stern Review in Hindsight

Early in the book, we noted that 'all models are built with assumptions'. Therefore, a model is only as strong as the accuracy and reliability of the assumptions made in them. An economist ought to question assumptions that are made in any model. Indeed, much of the disagreement between economists is not always about the nature of cause and effect but the extent to which the two are related, as the size of the effect may be dependent on the assumptions made.

We have mentioned that the assumptions made by Stern are crucial to the argument being put forward in assessing the value of the costs and benefits associated with taking action on climate change. Cambridge professor Sir Partha Dasgupta is one of a number of economists who reviewed Stern and raised some questions about the assumptions made in the Review. Professor Greg Mankiw, through his blog, noted, 'Partha Dasgupta reads the Stern Review of climate change and, like Bill Nordhaus, does not like what he finds.' William Nordhaus, Professor of Economics at Yale, has been researching global warming and climate change for many years. One of the main sources of concern of Dasgupta and Nordhaus are the assumptions of values associated with measuring the future costs and benefits compared to those of the present. Dasgupta notes that the discount rate assumed is low compared to those used by other economists.

Recall that in the first chapter of the book, we noted that rational people think at the margin. The concept of marginal utility is important in comparing satisfaction from consumption today and that of consumption by people in the future. One way to measure this is to take a measure of the addition to total utility (marginal utility) and provide an estimate of how this changes with respect to consumption over time. Some estimate can be made of this variable now and at some point in the future. Dasgupta refers to this variable as 'eta'. A focus of this variable is the extent to which people in the future are better off than people today. People in the 1970s, for example, would never have been able to imagine the increases in technology and consumption habits that we enjoy today. Dasgupta points out that the assumptions used in the Review suggest that the current generation should be saving around 97 per cent of its GDP for the future. At the time of writing, Dasgupta points out that the UK savings rate was about 15 per cent of GDP. He concludes, 'To accept [this] would be to claim that the current generation in the model economy ought literally to starve itself so that future generations are able to enjoy ever increasing consumption levels' (Dasgupta, P. (2007) Commentary on the Stern Review's Economics of Climate Change. qed.econ.queensu.ca/pub/faculty/garvie/econ443/debate/dasgupta%20commentary%20stern%20review.pdf, accessed 6 August 2025).

Other concerns expressed by economists are on the values that Stern puts on the costs of externalities. Assuming that carbon is a negative externality (some point to the fact every living cell depends on carbon and so to see it as a pollutant is not entirely accurate), there must be some way of putting a value on the cost of this negative externality. Again, working with the concept of the margin, what would the social cost of a marginal unit of carbon be? Different studies come up with different values for this social cost. Dasgupta and Nordhaus both point out that the conclusions that can be drawn from any analysis clearly depend on the value used. Dasgupta refers to the value of the social price of carbon, a measure of the damage caused by one extra unit (tonne) of carbon, reported by Nordhaus at US$13 per tonne. The Stern Review, on the other hand, values it at around US$310 per tonne. Amending the discount rate used in the Review in Nordhaus's model results in a social price of carbon at around US$150 per tonne. How the variables in climate models are defined, therefore, can have significant effects on the forecast outcomes.

Nordhaus has done further work on estimating the social cost of carbon and in 2017 he published a paper which estimated the cost at US$32 per tonne. The paper noted, however, that the uncertainties around the knowledge of the effects of carbon and how these are accounted for in different models used for calculating the social cost of carbon (SCC) mean that there is likely to be 'extremely large structural uncertainty about the SCC even in a single model' (Nordhaus, W. D. (2017) Revisiting the Social Cost of Carbon. *PNAS*, 114(7). www.pnas.org/doi/10.1073/pnas.1609244114, accessed 6 August 2025).

In a subsequent paper published in 2024 by Barrage and Nordhaus, the SCC was cited as $66 per tonne. The authors also note, 'To meet the 1.5°C target, emissions would be required to fall virtually to zero in the next 5 years. This would entail either a deep depression (output declining by around 75%) or an implausibly sharp increase in emissions reductions (by at least 50% within a decade). The scenario is so far from what any economic model can hope to capture realistically that it is best thought of as infeasible.' (Barrage, L. and Nordhaus, W. (2024) Policies, Projections, and the Social Cost of Carbon: Results from the DICE-2023 Model. *PNAS*, 121: 13–18.)

Ten years after the publication of the Stern Review, Climate Central, an independent organization of leading scientists and journalists researching and reporting the facts about our changing climate and its impact on the public, published an article that asked a group of climate economists to offer an appraisal of Stern's work. The general view was that the Stern Review was an important piece of work in that it helped focus attention on the economic issues as well as the scientific ones. It gave a clear view of the consequences of action and inaction and the extent to which both would present significant challenges. Time has moved on and so has the debate. Some of the respondents interviewed noted that the debate was now about how to achieve a low-carbon economy and how technology and innovation had begun to address some of the challenges faced. However, while there was some optimism expressed about the future, there was also a considerable degree of caution expressed about the size of the challenges that exist. Technically, the idea of limiting global warming to 1.5 degrees Celsius by 2050 was possible, albeit noting the point raised by Barrage and Nordhaus above. However, there were questions about the political will to achieve this target.

The focus on 1.5 degrees came from the Intergovernmental Panel on Climate Change (IPCC), which produced a report in 2018 on the impacts on global warming of the average global temperature rising 1.5 degrees above pre-industrial levels. The IPCC notes, 'Human activities are estimated to have caused approximately 1.0°C of global warming above pre-industrial levels, with a likely range of 0.8°C to 1.2°C. Global warming is likely to reach 1.5°C between 2030 and 2052 if it continues to increase at the current rate.' (www.ipcc.ch/site/assets/uploads/sites/2/2019/06/SR15_Headline-statements.pdf, accessed 6 August 2025).

The IPCC notes that this estimate is provided 'with high confidence'. The implications of this would mean more extreme weather events, a rise in sea levels, but a lower loss of biodiversity and species through extinction than if the average temperature rise were above this level. Regardless, even a rise of 1.5 degrees would be likely to see problems arising for food security, water supply, livelihoods and economic growth. The focus on agreeing targets to try to limit global warming to 1.5 degrees by 2050 have been central to the 'Conference of Parties' (COP) summits at the annual meetings over the last few years.

CRITICAL THINKING POINT Berkeley Earth is an independent non-profit organization with the aim of making climate and air pollution data open and accessible to inform the debate on global warming. In one publication it notes:

'Are you a climate change skeptic? You should be. With so many people ignoring the science, it's important to distinguish facts from alarmist statements.'

Critically analyze this statement.

(Source: berkeley-earth-wp-offload.storage.googleapis.com/wp-content/uploads/2022/12/03232411/skeptics-guide-to-climate-change-1.pdf, accessed 6 August 2025.)

The COP Summits

The United Nations Framework Convention on Climate Change (UNFCCC) has been set up to coordinate and support the global response to the threats from climate change. It seeks to support numerous bodies and governments in implementing the Paris Agreement of 2015. Almost all countries on Earth are parties to the convention and are represented at an annual meeting called the 'Conference of Parties' or COP. At these events, progress on meeting the Paris Agreement is discussed and agreements are (hopefully) reached on measures to support progress on achieving the aims of that agreement. The COP21 summit in Paris resulted in the so-called Paris Agreement, whereby every country committed to working together to try to achieve a global warming target of less than 2.0 degrees Celsius and to seek to aim towards 1.5 degrees Celsius. Each country agreed to produce plans outlining how they would reduce GHG emissions, referred to as 'Nationally Determined Contributions' (NDCs) and that they would update these plans every five years. At the time of writing, the most recent COP meeting was held in Baku, Azerbaijan. COP29 took place against a backdrop of increased geopolitical tensions and results were seen as limited. However, two important outcomes focused on a finance goal, whereby developed nations would provide funds amounting to US$300bn a year by 2035 to the developing world. This was far less than the developing world argued for. The second key outcome was around agreement on rules for carbon markets to help them function more efficiently.

Other aspects of the negotiations were seen as being less positive with disagreement among those representing developing and developed countries about the commitment to limiting the rise in global temperature to 1.5 degrees Celsius.

CONCLUSION

There is widespread agreement that our planet faces significant challenges in the years ahead. There is also general agreement that time is running out to have an effect on the potential outcomes that might occur if emissions are not cut and average global temperatures rise above 1.5 degrees Celsius before 2050. There are still many who feel that we are not collectively doing enough to prevent global catastrophe. In the twenty-first century there has been an increasing recognition of the need to think about how we behave as individuals, as firms, as governments and as a global community. There is a parallel to be drawn between the forecasts of Malthus in the latter years of the eighteenth century and those of today. We have to try to take into consideration the innovations in technology that may arrive in the coming years, which may revolutionize the way we produce, consume and behave, and how we generate and use energy. There may be developments in finding ways of using carbon dioxide in some way that can offset emissions levels. The future is full of unknowns, but economists, along with those in other disciplines, will be at the forefront of the research into not only how we might reduce GHGs but also how we might manage our resources more effectively and efficiently. It will be a story that will continue to unfold as the years progress. Governments, firms and individuals will come under increasing pressure to take action and change behaviour to protect and preserve the planet we inhabit, as well as look at ways in which we can improve living standards around the world.

SUMMARY

- Sustainability looks at how we use resources today to satisfy wants and needs in a way which does not compromise the ability of people in the future also being able to satisfy their wants and needs.
- A key issue in sustainability is the extent to which we can accurately price the impact on the environment both today and in the future.
- There are four important questions that need to be answered in relation to sustainability – balancing current and future needs, measuring intertemporal choices, defining what we mean by 'efficiency', and who should bear the costs and gain the benefits of the design and implementation of changes in behaviour to achieve sustainability.
- Many firms are now taking an increasing interest in, and recognizing, their role in sustainability.
- Socially responsible investing refers to the process whereby individuals and firms with funds to invest make decisions based on the ethical and sustainable credentials of the investment.
- Efficiency can be viewed in different ways: productive and technical efficiency, allocative efficiency and social efficiency.
- Climate change is increasingly seen as being the single most important challenge to humankind. It refers to the effect on the climate of human activity primarily through the generation of GHGs which are contributing to the warming of the planet.
- The Stern Review published in 2006 was one of the first attempts to economically quantify the effects of human activity on climate.
- The Stern Review was generally seen as being an important contribution to the general debate around climate change, but some economists questioned the assumptions used in the modelling in the Review.
- One of the challenges of implementing change to reduce the impact on climate and the environment is the difficulty in assessing costs and benefits now and in the future. Equally, countries disagree on who should bear the major responsibility for reducing GHGs.

IN THE NEWS

Climate Change

In January 2025, the Copernicus Climate Change Service (C3S) reported that 2024 was 'the warmest year on record globally, and the first calendar year that the average global temperature exceeded 1.5°C above its pre-industrial level'. Carlo Buontempo, Director of the C3S, was quoted as saying, 'All of the internationally produced global temperature datasets show that 2024 was the hottest year since records began in 1850. Humanity is in charge of its own destiny but how we respond to the climate challenge should be based on evidence. The future is in our hands – swift and decisive action can still alter the trajectory of our future climate.'

(Continued)

Samantha Burgess, Strategic Lead for Climate, from the European Centre for Medium-Range Weather Forecasts (ECMWF), added, 'Each year in the last decade is one of the ten warmest on record. We are now teetering on the edge of passing the 1.5°C level defined in the Paris Agreement and the average of the last two years is already above this level. These high global temperatures, coupled with record global atmospheric water vapour levels in 2024, meant unprecedented heatwaves and heavy rainfall events, causing misery for millions of people.'

The reported increase in the incidence of extreme weather events seems to provide obvious evidence of climate change, yet reaching agreement on how to tackle it remains challenging.

At the time of the publication of this report, Los Angeles (LA) in the United States was experiencing significant wildfires which killed dozens of people and wrought extensive damage to large areas of woodland and housing. Reports were not slow to make a link between the fires in LA and climate change. CarbonCopy, a platform that curates content on the climate and energy, noted that 'several studies' had shown climate change was a significant cause of the LA fires. The reasoning given was that the region had received far less rainfall than normal resulting in the land and vegetation being exceptionally dry. When fires break out, the sparks and embers ignite surrounding areas. The Santa Ana winds, a natural phenomenon in the region around the autumn/winter time, helped to fan the flames further. The winds were strong in the latter part of December 2024 and made the task of containing the fires very challenging.

According to the editorial team publishing the report in January 2025, 'California had its hottest June and July and the second hottest October, with many of the hot days scientifically linked to climate change. 2024 was the hottest year on record globally, due to climate change. This heat and lack of rainfall left the vegetation tinder dry when the Santa Ana winds started. Climate change is thus increasing the probability of the strong winds and dry conditions overlapping, which together can intensify fires.'

Critical Thinking Questions

1. In assessing reports such as those produced by C3S and CarbonCopy, what further information would you want to gather?
2. Look at the quote provided from the director of C3S. Given the challenges of reaching agreement at COP meetings, as noted in this chapter, why might an appeal to the use of evidence be problematic in seeking to meet the terms of the Paris Agreement?
3. Consider private and public solutions and comment on their applicability to the problem of climate change.
4. To what extent do you think it depends on who is affected as to the urgency of global action on climate change?
5. Given the continued challenges outlined in this article, to what extent do you think that the conclusions of the Stern Review are being played out? Have economists been right in casting doubt on some of the assumptions in the models used as part of the Review?

References:

climate.copernicus.eu/copernicus-2024-first-year-exceed-15degc-above-pre-industrial-level, accessed 6 August 2025.
carboncopy.info/several-studies-say-climate-change-behind-the-wild-fires-ravaging-california/, accessed 6 August 2025.

QUESTIONS FOR REVIEW

1 What do you understand by the term 'sustainability'?
2 Outline the four key questions related to sustainability.
3 What do you understand by the term 'greenwashing'? Can you find an example of 'greenwashing'?
4 What is socially responsible investing and what benefits do you think it brings in relation to meeting sustainability targets?
5 Define and give examples of four different measures of efficiency. Which do you think is the most appropriate definition in relation to achieving sustainability?
6 What do you think are the three most salient findings of the Stern Review from the key points list given in this chapter?
7 How do the assumptions made in the Stern Review highlight the difficulties faced by policymakers in formulating policy to manage climate change?
8 Comment on the views expressed by Dasgupta and Nordhaus on the Stern Review. Do their comments reduce the value of the Stern Review?
9 The estimates of the effect on the planet of average global temperatures rising by 1.5 degrees Celsius are given by the IPCC with 'high confidence'. What do you think 'high confidence' means in this context and how reliable do you think this is in relation to decision-making on future actions on climate change?
10 What are the main challenges faced by the UNFCCC in securing agreement and action on meeting the goals of the Paris Agreement?

PROBLEMS AND APPLICATIONS

1 Is it possible to measure the costs and benefits to people at some point in the future? If so, how long in the future should such a measurement attempt to go?
2 Economists develop models to help them think about the world and make decisions. In the light of the context of climate change and what you have read about the Stern Review, discuss some of the benefits and limitations of economic modelling in relation to sustainability and climate change.
3 Should we be concerned that people in 100 years' time will be marginally worse off if we did nothing about carbon emissions compared to if action is taken now?
4 Some analysts have pointed out that average temperatures in particular regions of the world, and within those regions, vary tremendously yet humans are able to adapt and survive. Does this suggest that we should not be concerned about climate change?
5 In the late eighteenth century, Malthus predicted disaster befalling humankind. His immediate predictions were wrong. Are there lessons we can learn from Malthus and the subsequent events of history that can be applied to the issue of climate change?
6 Do the analyses from Dasgupta, Nordhaus and others suggest that climate change is not something humans should be concerned about?
7 'The risk of human catastrophe as a result of climate change is dwarfed by other more pressing problems including poverty, water resources, global terrorism, the potential for nuclear conflict and biological warfare/terrorism amongst others'. To what extent do you agree with this view? Explain your reasoning.
8 'The difficulty is that reducing emissions is an extreme "global public good", meaning that no single nation can capture for itself a substantial part of the benefits from its own emission reductions'. To what extent do you think this characterization of reducing emissions is the reason for the difficulties that have been experienced in nations agreeing to global agreements on carbon emissions?
9 What relevance has game theory to the problem facing governments in reaching agreement on measures to tackle climate change?
10 To what extent would you agree with the view that summits like the COP meetings produce lots of empty words and no action?

GLOSSARY

actual spending, saving or investment the realized or *ex post* outcome resulting from actions of households and firms
adaptive expectations a model which states that individuals and organizations base their expectations of inflation in the future on past actual inflation rates
aggregate demand curve a curve that shows the quantity of goods and services that households, firms and the government want to buy at each price level
aggregate risk risk that affects all economic actors at once
aggregate supply curve a curve that shows the quantity of goods and services that firms choose to produce and sell at each price level
amplitude the difference between peak and trough and trend output
annual chain linking a method of calculating GDP volume measures based on prices in the previous year
appreciation an increase in the value of a currency as measured by the amount of foreign currency it can buy
asymmetric shocks a situation where changes in aggregate demand and/or supply differ from one country to another
automatic stabilizers changes in fiscal policy that stimulate aggregate demand (AD) when the economy goes into a recession, without policymakers having to take any deliberate action
autonomous spending or autonomous expenditure spending which is not dependent on income/output

balance of payments the official account of international payments for the import and export of goods, services and capital
balanced budget where the total sum of money received by a government in tax revenue and interest is equal to the amount it spends, including on any debt interest owing
balanced trade a situation in which exports equal imports
barter the exchange of one good or service for another
birth rate the number of people born per thousand of the population
bond a certificate of indebtedness
brain drain the emigration of many of the most highly educated workers to wealthier countries
budget deficit where government tax revenue is less than spending and the government has to borrow to finance spending
budget surplus where government tax revenue is greater than spending because it receives more money than it spends
business cycle fluctuations in economic activity such as employment and production

capital the equipment and structures used to produce goods and services
capital flight a large and sudden reduction in the demand for assets located in a country
capitalist economic system a system which relies on the private ownership of factors of production to produce goods and services which are exchanged through a price mechanism and where production is operated primarily for profit
catch-up effect the property whereby countries that start off poor tend to grow more rapidly than countries that start off rich
central bank an institution designed to regulate the quantity of money in the economy
***ceteris paribus* (other things equal)** a term used to describe analysis where one variable in the model is allowed to vary while others are held constant
classical dichotomy the theoretical separation of nominal and real variables
coincident indicators indicators whose changes occur at the same time as changes in economic activity
collective bargaining the process by which unions and firms agree on the terms of employment
commodity money money that takes the form of a commodity with intrinsic value
common currency area a geographical area throughout which a single currency circulates as the medium of exchange
comparative statics the comparison of one initial static equilibrium with another
competitive market a market in which there are many buyers and sellers so that each has a negligible impact on the market price
complements two goods for which an increase in the price of one leads to a decrease in the demand for the other
compounding the accumulation of a sum of money in, say, a bank account, where the interest earned remains in the account to earn additional interest in the future
constrained discretion a monetary policy framework which acknowledges a clear goal (or target) but allows policymakers the freedom to respond to economic, financial and political shocks using all the data available and their collective judgement
Consumer Prices Index a measure of the overall prices of the goods and services bought by a typical consumer
consumption spending by households on goods and services, with the exception of purchases of new housing
contraction when real output is lower than the previous time period
cost of living how much money people need to maintain standards of living in terms of the goods and services they can afford to buy
cost-push inflation a short-run cause of accelerating inflation due to higher input costs of firms which are passed on as higher consumer prices
countercyclical a variable that is below trend when GDP is above trend
counterfactual analysis based on a premise of what would have occurred if something had not happened
creative destruction the process where new technologies replace old ones and new skills are needed which render existing skills obsolete
credit default swap a means by which a bondholder can insure against the risk of default
credit risk the risk a bank faces in defaults on loans

cross-price elasticity of demand a measure of how much the quantity demanded of one good responds to a change in the price of another good, computed as the percentage change in quantity demanded of the first good divided by the percentage change in the price of the second good

crowding out a decrease in investment that results from government borrowing

cryptocurrencies peer-to-peer networks facilitating transactions between users without an intermediary such as a bank

currency the paper banknotes and coins in the hands of the public

cyclical deficit a situation when government spending and income is disrupted by the deviations in the 'normal' economic cycle

cyclical unemployment the deviation of unemployment from its natural rate

death rate the number of deaths per thousand of the population

deflation a fall in the price level over a period occurring when the inflation rate is less than 0 per cent

deflationary gap or output gap the difference between full employment output and expenditure when expenditure is less than full employment output

demand curve a graph of the relationship between the price of a good and the quantity demanded

demand deposits balances in bank accounts that depositors can access on demand, for example by using a debit card

demand schedule a table that shows the relationship between the price of a good and the quantity demanded

depreciation a decrease in the value of a currency as measured by the amount of foreign currency it can buy

depression a severe recession

deterministic trends trends that are constant, positive or negative, independent of time for the series being analyzed

discount rate the interest rate at which the Federal Reserve lends on a short-term basis to the US banking sector

disinflation the reduction in the rate of inflation

diversification the reduction of risk achieved by replacing a single risk with a large number of smaller unrelated risks

double coincidence of wants a situation in exchange where two parties each have a good or service that the other wants and can thus enter into an exchange

economic activity how much buying and selling goes on in the economy over a period of time

economic agents an individual, firm, government or organization that has an impact in some way on an economy

economic growth the increase in the amount of goods and services in an economy over a period of time

economic system the way in which resources are organized and allocated to provide for the needs of an economy's citizens

economically inactive people who are not in employment or are unemployed due to reasons such as being in full-time education, being full-time carers or raising a family

economics the study of how society manages its scarce resources

economy all the production and exchange activities that take place

effective demand the amount that people are not only willing to buy at different prices but what they can and do actually purchase

efficient markets hypothesis (EMH) the theory that asset prices reflect all publicly available information about the value of an asset

elasticity a measure of the responsiveness of quantity demanded or quantity supplied to one of its determinants

empirical research knowledge generated through observation and experience of measurable phenomena which allow conclusions to be drawn, supported by verifiable evidence

endogenous growth theory a theory that the rate of economic growth in the long run is determined by the rate of growth in total factor productivity. This total factor productivity is dependent on the rate at which technology progresses

endogenous variable a variable whose value is determined within the model

equilibrium or market price the price where the quantity demanded is the same as the quantity supplied

equilibrium quantity the quantity bought and sold at the equilibrium price

equity the property of distributing economic prosperity fairly among the members of society

European Central Bank (ECB) the overall central bank of the 20 countries comprising the European Monetary Union

European Economic and Monetary Union the European currency union that has adopted the euro as its common currency

European Union a group of democratic European countries committed to working together for peace and prosperity

eurosystem the system made up of the ECB plus the national central banks of each of the 20 countries comprising the European Monetary Union

exogenous variable a variable whose value is determined outside the model

externality the cost or benefit of one person's decision on the well-being of a bystander (a third party) which the decision maker does not take into account when making the decision

falsifiability the possibility of a theory being rejected as a result of the new observations or new data

fiat money money without intrinsic value that is used as money because of government decree

financial intermediaries financial institutions through which savers can indirectly provide funds to borrowers

financial markets financial institutions through which savers can directly provide funds to borrowers

financial system the group of institutions in the economy that help to match one person's saving with another person's investment

fintech financial technologies used in the financial services industry, including mobile payments, transferring money, loans, fund raising and asset management

fiscal federalism a fiscal system for a group of countries involving a common fiscal budget and a system of taxes and fiscal transfers across countries

Fisher effect the one-for-one adjustment of the nominal interest rate to the inflation rate

foreign direct investment capital investment that is owned and operated by a foreign entity

foreign portfolio investment investment that is financed with foreign money but operated by domestic residents

frictional unemployment unemployment that results because it takes time for workers to search for the jobs that best suit their tastes and skills

full employment a point where those people who want to work at the going market wage level are able to find a job

fundamental analysis the study of a company's accounting statements and future prospects to determine its value

future value the amount of money in the future that an amount of money today will yield, given prevailing interest rates

GDP at constant prices gross domestic product calculated using prices that existed at a particular base year, which takes into account changes in inflation

GDP at current or market prices gross domestic product calculated by multiplying the output of goods and services by the price of those goods and services in the reporting year

GDP deflator a measure of the price level calculated as the ratio of nominal GDP to real GDP times 100

generalization the act of formulating general concepts or explanations by inferring from specific instances of an event or behaviour

geographical immobility where people are unable to take work because of the difficulties associated with moving to different regions

gig economy a labour market in which workers have short-term, freelance or zero-hours contracts with employers and where workers are more akin to being self-employed than employed

globalization the growth of interdependence among world economies usually seen as resulting from the removal of many international regulations affecting financial flows

gold standard a system in which the currency is based on the value of gold and where the currency can be converted into gold on demand

government deficit a situation where a government spends more than it generates in tax revenue over a period

government spending spending on goods and services by local and national governments

Great Moderation (The) the period of economic stability characterized by relatively low inflation, high employment, low unemployment and stable and persistent growth

greenwashing the suggestion or implication that a product or service is sustainable, environmentally friendly, eco-friendly or 'green' that may be misleading or false

gross domestic product (GDP) the market value of all final goods and services produced within a country in a given period of time

gross domestic product (GDP) per capita the market value of all goods and services produced within a country in a given period of time divided by the population of a country to give a per capita figure

gross value added the contribution of domestic producers, industries and sectors to an economy

hyperinflation a period of extreme and accelerating increase in the price level where the monthly rate exceeds 50 per cent

hypothesis an assumption, tentative prediction, explanation or supposition for something

hysteresis the lagging effects of past economic events on future ones

idiosyncratic risk risk that affects only a single economic actor

income elasticity of demand a measure of how much quantity demanded of a good responds to a change in consumers' income, computed as the percentage change in quantity demanded divided by the percentage change in income

indexed the automatic correction of a money amount for the effects of inflation by law or contract

inferences conclusions or explanations derived from evidence and reasoning

inferior good a good for which, *ceteris paribus*, an increase in income leads to a decrease in demand (and vice versa)

inflation an increase in the overall level of prices in the economy

inflation rate the percentage change in the price index from the preceding period

inflation tax the revenue the government raises by creating money

inflationary gap the difference between full employment output and actual expenditure when actual expenditure is greater than full employment output

informationally efficient reflecting all available information in a rational way

interest elasticity of demand and supply the responsiveness of the demand and supply of loanable funds to changes in the interest rate

intertemporal substitution effect the response of economic actors to changes in the interest rate by changing consumption and savings decisions

interventionist supply-side policies policies focused on improving the working of markets through investing in infrastructure, education, and research and development

investment spending on capital equipment, inventories and structures, including household purchases of new housing

investment or mutual fund an institution that sells shares to the public and uses the proceeds to buy a portfolio of stocks and bonds

involuntary unemployment where people want work at going market wage rates but cannot find employment

job search the process by which workers find appropriate jobs given their tastes and skills

labour the human effort, both mental and physical, that goes into production

labour force the total number of workers, including both the employed and the unemployed

labour force participation rate (or economic activity rate) the percentage of the adult population that is in the labour force

Laffer curve the relationship between tax rates and tax revenue

lagging indicator an indicator whose changes occur after changes in economic activity have occurred

land all the natural resources of the earth

law of demand the claim that, other things equal (*ceteris paribus*) the quantity demanded of a good falls when the price of the good rises

law of supply and demand the claim that the price of any good adjusts to bring the quantity supplied and the quantity demanded for that good into balance

law of supply the claim that, *ceteris paribus*, the quantity supplied of a good rises when the price of a good rises

leading indicators indicators which can be used to foretell future changes in economic activity
liquidity the ease with which an asset can be converted into the economy's medium of exchange
liquidity risk the risk that a bank may not be able to fund demand for withdrawals

macroeconomics the study of economy-wide phenomena, including inflation, unemployment and economic growth
macroprudential policy policies designed to limit the risk across the financial sector by focusing on improving 'prudential' standards of operation that enhance stability and reduce risk
marginal changes small incremental adjustments to a plan of action
marginal propensity to consume the fraction of extra income that a household consumes rather than saves
marginal propensity to save the fraction of extra income that a household saves rather than consumes
market a group of buyers and sellers of a particular good or service
market economy an economy that addresses the three key questions of the economic problem by allocating resources through the decentralized decisions of many firms and households as they interact in markets for goods and services
market failure a situation where scarce resources are not allocated to their most efficient use
market for loanable funds the market in which those who want to save supply funds, and those who want to borrow to invest demand funds
market-orientated supply-side policies policies designed to free up markets to improve resource allocation through more effective price signals
market power the ability of a single economic agent (or small group of agents) to have a substantial influence on market prices or output
medium of exchange an item that buyers give to sellers when they want to purchase goods and services
menu costs the costs of changing prices
microeconomics the study of how households and firms make decisions and how they interact in markets
migration rate the difference between the number of people entering a country from abroad and the number leaving
model of aggregate demand and aggregate supply the model that some economists use to explain short-run fluctuations in economic activity around its long-run trend
monetary neutrality the proposition that changes in the money supply do not affect real variables
monetary policy the set of actions taken by the central bank to affect the money supply
money the set of assets in an economy that people regularly use to buy goods and services from other people
money market the market in which the commercial banks lend money to one another on a short-term basis
money stock the quantity of money circulating in the economy
money supply the quantity of money available in the economy
multinationals organizations characterized by having operations in a number of countries although their main headquarters will be in one country – normally the country in which the firm originally developed
multiplier effect the additional shifts in aggregate demand that result when expansionary fiscal policy increases income and thereby increases consumer spending

national debt the accumulation of the total debt owed by a government
national saving (saving) the total income in the economy that remains after paying for consumption and government purchases
natural rate hypothesis the claim that unemployment eventually returns to its normal, or natural, rate, regardless of the rate of inflation
natural rate of output the output level in an economy when all existing factors of production (land, labour, capital and technology resources) are fully utilized and where unemployment is at its natural rate
natural rate of unemployment the normal rate of unemployment around which the unemployment rate fluctuates
natural resources the inputs into the production of goods and services that are provided by nature, such as land, rivers and mineral deposits
neo-classical synthesis the idea that markets can be slow to adjust in the short run due to sticky prices and sticky wages but revert to long-run classical principles which could be aided by appropriate use of fiscal and monetary policies
net capital outflow the purchase of foreign assets by domestic residents minus the purchase of domestic assets by foreigners
net exports spending on domestically produced goods and services by foreigners (exports) minus spending on foreign goods by domestic residents (imports)
nominal exchange rate the rate at which a person can trade the currency of one country for the currency of another
nominal GDP the production of goods and services valued at current prices
nominal interest rate the interest rate as usually reported without a correction for the effects of inflation
nominal variables variables measured in monetary units
non-accelerating inflation rate of unemployment the rate of unemployment in the long run, consistent with a stable rate of inflation
non-stationary data time-series data where the mean value can either rise or fall over time
normal good a good for which, *ceteris paribus*, an increase in income leads to an increase in demand (and vice versa)
normative statements claims that attempt to prescribe how the world should be

occupational immobility where workers are unable to easily move from one occupation to another
Okun's law a 'law' which is based on observations that to keep the unemployment rate steady, real GDP needs to grow at or close to its potential
open market operations the purchase and sale of non-monetary assets from and to the banking sector by the central bank
opportunity cost whatever must be given up to obtain some item; the value of the benefits foregone (sacrificed)
optimum currency area a group of countries for which it is optimal to adopt a common currency and form a currency union

outright open market operations the outright sale or purchase of non-monetary assets to or from the banking sector by the central bank without a corresponding agreement to reverse the transaction at a later date

peak a point where related economic variables begin to decline
Phillips curve a curve that shows the short-run trade-off between inflation and unemployment
planned economic systems economic activity organized by central planners who decided on the answers to the fundamental economic questions
planned spending, saving or investment the desired or intended actions of households and firms
positive statements claims that attempt to describe the world as it is
present value the amount of money today that would need to be invested using prevailing interest rates, to produce a given future amount of money
price elasticity of demand a measure of how much the quantity demanded of a good responds to a change in the price of that good, computed as the percentage change in quantity demanded divided by the percentage change in price
price elasticity of supply a measure of how much the quantity supplied of a good responds to a change in the price of that good, computed as the percentage change in quantity supplied divided by the percentage change in price
price level a snapshot of the prices of goods and services in an economy at a particular period of time
private saving the income that households have left after paying for taxes and consumption
procyclical a variable that is above trend when GDP is above trend
producer prices index a measure of the prices of a basket of goods and services bought by firms
productivity the quantity of goods and services produced from each hour of a worker or factor of production's time
public saving the tax revenue that the government has left after paying for its spending
purchasing power parity a theory of exchange rates whereby a unit of any given currency should be able to buy the same quantity of goods in all countries

quantity demanded the amount of a good that buyers are willing and able to purchase at different prices
quantity equation the equation ($M \times V = P \times Y$), which relates the quantity of money, the velocity of money and the currency value of the economy's output of goods and services
quantity supplied the amount of a good that sellers are willing and able to sell at different prices
quantity theory of money a theory asserting that the quantity of money available determines the price level and that the growth rate in the quantity of money available determines the inflation rate

random walk the path of a variable whose changes are impossible to predict
rational the assumption that decision-makers can make consistent choices between alternatives and do the best they can given their situation
rational expectations the theory according to which people optimally use all the information they have, including information about government policies, when forecasting the future
real exchange rate the rate at which the goods and services of one country trade for the goods and services of another
real GDP the production of goods and services valued at constant prices
real interest rate the interest rate corrected for the effects of inflation
real money balances what money can actually buy given the ratio of the money supply to the price level $\frac{M}{P}$
real variables variables measured in physical units
real wage the money wage adjusted for inflation, measured by the ratio of the wage rate to price $\frac{W}{P}$
recession a period of declining real incomes and rising unemployment. The technical definition gives recession occurring after two successive quarters of negative economic growth
refinancing rate the interest rate at which the European Central Bank lends on a short-term basis to the euro area banking sector
regulatory capture a situation where regulatory agencies become unduly influenced and dominated by the industries they are supposed to be regulating
relative price price expressed in terms of how much of one good has to be given up in purchasing another
repo rate the interest rate at which the Bank of England lends on a short-term basis to the UK banking sector
repurchase agreement the sale of a non-monetary asset together with an agreement to repurchase it at a set price at a specified future date
risk the probability of something happening which results in a loss or some degree of hazard or damage
risk averse exhibiting a dislike of uncertainty

sacrifice ratio the number of percentage points of annual output lost in the process of reducing inflation by 1 percentage point
Say's law an argument that production or supply is a source of demand, that supply creates its own demand
scarcity the limited nature of society's resources
Schengen area 29 countries, including Iceland, Liechtenstein, Switzerland and Norway, who have agreed to allow free movement between their countries with no passport and border controls
securitization the packaging of mortgage-backed securities into pools of debt and selling them on
shoe leather cost the resources wasted when inflation encourages people to reduce their money holdings
shortage a situation in which quantity demanded is greater than quantity supplied at the going market price
Single European Market a (still not complete) EU-wide market throughout which labour, capital, goods and services can move freely
socially responsible investing investment decisions that take into account sustainability, ethical and governance factors
sovereign debt the bonds issued by national governments to finance expenditure
spread the difference between the average interest banks earn on assets and the average interest rate paid on liabilities
stagflation a period of falling output and rising prices

standard of living refers to the amount of goods and services that can be purchased by the population of a country. Usually measured by the inflation-adjusted (real) income per head of the population

stationary data time-series data that has a constant mean value over time

steady-state equilibrium the point in a growing economy where investment spending is the same as spending on depreciation and the capital–output ratio remains constant

stochastic trend where trend variables change by some random amount in each time period

stock (or share or equity) a claim to partial ownership and the future profits in a firm

store of value an item that people can use to transfer purchasing power from the present to the future

structural deficit a situation where the deficit is due to a government 'living beyond its means' that is spending persistently more than its income

structural unemployment unemployment that results because the number of jobs available in some labour markets is insufficient to provide a job for everyone who wants one

sub-prime market individuals not traditionally seen as being part of the financial markets because of their high credit risk

substitutes two goods for which an increase in the price of one leads to an increase in the demand for the other (and vice versa)

supply curve a graph of the relationship between the price of a good and the quantity supplied

supply schedule a table that shows the relationship between the price of a good and the quantity supplied

supply shock an event that directly alters firms' costs and prices, shifting the economy's aggregate supply (AS) curve and thus the Phillips curve

surplus a situation in which the quantity supplied is greater than the quantity demanded at the going market price

sustainability the capacity of economic activity to produce goods and services for current use that does not compromise the ability of future generations to also meet their economic needs

systemic risk the risk of failure across the whole of the financial sector

technological knowledge society's understanding of the best ways to produce goods and services

theory of liquidity preference Keynes' theory that the interest rate adjusts to bring money supply and money demand into balance

time-series data observations on a variable over a time period and which are ordered over time

total expenditure the amount paid by buyers, computed as the price of the good times the quantity purchased

total revenue the amount received by sellers of a good, computed as the price of the good times the quantity sold

trade balance the value of a nation's exports minus the value of its imports; also called net exports

trade deficit an excess of imports over exports

trade-off the loss of the benefits from a decision to forego or sacrifice one option, balanced against the benefits incurred from the choice made

trade openness the ratio of exports plus imports to gross domestic product

trade policy a government policy that directly influences the quantity of goods and services that a country imports or exports

trade surplus an excess of exports over imports

transfer payment a payment for which no good or service is exchanged

trend the underlying long-term movement in a data series

trough the point where related economic variables begin to rise

unemployment insurance a government programme that partially protects workers' incomes when they become unemployed

unemployment rate the percentage of the labour force that is unemployed measured by dividing the number of unemployed by the labour force and multiplying by 100

union density a measure of the proportion of the workforce that is unionized

unit of account the measure people use to post prices and record debts

value chain all the processes that a firm is involved with which add value

velocity of money the rate at which money changes hands

voluntary unemployment where people choose to remain unemployed rather than take jobs which are available

wealth the total of all stores of value, including both money and non-monetary assets

INDEX

LIST OF FORMULAE

Chain-Weighted GDP Deflator:

Chain-weighted GDP deflator in Year X =

$$\frac{\text{Nominal GDP}_{\text{Year X}}}{\text{Real GDP at year X average prices}} \times 100$$

Comparing Inflation Over Time:

$$\text{Amount in today's curency} = \text{Amount in year t currency} \times \frac{\text{Price level today}}{\text{Price level in year t}}$$

Consumer Prices Index:

$$CPI_{\text{year } t} = \frac{\text{Cost of basket of goods in year t prices}}{\text{Cost of basket of goods in base year prices}}$$

Cross-Price Elasticity of Demand:

$$\text{Cross-price elasticity of demand} = \frac{\text{Percentage change in quantity demanded of good 1}}{\text{Percentage change in the price of good 2}}$$

Deviation of Output from the Natural Rate:

$$Q = NRQ + a(APL - EPL)$$

Expectations Augmented Phillips Curve:

$$\Delta p_t = E_t \Delta p_t + 1 + (NR_t - RU_t)$$

Gross Domestic Product (Expenditure Method):

$$GDP\ (Y) = C + I + G + NX$$

GDP Deflator:

$$\text{GDP Deflator} = \frac{\text{Nominal GDP}}{\text{Real GDP}} \times 100$$

Growth Rate of Real GDP:

$$\text{Growth rate of real GDP in year } t = \frac{(GDP_t - GDP_{t-1})}{GDP_{t-1}} \times 100$$

Income Elasticity of Demand:

$$\text{Income elasticity of demand} = \frac{\text{Percentage change in quantity demanded}}{\text{Percentage change in income}}$$

Inflation Rate between Consecutive Years:

$$\text{Inflation}_{\text{year } t} = \frac{(\text{Price index}_{\text{year } t}) - (\text{Price index}_{\text{year } t-1})}{(\text{Price index}_{\text{year } t-1})} \times 100$$

Implicit GDP Deflator:

$$\text{Implicit GDP Deflator} = \frac{\text{Nominal GDP}}{\text{Real GDP}} \times 100$$

Labour Force Participation Rate:

$$\text{Labour force participation rate} = \left(\frac{\text{Labour force}}{\text{Adult population}}\right) \times 100$$

Marginal Propensity to Consume:

$$MPC = \frac{\Delta C}{\Delta Y}$$

Marginal Propensity to Save:

$$MPS = \frac{\Delta S}{\Delta Y}$$

Marginal Product of Capital:

$$MP_K = \frac{\text{Change in the quantity of output } (\Delta Q)}{\text{Change in the quantity of capital } (\Delta K)}$$

Marginal Product of a Factor:

$$MP_F = \frac{\text{Change in total product}}{\text{Change in quantity of the factor}}$$

Marginal Product of Labour:

$$MP_L = \frac{\text{Change in the quantity of output } (\Delta Q)}{\text{Change in the quantity of labour } (\Delta L)}$$

Market Equilibrium:

Market equilibrium occurs where $Qd = Qs$

Multiplier (*k*):

$$\text{Multiplier} = \frac{1}{(1 - MPC)}$$

$$\text{Multiplier} = \frac{1}{MPS}$$

$$k = \frac{1}{MPS + MPT + MPM}$$

$$k = \frac{1}{MPW}$$

Net Capital Outflow:

Net Capital Outflow = Purchase of foreign assets by domestic residents − Purchase of domestic assets by foreigners

NCO = NX

Net capital outflow = Net exports

Net Exports:

$NX = X - M$

Nominal Exchange Rate:

$$e = \frac{P^*}{P}$$

Opportunity Cost:

$$\text{Opportunity cost of good } y = \frac{\text{Sacrifice of good } x}{\text{Gain in good } y}$$

Price Elasticity of Demand:

$$\text{Price elasticity of demand} = \frac{\text{Percentage change in quantity demanded}}{\text{Percentage change in price}}$$

Mid-Point Method:

$$\text{Price elasticity of demand} = \frac{(Q_2 - Q_1)/[(Q_2 + Q_1)/2]}{(P_2 - P_1)/[(P_2 + P_1)/2]}$$

Point Elasticity Method:

$$\text{Price elasticity of demand} = \frac{P}{Qd} \times \frac{1}{\frac{\Delta P}{\Delta Qd}}$$

$$\text{Price elasticity of demand} = \frac{P}{Qd} \times \frac{dQd}{dP}$$

Price Elasticity of Supply:

$$\text{Price elasticity of supply} = \frac{\text{Percentage change in quantity supplied}}{\text{Percentage change in price}}$$

Mid-Point Method:

$$\text{Price elasticity of supply} = \frac{(Q_2 - Q_1)/[(Q_2 + Q_1)/2]}{(P_2 - P_1)/[(P_2 + P_1)/2]}$$

Point Elasticity Method:

$$\text{Price elasticity of supply} = \frac{P}{Qs} \times \frac{1}{\frac{\Delta P}{\Delta Qs}}$$

$$\text{Price elasticity of supply} = \frac{P}{Qs} \times \frac{dQs}{dP}$$

Production Function (Assuming Two Factor Inputs, Land and Capital):

$Q = f(K, L)$

Productivity:

$$\text{Productivity} = \frac{\text{Total output}}{\text{Units of the factor}}$$

Real Exchange Rate:

$$\text{Real exchange rate} = \frac{(\text{Nominal exchange rate} \times \text{Domestic price})}{\text{Foreign price}}$$

$$\text{Real exchange rate} = \frac{(e \times P)}{P^*}$$

Real GDP:

$$\text{Real GDP} = \frac{\text{Nominal GDP}}{\text{GDP Deflator}}$$

Real Interest Rate:

Real interest rate = Nominal interest rate − Inflation rate

$r_t = i_t - \pi_t$

Real Money Balances:

$$\text{Real Money Balances} = \frac{M}{P}$$

Real Wage:

$$\text{Real Wage} = \frac{W}{P}$$

Relative Price:

$$\text{Relative price} = \frac{\text{Nominal Price } X}{\text{Nominal Price } Y}$$

Sacrifice Ratio:

$$\text{Sacrifice ratio} = \frac{\text{Euro cost of loss of production}}{\text{Percentage change in inflation}}$$

Saving:

$$\begin{matrix} S & = & I & + & NCO \\ \text{Saving} & = & \text{Domestic investment} & + & \text{Net capital outflow} \end{matrix}$$

Slope of a Demand Curve:

$$\text{Slope} = \frac{\Delta P}{\Delta Qd}$$

Taylor Rule:

$r = p + 0.5y + 0.5(p - 2) + 2$

The Equilibrium of the Economy:

Planned $S + T + M$ = Planned $I + G + X$

Unemployment Rate:

$$\text{Unemployment rate} = \left(\frac{\text{Number of unemployed}}{\text{Labour force}}\right) \times 100$$

Unemployment rate = NRU − a(Actual Inflation − Expected inflation)

Velocity of Circulation:

$$V = \frac{(P \times Y)}{M}$$